Companions Without Vows

Companions Without Vows

Relationships Among Eighteenth-Century British Women

BETTY RIZZO

The University of Georgia Press   Athens and London

This book has been supported by a grant from the National Endowment
for the Humanities, an independent federal agency.

Designed by Sandra Strother Hudson
Set in 10 on 13 Linotype Walbaum by Tseng Information Systems, Inc.
Printed and bound by Maple-Vail

The paper in this book meets the guidelines for permanence
and durability of the Committee on Production Guidelines for
Book Longevity of the Council on Library Resources.

Printed in the United States of America
98   97   96   95   94   C   5   4   3   2   1

Library of Congress Cataloging in Publication Data

Rizzo, Betty.
Companions without vows : relationships among eighteenth-century
British women / Betty Rizzo.
p.   cm.
Includes bibliographical references and index.
ISBN 0-8203-1541-9 (alk. paper)
1. Single women—Great Britain—History—18th century—Case
studies.   2. Women—Employment—Great Britain—History—18th
century—Case studies.   3. Fellowship.   4. Marriage—Great Britain
—History—18th century.   5. Benefactors—Great Britain
—History—18th century—Case studies.   6. Upper classes—Great
Britain—History—18th century—Case studies.   I. Title.
HQ800.4.G3R58   1994
306.81'0941'09033—dc20   92-45141

British Library Cataloging in Publication Data available

Title page: "Iphigenia's Late Procession from Kingston to Bristol."
Elizabeth Chudleigh shown with three companions, a clergyman,
a physician, and an apothecary, 1776. Courtesy Print Collection,
Lewis Walpole Library, Yale University.

To Bee and Frank,
veterans of a sixty-eight-year good companionship

Contents

Acknowledgments

THE FIRST ACKNOWLEDGMENT for this book must be to my friend and former editor, Robert Phillips, who suggested it be written and nursed it through more versions than either of us at first contemplated. The book would never have been written or published without his interest and efforts. Mary Margaret Stewart and Calhoun Winton invited the conference paper from which the book developed. Many people read all or part of the book in its various stages, and I am especially grateful to Janice Thaddeus, Joanna Lipking, Elizabeth Brophy, and Jerry Beasley for their careful readings and many useful suggestions and strictures. Jane Marcus, Marylea Meyersohn, Mary Margaret Stewart, and Carolyn Woodward read specific chapters and were also very helpful.

Friends who helped essentially with problems of research also made the book possible. These include Mary L. Robertson, Curator of Manuscripts of the Huntington Library; Cynthia Comyn of the London College of Heralds; Dr. Frances Harris and Dr. C. J. Wright of the British Library Manuscript Division; Marie Devine, Joan Sussler, and Anna Malicka of the Lewis Walpole Library of Yale University; and Barbara Dunlap of the library of The City College of New York. I should also thank Peter Day of the Devonshire Collections, Chatsworth, for the many copies he provided, and Lars Troide for generously sharing manuscript materials from the Burney Papers project. It would not be possible to produce a book of this kind without the ready assistance and support all these have generously given. To my friends John and Cynthia Comyn I owe a special debt of gratitude as well, for unstinting hospitality and kindness; to her other virtues should be added the unfailing willingness of Cynthia Comyn to interrupt her own researches to look up yet another will for me in the Public Record Office. Rather than listing her name repeatedly in the notes, let me thank her here. Two descendants of Frances Greville's provided invaluable assistance: Mary Duchess of Roxburghe let me have copies of Greville's notebook of poems and unfinished novel and granted permission to publish portions of them; Quentin Crewe gave important information and advice. Mary Margaret Stewart lent me manuscript materials from her archive on Caroline and

Henry Fox; and she, Robert Bataille, Lillian Feder, Sidney Feshbach, Mary Jackson, James May, Mitzi Myer, Beverly Schneller, Judith Stanton, Janet Todd, and Sue Zalk all provided enlightenment at crucial points. Mrs. Anne (now Lady) Boulton gave valuable research assistance. Others who helped are acknowledged in the notes.

I want to endorse, as Margaret Doody has done in *Frances Burney: The Life in the Works,* Janice Thaddeus's point, made in conference papers at the University of Hartford and at Hofstra University in 1985, that Frances Burney should be known by that name and not by the diminutive name used only by her family. I only wish it were possible to identify and list here all the other ideas and insights to which I have been helped by other scholars.

The New York Public Library, the libraries of the City College of New York, Columbia, Harvard, and Yale Universities—particularly the Sterling, the Beinecke and the Lewis Walpole Library at Farmington of Yale—the British Library, and the London Public Record Office have been constant resources. Archivists in the English County Record Offices have always been helpful when I have written; I have tried to acknowledge their important assistance in my notes and apologize now for any omission. The owners of the many manuscripts quoted here are acknowledged in the bibliography, but I thank them again.

Collecting illustrations can be a taxing problem and I have many archives and archivists to thank for the illustrations. I want especially to mention the inspired guidance of Joan Sussler, and the help of Christopher Gatiss, formerly of the Courtauld Institute, Sarah Wimbush of the Courtauld, Jayne Shrimpton of the National Portrait Gallery, and Nancy Schmugge of the Pierpont Morgan Library.

I cannot sufficiently thank Nancy Grayson Holmes and Karen Orchard of the University of Georgia Press for their initial warm appreciation of this book and their subsequent deft handling of its production, which included their provision of Kelly Caudle's and Trudie Calvert's expert editing.

Finally, I acknowledge that in its earliest stages I read too much of the manuscript aloud to my husband, Ray, and to my daughter, Jennifer Magnani, that their responses were enlightening, and that because they continued to listen with interest, I continued to write.

Companions Without Vows

Chapter One

COMPANIONSHIP: A RANGE OF POSSIBLE CHOICES

A BOOK about women's relationships with one another in eighteenth-century England probably has to focus, as does this one to a considerable extent though not exclusively, on a network of middle-to upper-class women who left a significant body of writing, in letters, memoirs, and fiction. My investigations focused on such women and their lives, using whatever materials I could find, but particularly their discourse about themselves, each other, and the conditions—social, economic, and psychological—in which they lived. Women less literate, of any class, who have left no such discourse, must be investigated in other ways than I have done. My purpose has been to focus on the depth, the richness, the diversity, and sometimes the perversity of some relationships between women, which may also cut across economic and social lines.

The relationship I am most interested in investigating was institutionalized and therefore both common and well recognized at the time—the companionate relationship, that of the employer (known in the eighteenth century as the mistress, or, ironically, the patroness) and the humble companion. To any serious investigator, it soon becomes apparent that in several significant ways the companionate relationship of the eighteenth century mirrored the marriage relationship and was often identified with it. And so women's relationships with men cannot be excluded from secondary consideration here.

The histories in this book will show that, as is true of marriages, a great many variations were possible in companionate relationships. The autonomous mistress had the same powers over her companion that the husband had over his wife. She could choose either to exercise those powers autocratically, as she had probably seen her father and husband do, or to work out an equitable arrangement such as she herself would

1

have liked to experience in her dealings with men: that is, she could do either as she had probably been done by or as she would like to have been done by. Particularly if she chose the latter course, but even if she chose the former, she was making an oblique comment upon what was for her the marriage problem.

For men, marriage was not a problem in the sense that it was for women. The men whose comments about companionate relationships are explored here usually demonstrated a sense that the conventional marital model of the time—controlling husband and amenable wife— was perfectly satisfactory by expressing their approval of the amenable humble companion and certifying her as the ideal candidate for marriage. Conversely, the autocratic or tyrannical mistress became, in these men's writings, proof that women should not be trusted with authority over others, though the justification or rationalization for refusing authority to women changed gradually during the century as the ideology about woman's nature changed: men believed earlier in the period that women could not be given authority, though they might lust for it, because God had created them too irrational and passionate to wield it properly, and later in the period because they were by nature submissive and subordinate. Often conflicting, yet alone or in combination invincibly strong, these pious and "rational" justifications for making most of women's choices for them persisted long past the eighteenth century. Men commonly recognized the high-handed, even sadistic, behavior that wives often endured at the hands of their husbands as tyrannical only when replicated in the mistress-companionate relationship or when the tyrant was a woman rather than a man. The companionate relationship of the eighteenth century cannot be fully understood without reference to its consistently recognized and often invoked analogy to marriage. Discourse about it by either gender is therefore often also a tacit discourse about marriage.

It is for this reason that discussion and analysis of fictitious companionate relationships from literature by both women and men have been included in this book along with women's writings about their real-life companionships and my own histories of those companionships. A comparison of literary considerations of the subject shows that women's writing explores comforts and corruptions of mistress-companionate relations of which men's writing indicates comparative unawareness. Contemporary works by women provide by far the more perspicacious analyses of this subterranean world, which was their daily environment. When I have mingled fictional presentations of companionship with actual companionships, it is to illuminate the awareness of eighteenth-century writers of the subject and the gendered difference of their perception of it.

Reinforcing the parallel between marriage and companionship was the similarity of duties performed by wife for husband and by companion for wife in middle- and upper-class society. In Charlotte Smith's *Old Manor House* (1793), the tasks of Mrs. Rayland's companion Mrs. Lennard were

> to sit with her in her apartment when she had no company; to read the newspaper; to make tea; to let in and out the favourite dogs (the task of combing and washing them was transferred to a deputy); to collect and report at due seasons intelligence of all that happened in the neighbouring families; to give regular returns of the behaviour of all the servants . . . ; to take especial care that the footmen and helpers behaved respectfully to the maids . . . ; to keep the keys; and to keep her mistress in good humour with herself.[1]

These were not physically laborious services but essentially servile ones. The labors of the upper servant mediating between employer and his or her possessions, lower servants, children, neighbors, and society, they signalized the need for white-collar wives as a result of the gentrification of society. A person performing such functions had always to be conscious that her position was not autonomous but contingent.

This analogy between the companionate relationship and marriage may help to illuminate the discussion about the ideal of companionate marriage in the eighteenth century as promulgated by Lawrence Stone.[2] The term *companionate marriage*, referring to a companion in the sense of the woman's or humble companion—not an equal at all—acquires an ironical inflection. Often, even usually, an acknowledged social equal (that is, with reference to the status of the males from whom she derived), a wife, unlike the servants, was permitted inclusion as a social presence, but both wife and humble companion functioned in the household hierarchy as subservient handmaidens—as "upper servants," as so many women were to complain. Mary Delany wrote in 1759, "The wife is only considered as a head servant in the family, and honoured with the head of the table, only that she may have all the trouble of carving, as well as the care of supplying that table, so that her lord may not descend to any domestick drudgery. Our Maker created us 'helps meet' which surely implies we are worthy of being their companions, their friends, *their advisers*, as well as *they ours*."[3]

If companionate marriage resulted from the increasing prevalence in

the home of a husband and wife in an increasingly isolated confrontation and from their adjustments to this situation, the subservience of
wives still caused many women who had any choice to eschew this form
of companionship. Elizabeth Montagu, once she had achieved liberation through widowhood, was one of these. Writing to Elizabeth Carter
of the second marriage of a friend, she said, "I always thought her
the perfection of the female character, formed to become the domestic
situation and disposed to obedience. She could not stir till she received
the word of command. I really believe she was just like Eve before she
eat the apple. . . . She would have preferred her husband's discourse
to the angels. I am afraid you and I . . . should have entered into some
metaphysical disquisitions with the angel. . . . We can think for ourselves and also act for ourselves." She added, "When I was a wife I was
obedient because it was my duty, and being married to a man of sense
and integrity, obedience was not painful or irksome, in early youth a
director perhaps is necessary if the sphere of action is extensive; but it
seems to me that a new master and new lessons after ones opinions and
habits were formed must be a little awkward, and with all due respect
to the superior sex, I do not see how they can be necessary to a woman
unless she were to defend her lands and tenements by sword or gun."[4]

Hester Thrale, who had cause to lament that after a first-class education under the tutelage of Arthur Collier—that remarkable educator
of remarkable women[5]—she had become a breeder and upper servant
to the rich brewer Henry Thrale, once expressed her own sentiments by
imagining the hypocrisy forced upon country gentlewomen:

Well then Philosopher—if thou hast a Daughter, Shall She become a quiet
Country Gentlewoman? keep her Pickles from Mother, and Conserves from
Cloud? narrow her notions to petty Scandal, foment Election Quarrels in the
County, pot the Hares her Husband brings home from Hunting? watch him
when he is drunk that the Liquor may not choke him? & as he lies fast asleep,
cheat him of a few Guineas by bringing him in falso Acc[ts] of Sugar &c for
Family uses, in Concurrence with her own Maid & Housekeeper who came
with her at Marriage-Day. . . . When such is Life however—& who can deny
that such it is?—Can one help being a Misanthrope?[6]

Mary Astell had suggested earlier in print that for their own good,
women ought to avoid marriage and its victimization.[7] Astell's out-
spoken protest may have been feasible during the joint reign of William
and Mary and the reign of Anne but not after the death of Queen Anne
in 1714: in her appendix to *Some Reflections upon Marriage* Astell denied "the natural inferiority of our sex," "it being sedition at least, if

not treason, to assert it in this reign." As Ruth Perry has noted, Astell's last publication appeared in 1709, and she may well have understood subsequently that the period for debate had all but concluded, that her struggle was lost.[8] Direct critiques of marriage by women by no means disappear, but after midcentury they tend to appear more in private letters than in published works,[9] and the published critiques tend to be expressed more by implication than overtly. Consequently, the tensions arising from male-female relationships are sometimes best elucidated in private records.

In relation to women's indirect public commentary, a great deal of important work on the implicit second or woman's plot in the novel has recently been accomplished.[10] One overt woman's plot, that of Elizabeth Griffith's play *The Platonic Wife* (1765) was condemned probably because its heroine stubbornly insisted upon equality of treatment in her marriage and eventually obtained it. In this play the morally dubious Lady Fanshaw openly condemns marriage: "Next to the felicity of widowhood is that of being separated. However, there are, my dear, some material differences: While the tyrant lives to whom we have been bound, we never can forget we have been slaves."[11] But because Lady Fanshaw is morally discountable, her statement is too; and messages thus indirectly propounded were rarely noted. In any case, the play promptly vanished forever from the boards.

An example of the publicly unbroachable is the distaste, even horror, of married women at the prospect of perpetual pregnancy, which women considered a primary reason not to marry or to marry late. It was never broached in print, for having children was the obvious first duty of women. According to Elizabeth Brophy, it was apparently not even discussed by women in their letters and journals (p. 168). Discussion of contraceptive methods, an engrossing subject to women, was never published in the women's magazines, nor is any work to improve such methods know to have been under way. Though one can find women writing to each other significantly of young married women suffering miscarriages after imprudently riding horseback or traveling at length by coach over bumpy roads, recognition of the problems of the risk of death in childbirth, the loss of women's looks and freedom, and the various entrapments associated with motherhood belonged to women's private, even solely personal, sphere and were not available for consideration by women writers. These taboo subjects were some of the "not-saids" defined by Terry Eagleton as contributing importantly to the definition of an ideology.[12]

Hester Thrale could confide in her mother about her distress over her perpetual pregnancies and the deaths of her children between her marriage in 1763 and her mother's death in 1773. She confided a little of what she felt in her "Children's Book," writing as her mother was dying, "Nobody can guess what a Winter this has been to me, & big with Child too again God help me!" But her more honest comments came only after the end of the century. In 1817 she wrote of Princess Charlotte's fatal lying-in, "Every Female must feel not only afflicted, but indignant at one Express coming here after another, telling us all how Charmingly the Business was going on—a Charming Labour truly of *48* Hours *Agony!*" And in 1819 she tersely summed up the "pleasures" of her marriage, which, she said, "consisted in holding my head over a Bason Six Months in the Year."[13] Even from Hester Thrale, such honesty was possible only after the century had ended.

The question of women's equality to men was also rarely directly broached, but issues tangential to it that were broached included the right of women to a claim to rationality as well as sensibility; the importance to women of an education of their reasoning capacities; and, to be explored in this book, the perniciousness of the hierarchically structured mistress-companionate relationship (also read marriage).

If during most of the eighteenth century a woman writer could no longer, like Mary Astell, very easily directly advise other women not to marry because husbands were tyrants, she could and did point not only to the painful subservience of humble companions but also to the deleterious effects of their subservience on the characters of humble companions—the truly hidden cost of marriage. Frances Burney, who well understood the correspondence between the institutions of marriage and companionship, was particularly interested, as her fiction shows, in the damage done the companion's character because of the deviousness forced upon her, damage hideously exemplified in her own life by her stepmother and by her superior at court, Mrs. Schwellenberg, both of whom were middle figures in triadic relationships between a superior above and an inferior (unluckily Burney herself) below. If this subject could not easily be directly addressed, it could be indirectly, and subversively, exposed in fiction. The conduct books proclaimed that woman was *naturally* submissive so how could damage be done to the woman of whom submission was required? In exposing the moral hypocrisy of such seemingly submissive female figures as humble companions, women could simultaneously suggest their own independent spirit and expose the cruel and self-serving immorality of their oppressors. The figure of the companion could express either the helplessness or the de-

viousness of the wife; the figure of the tyrannical mistress could sym-
bolize the husband but at the same time announce that because women,
too, given the opportunity, could be tyrannical oppressors, they were not
really submissive by nature. If that were the case, then a woman who
secretly knew that she was not submissive at least did not have to be
ashamed of being unnatural. And the figure of the mistress, if she were
not tyrannical, could suggest an alternative model for marriages. These
points will be demonstrated later in discussions of the work of Sarah
Fielding and Sarah Scott.

Male writers, like Arthur Murphy and Samuel Foote, naturally failed
to detect the nuances of the mistress-companion relationship, tending
rather to stress the similarity between properly subservient companions
and the best of wives. In this respect they were of a mind with the author
of a letter published in the *London Magazine* in April 1751, which described the ordering up of a suitable wife from England by a merchant
in Jamaica. Invoiced as one of the recommendations of the chosen one
was that she "had no subsistence but from a cross old aunt, who gave
her a great deal of uneasiness," and that she had lived with this intoler-
ably peevish aunt for three years "and had not during all that time given
her said aunt the least occasion of complaint." The merchant's judicious
choice of this practiced toady resulted in a marriage that proved "the
most fortunate that had happened in that island for many years."[14]

Hester Thrale wryly recounts a tale about a woman who served for
years as a humble companion to win her Jacob that underscores the
value of humiliation training for a wife. A Welsh lady with a fortune
of £8,000 fell in unrequited love with a clergyman named Myddelton.
While he was abroad she coaxed his mother to take her in as a paying
guest by offering twice as much board as necessary, and she attended
her hostess in her last illness "with the assiduity of a Servant expecting
a Legacy, and with the affection of a dutyful & amiable Child." The
clergyman was so touched that he permitted the woman to live on in the
house with his sister, whom she served as companion and housekeeper.
He came to visit on occasion, and at last one evening he told her he
would marry her the next morning. She fell down in fits from which he
caressed her into recovery, and they were indeed married the next day.[15]
The passive aggression of the Welshwoman and the capitulation of the
clergyman illustrate one of the hopeful themes of eighteenth-century
women writers: if women suffer in virtuous patience long enough, their
husbands may be converted to a full appreciation of them.[16]

The all-suffering humble companion was the mirror image of a much

admired wife, the saintly Amelia of Fielding's novel, who, if she could
have functioned as her husband's adviser (as Delany put it) and had
the power to enforce her advice, would have prevented all the distresses
that ensued, but who had to suffer in patience while her errant and
headstrong, albeit good-hearted, husband learned for himself. When
Frances Burney discovered in 1786 that her position at court as second
keeper of the robes to the queen required her to function as companion to the truly dreadful Mrs. Schwellenberg, first keeper, she resigned
herself by likening the relationship to that of the most sacred commitment: "I am married, my dearest Susan—I look upon it in that light—
I was averse to forming the union, and I endeavoured to escape it; but
my friends interfered—they prevailed—and the knot is tied. What then
now remains but to make the best wife in my power? I am bound to it
in duty, and I will strain every nerve to succeed." [17]

All insults a wife received from her husband had to be endured. One
day when Burney planned to absent herself in the evening, Schwellenberg refused to help her to any food at dinner. "I had no way to compose my own spirit to an endurance of this, but by considering myself
as married to her, and therefore that all rebellion could but end in dis-
turbance, and that concession was my sole chance for peace! Oh what
reluctant nuptials!—how often did I say to myself—Were these chains
voluntary, how could I bear them?—how forgive myself that I put them
on!" (3:347).

The ease with which Burney and others drew the parallel between
marriage and close relationships between two women suggests that to
their minds sexuality was far from the most important aspect of marriage: what bore on Burney's mind was the power structure encapsu-
lating the marriage "partners." To Burney's friend Stephen Digby, too,
the important point was Burney's thorough breaking-in: " 'How well
you will be trained in by Mrs. Schwellenberg—if you come to trial!' Ah!
thought I, the more I suffer through her, the less and less do I feel disposed to run any new and more lasting risk!" (4:234).

Jane Austen in *Emma* (1816) plays on a similar theme. Emma's governess, now her companion, Mrs. Weston, "had been a friend and companion such as few possessed, intelligent, well-informed, useful, gentle,
knowing all the ways of the family, interested in all its concerns, and
peculiarly interested in herself, in every pleasure, every scheme of
her's;—one to whom she could speak every thought as it arose, and who
had such an affection for her as could never find fault." [18]

Mrs. Weston as companion was playing the wife even to the point of listening to "every thought as it arose," thus abnegating her own natural thought processes. Mr. Knightly later reproaches her: "You were preparing yourself to be an excellent wife all the time you were at Hartfield. You might not give Emma such a complete education as your powers would seem to promise; but you were receiving a very good education from her, on the very material point of submitting your own will, and doing as you were bid" (p. 38).

Janet Todd has commented that in these passages Mrs. Weston put up with altogether too much, playing the wife instead of the governess, and that the dangers of playing another woman's husband or of experiencing vicarious wifehood through the other woman had not occurred to Emma.[19] She adds that Emma also insisted on regarding her protégée Harriet almost as a wife and that she echoed many a husband in her patronizing exclamation, "Dear Harriet! I would not change you for the clearest-headed, longest-sighted, best-judging female breathing" (p. 284).

Indeed, Emma's assumption of male prerogative has often been noted. Lionel Trilling thought she was extraordinary because "she has a moral life as a man has a moral life."[20] He apparently means that Emma views herself as a person entitled and empowered to make her own choices. Marylea Meyersohn has commented on her "abuse of her linguistic power over the dependent women"—Harriet, Miss Bate, Mrs. Elton—and identified Emma's discourse as "male" in its wit, brevity, intelligence, and tendencies toward abstract reasoning and toward reinforcing the reader's uncomfortable awareness of her alienation from other women.[21] In this novel Austen seems to have explored the question of what might become of an attractive young woman who assumes all the prerogatives of a man—the right to reason for herself, do and say as she likes, and plan others' lives for them. When the book is read in this way, Emma's acceptance of her own mistaken effrontery and of Knightly as mentor is painful, representing the defeat of the heroine of an antimarriage plot.[22] Emma, like Tom Jones, has made a full complement of apprenticeship errors, but Tom matures to judge rightly and to take command of himself and his family, whereas Emma "matures" by accepting, with apparent relief, a loving mentor.

The incompatibility of roles of a woman who was both wife of a husband and mistress of a companion was not lost to Henry Fox and his wife, Lady Caroline, as demonstrated in an uneasy but comic colloquy of letters in 1749. Fox, a political power but a social upstart—his father had begun life as a footman and risen to be paymaster of the forces—had eloped with the daughter of the powerful Duke of Richmond. Lady Caroline had been in love; Fox was influenced by his father-in-law's enormous political influence and his wife's being the great-granddaughter of Charles II. Because of her lineage and her sacrifice in marrying him—after the elopement her parents cut her off for four years—Fox was a particularly considerate husband, unusually communicative to his wife and solicitous of her advice on political affairs.[23] In 1749 Lady Caroline was in Bath drinking the waters for her health; for the period of her stay she had borrowed Miss Cheeke, the customary companion of Fox's sister-in-law Lady Ilchester of Red Lynch.

In her first letter Lady Caroline apologizes for having opened some of her husband's letters and then announces, "Miss Cheeke and I shall do very well together only she is too complaisant and wont do her own way enough it w^d make it pleasanter to me if she w^d but I believe she is used to study other peoples way."[24]

Here was a compliment to her own amenability at the expense of his near relations, and Fox's consequent observations elicited a flood of self-justification from his wife:

I agree with you Miss Cheke's fault is a good fault but I had rather she had it not for I dont love people should feel themselves toad Eaters because I dont put any body on that footing with me but I find you dont take my meaning right with regard to you when I want you to be complaisant to me in any thing tis not for the sake of doing any one particular thing but because I like you should love to please me and when I'm vex't at your not being of the same opinion about any thing tis because when I love any body vastly I allways wish them to think as I do. But you mistake me vastly if you think I like an humble companion. at first Miss Cheke thought it necessary to tag every where after me and to fast till I breakfasted but I have insisted upon her eating some breakfast before me in a morning for tis impossible any body can chuse to fast 2 hours after they are up now I know she likes Lying a bed but I can't persuade her not to get up for to go with me in a morning these are the sort of things I mean and I believe youl agree with me t'would be pleasanter to have any body take their own Way in such things but I believe she does not dare at Red Lynch but you are quite out when you name any indifferent persons behaviour and yrs because I think it a very different thing and whats very agreeable in one is not at all so in another. . . . I don't like that because I often quarell with you about a triffle you should imagine I like people should be slaves to me and have no will of their own I'm vastly mad with you for thinking such a thing of me for I assure you tis the only thing I disliked in Miss Cheke and she is vastly mended by finding I dont desire it I have no patience that you should compare her and you.[25]

When Fox jovially charged his wife with loving a humble companion, she understood very well his hint that she was not always a submissive wife, and after her adieus she reverted to her reproach: "You never used to accuse me of liking a humble companion."

MOST HUMANS exhibit both tyranny and benevolence. The choices that two women alone in a relationship were empowered to make were of course to be made not in a vacuum but in an intellectual and social climate within which the available options were already defined. In the course of the eighteenth century, tyranny and benevolence were established as important terms in a polarity and as important human attributes. Following the Glorious Revolution of 1688, it had become more or less the duty of every Englishman to extirpate tyranny. But tyranny must be identified before it can be extirpated, and its definition and local identification were problematic. To locate tyranny in the camp of one's enemy became a standard political strategy, for to identify the behavior of one's opponents as tyrannical nearly accomplished one's work. But the term, encountered everywhere, was hard to fix definitively. For example, the Americans perceived the English government as tyrannical to them, and the English Opposition agreed, but Samuel Johnson published his own influential refutation, *Taxation No Tyranny* (1775). And if a consensus about the definition of tyranny was difficult to achieve in the political sphere, the suggestion that wives were the victims of male tyranny was an idea—like the idea that slaves were victims of tyranny— for which the time had only barely arrived.

The tyranny of the overweening monarch who threatened the prerogatives of privileged males would naturally be far more easily recognizable in eighteenth-century culture than would be the tyranny of the father of the family who threatened the prerogatives of his wife, children, and servants. Yet the patriarchal prerogative was identified as tyrannical regularly, if cautiously, during the century. Not surprisingly, it was outsiders and impatient sons who registered the insight. A rebellious clergyman's son, the publisher John Dunton, in 1705 expressed his opinion that the heads of some households "are no better than domestic tyrants, and the perfect enemies to peace withindoors." [26] The concept of domestic tyranny was therefore already in circulation at the start of the century and was commonplace enough to provide the conflict between father and son in comedy plots to the end of the period, when the idea that husbands were tyrannical to their wives was still not entertainable by males and any contest between them certainly not regarded—unless by the ground-breaking Elizabeth Griffith—as the subject of comic conflict, to be happily resolved at the curtain by the triumph of the suppressed. Obviously, by the establishment, males could be recognized as the victims of tyranny long before females, traditionally defined as born to be subjected, could. Charles ("Louse") Pigott, the politically radical author of *The Female Jockey Club* (1794), a satirical review of fashionable women, was a man raised in the establishment but a supporter of the principles of the French Revolution who complained, "Let us now proceed to consider the nature of power, and we shall discover its baneful effects to be equally pernicious, and universal. Wives often set no bounds to the controul they have assumed over their husbands. Mistresses never fail to abuse the dominion they hold over their lovers, when they have once gained an ascendent, becoming the veriest Tyrants; and where does history record a Monarch or a Statesman who has not more or less, been debauched by its seductions?"[27]

The radical Pigott's conception of the location of the abuse of power is breathtaking and instructive. He betrays a universal inclination to identify as tyrants only those who interfere with one's own autonomy and prerogatives; hence his particular examples of tyrannous abusers of power are monarchs, wives, and mistresses. The power to define tyranny for a culture rests with the empowered. Thus in the discourse quoted and discussed in this book, women will often call men tyrants, but men will reserve the term for women who challenge any part of their own prerogative.

Benevolence was a quality much more clearly defined and recognized. The concept of benevolence was popularized by Shaftesbury in his *Characteristics* (1711), in which he postulated that social love was a natural human attribute that humans naturally enjoy practicing. Besides the natural or social affections, which included love for morality and justice, and led, in their exertion, to happiness, the human being was also endowed with necessary self-affections, such as love of life, resentment of injury, ambition, love of praise, and rest, all of which, however, in excess led to selfishness and unhappiness. For Shaftesbury this second group was not vicious (except, of course, in excess), but there was a third group of entirely vicious affections, including inhumanity and tyranny, which made their indulgers malign and utterly miserable; though Shaftesbury recognizes all three of these "affections" or passions as endemic to humans, he labels this third group "unnatural."[28] According to this scheme, each individual ought to regulate his or her own passions, balancing the first and second kind properly (remembering that happiness resided principally in the exertion of the social affections), and extirpating the third kind, which would produce utter self-misery. It was a useful and influential social prescription, which should be borne in mind when considering the moral decisions and the writings of the women investigated here.

We would recognize, as did Shaftesbury, that benevolence, selfishness, and tyranny are not incompatible in the same person, who may act upon all of these endemic impulses in the course of an hour. As the period wore on, however, benevolence was to become closely associated with sensibility, that empathetic response to the feelings and needs of others.[29] And although in the latter half of the century sensibility became a fashionable quality for both genders, it was increasingly assigned particularly to women. One who was truly benevolent and had true sensibility could not practice tyranny at all. Women were by nature endowed with sensibility, it became convenient to assume, which enabled them to serve men effortlessly and "naturally." To oversimplify the case, then, a woman who found herself empowered over another socially equal adult —her companion—could, possibly for the first time in her life, elect to play one role or the other, the domestic tyrant or the benevolent friend.

To play the tyrant, however, in the latter part of the century, a woman had to ignore the prescriptions of the conduct books, which certainly did not alone incorporate, but which conveniently concentrated, contemporary thinking about the proper role of women of the middle and upper classes, that is, women of whom actual hard labor was not required. Dorothea, the daughter of Dr. John Gregory, will figure importantly in chapter 6, so his influential conduct book, *A Father's Legacy to His Daughters* (1774), may serve as an example of these works.

Although Gregory writes in affectionate and seemingly liberal terms to his daughters, asserting that he has always considered women as companions and equals to men rather than as domestic drudges or the slaves of pleasure, he endorses a view of woman's "naturally" submissive and retiring nature that he himself belies in the strength of his caveats against all behavior that was unsubmissive and unretiring. (For emphasis, I italicize the words *nature* and *natural* in the following references.) "*Nature* has made you to blush when you are guilty of any fault, and has forced us to love you because you do so": here the reward for remaining childishly bashful, for failing to achieve a mature self-assurance, is "love," by which Gregory means no more than approval. He assures his readers that "extreme sensibility" is particularly engaging in women.

Also *natural* to women, he believes, are their love of dress, their vanity and love of admiration, and their reserve in regard to revealing their attachments to men before the men in question have declared themselves. "*Nature* has not given you that unlimited range in your choice which we enjoy, she has wisely and benevolently assigned to you a greater flexibility of taste on this subject." Thus woman *naturally* accommodates herself to the man who has chosen her: in the great world women have their choices dictated to them. Apparently woman's *natural* love of admiration will ensure that the attachment of any man will fix first her gratitude and then her love.

Delicacy, though, is the perfection of women to which Gregory frequently reverts. A retiring delicacy that avoids the public eye is one of the chief beauties of the female character. The modesty so essential in the sex "will *naturally* dispose you to be rather silent in company." In compensation, Gregory suggests his daughters may notify the world they are not dull by showing expressive countenances, for "one may take a share in the conversation without uttering a syllable." They must not demonstrate wit, for it is seldom found united with softness and delicacy; humor is often a great enemy to delicacy; even good sense should not be displayed; and learning must be kept a profound secret from men, "who generally look with a jealous and malignant eye on a woman of great parts and a cultivated understanding." Good health in a woman is an obvious boon, but the idea of female softness and delicacy is so associated with a correspondent delicacy of constitution that "when a woman speaks of her great strength, her extraordinary appetite, her ability to bear excessive fatigue, we recoil at the description in a way she is little aware of." [30]

Lest his daughters now suspect that he wishes to strip them of their true natures and make them entirely artificial, Gregory protests that he wishes them "the most perfect simplicity of heart and manners. I think you may possess dignity without pride, affability without meanness, and simple elegance without affectation."

Such conduct books—and Gregory's is not atypical—made it difficult for a woman to play any part but that prescribed; they limited a woman's ability to express her strengths and powers, to make choices, to define goals and pursue them aggressively, to be creative. Gregory, an eminent university professor and a man at home in aristocratic circles, is confidently defining natural woman so that if women were to display such honest attributes as wit, humor, learning, good sense, or robust health, they must appear "unnatural." What does his stated ideal of woman as companion and equal amount to if woman is already defined as in every way not equal to man but an agreeable and unthreatening complement? As for the women, what one could not display, it would seem one was rather unlikely to labor very mightily either to acquire or to maintain. In fact, however, a considerable number of eighteenth-century women, associating the learning reserved to men with their purported superior mental abilities, proved their own equality privately to themselves by acquiring considerable classical knowledge and made forays into the fields of philosophy and history as well. But the evidence of their proof was, as Gregory enjoined, kept private, perhaps circulated only among communities of women. Thus women discreetly fell in with Gregory's advice that if one of them did happen to have to any great degree any of those attributes he considers unlucky—attributes which in men would be such positive assets—that possession enjoined secrecy—and hypocrisy and deception—upon them.

In summation, if a woman should not even display her "good sense" to society, if in particular she must not exhibit it to men, Gregory is admitting that women can reason but that men do not wish to know that they can reason and that women must therefore not appear to reason. The results of such instruction were threefold: many women avoided developing good sense, which might interfere with their being "loved"; developing "reason" was not an object of girls' education as it was of boys'; and women who did attempt to develop their reason—and to study the classics—did so privately and avoided exposing the result, thus allowing evidence of their intellectual equality to be ignored or treated as anomalous.

The undercurrent of uneasiness about seeming to recommend "hypocrisy"—a theme in both Gregory and the next work discussed—was always present, for it was all but apparent that hypocrisy was constantly being enjoined on women despite the comforting pretense that women were "naturally" formed in the mold Gregory advocated. As women's bodies were deformed from the age of two by metal stays that contracted their upper torsos (and rendered their health attractively delicate), so their minds were deformed by the injunctions to remain silent and silly. The conduct books, then, obviously helped to define one of the choices presented to all women: how far should they attempt to imitate the new prescription for "lovable" womankind?

Gregory included a final prescription for trivializing the lives of women. He recommended ladylike work—needlework, netting, knitting, and so on—not because it was natural, but because it was useful, for though he judged its intrinsic value to be trifling, he recommended it for enabling its executants to judge the work of others fairly and to fill up the "many solitary hours" necessarily spent at home because gadding about was to be discouraged. He thus condemned genteel women of all ages to hours of solitary work, which they were told was of small value, only to avoid their seeking pleasure, education, or any other form of fulfillment.

In the tenderest, most loving of tones, between what he deems natural to women and what he deems delicate in them, and promising them the admiration they desire if they will conform to his prescriptions, Gregory has recommended almost every possible disadvantage to his daughters. If a woman believed she could achieve approval only by being all that Gregory advocated, it is no wonder that she tried to fit the pattern. If a man of sensibility like Gregory could thus use the softest arguments to persuade women to play submissive, anemic, ignorant little girls, promising them that if they remained petlike they would be petted, what treatment of women was not to be expected of overt tyrants?

Dr. Tyrold's letter to his daughter Camilla—supposed to be the work of a beneficent clergyman of Gregory's type, but actually, of course, the work of Frances Burney in her novel *Camilla* (1796)—was sufficiently orthodox to be bound at least once with Gregory's own conduct book.[31] Tyrold's letter, though addressed to a particular young woman at a particular crisis—he fears Camilla will prematurely reveal to Edgar Mandlebert that she loves him—follows Gregory in this and most other salient points. The letter deals with the necessity of educating or forming a young woman in minimalist fashion to leave her sufficiently malleable to oblige her husband, whoever he may be. A woman, says Tyrold, begins life involved in all the worldly accidents of her father and continues by being involved in those of her husband (p. 356). The difficulties arise because she is in this "doubly appendant" state and it is all but impossible for her first accommodations to pave the way smoothly for her last. Any education may in these circumstances be disastrous, and Tyrold informs Camilla that she has therefore been brought up "with as much simplicity as is compatible with instruction, as much docility for various life as may accord with invariable principles, and as much accommodation with the world at large, as may combine with a just distinction of selected society" (p. 357). That is, any man requires that his wife has received some instruction, learned some sense of principle and some appreciation of his proper place in the world, but simplicity (or ignorance), docility, and accommodation are equally valuable, if not preferable, attributes. Furthermore, "Since Man must choose Woman, or Woman Man, which should come forward to make the choice?" (p. 358). Anticipating no debate on this point, Tyrold next proceeds to show that Camilla, aided by good sense and delicacy, must suppress her predilection, that she must "obtain a strict and unremitting control" over her passions (p. 359), and that this technique of suppression, once mastered, is to be practiced for the rest of her life.

Aware, like Gregory, that he comes dubiously close to advising hypocrisy to Camilla, Tyrold expatiates on the difference between hypocrisy and discretion. "The first is a vice; the second a conciliation to virtue. It is the bond that keeps society from disunion; the veil that shades our weakness from exposure" (p. 361). This sounds very well but means that "society" requires women to play submissive roles throughout life and that women's deviation from the role will be labeled as exactly what it is not—"weakness."

Though it appears to follow the conduct book tradition, I read this letter as a bitter piece of irony. First, it is the hypocrisy of Camilla's pretense that she does not love Edgar that precipitates the gothic horrors of the last volume of the novel, including the imprisonment for debt of the sententious Dr. Tyrold—who at that point would have been only too delighted to hear of his daughter's engagement to Edgar, an engagement that certainly would have occurred had it not been for his instructions. His own punishment, it would seem, represents Burney's assessment of the practical as well as the moral value of his advice.

Burney also comments bitterly on the failure to educate the young adequately. Sir Hugh, who controls their education, is good-humored but foolish, and the governess he has chosen, Miss Margland, a woman of hypocritical character who manipulates the world to get what she wants, a woman totally incapable of teaching learning or morality, is matched by the boys' tutor, Dr. Orkborne, who is so selfishly abstracted by his own endless preparations for publication that he never thinks of anyone else. The titles of two chapters in volume 1 underscore Burney's point: "Schooling of a young Gentleman" and "Tuition of a young Lady." Most of the products of these two instructors are quite feckless, and though Camilla left Miss Margland's tuition at the age of ten and thereafter benefited solely from her parents' guidance—nothing whatsoever is said of the curriculum they provided her—she might possibly have made better choices had her first tutress been a competent guide. Given Tyrold's remarks about her upbringing, however, one suspects that a competent governess may not have been wanted. Camilla's minimalist education and her "nature," which may well be the result—

marked by an airy thoughtlessness which is "a source of perpetual amusement" to her family (p. 51)—are conceivably to blame for her moral uncertainty as how to proceed in a series of difficult straits, for she *is* faced with a long series of difficult choices and makes a series of significant errors. Women are deliberately not educated, says Burney bitterly—who received no formal education—and see the result. The letter of Dr. Tyrold, taken at face value, was very popular in its time and, continuing to be read literally, has since contributed to a view of Burney as a cowardly conservative. It should instead be read as an example of the oblique technique forced upon women writers and as a parody of Gregory designed to show the pernicious effect of *not* equipping young women to make informed decisions and of the crippling of them even by their loving fathers so as to wrench from them the power of choice that should be theirs.

The conduct books, then, put pressure on women to stress their sensibility, to conceal their sense and ability to reason, to remain deferential and contingent. These pressures should be remembered when we consider the choices the women investigated in the following chapters made when they were free to make choices in their relationships with companions. Perhaps the extent of these pressures can be better assessed through resorting once more to the radical Charles Pigott, who, in *The Female Jockey Club*, vindictively characterizes and blames the bluestocking Lady Lucan as a hypocritical pretender to sensibility, "her sensations so delicately acute, that the slightest accident terrifies her out of her little wits. She faints at the approach of a mouse; if surprised by the sight of a black lobster, she screams unmercifully, and over the fictions of woe, she will shed innumerable tears; while she can behold with more than stoical composure, with frozen apathy, the deepest scenes of real distress."[32] Moreover, Lady Lucan, though thoroughly irrational, pretends to rationality. Her tongue, in eternal motion, expresses little, and she poses pretentious questions impossible to answer. She is guilty on two counts: she lacks the true womanly sensibility that she pretends to have, and in an unwomanly fashion she pretends to an intellectuality she also does not possess. She ought to have possessed sensibility and ought not to have pretended to intellectuality, so as a woman she is a complete failure.

THE EIGHTEENTH CENTURY had its own way of looking at what we call altruism: it was the product of sensibility, and it was called benevolence.[33] La Rochefoucauld had suggested the existence of nothing but self-love. I have noted Shaftesbury's influential endorsement of social love as endemic to human nature. In 1740 in his *Inquiry Concerning the Principles of Morals*, David Hume sounded what is perhaps a middle note when he suggested that every individual had both self-regarding and other-regarding desires but that those who practiced other-regarding behavior were also selfishly pleasing themselves. This point of view, carried further to claim that humans had *only* self-regarding impulses, has often been used to detract from the sum of moral virtue that might otherwise have been considered inherent in self-sacrifice. Theorists about altruism have continued to alternate between one or other of these views. William Godwin in 1793 adopted Shaftesbury's terms, noted the authors aligned on either side of the question, and opted for the real existence of human benevolence.

The recommendation of sensibility to women derives from this debate. But several more recent views of altruism also cast insights back concerning the choices available to eighteenth-century women in regard to their relationships with one another. The theory of Anna Freud that children learn to use different defense mechanisms against pain postulates that both aggression and altruism are such defenses.[34] Through identification with the aggressor the victim alleviates anxiety and fear by *becoming* the aggressor. I am not aware that this concept has yet been broadly applied to problems of gender and the victims of patriarchy, but Lillian Feder has suggested its broad application to explain a whole society's endorsement of a punitive leader.[35] Freud's theory of identification with the aggressor usefully illuminates the tyrannical practices of some women once they are empowered over others.

The women discussed in this book seem to exhibit examples of two different kinds of identifiers with aggressors. One kind appears to commit a premature suttee so as to submerge herself in a male, become his extension, his right hand, his agent, thus both acquiring his power and avoiding the pain of knowing herself as a separate, inferior being. Such women are Clarissa Howe's sister and Mother Sinclair in Samuel Richardson's *Clarissa*, the wicked Jewkes in his *Pamela*, and Mary Delany's sister-in-law (chapter 8). Other women so determinedly imitate male tyrants and internalize them that they have become tyrants on their own account. Such women, typically liberated by financial independence and spinsterhood or widowhood, are Lady B. in *Pamela*, Aunt Western in Henry Fielding's *Tom Jones*, and Elizabeth Chudleigh (chapter 4).

But Anna Freud diagnosed a second possible mechanism of defense:

altruism. For her, altruism involves "the surrender of instinctual wishes to an object better qualified to fulfill them" (p. 131). The altruistic person who desires the happiness of personal fulfillment but cannot attain it finds happiness instead in helping other people whose problems are easier to solve. In formulating this conception of altruism as a self-suppressing strategy, even a form of symbolic suicide, Anna Freud denies Shaftesbury's or Godwin's conception of benevolence as a natural human trait and confirms the psychoanalytical bias toward an explanation of altruism that makes it always basically selfish. Her explanation of altruism is particularly unennobling.

Recent students of altruism, however, have made other points that are interesting in regard to eighteenth-century women's choices, which, as we will see, leaned significantly, as the century progressed, toward what we would call altruism. Altruism is seen in evolutionary theory as self-sacrifice for the benefit of others, but in actual practice as requiring the added component of a subjective intent to make the sacrifice. It is a regard for the interests and welfare of others, the direct opposite of aggression, which is a form of hostile encroachment on others. One question relevant to this discussion is whether it is not to the advantage of social groups to assign altruistic behavior to certain members, thus increasing the fitness of the group as a whole (much recourse to beehive and ant society models). From this viewpoint, women and clergymen could be the ones assigned the burden of altruism or care-giving, leaving the bulk of the male population to carry out aggressive behavior necessary for group survival. Another persisting question is whether any such quality as genuinely unselfish altruism exists. Emile Durkheim considers altruism to be as deeply rooted as its opposite in our natures but considers that as there is egoism in our altruism, so there is altruism in our egoism.[36] M. T. Ghiselin has postulated that opportunism and exploitation underlie every seemingly altruistic act in nature: "Scratch an 'altruist,' and watch a 'hypocrite' bleed."[37] If this were so, then every nurturing woman would be a hypocrite. J. Philippe Rushton, however, postulates the existence of a truly altruistic personality, a personality more mature, more integrated, and perhaps more highly evolved than others. It is certainly this kind of person that Sarah Scott, Lady Bab Montagu, Sarah Fielding, Frances Burney, Frances Greville, Lady Spencer, Molly Carter, and other of the women considered here were trying to be:

He or she has internalized higher and more universalized standards of justice, social responsibility, and modes of moral reasoning, judgment, and knowledge, and/or he or she is more empathetic to the feelings and sufferings of others and able to see the world from their emotional and motivational perspective. . . . This person is likely . . . to engage in a great variety of altruistic behaviors . . . giving . . . comforting . . . reassuring. Altruists also behave consistently more honestly, persistently, and with greater self-control than do non-altruists. . . . This person will have a *reputation* for being altruistic among his or her peers and colleagues. . . . [She] is likely to have an integrated personality, strong feelings of personal efficacy and well-being, and what generally might be called "integrity." [38]

Sarah Scott and her friend Lady Bab Montagu certainly seem the quintessential representatives of this type, a type that obviously had to have not only strong sensibility but a well-developed moral sense, clear reasoning powers, and the freedom to make moral choices.

In regard to the altruistic women of this book, Carol Gilligan's thesis in her two books, *In a Different Voice* and *Mapping the Moral Domain*, [39] should also be mentioned: weren't these women in fact using a different standard such as the one Gilligan suggests, one that made moral choices dependent upon which ones hurt the fewest people? Finally, Nancy Armstrong notes that by the beginning of the nineteenth century "the two forms of desire—acquisitiveness and altruism"—had been gender-assigned, with doing good to others assigned, of course, to women, and had by that time "thoroughly reorganized sexual relations." [40]

A glance at Sarah Scott's utopian novel *A Description of Millenium Hall* (1762) will help establish the mental accommodations to some of the influences of her time made by a woman of the period who was economically independent, morally mature, free to make her own choices, and desirous of making the world a better place for its victims. Scott was not born an altruist; she became one after a series of misfortunes (chapter 13). In her book almost every imaginable kind of tyranny is remedied in a utopia administered by women; such victims as animals, the deformed, and the poor are all befriended and find a place. Industries are founded to employ them and villages to house them. The tyranny of marriage, however, is little touched upon. Millenium Hall is administered by a group of five women, all of whom have had sad experiences with men; but only one of these is an actual husband, and his worst tyranny is his determination to separate his wife from her cherished friend. The Hall shelters single gentlewomen who could not have managed alone so that marriage is banned in this heart of the community; but Scott writes that the community was formed (unlike Astell's early one, designed to enable women to remain single) to save women from the degrading fate of *humble companionship*. Obviously there was by 1762 a taboo of some force on speaking out in print against marriage for women. Consequently, no mention is made of the problem of battered wives or children, surely a matter for serious concern at the time.[41] Sarah Scott had no intention of taking on the patriarchs in regard to marriage, and she used the institution of humble companionship in the place of marriage in this book, attacking it vigorously, claiming that the Hall was founded to provide women with a better alternative. Furthermore, the women who run Millenium Hall justify their single state to their male visitors because they could not have undertaken their work had they been married and at the disposal of their several husbands. Scott was an altruist; she wanted to ameliorate the lot of the victims she had always seen around her; she and her circle planned a utopia that would ameliorate the lot of victims; but they were unable, unlike Astell, openly to recommend the single life for women who wanted to accomplish anything beyond the superintendence of a house and family, and thus they had to speak in parables. Apparently one of the most important, perhaps *the* most important, unbroachable subject for women of the period was their desire for equality in marriage.

WOMEN CAN BE FOUND working in combination with each other again and again in this book. Those combinations that together chose the first term of the dichotomy outlined above—that is, tyranny, or self-regarding behavior, or identification with the aggressor, or the desire for acquisition (granted that these are terms in similar, if not identical, dichotomies)—no doubt realized certain benefits. In this group are Sophia Baddeley and Elizabeth Steele (chapter 9), the Parrs, mother and daughter, and the fictitious Mitissa and her maid (chapter 7). Generally speaking, their aggression was turned outward upon the world of men; to each other they appear to have acted with kindness, consideration, and the close-knit loyalty of coconspirators. They may have experienced a sense of increased power, of shared endeavor, of strengthened purpose. But their fates suggest that few such conspirators, certainly not these, prospered for long. For their economic designs upon their masters they were punished as examples.

Women who in pairs or groups opted for the opposite terms of the same dichotomies—that is, benevolence, other-regarding behavior, altruism, or the desire for it—were far more prosperous, especially in regard to self-development and growth. Could this have been only because instead of being cut off in their careers, they were allowed to continue in them? Does it mean that by the kind of hothouse pruning and training John Stuart Mill describes,[42] they were discouraged from one reaction to their political situation, encouraged in another, and molded into care givers? In any case, they reaped comparatively few financial rewards by combination but were often greatly strengthened by it. Frances Greville drew support from Lady Spencer; Spencer had a wide network of charitable co-workers. Lady Clarges and Molly Carter each nurtured the other into important self-growth. And the Bath community of women (chapter 13) is one of the most important of women's groups ever to have existed; it generated ideas and books that never could have emanated from single isolated women.

After having studied combinations of eighteenth-century women for several years, it is my opinion that, more than men, women were by the second half of the century likely to come together for tacitly or avowedly altruistic purposes, that combinations of women, unable to meet for aggressive purposes (as in regiments), unlikely to meet for overtly deliberative purposes (as in judicial or governmental bodies), condemned to meet only for social purposes, had begun to discover in charitable societies and purposes a challenging as well as acceptable use for their talents.

When the cluster of contemporary women, all born about 1720, are considered here—Elizabeth Chudleigh, Elizabeth Montagu, Frances Greville, Sarah Scott, and Elizabeth Vesey—it appears that for them a variety of models of behavior were still accessible. For women born after midcentury, like Frances Burney, Dorothea Gregory, and Louisa Clarges, there were fewer options, and the one model proclaimed "natural" to women by John Gregory had become almost obligatory, as had the burden of benevolence.

Related to the question of whether women were increasingly choosing altruism as their official mode during the century—which they were—is the question of their attitude to hierarchy, a question crucial to the choices they made in the arrangements of their combinations. Both equality and altruism are ideals more attractive, even more imaginable, to people used to thinking of themselves as politically inferior rather than superior. I hope I will demonstrate here that, in their portrayals of companionship combinations, many women writers, unlike most male writers, consistently indicated the moral corruption bred in both superior and inferior by hierarchically structured relationships. That in spite of their recurrent demonstration women writers of reputation did not then call openly for an end to inequality between genders, classes, or races can best be understood as an effect of their having to a great extent chosen the tactics of indirection and gradualism because they wanted to be published and read.[43] William Godwin, whose awareness of the moral damage to both the upper and the lower orders in a hierarchical society must to some considerable extent have derived from the work of such women as are considered here, was able in his *Enquiry Concerning Political Justice* (1793) to demand social equality for all as a necessary remedy. But Mary Wollstonecraft, in her *Vindication of the Rights of Woman* (1792), still asks only for equal education for women and asks it only to increase benefits to men and their children. Nevertheless, I hope it will become apparent to readers of this book that writers such as Frances Burney, Sarah Fielding, Jane Collier, Sarah Scott, and Charlotte Smith were often positively, and considerably more than has been recognized, subversive and effectively subversive of the prevailing ideology of the time. Such women were quietly experimenting with alternative models for relationships, for different ways of regarding others and even for ameliorating society.

There are, after all, at least three ways of looking at the increasing incidence of altruistic middle- and upper-class women in the course of the eighteenth century. First, it may reflect a passive acquiescence to a newly assigned role intended to differentiate the genders by removing women as much as possible from competition with men. Second, it may reflect an accommodation by women who saw in it a new opportunity to exercise unopposed and publicly, as well as privately, their talents for organization and leadership. But finally, for some women it offered scope for devising alternative and improved methods of governing social affairs, which also exposed the old patriarchal systems to reappraisal.

Chapter Two

THE SOCIOECONOMICS

A Widow Lady, free from all Incumbrences, having been rather unfortunate in her Connections, regarding Circumstances, would be happy to recommend herself to a Lady as a Companion, or, if required, to superintend the Family, having kept House herself; she is in every Respect qualified for such an Undertaking, and makes no Doubt of acquitting herself to give entire Satisfaction; her Disposition is naturally chearful, and she flatters herself she may be agreeable to any Lady whom this may suit, and will do her the Favour to enquire after her. She is to be heard of at Mrs Saunders's, No 99, Cheapside, Tomorrow or Thursday.
—*Daily Advertiser*, Tuesday, June 16, 1772

Wanted, a well-bred young Gentlewoman, as a Housekeeper and Companion (but not a Mistress) for a Man above 40, as Trust and Confidence will be reposed it is hoped none but of unblemished character will answer this. A line directed to A.B. at the Duke-Street Coffee-House, facing the Chapel, Lincoln's-Inn Fields, signifying where the Party may be spoken with, will be attended to.
—*Daily Advertiser*, Tuesday, June 23, 1772

A Young Widow, about 28, whose Circumstances oblige her to have Resource to Servitude, would be happy to wait on an elderly Lady; she thinks herself capable of undertaking the Place of a Nursery-Maid, where there are not many children; can work well at her Needle, understands getting up small Linen, and can bear Confinement; her Strength will not permit her to undertake any Thing that is laborious; she has been genteely brought up, and can have an undeniable Character. Please to direct for A.B. at No. 2, Falcon Court, Lothbury.
—*Daily Advertiser*, Tuesday, June 30, 1772

Wanted by a Widow Gentlewoman who has no Family, any decent sober Woman to live with her, who can maintain herself as to board, and will keep a small Apartment in order; she may have Lodging and Fire for her Trouble. Any Person this may suit, who can be well recommended and likes Retirement, please to leave a Line, where she may be seen, for A.B. at Mr. Botvyle's a Tinshop, No 122, Fleet-Street.   —*Daily Advertiser*, Tuesday, July 7, 1772

A Widow Lady about 40, of Family, Character, and Education, would like to superintend a single Gentleman's Family that is but small, and who is a Man of Good Morals, and not under the same Age. The Lady expects to be treated as a Friend and Companion, as no Salary is required unless the Gentleman has Children, and should like the Lady to act in the Capacity of a Governess, being properly qualified to undertake the Care of Young Ladies; has no Objection to Town or Country. Please to enquire for J.B. at No. 14, Cloak-Lane, Queen-Street, Cheapside, from the Hours of Eleven to Four; or Letters directed (Post-paid) to J.B. at the said Place shall be immediately answered.

—Daily Advertiser, Tuesday, July 7, 1772

A Gentlewoman with a small income, whose Husband is abroad, for the Sake of Company and being employed, would be glad to superintend an elderly Lady's or Gentleman's Family, in the Capacity of a Companion at leisure Hours: No other Gratuity is required than genteel Treatment; Age about 30; if the Country more agreeable. Please to inquire of Mr. Hall, Linnen-Draper, in Parliament-Street; or a Line left there directed for H.S. shall be answered immediately.

—Daily Advertiser, Tuesday, July 14, 1772

A Young Person genteely educated and of undoubted Character, is desirous of being a Companion to a Lady, or Governess to a Young Lady, she can speak French, and other genteel Accomplishments; and as it is not for lucrative Views, should not chuse to be ranked as a Servant; no Objection to travel. Please to address a Line for A.E. at Mrs. Bennet's, in Devonshire-Street, Queen Square.

—Daily Advertiser, Thursday, July 16, 1772

A MONTH'S NEWSPAPER ADVERTISEMENTS, from June 16 to July 16, 1772, inserted by persons requiring companions or applying for such posts, well indicates the difficulty of defining the position. The *Oxford English Dictionary* gives as its seventh definition of *companion,* "A person who lives with another in need of society, and who, though receiving remuneration, is treated rather as a friend and equal than as an inferior and servant. (Now usually of women.)" But the position admitted of a host of variations. A female companion might attend a gentleman; she might be either a woman or a lady; and she often doubled as housekeeper, governess, lady's maid, nursery maid, paying guest, or (despite the denial of the gentleman who advertised above) mistress. In the middle class she usually doubled as something. The motherless girl required a companion who could also function as lady's maid and governess; the bachelor or widower required a companion-housekeeper. These companions often filled the important functions of absent wives or mothers. An older woman alone might also require a companion-housekeeper.

Only in the upper classes, which had separate servants for each function, does one find the pure humble companion, thoroughly genteel, dedicated to pouring out tea, reading to and walking with her employer, and unburdened by those reponsibilities of the lady's maid, the washing out of lace and the making up of small linen.

The more genteel the companion, the more incapacitated she was from performing the functions of paid servants and from receiving a salary so that the genuine distressed lady was more at the mercy of her benefactors than was the lowly servant girl. If dismissed, she was only a little less handicapped in her ability to find a new position than the wife. Her great object was to find a home—anyone's—to live in as a humble member of the family, and for a home she was willing to make herself useful at all hours. She was constantly in danger of the degradation of being asked to perform tasks beneath her station, of being snubbed, but a salary would have been an intolerable insult, a clear statement of her social inferiority. Thus in her dependency she was in a precarious position: without the right to remain under the family's protection except as she gave satisfaction from hour to hour and without the dependent daughter's modest right to a share of the family resources.

The reader of eighteenth-century newspaper advertisements for servants and places learns much about the family arrangements of the time; there was, for instance, a social scale for governesses ranging upward from those who also functioned as lady's maids to those who also functioned as companions and were fit company for the family. So it was too with companions. But as each marriage differs in some particulars from all others yet discovers general patterns, so with companionships. Some of the types of employer-companion relationships will be explored in this book, and the differences between the various relationships will be considered.

In the eighteenth century, women seeking posts as cooks, housekeepers, and lady's maids are many, while women seeking posts as companions are comparatively few. Doubtless most indigent gentlewomen were accommodated in the homes of relations where they may have been better off than in the homes of strangers, though in both cases they were, like the young widow of the third advertisement above, reduced to a "resource to servitude."

But in fact there *was* a need for companions in the middle and upper classes. Only working-class women could live solitary lives even at home, let alone out-of-doors; genteel women were to be found in braces or swarms. The companionship of husbands did not even enter the question; separate gender-determined assignments of both work and play made male-female companionship occasional, easy to avoid, even challenging to arrange. Middle-class husbands in trade or the professions worked long hours and took their diversion in all-male clubs meeting in the evenings in taverns. Well-to-do husbands often dined away from home and enjoyed regular rounds of diversion with their peers and their mistresses, often in groups. They left the running of their homes to their wives and in the country absented themselves to tend their estates or to hunt. Wives and husbands habitually made their visits separately, received them separately, went to diversions separately, and often made extended country visits separately. Husbands went to their clubs nightly while their wives went out to receptions, card parties, or the theater.[1] The problem for these wives was that if they did go out, they had to go accompanied in some manner. Her own footmen and chair might do for an evening engagement, her maid might do for shopping, but a woman needed the social endorsement of her peers, and she could not take her maid to the theater. A reliable companion always at hand was a great convenience.

In fact, a respectable woman without a sympathetic companion was seen as disadvantageously incomplete, and thus we find Richardson's heroine Pamela sending for Mrs. Jervis, and Smollett's heroine Lydia Melford sending for her schoolfellow on the approach of their weddings, apparently in genuine (or conventional) distress for want of proper female support. Henry Tilney in *Northanger Abbey* describes his sister as uncomfortably circumstanced at home because she is the only woman in the family and has no companion,[2] and it is part of the growing indictment of General Tilney that he is indifferent to her situation, which he is willing to ameliorate only when he wants to invite Catherine for a visit. But he then proceeds to isolate Catherine as well, even to the extent of sending her away unprovided for and by herself, so that she finds herself alone as she has never been before in her life—and copes very well. General Tilney is such a villain that he ignores the patriarchal rules about women, which respect the principle of noblesse oblige: if you infantilize women to the point that you have to take their fortunes from them, then you are also obliged to look after their physical well-being. But through selfish neglect he inadvertently does Catherine a great service by allowing her to test herself.

When women in novels of the period do go out alone, it is often a mark of purpose so strong that it overrides convention, a moment of strong moral conviction in the heroine, in which she knows she must act.

One thinks of Catherine Morland, usually in company with *someone* at Bath, indoors or out, hurrying alone "in great agitation, as fast as the crowd would permit her," to inform the Tilneys that she intends to keep her engagement with them (pp. 101–2); of Evelina almost stealing from Mrs. Beaumont's house in Bristol to meet Mr. Macartney alone, though it is with fear and trembling that she opens the garden gate and though her action strongly excites Lord Orville's curiosity.[5] But even if born of desperate need and moral conviction, such adventures, which flout convention, can lead to distresses: Sarah Scott's heroine Cornelia, forced to flee from home alone (*Cornelia*, 1750), suffers all the gothic assaults. (When Scott reworked this theme in 1754, her heroine Leonora took companions with her.) The heroine of Amelia Opie's *Adeline Mowbray* (1804) is exposed to various forms of insult when she goes, even with a boy escort, to consult a lawyer. And such adventures can be associated with deeper troubles: novelists at the end of the period regularly explored the crucially interesting question of how women might fare alone, and their heroines all encountered difficulties. Sometimes, like Juliet, heroine of Frances Burney's *Wanderer* (1814), or Ellen Percy, heroine of Mary Brunton's *Discipline* (1815), they elected the test of solitary adventure and responsibility for their own maintenance, suffered great tribulation, and survived, having acquired a sobering knowledge of the world otherwise reserved for men. Sometimes, as in the case of the kidnapped Laura Montreville, heroine of Mary Brunton's *Self-Control* (1811), they entered the solitary adventure involuntarily, but survived, with the same heavy boon of knowledge. The worst kind of isolation, however, that of Frances Burney's heroines Cecilia and Camilla at the end of their respective adventures, is symptomatic of breakdown under the burden of patriarchal indifference and rejection and involves almost mortal distress; the cards have been so stacked that these heroines were unable to survive alone. However they resolved it, women writers were much concerned about the question of women's ability to manage on their own.

The comic exegesis of this social situation is Mrs. Mittin in *Camilla*, who has two modes of disguise, one genteel, one working woman, so that when she wants to save expense by trudging it alone on foot, she whisks on the working woman, becoming in the process invisible to her fine friends, but in her genteel aspect she travels like Camilla, decorously, in a group. Burney develops more seriously in *The Wanderer* the point that lower-class disguise offers liberation of a kind to the genteel woman, and conversely, that the genteel woman is imprisoned by convention. Juliet in *The Wanderer* adopts a working-class disguise to escape from France and a series of working-woman disguises in England. Because she must live in isolation, her assumption of working-class status is almost a necessary convenience quite apart from the requirement that she support herself. To underline this theme of the genteel woman's need of disguise to escape restriction, Elinor Joddrel, more daring and less prudent, adopts the dress of a man.

In actuality, of course, women could and did live "alone," but this was possible only when they had sufficient income to maintain a proper staff of servants, ideally, a housekeeper, two maids, and a footman. The footman would offer sufficient protection both indoors and out to a woman of mature years. But a handsome young woman would not have been considered safe alone even in her own establishment. Probably a significant number of older women lived alone, though the "many old maids who inhabit Milman Street and Chapel Row," "the little knot of unmarried females turned fifty round Red Lion Square" mentioned by Hester Thrale, may some of them have been living in pairs.[4] She considered these women, however, less fortunate than a community of nuns, though she did think of them as also living in community. Even so she suggests that, because these lone Englishwomen might be robbed or insulted by servants in the decline of life, or ruined by runaway agents, bankrupted bankers, or roguish stewards, the nuns were safer and luckier. Having a companion was the most efficient way to obviate all the difficulties posed by the requirement that women live and travel in companies.

Moreover, married women also needed companions. Familial social responsibilities were relegated to wives so that women of position needed consultants. The social arrangements of a family could be very important, and the wife—guided by her husband's wishes—made decisions about who to visit and cultivate, when to cease acquaintance, who to entertain, and who to introduce to her children. The daughters' marriages, like the sons', were of great importance, and it was the mother who was credited with any coup.[5] Friends, likely to have rival agendas, could not often be relied upon as allies, and women needed faithful coadjutors as fellow conspirators, deputies, consultants, confidantes, social secretaries, and supports.

Companions could also run errands, convey messages, and soothe domestic turmoils. They were there to dine when company was wanted, to fill in at a card table, to play and sing, and to provide music for dancing or to fill in a set as needed. They could be counted upon to regard themselves as contingent creatures with every genteel accomplishment, including that of knowing when to make themselves useful and when to retire gracefully.

Finally, they could function as receptacles of personal confidences, as did the companion of Lady Tempest (modeled on Lady Townshend) in Francis Coventry's *History of Pompey the Little* (1751). Of Lord and Lady Tempest Coventry writes:

> They sat down to Meals with Indifference; they went to bed with Indifference; and the one was always sure to dislike what the other at any Time seemed to approve. Her Ladyship had Recourse to the common Expedient in these Cases, I mean the getting a Female Companion into the House with her, as well to relieve her from the Tediousness of sitting down to Meals alone with her Husband, as chiefly to hear her Complaints, and spirit her up against her Fool and Tyrant; the Names by which she usually spoke of her Lord and Master. When no such Female Companions, or more properly *Toad eaters*, happened to be present, she chose rather to divert herself with a little favourite Dog, than to murder any of her precious Time in conversing with her Husband.[6]

Such companions as Lady Tempest's kept close company with their mistresses, and not for their own happiness but for the sake of the pride of their mistresses they were politely acknowledged to be of equal class, just as wives were acknowledged to be of equal class with their husbands. Because they could not be stigmatized as the recipients of salaries, companions usually had to be provided for by judiciously and sometimes injudiciously bestowed gifts, and making their needs known must have been a matter of exceedingly delicate negotiation.[7] Because they lived in the house as social equals, they inevitably took on the coloration of dependent family members. The family member most serviceable in the home was the wife, and it therefore followed logically that women often treated their companions as wives were treated, that women with companions were in a sense women who had *found* wives.

The compelling social reasons for women to live in groups rather than singly were strong in themselves, but even more compelling were the economic reasons. Only the luckiest of unattached women could have afforded at that time to live in comfort on their own. The necessity, if the family and its power were to come first, was that most of the money and property had to be concentrated in the possession of the eldest son; then, if all went well, the women and the younger sons could benefit from the family shelter. Neither, however, could be spared sufficient endowments of money to bestow independence. Younger sons were more fortunate: they got a start in the services or the professions; the family interest could help them onward; and they might marry profitably. The daughters could do nothing for themselves except endeavor to marry profitably by capitalizing on their dowries. Those who wasted their opportunities might pay heavily and sometimes had only themselves to blame.

An examination of the affairs of two of the daughters of George Montagu, Earl of Halifax—Ann, who married, and Barbara, who did not—shows how the settlements made on daughters could be used to advantage. The earl was not rich, having gambled away much of his substance, and he had six daughters and a single son. The daughters were assigned £5,000 apiece, a modest sum for an earl's daughter, though not to their brother, who had to find and relinquish £30,000 to portion them off, a sum now worth at least $3 million.[8]

The brother, George Montagu, the second earl, solved his problems by marrying in 1741 the heiress of an ironmonger with £100,000, though to marry her he had to change his name to Dunk. He does not thereafter appear to have been a benefactor to his one unmarried sister, and, perhaps significantly, she seems never to have lived with him.

Ann Montagu took her £5,000 to her marriage with Joseph Jekyll; they had one daughter, and Jekyll predeceased his wife. At her death in 1766, quite apart from the estate, Dallington, which went to the daughter with many of the family valuables, Lady Ann Jekyll left £7,500 in stocks and bonds, a furnished house in Brook Street, and many other effects still to be sold.[9] Marriage had multiplied her talents, though largely because she had had no son.

Had her sister Barbara invested her £5,000 in the safe government bonds known as the three or three-and-a-half percents, she would have had an annual income of about £150, on which she must have lived like a pauper compared to Lady Ann Jekyll. With such an income she would ordinarily have been obliged to live under her brother's roof or that of one of her sisters. But she was in ill health all her life, and besides not wishing to burden any of her connections, to whom she could have been of little assistance, she was in best health at Bath. Some people who knew they would never marry converted their money into annuities, and Montagu, who was not, as they then termed it, "a good life," might have doubled her income by doing so. She probably consulted her brother, for money sunk into an annuity was indeed "sunk," or lost to the family. Her brother appears to have solved this problem by buying with her an annuity for two lives, hers and his, toward which she probably paid £2,000, for at her death she was possessed of an annuity worth £100 a year, which reverted to him, and £3,000.[10] If she had indeed purchased the annuity with her missing £2,000, she received 5 percent on her investment during each year of her life, not a bargain because she had lost the capital sum. In any case, her income was probably just under £200 a year, and with it she maintained herself at Bath, living the simple life of an invalid, when fortuitously Sarah Scott, who had even less of her own, joined incomes with her (chapter 13).

Luck was always a factor. The first earl had provided in his will that, should any of his daughters die before the age of twenty-one or before marriage, their portions were to be divided among the other unmarried daughters. Had Lady Mary Montagu, who died in 1743, only three years after marriage, died before marriage, Barbara, the only daughter still unmarried, would have had £10,000, a more adequate fortune for an earl's daughter.

But it was never intended that women should be provided with money sufficient to allow them to live independently; they were always intended to be dependent on father, husband, brother, or son. Had Lady Ann Jekyll had a son, he would have inherited the estate and other effects on his father's death, his sister would have had only a stipulated marriage settlement, and his mother would have had her widow's jointure, probably of about £500 a year.[11] This return of almost 10 percent on her fortune, though awarded only on her husband's death, far exceeded the return an unmarried daughter saw on the same investment. The dowry, often paid down in cash or conveyed in land, was worth a great deal; husbands took the cash and paid a moderate interest in pin money (or spending money) to their wives.[12] The widow's jointure was a problem to be confronted by their heirs.

Obviously, in addition to the social pressure, the financial pressure on women to marry was great. A carefully contracted marriage represented by far the best return on their fathers' investments in their behalf. Louisa Skrine, the illegitimate daughter of a rich apothecary's son and a courtesan, with a dowry of £8,000, made a brilliant marriage to Sir Thomas Clarges; he died young and left her a large fortune, and in her will she disposed of almost £40,000 (chapter 12). Elizabeth Montagu, with a dowry (probably) of £1,000, married an older man of fortune who left her all he had, which provided her an income of between £7,000 and £10,000 a year (chapter 6). Her sister Sarah Scott married a poor man for love, separated from him, and lived on the edge of penury all her life (chapter 13). A woman who did not look for an advantageous marriage was counted foolish; a woman who rejected an advantageous offer could not expect such luck a second time but could expect forever after to be counted responsible for her own misfortunes. It was within this context that Frances Burney had the courage to refuse the unobjectionable and comparatively prosperous Thomas Barlow (chapter 4) and Dorothea Gregory the courage to refuse Matthew Montagu (chapter 6); those who found them foolish had the comfort of seeing that they never did grow rich. But a careless marriage for love could involve a woman in a lifetime of deprivation. Not many women had the luck or the sangfroid of the great heiress to £50,000 or £60,000 a year, Mary Edwards, who was apparently married in 1731 at the Fleet to Lord Anne Hamilton, a rake and wastrel, and who, when he began to waste her money, paid to have the marriage expunged from the books.[13]

Thus economics even more than social convention dictated whether a woman could live alone. To set up alone would mean a drop in the standard of living of any lady. A dowry of £10,000 was the sum that could be regarded, minimally, as a good fortune; it was the conventional dowry of a duke's daughter, who might be calculated to bring a great deal to the marriage in influence as well. At the usual safe rate of interest, such a fortune would have yielded its possessor an annual £300 or £350, an income equivalent to $30,000 or $35,000 in today's currency. On that income she could not have maintained a house and staff, dress, and a carriage in London. Therefore, even were her fortune actually in her possession (which was not likely, for a woman ordinarily lived on a stipulated allowance until she married, when her fortune was paid into her husband's hands), she would have had the options, if she did not marry, of sharing housekeeping with family or friends, of living with a brother or sister, or of moving quietly out of London and forgoing most of the privileges of society she had formerly enjoyed.

When Agmondesham Vesey died in 1785 and failed to remember his wife in his will, so that she was left with her jointure, the lease on her London house, and the income of her companion, Mrs. Handcock (chapter 10), Mrs. Vesey's friends calculated the combined income of the two women at about £800 and agonized that the ailing Vesey would probably not be able to afford her own carriage. Probably an income of £1,000 was the minimal requirement for the maintenance of a full London establishment. Burney's Cecilia paid £250 a year just for the privilege of boarding and lodging with the fashionable Harrels. Presumably that payment entitled her to the use of a carriage. But she still had the expensive item of dress to pay—a court dress could cost £50—servants to keep, and sums for such perpetual expenses as books, subscriptions, vails (or obligatory tips to the servants of hosts), gifts, and charities to disburse, all of which must at least have doubled the basic sum she required, and this without the comfort of her own establishment.

Anne Boone, an unmarried woman well-known in society, lived in Tunbridge instead of London, for one could live more economically at Tunbridge or Bath, and one's friends would come there at their own expense. In 1782 she was left money that provided her with about £600 a year to live on, "so that she may do very well," reported Caroline Howe to Lady Spencer. She was also left a house in Tunbridge, into which she quietly settled, and a house in London, which she let.[14] Lady Spencer's response was that £600 a year with a house of her own would do very well for a single woman if she was careful, though she thought that Boone gave away a lot in charity. Apparently, even with her own house in London and £600 a year, Boone did not care to try to keep up.[15]

Sarah Scott faces all such vulgar economic considerations in *Millenium Hall;* she is perhaps the most precise of all the women novelists about women's need for money and understands that the lack of money underlies most of the difficulties women experienced. Miss Selvyn, one of the founders of the Hall, had been unable with a fortune of £3,000 to live in London with convenience,[16] and women with fortunes of £2,000 (or $200,000) sought admission to the community, "the expensive turn of the world now being such, that no gentlewoman can live genteelly on the interest of that sum" even out of London (pp. 87–88).

One can check these calculations by the case of Hester Greville, the unmarried sister of an heir to many estates, Fulke Greville, who lived in princely fashion and squandered all he could lay his hands on. After he had ruined himself, his wife, his children, his mother, and his sisters, Hester still possessed £3,200 in the three-and-a-half percents, the income from which could not maintain her in the quiet suburban establishment—for they had long since had to give up London society—that she had shared with her mother. Her married sister, who had procured a place for herself in Princess Amelia's court, obtained for her one of those apartments at Hampton Court set aside for genteel sufferers, where she quietly and penuriously lived out her existence.[17]

Many of the women at Millenium Hall could not have maintained themselves there. On entering the community, the women contributed their fortunes; in return they received their board and lodging, all the amenities, and £25 pocket and dress money annually. Visitors to the community who had not been accepted as permanent members paid £100 a year and in addition provided their own pocket and dress allowance. Simply to be able thus to afford visitors' expenses of approximately

£125 a year, women would have had to possess fortunes of about £4,000. If they were accepted as members of the community, however, they might enter with far less, some with no more than a hundred pounds, others with £2,000 or more.

Scott repudiated the idea of marriage for women who had any work to do in the world; the women who ran the Hall community were all single. But apparently unwilling to attack marriage openly, she saved her *avowed* detestation for the complementary expedient of becoming a humble companion; that position, she stated publicly, was degrading and morally corrupting. The Millenium Hall community was in large part conceived from compassion at the wretched fate of those

who from scantiness of fortune, and pride of family, are reduced to become dependent, and to bear all the insolence of wealth, from such as will receive them into their families; these, though in some measure voluntary slaves, yet suffer all the evils of the severest servitude, and are, I believe, the most unhappy part of the creation. Sometimes they are unqualified to gain a maintenance, educated, as it is called, genteelly, or, in other words, idly, they are ignorant of every thing that might give them superior abilities to the lower rank of people, and their birth renders them less acceptable servants to many. . . . Possibly pride may still oftener reduce these indigent gentlewomen into this wretched state of dependance, and therefore the world is less inclined to pity them. (p. 82)

All that Scott said was equally applicable to wives. Like Astell, who had earlier designed a community for single women, Scott was subtly suggesting that communities of women could provide an alternative to marriage and voluntary servitude. She was thinking of both wives and humble companions when she observed that a common attribute of humble companions was a pride that would not allow them to seek out some lower but more useful form of employment.

If we are despised for casual deficiencies, we naturally seek in ourselves for some merit, to restore us to that dignity in our own eyes, which those humiliating mortifications would otherwise debase. Thus we learn to set too great a value on what we still possess, whether advantages of birth, education, or natural talents; any thing will serve for a resource to mortified pride. . . . To persons in this way of thinking, the pride which reduces many to be, what is called with too little humanity, toad-eaters, does not render them unworthy of compassion. Therefore for the relief of that race they bought that large mansion. (pp. 82–83)

Anything will serve for a resource to mortified pride. The debased wife takes pride in the stateliness of her husband; the debased companion takes pride in the glories both of her own lineage and of that which now offers her a refuge. Scott's remedy is for the woman to step down in station and find self-esteem in useful work. Implicit in her prescription is a judgment that station is not the important index to worth, hierarchy not sacred.

When at Millenium Hall the plight of Lady Mary Jones on the death of her aunt, who has supported her, is discussed, the expedient of Lady Mary's going for a companion is denigrated: "She saw no resource but in the pride of some insolent woman, who would like to have a person of her quality dependant on her; a prospect far worse than death" (p. 148). Scott would have rendered the same verdict on a loveless marriage.

Though the tyranny of marriage is rarely directly addressed in this book, it is an important theme of the novel. And it is feasible whenever the institution of companionship is denigrated to read therein a denigration of the usual form of marriage. Scott, in her description of the pride of companions, comprehends the pride of wives like her sister Elizabeth Montagu, who, both humiliated and depreciated, yet took solace in their origin from impressive fathers and their connections to impressive brothers or husbands. They were "voluntary slaves" suffering "all the evils of the severest servitude," many of them too ignorant, and educated too genteelly (idly), to be useful.

Scott's point was the result of deliberations made in a community of women and inspired by one original thinker, Sarah Fielding, a member of Scott's Bath circle, an extraordinary Bath group of women in the 1750s and 1760s. There was a great deal of mutual influence among them, but as we will find in chapter 3, it is Fielding who first conflates the situations of companionship and marriage. In her *History of the Countess of Dellwyn* (1759), Miss Weare, left at twenty-one with an inadequate provision, from pride as much as from incapacity, first spends her capital to maintain herself, hoping a husband will rescue her, then accepts an invitation from the divorced and discredited Lady Dellwyn to accompany her to France. At first agreeing only to attend her mistress abroad, she at last consents to return to England with her, thus accomplishing the complete ruin of her own reputation. Fielding's quarrel with Miss Weare's behavior is that she has preferred to blast her reputation rather than to quit her rank and living standard. Her first solution was to find a master, her second, a mistress, but in either case she sought nothing but a provider from whom she could extort a fashionable maintenance by ministering subserviently, and in the case of marriage as in the case of companionship there would have been no pretense of making a moral choice; there was no consideration but expediency. The suggestion of both Fielding and Scott is that poorly educated genteel women marry and take positions as companions from an unworthy desire to continue to live as they did in their fathers' houses, but that if they would put away their pride, they might find independence and self-sufficiency in a lower sphere.

Carolyn Woodward has pointed out that in this novel Fielding follows Mary Astell and precedes Scott in proposing what became the Millenium Hall scheme when she writes of a couple who "hired a large House as a Receptacle for Gentlewomen, who either had no Fortunes, or so little that it would not support them. For these they made the most comfortable Institution . . . [and] provided [them] with all Conveniences for rural Amusements, a Library, musical Instruments, and Implements for various Works." [18]

Woodward has noted Fielding's tendency to form communities of women—particularly with the Colliers—and also identifies a women's community in *The Adventures of David Simple*. There is every indication that Fielding was an important originating force behind the Bath community, its ideals, and actions. But Jane Collier (see chapter 3) was an important influence on Fielding. Woodward has also pointed out that it was after Fielding had worked with Collier on *The Cry* (1754) that the focus of her work shifted to women's lives. [19]

Many women besides Scott and Fielding understood that it was bad for the character of a woman to toady. Amelia Opie, in her serious investigation of marriage in *Adeline Mowbray*, includes as an important component of the plot the devious, selfish behavior of Miss Woodville, Mrs. Mowbray's companion, a dog in the manger who from fear of losing her place and her influence suppresses Adeline's letters to her mother, keeps them separated for years, and is therefore instrumental in causing Adeline's death. This young woman's ruling passion is avarice, her greatest talent, cunning. [20] The mother and daughter, doubles, are kept from union by this scheming and self-serving inferior. Most women knew, if men did not, that enforced submission, even for the course of a lifetime, does not produce genuinely altruistic character, however altruistic the suppressed may be forced to appear.

Among other significant features of life at Millenium Hall is that the system among the inhabitants is determinedly egalitarian rather than hierarchical: no gentlewoman need ever feel, once she has acceded to the rules of the community, that she is not equal and autonomous within that community. The women share drawing room and dining room, housekeeper and servants, musical instruments, books, and gardening equipment, but each has her own room. Regular attendance is required only at morning and evening prayers and at meals. Gardening is encouraged. Medical expenses are paid. Dress is to be plain and neat but neither individualistic nor uniform. Each woman for a week at a time presides over the table and takes responsibility for running the establishment. The votes of three-quarters of the members are sufficient to expel those who will not conform to the rules, and if dismissed, a lady has her fortune returned to her, for only the income is employed during her stay.

The strictures are obvious: the life is designedly celibate; amusements, concerts, and conversation must all be found within the community; routine must be regulated by the community schedule. But compared to the life of a lady's companion or a wife, the community life is paradisiacally free, each woman able to think her own thoughts and tend her own needs, serving the needs of others only as much as she wishes.

Scott has been faulted because the community is not fully egalitarian; class differences are preserved, and the ladies are waited on by servants. Scott's vision, however, was not of a democracy but of the liberation of her own class of women from the servitudes of companionship and marriage. That was a sufficiently difficult object, and to publish and disseminate her book she had to veil half of her intention. The ladies at Millenium Hall have no galling superiors, and they maintain equality among themselves. Tyranny to servants is unknown there; the servants live utopian lives, but they remain servants. Although many kinds of tyranny are rectified at Millennium Hall, it is obvious that Scott's heart lay principally in removing the tyrants from the lives of women of her own kind.

Utopias rarely work in practice, and when Scott had a chance in 1768 to try her scheme on a very limited scope, the community of about four women lasted scarcely six months (chapter 13). But what is extraordinary is not that it did not work but that Scott and her friends opposed, in life as in literature, what they considered wrong in their own society with a countersociety. Her book contrasts quasi-gothic tales of patriarchal victims who have found refuge in the Hall with the rational discourse of the projectors of the community, amending, correcting, and certifying a new life. The book is at once an anatomy of the tyrannies of her culture and a system of remedies.

Scott's book could not have been proposed or developed without the collaboration of the Bath community of women consisting of Scott, Lady Barbara Montagu, Sarah Fielding, Elizabeth Cutts, Mrs. Arnold,

Mrs. Adams, Margaret Riggs, Margaret Mary Ravaud, and others—a community that supported its members morally and financially and that raised their self-esteem, consciousness, and efficacy.

Companions in general, though in above-stairs service, are rarely memorialized except in fiction. Some of those who appear in the following chapters are drawn from fiction, some resurrected from journals and letters. But history is filled with silent humble companions now forgotten. Once in a while a single reference to a companion emerges and we hear of the Duchess of Ancaster's Miss Tutting of Newmarket, "marked with claret quite over one side of her face,"[21] of Lady Ann Jekyll's Miss Roberts, who lived "just like a toad under a harrow,"[22] of the daughters of the Duke of Argyll's Jenny Cockburn, suffered in the summer months "to snuff the candles, ring the bell, go and come, and be their *souffre-douleur*, the lawful receptacle of all their complaints and ill-humours."[23] People who knew and observed such women every day as seldom paid them attention as they did those other appurtenances—footmen and dogs. That comparison is inapt, though, for it was the fashion of the time to compose and publish dog epitaphs, but I have found only one epitaph ever for a lady's-maid companion (chapter 11).

Chapter Three

SATIRES OF TYRANTS
AND TOADEATERS: FIELDING
AND COLLIER

THE TOADEATER—certainly a common type of humble companion—is often, and sometimes unjustifiably, first thought of when the subject of humble companionship arises. The word *toadeater* as applied to a political lackey (or toady) was new when in 1742 Horace Walpole called Harry Vane "Pulteney's toadeater."[1] Sarah Fielding, using it two years later in *The Adventures of David Simple* (1744) in its sense of a humble companion, defined it: "It is a Metaphor taken from a Mountebank's Boy eating Toads, in order to show his Master's Skill in expelling Poison. It is built on a Supposition . . . that People who are . . . in a State of Dependence, are forced to do the most nauseous things that can be thought on, to please and humour their Patrons."[2] The close connection between the political and the domestic application of the term is reinforced by the adaptation of the term *patron* to *patroness* in describing the employer of a domestic toady.

Though references to miserable humble companions are certainly to be found earlier, with the word *toadeater*, or *toady*, now available to describe the humble companion, the toadeater aspect of companionship could be even more readily recognized. Companions presented by earlier women writers were often sturdy and independent creatures or scheming adventuresses defying economic or social barriers in their determination to rise. Delariviere Manley in her autobiographical *History of Rivella* (1714) describes her six-month period as "favorite" to the Duchess of Cleveland as one in which she was afforded every indulgence; when the fickle duchess replaced her, she departed in dignity, after delivering a fine public reproach, to join a friend in the country and to commence her playwriting career by writing two subsequently pro-

41

duced plays.[3] The companion in her tale "The Physician's Stratagem" (1720) is a devious and feisty inferior whose submission to her mistress, a count's daughter, is feigned. After having been seduced by the family physician, she takes her revenge by drugging her mistress so that the physician can secretly impregnate her and then win the family's gratitude by marrying the disgraced girl.[4] This misfortune destroys the parents and renders their daughter miserable but profits the companion, whom the physician sells into servitude, nothing.

Another companion, Desideria, a gentlewoman of "Wit and Wantonness, but little Fortune," because of her gay humor and jauntiness, is welcomed into their homes for two or three months at a time by one great lady after another, where she "liv'd a Life very much to her Mind, in the midst of Balls, Visits, Musick, Intrigues and Admiration."[5] She dupes a middle-aged soldier into marrying her but is caught in an intrigue, whereupon her husband kills her lover and immures his body in company with his ungrateful wife and her own companion. These companions, victims of the conventional sad fate awaiting disloyal subordinates, are not toadeaters, and Manley is an early example of the woman writer who understands the anger and revenge stimulated by the enforced social and economic inferiority of such women and hypocritically covered by manipulative charm.

The term *toadeater*, once introduced in its domestic application, soon became familiar. In 1746 Horace Walpole wrote from Windsor, "I am retired rather like an old summer dowager; only that I have no toadeater to take the air with me in the back part of my lozenge coach, and to be scolded."[6] Francis Coventry referred in his 1751 novel *The History of Pompey the Little* to "Female Companions, or more properly *Toadeaters*."[7] This sudden appearance of the word, used first in a political application, then almost immediately in a domestic one, must coincide with an increased consciousness of tyranny, or tyrannical power structures, in political and domestic contexts; and in both cases the contempt, though ostensibly turned upon the subjected ones, is contrived to discredit the tyrants who exact such humiliating servitude. An awareness of tyranny awakens most readily when one scrutinizes the advantages of one's oppressors or adversaries, and Walpole, son of an arch-tyrant (as he showed when he wrote *The Castle of Otranto* [1759]), had as little tolerance for his father's adversary William Pulteney (a good friend of Elizabeth Chudleigh and Elizabeth Montagu—see chapters 4 and 6) as for imperious old dowagers, just as Sarah Fielding had no tolerance for the companionship relationship. Political tyranny would continue to be recognized in the administrations of one's opponents, domestic tyranny in the power, however limited, of those who opposed one's will at home.

From 1744, when Fielding published *The Adventures of David Simple*, to 1814, when Frances Burney published *The Wanderer*, the figure of the humble companion as toady was subjected to considerable scrutiny in works of literature. In Fielding's novel *The History of the Countess of Dellwyn*, the companion, Miss Weare, considers marriage and companionship to be the only two options open to a lone young woman of no fortune, and the terms in which the two are discussed in *The Adventures of David Simple* strongly reinforce the notion that Fielding conflated these two resources as very similar in their degrading demands. Her hero, David Simple, is traveling the world in search of a true friend, when in the course of his adventures and education Cynthia is introduced to his notice as a companion so ungrateful that she has schemed to marry her patroness's seventeen-year-old nephew—an untrue allegation. When her patroness has sent her from the room on an errand and then vilified her, another lady describes the ingratitude of her own companion:

When she came to be old enough to be capable of being of service, she only desired the Wench *to keep her House,* to *take care of her Children,* to *overlook all her Servants,* to be *ready to sit with her when she call'd her*—with *many more trifling things;* and Madam grew out of humour at it, altho' she never put the Creature at all on the footing of a Servant, *nor paid her any Wages as such,* but *look'd on her as her Companion.* Indeed, (continued she) I soon grew weary of it; for the Girl pined and cried in such a manner, I could not bear the Sight of her. I did not dare to speak to the Mynx, which I never did but in the *gentlest Terms,* only to tell her what a *Situation she was in,* and how unbecoming it was in her to think herself on a footing *with People of Fortune;* for that she was left by her Father on the World, without any Provision, and was beholden to me for every thing she had. And I do assure you, I never talk'd to her in this manner, but she had *Tears in her Eyes* for a Week afterwards. (pp. 99–100)

David Simple has the curiosity to inquire into Cynthia's history and circumstances and learns from her that she had a fortune of £2,000 with which her father designed she would make a financially advantageous marriage. She describes to David her suitor's proposal and her own response:

I am none of those nonsensical Fools that can whine and make romantick Love, I leave that to younger Brothers, *let my Estate speak for me; I shall expect nothing from you, but that you will retire into the Country with me, and take care of my Family. I must inform you, I shall desire to have every thing in order; for I love good* Eating and Drinking, *and have been used to have my own Humour from my Youth, which, if you will observe and comply with, I shall be very kind to you, and take care of the* main Chance *for you and your Children.* I made him a low Court'sey, and thanked him for the Honour he intended me; but told him, I had no kind of Ambition to be his *upper Servant;* Tho', indeed, I could not help wondring how it was possible for me to escape being charmed with his *genteel Manner* of addressing me. I then asked him how many Offices he had allotted for me to perform, for those great Advantages he had offered me, of suffering me to humour him in all his Whims, and to receive Meat, Drink and Lodging at his hands; but hoped he would allow me some *small Wages*, that I might now and then recreate myself with my *Fellow-Servants.* (p. 109)

Both the patroness of the companion and the suitor for a wife require someone to manage the home, the table, the servants, and the children; both expect to be thoroughly humored at all times; neither recognizes the servitude imposed or compensates it with wages. For her plain thinking and plain speaking, Cynthia is disinherited by her father, and at his death she must become a lady's companion. At first her treatment is bearable, but

by that time I had remained with her two or three Months, she began to treat me as a *Creature* born to be her *Slave:* whenever I spoke, I was sure to offend her; if I was *silent*, I was *out of humour;* if I said anything in the softest Terms, to complain of the Alteration of her Affection, I was *whimsical* and *ungrateful.* I think it impossible to be in a worse Situation. She had raised my Love, by the Obligations she had confer'd on me, and yet continually provoked my Rage by her Ill-nature: I could not, for a great while, any way account for this Conduct: I thought, if she did not love me, she had no Reason to have given herself any trouble about me; and yet I could not think she could have used one for whom she had had the least Regard in so cruel a manner. At last, I reflected, it must be owing to a love of *Tyranny*, and as we are born in a Country where there is no such thing as public, legal Slavery, People lay Plots to draw in others to be their Slaves, with the pretence of having an Affection for them. (p. 115)

In both marriage and companionship, that is, women may be drawn in, under the false presumption that they are regarded and loved, to become slaves to lovers of tyranny. Their finest feelings of obligation are violated.

You cannot imagine what I felt; for to be used ungratefully, by any one I had confer'd Favours on, would have been nothing to me, in comparison of being ill used by the Person I thought myself obliged to. I was to have no *Passions*, no *Inclinations* of my own; but was to be turned into a piece of Clock-work, which her Ladyship was to wind up or let down, as she pleased. (p. 116)

In fact, it is the patriarchal family that is at fault.

I know not to what Malignity it is owing, but I have observed, in all the Families I have ever been acquainted with, that one part of them spend their whole time in oppressing and teazing the other; and all this they do . . . to shew their Power: While the other Part languish away their Days, in bemoaning their own hard Fate, which has thus subjected them to the Whims and Tyranny of *Wretches*, who are so *totally void of Taste, as not to desire the Affection of the very People they appear willing to oblige.* (p. 117)

I know of no other such analysis of the family in this period. Because Fielding had an important influence on Jane Collier, author of the locus classicus of the discussion of domestic tyranny, it is important to identify Fielding's ideas that a love of tyranny seems almost endemic to humans and that those who have the power in a family or a relationship will use it to impose misery on those who have not. Education was the tool that would, she hoped, abolish tyranny and encourage benevolence, as she demonstrates in *The Governess* (1749). Her friend Jane Collier shared her views.

Sarah Fielding and Jane Collier were girlhood friends in Salisbury, Sarah born in 1710 and Jane probably in 1714. Jane was one of the daughters of Arthur Collier, a learned but improvident Salisbury divine. Her brother Arthur, later a doctor of common law, specialized, in his earlier impecunious years and his later, in educating women in the classical languages and literatures. In educating his sisters and Fielding, he was apparently preparing them to become governesses. The two Collier sons were provided with professions, Arthur in the law and Charles in the army; but on their father's death in 1732 the two girls, Jane, aged seventeen, and Margaret, fifteen, were virtually unprovided for.[8]

In 1748 the sisters were in London living with their brother Arthur in Doctors' Commons, but their situation with him was evidently not satisfactory. Thereafter Margaret frequently lived with the family of Henry Fielding as governess to his daughters, and Jane was often with that of Samuel Richardson and by early 1750 was functioning as governess, companion, and friend. In February 1750 Richardson wrote to Lady Bradshaigh that he had walked with Miss Collier and his daughter Patty to North End, and shortly he informed her—she was suspicious of learned women—that Miss Collier was indeed an example "that women may be trusted with Latin and even Greek, and yet not think themselves above their domestic duties."[9] Collier was still with the Richardsons when she wrote *An Essay on the Art of Ingeniously Tormenting* in 1753, published in April by Millar. Generic satire by women is comparatively rare, and Collier's is fine satire, sustaining a witty, ironic appeal to reason. It has been suggested that Richardson assisted in the composition, but satire was not his forte. Martin and Ruthe Battestin have discovered another claimant to having rendered substantial assistance, an old family friend of both Collier and Fielding, James Harris.[10] Richardson and Harris may have reviewed the manuscript and offered suggestions, but Collier's major assistance came from Sarah Fielding, who had made a close study of tyranny, had already expressed the important idea of the book, and was to collaborate with Collier on an allegorical and satiric novel, *The Cry*, in 1754. Collier's early intimacy with Fielding and their collaboration establish Collier as an important influence on the Bath community of women, though her early death—she was dead by 1755—may have precluded much personal contact with most of the community members.

Collier's model for the *Essay* was Jonathan Swift's *Instructions to Servants* (1746), which tells servants how to do their worst. Swift writes from the establishment point of view, Collier from the nonestablishment. Her first chapter, "Instructions to Masters and Mistresses, concerning their Servants," turns the tables, informing us satirically of the torments inflicted upon the serving class. The second chapter, the longest and most detailed in the book, "To the Patroness of a Humble Companion," is the fruit in part of her own experience, in part of her consultations about their mutual positions with Sarah Fielding, who undoubtedly influenced her opinions and edged her satiric sword. Decorously and elegantly Collier claims her right to her subject in a closing fable attributing a poem about the agony of being devoured to the lamb rather than to the lion, leopard, or lynx because "it is from suffering, and not from inflicting torments, that the true idea of them is gained."

Collier begins the book by noting Fielding's point that the love of tormenting is endemic among humans, adding that it must be either implanted in our natures or inculcated very early. Fielding and Collier believed that even if the trait of tormenting were implanted, education could help a great deal to curb tyrannical propensities; else they would probably not have written. Much of the work of the Bath group would have been pointless had love of tormenting been irrevocably implanted in our natures; they appear to have considered that the tendency to tyranny was present but that a proper education could control it. In regard to the proper education of children, in her chapter "To Parents," Collier advises, "If you see them possessed with a due degree of obstinacy, wilfulness, perverseness, and ill-humour; if you find, that the passions of pride, cruelty, malice, and envy, have, like rank weeds, flourished, for want of rooting up, and overwhelmed every spark of goodness in the mind; then may you (as my true disciples) rejoice in having so far done your duty by them, as to have laid the proper foundation for their becoming no small adepts in this our useful science." Education could help, and her satire is essentially educational.

By providing careful analyses of the abuses practiced by those in power against the powerless, Collier's satire is calculated to shame the punishers of the weak into adopting the more beneficent ways to which they were already hypocritically pretending. She begins her examination of the treatment of humble companions by wondering, since the love of tormenting is so prevalent, why more families do not take advantage of those well-educated but indigent daughters of the services and the clergy who make such splendid victims. They are, she points out to potential mistresses, much more vulnerable than servants: unlike servants, they receive no wages and are always on hand "to receive every cross word that rises in your mind"; like servants, they must bear the insults of mistress, dogs, cats, parrots, and children, but they must bear the insults of the servants too. They are thus the ideal victims of tyranny.

The companion-as-victim, however, must be carefully chosen. Well-born and well educated she must be, and "the more acquirements she has, the greater field will you have for insolence, and the pleasure of mortifying her." The best choice will be one who has lived happily with tender and indulgent parents, has a tender heart and a meek and gentle disposition, "for if she has spirit enough to despise your insults, and has not tender affections enough to be soothed and melted by your kindness (which must be sparingly bestowed), all your sport is lost." Finally, the patroness must make a choice either of a companion of good sense but plainness or deformity or of one with beauty but a weak capacity; a companion with both good sense and beauty would be too formidable a target.

Collier then provides intricate directions for tormenting in either case. If the companion is a weak-minded beauty, you are to call her nothing but Beauty, Pretty Idiot, Puppet, Baby-face, and the like, accuse her of flirting with the servants, and when she weeps, ask her in what romance she has learned that tears are becoming. You are to attack both the girl's weak points and her strong ones—and are always to accuse her of having sweaty feet and a nauseous breath. If the victim denies this last, you are to say,

"Oh to be sure! you are too delicate a creature to have any human failings! you are all sweetness and perfection! well, Heaven defend me from such sweet creatures!" Then changing your tone and looks into fierceness, you may proceed: "I tell you, Madam Impertinence, whatever you may think, and how impudently soever you may dare to contradict me in this manner, that all your nasty odious imperfections, have been often taken notice of by many people beside myself, though nobody had regard enough for you, to tell you of such things.—You may toss your head, and look with as much indignation as you please; but these airs, child, will not do long with me.—If you do not like to be told of your faults, you must find some other person to support you. So pray, for the present, walk off to your own apartment; and consider whether you choose to lay aside that pretty, becoming resentment of yours; or to be thrown friendless, as I found you, on the wide world again.—You must not be told of your failings, truly, must you! Oh I would not have such a proud heart as thine in my breast, for the world! Though, let me tell you, Mistress Minx, it would much better become my station, than yours."

When the girl has gone away to her room, to prevent her leaving and escaping your ministrations, send your maid with sweetmeats, fruit, or anything she likes to report how kindly you have spoken of her and to coax her downstairs again. Then offer new clothes, a pleasant jaunt, or any pleasing indulgence and continue your kindness until the girl begins to blame herself and is ready for the next round of torment. The alternation of cruelty with occasional kindnesses, all without reference to the girl's behavior, is a positive necessity.

Collier's detailed instructions continue: If the companion is plain and of good understanding rather than a dull beauty, the mistress is to say she hates anything about her not pleasant to look at and is to accuse her of being a wit at least a hundred times a day. The companion should be induced to say that she is not greatly concerned about her plainness, and then, if she dresses well, she can be accused of vanity; if ill, she can be called "trollop, slattern, slut, dirty beast, &c." The patroness is often to observe "that all Wits are slatterns;—that no girl ever delighted in reading, that was not a slut;—that well might the men say they would not for the world marry a WIT." But she is also to remember that the more understanding the companion has, the more her chains have to be gilded over with real indulgences, and she must ever be shown great tenderness and affection before company so that if she departs, she can be accused of the highest ingratitude. Then, "Remember to keep her as much in your sight as possible; because the only chance of comfort she can have, is in being out of your presence."

In dealing with both kinds of companions, the patroness must note how the girl tries to please her and never appear pleased; if the companion is very obliging, she is never to be told what is wanted so that she can be stormed at when she does not guess. The patroness is to develop foibles, such as hatred of noise, so that the girl will often have to transgress; and she is never to listen to the girl's defenses after the servants or members of the family have complained against her. Finally there is the fine game of compassion: the patroness is to talk to her of her parents and her loss; dissolve her into tears with which she mingles her own; announce herself a second parent and protectress; then suddenly grow into a rage with her over nothing "to make the girl more sensible than before of the loss of indulgent parents, by the cruel reverse she now so strongly experiences."

In contrast to this excellent and experienced advice, Collier's chapter on husbands is brief and uninspired. She makes no attack on marriage, never suggests that it may be deleterious to women. Though she attacks tyranny in many forms in this book, she is the most cursory with the tyranny of husbands and is careful to name abuses that are either admittedly egregious or comic and not pernicious. First, she exempts from her discussion husbands in low life, who, she says, quickly break either their wives' bones or their hearts; next she exempts those in high life, who keep mistresses and ignore their wives entirely. Thus with jests, which nevertheless manage to suggest that there are no marital relationships worth consideration in the top and bottom sectors of society, she avoids confronting her subject. Concentrating then on husbands in middle life, she suggests that the husband may take the maid for a mistress; may smoke if it makes his wife sick; may express displeasure with all that comes to his table and praise all that he has eaten elsewhere; and may always come home in an ill humor. Such humiliation techniques are designed to convince the wife that she is unattractive, powerless, incompetent, and unappealing, but they are nothing compared to the subtle tactics practiced by the patroness. The latter, more refined psychological torments, however, were probably recognized by many a wife as those used by her husband upon herself, despite Collier's prudent restraints. It took only a little consideration to recognize that no matter how great the wife's fortune had been, marriage reduced her to, at best, an allowance dependent upon her good behavior and thus she was not so different from the companion: like the companion she received no wages; she was in fact her husband's humble companion. It was no secret that women were commonly rewarded with marriage for their ability to bear humiliation, as a backward glance at the marriage choices of the Reverend Mr. Myddelton and the Jamaican merchant and the remarks about marriage of Delany, Thrale, and Montagu demonstrate (chapter 1). A recent

popular book on male misogyny lists the strategies for torture available to Collier's patroness in a checklist designed to enable women to
determine whether they are involved with misogynists: the nine points
covered include the empowered one's assumption of the right to control;
devaluation of the inferior's opinions, feelings, and accomplishments;
yelling, threatening, or withdrawing into angry silence when displeased;
reducing the inferior to "walking on eggs" to avoid offending; switching from charm to rage without warning; and blaming the inferior for
everything that goes wrong.[11] The recognition in both systems of the
importance of the strategy of arbitrary alternation of cruelty and kindness (in Susan Forward's system "switching from charm to rage without
warning") in maintaining the inferior's confusion, insecurity, and vulnerability is striking as is the equal importance of devaluation, the belit-
tling of the inferior's strong points, and the mockery of her weak points.

Comedy, said Horace Walpole, is addressed to those who think,
tragedy to those who feel. Satire like Swift's derives its point from the
fact that if one puts feeling or sensibility out of the question and uses only
the measure of reasonable expedience, programs like that of the Modest
Proposer are sensible and practical; but such satire seriously calls into
question the use of no measure but that of reasonable expediency. So
with Collier's satire: if we accept her proposed first premise that the love
of tormenting is basic to our natures and that it is good to gratify it—
a perverse negative expression of the Shaftesburian premise that love
of benevolence is basic to our natures and that it is good to gratify it—
then her instructions follow as eminently helpful and inspiriting.

Following the publication of Collier's *Essay* in April 1753—and its
considerable success—Charles Hanbury Williams, the politician and
wit, contributed an essay to the fashionable periodical the *World* on September 13, 1753, that was almost certainly inspired by Collier.[12] It purports to be the account, written by herself, of Mary Truman, the widow of
an affluent tradesman, left with no more than £1,000, which, placed in
the hands of a friend (rather than in safe government low-yield bonds),
give her £40 a year on which she retires quietly into the country. There
an old lady of great fortune, Lady Mary, takes a fancy to her and insists
she come live with her. In the first year all goes well, but then the failure
of the friend into whose hands the widow had placed her money ruins
her, and she becomes truly dependent. She informs Lady Mary that she
will now indeed be in need of all those proffered presents which hitherto
she has refused, and on the instant she becomes plain "Truman." She is

threatened when she breaks a teacup: "Do you think I can afford to have my china broke at this rate, and maintaining you into the bargain?"

Truman is now no longer a friend, but a *complaisante*, or humble companion, and a toadeater. She is constantly employed in fetching, carrying, ringing the bell, filling the pot, stirring the fire, calling servants, bringing water, and administering medicines. No one but she can please at preserving, pickling, and pastry. She makes up the linens, mends, washes lace, makes butter and cheese, and is scolded when any of this is improperly accomplished. The servants now refuse to respect or serve her, and at table she is forbidden to taste any dish that might appear again cold or hashed—beef, ham, venison, fowl, brawn, or sturgeon. She is allowed no wine, punch, or fruit. She is clothed in Lady Mary's old clothes and thus offends the lady's maid. She must ride backward in the daily airings, though it makes her sick. She must tend the favorite animals and is blamed for their accidents and illnesses. She is the only attendant allowed in her employer's illnesses and must have a perfectly sound tooth drawn to encourage Lady Mary to give up a rotten one. She must prepare and taste all physics, water gruels, and the camomile tea that Lady Mary takes (in contemporary terms) as a vomit, at which Truman must officiate, ruining her clothes in the process. Even Truman's moral autonomy is stolen: Lady Mary tells lies to company and makes Truman attest to their truth and forces Truman to judge her right in all contests so that the neighbors too detest her.

Williams made an important point about the violence done Truman's integrity when, against her own moral judgment, she is forced to support Lady Mary's erroneous views. But though he noted this violence, like Collier he failed to face squarely the truly deleterious effect of toadyism on the character of the toady, when she has at last become no longer indignant about such violation and no longer cares for the truth. Nor had Sarah Fielding employed that theme in *The Adventures of David Simple*. It may have been introduced by Fielding in 1759 in *The History of the Countess of Dellwyn* with the character of Miss Weare. That forced subservience to the moral judgment of the tyrant hurts the character of the oppressed was an important idea. It obviously meant that being a humble companion was morally injurious, and it implicitly meant that being a wife was equally so. Though women authors were subsequently to be consistently concerned with the evil effects of toadyism on the subordinated partner, in 1753 no such inferences distinguished Collier's work from Williams's essay. Nevertheless, there is a discernible gendered distinction between their approaches. Williams's tale is cautionary, exposing a wrong version of woman, that is, a woman given complete autonomy who then shows herself unworthy of that autonomy. Lady Mary's change of attitude toward Truman occurs instantaneously at the precise moment when Truman loses the power to leave her and when a woman of proper sensibility would have become most benevolent and kind. Williams recognized the propensity of humans to curb their autocratic and tyrannical tendencies when they have no power to express them and then to express them on the instant when the occasion arises—but he appears to be assigning that propensity only to women. His essay is characteristically midcentury in the suspicion it casts on the irrational nature of woman, a creature not to be entrusted with authority but not yet defined as by nature docile and altruistic. Williams would instead support the more realistic thesis that if docility in women is desired, it must be imposed early, and the imposition sustained wherever and whenever possible. His essay, though comic, suggests that women like Lady Mary (who incidentally may share some character traits with his own estranged and independent wife, Lady Frances, who had recovered her own fortune after having contracted venereal disease from him) should not be empowered to the point of anything resembling autonomy; he implicitly warns men to correct the vicious tendencies of women toward domination. Collier's book, by contrast, dealing with tyrants of both sexes and many kinds, is a warning to humankind to recognize and curb its endemically vicious tendencies. And in general from this point onward male authors dealing with the topic of humble companionship were to attack the termagant mistress and depict the victimized companion as an angel of complaisance; it was a splendid way of endorsing the ideal of complaisant womanhood.

Sarah Fielding and Collier both were endorsing the Shaftesburian or sentimental system, which assumes that sympathy and benevolence toward others are potential characteristics in all humans. They would not have bothered to protest against domestic tyranny had they not thought so. In this regard at least they fulfilled the growing expectation that women exalt sensibility as the highest human attribute. At the same time they suggested that when men and women reached this highest form of consciousness, they would be recognized as equals in such important matters as moral judgment and emotional relationships. Williams, however, endorses no such system, which would do away with male prerogative. His agenda is to underscore the unnaturalness *in a woman* of tyrannical behavior. If Lady Mary had been a husband and

Truman his wife, much of that tyrannical behavior would have appeared entirely normal. Any wife was expected to attend her husband at all hours, to see to the pickling and preserves, to nurse him in illness, to support him in company. Lady Mary's more extreme abuse, such as the denial of food and the drawn tooth, would therefore show up the inappropriateness of allowing a woman to assume a male's prerogative.

The great question, addressed by Fielding and Collier, was whether human nature was such that anyone could actually enjoy the moment-to-moment business of humiliating and hurting an assigned inferior, rendering the inferior's entire life miserable. The answer of both women was yes, but their efforts demonstrate that they considered the situation remediable by implementing the development in people of altruism to temper their aggressiveness. Collier's satire, which includes a chapter addressed to wives with instructions on tormenting husbands and a long chapter to parents explaining how to torment their children—demonstrating a very early consciousness of the abuse of parental power—proves that she considered tyranny a problem endemic to the human condition. Unlike Williams, who fully enjoyed his own privileges, both women sought to abolish tyranny, to educate it away.

Sarah Fielding's Miss Weare had demonstrated the bad effects of toadyism on the subordinate, an important aspect of the problem of tyranny, by the time Scott took up the subject. Forced to countenance and abet a morally despicable employer because of a refusal to give up the comforts she provided, Miss Weare becomes cowardly and dishonest in every particular. She has given up her own moral standards and autonomy. This insight into the damage done the character of the companion (or wife)—no deferential angel, as these women see, though she may act the part—is often thenceforward an important component of discussions of companionship by women. Sarah Scott deals with it in general terms in *Millenium Hall*; and in its sequel, *The History of Sir George Ellison* (1766), she carefully anatomizes not only the torments visited upon a companion but also the damage inflicted upon her character.

In the latter book her nameless companion, the orphan daughter of a clergyman, goes first to Mrs. Smyth, who lives well and keeps much company. Mrs. Smyth expects her protégée to keep busy doing trifling services and to flatter perpetually. "She would frequently . . . reduce me either to give the lie to my own conscience, or put an absolute affront on her vanity." [13] She asks her companion's opinion only to hear her own commended, and when she is not so gratified, she begins indignantly to expatiate "on the odiousness of a contradicting spirit; hint that conceit and obstinancy never failed making people disagreeable, as they led them to oppose every opinion but their own, and to think none wise but themselves" (1:303). If any company differs from her in opinion, the companion is applied to for a defense, which she has not the courage to refuse, though her blushes and confusion reveal her cowardice to all. Mrs. Smyth expects her to dress well and to hire carriages in which to travel "because it was not proper a young person who lived with her should appear in so ungenteel a light" as to walk. She is put to further expense filling in at card tables (1:305–6). Therefore, on Mrs. Mayer's invitation to come to her, she leaves Mrs. Smyth.

Mrs. Mayer pretends to benevolence. She has protested that her greatest pleasure is in using her large income to assist her friends. But soon the companion is oppressed by presents of which she has no need and which are too fine for her condition. In addition, Mrs. Mayer has an uncertain temper, and when she is out of temper, "every accident offended her; on these occasions she would reproach me with ingratitude, and enumerate the favours I had received from her. She would even cast oblique reflexions on me as being mercenary in accepting obligations" (1:311). Mrs. Mayer has a giving hand but not a generous heart. She is proud, and she alternates her violent behavior and her calm kindness, growing angry when her companion rejects unwanted presents that she knows she will later be reproached for having accepted. The companion is to learn "that of the many who give, few are really generous," for "vanity, a good natured but transient desire to please, and various other motives, frequently produce the same effects" (1:312). This companion is able not only to analyze the character of Mrs. Mayer but also, finally, to perceive her own moral danger. She has sometimes resolved "to leave Mrs. Mayer, and stand no longer indebted for a subsistence to any thing but my own industry"; she has sometimes only determined "not to be prevailed with to accept any presents beyond what was absolutely necessary for my proper appearance in her house" (1:313). In her weakness she is trapped between Mrs. Mayer's cruel outbursts and returning kindness—that classic alternation. She has become unequal to the implementation of both her first plan and her second, for when Mrs. Mayer offers useless presents, she refuses them until they are offered in anger, whereupon "my spirit then sunk, and cowardice made me take what my heart rejected" (1:313). This weakness, or "disagreeable and fluctuating state of mind; too proud to bear humiliation without severe pangs, and yet so enslaved by gratitude and cowardice, that I had not power to free myself from it" (1:314) is dissipated only when she hears of Millenium

Hall and applies for admission. There she finds true generosity that is easy to accept and genuine self-respect at last.

In this tale, which seems to suggest that no patroness of a companion will be able to prevent the companion's feeling the burden of dependency and that no patroness will find it easy not to take advantage of that dependency, Scott again, as in *Millenium Hall*, affirms her dislike of companionship as a solution for dependent gentlewomen and once more suggests the deleterious effect on the character of such dependency. In doing so she also suggests that the proclaimed flaws of the female character—weakness, inconstancy, hypocrisy, immaturity—are not so much natural as acquired. Scott's full view was that the situation of the empowered linked with the powerless is almost inevitably meretricious and tends to lead to some permutation of tyrannical behavior on the part of the empowered one and of some reprehensibly weak and manipulative behavior on the part of the powerless.

Male authors using the termagant-toady combination, however, continued, like Williams, to perpetuate the model of the unwomanly harridan and the pure angelic victim, who became an idealized version of womanliness. Two interesting versions of this pair, virtually unchanged from Collier's and Williams's presentations, are found in Samuel Foote's unproduced farce "A Trip to Calais" (1775) and in the comedy for which Arthur Murphy almost certainly borrowed Foote's characters, *Know Your Own Mind*, produced at Covent Garden in February 1777. Foote would probably not have found the subject particularly interesting had it not been relevant to his attack on Elizabeth Chudleigh, the bigamous Duchess of Kingston and a notorious misuser of companions. But once he had elected the subject, he fell back for much of his material upon the two 1753 loci classici.

"A Trip to Calais" was originally written to exploit the notoriety of the duchess's trial for bigamy in 1775, and her wicked misuse of her companion is part of the indictment of her character. Lady Kitty Crocodile is in Calais with her companion, the beautiful and gentle Lydia Lydell. She is approached by the relations of the unruly Jenny Minnikin, daughter of a London tradesman, who has eloped to Calais with her father's apprentice, and is asked to use her influence to get Jenny discharged from the convent where she has taken refuge to escape their pursuit. Lady Kitty is in excessive and hypocritical grief for the recent death of her husband, on the lookout everywhere for amour, and insistent that no male visitor take notice of her companion; she is every man's nightmare of the sexually voracious and aggressive woman. While she torments her companion—and ingenious as she is, she can invent no torment not recommended by Collier—she and Jenny Minnikin recognize each other as kindred spirits so that when Lydia at last departs with her suitor Colonel Crosby and Lady Kitty's maid Hetty, Hetty is able to respond to Lydia's concern for Jenny, now disengaged from her suitor and engaged as Lady Kitty's new companion: "You may discard your fears about her! unless I am mistaken, they are very properly matched, and will prove a mutual plague to each other. But, should it be otherwise, there seems to be a kind of dramatic justice in the change of your two situations: You, Miss, are rewarded for your patient sufferings, by the protection of a man of honour and virtue; whilst she, rebellious to the mild dictates of parental sway, is subjected to the galling yoke of a capricious and whimsical tyrant!" (p. 90).[14]

Foote, no lover of women, ameliorates his caricatures of Lady Kitty and Jenny, willful, destructive, and oversexed, with his portrait of Lydia, impossibly mild and full of sensibility and inflexible moral standards. At her entrance Lydia explains that her relations, seduced by Lady Kitty's promises, have entrusted her to her patroness's care expecting for her some permanent establishment—that is, marriage. Now that patroness wants only to rid herself of her burden and so tries to force her "to some indiscreet act of impatience, as an apology for the breach of her faith" (p. 54). Meanwhile, Lady Kitty affects in public to treat Lydia with particular regard and attention, while in private teasing, torturing, and mortifying her; she drives Lydia to tears by charging her with having ogled and thrown out lures to her husband and having laid traps in Italy to ensnare "Prince Pincossi and Cardinal Grimsky." "I never durst carry you with me to any conference I had with the pope, for fear you should be trying some of your coquetish airs upon him" (pp. 56–57). More annoying, Colonel Crosby, "the only decent man in town," has transferred his devotion from Lady Kitty to Lydia (p. 57). Lydia begs only to be sent, under adequate escort, to her mother, but Lady Kitty refuses: "You want to persuade people, that, through caprice, grown tired of your company, I have the cruelty to throw you at once upon the wide world" (p. 58). While Lydia is weeping, Colonel Crosby enters and Lady Kitty carries on a double conversation: "The poor child has just received a letter from her mother, one of the best kind of women that ever was: Dry up your tears, Lydia, my love!—You sullen, sulking, stomachful slut!—Poor Mrs. Lydell has but very bad health, Colonel Crosby; and the dear girl, who is indeed a most affectionate dutiful daughter—Go up to your room, you pouting, perverse, little vixen—You see, Colonel!

but be comforted, Lydy, my dear! though you should lose your mother, you should be certain of finding a mother in me" (p. 59). Hetty gives a character of her mistress: "In hypocrisy, she would be an over-match for a methodist. . . . And as to cruelty, there never was so ingenious, so refined a tormenter: The Fathers of the Inquisition themselves, would be proud to receive instructions from her" (p. 66).

At last, Hetty, Lydia, and Colonel Crosby settle their affairs and depart together, very *comme il faut.* Jenny determines to marry neither her apprentice lover nor her parents' choice of a husband but instead to throw in her lot with Lady Kitty as her companion. Thus the two termagants are mated not with men but to each other, in a tacit and comic admission by Foote that companionship is indeed a form of marriage and that they have made a fitting match, as have the virtuous Crosby and the sentimental Lydia.

The piece's genuine funniness, its farcical caricatures, may mitigate its dark misogyny, but misogynistic it certainly is. In Foote's hands Collier's thesis that tyranny is a pleasure endemic among humans is forgotten. No tyrannous male balances Lady Kitty, no willful young man balances Jenny Minnikin, and no Bluebeard of a male balances Jenny's marrying aunt, Mrs. Clack. The termagant-toadeater combination is used to extol the virtues of the helpless and passive Lydia as a model of womanhood and to indict the powerful, controlling Lady Kitty as a woman who has forgotten her proper place and is ill-equipped to handle the wealth and power she commands.

The duchess's resentment prevented the staging of Foote's play in 1775, and instead in 1776 he staged *The Capuchin,* a version that omitted Lady Kitty.[15] Their quarrel hastened the illness that caused his retirement from the theater in January 1777. At that time Foote signed all his dramatic properties over to George Colman at Covent Garden; he was no longer responsible for whatever was done with them. "A Trip to Calais," still neither published nor produced, was in Colman's hands and I think must, with Foote's permission, have been mined by his friend Arthur Murphy, who on February 22, 1777, produced at Covent Garden his own successful comedy, *Know Your Own Mind,* which featured a termagant-toadeater pair called Mrs. Bromley and Miss Neville, reminiscent of Foote's pair, and a wit named Dashwou'd complimentarily modeled on Foote.[16] The play was therefore a Parthian shot at Chudleigh, exposing her tyranny and proclaiming the essential decency and kindness of Foote.

Murphy's play, an adaptation of *L'Irrésolu* by Philippe Nericault

Destouches, had been written originally in 1760 without the termagant-toadeater pair, and Murphy was fully capable of adapting them, wasted in Foote's farce and excised from *The Capuchin*, to advantage in the few weeks between Foote's retirement and his own opening.[17] Murphy's full-length comedy, however, is better composed and better balanced than Foote's short farce. The subject of the tyrannous and the benevolent capacities of humankind was in the air, and the question of how to bring up a son—tyrannically or sentimentally—is posed through the contrast between two brothers, one of whom has reared his son despotically, the other permissively and lovingly. The Widow Bromley, in the style of Foote's Lady Kitty and with the same relationship to her companion, the lovely, helpless, and virtuous Miss Neville, is paired with another despotic woman, Madame La Rouge. But these two female despots are outnumbered by Mrs. Bromley's exemplary nieces, Lady Bell and Lady Jane, and Miss Neville. In the end the three young ladies engage themselves to three suitors, Miss Neville receiving Sir Harry Lovewit as her just share.

Murphy acknowledges his debt to Collier in two speeches that refer to the art of tormenting.[18] He balances his female despot with the male despot Captain Bygrove and similarly balances the disruptive, plotting characters Malvill and Madame La Rouge, thus endorsing Collier's thesis that tyranny knows no gender. He also includes a sample of parental tyranny. But Murphy has located domestic tyranny as inflicted by the father upon the son and by the mistress upon the companion. Tyrannical fathers have always been familiar on the comic stage—sons are very conscious of paternal tyranny—and so he has done nothing new. He has certainly not provided a demonstration of a husband's ordinary domestic tyranny to his wife. But he has provided a sentimental conclusion in which insight into former errors reforms not only the rakish lover Millamour, who vows future fidelity to Lady Bell, but also the tyrants Captain Bygrove and Mrs. Bromley, the latter of whom confesses, "I now see, that to demand in return for favours conferred, an abject spirit, and mean compliance, is the worst usury society knows of" (p. 177). Thus the play follows Collier in establishing the general tendency toward tyranny in humankind (when empowered over others) and in presenting the possibility that education will produce conversion to more altruistic behavior.

Mrs. Bromley's treatment of Miss Neville follows a familiar course. She accuses Neville of dizening herself up in clothes borrowed from her patroness and rebukes her with a description of the country parsonage from which she has been rescued. When she has reduced Neville to tears, she uses Collier's recipe of tenderness: "I fancy I have been too violent. After all this sour, I must sweeten her a little.—Come, dry up your tears: you know I am good-natured in the main. I am only jealous that you don't seem to love me" (p. 44). Later she drives Miss Neville to tears, orders her to her room, and finally tells her to quit the house before Sir Harry rescues her by claiming her as his wife.

Murphy is not, however, interested any more than Collier was in demonstrating the deleterious effect of prolonged dependency on character. Miss Neville, like Miss Lydell, is a model of fine-principled integrity and, in the main, docility; but when she is too much put upon, she makes spirited speeches to Mrs. Bromley, of which the first is a sufficient sample: "Give me leave to tell you, madam, that when people of superior fortune, whom Providence has enabled to bestow obligations, claim a right, from the favour they confer, to tyrannize over the hopes and fears of a mind in distress; they exercise a cruelty more barbarous than any in the whole history of human malice" (p. 43).

The influence of Restoration comedy may have inspired the gender balance of the play, but the speeches about tyranny and persecution reflect Murphy's sensitivity to domestic tyranny. This was awakened no doubt by his own experience with a tyrannical uncle who designed him for trade; because of a mandate inherited from Foote it extended to an indictment of Chudleigh for the usurpation of a patriarchal role and thus to an understanding of the female companion's plight, but certainly not to an understanding of the plight of the ordinary wife.

Sir Harry: They are much mistaken, who can find no way of showing their superior rank, but by letting their weight fall on those whom fortune has placed beneath them.
Dashwou'd: And that sentiment, however I may rattle, I wish impressed upon all the patrons of poor relations, throughout his majesty's dominions. (pp. 176–77)

And however enlightened Murphy, who began life as a poor relation, was, the suggestion that dependency, as well as authority over others, undermines moral character remained for women to inscribe.

In the circumstances surrounding the evolution of the ideas of Fielding and Collier there is ample evidence to suggest that new insights such as the recognition that hierarchical social relations instigate moral damage in both the empowered and the powerless are often generated not so much by individuals as in community. For women the circumstances in which Fielding and Collier found themselves—they were educated equally to most upper-class men, in propinquity to each other, unmarried and partially dependent upon their brothers, and desirous of earning money and independence by writing—were extremely rare. The creativity of their response to these circumstances helps to elucidate the great handicap under which most women who were ambitious to write or to think labored, isolated as they were in domestic settings where they were expected to do womenly tasks, comparatively uneducated or self-educated, without contact with others like themselves.

Frances Burney was much occupied in her writings with an examination of the mistress-companion combination, and her Mrs. Ireton in *The Wanderer* (1814) is perhaps the most closely anatomized tyrannical mistress of them all. But before consideration of Mrs. Ireton, to the gallery of cruel patronesses and unlucky humble companions exhibited in this chapter will be added a close examination of the only known mass patroness, Elizabeth Chudleigh, Countess of Bristol and putative Duchess of Kingston, and her many hapless maids of honor.

Chapter Four

ELIZABETH CHUDLEIGH
AND HER MAIDS OF HONOR

ELIZABETH CHUDLEIGH's devastatingly triumphant and destructive career is probably best understood as inspired by the careers of the imperious court vixens in the pages of Delariviere Manley so it is not surprising that her initial courtship and subsequent abuse of her companions follow the pattern of the Duchess of Cleveland's in *The Adventures of Rivella*. The duchess was demonstrably Chudleigh's model. For Chudleigh, as for her close contemporaries Elizabeth Montagu and Frances Greville, there were both older Restoration models and newer models of sensibility to choose from and to combine, and Chudleigh's choice was absolute. She was neither a brilliant intelligence nor a reader, but she had clearly very early got the *New Atalantis* (1709) by heart. The models in the works of Manley of powerful, profligate, passionate, and willful women impelled the girl, already beautiful, irresistibly charming, passionate, and willful, into both profligacy and power. For Chudleigh the Restoration court ideology about women still worked when at twenty (in about 1740) she arrived at the court of the Prince of Wales.[1] When in 1776 at fifty-six she was tried for bigamy, her assumptions had become outré, her often self-conducted defense failed, and she escaped burning in the hand only because her despised husband had succeeded to an earldom. She had to flee England forever.

Chudleigh was neither self-reflective nor self-critical, and her analyses of herself, in her brief autobiography (written in 1786, two years before her death) might appear puzzlingly candid unless compared with parallel passages in Manley, which may reveal her model and her ideal:

From Manley on the Duchess of Cleveland:

Her Temper was a perfect Contradiction, unbounded *lavish*, and sordidly *Covetous*, the former to those who administer'd to her particular pleasures, the other,

61

to all the rest of the World, when Love began to forsake her, and her Charms were upon the Turn.[2]

From Chudleigh on herself:

She was both wasteful and penurious; the most enormous sums were constantly expended to gratify her love of display, at the same time that she refused to incur some trifling necessary expense in her household.[3]

From Manley on the Duchess of Cleveland:

Hilaria was *Querilous, Fierce, Loquacious,* excessively fond, or infamously rude. . . . The Extreams of Prodigality, and Covetousness; of Love and Hatred; of Dotage and Aversion, were joyn'd together in Hilaria's Soul. (*AR,* pp. 34–35)

From Chudleigh on herself:

"I would hate myself," she would say, "if I remained more than an hour in one tone of mind." (*Memoirs,* 1:221) The duke was simple, gentle, and retiring, whilst the lady was exacting, vain, and violent almost to fury. (*Memoirs,* 1:224) The duke's . . . wife . . . raised to the highest rank a subject could attain, became only the more arrogant and capricious. (*Memoirs,* 1:225)

And from the Baroness d'Oberkirch on Chudleigh:

She is proud and self-willed, opposed to almost all received maxims, and yet variable and inconstant both in her fancies and opinions. (*Memoirs,* 1:244)

Chudleigh's model was a female tyrant like Nourmahal in John Dryden's *Aureng-Zebe,* of whom her husband the emperor says, "A Spirit so untamed the world ne'r bore." Her whim was her will, which she instantly indulged, and she indulged rather than curbed her temper. In her attempt to buy her way out of her unfortunate marriage to Augustus Hervey and thus to establish herself above the law, she attempted no more than the earlier heroine Mary Edwards had achieved.[4] No less than Dr. Gregory's end-of-the-century disciples she was trapped in a deforming ideology, but she became far more conspicuous than they because her style, exhibitionistic and self-proclamatory rather than retiring, was by the 1760s identifiable as the counterideal of behavior for women.

To attempt to exculpate Chudleigh would be fruitless[5] for she often deliberately behaved like a monster. Her generosity, frequently noted by herself and by her beneficiaries, was directed not toward worthy, needy objects but toward those who best flattered and served her. Her passage through the world did not render it a better place. But contemporary accounts of her, written when Manley had to be read covertly and ideals of womanhood were radically different from Chudleigh's ideal for herself, were naturally censorious, and many compounded the censure with ridicule; extenuating details might therefore have been omitted. Some of her eighteenth- and nineteenth-century biographers could have been informed only at second or third hand, and some are clearly either interpreting or elaborating on sketchy information. With the registering of this caveat, I have no recourse but to report the record as it exists. And the character of this hero demands exploration at some length.

Chudleigh was the daughter of a younger son of Sir George Chudleigh and the well-known poet Lady Chudleigh, but from this famous grandmother she seemed to have inherited no notable literary tastes or talents. Her father, Colonel Thomas Chudleigh, married a cousin, Henrietta or Harriet Chudleigh, served in the 34th Regiment of Foot in the Marlborough Wars, and was rewarded with the post of deputy governor to Chelsea Hospital.[6] Here in the hospital gardens the young Chudleigh played with her brother—already an ensign in a regiment of foot—and the infant Horace Walpole, but in 1726, when she was about six, her father died and her mother took her two young children back to Thomas Chudleigh's small Devonshire estate—its income, according to one of her biographers, was £100 a year[7]—to rear them in genteel but straitened circumstances.

The patriarch was dead but had left behind a legacy of pugnacious and intrepid character. A witness told a tale in 1714 of being present at court when a man named Davenport stood by another named Alsworth and wondered aloud how anyone could have the impudence to come there that had drunk the Pretender's health. Alsworth inquired whether the reference were to himself. Davenport replied that "he knew best if he ever had, wch Alsworth deny'd. Coll. Chudleigh having an old grudge came up and affirm'd he had, so Alsworth went out with him; the Coll. kill'd him upon the spot fairly." The word "fairly" rings ironically, and the affair sounds like a murder plot. Colonel Chudleigh entered his son as ensign in Cavendish's Regiment of Foot perhaps on the very day he was born.[8] The mother, also a Chudleigh by birth and by temperament, was, in Walpole's unfriendly recollection, like her daughter, a "heroine." During her husband's governorship at Chelsea, coming home late at night in a coach followed on foot, a little tardily, by a patrol of two old Chelsea pensioners, she was awakened by three footpads, one of whom placed a pistol to her breast. Putting her head out of the window she coolly called to the pensioners, "Fire!", whereupon they shot and killed one of her assailants. With the body slung on behind the coach, she resumed her way to the hospital.[9] This woman, from whom Chudleigh had received a second measure of the brave, impetuous, and unreflective Chudleigh nature, provided both a model to build on and a champion to best.

Judging from Chudleigh's confidence about getting whatever she
wanted from men, her brother Thomas had probably also been bested
very early, but in any case, though he lived to inherit the family baronetcy in 1738, he had taken a commission in the army and he died at
Aix-la-Chapelle in 1741, aged no more than twenty-two. Probably his
gallant sister and his mother would also have realized their best selves
in active military service.

The formidable charm Chudleigh possessed, combined with her
beauty—she had beautiful blue eyes, dark brown hair, and a lily-white
skin—and autocratic nature, produced the likeness of a young prince,
exercising authority, developing her wit and verbal skills, and living the
outdoor life that made her an accomplished horsewoman and intrepid
traveler. In her autobiography she remembered her first years:

Reared at the country seat of her father, her childhood passed happily and innocently, and to this period she ever looked back with pleasure. She was surrounded by good and faithful beings, who never deceived her, but ever spoke
frankly the truth, and over whom she exercised an authority that gratified her
infantine pride. . . . One thing is certain, that from her earliest years Elizabeth
was remarkable for her wit and power of repartee, as well as for the elegance
and fascination of her manners. The peasantry on her father's estate said that
she was *charmed*, that the beasts would follow her without being called, and
that no person could know her without loving her. (*Memoirs*, 1:220)

In 1782, however, she was charged by an early biographer with having
not one but three ruling passions: ambition, vanity, and avarice.[10] The
judgment is justified, and all three passions probably originated in her
isolated, privileged, but straitened childhood, but it was her avarice, her
greatest passion, which she was most loath to recognize. Her avarice
accounted for her vast wealth, but she preferred to the end to pretend,
despite the way she used her possessions to keep her unfortunate acquaintances dangling after her, that her enormous power was the result
of her personal charms.

The autobiography shows many characteristic lapses from fact, some
designed to exalt the importance of her own family, and although Chudleigh claimed that her start in fashionable life, a position as maid of
honor at the court of the Prince of Wales, was obtained for her by her
family, it was in fact a gift from William Pulteney (the Earl of Bath in

1742 and more than thirty years her senior), reputed to have been one of her earliest lovers.

Pulteney was said to have met Chudleigh by accident while he was hunting. If so, it is easily conjectured that she, probably not yet twenty, deliberately put herself on horseback in his way. He was a great political figure but a notable miser, adept at benefiting others to whom he was obliged without disbursing from his own supplies—though not as adept as his pupil would become—and it was probably his idea that Harriet Chudleigh take a house at Chelsea and let lodgings to people of tone in temporary need of country air. Thus with small expense to himself, his protégée, now about twenty, in about 1740 was suitably established in comfortable proximity to the court. Pulteney had assigned himself the role of mentor to the captivating, witty, but comparatively uneducated girl[11] and designed for her a course of reading which, however, she refused to undertake. As she outstripped her mentors in influence, it was always she who set the tone wherever she went, and because of her announced prerogative to be perpetually changing, she was utterly unreliable in her relations with others. One biographer found her true to her maxim, changing friends as she changed her dress.[12] Following the failure of the reading course, says another, Pulteney "changed the scene, and endeavoured to initiate her in the science of economy instead of books."[13]

Whether or not he did teach her his science of economy, Chudleigh certainly perfected his art of conferring obligations at no expense to the obliger, and another art she perfected was that of acquiring and retaining gifts to herself. In 1740 or soon afterward Pulteney obtained for her the post as maid of honor to the Princess of Wales, at a stipend, probably, of £200 a year, and she would retain the post for an improbable number of years, even after the princess knew that she had married Augustus Hervey and produced at least two children. Wherever she studied "economy," she remained throughout life notoriously tight with money (unless she was spending it on herself or someone who benefited herself), did no one a good turn except at the expense of someone else, and consistently extracted present benefits in return for the promise of future ones.

In her autobiography Chudleigh touches honestly upon her unwillingness to spend on any other than herself,[14] on her love of display, and on her reckless courage, modeled after her mother's:

She absolutely adored her casket of jewels, always taking it with her in her carriage when she travelled, and armed with pistols prepared to defend it at the risk of her life. She was courageous even to rashness, and, instead of fearing, always felt a pleasure in braving the most terrific dangers. Once that she was attacked by robbers in Russia, she defended herself with great courage, and, with the assistance of her servants, put them to flight. . . . Her contempt for public opinion was no less than her fearlessness of physical risk. (*Memoirs*, 1:225–26)

Two recorded examples of her meanness should suffice. After her trial for bigamy in 1776 she presented her steadfast friend Dr. Schomberg, who had consistently befriended and supported her, a ring with a deep blue stone engraved "Pour l'Amitié" and surrounded with brilliants. One of the supposed diamonds had fallen out, and Schomberg took his ring to a jeweler who pronounced it not worth repairing because its value was no more than thirty-six shillings. When she departed for Russia in 1777 she attempted to secure friends there in advance by forwarding two paintings from the Kingston collection to Count Chernicheff. Later, on discovery that the paintings were by Raphael and Claude Lorraine, she tried to exchange them for others, and when that tactic did not work, in her will averred that the paintings had been lent rather than given.[15]

Chudleigh's eventful life was characterized by an upward climb toward vast wealth and power during which she was able to avoid assuming an exaggerated moral hypocrisy and to enjoy an impressive sum of self-indulgence. Her position as maid of honor to the Princess of Wales placed her at the center of the gay, young Opposition court of the prince and princess. At Leicester House and Kew she quickly gained an ascendancy over the princess. Still, the necessity of attending at assigned hours and the obligation to curb her imperiousness before the prince's family must have been galling to Chudleigh and strengthened her longing to become queen of her own court. In her early twenties, she was overpoweringly seductive to strangers: "Viewed superficially, and, by a transient acquaintance, she appeared irresistibly attractive," wrote a biographer in 1789, but "an intimacy dissolved the charm."[16] Almost at once on her arrival at court the young Duke of Hamilton fell in love with her. He was just off on his European tour but promised faithfully to marry her on his return. An aunt of hers, set against the match, intercepted his letters and, piqued by his seeming neglect, Chudleigh secretly—so as not to have to forfeit her court post as a "maid"—married the poor but fascinating Augustus Hervey on August 4, 1744. In the summer of 1747 at Chelsea—that is, at the home of her mother, always her staunch ally—she bore Hervey's son, who quickly died. By this time the spouses had come to loathe each other, and they agreed never to acknowledge their secret marriage.

The birth of the child had not, however, been so secret, and it occasioned Chesterfield's celebrated bon mot when, while playing whist with him, Chudleigh laughed at the report that she had given birth to twins: he replied that he never believed more than half of what he heard. The princess, however, continued to countenance her, and soon afterward, despite the strain between the two courts, George II himself fell in love with her. Another parsimonious man, he once, to Walpole's astonishment, actually paid thirty-five guineas from his own purse to buy Chudleigh a fairing, probably a watch and chain.[17] He was in love with her either before or upon the spot when she made her celebrated appearance as Iphigenia at a masquerade on May Day in 1749, so naked, Walpole said, "that you would have taken her for Andromeda,"[18] so naked, Elizabeth Montagu said, that as Iphigenia for the sacrifice, "ye high Priest might easily inspect ye Entrails of ye Victim the Maids of honour (not of maids ye strictest) were so offended they w[d] not speak to her."[19] The Princess of Wales, it was reported, threw her cloak over her, whereupon Chudleigh is said to have responded, "Those who have parts not fit to be seen, do well to conceal them; that is not my case. It is the blackest ingratitude to bountiful nature not to display the beautiful limbs she has formed."[20] The king, amused and entranced, refused to join the censure and a week later gave a jubilee masquerade specifically in her honor.[21] It was assumed that she had become his mistress. In December 1750 at a Drawing Room at St. James's he informed her that he had appointed her mother housekeeper at Windsor (at £800 a year) and against all precedent kissed her where she stood. "He has had a hankering these two years," Walpole commented discreetly.[22] A later source reported that she might have become official court mistress had she not displayed too much of a spirit of intrigue.[23]

These were the years of her great general ascendancy. Samuel Richardson encountered her at Tunbridge in August 1748 and reported her "a lively, sweet-tempered, gay, self-admired, and, not altogether without reason, generally-admired lady—She moved not without crowds after her. She smiled at everyone. Every one smiled before they saw her, when they heard she was on the walk." And everyone was in love with her. But Richardson's conclusion (in paraphrase) was that she had more the éclat of a mistress than the properly repressed charms of a wife.[24]

When charm failed, Chudleigh resorted to trickery and blackmail, and Hester Thrale in *Thraliana* records an anecdote of about 1760 that may be apocryphal but sums up public opinion about its subject—and produced a popular print of the period: "Miss Chudleigh being pressed to resign her Post as Maid of Honour soon after the Accession of George the 3[d] in favour of a Scotch Lady related to Lord *Bute* with whom as 'tis well known the Princess was supposed to be too intimate;—made her Highness this arch Answer; Votre Altesse Royale doit sçavoir, que chacun a son But; le mien est de servir votre Altesse Royale jusqu'a la fin de ma Vie—." [25]

But in 1751 she had already turned the good-natured weak head of Evelyn Pierrepont, Duke of Kingston. Kingston was good-looking, well-mannered, and not very clever; his horsemanship and dancing were irreproachable.[26] She was just in her thirties; he was forty. It is probable that in 1751 they produced a daughter, Elizabeth.[27] In January 1752 the duke sent away his longtime mistress, the French Madam de la Touche, who had ruined herself for him, and by the summer the pair had become a customary sight visiting her mother, now conveniently established at Windsor.[28] From this period Chudleigh was in command of the duke's great revenues, and she began to lease and embellish the house in Paradise Row, Knightsbridge, later, on her "marriage" in 1769, to be known as Kingston House, as well as the villa at Finchley and Percy Lodge near Colnbrook. Kingston House stood on Knightsbridge, and opposite to it was a private iron gate into Hyde Park by favor of the king. In the great house she gave lavish parties, often entertaining the ministers or envoys of foreign courts where subsequently she would be gratifyingly received. According to her French biographer, who seems intimately informed about Kingston House, Chudleigh received there in a print room, "papered by her own lovely hands with the prints of the best engravers in Europe" (translation from p. 146). He also claims that ministers met there to project affairs of state and avows that the plans that accelerated the loss of the colonies were hatched there, as were cabals to lose the patriots their places (p. 144). It was largely a male society. Though Chudleigh was never actually dropped from the great world, fashionable women went to her only to attend the great parties which she contrived to make so spectacular that no one could afford to miss them. By the 1760s the Kingston set, consisting of the duke's military friends and entourage, much inferior to him in station, and Chudleigh's set of companions, without additions from the polite world, was to be found in the various houses of the duke, including the ducal seat at Thoresby, which under Chudleigh's direction was being rebuilt from 1761 to 1771.

Chudleigh's expert assumption of male prerogative would have been incomplete had she not toured abroad. She undertook the first trip in early 1765, when she was forty-five, to pique Kingston, many thought, who had so far faltered in his devotion as to establish a milliner friend at Thoresby. Walpole informs us that she first beat her side until it was injured and then set off to drink the Carlsbad waters.[29] Cynical comment passed between Lord Chesterfield and his son, then resident in a minor diplomatic post at Dresden. "As for the lady," wrote that cynosure of *politesse* Chesterfield, "if you should be very sharp set for some English flesh, she has it amply in her power to supply you, if she pleases."[30] The trip was successful in every aspect: the Electress of Saxony fell at Chudleigh's feet, and Kingston discovered that he must have her back again. "It was a dangerous experiment that she tried, in leaving him so long," wrote Lord Chesterfield to his son; "but it seems she knew her man."[31]

Chudleigh had designed her own traveling coach, an emblem of her determination to dominate every detail of her life and to live like no other. A large trunk made to hold her wardrobe was set onto the spring of the forecarriage, and a seat with arms and back like an easy chair was set on top. In the carriage she carried her jewel case and her pistols. Within the carriage was a night stool open at the bottom and next to it a container for her favorite Madeira. When she intended to make use of the former, her male companions were instructed to mount the trunk to survey the country. That company on her first trip included a manservant; a Swiss hussar borrowed from the Marquis of Granby; her apothecary, Thomas Evans, to administer her vomits; Mr. Siprutini the musician; and her favorite companion, Miss Bate.[32]

Chudleigh's subsequent travels, as memorialized by her biographers, included a return to Saxony in 1766; a prolonged sojourn in Calais and Rome after the duke's death in 1773; and, after her trial and exile, wanderings from Calais to Rome to Russia to Paris, where she died in 1788. In addition, Jacques Casanova gives a circumstantial account of meeting her in Naples in 1770 at two semiorgiastic entertainments given by the Prince of Francavilla, at the first of which a naked priest and several pages cavorted in the water at the seashore, and at the second (pronounced tedious by Chudleigh) ten or twelve beautiful naked girls cavorted in a fountain. Casanova also arranged for an adventuress of his acquaintance, whose lover of seven years was in prison for debt, to join Chudleigh's train of companions "in the place of a Roman girl" on the return to England.[33]

The continuing inconvenience of the good health of Augustus Hervey —a person as robust and as inconsiderate as herself—so exasperated

Chudleigh, who wished to marry the duke, that in 1769 she applied for a nullity decree on the ground that there had been no marriage; probably the impecunious Hervey was paid by the duke to support Chudleigh's claims. In February of that year she was officially pronounced a spinster.[34] In March, in Lent (the bishop of London refused a license), Chudleigh married the duke. She was forty-nine and had been his mistress for eighteen years. According to Thomas Whitehead, the duke was motivated less, in his exemplary fidelity, by his enduring passion than by his having signed an agreement that whenever she should prove herself a single woman, he would marry her or forfeit £10,000 a year for her life (Letter I). *The Case of the Duchess of Kingston* claims the forfeit would have been a bond for £36,000, canceled by the duke after the wedding. Chudleigh may well have been remembering the Madam de la Touche when she forced the duke to such an agreement.

One respectable account claims that on marriage the duke settled £4,000 a year on Chudleigh, whose next object was to induce the duke to name her heir to his vast personal wealth and possessions, the wealth forever, the real estate for life provided she never remarry.[35] For her lifetime, at least, the duke and Chudleigh thus thwarted his expectant heirs, the sons of a sister. That there was no heir to the dukedom made her achievement feasible, but her greed was at last her undoing. When the duke died in 1773—harried, said Whitehead, into the grave—his sister, having turned up a witness to her original marriage, filed a bill of indictment for bigamy against Chudleigh at Hicks Hall. She was in Rome, where it was said she had converted the largest part of her inherited property to money and deposited it in the papal bank, and a sentence of outlawry was threatened against her. But she returned to contest and then to stand her trial for bigamy at Westminster Hall in 1776, when she was adjudged guilty, yet—to the chagrin of the duke's family—left for the moment in full possession of her inherited acquisitions.[36] Moreover, her luck had held: in March 1775 Augustus Hervey had succeeded as Earl of Bristol, and as a peeress she was exempt from being burned in the hand. Only hours before an order not to depart the country could reach her, Chudleigh escaped to France and was thenceforward an exile.[37] Until her death she wandered through the countries where the heads of state made her welcome—"It must be confessed," Chesterfield had said, "that she knows the arts of Courts; to be so received at Dresden and so connived at in Leicester-fields"[38]—and showered her with gifts in return for the promises she broadcast that everyone and anyone should be her heirs. She acquired more of those fabulous jewels that, being displayed to her greedy victims, made them the more eager to oblige her. Among her great friends and protectors at various times were Frederick the Great, the pope, the Electress of Saxony, and Catherine the Great. She lived in a state and with an attendance equaled only by royalty. Musicians, physicians, and stewards attended in her train; at her death she left in Russia four musician slaves, to be manumitted six years after her decease.[39]

Chudleigh had lovers, husbands, houses, stewards, and heirs in multiples, and it is not surprising that from the days of her prosperity with Kingston she kept on hand at all times a set of three to six companions whom she called, in imitation of the Princess of Wales, her maids of honor. Other society women did not frequent her house, and the companions made up an adequate feminine complement. But her behavior to these companions, which might have been considerate, instead was, after an initial honeymoon period, tyrannical in the best tradition of Collier. She would have no companion who was not young, beautiful, and accomplished; she dressed them all in vestal white; she used their presence to lure men to her houses but fell into a fury when men paid them attentions. She alone could be the object of admiration. She appeared to have adopted as her motto the warning of Astrea in the *New Atalantis* "that no Woman ought to introduce another to the Man by whom she is belov'd; if that had not happen'd, the Duke had possibly not been false" (p. 43). Her companions, who perforce lived with Chudleigh's duke, were therefore under the most stringent requirements of restraint in regard not only to Kingston but also to all other men.

These companions were gentlewomen of little to no means lured into place by Chudleigh's promise to "find them establishments" or otherwise to provide for them—that is, to marry or pension them. But they were not allowed to marry, and she is not known ever to have provided a pension for any of them.

Her behavior toward her companions was perfectly consistent with that of the sultan of a harem, and there is certainly a possibility that Chudleigh was a practicing lesbian.[40] In her twenties her two intimate friends were the rakish Lady Caroline Fitzroy Petersham and Elizabeth Ashe, with whom she vied in horsemanship as well as amours. It has been suggested that Petersham and Ashe on occasion frequented a lesbian bordello.[41] The possibility that Chudleigh took a sexual interest in her companions should not be overlooked. But she also exacted the homage and attention of men, and like Snow White's stepmother queen demanded that her stepdaughters remain prepubescent, that she herself remain eternally fairest of them all.[42]

When she hired a new companion, her instruction was, "Take care of the men; they will first squeeze your hand, next kiss you; growing bolder, they will attempt your bosom; which gained, they will try for *something else:* now you be a good girl, and remember my advice" (Letter X). This gross and insulting warning, with its implication that men could be interested in nothing but their flesh, was calculated to justify a tantrum on Chudleigh's part should she find anyone kissing the hand or gazing into the eyes of one of her maids.

The social strictures laid upon them must have been impossible for the most modest of companions to obey, and in addition domestic life with Chudleigh was taxing; her maids were often on duty. In the morning, if there were not a concert at home which they attended and to which they sometimes contributed, they all went out, for when Chudleigh went out *en duchesse,* her court went in attendance, though only to wait in a second coach while she made her calls. Mary Delany noted in 1771 that Chudleigh, who had "unsuccessfully tried all her charms to inveigle company" following her "marriage" to Kingston, "has her state coach following her wherever she bestows her presence, with three or four ladies (or rather *misses*) called her maids of honor."[43]

At dinner in mid-afternoon her companions had to witness, endure, and sometimes assist at the grossest of her rituals. Chudleigh was a great eater and drinker and had recourse to vomits in an attempt to preserve her beauty. Whitehead reported that when she drove in the park between breakfast and dinner, he had known her to order the carriage home five or six times for refreshments of tea, chocolate, sweet cakes, and Madeira (Letter XIII). Thomas Evans, her apothecary, lived with her and administered her vomits. Whitehead described the dinner table, at which Chudleigh would stuff immoderately, get up and go into the next room (leaving the door open, however), relieve herself with Evans's assistance, and return smilingly to beg the company's pardon for having just suffered a fit of gout of the stomach. She was then persuaded to eat or drink something, after which the duke ushered her, with her ladies, back into the next room, where she lay upon the sofa and snored, the ladies in attendance and the rest of the company uneasily subdued. Following her slumbers, she would reenter the card room with a white handkerchief tied round her head to relieve her headache, and if she did not lose at cards, she would, to the relief of all, manage to maintain her temper. When she lost, she might order the entire company from the house. In either case her manners were original: when she grew hot, for instance, she would rise from the table and fan herself by vigorously shaking her petticoats. The maids continued in attendance until bedtime. When there was a general entertainment after dinner, with tea and cards, the domestic music played the company upstairs into the drawing room, where the maids of honor attended to usher the ladies into Chudleigh's presence (Letter XIII).

Nor need attendance necessarily end there. After Chudleigh had retired with the duke, her maids were usually dismissed. Chudleigh had warned them never to enter her room unless rung for lest she shoot them with the pistols she kept by her bed.[44] But when the duke had denied Chudleigh one of the great sums she frequently extorted from him, she had his bed moved to another room, pleaded illness, and forced one of her companions to sit up with her all night. She continued this punishment for the space of a month so that he could not approach her until he had met her conditions (Letter XIII).

Chudleigh was passionately fond of music and devised a compromise between her penuriousness and her love of state and desire for a private band of music by hiring servants who could play an instrument or sing. Whitehead described a typical musical morning on a wet day at Thoresby and named the concert group: Mr. Markordt, a servant, presiding on the harpsichord as music master; Colonel Glover, a friend and a cousin of Chudleigh's, as first violin; Mr. Zun, groom of the chamber, as second violin; Whitehead, the duke's valet, as tenor; the favorite musician Siprutini on the violoncello; Mr. Lilly, footman, first horn; Mr. Presly, footman, second horn; Miss Bate, companion, soprano.

During the performance, Chudleigh, having set several pens to work in different languages, dispatched her correspondence with an ease Whitehead professed to admire. "She would talk likewise to Mr. Simpson, the architect, about some alterations, and yet be very attentive to the music; would often cry, 'Bravo! bravo, Miss Bate; do me the favour of singing that again. Mr. Main (the librarian) you write so and so. Mrs. —— you write, and you Miss ——, etc.'" (Letter XIII).

Of Chudleigh's much-abused companions, of whom there must have been many, six have been particularly memorialized. The earliest of these was Harriet Fielding, Henry Fielding's daughter and therefore, like her father, a cousin of the duke. For many years one of the regular diversions of Chudleigh and the duke had been attendance at the court of Sir John Fielding, Harriet's uncle, to hear the examinations of felons;

their coach was a familiar fixture in Bow Street. Chudleigh must have known Harriet as a child and promised her connections to give the girl a home and protection. Whitehead (who tends consistently to under-estimate age and who is speaking of the events of 1765, when Harriet was twenty-eight) writes:

Miss Fielding was of a good stature, about twenty years of age, a sweet tem-per, and great understanding; but in a deep decline. She had been a visitor and companion to Miss C. for some years. Colonel Montressor, who was between fifty and sixty years old [he was actually sixty-three] paid his addresses to her, and in a few months afterwards they were married; which so displeased Miss C. that she never saw them after. If the colonel had not married her I believe she would never have got a husband; being, poor lady, the colour of a ghost—a mere skeleton, with such coughings and spittings as would have turned the stomach of a coal-heaver. (Letter XI)

In the Christmas holidays of 1765, the Kingston set spent a month at Clinton Lodge, later Pierrepont Lodge, near Farnham, Surrey. Warner the harpist and Prosser the violinist played country dances. The first ball was held on Christmas Eve, and the entertainments continued every night for a month except on Sunday. Those present were Chud-leigh and her faithful cousin Bell Chudleigh (sometimes a companion), Miss Bate, Miss Fielding, Sir James and Lady Laroche, Captain and Mrs. Moreau and their son, the Reverend Dr. Cotton of Winchester and his son, Colonel Montresor, the governor of Tilbury Fort, and Master Richard Shuckburgh, Miss Bate's stepbrother.

During these prolonged festivities, Harriet Fielding became intimate with James Gabriel Montresor, a noted military engineer who had re-turned from America in 1762. Harriet Fielding, a veteran of the 1754 journey to Lisbon that had ended in her father's death, had very little money: her father's will had left her seven shares in his Register Office, and Ralph Allen on his death in 1764 had bequeathed her £100. On August 25, 1766, the couple married, after which the infuriated Chud-leigh never saw either of them again, though she must have known that Harriet was dying. She was buried in London at St. James's Church on December 11. Montresor was not readmitted to the Kingston set.[45]

As an accumulator of companions, Chudleigh found poor relations her great resource, and her will shows that her strongest loyalties were to her family. But she could not bear that a dependent should obtain supplies elsewhere than from herself or that any other woman in her household should be the recipient of admiration. She always remained entirely incapable of facilitating the marriage of a companion and perhaps (as Foote revealed) became most enraged when one attracted a serious suitor.

More comical than tragical were her efforts to destroy the amour of her companion Betty with the German footman Presly, who doubled on the French horn. Betty was a short, pretty girl whom Chudleigh had discovered in Plymouth in about 1765. Following the duke's death and after the loss of her favorites, Miss Bate and Miss Penrose, Chudleigh elevated Betty to the position of chief maid and took her on her third sortie into Saxony in the late 1770s. In the course of the journey Betty responded favorably to Presly's devoirs, though, said Whitehead, "he was as ordinary a man as ever you saw," and Chudleigh, informed by other members of the party, disposed of Presly through an elaborate device. She told him that she had left something at Calais for which he, the only person she could trust, must return at once, and she gave him a letter to deliver to her steward there. The steward found within his letter another which Presly was to deliver in all haste to the steward at Kingston House in Knightsbridge. In Knightsbridge the steward, Mr. Williams, opened his letter and found within it an order for Presly's instant discharge (Letter V). As Chudleigh was not again to return (at least openly) to England, she had effectually separated the lovers forever.

An anonymous biographer is the dubious authority for the tale of another maid both nameless and hapless. When Chudleigh left Rome in haste for Calais in 1775 on her way to stand trial for bigamy, she deposited her plate in a bank but left in her palace many valuables, a renegade Spanish friar, and a pretty young English girl described as prudent, handsome, rosy, plump, high-spirited, and good-humored. A cardinal of the church, much attracted by the girl, attempted by frequent visits to the house, ostensibly to inquire about Chudleigh, to corrupt her. The friar had his own designs, and the girl suffered from having neither the authority to forbid the two the house nor the right to desert her trust. At length the friar prevailed, after which he carried everything portable from the house and sold it. An account of this robbery (rather than the pressing invitation from the pope which she reported—indeed, she was never again welcome in Roman society) was the reason for Chudleigh's hasty return to Rome in May 1776. When she arrived—according to this account—she found the friar decamped and the girl about to become a mother.

The poor girl being questioned fell on her knees—She charged the friar with opening her chamber door and obtaining his ends by force—the lady answered what's that to me—you let him force open my escrutoir—"Alas," said the girl,

"I was naked and in bed"—"My linen is all gone!" exclaimed the lady—"Pity my condition," said the maid—"I have lost my candlestick," cried the lady— "That infernal friar," said the poor girl, sobbing, "has robbed the palace, by the living God" ejaculated the lady—and bursting into tears, lamented in terms the most pathetic, at which even the heart of the friar would have relented, the loss of a diamond buckle, left her by her dear duke.[46]

The literary parody of Laurence Sterne here (confined to this episode by the unknown biographer) helps to indict Chudleigh for her distorted values, the total failure in her of that sensibility so exalted by Sterne, her lack of empathy for the girl imperiled by herself who had been raped, abused, and ruined. Chudleigh's unnatural unwomanliness is further suggested by the hint that she herself had made sexual use of the friar— "I have lost my candlestick!"—and further differentiates her from her victim. Her hypocrisy remained to be indicted, but soon a message of condolence arrived from the pope.

"What I have lost, Sir," said the Countess of Bristol to his holiness's gentle-man, "is certainly of very considerable value; but virtue, Sir, is above all price; and his villany in taking advantage of the weakness of an innocent creature, is the cause of my distress—my jewels may be replaced; but her chastity, Sir! My noble lord bequeathed me a princely revenue, and I wish to make others happy with it—My unfortunate servant I took when a child, and meant to provide for her like a mother, . . . and having dispatched the messenger, returned to her de-luded domestic in as high a passion as she left her, swearing if she did not find the friar she would have her put to death by torture as an accomplice. (p. 33)

This imaginative rendition juxtaposes Chudleigh's true nature with her awareness of how she ought, by contemporary standards, to be re-sponding, making of her a consummate hypocrite who could play the woman of sensibility. Chudleigh knows exactly how she *ought* to re-spond to the situation and simply chooses not to. She is aware of what she *ought* to do with her fortune and how she ought to behave to her maid—but chooses not to. She stands indicted here not only for her monstrously selfish behavior but also for knowing better, for counter-feiting sensibility.

Perhaps the most pathetic tale of all is that of Elizabeth Skinner, an orphan born in about 1751 and left in a basket on the staircase to Harriet Chudleigh's lodgings at Windsor.[47] It was generally considered that this child, known only as Elizabeth, was Chudleigh's. Chudleigh's mother kept the infant until her own death in 1756; Chudleigh must have maintained her thereafter, for when she was no more than fifteen she was appointed a maid. During Chudleigh's second journey to Saxony, which commenced hastily in the summer of 1766 following the electress's urgent request for her return, Elizabeth was left at Thoresby with the duke, whose friends seized the opportunity to persuade him that, as what he most needed was an heir, he ought, in Chudleigh's absence, to marry and impregnate Elizabeth (or perhaps, more prudently, to impregnate and marry her). The duke refused—a weak-headed but decent man, he would have been unlikely to have married a girl whom he believed to be his own daughter—but Chudleigh's subsequent cruelties to the girl suggest that she learned the plot from her spies. Or had the girl actually served as the duke's mistress during Chudleigh's absence and then perhaps been informed by Chudleigh of his relationship to her? In any case, Chudleigh's subsequent mistreatment of Elizabeth was such, Whitehead reported, that she broke Elizabeth's heart. The day before her death in October 1770 she told Whitehead that she was very ill, "and, if she quitted this life, she hoped the duchess would behave better to her successor" (Letter V). She was buried in the churchyard at Perlethorpe, the register for which parish notes, "Elizabeth Skinner of Thoresby was buried on 15th October, 1770"—on the north side of the chapel, said Whitehead, which to him denoted a suspicion of suicide.[48] Chudleigh, at first shocked by Elizabeth's death, ordered a funeral and declared the girl should have a monument—but it was never erected.

Most important in Chudleigh's life, however, were Miss Bate and Miss Penrose, the last two companions to be considered here. Bate was the longer-lasting, the principal companion of Chudleigh's career. She was in place for many years before Chudleigh's marriage to Kingston and for a few years after. She traveled with Chudleigh twice to Saxony, in 1765 and 1766, was a fixture during the Kingston set years, and followed her mistress faithfully into marriage. She must have had an unusually complaisant character.

Bate was the daughter of Edward Bate, Esq. and Sarah Haywood Bate; when after her father's death in 1750 her mother married Colonel Richard Shuckburgh, Bate acquired two half-brothers, George Shuckburgh—later Sir George, a close friend of Chudleigh's for many years and one of her executors—and Richard Shuckburgh, from his childhood a plaything to Chudleigh, who took him to the theater, taught him speeches from the plays, and amused herself by bidding him repeat them to Garrick (Letter XI). Mrs. Shuckburgh enjoyed a widow's pension to her death, and Chudleigh, following her principle of doing for others what cost her nothing and benefited herself, managed (probably through the duke's influence) to get the pension continued to the daughter. Thus Bate was amply provided for without any cost to Chudleigh, who took the credit and probably suggested that the pension was to continue only at her own discretion. Bate had come to Chudleigh no later than at her mother's death.

Bate was probably one of those women about whom Fielding and Scott were most censorious, too genteel and proud to earn her living by departing from her station, for she could have been a professional singer. She had a remarkably fine and well-trained voice, both equal to and very like, Whitehead said, the voice of Arne's celebrated pupil Miss Brent, with whom she often sang at Chudleigh's entertainments. From the next room listeners found it impossible to distinguish one voice from the other; Bate also resembled Brent in stature and features. Her best-known renditions were "The Soldier Tired" and "I Know that my Redeemer Liveth" (Letter V).

Bate was so suitable a companion that she might have stayed with Chudleigh to the end had not Chudleigh become enraged at her by a codicil to the duke's will leaving her a small annuity of £60. What enraged her most is difficult to determine: that the duke had meddled in her domestic affairs; that he had shown interest in another woman at her expense; that Bate had acquired a small measure of independence; or that the £60 was money out of her own pocket. Whitehead charges that Chudleigh attempted to persuade her lawyer to add another codicil canceling this and other of the duke's small bequests (including one to Whitehead).[49] It is entirely characteristic of Chudleigh that, having become the duke's principal heir, she considered his naming a few other legatees unpardonable perfidy.

Chudleigh's resentment at the legacy at last forced Bate to retire to Bath with her pension and her annuity. Then she married the Reverend Mr. Williams of Lad-Dock near Truro, "whom she certainly," says Whitehead—joining the chorus of those who viewed companionship as the perfect preparation for wifehood—"makes happy, being mistress of an amiable temper and disposition" (Letter V).

Mary Penrose (1749–1840) had been a longtime subordinate companion and on Bate's retirement was promoted to first place. Whitehead says she was "a beautiful fine-grown young woman, about nineteen or twenty" (Letter V). She was considerably junior to Bate. Penrose saw Chudleigh through the death of the duke, the subsequent wanderings abroad, the trial for bigamy, and the flight to Calais. She was the daughter of the Reverend John Penrose, rector of Penryn, Cornwall; they were a notable family and related to Chudleigh.[50] Penrose has the distinction of having been named in the contemporary memoirs of Chudleigh as the model for Lydia Lydell in Foote's farce and as the informant who gave Foote Chudleigh's secrets. She was the first but scarcely the second.

That there was an informant who talked to Foote about Chudleigh is certain. In the spring of 1775 Chudleigh returned to England to stand trial, and for the remainder of that year her lawyers procured one delay after another so that the proceedings did not begin until April 1776. In December 1774 Foote was in Bath, where Whitehead, probably with the duke's legacy, had set up a music shop; on his return to London early in 1775, Foote apparently set about writing his farce.[51] That Foote's information came from Whitehead is far more feasible than that it came from Penrose. Whitehead, who had always detested Chudleigh and who now owed her a particular grudge for having attempted to cancel his legacy, probably contacted and sold his information to Foote, who specialized in topical subjects and the taking-off of well-known personages in his farces and who may well have planned to act the role of Lady Kitty Crocodile himself.

In the farce Lady Kitty, like Chudleigh, married in Lent and professes an inordinate grief for the loss of her husband. Her name, Crocodile, refers to the nature of her tears and to her predatory nature. Lady Kitty, like Chudleigh, is a friend of the pope's and lives in Calais. Chudleigh was charged with bigamy; Lady Kitty advises Jenny to marry both her suitors. Like Penrose, Lydia Lydell is a relative of her patroness and the daughter of a clergyman.

Two 1788 biographies of Chudleigh name Penrose as the informant. One notes that Foote received private information from a former inmate of Chudleigh's house and that suspicion had fallen on Miss Penrose, the disappointed recipient of many gracious promises. Another, deriving its information from the first, notes that Foote's informant was "Ponrose," "who having long been deceived by her grace's *promises*, was forced by necessity to convert her *secrets* into saleable commodities, and disposed of them to Foote for a sum of money."[52]

But Chudleigh never turned on the Penroses. Bate does not appear among the numerous legatees in her will, nor does any other identifiable former companion except Penrose. The Penrose family, however, is well represented. Before her death Chudleigh had bestowed various Kingston livings on members of the family, Fledborough in Nottinghamshire on Penrose's brother John in 1783, and two livings on Thomas Donnithorne, whom Penrose was to marry: first Cuckney, then Holme-pierrepont.

The actual legacies to the Penroses may have been more hollow. To John Penrose Chudleigh left her paternal Devonshire estate in succession after several other unnamed legatees,[53] but when he was about to attempt to claim it, he found it in the hands of the duke's nephews, it having been made over to the duke as part of his marriage settlement and they having inherited his real estate after Chudleigh's death. To Mrs. Donnithorne Chudleigh left all the plate and other effects (except the paintings) from her house in Paris; these were to be sold and the sum put into government stocks, the income from which would go to Penrose, the capital to be divided among her children when they came of age. Her house in Montmartre had turned out to be ruinous, involving Chudleigh in a lawsuit the loss of which was said to have occasioned the stroke that killed her; though she lived in another house in Paris, in the end Evelyn Medows, Kingston's nephew, got to the house immediately after Chudleigh's death and removed most of the valuables.[54] But whether or not Penrose actually received any legacy, Chudleigh apparently did not identify Penrose as Foote's informant and did not cut off relations with her former companion even though Penrose left Chudleigh after the trial—she was at home in Cornwall with her mother in 1778 and married Donnithorne in 1780. If the print of Chudleigh and her maids at the trial was done from life, the principal maid is Penrose.

Perhaps Chudleigh deserves a feminist plaudit for courage, for having wrested the most destructive of male prerogatives from the establishment, for having raised a question in the 1770s about the essential submissiveness and sensibility of the female nature. But she became a monstrous parody of male prerogative in her cruel determination to regard nothing but her own will, pleasure, and power, to subordinate all human relationships to the service of her ends, and to enjoy being tyrannical as evidence of her success.

There was no male prerogative that she did not assume and no feminine convention that she did not despise; perhaps herein lies her attraction for her recent biographers. Her mistreatment of the legion of her lovers, her plain speaking, her refusal to lie about her age, her rejection of refined manners, her drinking, her gargantuan appetite, her acquisition of princely riches, her travels, her courage, her use of firearms, and finally her treatment of other women as commodities all evidence a determined identification with the aggressor. In many ways she realized the heroine it was her ambition to play. She was the second woman (after Catherine Macaulay) to apply for a ticket to the reading room of the British Museum.[55] In her own name she raced a mare, Marie Antoine, at the Newmarket spring meetings in 1772 and 1773. Numerous stories attest to her manliness. When she was summoned from Rome to trial and found her banker loath to dispense the necessary travel funds (being, one biographer claimed, in collusion with her heirs at law), she waylaid him on his own front steps and forced him at pistol point to disburse.[56] She was a daring and accomplished horsewoman.[57] Her excessive drinking was done openly, and once in Prussia, after putting away two bottles, she fell flat on her face in Frederick's ballroom—though she remained thereafter his correspondent. She was a businesswoman, investing in a brandy manufacture in Russia and selling rabbits from her St. Assize estate. She prided herself, she said, on never departing from her word once it was given and never allowing her will to be disputed—even when "married" to a duke—and once in Bath, having determined to move the dying duke from lodgings engaged for a month and having announced that she would neither pay the full month nor see her will disputed, she at length sent the landlady a piece of plate worth ten times the sum owed. The motto of the Chudleigh coat of arms was, Whitehead said, "Aut vincit aut perit,"[58] and Chudleigh was determined to conquer or perish in the attempt.

As was true of the more disreputable rakes of the time, her friends in later years numbered none of the fashionable women, but her exploits were pardoned like men's, and society never truly ostracized her. The Princess of Wales retained her in her court for years. The king and queen, on her "marriage" to Kingston (which everyone knew then was bigamous), wore the marriage favors and received her at court, speaking to her as little as possible—but speaking to her. And when she gave a great party, everyone came. Walpole mentions a housewarming in Knightsbridge in June 1760 at which the garrets were decorated in Oriental fashion and used for gambling.[59] In May 1765 she gave a grand entertainment and ball in honor of the queen's birthday for "a numerous Company of the first Rank and Distinction," who were entertained by "a most curious Illumination of Fireworks, with Scenes and Pyramids richly painted and decorated with suitable Devices and Mottoes . . . exhibited in Honour of the whole Royal Family."[60] And Lady Mary Coke tells of a dinner in Knightsbridge for the Spanish ambassadress and other foreigners attended by Lord and Lady Hertford, the Duchess of Portland, and other notables in January 1769, and in May, following the marriage, a ball to which *everyone* came.[61] Chudleigh contrived through one clever scheme or another to extort countenance and when she came to judgment was not stripped of her possessions by her peers in favor of the duke's male heirs. Her whims were those of a Roman emperor: in her private yacht she sailed up the Tiber; she illuminated and entertained in the Colosseum.

One must respect her success if not her aspirations. But to view her as a female Dick Whittington would be to miss the point. Her treatment of the gentle and easily outwitted duke was apparently tantamount to a continuing torture, and her treatment of her companions was equally objectionable. In the court of her own mistress—the princess—the maids, supposed to be virgins, were permitted their amours and, in Chudleigh's case at least, marriage and pregnancy.[62] Her treatment of her own harem may have been the most patriarchal of all her behavior: every aspect of her companions' lives, including their sexuality and their affections, was at her disposal alone. From a heterosexual point of view, which may have represented her public face, she was the stepmother of Snow White or the fairy godmother of Rapunzel, freezing her captive maidens into perpetual prepubescent chastity that left her the one sexually active woman in an environment filled with men. In this regard her behavior is perfectly consistent: she was filled with rage when Montresor married Fielding, when Presly made love to Betty, when the friar impregnated the housesitter at Rome, when the duke's friends proposed Skinner to him for a wife, when the duke remembered Bate in his will. Penrose, too, we may assume from Foote's farce, was a victim of Chudleigh's jealousy. If sensibility could not provide women the tools for worldly success, Chudleigh's career suggests that unremitting tyranny (as Shaftesbury postulated) exacts its own enormous price.

It may, however, be instructive to examine the career of a woman of another generation, committed to the altruistic values of sensibility and therefore incapable of marrying for money or conniving at the acquisition of ascendancy over others—Frances Burney. In Burney we can explore not the tyrant but the victim of one monster of a tyrant and the creator of another. Burney, who was a genuine altruist, is examined next for the sake of the studies in tyranny her life and works provide.

Chapter Five

FRANCES BURNEY AND THE ANATOMY OF COMPANIONSHIP

THOUGH IN ALMOST ALL WAYS she was Dr. Gregory's ideal woman, Frances Burney also had a firm sense of self and a sound instinct for self-preservation. She had no appetite for self-immolation; her decisions to sacrifice her own happiness and deny her own inclinations were made consciously and at great expense. She tended to put the happiness of her father before her own, but even to gratify Charles Burney she would not make the sacrifices of marrying a dull suitor, dying in the queen's service, or giving up a man she loved who wanted to marry her. She lived by altruistic values but maintained a healthy balance between the demands of self-love and social, of others' and her own fulfillment, erring too dangerously on the side of self-sacrifice only once, in the great matter of her service to the queen. But when she undertook that service, she did not know a fact that would have humiliated her had she known it, that she had been judged and chosen as a *complaisante,* a toady upon whom that arch-toady Mrs. Schwellenberg could practice her own tyranny. Had she known, she would never have engaged. That she emerged from the royal net with an annuity and able to choose a companion of her own is some indication of her unusual strength of character; her life and her works illustrate that a healthy and mature altruist does not have to be an easy prey to tyranny. Yet, trapped by choices that her father made, she did fall victim twice, first to her step-mother and then to the terrible Mrs. Schwellenberg.

The Burneys, like the Colliers or the Gregorys, were the kind of family from which in the eighteenth century companions were naturally chosen: they were genteel, but they had no resources except the father's earnings, no money with which to render their sons independent or their daughters marriageable. Fortunately, individual family members had the graces to fit in anywhere, provided they were useful, but the polite world cared little for the family itself (drew the line at marrying into it, for instance), and its acceptance of Charles Burney the music teacher and Frances Burney the novelist in no way provided entrée for the others. Frances's sister Esther, a child prodigy on the harpsichord whose performances had procured her father the London teaching employment that enabled the family to return to London in 1760, was apparently, as a public performer, beyond the pale; a polite suitor to whom she had given her heart only toyed with her. (In *The Wanderer* Juliet narrowly averts this fate, which would have destroyed her prospects of polite marriage, by fainting before her public musical debut.) George Cambridge, whom Frances Burney loved, treated her in much the same fashion. James Burney, the seaman, who returned home late in 1780 with James Cook's last expedition, would have made a minor lion, but, unlike the rest of the family, was too gruff and unamenable—too honest, perhaps. Susan, Burney's favorite sister, would have done well had society had any reason to notice her, but it hadn't, and so she, barely known save in musical society, lived in social circles unlike those of her sister after 1778, when with the publication of *Evelina* Frances Burney became a personage.

Finally, Charles Burney had miscalculated when for a second wife he had married the widow Elizabeth Allen, who had passed as a belle and a literary lady in King's Lynn, but who in London was pronounced ridiculous, pretentious, and affected, with too youthful a taste in dress. Elizabeth Burney presided over the concerts in her house to which everyone came, but the polite invitations ordinarily arrived only for her husband and stepdaughter. Instead of indulging her uncertain and imperious temper over her husband's social engagements, she had to accept them because his success as a music master and as a petitioner for an important musical post depended upon his connections, but she managed to make her stepdaughter's life very difficult. Those who wanted to call on Frances Burney had perforce to call on her stepmother as well, but the pretense fooled few and certainly helped further to sour the disposition of the once socially ascendant Elizabeth Burney, particularly because her stepchildren enjoyed her discomfort. Charles Burney, Jr., wrote to Frances Burney in November 1781 (with some glee), "M.[rs] Thrale has never been once in S.[t] M[artin']s Street, since you went."[1] Elizabeth Burney in her turn lobbied at home to force her stepdaughters to become more notable housekeepers and employ themselves in household affairs,[2] a strategy that might effectually have stifled their talents and was luckily vetoed by their father.

The second-rate status and position as household butt of poor Elizabeth Burney is nowhere so clearly revealed as in her stepdaughter's wicked account, dating from about 1768, of her first interview with the formidable Frances Greville, who had been an intimate friend of the lady's predecessor:

> Mrs. Greville, as was peculiarly in her power, took the lead, and bore the burthen of the conversation; which chiefly turned upon Sterne's Sentimental Journey, at that time the reigning reading in vogue: but when the new Mrs. Burney recited, with animated encomiums, various passages of Sterne's seducing sensibility, Mrs. Greville, shrugging her shoulders, exclaimed, "A feeling heart is certainly a right heart; nobody will contest that: but when a man chooses to walk about the world with a cambric handkerchief always in his hand, that he may always be ready to weep, either with man or beast—he only turns me sick."[3]

In reality Frances Greville was a great empathizer, Elizabeth Burney was not, and the hypocrisy of much of the appreciation for the cult of sensibility is suggested in this passage. Yet despite her limitations, one cannot but feel some compassion for the provincial bride, who had probably memorized passages of Sterne's book to impress her important visitor. Following this experience, Frances Greville virtually dropped the acquaintance so that in this one unlucky audition, the new Mrs. Burney lost her chance of social acceptance among Greville's friends and, like Susan, had to cultivate a middle-class and professional circle. Her own three children by her first marriage turned out not very satisfactorily (more gall and wormwood), and probably she knew that her clever stepchildren congregated in a particular room upstairs for their favorite activity of "talking treason" against her and that they privately dubbed her "Dearest," "Precious," and "The Lady of the Manor." All this, however, went on "unknown" to their father; both wife and stepchildren were agreed that he must never be distressed—some indication of his ability to convince his family, particularly his daughters, that he required protection so he could get on with the truly onerous burden of supporting them all, at the same time pursuing his ambitions to acquire fame and some comfortable post and leave off giving music lessons from morning to night. Isolated and unappreciated, Elizabeth Burney took refuge in caprice, an uncertain temper, indifferent health, and increasingly large doses of laudanum.

Charles Burney had himself been a companion, but in his case the position had represented an undreamed-of elevation and had been the making of his fortunes; considering the Burney family situation, he could not be counted on to express an unqualified distaste for the relationship where his daughters were concerned—particularly if he saw an advantage for the family in it. Charles Burney had begun life not only with musical talent but also with a natural elegance and grace— his father had been an actor, dancing master, and portrait painter—and with a suppleness of character for which Hester Thrale once faulted him when she criticized a "quality dangler" (or society hanger-on) who had "lost that independent Spirit & lofty manner without which no Man can much please *me*—but in Burney I *pardon* the want on't."[4]

Charles Burney's charm and grace, coupled with his musical talents, had taken him far. In Shrewsbury he had been discovered by Dr. Arne, who was passing through from Ireland on the way to London, and had been adopted by him as an apprentice without his father's having to pay the usual fee of £100. Then the connoisseur Fulke Greville, desiring a musician fit to be a companion, auditioned him for both parts and carried him off to his estate, Wilbury, in Wiltshire, as well as to Bath, where he was treated as a social equal and acquired a social education that he always said had been the making of him. Greville had literally owned Charles Burney—had bought his apprenticeship articles from Arne—and however lucky her father considered that circumstance to have been, his daughter Frances did not wish to repeat it in her own career, either through marriage or through toadyism.

Her first experience as a companion, however, she could not elude. Both family politics and convention dictated that one of the stepdaughters must always remain at home with their mother, always on duty. Charles Burney was often out of the house teaching his music lessons for twelve hours or more a day, and the onerous garrison duty with his wife had to be rendered without complaint. Thus, after the success of *Evelina*, Burney could escape to the Thrale circle at Streatham, or to Chessington, the only place where she could write, only at the expense of the angelic Susan. The problem of Elizabeth Burney always remained a primary consideration, with the additional understanding that her husband was never to be vexed about it. In a letter of July 1781, for instance, Burney informs Thrale that had her brother Charles, expected after a long stay in Scotland, arrived, she might have returned to Streatham that very day, for Susan remained in town.[5] In April 1783 Thrale calculated that if Burney were to marry, then she herself might get even more of her company than before, for her stepmother was a greater tyrant than

any husband would be.[6] In 1781 Burney wrote Susan of her reluctance
to leave Chessington, where she was working on *Cecilia:* "I know but
too well the many interruptions from ill management, inconveniences,
& ill nature I must meet with when I go, will retard me most cruelly, &
keep me back."[7] The sisters were later to draw parallels between Elizabeth Burney and the dreadful Mrs. Schwellenberg, and judging from
Schwellenberg's behavior, it is probably fair to assume that without concern for Burney's comfort or wishes, Mrs. Burney insisted on her attendance for many hours of the day during which Burney had to wait upon
her stepmother's needs, pick up the dropped stitches of conversation,
soothe complaints, and bear the petty abuse resulting from Mrs. Burney's jealousy. When callers came, Mrs. Burney played reigning belle,
dominating the conversation, and Burney attracted attention to herself
at her peril.

Such training taught the perspicacious Burney what she might expect from marriage or companionship. In 1775, when she was twenty-
one, she attracted the attentions of Thomas Barlow, an unexceptionable
young man with good prospects.[8] He immediately assessed her as filled
with "Affability, Sweetness, and Sensibility," clearly the very and sole
qualities he required in a wife. This description was both a prescription
and a contract. What accommodation was to be provided the prospec-
tive Mrs. Barlow's acute intelligence, her keen sense of derision, her
fun, and her wit? These were not wanted; Mr. Barlow was an ordinary
young man who wanted to live an ordinary life. Everyone expected her
to accept Barlow—or at least to entertain the proposal seriously. If Burney refused him, her stepmother would resent the unnecessary drain
on the family finances of keeping her; her beloved father urged her not
to be *"peremptory"* in her refusal. Samuel Crisp, her mentor and second father, begged her to consider carefully: "Oh Fany this is not a
marrying Age, without a handsome Fortune! . . . Suppose You to lose y^r
Father,—take in all Chances. Consider the situation of an unprotected,
unprovided Woman—."[9] In an emotional scene with her father, Burney
obtained his permission to remain with him. At this time, I think, she
conceived the notion of protecting her integrity by writing for a living to
earn enough money to pay her own way and thus to justify her refusal to
marry. It was a heroic, almost an unprecedented idea. Certainly Crisp
saw her literary labors in these terms; for him, as she struggled over her
second novel, *Cecilia,* in 1780, she had become Rumpelstiltskin: "You
see how triumphantly she goes on. If she can coin gold at such a Rate,
as to sit by a warm Fire, and in 3 or 4 months . . . gain £250 by scribbling

the Inventions of her own Brain—only putting down in black and white whatever comes into her own head, without labour drawing singly from her own Fountain, she need not want money." [10]

Burney has frequently been charged with being the slave of decorum. Certainly she did all she could to avoid calling additional attention to herself after she had published *Evelina*. But had she been the slave of decorum, or even had she been truly willing to immolate herself for her father's pleasure, she would have married Barlow. Publishing a novel, no matter how secretly, was at that time for a middle-class dependent maiden a thoroughly indecorous move, but it preserved her independence. Just as Burney has been accused, her heroine Evelina has also been accused of obeisance to decorum; but Evelina too has a distinguished sense of self, the ability, like Burney, to act against convention. She acts indecorously at least three times when she knows she is right: she rushes to Macartney's chamber to save him from suicide; she goes to meet him alone in Bristol; and she disobeys her father's solemn injunction to leave his presence forever and talks him into a reconciliation with her. Judging situations for herself and acting upon her judgment constitute and certify Evelina's maturation, and if she had not achieved maturation, she would not have been worthy to marry Orville.

Evelina's final scene with her father was probably inspired by Burney's scene with her own father in which she wrung from him his consent for her not to marry. The Burney, then, who in 1779 faced Hester Thrale's determined effort to annex her as a companion, was no easy mark.

Had Burney never written *Evelina*, Hester Thrale would never have taken her up. To be fair, having met Burney only at her father's house on musical evenings, Thrale would have taken her for all affability, sweetness, and sensibility, for only *Evelina* revealed the acuteness, the sense of fun, the satiric and judgmental eye that so discerned and relished the ridiculous, that attracted Thrale and that, having once publicly revealed, Burney could not thereafter deny. Another part of Burney's value was that she was a lion, and Thrale, married to a rich brewer, needed lions at Streatham as much as she needed a friend. The publication of *Evelina* both embarrassed and liberated Burney, but at least she no longer had to pretend to be nothing but sweetness; if subtle punishments awaited her for having abnegated the role the patriarchy (and Barlow) wished to assign her, there were also heady rewards. And in Thrale she had found a powerful woman friend who properly appreciated her.

Thrale, whose mother, her last female friend, had died in 1773, needed a woman companion in ways which Burney, brought up intimately with beloved sisters, probably could not understand. Thrale had been confined to her two households with male companions and constantly sickening and dying children for years. On a tour to Wales in 1774 with her husband, her nine-year-old eldest daughter (whom significantly she had insisted on taking along), and Samuel Johnson, she wrote:

'Tis so melancholy a thing to have nobody one can speak to about one's clothes, or one's child, or one's health, or what comes uppermost. Nobody but *Gentlemen*, before whom one must suppress everything except the mere formalities of conversation and by whom every thing is to be commended or censured. Here my paper is blistered with tears for the loss of my companion, my fellow traveller, my Mother, my friend, my attendant . . . I hoped, and very vainly hoped that wandering about the World would lessen my longing after her, but who now have I to chat with on the Road? who have I to tell my adventures to when I return? [11]

Burney had her sisters and her brothers too; Thrale, married to a civil but unloving and unappreciative husband, mother of the even colder Queeney, and hostess to the cerebral Dr. Johnson, whose primary loyalties were to her husband, was not only without anyone to confide in but also emotionally without a reciprocating object.

The relationship with Thrale and the life at Streatham were wonderful for Burney, who was at once released for long periods from the oppression of her stepmother and exposed to the great world with all its varied scenes and figures. But at the same time there were disquieting resonances. Did Thrale, for instance, think she was acquiring Burney as Greville had acquired her father? Thrale, still much confined to home by domestic obligations and not yet thoroughly at home in the polite world, was constrained to find society in those who came to the villa at Streatham and had eagerly cultivated Charles Burney, her daughter's music master. Once a week he came, instructed her eldest daughter, Queeney, and stayed to tea; sometimes he dined. But the warmhearted, literary, and learned Thrale, though she could appreciate merit when combined with charm, was all the prouder of her own blue blood because she was married to a lowborn brewer with a business (and a detestable house too) in Southwark. Within her was a reserve of acerbity and cold penetration even toward those she loved. She recognized in Charles Burney that too accommodating affability that led him once to claim that Greville was the only friend he had ever lost to a quarrel.[12] The quick-sighted Burney saw the dilemma in the attractive advantages offered by Thrale: if she were supple and too accepting, too available, she would forfeit her benefactor's respect and become a companion in fact rather than a friend who made frequent visits. Burney was happy to make frequent visits, but they must be made at her own discretion and with regard to the complex needs of her family. Thrale, however, wanted a reliable and virtually full-time companion suited not only to the busy Streatham life but also to that of the London social scene and of the fashionable watering places, and she would never cease to repine and complain at each fresh defection by her perfectly qualified friend. The struggle that ensued between these two intelligent, tenacious, and high-minded women regarding the disposal of Burney's time, a struggle sometimes comic but always tension-filled, was the inescapable effect of their separate determinations as to the nature of their relationship.

At first depending upon Charles Burney's general willingness to oblige and upon her own sense (she did not see continued professional authorship as a serious option for a young woman) that Burney's best chance of an advantageous marriage would be through Thrale's efforts, Thrale probably anticipated no problem in acquiring the permanent companionship of her new protégée, to whom she could offer undeniably great advantages. On her side was the centuries-old convention of extrusion according to which families sent their children away for training: in the lower classes into apprenticeship or as servants, in the middle and upper classes to sea, to court, or to great houses. It was not usual for a child to cling to the family in the face of proffered advantage— or to be allowed to do so—and Thrale perhaps did not yet realize that to do just that odd thing and to maintain the measure of autonomy to which she was accustomed, Burney had already sacrificed her privacy and her modesty, sacrifices she did not now intend to render meaningless. Thrale intended to bring Burney out, dress her, procure her the opera and concert tickets she so coveted, introduce her, and eventually "establish" (marry) her. And unquestionably Burney from the start loved Streatham, with its sympathetic and learned mistress, its connection with her father, its interesting visitors, its resident mentor Samuel Johnson, its luxury, fine library, leisure, and walks.

Clothes were a vast problem for Burney all her life. Staying at Streatham must seriously have taxed her resources. Dresses were very expensive, and throughout her life Burney spent far too much time altering and refurbishing clothes and doubtless sewing her own undergarments and washing out her lace—functioning, that is, as her own maid.

Perpetual Dress requires perpetual replenishment, & that replenishment actually occupies almost every moment I spend out of Company. "Fact! Fact!" I assure you,—however paltry, ridiculous or inconceivable it may sound. Caps, Hats,

& Ribbons make, indeed, no venerable appearance upon Paper;—no more does Eating & Drinking;—yet the one can no more be worn without being *made*, than the other without being *Cooked*,—& those who can neither pay milliners, nor keep servants must either toil for themselves or go *Capless* and Dinnerless. . . . Now instead of Furbelows & Gewgaws of this sort, my dear Daddy probably expected to hear of Duodecimos, Octavos or Quartos!—Helas! I am sorry that is not the case.[13]

So Burney wrote to Crisp from St. Martin's Street in January 1780, but throughout her life she found herself obliged to dress for circles of society in which the other women were not much concerned about either the expense or the maintenance of their clothes. Even at court Burney had to use her small leisure after breakfast to work on dress for Kew (plain), Windsor (simple), court days (very particular), and royal birthdays (new) (2:396).

She must have been sorely tried by Thrale's proffered presents, only too aware of the ease with which she could have acquired her wardrobe at Streatham. Thrale did indeed with some difficulty make a few presents, but Burney recognized that to be clothed meant to be a *companion*, and, determined to remain independent, she stipulated for equal friendship or nothing. She would not and could not be always on call, often went home to stay in St. Martin's Street, and sometimes went to make long visits to Crisp at Chessington to work; for with *Evelina* a great success, Burney's own father and her "daddy," Samuel Crisp, were bent on her achieving independence through writing, and the pleasures of Streatham could only delay her setting about new work. Thrale chafed whenever Burney left Streatham; hungry for love and companionship, most of all for the understanding that only Burney could give, she wanted Burney always on hand and patently needed her once her husband's final illness began in late 1779. But before that, on August 15, 1779, she wrote in her journal: "Fanny Burney has been a long time from me. I was glad to see her again; yet She makes me miserable too in many Respects—so restlessly & apparently anxious lest I should give myself Airs of Patronage, or load her with the Shackles of Dependence—I live with her always in a Degree of Pain that precludes Friendship—dare not ask her to buy me a Ribbon, dare not desire her to touch the Bell, lest She should think herself injured—lest she should forsooth appear in the Character of Miss Neville & I in that of the Widow Bromley" (1:400).[14] On December 1 she wrote: "Fanny Burney has kept her Room here in my house seven Days with a Fever, or something that she called a Fever: I gave her every Medicine, and every Slop with my own hand;

took away her dirty Cups, Spoons, &c, moved her Tables, in short was Doctor & Nurse, & Maid—for I did not like the Servants should have additional Trouble lest they should hate her for't—and now—with the true Gratitude of a Wit, She tells me, that the *World thinks the better of me* for my Civilities to her" (1:413).

From April to June 1780 Burney was in Bath with the Thrales and accompanied them to Brighton in flight from the threatened extension to Bath of the Gordon riots. Thrale punctuated Burney's visit with a series of undated pleas to Charles Burney: "Your sweet Fanny is all my comfort"; "I *knew* I was right to make you lend me her; she is worth all my intreaties"; "I *must* keep your sweet Daughter two days longer." And from Brighton on June 19 she thanked him for Burney's friendly conversation, her sole support through her husband's illness and election troubles, and bargained to return her for a week to London but then to be permitted to take her back again to Brighton: "I must have her again or come back with a heart really broke." [15]

The very next day Burney herself wrote to her father almost apologizing for wishing to leave the Thrales, who she says, hoped to keep her in Brighton until changes undertaken at Streatham were finished, "& Streatham, I also find, has no chance of being finished these 2 or 3 Months,—yet they *take me on*, as if upon the original agreement!" Although she was determined to stay with her friend through any illness or trouble, she could never agree to accommodate her never-ending emotional need and make Thrale the first object in her life. Now that Henry Thrale was as well as could be, she longed to come home. "I have almost been an *Alien* of late,—nobody in the World has such a Father, such Sisters as I have.—nobody can more fervently love them,—& yet I seem fated to Live as if I were an Orphan;—for the World I would not offend this dear Family, whom I love with the utmost affection & gratitude, & who pour upon me kindnesses undeserved and unremitting,— but as I shall not even *wish* to leave them when they are in sickness or in sorrow, if I also stay with them when they are in Health & in Spirits, I am neither *yours* nor *my own*, but *theirs*." [16]

She told her father that courage had failed her and she had been unable to ask Thrale to let her return home; but at last she did so, and she departed. Thrale wrote in her journal on July 1:

Mrs Byron who really loves me [that is, unlike Burney], was disgusted at Miss Burney's Carriage to me, who have been such a Friend & Benefactress to her: not an Article of Dress, not a Ticket for Public Places, not a Thing in the World that She could not command from me: yet always insolent, always pining for home, always preferring the mode of Life in St Martins Street to all I could do for her:—She is a saucy spirited little puss to be sure, but I love her dearly for all that: & I fancy She has a real regard for me, if She did not think it beneath the Dignity of a Wit, or of what She values more—the Dignity of *Doctor Burney's Daughter*, to indulge it. Such dignity! the Lady Louisa of Leicester Square! in good Time![17]

Burney spent the rest of that year in St. Martin's Street, at Chessington, and, again, at Streatham, where Henry Thrale was once more alarmingly ill. It was largely at Chessington that by January 1781 she had contrived to finish a draft of the first two volumes of *Cecilia*. In that month, at last convinced that Burney, backed by the determination of her two daddies, intended to be a novelist and never would subside into a companion, Thrale announced her defeat: "What an odd Partiality I have for a rough Character! and even for the hard parts of a soft one! Fanny Burney has secured my Heart: I now love her with a fond & firm Affection, besides my Esteem of her Parts, & my Regard for her Father. her lofty Spirit dear Creature! has quite subdued mine; and I adore her for the Pride which once revolted me. There is no true Affection, no Friendship in the sneakers and Fawners" (1:470).

Burney had evidently convinced her of her own disinterested love and friendship by coming to her as a friend when she was needed. The temporary subsidence of Thrale's ambition to annex Burney also reduced Burney's resistance, and in March Thrale added, "I have at length conquered all her Scruples, & won her Confidence and her Heart: 'tis the most valuable Conquest I ever *did* make, and dearly, very dearly, do I love my little *Tayo*, so the people at Otaheite call a *Bosom Friend*. She is now satisfied of my Affection, and has no Reserves, no ill Opinion, no further Notion I shall insult her Sweetness: I now respect her Caution, & esteem her above all living women" (1:487).

In May, following the death of Henry Thrale in April, there was a setback: Burney bridled when a newspaper paragraph announced her apparent dependency: "Miss Burney, the sprightly Writer of the elegant Novel Evelina, is now domesticated with Mrs. Thrale in the same manner that Miss More is with Mrs. Garrick, & Mrs. Carter with Mrs. Montagu."[18] Because she was still needed, Burney stayed on, but she departed in early July, whereupon Thrale complained, "What a Blockhead Dr Burney is, to be always sending for his Daughter home so! what a Monkey! is not She better and happier with me than She can be any where else? Johnson is enraged at the silliness of their Family Conduct, and Mrs Byron disgusted: I confess myself provoked excessively but I love the Girl *so* dearly. . . . If I did not provide Fanny with every *weare*able, every *Wish*able indeed, it would not vex me to be served so; but to see the Impossibility of compensating for the Pleasures of *S*^{*t*} *Martins Street*, makes me at once merry & mortified" (1:502).

Thrale's assumption that Burney's time and attentions could be purchased seems to have endured, as did her struggle to preempt them. In November 1782 Thrale was identifying Burney with Gabriel Piozzi, with whom, in a new attempt to fulfill her emotional longings, she was now in love: both of her objects were resistant to annexation. "*Pride* is the prominent Fault in both their Characters: but both will mend of it: when their Situation in Life will be exalted—hers by her Ingenuity— his by his Merit & Talents. They are proud *now* because they are *poor*, and feel their Fortune below their Deserts. When they shall no longer have their Dignity to defend by perpetual Vigilance, they will be more humble, more gentle, & suffer that keen sense of Neglect never practised [by Thrale]—to offend them less, as they have less Reason to apprehend it" (1:551).

Thrale's growing preoccupation with Piozzi and her marriage to him in the summer of 1784 finally removed her from Burney's life, and Burney has been faulted for the conventionality of her disgusted response to that marriage (probably owing at least in part to her hurt at losing first place in her friend's affections, in part to a sense that unable to annex her as a companion, Thrale married Piozzi to annex him). But Thrale too had been for a long time equally unsympathetic to Burney's equally unconventional object; it would seem that each had wished the other to behave more conventionally.[19] The strength of Burney's character, the originality of her choice of life, the courage she evidenced in her refusal to marry and to be a companion have often gone unnoticed and should be understood. Burney does not belong to that group of independent and tough-minded critics of society, the community that included Collier, Fielding, and Scott; as Kristina Straub has noted, she rarely takes "the step into radical revision of the institutions that shape women's lives" though "she is acutely sensitive to the difficulty of finding self-worth within those institutions."[20] But it should not be surprising, given her experience, that like the Bath community writers she did see beyond the simple tyranny of the mistress and the simple victimization of the companion to the dreadful deterioration of character implemented in the companion by the degrading expedients she must employ to attain any object. It was this deterioration in her own character that, above all, she was resisting in her refusal to become either Mr. Barlow's or Mrs. Thrale's parasite. Burney's undeniable altruism was founded

not in a weak accommodation to or furtherance of the fortunes of some
other who should then protect her but in a firm sense of her own independence and her own power as sufficient to permit her to follow her
conscience and purposes. She was an equal match for the older, more
experienced, energetic, spirited, and far richer Thrale; her heroines too
endure without capitulation. For Burney, endurance is more an active
than a passive strategy and is sometimes the only strategy possible.

Burney was a comprehensive reader and knew the work of Fielding
and Scott; to some extent she must have followed their lead in the literary treatment of humble companions. From the variation of her own
behavior it is also patent that she reacted against the suppleness of her
beloved father's character and his notable complaisance to the great,
and therefore to some extent her critique of the character of the companion was founded as well on painful observation of him. But her most
important model was her stepmother. Elizabeth Burney exemplified the
inauthenticity of induced altruism, a hypocritical sensibility forced by
societal pressure. With no firm moral character of her own, she had become expert at the kind of support and love with which women without power are wont to spur on their husbands so they can brave and
contest the world vicariously. Self-interest was her only interest; and
she excused her misbehavior, occurring only where it could safely be
expressed, as an expression of her unhappiness at the misbehavior of
others. With her second husband as, no doubt, her first, Elizabeth Burney was a consummate identifier with the aggressor. And therefore,
though to her husband she was kind, ingratiating, and accommodating,
to her stepchildren she was often tyrannical and capricious. Dr. Burney
never officially "knew" the problems of his household, for both wife and
children protected him, allowing him to go about his necessary labors.
But at home his daughter observed the common political triad of husband, wife, and children, the wife, a Janus figure, acting the double part
of toady and tyrant.

For instance, in August 1781 Burney returned from Streatham to St.
Martin's Street believing that as her mother (as she was always called)
intended going to Chessington, she herself was needed to attend on her
father. But when she arrived, her mother announced she had no intention of going, "& that if such alone was my reason for returning, I
had better go back again to Streatham." Burney, who seems unaware
that she had injured her mother's feelings by indicating no desire to return to her, was tempted to take her at her word but decided instead to
make a promised week's visit to her sister Esther. When she called on

Esther an hour later, however, she found that her mother had just been to say that as Fanny had come, she meant to go to Chessington five or six days thence, thus preventing both the visit to Esther and the return to Streatham. Burney confided to Thrale, "I dare not expostulate, & indeed I am fully satisfied that it is every way best to forbear, since the same bright act of tormenting which is now exerted merely to gratify general spleen, would then be exercised purposely to satisfy anger from particular spite. At present she has none against *me*, but what I share in common, I believe, with the whole Human Race." [21] In this way the Burney siblings (and Samuel Crisp) habitually spoke of Dearest. Burney's brother Charles wrote to Burney in November 1781, for instance, "Madam is as spiteful as usual—The Devlish Particles in her composition, act with their usual powers." [22]

It was the tyranny to herself and to her sisters that Burney no doubt found most obtrusive, but even more disturbing must have been the assumed and hypocritical sensibility exposed in Burney's account of her stepmother's unsuccessful attempt to woo Frances Greville. From the muttered asides of her stepchildren (seconded by those of Crisp, Thrale, and Johnson), Elizabeth Burney emerges as insincerely submissive when necessary and sycophantically friendly for her own ends, capricious and inconsistent, unreliable, untrustworthy, vengeful, sadistic, incapable of empathy for others or of genuinely moral or altruistic behavior, but displaying her aggressive side only to her victims, while to her husband, who liked her, she was agreeable, if loud and noisy when in spirits. She demanded constant consideration. Her character exemplifies that of the tyrant mistress more subtly and more in detail than the characters created by Collier, Williams, Foote, and Murphy: probably an early victim of familial tyranny and never given the opportunity to develop a moral dignity or a sense of autonomy, she had been spoiled in Lynn by her undisputed superiority of beauty, wealth, and literary taste. She played, when necessary, a submissive female role, but not to her children. Males who had an investment in believing women to be "naturally" submissive or who believed tyrannical women required punishment into submission did not recognize the pattern of hypocrisy into which such women slipped, but Burney anatomized it in the second and third of her novels.

Certainly she raised the problem of dependence in *Evelina*, where upon her emergence into society Evelina is labeled "a kind of toadeater," [23] where she is something of a toadeater to her grandmother, Madame Duval, where she provides, in relation to such personages as

Sir Clement Willoughby and Lady Louisa Larpent, a splendid example of how one is treated when one is nobody, and then again somebody, yet of how a dependent female may still behave with moral dignity. The other face of dependency for adult females, marriage, is also sketched in *Evelina* through the destructiveness of the marriages of Evelina's grandfather and mother and that of Mrs. Mirvan, not to mention that yet to come of Lady Louisa, whose cynical lover Lord Morton mutters that the wooing will not last long. The destructiveness of marriage is revealed even in the nonmarriage that makes Macartney illegitimate and the whores of the public gardens whores. So Mr. Smith's grudging admission to Evelina that she may consider him attainable and Madame Duval's seeming presentation of young Branghton as a candidate constitute even more of a threat to Evelina than Willoughby's attempted abduction. But Burney did not address the subject of humble companionship directly until she wrote *Cecilia*, published in 1782 and written during the period of her conflict with Thrale about the definition of their relationship. In that novel Miss Bennet, the sycophantic companion of Lady Margaret Monckton, may reflect Burney's fears for her father's character and her own but is in some ways—in her frightening lack of true sensibility, her hypocrisy, her lack of regard for truth—a psychological portrait of her stepmother. Miss Bennet was also cringing and fawning. She "was low-born, meanly educated, and narrow-minded; a stranger alike to innate merit or acquired accomplishments, yet skilful in the art of flattery, and an adept in every species of low cunning. With no other view in life than the attainment of affluence without labour, she was not more the slave of the mistress of the house, than the tool of it's master; receiving indignity without murmur, and submitting to contempt as a thing of course." [24] We are told of her "fawning courtesy" (p. 532), her "mean sycophancy" (p. 719), and her "parasitical conversation" (p. 722). Had she been a character in *Evelina*, Burney would have derived low humor from her speeches, but the only time we ever hear Miss Bennet's actual voice is when she interrupts Cecilia's wedding to Delvile by claiming to be aware of a just impediment. Her "I do!" (p. 626) is a theft of Cecilia's own vow, and after it Cecilia's greatest trials begin.[25] Miss Bennet is too evil for comedy. Here the observable submission of the humble companion is shown to be a dreadful self-serving hypocrisy under cover of which Lady Margaret is eventually done to death. Elizabeth Burney too was celebrated by her stepchildren as evil, beyond a joke, for her "Devlish Particles."

There is no Villars in *Cecilia* and no Orville. Even the father figures,

Cecilia's uncle and her three guardians, are unworthy of guiding and certainly do not guard her; husbands are equally wanting. Mr. Monckton long plans to murder and eventually does murder his wife; Harrel fails to justify his own privilege as guardian of the family wealth and destroys his riches, the happiness of his wife and Cecilia, and finally himself; the Delviles, doubly connected as cousins and spouses, separate. Instances abound in the book of the misemployment of power by parents, guardians, and the rich over those whose fates they control; but marriage is the most suspect institution of all, and even Mortimer Delvile, though Cecilia comes to love him devotedly, is a woefully inadequate protector, a maker of costly errors. The interrupted marriage of Cecilia and Delvile punctuates the center of the action like a mock conclusion that cannot conclude; but because of male pride the real marriage leaves Cecilia more vulnerable than ever. It would seem that Burney, just thirty when the book appeared, had learned the lesson that she must henceforth rely upon herself but had entirely reasonable doubts about her ability to manage, given the circumstances in which women struggled.

Before she wrote another novel, Burney was at last fairly caught, though it took the queen to do it. Samuel Crisp had died in April 1783, reassured that his protégée would be able to support herself by her pen; the Chessington days were over. The Streatham idyll ended in 1784 with Thrale's marriage to Piozzi, the end punctuated somberly by Johnson's death in December. Burney had been glad in the summer of 1784 for the opportunity to visit new friends, the Lockes of Norbury Park, but in the summer of 1785 made the fatal decision to leave that place to nurse her ailing friend Mary Delany, now eighty-five, in London. Delany (chapter 8) had spent a lifetime without enough money. Her friend and patroness the Duchess of Portland had died that summer, and Delany fell ill with grief and worry. She had been managing by spending the winters in her own London house, the long summer months with the duchess at Bulstrode. The duchess, unaccountably, had failed to provide for Delany in her will so that everyone was delighted when the king and queen stepped forward, offering a house in Windsor and a £300 pension. Delany was ensconced there, a grandmotherly companion to the royal family, someone they could visit comfortably, unofficially, even unannounced—though the situation can't have been particularly comfortable for Delany. Now nothing seemed more natural than that one of Delany's first guests at Windsor, in November and December of 1785, should be Burney, who had so generously left her friends to look after Delany in the summer.

Burney was only thirty-three to Delany's eighty-five, but the women were similar: gifted, poor, agreeable, accommodating, and self-respecting. When the king and queen dropped in to meet Burney, they were already all too aware of her possibilities. If Burney recognized the net being spread, she was also dangerously willing to give her father joy of it: writing to him of this royal interest in her, she said, "I have really the grace to be a little ashamed of scribbling this, but I know I can scribble nothing my dear father will be more curious to hear."[26] Indeed, to Charles Burney the news was sweetly gratifying. Though the king and queen were kindly disposed to him, he had never been the recipient of royal favor and for years had coveted the post of master of the king's band.[27] The entire family believed that their sister's proximity to the royal family could jog the royal memories, if not in favor of their father, then for Jem the sailor, whose career was in a backwater and who ardently desired a ship to command, or for their brother Charles, who now needed a special dispensation to be ordained. Charles Burney swiftly convinced himself that a post with the royal family, perhaps to wait upon one of the princesses, must be as delightful for his daughter as it would be for himself and Jem and Charles. The success of *Evelina* and *Cecilia* had been a vast satisfaction to him, but it was nothing to the prospect of having his daughter at court in a post sought by women of the bluest blood and the most influential connections and bestowed upon her only because she was preferred and distinguished, for her merit alone, above the rest.

But the king and queen were neither so entirely gracious nor so discerning. The post that needed filling, that of the second keeper of the robes to the queen, required a genuine toady and would never have done for a fashionable woman who wanted a comfortable post about the court. The keeper of the robes was Elizabeth Juliana Schwellenberg, now about fifty-eight, who had come from Mecklenburg with the queen in 1762 and as her closest confidante had enormous political power. The second keeper, Mrs. Haggerdorn, had also come from Mecklenburg, had functioned all those years as Schwellenberg's victim, was now retiring, and needed replacing. Not the least of Burney's humiliations during her five years at court must have been her realization that to the queen she—powerless, in a sense unfamilied, humble, and amenable—appeared, as she had to Thrale, the perfect, pliable choice. But once caught, she must seem, publicly, to be all affability, sweetness, and sensibility.

The offer came in late May or early June 1786. Dr. Burney was be-

side himself, taking it as all the more a tribute to the family that the post
was to be in the service of the queen. His daughter prepared herself like
Esther for the sacrifice. On an early visit to Delany she had observed
of the king and queen, "Here, at Windsor, it seems an absolute point
that whatever they ask must be told, and whatever they desire must be
done" (2:327). She was to discover the truth of her observation.

The Burneys had neither the connections at court nor the caution to
inquire about the post, and they all, apparently, envisioned Burney attending upon the queen like one of those aristocratic ladies who still had
every right to their private lives, to access to their families and friends.
Burney was to have apartments in the palace, a place at Schwellenberg's table, a maid, a footman, and £200 a year. She had barely arrived
at Windsor in July 1786 when she learned the truth about her situation,
which could not have been more constrictive or unpleasant.

Having risen at six each morning and dressed in morning gown and
cap, she was to await the first summons, by bell, of the queen at about
7:30. The summons by bell was a horror to Burney: "It seemed so mortifying a mark of servitude" (2:400). Schwellenberg never appeared in the
morning, and Mrs. Thielky, the wardrobe woman, and Burney dressed
the queen, Thielky handing Burney the clothes and Burney putting them
on. Burney then returned to her own room to breakfast, the best part of
her day. At nine she applied herself to work on her own dress, and her
time was her own until, at quarter to one, Schwellenberg and Burney attended the queen. They adjusted her powdering things; the hairdresser
did her hair while they stood in attendance; then they dressed her. From
three to five Burney was again at liberty. At five she joined Schwellenberg for dinner; but only the first keeper, it appeared, had the right to
invite guests. After dinner there was coffee in Schwellenberg's rooms,
and Burney soon found that she evaded this attendance at her peril. At
eight the ladies went down again to the dining room and poured tea
for the gentlemen attending the king or invited for the evening. After
tea, at about nine, an equerry conducted them all to the concert room.
If Schwellenberg was alone, Burney was forced to stay with her until
about eleven, when she had a little supper in her room and then was
summoned between eleven and twelve to the queen, who was undressed
in about twenty minutes. Burney could scarcely have had six hours of
sleep before her morning duties again commenced (2:396–97).

Burney was therefore little in the company of the queen but very much
in the company of Schwellenberg, for about six hours a day, through
all the social hours of dinner, tea, and the evening. She seems to have

recognized Schwellenberg's power with the queen but never to have acknowledged that the queen must have known exactly how Schwellenberg behaved to her and indeed took Schwellenberg's part. She had arrived at a familiar situation, and just as she had protected her father by never complaining to him about her stepmother, so she now took pride in protecting the queen by never revealing the extent of Schwellenberg's cruelty. But in fact she had been the queen's gift to Schwellenberg, her dearest friend; and throughout the whole sorry relationship, both the queen and her first keeper exhibited the most profound contempt for the profession of letters, the English middle class in general, and the Burney family in particular.

Had Burney been able to flatter Schwellenberg, explain her family's needs, and make her applications through her, she probably could have attained much. Schwellenberg was the known route to the queen's ear; but Burney never took that route, never acknowledged the particular collusion of the two. "Cerbera" was one of Burney's terms for Schwellenberg, to whom she soon learned to her horror that she was intended to be a toady: "I saw myself expected by Mrs. Schwellenberg, not to be her colleague but her dependent deputy! not to be her visitor at my own option, but her companion, her humble companion, at her command! This has given so new a character to the place I had accepted under such different auspices that nothing but my horror of disappointing, perhaps displeasing, my dearest father, has deterred me . . . from soliciting his leave to resign" (3:9–10).

The queen, by contrast, she found "all sweetness, encouragement, & gracious goodness to me—& I cannot endure to complain of her old servant." Burney was still deluded when she wrote again, "Little does the Queen know the slavery I must either resist or endure. And so frightful is hostility, that I know not which part is hardest to perform" (3:11). It had taken royalty to subdue her, but Burney had at last fallen almost into the condition of Scott's anonymous humble companion.[28] Throughout Burney's five years of agony, the queen never once intervened for her, and once, when Burney ventured to complain, she defended poor Schwellenberg. Yet—was it sheerly politic to do so, or because the queen stood in the position of Dr. Burney in St. Martin's Street?—Burney never accused her of complicity with her first keeper, writing in December 1790 of the king that he might, she thought, "surmize my cruel Hours of *leisure*—so piteously exhausting to all existence. The q—— I think is not aware of their undermining labour to Health and Peace."[29] The queen, *I* think, was an excellent actress.

Schwellenberg was an arch-tyrant and, for Burney, Elizabeth Burney's "exactest Fellow,—gloomy, dark, suspicious, rude, reproachful." [30] "O Heaven!—how depressing,—how cruel to be fastened thus again on an Associate so Exigeante, so tyrannical, & so ill disposed!" [31] But this was her stepmother empowered without hindrance, with no kind father to enjoin even a hypocritical sensibility. Susan Burney noted in her 1789 journal that Schwellenberg "has the heart and temper of a Fiend, wth the grossness & undissembled violence of the lowest & most vulgar of mankind—she seems to be that sad counterpart of which she so cruelly & continually reminds us." [32] There were, wrote Burney, the "foul fiends of Jealousy and Rivality in my colleague; who, apparently, never wishes to hear my voice but when we are *tête-à-tête*, and then never is in good humour when it is at rest" (2:433). Burney's function even in company was to amuse Schwellenberg, never others and never herself. She was particularly humiliated to be forced to inform her own visitors that she had no right to invite them to dinner.

"No one is wished to be noticed, when we are in society, except the Lady of the Manor [a name formerly bestowed on Elizabeth Burney].... No visitor fares so well as when I put myself most out of the way" (3:377). One caller, stealing into Burney's room for a book, begged her visit go unmentioned, for "I should never be forgiven if it was known I called for a moment!" and added, "If she should hear me here she'll never forgive it, and she's always listening what voices she can hear in your room" (4:104–5). Every situation was uncomfortable and many were perilous.

When Schwellenberg was ill and could not preside at the tea table, the gentlemen lingered for an hour instead of dispersing in the usual five minutes. Schwellenberg, alone and awaiting Burney's attendance, was bitter in reproach (4:110–11).

But at her worst, Schwellenberg was practically murderous. In November 1787 in the coach to town for the Drawing Room, Schwellenberg insisted, as was her wont, on lowering the window on Burney's side; the sharp wind inflamed her eyes and made her ill (3:336–37). Protests on the return trip produced "Oh, very well! when you don't like it, don't do it. what did the poor Haggerdorn bear it! when the blood was all running down from her eyes!" (3:340). In March 1789 the scene was repeated. The piercing wind cut Burney's face and she put up her muff. This implied protest so incensed Schwellenberg that she vehemently declared that " 'she never, *no never*, would *trobble any won* to air with her again, but always go selfs.' " By evening Burney had a violent cold and painful neuralgia. When the queen saw her unwell, Burney ventured to tell the episode of the glass, and the queen "instantly said she was surprised I could catch cold in an *airing*, as it never appeared that it disagreed with me when I took it with Mrs. Delany" (4:268).

At Kew, where in the mornings Burney was accustomed to await the arrival of a summoning page in a parlor considered by Schwellenberg to be exclusively her own, Schwellenberg had the parlor door locked, constraining Burney to a long wait in a cold, damp passage. Her shivering attendance on the queen occasioned an explanation and the opening of the parlor for more general use but also resulted in dreadful punishments for the informant.

Knowledge that she had become the toady of a mistress infinitely more unkind than Thrale was so painful to Burney that she resorted to the marriage trope to interpret her condition and thus induce resignation: "I am *married*, my dearest Susan. . . . What then now remains but to make the best wife in my power?"[33] But even after five years of battering at court, Burney had enough strength to extricate herself when she realized that otherwise she would soon die in service. In the end, though, it was touch and go: "My loss of health was now so notorious, that no part of the house could wholly avoid acknowledging it; yet was the terrible picquet the catastrophe of every evening, though frequent pains in my side forced me, three or four times in a game, to creep to my own room for hartshorn and for rest. And so weak and faint I was become, that I was compelled to put my head out into the air, at all hours, and in all weathers, from time to time, to recover the power of breathing, which seemed not seldom almost withdrawn" (4:436).

In the autumn of 1790, contemplating her withdrawal from court if she should live, Burney screwed herself up to make requests for James and Charles. In October she "perpetually brought in my wishes for poor James, though without avail" (4:428). Nothing had been done for her father or for James. Charles's disgrace at Cambridge for stealing library books and the subsequent refusal of the bishop of London to ordain him might be ameliorated if he could obtain a Lambeth doctorate as a mandate degree; with the degree, he might win the Charterhouse headmastership, about to fall vacant. Burney, summoning up all her courage, humiliated herself by explaining the whole unpleasant affair to the queen, who, the family hoped, would be moved to request the archbishop of Canterbury to grant the degree. The queen, probably concealing her annoyance that Burney was still unwilling to observe protocol by approaching her through Schwellenberg, did speak to the archbishop, but in such fashion that the petition was refused.[34] That denial may well have been owing to Schwellenberg, to whom Burney stubbornly refused to apply for any benefit.

Burney waited to resign until her petitions had failed. In December, when Schwellenberg learned that her departure was to be permanent, that the queen's counteroffer of six weeks' leave to allow her to regain her health had been refused by Burney and her father, the response was characteristic: "She was too much enraged for disguise, and uttered the most furious expressions of indignant contempt at our proceedings. I am sure she would gladly have confined us both in the Bastile, had England such a misery, as a fit place to bring us to ourselves, from a daring so outrageous against imperial wishes" (4:446–47).

It seems probable that both the queen and Schwellenberg, miscalculating the lackeyism of the Burneys, had believed Burney would not stir until she had obtained what she had come for. The basic error was Schwellenberg's. Burney's determined departure gave the pair new respect for her, and Schwellenberg thereafter was always courteous. When the queen understood that Burney really would go, and go unconditionally, she came through unexpectedly and fairly: nothing for Burney's father or brothers but a pension for herself of £100. On July 7, 1791, at the age of thirty-nine, Burney was all at once both free and possessed of an income of her own. That income, minimal though it was, ensured that she would never again be a burden on her father, that she need write no more, that she was free to visit family and friends at her own expense. It must have seemed to Burney, as she slowly recuperated from the strain of the past five years, and to her family, that her adventures were over.

A year and a half later, however, at Norbury she met Alexandre d'Arblay, a handsome, aristocratic, and penniless émigré. His lands had been confiscated, and he was a Roman Catholic. In France he would never have thought of marriage to a portionless Protestant bourgeoise novelist. But they were attracted to each other and, feminized (that is, disadvantaged) by his misfortunes, d'Arblay became an equal companion to his wife. Thus she survived to find at last the friend sought by David Simple, and, like the true altruist, once empowered, she practiced no tyrannies.

The portrait of a timid and fearful Frances Burney is a misrepresentation that should be laid to rest.[35] To marry d'Arblay, Burney had to offend and defy her father. Burney's old protectiveness of her father had probably come entirely to dominate her attitude to him by the time she left court. In the tragedies she wrote in the court years, she persistently drew her father figures not as protectors but as dependents of whom her heroines had to take care through great self-sacrifice.[36] These father images are noble and loving but sometimes bad advisers to their daughters, incapable of protecting them, needy of their sacrifices. In d'Arblay Burney had found a very similar man.

She would probably not have written another novel, for instance, but £100 was not a noble sum to live on, and the couple needed a home, particularly after their son Alexander was born in 1794. Burney wrote *Camilla* (1796) to provide the house, which in fact it did.

The humble companion in *Camilla*, Miss Margland, is another scheming toady, this time a comic figure treated satirically, though with malevolent overtones. Nominally governess to the young women of the family, she is actually serving as their companion and chaperone. She is a woman of family and fashion, "reduced, through the gaming and extravagance of her father, to such indigence, that, after sundry failures in higher attempts, she was compelled to acquiesce in the good offices of her friends, which placed her as a governess in the house of Sir Hugh."[37]

Margland suffers from the defects of character attributed to companions by Fielding and Scott. "Her former connections and acquaintance in high life still continued to be the stationary pride of her heart, the constant theme of her discourse, and the perpetual allusion of some lamentation and regret" (p. 53).

Margland, like Miss Bennet, is in quest of an establishment for herself and counts on the beautiful but shallow Indiana to marry Edgar and provide for her. She therefore obstructs and long delays the understanding between Edgar and Camilla. Margland has no moral life whatsoever. She is also void of taste and resources for the country—and in this long novel there is no visit to London—and has languished there for twelve years. By playing on Camilla's better nature to make her eschew Edgar in Indiana's behalf, Margland indirectly helps to bring about the catastrophic events of the latter part of the book. She is a stupid woman, gravitating to those she can manipulate, a selfish woman interested in Indiana only because she can be managed. But she remains unpunished. Serenely unaffected by all that has occurred, she at last obtains her wish; she is not, as one would expect, repudiated by the ungrateful Indiana, for she remains necessary to the pupil she has corrupted as "the constant adulatress of her charms and endowments" (p. 909). The terrible events of the book scarcely disarrange her hair, for, as Burney means to tell us, such a woman, being without sensibility, is virtually untouchable, impenetrable. Lest any woman think the lack of sensibility an asset, Miss Margland, in succeeding in attaining her pitiful object, is a cautionary example.

Margland has no real power of her own and thus is confined to manipulation and constrained to hypocrisy. A toady herself, she practices her tyranny subtly though no less effectively for that. The men in her universe seem completely unaware of her malevolent feelings and her influence, reading her as a properly subjected and in no way unusually limited woman.

Marriage, too, that other face of female dependency, is again savaged in this novel, though one marriage, that of Camilla's parents, stands as the most idealized in all Burney's fiction. The Tyrolds live together, talk together, act together, and respect each other's opinions and decisions; Mrs. Tyrold is such an active and practical partner that though most mothers must be removed from the scene by death, she departs for the Continent on family business early in the novel. But Camilla is, like Evelina, besieged by unworthy claimants. The action is in large part precipitated by the misogynistic tutor Marchmont, who, having been twice unhappily married, persuades his pupil Edgar Mandelbert (like Mortimer Delvile, a rather shaky reed) to study Camilla thoroughly before declaring himself. The comic vulgarian Dubster, too, has had two marriages which he assesses only in terms of the money they have brought in. The feckless and destructive brother Lionel is delighted at the prospect of selling Camilla to a husband who can pay his debts, and he has to flee to the Continent after being named correspondent in a divorce case. The crippled sister Eugenia is abducted, for her fortune, by the ironically pseudonymously named Bellamy, who then nearly murders her. The silly young Miss Dennel marries recklessly for an establishment and independence and then finds that her autonomy is more straitened than ever: "I'm sure if I'd known I might not do as I like, and come out when I'd a mind, I would not have married at all!" (p. 783). In such a world, in which marriage tends to murder the wife either literally or psychologically, the Tyrolds' marriage stands not as the norm but as a rarity that is also an attainable possibility. This is the only one of Burney's novels that incorporates such a possibility into the text before the heroine's marriage at the end, thus validating the *possibility*, at least, of a good marriage, and for it we may probably consider the good General d'Arblay responsible.

But in her last novel, *The Wanderer* (1814), Burney portrays the great female tyrant Mrs. Ireton, an autonomous monster based on the worst aspects of Elizabeth Burney and Schwellenberg. Mrs. Ireton, we are to assume, has put in her time as a wife and earned her privileges as a tyrant.

Mrs. Ireton is one of the three Furies of the book, the older women who persecute the heroine, Juliet, in the name of patriarchy—all the more terrifying because they have totally bought into the benefits of patriarchal privilege. She is probably the most memorable of all fictitious mistresses to a humble companion, and this time the mistress, not the companion, is the monster.[38] In this book Burney is able to wreak revenge on her stepmother and Schwellenberg without regard to the deleterious effect on the companion's character because Juliet—like her author—never capitulates, always quietly resists the moral rot that is the ordinary companion's fate. One can scarcely better Collier's instructions to such a patroness, and Mrs. Ireton is a faithful and deliberate follower.[39]

Burney takes full advantage of her opportunity with Ireton, painting the tortures she inflicts on her victim in scene upon scene, conversation upon conversation, and humiliation on humiliation. Ireton drags Juliet to Arundel Castle to look after her unpleasant dog and denies her a chance to see the interior; she summons her to sit in company but denies her refreshments; she perpetually drenches her with deluges, drownings, of words, as on their first interview when Juliet is about to leave: "Whither are you going, Mrs . . . what's your name? . . . I have not paid you sufficient attention, perhaps?—Nay it's very likely. I did not run up to receive you, I confess. I did not open my arms to embrace you, I own! It was very wrong of me, certainly. But I am apt to forget myself. I want a flapper prodigiously. I know nothing of life,—nothing of manners. Perhaps you will be so good as to become my monitress? 'Twill be vastly kind of you. And who knows but, in time, you may form me? How happy it will be if you can make something of me!" (p. 457).

Happy indeed it would be, but rarely does the tyrant succumb to the superior moral virtues of the victim, either in companionship or marriage, and it is very much a tyrannical marriage that Juliet is fleeing. Marriage creates a subtle villainy throughout this book. Little Selina is first introduced by Elinor Joddrell as "a sister of mine, a conceited little thing, who is just engaged to be married, and who is wild to see you; and it is a rule, you know, to deny nothing to a bride elect; probably, poor wretch, because every one knows what a fair way she is in to be soon denied every thing!" (p. 44).

Marriage is not only the institution from which Juliet flees, it is also the institution in which males like Ireton's son and Sir Jasper Herrington have all the prerogatives of choice. There is no happy union in the entire novel. Most of the characters are single, but Gabriela, who is married and who merits happiness, is solitary and unappreciated. The novel is about the narrow resources available to women alone, and women's loneness is emphasized by Burney's giving only negative examples of marriage: it is not an actual resource. The feminized hero Albert Harleigh is a rare phenomenon; there is no other man like him in the book and very few if any on the street. In one sense he is an image of the integrated male, endowed with reason and sensibility, the man who dares give up tyrannicizing. In another sense he is an idealized version of d'Arblay, and the trials of Juliet are a symbolic version of the sorrows of Frances Burney. Both women seized their few advantages, resisted all they could, and endured. Both were lucky but also invincibly brave.

Altruism requires character of the kind that Burney possessed. Such character is not likely to be produced in people forced from infancy into submission; such forcing is likely to produce instead an Elizabeth Burney, a Schwellenberg, or an Ireton. It is useful here to consider Samuel Crisp's recollection of the young Burney, aged about sixteen: "Do you remember . . . how you used to dance Nancy Dawson on the grass-plot, with your cap on the ground, and your long hair streaming down your back, one shoe off, and throwing about your head like a mad thing?"[40] This image better expresses the real Burney than does the decorous aspect she wore in public to avert undue notice. Everything known about Burney's childhood suggests contact with kind and nurturing adults, very little pressure or obloquy on a child remarkably slow to read, and plenty of opportunity for wild and creative games in which she was a leader among her siblings, for scribbling literary inventions on every scrap of paper she could find. Her true mother was loving, her father to an unusual extent a friend, companion, teacher, and guide. But the child with a firm sense of self must also learn to identify and empathize with others or she may become a Chudleigh. For the Burneys there were shared sorrows such as the death of the children's mother. It is perhaps most instructive in this regard that throughout her life, despite her genuine sensibility, Burney was not habitually the victim of aggressors; she was usually able to defend herself. An important part of her defense for many years was the eschewal of companionship and marriage. The court was an unusual trap into which she was seduced by the desire to please her father and to help her family and by her ignorance of what the position entailed. But from this trap she was able to extricate herself, reassuming control of her own life.

Consideration of the problem of the altruist—how one can remain benevolently connected to one's fellow creatures without being destroyed by them—is endemic to eighteenth-century fiction but was a theme of particular importance to Burney, who examined different aspects of the problem in her four novels, engaging in an ongoing examination of and speculation about it. That is Evelina's—and Villars's—problem. Evelina is Villars's third cast: Evelina's grandfather and her mother, both Villars's responsibilities, both good and too defenseless, have gone out into the world and been destroyed by Madame Duval and her all too willing coadjutors, who thus represent all the selfish and egotistic forces who will destroy the defenseless virtuous. Now Evelina must try, and riding on her effort are not only her own safety and happiness but also a justification of Villars's techniques of instruction, of the possibility of being virtuous at all in the world as it is. Resistance and endurance are Evelina's as well as Burney's strategies. Resistance may be unvoiced, except in the letters to Villars, expressing criticism of social usage and individual character and behavior. It may also, when necessary, be decisive, as when Evelina raises her voice to stop the carriage in which Willoughby is abducting her. It may even be indecorous, as in the above three examples of Evelina's firm action. The point is that Evelina usually knows—no doubt because of her training—when to resist, and her resistance is successful because she also knows how to endure. Too much has been made of the "passivity" of both Burney and Evelina, as well as of the fact that Burney does not remedy social ills. Short of writing a utopia or a feminist tract, how could she remedy them when they existed, when she so clearly understood them, when she was trying to solve the problem of how to cope with the situation as it existed? In *Evelina* Burney gives it as her youthful opinion that young women can cope. Evelina, the litmus paper that shows up all the rest, *does* discover one other (apart from Villars) worthy of herself; *does* return, triumphant from the field and vindicating his faith, to her guardian; *will*, in combination with Orville and thus in safety, thereafter leaven the world.

But it was a bit too easy, too much of a fairy story, for a realist. The heroine of her next novel, Cecilia, is a great heiress, as well as a beautiful orphan. This time everyone knows who she is, and everyone is after her money. When Evelina is snubbed, she at least knows why; when Cecilia is courted, she can't be sure. On the assumption that she will marry and acquire a financial manager, Cecilia has never been taught to handle money. She is naturally altruistic but cannot control her benevolence, willing to alleviate every suffering, and although her guardian Harrel finds her impossible to sell in marriage, he is able to extract most of her £10,000 by appealing to her sympathy and threatening suicide—a useless sacrifice on Cecilia's part, for he is ruined and commits suicide anyway. Cecilia is a classic portrait of the altruist as victim; with all the necessary sensibility but little of the necessary judgment, she has not been properly prepared for her responsibilities. The rude shocks and punishments of the book are all calculated to teach her wisdom and discretion, for her heart is always perfect, and she must learn the variety of ways in which other hearts are imperfect and how best, in an imperfect world, to apply her assets and protect herself.

Camilla repeats Cecilia's mistake of injudicious altruism: it is her giving to her brother Lionel, who can never be sufficiently supplied, that precipitates all the financial disasters of her family and brings her father to debtors' prison. Her heart and her sensibility are impeccable, but she must learn how to defend herself and those she loves from such predators as Lionel. (Burney herself paid heavily for this lesson; it has been said that she gave her brother Charles, a dreadful spendthrift and a model for Lionel, the profits of *Evelina* after his debacle at Cambridge, when his father cut him off. Those profits would have done much for Burney but would have been thoughtlessly dispersed in a moment by Charles/Lionel.[41])

In *The Wanderer* Juliet has begun the action by self-sacrifice, marriage in France to an unworthy tyrant to preserve the life of her guardian. She performs the complex act of saving herself and the guardian by fleeing incognito to England, where she must remain incognito until she receives word that her guardian too has escaped. But in her escape to England she has lost all her money. The travails through which she finds her way and manages to support herself are therefore one prolonged and determined act of heroic altruism. Juliet has very little to learn about discretion; she is already an integrated personality, a genuine altruist, who must discover the difficulties a woman of refined reason and sensibility faces when she must earn her own living. But Burney insists that a heroic object is appropriate to and attainable by a woman who resists and endures; and as Villars instructs Evelina, so the bishop-guardian instructs Juliet (both women, I fear, thus drawing authority for their fortitude from a male guardian). Villars writes, "you must learn not only to *judge* but to *act* for yourself," whereupon Evelina immediately sets out on her course of three decisive actions; he later adds, "fortitude and firmness, when occasion demands them, are virtues as noble and as becoming in women as in men; the right line of conduct is the same for both sexes" (pp. 164, 217). The bishop encourages Juliet: "Where occasion calls for female exertion, mental strength must combat bodily weakness; and intellectual vigour must supply the inherent deficiencies of personal courage; those, only, are fitted for the vicissitudes of human fortune, who, whether male or female, learn to suffice to themselves. Be this the motto of your story" (p. 204). It is an important motto of Burney's oeuvre. The quiet heroism with which she later endured her mastectomy[42] is only the consistent application of a habitual heroism that insisted on her right to altruism and self-defense. Burney is an important example of how a mature altruist may survive in a world full of people with tyrannical natures; her work often poses the same question.

We have next to consider Elizabeth Montagu, the famous bluestocking, who chose an entirely different, and more conventional, route to autonomy. (One might well ask why, when Montagu functioned for years as a captain of commerce, she should be known only as a hostess.) Burney was never fond of Montagu, who, not so incidentally, thought the comic characters in *Evelina* unnecessarily low, and whose altruism was well publicized but somewhat suspect, who like Chudleigh joined and outpatriarched the patriarchs, and who dictated the terms of their lives to her dependents.

Chapter Six

PARENT AND CHILD:
MONTAGU AND GREGORY

THE CELEBRATED BLUESTOCKING HOSTESS Elizabeth Montagu was far more than an inspired hostess. Throwing literary parties was only the social expression of her aspirations. Beginning like Chudleigh—her close contemporary—as a beautiful girl with social entrée and slender means, Montagu was even more successful than Chudleigh in turning herself into a perfect patriarch and maintaining her prerogatives. She was a very thin velvet glove over a steel hand that successfully executed, for the time, almost incredible achievements. Like Chudleigh she wrested her wealth from a man, her husband. While her husband lived she was an executive arm to him, with—an expression she was later to use ironically—no will of her own. On her own she became a notable captain of industry and something of a domestic tyrant.

Although her principal companion, Dorothea Gregory, was considered by all the world to be her adopted daughter, and although the relationship between the two women was very like that of mother (or, later, father) and daughter, at the same time Dorothea played the role for Montagu that for more than thirty years Montagu had played for her rich, elderly husband: that is, with superb efficiency and acting willessly as an executive hand, she consulted and advised, made domestic arrangements, parlayed with servants, tradespeople, and tiresome relations, wrote countless letters, listened, agreed, soothed, brightened, softened, and was always on call to serve in any capacity needed. If toward Edward Montagu his wife played the role of consort conflated with that of daughter, toward Montagu herself Dorothea played the role of daughter conflated with that of consort. Both Montagu and Gregory, seen only in their social roles, fail misleadingly to display those formidable executive abilities that would clash spectacularly in their struggle over Gregory's marriage.

Even more at issue, however, than the question of whom Gregory was to marry was Gregory's rejection of Montagu as the model for her own career. In their earlier relationship Montagu must have appreciated Gregory's complaisance, while she herself played the brilliant star. Later, through marriage to Montagu's nephew and heir, Montagu offered Gregory—besides a surrogate marriage to herself—a succession to her own success: Gregory was to marry the nephew and subtly to direct his affairs (always with reference to Montagu) as Montagu had directed her own husband's and was to have her own chance of succeeding to perfect power. In other words, Matthew Montagu was Montagu's ostensible successor, but her true successor was to be her surrogate daughter, Gregory. Gregory's rejection of the proffered opportunity—of which marriage to the unobjectionable nephew was probably the least part, while the greater part would have been her endorsement of Montagu's life choices—was a devastating blow to Montagu's self-opinion and conceit. Gregory's refusal meant that she had not, all the time, been playing the part of subordinate while longing for the role of starring autocrat. Where Montagu pretended to altruism, Gregory, who had long been acquainted with all her splendid attainments, instead chose life with a poor but morally admirable man, sacrificing all the luxuries and comforts Montagu could offer to play the genuine altruist—and thus slapping her benefactor by rejecting her and her way of life. Gregory's rebellion and defection proved one of the very few defeats of Montagu's truly brilliant career, a defeat from which she never really recovered and one she never forgot or forgave. She never offered Gregory any alternative method of "establishment." Her responses to Gregory's rejection help to reveal Montagu's essential nature—resolute, resourceful, utterly determined, hard, and vindictive.

Dorothea Gregory was at the start the perfect humble companion—it was, after all, her father, Dr. John Gregory, who wrote the book. Sprightly, intelligent, and attractive—not unlike the young Montagu—she was the motherless daughter of an Edinburgh family that relied entirely upon the professional earnings of her father, an eminent professor of the theory of medicine at the university. The Gregorys, like the Burneys, belonged to that new professional middle class of people acceptable in polite society but without resources for the establishment of their children. "I have always been accustom'd to see my dearest friends

& nearest Relations marry without having it in their power to provide for a family," Gregory was to write to Montagu in 1783.[1] The daughters of such families were now to be added to those daughters of the clergy, the army, and the navy whom Collier recommended as ideally suitable for toadeaters.

Gregory had other recommendations. Her mother, Elizabeth Forbes, a cousin of Montagu's, was the daughter of Sir William Forbes and his wife, Dorothy Dale, the latter a woman celebrated for having lost £20,000 in the South Sea Bubble; as a person wellborn but of small fortune, Elizabeth Forbes had been suitably married to a promising physician. Through her mother, Dorothea Gregory was seventeenth in direct descent from Edward I, Robert Bruce, and Philip IV, certainly a matter of consideration to Montagu. John Gregory had enjoyed a long friendship with Montagu and her husband following his marriage to her cousin Forbes in the 1740s.[2] Edward Montagu, a gifted amateur mathematician, found him compatible, and, having made a friend of him, invited him to stay at times with the Montagus.

Dorothea Gregory was born in 1754;[3] the Montagus stood godparents to her younger sister. In 1766 John Gregory, a widower since 1761, came down to Denton, the Northumberland estate of the Montagus, and then escorted his hostess on a tour back to Scotland. In Edinburgh she discovered that John Gregory was esteemed and loved, that his children were also "loves."[4] The father with his two captivating daughters returned to Denton with Montagu, and when Gregory returned home, his daughters remained to visit. Montagu, who had been childless since the death of her baby son in 1744, eventually and reluctantly relinquished her "dear dear little friends."[5]

Before settling on Dorothea Gregory, Montagu entertained a variety of genteel young women on long visits: the sister of Christopher Anstey, who, however, unluckily died about 1760, was one; Mary Wilkes, the daughter of the celebrated John Wilkes, was another; and her own homeless sister Sarah, never, however, sufficiently amenable, was a third. The idea of selecting and rearing a child to become a suitable companion must have occurred to her when she encountered the charming, motherless Gregory girls. With pools of orphaned and unprovisioned children available everywhere, it was a popular idea of the time, like estate improvement. Lady Spencer was to oversee the satisfactory production of her favorite companion, Miss Preedy (chapter 11); Lady Bertram in *Mansfield Park* reaped a reward in her decline for having nurtured Fanny Price as a humble protégée; and the celebrated Thomas

Day's scheme of rearing two grateful foundlings so as to marry the one he deemed best for the purpose was not so outré in its time. Montagu, however, never considered taking in both motherless girls, one of whom in any case their father required, and therefore took the elder—a cruel separation for the girls but a necessity if she was to mold Gregory anew for her own purposes. In September 1770 Hester Chapone and Montagu traveled to Edinburgh to visit the Gregorys, and once again Gregory and his daughters returned with the party to Denton. Dorothea was fifteen, and now—or soon afterward—the final arrangements were made.

In taking Dorothea from her family into a new and much more luxurious way of life, Montagu must have made the usual promise to be responsible for establishing her ward—that is, for either marrying her off, with the provision of a modest fortune, or, if she did not marry, for providing her with an independence, probably in the form of an annuity. How could she have foreseen that Gregory was to become so essential and so dear to her that she could not bear to part with her? John Gregory, on his part, would have had his reservations about the change in his daughter's style of living—no doubt he gave her private instructions not to let her head or heart be turned—but ultimately he knew that he had no right to stand in the way of such proffered advantages. The parting was effected before May 1772, by which date Gregory was with Montagu at Tunbridge. Only seventeen, she was already a favorite with the Montagu circle, judged pretty, intelligent, and a shrewd observer.

The death of John Gregory in 1773 must have sealed the relationship; now there was no one else to whom Gregory could turn except her brother James, who was struggling to rise in the medical profession. John Gregory's posthumous and successful *Father's Legacy to His Daughters*, edited by his son and published in London in 1774, may have provided both girls with small annuities—Gregory had £50 a year of her own—and have thus proved a double legacy. The strictures on feminine decorum, if faithfully observed by Gregory, would make her the perfect companion.

Gregory was thus for Montagu a most valuable acquisition. In her letters during their ten happy years together Montagu habitually refers to her companion as "gentle Greg," "little Greg," or "fair Gregory." She makes far less stir about Gregory's great competence, founded on sturdy Scottish self-reliance and practiced both at home in Edinburgh, where she must to some extent have replaced her mother, and with the Montagus, where her benefactor expected of her the same extraordinary services she herself provided her husband. Gregory was an agent in domestic business, a sympathetic confidante, and a vivacious social companion. She was to become an intrepid charioteer, driving Montagu on long excursions between estates. She was resourceful, trustworthy, and firm; her heart, said Montagu, was "one perfect chrysolite, no flaw, no imperfection in it."[6] Frances Burney's portrait of her in 1780, when she was twenty-five, demonstrates that in society she disguised most of her assets—including, naturally, her notable common sense—just as her father had directed, displaying most prominently a girlish sense of fun that was *very* girlish for a young woman of her age. Encountering Gregory at Bath, Burney suggested to her that a character in a new book resembled their mutual friend William Seward, and together they projected a plot to copy out the character and send it to him anonymously. "I will send it first to a friend of mine who shall put it in the Post Office many miles away from both of us, & where he cannot suspect us," offered Gregory.[7] A week later they met again and Gregory raved on about the plot until Burney noted, "It is but a silly scheme, & I am already sick of it" (April 10, 1780, Berg Collection). Nevertheless, Burney, in Bath as friend and companion to Hester Thrale, probably entertained a strong fellow feeling for Gregory; she confessed that Gregory had become her most intimate acquaintance there, "& I find her far more agreeable than I believed she could have been."[8] "She is frank, open, shrewd, and sensible, and speaks her opinion both of matters and things with a plumpness of honesty and readiness that both pleases and diverts me. . . . And . . . she has never made me even a hint of a compliment" (1:353). Soon afterward Gregory wrote an undated note from Hill Street in London asking Burney how she could have known her whereabouts the evening before: "You shall not escape a *pinch* for your penetration into Characters."[9]

Besides her playfulness, Gregory displayed frankness and "shrewdness"—a quality even more compromising than cleverness—that were not particularly girlish. And in addition, she had made up her mind to emulate Montagu neither in scholarship nor in wit. She found Montagu's delight in the limelight unattractive. Her son was later to repeat her endorsement of a friend's judgment that "he had no objection to blue stockings, provided the petticoats were long enough to conceal them."[10] For all that, her son reported, her conversation was highly varied and animated, and she had great readiness and talent for repartee, strong good sense, a masculine understanding,[11] a determined will, and a pronounced sense of humor. Horace Walpole thought her—in contrast, no doubt, to Montagu—a "natural," meaning unlabored and unartificially delightful; and her friend Lady Louisa Stuart, with the same contrast in mind, called her "the perfection of strict truth, blunt honesty, and clear understanding," adding, "She verified the old Scotch proverb—'An ounce of mother wit is worth a pound of clergy.' "[12] Although Montagu probably interpreted the difference between herself and Gregory favorably to herself, as evidence of the uniqueness and inimitability of her own genius, Gregory, by her adopted diffidence, may actually have been making an unfavorable judgment on Montagu's love of self-display.

Gregory's position in the Montagu establishment, ostensibly that of an adopted daughter, became uncomfortably equivocal as she became noticeably marriageable. She was never adopted; Montagu's nephew Matthew Robinson was adopted, in 1776, following the death of Montagu's husband and four years after her acquisition of Gregory. Robinson, born in 1762, was her principal heir, and he took the Montagu name in 1776. It was understood that Montagu was to provide for Gregory in some way, but how? And if she were to marry, what were her pretensions? Montagu proclaimed no large fortune, without which no brilliant match would have been proposed, and although it might have been assumed that, should an appropriate modest match be proposed, Montagu would have provided a modest dowry, nothing of that sort transpired. Indeed, in 1777 Gregory fell in love with an unestablished young man, apparently wished to marry him, and saw him summarily dismissed by Montagu. Was she behaving selfishly, or was the young man suspected of being a fortune hunter, testing the waters? After that, no further applicants have been noted. Whether Montagu had already conceived the plan of marrying Gregory to her nephew (eight years the junior) and thus of binding both of them closely to herself for her lifetime is unknown but conceivable.

At this point, Montagu had become, in her widowhood, a patriarch. She saw no reason, so long as she herself had what she wanted—money, power, adulation—either to disturb or to reform the universe. On her husband's death in 1775 she had succeeded to an empire. In 1783 in Yorkshire alone she oversaw five hundred miners toiling in her pits, sixty reapers in her cornfields, and a brick, tile, and tar manufactory.[13] Her social system was to look after her workpeople adequately and to give them spectacular annual treats. The chimney sweeps of London were in a way the product of her coal mines, the emblems of her prosperity, and she gave no thought to alleviating their miseries except that in her later years every May Day she gave them a fete—roast beef and plum pudding—on the lawn of her Portman Square mansion. She habitually gave such parties; through them she saw her workpeople in the most expansive and grateful of moods and imprinted herself graciously upon their memories. In June 1775, for instance, she gave dinners on two successive days to the tenants of her Yorkshire estates and their families, the menu at one including "a brood of fine chickens, at the top a great sirloin of beef, at the bottom a loin of veal on one side and leg of mutton on the other, a ham and pigeon pye in the middle, with ducks and geese, tarts, cheesecakes, pudding, pease &c. to fill up chinks" (1:202–3). The style was well calculated to rear up the new generation of tenants in a proper appreciation of her greatness. To the haymakers "with their little families" at Sandleford in Berkshire in 1782 she gave a supper: "The appetite with which they eat, the jollity with which they laughed and sung showed me, I had not ill bestowed my meat and drink" (2:121). In 1787 at Sandleford she celebrated the king's birthday by inviting hundreds of schoolboys and their masters to a dinner of roast and boiled beef, mutton puddings, and pies served up on long tables in her grove and then gave a supper that same evening to her workpeople; the next month in July she gave a feast for Sunday school children (2:210–11). Unlike her sister Sarah Scott, Montagu saw nothing wrong with the system up which she had clambered to a position unprecedented for a woman.

Charles Pigott, in *The Female Jockey Club*, belabored Montagu for this approach to charity: "We . . . cannot discover any transcendant charity in a *public, ostentatious* expenditure of a few pounds *once a year*, out of an immense property, which bestows on the *Lady's dear self* every indulgence, and luxury *all the year round*. What a profanation of terms to call this charity; to bestow plenty one day, that famine may be more cruelly felt the next. . . . To behold these little victims of an arbitrary Brute, regale themselves to-day, without procuring them the same consolation . . . to-morrow, must excite pain, rather than pleasure, in a truly *sensible*, compassionate heart." [14]

Montagu was born beautiful, clever, and precocious, though not quite so precocious as people thought; her actual birth date was not 1720, as she caused to be recorded, but 1718.[15] She was the elder by two years of the two daughters of Matthew and Elizabeth Drake Robinson; there were seven brothers. As children the two girls were thought to be all but indistinguishable. Elizabeth, for her sprightliness, was called Fidget, and Sarah, for her resemblance to Elizabeth, was called Bridget, or Pea. Matthew Montagu has written that in her youth his adoptive mother was a beauty "most admired in the peculiar animation and expression of her blue eyes, with high arched dark eyebrows, and in the contrast of her brilliant complexion with her dark brown hair. She was of the middle stature, and stooped a little."[16] Sarah must have had similar charms before she had smallpox in 1741. The girls were gifted writers and enjoyed an unusual upbringing. Matthew Robinson, their father, had great wit and was bored by the country to which, with his large family, he was principally confined; his recourse was to stimulate his children to those exertions of wit and ingenious argument he might otherwise have enjoyed at his London club. In response to his unusual encouragement, Elizabeth proved his particular pride, and he fostered in her those sallies of humor which, reported her nephew, "by grave readers may be thought to form too large a part of her early correspondence" (1:4–7). The Robinson girls also profited from the attentions of their grandmother's second husband, the scholar Conyers Middleton, who took a great interest in their education.

Sarah may always have been more serious; Elizabeth had an invincible optimism that prompted someone, when she was a child, to inquire curiously why she always looked so glad.[17] Her happiness may well have resulted from the absence of those lessons in submission ordinarily practiced upon girls and from her father's approval of her natural bent toward wit. Still, she had obstacles to surmount. Her mother, who died in 1746, had been ill and unequal to taking her and Sarah about. But Elizabeth met Lady Margaret Cavendish Harley and became her favorite correspondent; after Lady Margaret married the Duke of Portland in 1734, Elizabeth for some years functioned, on long visits, as friend and companion at Bulstrode and for one or two London seasons.

Functioning as the acknowledged friend and companion of the duchess was not unduly humiliating to a young woman with a thousand pound portion.[18] But Montagu had every intention of improving her position; an advantageous marriage was the next step. In London with the duchess in 1740, at a party at Lady North's where the guests were displaying their new birthday clothes,[19] Montagu saw and admired George Lyttelton.[20] He was a tall, gawky, scraggly person, altogether unprepossessing in appearance, and so it was undoubtedly his conversation she admired, while he was taken by her beauty and her wit. Soon after their meeting she sent her sister some of his verses and wrote, "Either I am very partial to the writer, or Mr. Lyttelton has something of an elegance in all his compositions, let the subject be ever so trifling."[21] They were to be lifelong friends, but whatever their feelings for each other, a poor expectant lord could not marry a negligible fortune; and in June 1742 Lyttelton married the beautiful and amiable Lucy Fortescue. In the meantime, Montagu had caught the eye and soon engaged the heart of fifty-year-old Edward Montagu, a grandson of the first Earl of Sandwich, the owner of rich Northumberland coal mines and the heir to still greater wealth. Her eminent companionship abilities, as demonstrated by her connection with the duchess, must have recommended her as a good wife for his old age; but he could hardly have guessed that he was also acquiring a business agent. They married in August 1742.

If, as seems likely, Montagu had loved Lyttelton, she soon enough came to believe in the fortuitous nature of her own marriage. Her husband, like her father, acknowledged her superior qualities (as long as she was properly submissive toward him) and accepted her, as he grew older and more infirm, as his executive arm in everything. In the course of her thirty-three-year marriage she moved resolutely toward the command of an empire of wealth and power.

Yet the persisting friendship between Montagu and Lyttelton may have been in part romantic. Lyttelton moved to Hill Street, where the Montagus lived, in 1749. In November 1759 Horace Walpole, no admirer of Montagu, noted a remark of her sixteen-year-old postilion: "I am not such a child but I can guess something: whenever my Lord —— comes to my lady, she orders the porter to let in nobody else, and then they call for a pen and ink, and say, they are going to write history." [22]

At the least there was a serious attachment between the two. When Lyttelton died in August 1773, Elizabeth Vesey was frightened for her friend: "I tremble for you my D^r friend the letter I received from you last night sais you are not well & this stroke will be felt for Heavens sake write to to [sic] me. . . . What ever you write shall never be seen by mortal as my Heart is open to you I can not bear a looker on & believe you feel the same." Reginald Blunt has suggested that Montagu may also have had a tenderness for Sir James Macdonald, the brilliant young Scotsman who died in Rome in July 1766, aged only twenty-four. Like Lyttelton, Macdonald was unprepossessing in appearance, solid in character, good-hearted, and a delightful conversationalist. On his death, too, Vesey exhibited alarm for Montagu: "My d^r Mrs Mountagu if you have any Charity write to one who feels every accident that can distress you not even Mr Vesey (I will promise you) shall see y^r letters I am frighten'd at what the sensibility of y^r Heart and y^r constitution may suffer." Possibly Vesey and Montagu, each married to a man with whom romance was out of the question, had agreed that love and marriage had no natural connection and that love dwindles while money grows; for Vesey's excuse for Gregory's final defection in 1784 to marry a poor man would be that she had "only been mistaken in believing that Love is an evergreen."[23]

Possibly Montagu had known passion and considered it had no place in marriage; that would help to explain her fury when Gregory insisted on giving up the prospect of an advantageous marriage for nothing but a predilection. But some of Montagu's friends thought her simply lacking in passion. Mrs. Chapone called her "an ignoramus in love."[24] Burney thought the defect so serious that it prevented others from loving her and wrote to Hester Thrale in 1781, "Mrs. Montagu, as we have often agreed, is a Character rather to respect than love, for she has not the *don d'aimer* by which alone love can be made fond or faithful."[25] We cannot know, therefore, whether Montagu twice demanded that Gregory sacrifice her heart from ignorance of what she asked, from a conclusion that the men were unworthy, from experience that had proved money the greatest good, from a mean-minded desire to make Gregory give up what Montagu had never enjoyed, or from a selfish desire to keep her in attendance upon herself. Her motives may have been a combination of all these.

Certainly Montagu had put in her own submissive time and saw no reason why Gregory should not do the same. Edward Montagu, growing old in the first decade of his marriage, was often captious, fractious, demanding, and suspicious. Montagu herself, who understood her wifely role and played it as a role, was in turn obliging, obedient, and grateful. Gratitude, in fact, flowed unceasingly from her toward her husband, an essential unguent in the relationship. Her letters often close with a dose of it: "Your most faithful, affectionate, and grateful wife"; "with the greatest love, esteem, and gratitude, I am most affectionately yours."

She understood that a wife must be perfectly complaisant. Not only did she embrace her own responsibility, but she impressed the role on younger women. She wrote to Lyttelton in 1758 of his thirteen-year-old daughter, "If she pleases herself she is not very sollicitous whether she pleases others. . . . She does not know how much the amiableness of a Woman depends on trivial things." But when the girl was fifteen, her proud father informed Montagu: "I did not know her domestic virtues before, but I assure you they are very great. She seems to have no mind of her own; she is soberly cheerful; she envies nobody, backbites nobody, troubles nobody."[26] This was a mighty advance in two years—and Montagu was the mentor.

For the thirty-three years of her marriage, Montagu was a model wife. She kept three great establishments running—at Denton in Northumberland, at Sandleford in Berkshire, and in London. In 1768 at Sandleford alone there was a staff of thirty. She cosseted and cared for her husband, an ailing asthmatic, and kept him alive to the good age of eighty-three. She entertained splendidly. She served as her husband's secretary and business agent. Unluckily, in 1744, her one child, a son, aged only fifteen months, had died, and there were no other children; but in this, as in everything, she had done her duty. Her husband was proud of her successes and had no objection to the famous conversation parties that by 1750 she had instituted in Hill Street. She specialized in parties at which the wit flew, invited all the current authors, and kept the current publications in her drawing room. The whole was an arena designed for the exercise of her own conversation and wit. But she had no intention of figuring only as the hostess of authors; she was an accomplished author herself, as much approved as any of them. Remarkably, her husband had no objection to the publication of some of her writings—first, three clever dialogues tucked anonymously into Lyttelton's *Dialogues of the Dead* in 1760 and then the famous *Essay on the Writings and Genius of Shakespeare* in 1769. Neither had he any serious objections to her quitting him to attend to her ailments—not surprisingly, she suffered from chronic stomach disorders—but in the beginning, at least, she also went to remedy her childlessness for long periods at Tunbridge or Bath.

She was as gifted a business agent as she was an estate manager, and as Edward Montagu failed in the 1760s, she began to travel in his behalf between the estates, seeing men of business and making decisions, which, she always noted, were precisely those decisions he himself would have made. In those days, officially she—like Lucy Lyttelton—had no mind of her own. Her husband had early made a will in her favor, and in his final will he left her all except a £3,000 bequest to her nephew Morris. His own relations went unregarded, nor did he leave her his possessions only for life, after which they would revert to his closest male relative; his three estates, his income (variously estimated at £7,000 to £10,000 a year) were hers unconditionally. How had she accomplished this?

When he lay dying, Montagu assured her sister that there would be no testamentary changes: "You are very kind in what you hint at; there is no danger of that while his understanding keeps clear; if he should grow partly childish he might be wavering in this point, but his opinion and his good will are too much fixd for him ever to alter them, indeed his esteem for me and his humour seem to be well matched: they have been fighting these 20 years, the esteem never subdued the humour, nor the humour the esteem."[27] Montagu would seem to suggest that by nature her husband grudged admiration to her but that her attributes, compelling admiration, held nature at bay. Such an estimate of her situation must have rendered her marriage, the long novitiate of her power, an exacting trial.

Clearly she was committed to the object of ruling one day and, just as clearly, to attain that end, she had to play a part that was all submission. That is, she was in the precise hypocritical position which Sarah Fielding and her own sister, Sarah Scott, identified as most damaging to the moral character of woman. Had their observation of her helped to confirm their conclusions? Her immediate task during her marriage was to reassure her husband in every possible way that his wishes were sacred, that even after his death his desires would be executed by his vicar on earth exactly as if he were there to see to it himself. Occasionally she can be overheard saying so. On a visit in his behalf to Yorkshire, for instance, having discovered that a condition of her uncle's will—the provision of an annual feast for the people of an almshouse he had endowed—had fallen into abeyance, she ordered beef, bread, and ale for each inmate at her (husband's) expense, and wrote to him: "Indeed one may say the feast on his Birthday does not now do him any good, however I am very scrupulous in articles of this kind, for if these sort of things make ye pleasure of the Living, it is an injury to Society to suffer the Will of the Dead to be neglected, since all will fear the same treatment when they are dead. . . . I am sure your noble mind will approve my sentiments on the subject."[28]

Her greatest point, of course, had been carried when he allowed her to be his business agent. There could be no danger during her marriage of Montagu's becoming a mere emanation of her husband, unable—like Vesey, for instance (chapter 10)—to live free of his repressive direction. Montagu was always fiercely herself and had her own methods of dealing with her husband's repressive measures. It would never have answered to have attempted to subdue him entirely, as Chudleigh did her duke. Instead she manipulated him. Glimpses of the politics of the marriage can be found in her letters. In September 1762, for instance, during a visit of her close friend Lord Bath at Sandleford, she

started ye thought of going to Spa instead of Tunbridge this summer, which we all talk'd of some time, with great alacrity, except Mr. Montagu, who prudently threw in ifs and buts, doubts and quandaries. As I never love to labour a point till ye time comes near, I said no more of it. . . . A little after Xmas his Lordship in a laughing manner attack'd Mr. M: on ye propriety or indeed necessity of my

going to Spa for my health, and less dislike was expressed than I expected, so
now and then, tout doucement I used to say, my dear, if we go to Spa—to which
my dear answerd, I have not told you that we shall go to Spa.[29]

Agmondesham Vesey, too, refused to make travel plans with his wife:
the withholding or the alteration of plans is a common means of keeping
subordinates disadvantaged and mindful of their contingent positions.
In this case Edward Montagu, now seventy, perhaps dubious about the
exertion and expense entailed by such a journey, probably fearful of
ridicule at a fruitless quest for an heir, yielded at last to the formal request of Lord Bath, who had, by his solicitations, thus acknowledged
the husband's prerogative.

A refusal to accommodate the elderly Lord Bath might have exposed
Edward Montagu to social criticism, to which he was sensitive, and his
wife became expert at manipulating him through this weakness. She
could easily acquit him of all blame herself while conveying to him that
others might blame him. In 1772 the couple was at Sandleford, Montagu to go on alone to Hill Street, when Frances Boscawen desired her
to come on a visit to Hatchlands, in nearby Surrey. The visit could, as
Montagu wrote to her sister, make no difference to her husband, for she
was to be absent from him in any case and the London staff would be un-
disturbed by her departure. But her husband complained that she had
rambled enough for one summer, "so I told him I was sure Mrs. Boscawen wd not desire me to come against his inclination, and his refusal
was an excuse for me, and it was very well and I wd write and let her
know that I had so good a reason for not keeping my promise." Threatened with the exposure of his unwillingness to oblige the widow of one
of the nation's heroes, Edward Montagu countered with an offer of three
days' leave. His wife replied that three days would incur great fatigue
upon herself and no pleasure on her friend, and reluctantly he bestowed
upon her a week. "I was determined either to have my pleasure or give a
signal mark of my obedience and his noble exertion of prerogative. Do
you not admire these lovers of liberty! What do the generality of men
mean by a love of liberty but the liberty to be saucy to their superiors,
and arrogant to their inferiors, to resist the power of others over them,
and to exert their power over others. I am not sure that Cato did not
kick his wife. . . . But these Lords of Creation must be lordly."[30]

In August 1774, when her husband was visibly failing, Montagu wrote
to Elizabeth Carter that she awaited his pleasure in the matter of a pro-

jected journey northward. She did not venture to ask his plans; he did not vouchsafe.

In the mean time your Friend is one of those good creatures that has not a Will of her own. No word, no phrase, no syllable intimating a wish escapes her. As our Friend Mr. Harris assumes, that every sentence will be a sentence of assertion or Volitions, I think it does not become the humble character of a Wife to utter any sentence at all on so important a subject as a journey; and now my dear Friend I hope I am as good as you could wish, and I wish you were married, and had a Husband who wanted to go into Northumberland when he could not go 30 miles, and then I shd know whether you were the same sweet, passive, quiet thing as I. When his Honour gives a distant hint of a journey, I answer only with my head, an humble bow, no assertions, no volitions. How headstrong, how petulant are some Women! How they reason, how they argue, and lose their points by the force and acuteness of their logick. It is strange that so often a Woman has a Will of her own, which is petty treason, and ought to be capitally punished. You will perceive by my nonsense that I am well and in good spirits.[31]

Montagu handled her husband's morose temper to the end, glad of it at last because it tempered her grief at his dissolution. "I am glad illness does not so far soften his temper as to make him speak tenderly to me; peevishness hurts my ear, tenderness from a departing friend wounds the heart," she wrote.[32] The concluding sentence or sententia is characteristic of her style, conversational, no doubt, as well as literary. First, she speaks her mind; then, just as she tossed placatory and incongruous bows and diamonds upon her person, so she tosses placatory diverting bows onto her discourse: "I am not sure that Cato did not kick his wife"; "You will perceive by my nonsense that I am well and in good spirits." Montagu has been talking less nonsense than treason. How much resentment did women like her suffer in reading such ordinary stuff as James Harris's simple definition of a sentence as being expressive either of assertion or volition and recognizing that as properly unassertive and unwillful women, they had no property in the sentence at all. If Montagu's career, already brilliant, had ended here, we should have lamented her wasted talents.

Her first and less serious fault was an uncontrolled vanity. Vanity and the obsessive desire to display herself lay at the root of her bluestocking or conversation parties. Probably because of her overweening ambition to singularize herself, perhaps to recover what she had been to her father, her parties never quite came off. She was to note Vesey's ability, despite her preoccupation with the breaking up of the conversational circle, to fuse the occupants of her room into a whole. Her own parties were the opposite: the conversational semicircle remained rigidly unbroken, but the component parts never melded. She lacked, Lady Louisa Stuart said, the "art of kneading the mass well together. As her company came in, an heterogeneous medley, so they went out, each individual feeling himself single, isolated, and (to borrow a French phrase) embarrassed with his own person. . . . Everything in that house, as if under a spell, was sure to form itself into a circle or semicircle."[33]

One went to Montagu's not to be a success, as one went to Vesey's, but to see the lions and to admire Montagu's wit and learning. Over the years her style scarcely changed. Fulke Greville, probably with assistance from his wife, who was never fond of Montagu, painted a verbal portrait of her in the mid-1750s as a magnificent and voluble talker who took small notice of logic and had no sense of audience and no sensitivity to others, disputing on opposite sides of the question on Monday and Tuesday, telling cant jokes of one set to uncomprehending members of another and "a sentimental story to a civil listening country farmer." He made early mention of her oft-noted failure of taste in dress, her appearance without buckles to her shoes, in ribbons chosen by her maid and flung promiscuously upon her, in a gown the effect of which was totally destroyed by the wrong accessories.[34] How much criticism came from males who resented her free use of her brilliant conversational powers is difficult to judge. It seems to have been the fashion to attend her parties and flatter her to her face, then mock her, because of her insatiable appetite for flattery, behind her back. Twenty years later, in 1776, Nathaniel Wraxall described her after her husband's death, always cheerful and spirited, leading the conversation, "but her manner was more dictatorial and sententious than conciliating or diffident. There was nothing feminine about her; and though her opinions were usually just, as well as delivered in language suited to give them force, yet the organ which conveyed them was not soft or harmonious." That is, he found her unwomanly. He also found her "destitute of taste in disposing the ornaments of her dress," though she still persisted, he complained, in tastelessly ornamenting her emaciated person with her diamond necklaces and bows. "I used to think that these glittering appendages of opulence sometimes helped to dazzle the disputants whom her arguments might not always convince or her literary reputation intimidate."[35] In the salon Montagu was never diffidently cautious of assertion. Her logic may have improved over the years, but her feminine submissiveness died entirely.

But though much of the detraction she suffered was by our own standards undeserved, some she probably did deserve. Her overweening vanity and appetite for incense are too well documented to be entirely a misconception on the part of her critics. Montagu's sister Sarah Scott, in *A Description of Millennium Hall*, patently critiques her in the character of Lady Brumpton, a person known to have been ridiculed as a genius and learned lady but from whose set the youthful Lady Mary hopes for improving conversation, in the end gaining nothing but a confusion of scraps of miscellaneous reading. Lady Brumpton's ruling passion is vanity: "The adulation which she received with too much visible complacency, inspired her with such an opinion of herself, as led her to despise those of less shining qualities, and not to treat any with proper civility, whom she had not some particular desire to please, which often gave severe pangs to bashful merit, and called her real superiority in question; for those who observed so great a weakness, were tempted to believe her understanding rather glittering than solid." Lady Brumpton was easily imposed upon by anyone who used an excess of flattery. The turn of conversation in her house was ridiculed in every other company, "and indeed it was capable of being so; the extreme endeavour to shine, took off from that ease in conversation which is its greatest charm. Every person was like a bent bow, ready to shoot forth an arrow; which had no sooner darted to the other side of the room, than it fell to the ground, and the next person picked it up, and made a new shot with it." [36] The most telling part of this indictment may reside in the name: Lady Brumpton, in Richard Steele's comedy *The Funeral* (1701), is an unfeeling and manipulative wife who has worked her hypocritical arts on her husband to become both his principal heir and the guardian of and dictator to his wards.

Scott's exposure of her sister, whatever her motive, demonstrates the ideological differences between them at this point and helps to explain the somewhat formal relationship they maintained in later years. But many others took up the theme of Montagu's towering vanity. In 1786 Richard Cumberland lampooned her in an essay as Vanessa, who "in the centre of her own circle sits like the statue of the Athenian Minerva, incensed with the breath of philosophers, poets, painters, orators, and every votarist of art, science, or fine speaking." [37] He identified vanity as the mainspring of her actions, the reason for her patronage of art and her charities. She required outrageous flattery, he said, and depicts a guest producing the unction in her presence and cynically deriding her in her absence. For her own aggrandizement she displayed every new publication in her salon and had the authors on hand. (In a later paper he made amends by suggesting that her basic good nature shone unimpeded when she was not on display.) [38]

The unkindest portrait of all was provided by James Woodhouse, the peasant poet whom she befriended, patronized, and kept for twenty years as her steward. A long section, "Patroness," in his autobiographical poem *The Life and Lucubrations of Crispinus Scriblerus*, expatiates on his relationship with Vanessa, a woman marked by her pompous spirit, sparkling wit, and hunger for praise, and analyzes her reasons for bestowing favors:

> Ah! 'twas not perfect heart, but pregnant head!
> 'Twas hungry Pride, still hoping to be fed!
> 'Twas Ostentation gaping for a bit
> Of clownish Wonder, or of country Wit—
> 'Twas Affectation starv'd for flattering strain;
> 'Twas Vanity—the vainest of the Vain!
> Alas! 'twas Cunning, weaving specious wiles,
> With smooth expressions, and well-polish'd smiles—
> False proofs of fondness and a forg'd pretence;
> While hollow promise pledg'd rewards immense;
> To furnish Manhood with most plenteous meed,
> And raise old Age beyond the reach of Need! [39]

After twenty years of service, Woodhouse was dismissed by Montagu because of religious and political differences and was left unpensioned, unprovided for.[40] Interestingly, his dismissal followed Gregory's by only a year or two. Could it be that Montagu, once kindhearted, in her last years hardened in her autocracy, giving up the inconvenient sensibility that interfered with the joys of tyranny?

But Montagu's greater sin, greater than that of vanity, was willfulness. Perhaps she had always expected to direct the affairs of younger female relations. In the late 1740s, when she was unable to talk her sister Sarah out of marrying George Scott, a coolness arose between them, and the Duchess of Portland advised Montagu that though Sarah might wish to obey her in other respects, she could not control her affections.[41] In 1777, when Gregory fell in love, she proved more amenable on Montagu's representation that the affair was a great mistake. On this occasion Elizabeth Vesey at least appeared to have sided entirely with Montagu, writing to her of Gregory in 1778, "How she loves you! and how pleasant it must be to you to see the heart you have snatched from a shipwreck so entirely devoted to you; it tells so much for both; my eyes fill."[42]

Matthew Robinson Montagu also proved consistently amenable. William Seward told Thrale and Burney in 1779 that Montagu tyrannized over Matthew, then seventeen, offering as evidence Thrale's story that when Matthew knocked too hard at a door, Montagu sent him a reproving message by a servant bidding him stay till he had a door of his own to knock at so.[43] But Montagu depended on her two young people:

> I look upon it as one of the best rewards of a blameless life, to be able in ones old age to give Countenance and protection to deserving young Persons; the good one imparts to them is strongly reflected back again. Through my little Nephew and my fair Gregory, I enjoy a thousand little pleasures, that I could no longer taste in my own Person. As one has a tenacious love of this present life, this present World, it seems to me as politick to form attachments to the fate and fortunes of young Persons, as to ensure ones ticket in a Lottery. While theirs is in the Wheel, I think myself interested, tho my own should be a blank.[44]

Certainly, when in 1772 she took Gregory in, she was resolved to treat her like a daughter and not like a companion, the very idea of which she herself, who had so narrowly avoided that role with the Duchess of Portland, had every reason to loathe. When in 1765 a friend suggested to Montagu that Hester Chapone might be just the right companion for the Duchess of Beaufort and could improve the duchess's daughter in her studies, Montagu replied that Chapone, who had a tiny income of her own, a fond brother, and an uncle who was bishop of Winchester, would be unlikely to "accept of service on any terms whatever." For companions, service meant "a condition, in which, if they do not converse with Ladies women . . . they would be reckond proud and impertinent. The dapper butler, the spruce groom of the chambers, the House Steward and the friends of all these people must be her future companions, and one had rather live on bread and water than in the tittle tattle and gossipry of that set of people. . . . I must own I should as soon keep a person to blow my nose as to amuse me."[45]

About the same time Montagu thought Mrs. Chapone's sister-in-law Kitty Chapone, a young woman without provision, would be lucky to obtain a good place as a governess. "Every condition of life has its evils, a dependent one many, and especially that of an humble companion. . . . How few people, who for want of an independent subsistence have been forced to enter into a family in the quality of nurses to old ladies, or companions to country gentlewomen, have not suffered more indignities and mortifications than belong to servitude itself!" A situation as governess, she concluded, would be preferable to living "as companion to some old maiden whose peevishness has driven from her all who are able to subsist without her, or some ancient matron who is too blind to write her own letters, too deaf to understand her family, or so lame she wants to be led from one room to another." [46]

Montagu had no intention of treating anyone like that, and besides she had different needs. She needed a companion for social occasions just as the duchess had needed one, and she liked having a young woman in the house, someone like her younger sister before her sister began having critical notions. Dorothea Gregory was a young woman of family, and Montagu, who was sensitive to the plight of the humble companion, took her in determined to treat her as a relation and as a surrogate child—and to do so visibly.

The childless Montagu and the motherless Gregory truly loved each other and enjoyed ten good years together, though we can assume that during these years Gregory gradually established her own separate standards and held her peace about them. After the death of Edward Montagu, Gregory was there to abet Montagu in the fulfillment of certain aspirations: Montagu had wished to travel—to triumph, perhaps, as so many Englishwomen had—in France, and the pair spent the autumn of 1775 in Montauban, the summer of 1776 in Paris. It was never certain which Englishwomen the unpredictable French would take up, but Montagu had no great success and did not repeat the experiment. Instead she began extensive building at Sandleford and the erection of a great palace in Portman Square intended to house an illustrious progeny. She continued to oversee her collieries and estates and to entertain more lavishly than ever. And for a time, after Gregory's love affair, all seems to have become smooth again. But in 1777 Gregory was twenty-three, and by 1782 she was twenty-eight and still had not been "established."

The summer of 1782 may have been the moment when the affairs of the small family—Montagu, Gregory, and Matthew Robinson Montagu (now nineteen)—grew critically troubled. At Easter they had moved into the new Portman Square mansion and had celebrated with a series of housewarmings and parties. Montagu, in excellent health and spirits, always abetted by the redoubtable Gregory, enjoyed her varied building and business projects. Painting at Sandleford delayed her departure from town until mid-July, but the pleasures of the new Montagu House did not pall; in place of country walks, at night she would send away the candles and take a moonlight walk in the new dining room. Gregory delighted during the day to sit there and look over the Hampstead Hills and watch "the setting sun play on the grand lustre" (Blunt 2:119). When at last they moved on to Sandleford, the haymakers were to be entertained, as were the workpeople who were embellishing the "pleasure ground" under the direction of Capability Brown, transforming it into "sweet pastorals and gentle elegances" (2:123). The party consisted of Matthew and his tutor, Mr. Gilbank, Gregory, and Montagu. The men rode in the mornings and then studied; Gregory drove Montagu about in the whiskey and returned home in time for Montagu to give domestic orders and regulate the workwomen embroidering the feather hangings for the famous Feather Room in Portman Square and for Gregory to read for an hour before dinner. They dined at four, took coffee, then tea, and walked till sunset, after which the "young folks" walked till nine, studied till ten, and supped together while Montagu supped privately in her dressing room, leaving her young people "to indulge that innocent gaiety of conversation so becoming at their time of life" (2:122–23).

The intimacy between Matthew and Gregory was stultifying and enforced. It would seem that the erection of Montagu House had set Montagu upon pursuing her plan of founding a family to inhabit it. Matthew was very young, but Gregory was not, and now was the time, if Montagu meant to marry them, to be about it. At this period Matthew, who was generally amenable, developed a "fondness" for Gregory. For Montagu the plan had many advantages. Though one could always use more money, there was money enough in the family, and Matthew's marriage to Gregory would ensure that only the tutor would have to go, no unfamiliar bride would object to Montagu's continuing to queen it in Montagu House, Gregory would continue to implement her mother's many projects, and Montagu herself would never be lonely but would increase her ménage with a series of those delightful children she always so purported to enjoy.

In his autobiography, Gregory's son writes that Montagu warmly pressed his mother to marry Matthew Montagu. Gregory, who was fond of Matthew as a younger brother but could not think of her patroness's tame object as a man to marry, was unable to fall in with the scheme. Despite the years with Montagu, she remained at core a practical Scotswoman with the Gregory temperament. She wished neither to marry Matthew nor to live forever paired with him as Montagu's vassal. At the end of that summer she discovered a necessity to travel to Edinburgh, on the occasion of the marriage of her brother James, and was lucky enough to procure an escort in her brother William.

Gregory left Sandleford in early October and wrote to Montagu on October 7 from Portman Square ("My Dearest Madam if I am not very much mistaken"). Her letter illustrates her calm competence, her

matter-of-fact frankness on sensitive matters, and above all the services
she provided Montagu. On her arrival at Montagu House, she had at
once dispatched some partridges to Mrs. Walsingham and had been sure
to pay the carriage. She had dispatched another letter to a nephew and
more partridges to Matthew's mother, Mrs. Robinson (an unpleasant
woman who at least quasilegitimately resented the alienation from herself of her son's affections), " 'tho not without terrible apprehensions of
its bringing on a visitation but thank my stars she was not at home." She
advised Montagu to send letters earlier to Newbury to catch an earlier
post if she should require an immediate answer. She had received a call
from Sir William Robinson, who advised her and Woodhouse to bottle
some of the new claret in pint instead of quart bottles: what was Montagu's pleasure? She had sent letters from Montagu on to Capability
Brown and from Sarah Scott to Mrs. Hawkesworth and had delivered to
Woodhouse "all the directions you intrusted me with & all the notes &
comments I could make upon them by which I hope I have not obscur'd
their meaning." And she reported a problem about frames for copies in
the gallery of Sir Joshua Reynolds's *Faith, Hope,* and *Charity.* As an executive arm she was a treasure; but if she sometimes thought of having
her own home to manage, who can blame her? Montagu, however, who
had been all submission until she was fifty-seven and who saw no occasion for Gregory's attaining independence at half that age, continued to
view herself as both Matthew's and Gregory's munificent benefactor.

By mid-October Gregory was in Edinburgh. Sarah Scott was taking
her place at Sandleford, and the agreement was that Gregory should
return by the time Parliament convened. But although Gregory wrote
weekly letters full of love, concern, and gratitude—it was now her turn
to sign her letters "your most much obliged & most grateful affect."—
one eventuality after another intervened to forestall her return.

At first confessedly homesick for her life with Montagu, Gregory may
soon have felt a reattachment to an earlier way of life with its advantage of a sturdy sense of independence. But on November 2 she wrote
reassuringly: "Happy as I am in the society and affection of my friends
here I feel that I shall never be able to regard my present situation as
any thing but an honourable exile from that home which your tenderness has taught me to look upon as my own and well does my gratefull
affection for you serve to favour the deceit and my reason finds it difficult to persuade my heart that this is my native home" ("how good and
kind it is in you"). Still, Gregory makes the point that Edinburgh *is* her
native home, that she has no real right to consider Montagu's homes her

own. And although she does not mention it, she had already met the attractive, intelligent, and promising Archibald Alison, then twenty-six, a native of Edinburgh and an intimate friend of her brother—entirely acceptable as a suitor had he been able to support a family.

Montagu failed to preserve all of the letters sent her, week by week, from Edinburgh; did she destroy those of November 16, 23, and 30 and December 31 because they mentioned Alison? None of the surviving 1782 letters—those of October 19 and 25, November 2 and 9, and December 6, 14, 21, and 24—mention him. The critical letter announcing Gregory's engagement to Alison is among those missing. The letter of January 7, 1783, is a response to Montagu's incredulous displeasure at the news.

Your goodness my Dearest Madam in so soon writing me your sentiments at large on the interesting subject which I grieve to see has given you so much uneasyness quite overpowers me—all I can do in return for all your kindness is to assure you of the gratitude of a heart which whatever may be its weakness in other respects knows how to feel and value the interest you still take in its happiness. you may rest perfectly satisfied that the promise I made you in my last letter My Dear Madam shall be faithfully perform'd. I have already given you & my friends here too much uneasyness to harbour a wish that coud tend to your or their further disquiet and I pray heaven you may rather have to lament my death than any further imprudence on my part—I may be unhappy myself but I shall not render you so and whatever I may suffer under the restriction that your wisdom imposes I shall submit with patience and without a murmur. ("your goodness my dearest Madam")

Gregory was about to render Montagu more unhappy than, probably, she had ever been in her life. That her own family were displeased by the engagement was only a pretense to avert Montagu's possible anger from them; in reality, as close friends of Alison's, they were pleased. But no doubt they advised Gregory prudently to conciliate Montagu if she could, for Alison, a newly ordained clergyman, had no living of his own and had just been instituted as curate at Brancepeth, Durham, at a salary of £50 a year.[47] The restrictions Montagu in her wisdom had imposed were that the couple should defer their engagement until Alison had procured preferment, that Gregory should return to her under a pledge not to see him, and that for her nephew's sake—lest he imbibe the atmosphere of filial disobedience—the whole matter should remain a secret from him. There were, of course, other reasons for keeping the affair a secret from Matthew.

Montagu also demanded that Gregory return home. In the same letter of January 7, however, Gregory posed the problem of finding a suitable traveling companion. If Montagu truly wanted her at once, she might take her sister's maid with her and send her back again, but this would be paying for three travelers instead of one and would cost her £30 (of her annual income of £50). Once again she thanked Montagu "for all the indulgence you have already shewn me and for the sweet assurance of continuing to me thro' life that friendship without which I feel I could not enjoy life itself. I intend to write to Mr Montagu as soon as I am able and you may depend upon it, it shall be in a such way & so much in my usual stile that it will not be possible for him to take *any suspicions.*"

Gregory longed for mercy and kindness. Want of sleep, she told Montagu, and a continual pain in her forehead and temples made it almost impossible for her to hold up her head, and she had taken twenty-five drops of laudanum two nights before without its having induced sleep. "But I hope soon to get better now." She was to learn that Montagu would as soon see her dead as married to Alison. Despite potent threats on both sides—illness or death on Gregory's part if thwarted, cessation of friendship on Montagu's part if thwarted—the contestants were to remain inflexibly embattled during the ensuing eighteen months.

Gregory's tactics were those available to dependent women: illness, headaches, sleeplessness, loss of appetite, threats of dying, swoons like that into which she fell when Montagu's first letter of reaction arrived. To all this she added such arguments as seemed hopeful: that Alison was born a gentleman, that the life she would lead with him was only that to which her family was accustomed. Her brother could scarcely object to the situation, once Alison had procured a living, for

It is *exactly his own situation* for if my Brother was to die at present he could not leave a single sixpence to his wife & tho' he has a fair chance of rising in his Profession there is not the least chance of his being able to *save* money for many years and if his wife bring him Children they must all if he die young be left unprovided for—but this neither makes *him* nor *her* unhappy, because in that respect they are exactly on a footing with most of their friends and if you consider my Dear Madam that I have always been accustom'd to see my dearest friends & nearest Relations marry without having it in their power to provide for a family you will not be so much surpris'd at my being willing to trust in Providence that the person who could best provide for a family would not be the first to be taken from it. ([Feb.] 15, [1783], "My Dear Madam, altho' I wrote to you two days ago")

Gregory would not openly charge that Montagu was demanding that she live up to the standards of her adoptive family without actually defining her as part of that family. Had she after all, like the two wards of

Thomas Day, been reared only as a match, a convenience? But Thomas Day's wards, though neither married him, at least were provided for; and it must have seemed to Gregory's family that, if only because of public opinion, Montagu must acknowledge her companion's service with an annuity when she married.

It would also have been easy for Montagu to have found Alison preferment and to have provided Gregory with a settlement for herself and her children. But instead she was assuring all her acquaintance that this would never be. Her acquaintance, aware that Alison was a suitable match, that he was no fortune hunter but would take Gregory with no fortune at all, thought her far too rigid and harsh. Still, it was a parent's prerogative to approve a match, and for a year Gregory waited, hoping for approval.

In March Gregory had still failed to return, and Montagu was promising her a full restoration to favor provided she would come back and not correspond with her lover. Gregory had responded properly: "Whatever satisfaction I might derive from hearing from him I must ever greatly prefer the happiness of being with you and sh^d feel much more severely the being deprived of the latter pleasure" (March 22, 1783, "You have misunderstood me my dearest Madam").

At the beginning of April Gregory at last set out for London with her sister's maid. She had agreed that her understanding with Alison was a secret; she had obliged Montagu by writing several times as usual to Matthew; and it was understood that she would neither correspond with Alison nor mention him to Montagu. Montagu obviously hoped to conquer by attrition.

Montagu worked very hard to make that summer particularly charming. In July they were at Sandleford, Matthew with his friend Lyttelton, the former lord's nephew. Montagu was overly sanguine, for Vesey wrote that month from Clarges Street: "All wishes for Montagu & Gregory [the young couple]—I too good [sic] give a fete champetre in Clargis Street by dining in the Hall & dressing the Stairs and Windows into the Pulteney Garden with flowers if Gregory will call for the wedding fete she shall have one" ([July 1783], "my dear Friend you have order & regularity"). It is unlikely that Gregory saw this letter.

It was the year of Matthew's twenty-first birthday. In August Gregory drove Montagu three hundred miles to Denton in their whiskey, the post chaise following with relay horses. They visited Blenheim, Warwick Castle, and Coventry. At Denton Montagu described herself as queen bee of a great beehive—coalpits, wheat fields, and a manufactory, all as prosperous as possible.[48] She had a new colliery and a new estate for which she had paid £36,000, and she was busy with her stewards contriving new leases for her farms—how could Gregory fail to be impressed? Matthew went visiting on his own, without his tutor but with a valet and two horses—"a fine thing to be one's own master," commented Montagu.[49] He was also beginning to learn the business of the collieries.

Gregory did not capitulate. In October, unwilling any longer to make herself and Alison unhappy by the interdiction against letter writing and with his arrival in London in search of preferment imminent, Gregory raised the subject once more with Montagu—perhaps when Montagu thought the affair had ended. Terrible scenes ensued, such scenes, Gregory wrote the next year, as she hoped never again to see or experience, "very disagreeable altercations" (May 23, 1784). Exactly what Gregory saw was never recorded, but Montagu noted that at one point Gregory "fell into hysteric, then fainting fits, and lay as it were dead for some minutes. I saw then she would marry immediately if I did not allow her to see him a few times, as he was then in London, and by this compliance I should retard her indiscreet marriage; so I consented." [50] As a result of these scenes, Gregory won consent to correspond with and to see Alison when he was in London. As she later confessed to Montagu, he came several times to Portman Square as "Mr. Gordon," a deception adopted so as not to scandalize the servants. Even more important, Gregory had won from Montagu the concession that, should Alison win preferment on which the couple could live, Montagu would consent to the match.

The truth about the sad denouement of this conflict is difficult to establish. On April 4, 1784, Gregory hurried back to Edinburgh to the deathbed of her sister-in-law, who within hours of her arrival expired of consumption. On May 7, Gregory wrote to Montagu to convey convincing reasons why she could not leave her bereaved brother for several months (May 7 [1784], "altho' I have time to write"). But on May 23 she wrote again demonstrating that she had employed her time in Edinburgh arranging business matters and seeking preferment for Alison and that as a result she would soon leave her brother after all (May 23 [1784], "my dear Madam The Subject of this letter"). She had learned from Montagu how to manage practical worldly affairs.

She had acquainted William Nairn, one of her guardians, an advocate and a man of business, with her situation.[51] Nairn was an agent— the "factotum" Montagu later said sneeringly—of William Pulteney, the immensely rich heir of Lord Bath,[52] and he took it upon himself to consult Pulteney, who, with many estates, presumably had many a living to bestow. In her letter of May 7, Gregory had informed Montagu that Pulteney had a living of £150 to give them, which combined with her own £50 would provide a start, but that he was inquiring as to Montagu's opinion of the match. Gregory had told him that, although Montagu had steadily opposed it, she had promised her consent should Alison receive adequate preferment.

William Pulteney visited Montagu and obtained her leave "to pursue his intention with regard to Mr Alison." In a letter of June 5, Gregory thanked Montagu for this kindness,

which considering your disapprobation of the Match I look upon as a mark of the Superiority of your Mind—from what he tells me of the conversation he had with you I should now be convinced if I had ever had any doubts of it that you have acted from affection to me in the whole of this affair but I always knew the motive was friendly tho' I felt the impossibility of being sway'd by it—I beg leave also to assure you that I enter most fully into your reasons for not chusing to give any assent or approbation to my conduct on account of your Nephews and Neices but I trust you will permit me to Love and respect you as long as I live.

Despite Pulteney's offer of a living of £150, Montagu had after all, apparently, withheld the promised "assent or approbation." The question was, Had she somehow got round Pulteney? What followed remains a tangle. Sarah Scott sent Montagu at Sandleford an account that came from a friend of Gregory's brother.

Miss Gregory with her Brother or Brothers, Mrs. Gordon, and I believe Mr. Nairn set out from Scotland to be married at Mr. Alison's Parish Church in Northamptonshire. At the last stage before they reachd it Mr. Pulteney met them, and when they set off he took Miss Gregory in his Chaise. As they proceeded he informd her he had fail'd in his endeavours to procure Mr. Alison a Living, but presented her with a draught on his Banker for £150 and with a settlement of the same sum yearly, for her to draw on the same Banker for till he could get him a living. To this he added notes for £150 for her wedding cloathes; and a special License, with which they were married at a house of his at Sudborough, where they are to dwell.[53]

Montagu's reply was not charitable:

I am afraid that great part of Dr. Gregory's story is a farce, I have too much reason to believe all the parties knew Mr. Pulteney had not any living to give before they set out for Sudborough, and that all that was advanced on the subject of the living, was a lye to draw me in to give countenance to a disgraceful proceeding. . . . The whole proceeding of poor Mrs. Alison has much afflicted me, being so unworthy of her former conduct, but I beg you not to mention what I have said, as I shall keep distance and silence, but the attempt to draw me in to give my consent to the marriage on a false pretence of Alison's having a Living was abominable in the Gregorys, and very sly in Mr. Pulteney.[54]

Had there been a living? If so, why was it withdrawn? The ascertainable facts are that Alison, after taking a civil law degree at Oxford, had only just been ordained in September 1782, when he was named curate at Brancepeth. Gregory and Alison were married by special license at Thrapston, Northamptonshire, on June 19, 1784; the witnesses were her sister Jean Gordon and William Pulteney. Pulteney may very well have believed that he had obtained the promise of the living of Sudborough for Alison; the incumbent died immediately afterward, on July 1. The advowson of the living, however, was held by Robert Lowth, bishop of London, not by Pulteney himself, and when Pulteney met the wedding party he may have just learned that the living, instead of going to Alison, had been unexpectedly awarded to Edward Jones, who held it from 1784 to 1786. In 1784, then, Alison, instead of receiving the living, as he had expected, was named curate of the parish.[55]

Had Montagu learned what the anticipated living was to be and reached Robert Lowth herself to interfere? And had Pulteney, in shocked disapproval, done what he could to redeem the situation? The Alisons paid sufficiently for their haste to marry. Alison remained in place as curate at Sudborough; the tithes that made up his income came to about £25 a year. Pulteney found him no advancement; in 1786 Lowth's son succeeded to the Sudborough living for four months, followed by two more incumbents in the same year. The Alisons lived on in the Sudborough parsonage that had been procured for them, with their accumulated income of about £225 from Pulteney's gift, Gregory's annuity, and the curate's tithes. And so they might have lived out their lives had not Alison used the time to write his *Essay on the Nature and Principles of Taste*, which, published in 1790, was highly praised.

There may well have been a conspiracy to punish Alison. A letter from James Beattie to James Gregory in June 1790, following the publication of the *Essay*, reveals that Lord Hailes, acting for Bishop Hurd, had applied to him for a character of Alison and that Montagu herself (perhaps signaling a revocation of her ban) had expressed her approbation of the book in the strongest terms. "It was a matter of very general regret, that Mr. Alison had been so long in a state of dependency on Mr. P——y," Beattie reported.[56]

In any case the ban was lifted; Pulteney suddenly bestowed upon

Alison the perpetual curacy of Kenley in Shropshire, then in 1794 the vicarage of High Ercal, and in 1797 the rectory of Rodington. Alison was also appointed in 1791 to a prebend in Salisbury. The family, now enlarged by several children, lived in Kenley until 1800, then moved to Edinburgh, where Alison became minister of the episcopal chapel Cowgate. Altogether they had four daughters, and of their sons, William Pulteney Alison was a noted physician, Sir Archibald Alison a noted historian. Gregory lived until 1830, Alison till 1839.

Gregory's relationship with Montagu mended a little and slowly. Horace Walpole had taken Gregory's side: "Her conduct has been noble and reasonable—her patroness's, in my opinion, preposterous at least."[57] Elizabeth Vesey always corresponded lovingly with Gregory. Montagu waited until Matthew had been happily established. In June 1785 she married him to Elizabeth Charlton, an amiable heiress worth at least £40,000 and of a complaisant character. Montagu drove off from the church with them, and soon they were all established together at Sandleford. But somehow in the end they did not all live together. There were, however, four sons and six daughters, and at last, somewhat appeased, Montagu melted sufficiently to send Gregory a wedding present. But she had no further use for Mrs. Alison.

Various social comments on the affair remain. Caroline Howe wrote to Lady Spencer in March 1785 reporting the engagement of Matthew Montagu: "Mrs. Montagu in earnest wished him to marry Miss Gregory, who was *only* 10 years older than him, what a very wrong thing as well as strange! One of her friends supposes it was that Miss Gregory might never quit her; and now she neither sees her nor corresponds with her; I do not know her present name."[58] The astute Walpole saw how Gregory had profited from the relationship and wrote of her in 1789, "She has great merit, sense, and spirit, acquired all the good of her mistress the learned Aspasia, and none of her pretensions and affectations, of which I doubt she was a little weary, though nobody could behave with more respect and gratitude for really great obligations."[59]

Gregory had indeed acquired all the good of Montagu: her independence, her resourcefulness, her knowledge of the world. According to Lady Louisa Stuart, she had also been gifted with a great deal of humor, had "enjoyed like a comedy much that passed before her eyes," yet would never permit Lady Louisa, who "had sometimes a mind to laugh," to utter a derogatory word.[60] It was not, however, only the risible vanity and pretensions of Montagu that troubled Gregory. She had seen Montagu in the last three years of her marriage and knew the hypocrisy of her submission, her manipulation of her husband. She did not want to fall heir to the great Portman Square mansion. She could not have modeled herself after her foster mother, and only by doing so could she have married Matthew. Her rejection of Matthew was really a rejection of Montagu; this was probably what Montagu could not forgive.

The young couple had the humiliating experience of living for six years on the charity of Pulteney, but they took the best and cleverest way to revoke their banishment. Was it Gregory's idea that Alison should write a book, exactly the kind of book that Montagu liked best, the author of which she would ordinarily eagerly have sought for her salon? (Did Gregory, perhaps, even help with the book?) With the publishing of that book, Montagu was publicly embarrassed for all she had said about the unsuitability of Gregory's choice; she not only had to approve it and him, but she knew people blamed her for having refused to approve him before. From that time she had to see him recognized and rewarded.

Montagu may have begun life with sensibility, but sensibility can be lost or overlaid, and to become a genuine altruist she would have had to give up her ambitions. Even as it was, with all her attention to the main chance, had her husband had a brother with promising sons, had her own son lived, she would never have succeeded to the money and power. Capitalizing on her luck, falling in with the main chance, she became a patriarch, and as a patriarch she consulted only her own pleasure in the matter of Gregory's establishment. But she had violated, or come very near to violating, the rules for patriarchs in regard to the marriages of their daughters: Gregory was not to marry without her consent, but she had no right to force a marriage Gregory could not accept. Ostensibly Montagu simply remained adamant about refusing to accept Alison, and thus far she was within her rights; but actually, as everyone knew, she never considered Alison because she wanted Gregory to marry her nephew. It was this aspect of the affair that ranged her friends on Gregory's side.

Chudleigh, Montagu, and some lesser, some fictitious, tyrants have served here as illustrations of patriarchal persecutors of their dependents. Were there no devices by which these dependents (whether companions or wives) could strengthen their own positions and achieve more power and better treatment? In the ensuing two chapters I investigate the means by which dependents could strengthen their positions. Essentially these means were twofold: companions, whose basic utility was social, could enhance their value by offering their superiors additional economic or sexual advantage.

Companions and wives were generically dispensable and replaceable. Their departures or deaths might entail inconvenience, as did the departures of all upper servants, but new wives and new companions could be found without much ado. There were, however, exceptions. Elizabeth Montagu went to extreme lengths in an effort to keep Dorothea Gregory with her permanently. The reason seems not so much that she "loved" Gregory, not that Gregory was a charming social companion, but that the practical and notable Gregory was essential for helping her execute her ambitious plans, was, in fact, the secret of her remarkable efficiency. With her and after her husband's death, Montagu traveled, extended her business empire, buying new land and opening new enterprises, rebuilt Sandleford, and erected the great mansion in Portman Square. Matthew Montagu never inspired such projects, and after Gregory's departure, Montagu's enterprise slackened. Sexual power over the patriarch might provide anyone with strong temporary advantage, but being of significant economic use—like Gregory and like Anne Milward Fannen in the next chapter—procured the dependent more lasting power.

Chapter Seven

DEPUTY LABOR: EMPOWERING
STRATEGIES I

INITIATION INTO the economic mysteries of the culture brought empowerment, but it has been argued that women lost power in the years before the eighteenth century as they became less productive in the family; and as productivity moved progressively more and more out of the home while women stayed in it, they were further marginalized. Enforced nonproductivity in terms of earned income of even those women who looked after the household, the children, and the elderly in every waking moment lowered their status and minimized their power. To be directly useful economically a women had several routes, none of them readily available to gentlewomen. They could assist husbands who had shops or businesses; they could be employed as upper servants or as management in shops or businesses; they could be—but infrequently were—involved in managing the family estates.

Women who were perceived as idle and privileged wives, seeking nothing but their own amusement, were usually also attending to the family business by networking more or less effectively, as well as bringing considerations to marriage of dowries and influential male relations that might raise their prestige and increase their consequence.[1] But the idle humble companions who did nothing but wait on idle wives were nothing but displays of patriarchal power, owned objects, and therefore objects of contempt. Companions who were economically serviceable, however, could enjoy greater respect and security, even if combined with lower social status. The more empowered companions were often those who had other job titles as well and more useful but menial occupations that conferred salaries. The title and salary of housekeeper-companion (a functionary common in the small establishments of widows) mightily reduced the companion's social status—she would be less likely to sit in the drawing room with the guests and might in larger establishments be relegated to the servants' hall—but would increase her importance and independence. If a house ran smoothly and the mistress was pleased, the companion-housekeeper, perhaps demoted in class but no toady, was needed, constantly consulted, and better treated than the run-of-the-mill toady who clung to her genteel, nonlaboring status. The toady who persisted in remaining genteel without the necessary affirmation of father, husband, or brother was in essence a comic, pathetic, and inauthentic figure.

Conversely, wives or companions who gained admission to the administration of the economic machinery of the family unit became much more relevant, significant figures. Precisely for that reason, admission was difficult to achieve, and such breaching of the barriers as that achieved by Elizabeth Montagu was rare. Few women like Montagu learned to run their husbands' empires; few women like Johnson's Mitissa even learned to administer their husbands' estates. The power of Charlotte Smith's Mrs. Lennard also resides in her estate-managing abilities, as her powerlessness is signalized by her new husband's seizing the management. The admission of women into the economic secrets of their households—the secrets of the estates or businesses that provided the income—was a delicately nuanced process producing a great deal of tension without being directly or publicly addressed. Caveats against admitting them were subtly registered. Evidences of the tension can be found, however, when women occasionally upset the balance of power. The problem was that to be certain of maintaining their power, the male proprietors of the sources of production had to remain in charge as stewards. But privilege offers, with expanded opportunities to enjoy oneself, the opportunity to delegate responsibility and let others do the work. Occasionally women such as Elizabeth Montagu or Smith's Mrs. Lennard signalized themselves as the most appropriate delegates. Once women were in positions as stewards, they had the option offered all stewards, to be faithful or secretly to feather their own nests.

The four examples provided in this chapter, the first two from life and the second two glosses on life from literature, help to demonstrate the importance to a woman's status of her being privy to the economic system of her household. To the close observer they must also provide evidence of the opportunities and dilemmas confronting the women for whom implicit obedience was not the only option, for whom chances arose to take action in their own interest, to put something aside for themselves, and who had to make decisions about the extent of their

loyalty in serving their superiors. The temptation to subvert, even in
the smallest degree, must always have been present—wives and housekeepers often played booty with the housekeeping money—but how
much subversion in the larger world of the family income was politic?
Evidently as long as the superior remained hoodwinked, any amount
was safe (as Lennard found); but once discovered, wrath and reprisal
could be terrible (as Mitissa found). Still, to those who had comparatively nothing, the risk may have seemed worth it. The conclusion to be
reached, however, was that it was far safer to cooperate with rather than
attempt to outreach one's superior.

It is difficult to put together the life story of a servant girl of the period,
and assuredly the story of Anne Milward Fannen, a Sussex girl of the
yeoman class, is recoverable to some extent only because she rose to become a woman of substance. Still, the absence (with one exception) of
letters in which we might have heard her own voice, so that we learn
about her from others, distances her from us significantly. Beginning
probably as a nursery maid in the house of the great second Duke of
Richmond, she became lady's maid, housekeeper, and surrogate mother
and friend to his daughter Caroline, later Lady Holland, demonstrating
how much opportunity for self-development there could be for an intelligent, efficient, and loyal servant in a great establishment. Because of
the unusual generosity of Henry Fox, Lord Holland, we can postulate
that for Fannen, at least, self-love and social were usually the same—
that is, that to prosper, she had only to be loyal to the family with which
she had rather daringly thrown in her lot. But to seize this opportunity,
she had had dramatically to betray the trust of her almost feudal lord,
the Duke of Richmond, by assisting his daughter to elope with a suitor
rejected by her parents. She was probably heavily indemnified in advance to take this risk, but even at that her risk was considerable, and
her subversion, for whatever motive, of the stuff of which the night-
mares of great lords were made.

In lesser families of the aristocracy, a lady's maid, who had the most
prestigious position available to a woman servant, would probably remain a lady's maid all her life. But service in the most expansive establishments could resemble the modern civil service (as Lord Holland,
whose father had begun life as a footman, well knew). Anne Fannen
began as the daughter of a yeoman's family that had probably been tenants of, and provided servants for, the princely Lennoxes of Goodwood
for many years.[2] She was born Anne Milward in or before 1708 and had
performed humbler probationary services, probably as nursery maid,

for some time before, by at least 1740, she became lady's maid to Lady Caroline, then seventeen and the eldest daughter of her family.

Lady Caroline Lennox was the eldest of five daughters in a family that regulated its daughters carefully; while their politically powerful and very rich father lived, marriage to one of them was equivalent to marriage with a princess. Fannen was with Caroline in 1741 and enough a personage and a favorite for Caroline's friend Ann Pulteney to add, when writing, her "cmp.^{ts} to Mrs Milward."[3] Such notice suggests that Fannen had an unusually pleasing personality and that she was of considerable importance to Caroline. Whether or not she had been with Caroline in the nursery, she had by this time certainly begun to provide welcome mothering to the sensitive and insecure young girl whose own young mother was occupied with running two great households in which entertaining was unusually extensive, ministering to a uxorious husband, and producing still more children, the last, Cecilia, born in 1750.

Mrs. Milward, as Caroline generally called her (often even after her marriage) was fully in her mistress's confidence during the trying period leading to her elopement on May 3, 1744, with Henry Fox. To judge by his subsequent confidence in her, she was suborned by Fox, who needed an accomplice in the Richmond household. In fact, her brilliant career with the Hollands had its origin here. Caroline Lennox was a good and honorable girl; it is unclear how Fox obtained her inalienable affections, but once he had them he induced her to elope only by appealing to her generous nature to save his suffering health. How had he managed even to make love to her? With the rest of political England he had the entrée to Richmond House in London, and somehow during the winter of 1743–44 he and Caroline reached an understanding. Caroline was twenty, Fox thirty-nine, immensely clever and unscrupulous, from a family derived from nobody, which had already made scandalous use of women to implement their fortunes. There were unpleasant tales about Fox's personal life. He had wasted his inheritance. The duke and duchess regarded him as an upstart, a scoundrel, a wastrel, an opportunist, and simply out of the question.

The affair was dangerous, exhausting to everyone but particularly to Caroline, who never recovered from it. Fox declared himself to her, and she gave him permission to propose himself to her parents but assured him she could do nothing to make them uneasy. Waiting until she had turned twenty-one in 1744, Fox approached the duke, who, presuming too much upon his political power, challenged Fox by ordering him to think no more of a course that would prove his ruin.

Fox next, infuriatingly, attempted to win his point by assuring the parents of their daughter's maturity—"serious, considerate, sincere, older far in Mind than in Years, with a Heart so tender but as firm too as ever yet was form'd"[4]—and that her love for him was immutable: "Long and constantly observant of ev'ry Movement of her Heart, the most unaffected and sincere that ever was, I know (what she now knows but never knew till she was bid to get the better of it) its attachment to be unalterable."[5]

At a period when any violent attachment of a young woman to a man not approved by her parents (or even approved by her parents) was interpreted as unseemly sexual passion, at a period when a young woman was not supposed even to love until an acceptable suitor had proposed for her, this declaration on Fox's part was at least indelicate and was probably interpreted by the Lennoxes as characteristically caddish. They responded by attempting to introduce a suitor of their own choice. Lady Caroline excused herself from the intended interview—probably with assistance from Fannen—by shaving off her eyebrows.[6]

Fannen must have considered well before throwing in her lot with Caroline and Fox against the interdiction of the powerful duke and duchess. Had the lovers been defeated, Fannen would have found herself out of employment and in disgrace without a reference; her family might have suffered; and her decision flew in the face of generations of Milward loyalty to and benefits from the Richmonds. Her motive may have been in part from loyalty to her mistress, in part a response to the charm of Henry Fox, the most persuasive man in English politics (as well as the boldest briber), and in part her willingness to gamble that Fox and Caroline, with whom her opportunities would be much enlarged, would survive together and prosper. Complicated adjustments were no doubt made to protect her family, and her sister Betty Milward probably left the Richmonds and came with Fannen at the time of the elopement. Fannen was the one figure crucial to the affair; had she informed the Richmonds of the couple's meetings and subsequent plans, the marriage might easily have been prevented. Henry and Caroline Fox were never to forget this.

Fox's claim that his health suffered dangerously from the lovers' enforced separation, by playing on Caroline's sensibility, her vanity, and her sense of self-importance all at once, persuaded her into an elopement. On Saturday night, April 28, 1744, her fateful plans already laid, Caroline wrote to him: "I know the step I am going to take is a wrong one and an undutifull one in regard to my parents; I shall be blamed and abused by all the world, but I own the thought of your being so miserable (as you seem'd this morning) for seven, or eight months together has got the better of all the reasons I c^d alledge against being in so great a hurry." Her mother had forbidden her to see Fox again, and she fears her parents will never forgive her. She adds, truthfully, "I dread any thing that looks like deceit"; but she persists in her arrangements. She plans to leave early one morning after a ball, when all the family is asleep.[7]

Fannen accompanied and supported her through the events that followed. On May 3, no doubt early in the morning, Caroline slipped out of Richmond House and was privately married to Fox at the house of Sir Charles Hanbury Williams in Privy Garden, in the presence of Williams and the Duke of Marlborough—Fox was clever enough to persuade these impeccable witnesses to brave the Richmond wrath. The parson was kept in ignorance of the identity of the bride and groom. Then Caroline (still no doubt under the escort of Fannen) slipped home again. On the ninth the Richmonds were to give a great ball attended by the Prince of Wales and on the eleventh were to depart for Goodwood. But on the eighth at ten in the morning Caroline (and doubtless Fannen) left home and at noon joined Fox but not at his own house.[8] Fox sent a note to her parents informing them of the marriage and asking that Caroline be allowed to stay with them until their departure and leave home as though just married. The proud duke and duchess, unwilling to appear overreached or to countenance such independent behavior in the eldest of their daughters, refused to cooperate or to be reconciled with Caroline and Fox. They were to remain inflexible for four years.

Fannen's fortune was made by this affair; Caroline was its major victim. She was torn from the marriage's outset by a longing for her family, a sense of the unworthiness of her action, pain at the ostracism she experienced from those with anything to fear or gain from her parents. (Her aunt Lady Albemarle, for instance, in Bath in 1748, dependent upon Richmond's bounty, publicly refused to recognize her.) Almost at once Caroline began to suffer from the stomach disorders that remained with her until she died of cancer at fifty-one. Delicate health and an unnatural gravity of spirit became habitual with her, and she developed a diffidence, a desire to stay snug at home, that was strikingly different from the brilliance in society of her sisters. Fannen, always more a presence than her natural mother, was now more important as a mother figure than ever and remained faithful through all these trials.

After the marriage, the two were almost inseparable. When the Foxes were planning to stay at Cheltenham in the month after marriage (Caroline was probably already ill and, though they did not yet know it, pregnant), Fox asked his friend Charles Hanbury Williams to arrange lodgings with two rooms for themselves and one room for two maids.[9] Thereafter Fannen was her maid and faithful companion, traveling with her to Bath on annual visits toward the end of each year. Fannen was with Caroline a great deal more than Fox was, and Fannen and Lady Caroline over the years became significantly "we." Lady Caroline wrote from Bath in early 1748, when Ste was two, "Ste is very busy ten times a day learning his letters he says he is a good *Buoy* and will learn so we hope that in about two Years if he goes on as he does now he may possibly have learnt all the Alphabet."[10]

Three days later Caroline wrote her husband with news of a surprising confession of her companion's: on January 17, the Sunday before they had set off for Bath, the faithful Milward had quietly married Fox's recently acquired steward, John Fannen, a man several years younger than her own forty-odd. Because it was not then usual to countenance the private lives of one's servants, Caroline's real fear was that the Fannens would have to leave them; and she was considerably dismayed, as one is dismayed by the remarriage of a parent, and bewildered as to why Fannen would do such a thing, which she probably interpreted as an act of betrayal to herself. To Fox she confided that she would never have thought "she w^d have been guilty of any thing so silly at her Age."[11] Privately she must have considered it an insubordinate act, undertaken as it was without consultation or permission; she, who had confided everything of her affair to Fannen, had been shut out in Fannen's affair, and the new couple had obviously constructed a new alliance that superseded the old ones.

Fox himself characteristically focused on the comical question of consummation and wrote instructing Caroline to investigate the details. Caroline answered so as to forestall his calling her prude but in defense of Fannen's dignity: "I can't possibly find out any thing its a subject I don't love talking to people of & if I did she w^d not satisfy my Curiosity, tho I love queer jokes in General I dont love talking stuff in a grave stupid way to another Woman but shall be much entertain'd to hear you plague her when we meet again."[12]

Certainly the Foxes were in no position to fuss about the stolen match, but Caroline was displeased at Fannen's defection and told her husband that to her it was no joke: "I have no notion of *all that* at fourty Year Old and am rather sorry she is married I cant possibly find out what you w^d know if I attempt it; and dont at all care to attempt it because she w^d

be Mad." [13] Fox, however, applied to John Fannen, who provided some (disingenuous, as it turns out) satisfaction. Fox wrote, "There was Consummation, She went down after We were in bed into His Room. My Bro. says I should have sent Him to Bath on the first Notice." [14]

It now became less a question of whether the Foxes would keep the Fannens on than a question of whether the Fannens would remain in posts that required them sometimes to live apart or of where their first loyalties would lie. Henry Fox must also have considered that by this period both the Fannens knew a great deal more about his affairs than he should choose to have divulged; his negotiations with John Fannen must have been conciliatory. Fannen herself tactfully resolved the question in a letter to Fox:

Feb. 4, 1748

S^r

I am very thankfull for the honour of your kind letter, and believe you intend me the liberty of answering your questions, I was married a Sunday before I set out for Bath in the City, my sister knew of it, who was the only person except Mr Fannens uncle.

I shall be very glad to see Mr Fannen if you think proper to send him but I am sure he will do a great deal better than Joe, and take Care that your Cloths and linnen are well air'd, which is of great Consequence to your health, and to every body that knows you, (thank god I do) I am very happy your not displeased that I did not ask leave My only reason was to escape Joke & questions, for as my lady and you both agreed in approving of Mr Fannen as a servant, I thought you wou'd not be angry at my Choice of a friend

    I am S^r with the greatest
    respect your Most
    dutifully most
    faithfull humble Servant
        Anne Fannen [15]

Where else would the Fannens have been able to earn their living? They knew where their bread was buttered—Fox was extraordinarily generous to his friends—and they hastened to reassure their employers that service to them still came first. Anticipating no further inconvenience, everyone now settled back in relief. Fox wrote to Lady Caroline once more: "You ask me my Thoughts of their Marriage. In the first Place I never wonder at a Marriage, In the next I am always inclin'd to esteem People that dare please themselves. So, upon the whole You see I approve it." [16]

Fannen's status in the family was such that she was sent a congratu-
latory note by Lady Caroline's sister Emily, Countess of Kildare. And
on March 1 Caroline wrote to Fox requesting that John Fannen bring
their horse Old Bald to Bath so that Ste could ride, thus contriving to
unite the nuptial pair.[17] Fox, scenting fun, joined the party.

Caroline would have suffered a terrible blow, like a second loss of
her mother, had she lost Fannen, and Fox would have suffered inconvenience at the loss of her husband, but now nothing material seemed
changed. Something, of course, was changed: the Fannens in alliance
were strengthened and between them must have known more about
their employers than their employers themselves may have known. If
they had wished to make off with more than just perquisites, certainly
their opportunities were broadened.[18] The Foxes must have known they
were taking that risk, and Caroline lost her comfortable sense that Fannen was hers and the children's alone. But the worst the Foxes probably
never discovered, and that was that the Fannens had sadly hoodwinked
them. They had married not on January 17 but on July 21 the preceding summer, at St. George's Chapel, the marriage factory in Mayfair,
and had all the while been colluding together.[19] Just as Lady Caroline
had done, Fannen had slipped away—but without reciprocating confidence. No doubt the pair enjoyed the joke of Fox's prurient interest
in what was for them old news. Here is evidence that the Fannens had
their own agenda, which, whatever the extent of their loyalties to the
Foxes, they undoubtedly had.

A servant like Fannen was carefully prepared for each advance in
station. Whether or not she had begun as a nursery maid, to become a
lady's maid she had to be schooled in hairdressing, the mysteries of a
lady's toilet, taste in dress, and the making up of small linen. She had
learned to read and to write competently and for some time had been
Lady Caroline's reader because her mistress suffered from ailments of
the eyes. In the autumn of 1749 Fannen was not well enough to travel to
Bath, and her sister Betty Milward took her place; it was apparently necessary to take both maid and companion to replace Fannen so that Miss
Cheeke, the companion of the family of Fox's brother, Lord Ilchester,
came too. Fannen, left in charge of Ste at home, was granted extraordinary, more than grandmotherly powers: Caroline, writing to Fox on
September 23, tells him she has given "Milward" the power to counter-
mand even his own concessions to Ste, for she fears Fox will allow Ste
to ride out onto the public roads.[20]

In 1750 and 1751 Fannen went to Bath, and when she left there in

February 1751, Lady Caroline wrote "I feel very much forlorn I have nobody that loves me now with [me] I actually am like a Child in that respect if I am without You Ste, or her I feel as Charles does without Nurse."[21] But in 1755, 1756, and 1758 Miss Cheeke was Lady Caroline's Bath companion; Fannen had been advanced to the post of housekeeper and overseer of the children at home.

In 1748 the Richmonds had at last softened and there was a reconciliation. Caroline was briefly happy (so was Fox). But there was scarcely enough time to make up the years of estrangement for in August 1750 the duke suddenly died. Lady Caroline was able in some sense to make it up with her mother, who was grief-stricken and died a year later. Sarah Byng Osborn wrote "Mr. Fox has behaved like an angel to her: shared all her afflictions and troubles. Such melancholy scenes have been there. . . . The daughter married to ambitious views [Emily] is a thorn in her side, while that which disobliged her, and was never to expect forgiveness, turns out her great and only comfort, both her and him showing the greatest tenderness."[22]

In these years both Fannens were so effective in their roles that they could have been spared only with great difficulty. Throughout the 1750s John Fannen was not only Fox's steward and man of business but also his companion and reader. Anne Fannen ran the Fox household and was Caroline's executive and adjunct. While Fannen had grown and developed from one role to another, Caroline, once mature beyond her years, had in many ways remained a nervous and reticent girl, afraid to handle the many responsibilities, which Fannen therefore assumed. The different developments of the two women were not unconnected; we will encounter the same pattern with Elizabeth Vesey and her companion Mrs. Handcock (chapter 10). Nancy Chodorow has described the development of girls as different from that of boys: girls ordinarily do not reject their mothers but remain throughout childhood and puberty in a bisexual triangle with mother and father, usually making a sexual resolution in favor of men but not an emotional one.[23] Her analysis usefully illuminates several of the eighteenth-century relationships considered here, for at that period, it has been observed, women even more commonly than today formed their emotional connections with other women.[24] Lady Caroline eloped not only with Fox but also with Fannen; moreover, Fox, born in 1705, was only four years younger than the duke and was at most a year or so older than Fannen. Caroline Lennox may therefore be seen to have eloped with and married surrogate parents, two people who purported to care for her more than her own parents did and who gave her a great deal more attention. Fox and Fannen always continued to look after her, and the effect on her was that she remained, as Elizabeth Vesey did, a virtual child.

Lady Caroline never became a manager. It was Fannen who undertook the delicate, difficult, and seemingly endless commissions for Lady Emily, who in Ireland was furnishing and decorating a great house and who was also intent on being the first to show off all the latest London fashions. Fannen arranged lodgings for the Earl of Kildare, Emily's husband, when he came to London. When the ten-year-old Charles Fox was ailing in August 1759, Lady Caroline thought it very funny that it was Fannen who, through a friend who was steward to Lord Tylney, got Charles the use of Tylney's palace in Wanstead for his convalescence; clearly a network of powerful stewards was operating. Lady Caroline describes Charles ensconced in his borrowed establishment with his friend Peter Brodie and his man, a dozen servants of Lord Tylney awaiting his orders. "The best of it is too Lord Tylney and Mr. Fox are hardly acquainted."[25]

Connections between the Foxes and the Fannens proliferated. When the Fox boys and the sons of Lady Emily went to Eton, they were put in the charge of Betty Milward in a house taken for her. Fannen herself acquired a civil appointment as office keeper of the War Office[26]— not bad for a former nursery or lady's maid. Fox, an extravagant taker of spoils and a generous distributor of them to useful friends, no doubt either used her name to pocket her salary himself or was paying the Fannens for services.

Caroline was an apprehensive mother but not very competent. Though the eldest daughter, she had been unequal to the charge of overseeing the childhoods of her two youngest sisters after her mother's death. By the duchess's will they had gone to Lady Emily in Ireland. But they were to come to Caroline in London when it was time for them to enter society. Sarah, who joined the Foxes in 1759, was a problem her elder sister could not cope with, and Sarah found her elder sister puzzling: "She is just like a child and puts herself in such ways when her children don't mind her. . . . Her character is a riddle."[27] Surrogates had to take the debutante about, and Caroline, through her inability to take firm command, was indirectly an important contributor to the beautiful and lively Sarah's series of fiascos, her abortive romance with George III, her disastrous marriage to Charles Bunbury, her affair with Lord William Gordon, and her divorce. When Sarah married in 1762, it was Fannen who shopped for the trousseau. During their life together, Fannen grew at the expense of Lady Caroline, who remained in comparison timid and childlike, apprehensive and petulant.

When the Foxes (now Lord and Lady Holland[28]) went abroad in April 1763, they wanted to take both Fannens with them, for their companionship qualities all but outweighed their housekeeping abilities; but in the end the Fannens stayed behind in Kensington in command of Holland House, where, in addition to maintaining the establishment, they received the important shipments of purchases made abroad and dispatched some parts of them onward to favored recipients. Fannen wrote regularly to Lady Holland, sending her news of the household, family, and friends. She had her own charitable interests, expressing concern about the fate of the daughter of Lady Kildare's housekeeper, for instance, and reminding both ladies when something ought to be done for her.[29]

Fannen functioned as grandmother to the Fox boys, particularly to Ste, who opened himself most to her so that she could then report to his mother. After a rejected proposal to the beautiful daughter of Frances and Fulke Greville, Ste was finally engaged in April 1766 to Lady Mary Fitzpatrick and assured Fannen that he was not only the happiest of mortals but always should be so.[30] But then the next month in May Lady Holland noted in a letter to her sister that the Fannens, having grown infirm and old, had moved to their own small neat house

just of this side Kensington. He is still steward, and manages all, and she is to the full as great a comfort to me now as when she lived with me; her health is good and she will, with the quiet life she now leads, I hope be a stout old woman, and last years. I frequently walk to see her, sometimes one of my sons and I dine with her snug. She always comes if I want her, which I do when I want to alter, change or settle anything in the house with regard to servants' furniture, etc. I take more trouble myself since she left me, which is not the worse. Fannen is all morning employed writing for or reading the news to Lord Holland, and serves as secretary; dictating letters is one of Lord Holland's chief amusements.[31]

Thereafter Lady Holland often longed for Fannen in her absence. When she was ill in Naples in January 1767 she wrote to her sister, "How one misses somebody to nurse one and read to one in those illnesses. You have a great comfort with your dear girls about you in that respect, dear siss. Indeed at home I have Mrs. Fannen and Sal."[32]

Fannen, who had made an easy early retirement at the age of scarcely more than sixty to her own house, however, had little to regret. As pensioners of the generous Henry Fox, the Fannens would have had little need to steal in order to prosper, and Fox knew how to reward those

who had furthered his own fortune; but the Fannens must also have
had ample access to perquisites, acknowledged and unacknowledged.
Fannen outlived her husband and the Hollands too (who both died in
1774), and in 1776 Sarah Bunbury wrote her sister Emily in Ireland that
at Kensington Fannen, her sister Milward, and a Mrs. Leigrois all lived
comfortably together.[33]

During her years with the Hollands, Fannen clearly fulfilled many
more functions than her titles suggest. She was lady's maid, housekeeper, and companion, but she was also surrogate mother and grandmother, executive officer, confidante, adviser, social secretary, emissary,
shopper, reader, and nurse. The two women shared important memories unknown to their husbands. Besides her position in one of the great
houses and one of the great families of the time, Fannen also acquired
a husband, authority over a vast staff, the respect and love of the family,
a salary, and even a government sinecure.

All this was possible only because it had been in the interest of Fox
not only to have Fannen in place but to nurture her capacities. Lady
Caroline was a clinger, and Fannen's capacities gave him the freedom
he needed. With Fannen there, his wife had the security of both father
and mother figures in place. From this comfortable position, she played
the good and docile daughter, making amends for her one great rebellion. There was never any question of her playing the tyrant except in the
most petulant and childish way and without guile; she was a gentle and
loving if sometimes imperious child. Chodorow notes that girls, who do
not have to give up their identifications with their mothers, emerge from
their earliest relationships with their mothers with a basis for empathy
built into their primary definitions of self as boys do not.[34] Perhaps to
remain continually identified with the mother figure is to increase even
more the capacity for empathy, even though the identification under-
cuts the sense of self.

Fannen was favored because she could manage Lady Caroline's responsibilities and, by tending to his wife, shoulder some of Fox's as
well. Miss Cheeke, the genteel companion of the Ilchesters, who had
to be maintained in a style of life she could not afford, lived and died
poor even though she married. Fannen was also lucky in the essentially
generous nature of her employers; presumably she and her husband
achieved rewards for their services without having to resort to cheating
or an undue amount of manipulation. As a result, she was able all her
life to remain virtually cheerful, open, and honest and to prosper in the
continuing trust and goodwill of her employers.

A sanctionless alliance of women who think they can outreach the privileged, by contrast, tended to be punished and the punishment signalized as a lesson. I am taking the license here—not a great one—of treating mother and daughter in a closely confidential relationship as companions, which, in fact, they were. The case of Jane and Sarah Parr, wife and daughter of the eminent scholar Dr. Samuel Parr, known as the republican Dr. Johnson, is a telling example of this principle. Mother and daughter in this case figured as a pair of collusive companions who schemed to outwit the establishment to appropriate some of its wealth; they died, if not in the attempt, as a consequence.

Jane Marsingale, who married the famous scholar and pedagogue Dr. Samuel Parr in 1771, has had a markedly mixed press. Perhaps the reason is that she was equal to her husband in abilities but perpetually humiliated by his arrogant assumptions of natural superiority and not a woman to bear humiliation abjectly. Parr's marriage, undertaken at the time that he opened his own school at Stanmore, near Harrow (which school Parr had just left), was apparently instigated by his friend the eminent scholar Dr. Anthony Askew. "Mrs. Askew," wrote a knowledgeable friend, "was the intimate friend of Miss Marsingale, and the prudence of the young lady was supposed a necessary support to the young scholar in his establishment."[35] Jane Marsingale, born in Carleton, Yorkshire, in 1743, was the granddaughter of the respectable Timothy Mauleverer of Arncliffe, Yorkshire. Jane's mother had made a foolish marriage to Zachariah Marsingale of Carleton and died giving birth to her daughter, leaving her a small property which her Mauleverer relations prevented her father from appropriating. She had lived with a family in Derbyshire and then with the Askews, probably as a companion. Another version of the marriage, however, provided by the republican Charles Pigott, states that Jane Marsingale had been originally "the house-keeper of some obscure citizen's widow" and was a woman of sordid economies and cockney dialect, who "did not condescend to conceal her vexation at having chosen for her bedfellow a pedantic pedagogue, instead of an East-India Captain, who might have brought muslins and chintzes." The *Dictionary of National Biography* follows Pigott in suggesting that Marsingale was a cast mistress of Askew who had then fobbed her off on his unsuspecting friend.[36]

Apparently marriage to Parr, rather than chastening his wife, sharpened her adversarial instincts. Fairly or unfairly, she was described by one admirer of Parr as "an apt student in the art of ingeniously tormenting . . . self-willed, malicious, and only happy in inflicting pain." Another proponent of her husband noted, "Her sarcasms often wounded Parr's spirit, her want of temper diminished his domestic happiness, and her bitter and false representations sometimes tended to diminish his fame." The poet Tom Moore testified that in a rage against her husband, she hanged his favorite cat in his library.[37] To this testimony, Warren Derry adds that Parr took pride in his wife's intelligence, and Jeremy Bentham noticed nothing amiss in the Parr establishment, judging Mrs. Parr to be "a very sensible and intelligent woman." On still another side of the question, William Godwin's biographer noted that Dr. Parr "until stopped by the bishop . . . liked to relieve his aggressive instincts by personally butchering the cattle at the local slaughter house with an axe."[38]

The Parrs had two extremely intelligent and personable daughters, the eldest of whom, Sarah Anne, was her father's particular pride and her mother's particular confidante and friend. One man who knew her before her marriage described her as the cleverest woman he had ever known, "well informed, with a memory as remarkable as her father's, a lively imagination, and 'tremendous powers of sarcasm'." Her father described her in her 1810 obituary:

The brilliancy of her imagery in conversation and writing; the readiness, gaiety, and fertility of her wit; the acuteness of her observations upon men and things; and the variety of her knowledge upon the most familiar and most profound subjects; were very extraordinary. They who lived with her in the closest intimacy were again and again struck with admiration at the rapidity, ease, vivacity, and elegance of her epistolary compositions: whether upon lively or serious topics, they were always adapted to the occasion; they were always distinguished by a peculiar felicity and originality of conception and expression; and the genius displayed in them would most undoubtedly have placed the writer in the very highest class of her female contemporaries, if she had employed her pen upon any work with a deliberate view to publication.[39]

Sarah Anne was too clever, too outgoing, and too advanced in her opinions to find a husband easily. At twenty she had been engaged for some time to Charles Barker, a young clergyman, but the young man's mother had caused him to break off the engagement.[40] In 1794 at twenty-two she engaged William Godwin in argument and also sent him letters to an accommodation address, in one of which she expressed herself as so angry at him for not responding that "I could marry thee in downright spite, if I did not hold sacred the oath I swore six years ago never to marry—a wise man."[41] Signing herself "Anne," she continued to write to Godwin, who found her of considerable interest. Once in 1796 Godwin received twelve visitors, including Thomas Holcroft, Elizabeth Inchbald, Mary Wollstonecraft, and Samuel Parr and his two daughters.[42] Obviously, she moved in a gifted and radical set.

Dr. Parr had the peculiarity of imbuing all his actions, no matter how inconsequential, with an air of gravity, confidentiality, importance, and urgency. On one occasion, when he had sent for a friend in haste and closeted him in the locked library, his daughter Sarah on the spot penned a parodic letter—a piece of generic satire—supposed to express his invitation. The letter is long, but it conveys Parr's habitual tone of self-importance as well as his attitude toward women.

My Dear Sir,—Every well-constituted mind—and yours, I have abundant reason to esteem well-constituted—is stored with principles equally important to society and efficacious in procuring its own happiness. Among these principles, fidelity is constantly affirmed to hold the highest place; and so loudly and unanimously have mankind applauded the exercise of this virtue, that the idea of deceit is at least outwardly spurned by the very basest of mankind, and, to quote a trite though striking adage, there is honour even among thieves. Perhaps there is no situation in life more painful than to contain within one's bosom either joys or sorrows, without the power of participating with some person, upon whose truth and sympathy the heart may safely rely. Such is the lot of many. But I trust such misery will never be mine. Your prudence, your wisdom, your unstained fidelity, your unassailable secrecy, are my pledges; and I hasten to relieve my oppressed soul from a secret of the very highest possible importance; a secret, which my intimate acquaintance with men of the highest celebrity has alone enabled me to penetrate; a secret, upon which the fate of empires, if not of the whole human race, depends; a secret, of magnitude sufficient to convulse the mind of a stoic, however hardened by apathy; a secret, in short, too overwhelming in its effects, to be confided to a man less rigid in his moral principles, less blameless in the tenour of his conduct, less fortified against the power of temptation, or less proved by repeated and unfailing trials, than yourself. But, my friend, beware; and if you feel unequal to the trust I am about to repose in you, destroy immediately this paper, before you lead yourself into a snare, which will blast your own peace of mind for ever, and hurl the thunderbolt of destruction upon unoffending millions. Above all, keep the secret from all women. Mrs. John is a very worthy woman; I always praise her, though there is somewhat of a rebellious disposition in maintaining what she thinks right in her mind, which at times gives me great pain for your domestic comfort. You know, my friend, that women have no souls; that is, I mean, no souls except such as we choose to allow them. They are ignorant with respect to metaphysics and Greek—they are animals sent into the world to be a sort of medium between us, the faultless angels of creation, and the brutes of the field—they are to make our shirts, nurse our children, dress our dinners, wait on us when sick, try to amuse us when well, and serve as vents for those tyrannical and violent passions, which we dare not exercise on each other for fear of a beating. These are the proper duties of women, according to five thousand ancients, and ten thousand moderns; and nothing can so totally destroy the reputation of a man, as treating them with confidence or affection. Let me trust, then, my dear friend, that with your accustomed good faith, good sense, and good disposition to act as becomes a man, you will cautiously abstain from trusting to any of your own sex, and still more anxiously avoid to hint to any of the inferior female race, this secret. I am going to dine with the servants of Mr. Bromley, at the Falcon alehouse.

Hatton, May 16.   S. Parr[43]

This is an excruciating indictment of her father and gives some inkling of the quality and purport of her discussions with her mother. Apparently the pair had very early determined—when Sarah was sixteen, if she is serious—that she was not to repeat her mother's mistake of marrying a poor and wise man. She was to marry a man foolish and rich, on the mistaken assumption that he would be less likely to oppress the mentality and oppose the convictions of women. There is also the possibility that Sarah Anne Parr had seriously thought of life with William Godwin and now married out of pique. Against all his principles Godwin had married Mary Wollstonecraft on March 29, 1797, whereupon Sarah Parr had promised him the roasting of his life when next they met. But when they met, in June, Sarah herself had just married. Godwin visited the Parrs at the interesting moment of her elopement with a rich and foolish young pupil of the doctor's, John Wynne, aged eighteen. "I certainly regard Miss Parr as a seducer," wrote Godwin to Mary Wollstonecraft, "and have scarcely any doubt that the young man will repent, and that they will be unhappy. It was her & her mother's maxim, that the wisest thing a young woman of sense coud do, was to marry a fool; and they illustrated their maxim from their domestic scene."[44] Again,

He is a raw country booby of eighteen, his hair about his ears, and a beard that has never deigned to submit to the stroke of the razor. His voice is loud, broad and unmodulated; the mind of the possessor has never yet felt a sentiment that should give it flexibleness or variety. . . . John . . . has all the drawling, both of voice and thinking, that usually characterizes a clown. His air is *gauche*, his gait negligent and slouching, his whole figure boorish. [He and his brother are] as ignorant, and as destitute of adventure and ambition, as any children that aristocracy has to boast. Poor Sarah, the bride, is the victim of her mother, as the bridegroom is her victim in turn. The mother taught her that the height of female wisdom, was to marry a rich man & a fool, & she has religiously complied. Her mother is an admirable woman, & the daughter mistook, & fancied that she was worthy of love. Never was a girl more attached to her mother, than

Sarah Wynn (Parr). You do not know, but I do, that Sarah has an uncommon understanding, & an exquisite sensibility, which glows in her complexion, & flashes from her eyes. (pp. 103–4)

Responding to the youth and charms of the younger woman, Godwin put all the blame of insurrection on the older one. He was unable to evaluate the cost to these women of their domestic circumstances. He predicted a punishment for their scheme—"They have each, beyond question, laid up a magazine of unhappiness" (p. 104)—that was both wishful and accurate. The two women had failed to reckon with the strength of the system they had tried to outmaneuver.

The desperate coup they attempted was in part to attain some moral control over her life for Sarah Parr, but also, in important part, to attain control of some money. They guessed (wrongly) that once the elopement had forestalled the interference of his family, Sarah would be able to parlay with young John Wynne as no woman could parlay with Dr. Parr. But prerogative combined with stupidity do not feminize a husband; they only render him impenetrable.

Moral or economic control had to be bestowed upon women by men, not wrested from them, and it was bestowed only for the men's own purposes; it was fire that could not be stolen. The Parrs, mother and daughter, suffered Promethean endings. As Godwin predicted, the marriage failed. The first response of Wynne's parents was to suggest that the marriage be proved invalid; when Dr. Parr indignantly refused thus to stigmatize his daughter, they refused to give Sarah a marriage settlement, and Parr himself settled a provision upon her. Wynne, who turned out to have a violent temper, never took financial responsibility for his family, and his first two daughters were born at Hatton. Even Hester Piozzi, now a Welsh neighbor of John Wynne's father, Robert Watkin Wynne of Plas Newydd, Denbighshire, though she might well have delighted in Sarah (despite her republicanism), took the Wynnes' side: "One of our 'Squires sent his Boy there [to Dr. Parr] 18 years old to study Greek, and he came home with the House's Daughter *ten* years older than himself and She takes *Papa in tow* while he literally and figuratively Smoaks/ se macque the whole County and much amazes its Inhabitants. Lord! Lord! what Times these are! when as you say *nothing is high Treason.*" [45]

Sarah Wynne learned to her cost that poor and wise might be better than rich and foolish. The marriage was less successful even than Godwin had predicted. After Wynne inherited property on the death of his father in 1806, he continued to treat his wife brutally. In 1807 Sarah

Wynne left him, first tentatively and then permanently and, with her parents' cooperation, took lodgings in Shrewsbury, where, to obtain legal proof of her husband's refusal to support her, she intended to leave her landlord to sue her husband for her rent. Her health failed, she fell into a "deep decline," and went to Teignmouth to be nursed by her mother. In March 1810 Jane Parr had to travel to Shrewsbury in Sarah's stead to give evidence at the hearing of the suit of the landlord, *Grant* v. *Wynne* (the jury found for the plaintiff). Jane Parr, traveling back to her daughter at Teignmouth, met her husband at Birmingham, continued on in bitterly cold weather, caught a chill, and died at Teignmouth on April 9. Sarah returned to Hatton; in May her youngest daughter died, and in July Sarah died as well, a victim, as her father declared, to "the pressure of domestic sorrow." There are six bees on the arms of the Wynnes, and Parr lamented, "My family never partook of the honey of the hive; but the wound they gave was the sting of death."[46]

To his credit, Samuel Parr fought alongside his wife and daughter instead of supporting the honor and prerogative of the establishment; the inevitable result was that he suffered defeat with them. The deaths of Jane and Sarah Parr resulted from the pressure of the complex network of problems they themselves created, but even without their deaths, their punishment would have been obvious: Sarah acquired no comfortable establishment, only a sullen, stupid husband convinced that she had tricked him and that he owed her nothing. As Elizabeth Janeway has pointed out, the subordinate's awareness of the threat of punishment must regularly be reinforced by examples of punishment,[47] and here is a cautionary tale proving that a clever woman was no match for a stupid man, that women should not attempt to wrest benefits from men, and that those who interfere with the establishment and its agenda would suffer. Other women might think twice before making the same attempt. A pair of women working for their own empowerment against the empowered was unlikely to succeed.

Samuel Johnson had provided an early warning on this subject in his *Rambler* 35 (July 17, 1750), in which a mother-daughter-companion combination defraud the patriarch too indolent to run his own estate. Johnson's stipulated point in the essay is that men should not marry women solely for their fortunes, as his unfortunate subject has done, but he illuminates other questions.

The new wife, Mitissa, "was at least without [physical] deformity"; her manners were "free from reproach, as she had been bred up at a distance from all common temptations." Money being the object of both the suitor and the father, when the suitor fails to meet the father's exorbitant demands, Mitissa is sent to him to say he must meet them if he loves her, to burst into tears, and to call him perfidious and herself unhappy. Because the scene is a charade on both sides and he cares nothing for her, her appeal is without effect, a point she is swift to grasp. She next refuses to see him; he writes to her in feigned distress but refuses to yield on the question of settlements. In the end the father capitulates, informing his son-in-law that he likes him the better for having struck such a good bargain. Money has been everyone's sole object.

The marriage commences without illusions of preference on either side. Yet the husband is apparently surprised to learn that Mitissa, being equally as "prudent" as himself, has selfish views of her own and has married, like Burney's foolish young Miss Dennel in *Camilla*, for the purpose of being independent and having her own chariot. Having shaken off the father, she has no mind to wear the husband's shackles. With her she has brought to the marriage "an old maid recommended by her mother, who taught her all the arts of domestick management, and was, on every occasion, her chief agent and directress." This woman, accepted by the husband as one who would train Mitissa in the serviceable domestic way she should go, has actually been selected by Mitissa's mother as the agent of an underground operation designed to recover Mitissa's lost fortune.

With the help of her companion, Mitissa now sets about taking control of the establishment to which her fortune has so largely contributed. Together mistress and maid find pretexts for quarreling with and dismissing the husband's servants and then replace them with servants from the establishments of Mitissa's family and friends. The husband finds his staff uncontrollable and in perpetual conspiracy against him. Mitissa takes every occasion to wring money from him. She falsifies household accounts; she convinces him that times are so hard he must lower his rents, then with the assistance of the new steward takes commissions on the savings. Her jointure lies in lands she perpetually tries to improve at her husband's expense, and she once—to his utmost outrage—unsuccessfully seeks an injunction to prevent his devaluing them by cutting their timber and pocketing the profits. She enlists her parents in her projects so that they constantly reproach him for his ill usage and his failure to give his wife presents.

As Johnson recognized, Mitissa's responses from the start, though perhaps unusually resourceful, are actually no more than her husband deserves, for he ought to have married from personal inclination and bound his wife to him in mutual affection and respect. Her husband suffers from an indolence natural to the privileged and indulged; he has already once had to take his estates into his own hands because his income was injuriously lessened by a steward, and now he has allowed Mitissa to repeat the process. Though because of her husband's indolence she is provided with an unusual opportunity to take over the estate's management, she is expressing not an energetic desire to assist him and to improve their mutual interest but an active and spirited resistance to his decision to exploit her economically and reject her personally, emotionally, and sexually. Johnson recognizes that if she is mean-spirited, she is no more so than her mate. The immediate object lesson is that the husband ought to have chosen a woman for her character rather than her fortune and ought to have loved her—true enough. But a subtext warns against empowering a woman by letting her run the estate. Most obviously, there is a second lesson here that a man should look after his own affairs. Clearly it was this husband's duty to keep all the administrative power in his own hands, and if he had done so, he would have avoided the trouble he incurred.

The ultimate power, however, is his. After seven years of suffering (a proper patriarichal probationary period), he at last calls upon his wife's father, his natural ally, to remedy his wrongs. Once he has demonstrated Mitissa's frauds, he has no problem with her father, who, conscious that his first loyalty is to male prerogative, undoes all that his wife, daughter, and servant have accomplished. Having neutralized the father, the only other person who signifies in a legal sense, the husband now dismisses the steward, takes his business back into his own hands, puts his wife on a settled allowance—and turns her maid over to the constable.

Although he understands that it was the alliance of three women that had nearly undone him, he cannot punish his mother-in-law or his wife without embarrassing and dishonoring his father-in-law and himself, and so he confines his vengeance to the audacious and presuming maid who is now to learn in a court of law that one contests the prerogatives of the patriarchy at one's peril. The collusive steward is only dismissed; the collusive maid may well end in Bridewell as a method for punishing Mitissa and providing an object lesson to women.

Hester Thrale's exasperated "Well then Philosopher—", her reference to the sad and narrow life of the country gentlewoman who ends up cheating her husband of a few guineas "in Concurrence with her own Maid & Housekeeper who came with her at Marriage-Day," seems possibly to have been a forthright feminist gloss on Johnson's essay, par-

ticularly when it is recollected that one of the great sorrows and out-
rages of her married life occurred when her husband persisted in cutting the timber on her own beloved Welsh estate.[48]

Charlotte Smith, in *The Old Manor House* (1793), presents a study of
Lennard, housekeeper-companion to a termagant, Mrs. Rayland, which
anatomizes the damaging effect of a duplicitous stewardship on the
character of the hypocritically submissive manipulator, but surely incidentally also warns about the dangers of lazily delegating one's powers
of control: the same points covered by Johnson forty years earlier but
differently emphasized. The delegation each represents would appear
to be one of the signs of the prideful depravity of the privileged. Smith's
analysis of the hypocritical nature of subservient adulation is not new.
Smith's Mrs. Lennard is a daughter of Burney's Miss Bennet in her
hatred of her employer—both employers are blissfully unaware that
they are loathed, in large part because superiors don't have to empathize. But Lennard, unlike Bennet, labors in the absence of a controlling man and therefore can take full economic advantage of her position
and can end, it first appears, with all. One of the essential messages of
this situation, albeit carefully embedded, is that women are not created
as care-giving units and that insisting they are is dangerous. Lennard's
manipulation of Rayland is a great deal more laborious but essentially
of the same kind as her young husband's subsequent manipulation of
her. And both Lennard's and Rayland's blindness to the anger, contempt, and plots of their undoers, their fatal complacent proneness to
take lip-serving flattery at face value, is like the blind failure of understanding that males or any superiors may, at their worst, deliberately
and pridefully entertain toward their subordinates.

In Rayland and Lennard, Smith displays what by this time had become the standard termagant and the standard scheming toady, the
latter utterly destroyed morally by the devices to which she must resort
to survive and prosper. Lennard, like Fannen, profits from the willingness of her employer to have her work done for her, but there, it is to be
hoped, the similarity ends. Lennard, like Burney's Margland, has never
been anything but a hypocritical opportunist.

Although Lennard begins as housekeeper to Mrs. Rayland, she soon,
because of Rayland's proud inactivity, becomes "confidential servant,
or rather companion and femme de charge."[49] We can suppose she has
natural abilities at financial management; she is the daughter of a well-
to-do merchant who has educated her well, taught her "to expect high
affluence," and then lost his fortune. Rayland, who has a thorough con-

tempt for people in trade, is gratified to have Lennard beneath her in service, but in fact Lennard is the mental superior who, by her attention to business, soon governs her mistress entirely. "While the mean pliability of her spirit made her submit to all the contemptuous and unworthy treatment, which the paltry pride of Mrs. Rayland had pleasure in inflicting, she secretly triumphed in the consciousness of superior abilities, and knew that she was in fact the mistress of the supercilious being whose wages she received" (p. 10).

It is difficult to judge whether Smith considers Rayland or Lennard more deserving of the reader's contempt. The proud and indolent Rayland leaves all her business to Lennard, who controls her mistress easily enough by the application of flattery and by cutting her off as much as possible from the rest of the world. Thus each attempts to take advantage of the other. Smith carefully analyzes this process.

For instance, Lennard has demonstrated her own power by bringing into Rayland's home an orphaned grandniece, Monimia, to act as a miserable toady of her own; Lennard, the middle function of the three, gets to play both toady and tyrant. On one occasion Rayland's young male cousin Orlando, to attract Monimia's attention, has thrown a pebble through the window of the gallery where the three women are sitting. Lennard's first response is to hide the young man's interest in Monimia from Rayland by distracting her through the administration of a poultice of carefully compounded flatteries that begins with her noting that some people say the gallery is haunted and wonder that Rayland would cross it at night.

But I used to say, that you had such an understanding, that I should offend you by shewing any foolish fears; and that all the noble family that owned this house time out of mind, were such honourable persons, that none of them could be supposed likely to walk after their decease, as the spirits of wicked persons are said to do. But, however, they used to answer in reply to that, that some of your ancestors, Ma'am, had hid great sums of money and valuable jewels in this house, to save it from the wicked rebels in the time of the blessed Martyr; and that it was to reveal these treasures that the appearances of spirits had been seen, and strange noises heard about the house. (p. 16)

The passage gathers additional irony when it is later learned that the butler is all the time, unknown to either Rayland or Lennard, capitalizing on their smug preoccupation by running a smuggling operation in the house.

Having neatly abstracted Rayland's attention from the young people by addressing her pride in her own and her family's superiority of pedigree, moral rectitude, wealth, and loyalty, and having then ushered her out of the room, Lennard next turns to Monimia in her second character as tyrant, extracts a true account from her, and then brutally boxes her ear. The demonstration of her double true character has been economically drawn.

By gradually taking all the business of the house from the hands of the all-too-willing Rayland, Lennard becomes its true mistress, with duplicate keys even to the butler's private cellar. She functions as mistress of the revel at the annual tenants' and servants' ball in the great hall (pp. 175–76). She has a weakness for male attentions, and after Rayland has retired from the ball (abnegating responsibility as usual), instructing Lennard to oppose any impropriety, Lennard invites the advances of such handsome young farmers as require new leases or repairs.

When beautiful Monimia enters the household, she begins by taking some of the onus of attendance on Rayland upon herself but goes on to become the companion-servant of Lennard even in Rayland's presence. Lennard has begun the process of trying to become her mistress. With Monimia Lennard goes far beyond Rayland's contemptuous exploitation of herself and acts the part of Gothel to Rapunzel, literally locking the beautiful golden-tressed girl into a tower each night and seldom permitting her either to be seen by company or to leave the house. She is also almost unremittingly cruel to the girl. Lennard's pretensions to male admiration at the annual ball (and later her foolish marriage to a much younger man) suggest that like Chudleigh she was suppressing the sexuality of the girl to "prove" her own superior and enduring charms, which is why she is furious at the attraction between Monimia and the young Orlando.

Thus far Smith has illustrated the thesis of this chapter, indicating that she recognizes economic utility as one of the subservient's routes to prosperity. Perhaps because this is fiction and because Lennard has unjustly ousted Rayland's proper heir, she must also receive her comeuppance, but this is a separate action, ensuing upon Lennard's success and prosperity because, like Chudleigh when she used her duke's will to strip his legitimate heirs, she goes one step too far. But as in the real-life case of Chudleigh, that extra step is psychologically almost inevitable. As Rayland's age and indolence increase, so do Lennard's power and arrogance, until she has engaged the entire effort of the maid Betty to wait upon her as well as much of the time of Monimia. But because she has taken Rayland as her model, in her security she too grows indolent and more addicted to her own gratification (p. 135). Surrounded by easily outwitted mental or social inferiors, she begins to fancy her cleverness and power too much. She engineers her own destruction when Rayland's man of business dies and she insinuates an agent of her own into his place. At Rayland's death she inherits £10,000, valuable plate and jewelry, clothes worth hundreds of pounds, and farms yielding an income of £400 a year. If she exults that she has actually become the mistress who engaged her as a servant, reveling in her success, she fails to recognize her consequent vulnerability to people like herself. She therefore accepts the flattery of the nephew of her man of business at face value and marries him. But now that her opponent is a man and her personal attractions prove illusory, a pretense that they exist simply a method her clients have used to manipulate her, all of her valuable techniques for mastery are unavailing. Her husband uses her now furious and unrestrained termagancy to effect her virtual imprisonment and strips her of all with far less effort than she has expended to strip Rayland. Her final resort is to make an alliance with Orlando, the ousted heir, to save herself and, in order to strip her vicious husband, she restores Orlando to his inheritance. Poetic justice is served, and the unregenerate character of Lennard is fully explicated for the wise to note. Both in the first half of the book, detailing Lennard's rise, and in the last, detailing her fall, Smith has certified the importance of controlling the economics of the family income or estate as a method for gaining and exerting power. But controlling in actual fact rather than just in name or appearance is not easy. The butler's anarchic private smuggling enterprise, undertaken in the absence of discerning supervision, was going on all the time under both Lennard's and Rayland's noses. Not only Lennard but also her young husband went one step too far; he should have considered that once he had taken all from her, she could have her revenge without injuring her position by taking it all from him. One lesson here seems to be that power breeds a dangerous complacency and blindness. Another is that male and female power-seekers scarcely differ.

A comparison of Johnson's and Smith's emphasis in analyzing similar situations may be useful. Johnson presents a corrupted triad—master, wife, and companion, all morally flawed. Smith's mistress and companion are also flawed. But Johnson's emphasis is on the responsibility of the husband to be in effective charge of his own domain. It appears to be his fault if he provides too much temptation to lesser creatures. Mitissa, "bred up at a distance from all common temptations," was without reproach when she married, and the subsequent temptation was his fault. It is Johnson's assumption, as it was Henry Fielding's, that authority belonged with the upper-class male and that the primary reforms needed were to inspire those males to address their proper responsibilities. Johnson is interested in the depths of dishonesty to which the tempted Mitissa and her maid descend; he is unhampered by any such ideas as the natural submissiveness of women; but he is uninterested in Mitissa's descent into flattery and manipulation of her husband, the hypocrisy we saw in outline when her father sent her to sway her suitor about the settlement. Smith does not detail Lennard's money or estate dealings but instead closely anatomizes her manipulative strategies, her hypocritical fawnings contrasted to her real abusive nature; and we see much more explicitly the real damage done to the characters of both mistress and companion. Johnson's emphasis is on the political and economic damage ensuing from inappropriate stewardship, Smith's on the psychological damage ensuing from inappropriate distribution of power.

To some extent we have dealt here with opportunities for growth extended to subordinates. Though these subordinates have developed in particular ways, plainly, too, the subordinate who undertakes the master's economic enterprises grows and develops in response to the responsibilities imposed—but not otherwise. Elizabeth Montagu, Fannen, and Lennard grew in ability and power even as Edward Montagu, Lady Caroline, and Mrs. Rayland diminished—but each developed the abilities and skills required by the superior. Montagu learned to travel about alone and deal with attorneys, farmers, miners, and every kind of man of business because that was what her husband required; he did not, apparently, require a truly warm and affectionate companion, but, rather, he valued a wife who was admired by other people who mattered such as Lord Lyttelton and Lord Bath. Fannen became a notable manager of an enormous establishment but had to make do with other people's children and, for most of her life, other people's houses; she acquired a husband but no children of her own. Lennard did all the services her mistress was too lazy to perform, services not only domestic but also in a business way, involving leases and rents, but, living with the unsocial and grudging Rayland, never acquired any social skills. All three women developed in directions not chosen by themselves but afforded to them by others. The essential decency of Edward Montagu and the Foxes forestalled the development of obvious moral depravity in their dependents (though Sarah Fielding and Sarah Scott would not have absolved these entirely), whereas Rayland's tyrannical behavior produced hideous moral depravity in Lennard.

When Frances Burney's Dr. Tyrold pointed out that girls must be raised with a minimalist education so as to be delivered malleable into the hands of their husbands, (s)he was acknowledging that women will develop, no matter how straitened their opportunities. What the patriarchs intended was that women should develop in the ways that would suit and serve them and that they should not develop in certain inconvenient other ways. As John Stuart Mill was to note in 1869, "No other class of dependents have had their character so entirely distorted from its natural proportions by their relations with their masters." Conquered and enslaved races have been forcibly repressed, but what has not been crushed in them has been let alone, whereas "in the case of women, a hothouse and stove cultivation has always been carried on of some of the capabilities of their nature, for the benefit and pleasure of their masters." Other more inconvenient attributes of women "are burnt off with fire and disappear."[50] Mill might have added that when special needs arose, some of these more inconvenient attributes were allowed to flourish but only at the convenience of the master. There was always the unpleasant danger that these attributes—such as independent thought and the capacity for satire—might develop unbidden in ways that might lead women to outdo, rival, and challenge their masters. The struggle between tyrant and victim was therefore a permanent ongoing struggle that demanded eternal vigilance on the side of the tyrant. Development like Lennard's was probably as common as development like Fannen's. The provision to women of any unusual opportunity was accompanied by the risk of betrayal as well as by promised advantage to the master. And the dangers of letting women in on economic secrets or into the real power structure were being quietly canvassed.

For the subordinate, the important lesson to be extracted from examples such as the foregoing was that to be effectual, alliances of the weak had to be with the powerful rather than with other victims. To plot like the Parrs or like Mitissa and her maid against the empowered from a position of weakness was to invite defeat, humiliation, and punishment. But a firm alliance with the patriarch like that of the Fannens or Lennard, involving reassurance to him that it was his concerns that mattered and based on the ability of the subjected to provide something he needed, could not or would not provide for himself, and could not easily procure from someone else was the simplest route to sometimes vastly improved power. Even very limited access to the economic mysteries of the establishment provided enormous advantages; and it is not astonishing that such access in our own time has been hard won and was virtually denied middle-class and aristocratic women throughout the period when their contingency and serviceability were most valued.

Chapter Eight

AGENTS, RIVALS, AND SPIES: EMPOWERING STRATEGIES II

A WORKING OR ECONOMIC ALLIANCE with the empowered male could provide, as we have seen in the last chapter, a very considerable advantage to the companion (or to the wife). Either a confidential or a sexual alliance in which the inferior fulfilled another important need for the superior might advance either wife or companion, for a shorter period, further than an economic alliance. But an alliance, sexual or economic, with the patriarch against the wife was the strongest basis for advancement of all. The four companions considered in this chapter were, to some extent, and often greatly, advanced at the expense of their mistresses. Even though two of these four companions were already the social equals of the couples whose establishments they joined, such unattached women usually enjoyed only marginal positions in the families that received them. Jane Pendarves and Lady Elizabeth Foster, both estranged wives, both ostensibly companions to wives, would have had no positions at all to speak of had it not been for their services to the patriarch.

Three of the combinations of man, wife, and companion considered in this chapter are from life, and the fourth is from literature. This fourth once again provides a contemporary gloss on a familiar situation as to some extent the first does too, for Mary Delany inscribed her own history. Both Delany and Burney took the lowest view of the characters of those women who for their own advantage joined males to injure and drew their advantages from injury to their wives.

A wife's companion in the secret counsels of the husband, either as spy or as mistress, might readily advance in consideration over the head of the wife and would have no reason thereafter to desire a rapprochement between the couple. From her privileged position she might spy on the wife, elicit and betray her confidences, act as agent provocateur to compromise her, or influence her to the husband's advantage. She might take on a tincture of the superiority and self-importance of the man for whom she acted and with whom she identified. And thus the normal situation could easily be reversed, the companion empowered, the wife rendered comparatively powerless. The companion's circumstances were less stable, perhaps, than when she gained economic entrée into the establishment, but for the moment her power was proportionately greater. If the examples of Mitissa and the Parrs indicate that to plot with another woman was dangerous, the examples in this chapter suggest that plotting with the higher power in the household was considerably less so. The system, including its legal and moral components, all but guaranteed the punishment of women who conspired with one another, the rewarding of women who betrayed one another to men.

Mary Granville Pendarves Delany, famous in later life as Mrs. Delany, was in 1718 at age eighteen married by her uncle Lord Lansdown to his close friend and political ally the fifty-seven-year-old Alexander Pendarves.[1] She married against her will and honestly told Pendarves so.[2] "As to his person he was excessively fat, of a brown complexion, negligent in his dress, and took a vast quantity of snuff, which gave him a dirty look: his eyes were black, small, lively and sensible; he had an honest countenance, but altogether a person rather disgusting than engaging."[3]

Within a month of their marriage, Pendarves's nephew and heir was so obviously attracted to the young wife that Pendarves, who had never attempted to make himself agreeable (perhaps persuaded by his wife that he could not do so), turned gloomy, discontented, and sullen. Then, after two years of comparative sobriety, he also turned drunk, increasing his gloomy sullenness. His financial affairs worsened and he stayed home only when afflicted by gout, at which times he kept to his room and, able to bear no fire, kept Delany, shivering, sitting reading to him for three or four hours at a time.[4]

Pendarves had a sister Jane, two years his elder, who in 1717, the year before his marriage, had at the age of fifty-seven married an artful Scotsman in search of a fortune.[5] "Her judgment was by no means equal to her years; not that she wanted sense, but she was vain and imperious, excessively jealous, and inquisitive to the last degree of impertinence: she affected all the airs of a young woman of twenty-five" (1:61). Her cautious brother, apprised of her marriage, turned over two thousand pounds to the new husband but refused to pay the rest of her portion, whereupon "the cunning Scot walked off with his booty, and left the poor forlorn woman, to mourn his absence, for he had managed so well with her that she did not see the dupe she was" (1:61).

When Pendarves married, he told his wife of Jane's case, of his refusal to forgive her, and of her great distress. Delany begged that he be reconciled to his sister, at the same time requesting that he never insist upon their living together, for she was afraid of her new sister's meddling, governing temper. Pendarves promised her that his sister should never be imposed on her.

After two years of retirement in Cornwall, Pendarves reentered Parliament in January 1721 and took his wife to reside in unattractive and unfashionable lodgings in Rose Street, Hog Lane, Soho—where she found her sister-in-law ready ensconced. Delany's dilemma was now clear: she had a husband who neither honored his word to a woman (a phenomenon prevalent among gentlemen) nor trusted his wife in a fashionable district; and how very much he distrusted her could be judged by the compelling need for the presence of his sister, which had overridden his own detestation of her. But should Delany insist that her husband keep his promise, she might appear to have reason to wish to be unobserved. "I believe," she later wrote, "that if I had *insisted* upon Gromio's promise, that she should not live with me, I might have had her removed; but as I feared no spy, I would not put it into the power of her malice to say I did" (1:62). Delany's great-grandniece Lady Llanover adds a footnote to Delany's account to explain that at this period the servants were under orders to give a daily account of everywhere Delany went and that it was her knowledge that she was under suspicion that made her endure anything rather than ask for the removal of her duenna.

Hence the reluctant wife became the suspected outsider, and the despised sister became the valuable ally, elevated to the primary place in the household; nor was the sister, jealously guarding her position with her brother and jealous as well of Delany's youth, beauty, and graces, likely to have been eager to assuage her brother's suspicions. Imagine the domestic scene: the high-handed and easily offended sister demanding deference or reparation for unconferred deference at table at every meal; ensconced with her work in the drawing room and tacitly demanding hours of attendance; questioning engagements; proffering herself as a companion when Delany went out; monitoring, because always present, the calls of friends; poking among Delany's possessions and reading her letters; and presiding over the ring of informers who watched Delany's every move in and out of the house and delivered daily reports on her activities.

All her life Delany was the most lovable of creatures, but her sister-in-law would never have succumbed to kindness or grace or have believed either her integrity or her honor genuine. She needed only to remind her brother that Delany had married him—as she had told him herself—without love and with extreme reluctance. That Delany, once married, regarded her engagement as sacred her captor was incapable of comprehending and Delany incapable of descending to explain. Delany's failure to provide Pendarves with an heir must also have contributed to the contempt in which both her husband and his sister held her. Her honest expression of her feelings toward her husband had injured her with him; Montagu's regular asseverations of love for her own husband were far more effectual in winning confidence—and a legacy.

The weapons at Jane Pendarves's disposal no doubt effectually removed any possibility of the couple's arriving at a comfortable understanding, and they ensured that Pendarves would continue to avenge himself on his wife for his unrequited attraction to her. Meanwhile, Delany had further dangers to skirt: a fashionable aunt, who might have supported her, chose to mitigate Delany's misery by attempting to provide her with a lover; he and other admirers made attempts that might have compromised her. It transpired that Pendarves, now in his sixties, was being cheated by his steward and defrauded by his tenants; money was tight, and Delany was informed that her husband was supporting "some very near relations"—that is, illegitimate children (1:63). The end was of a piece with the beginning. Brother and sister quarreled, and at last the duenna departed. One evening in 1725 Pendarves came home ill, expressed a regard for his wife and her behavior, and said he hoped he might live to reward her. The next morning she found him dead—his face blackened—in bed. He had left her nothing but her jointure, perhaps about £200 a year. She was twenty-five and was straitened for money for the rest of her long life, or until 1788.[6]

Lord Lansdown had undoubtedly "protected" Delany by overseeing a marriage settlement which, as was usual, stipulated the amount of her jointure and settled money and estates on the children to be born of the marriage. But when no children were born, Delany was entitled, if not to inherit all, like Montagu or Chudleigh—far beyond reasonable expectation for a woman—at least to receive a considerable further sum in the form of an annuity. To have left his widow without sons to provide male protection or daughters to shelter her and with nothing but her jointure was a form of public insult, even of repudiation, from which Elizabeth Vesey, when similarly treated (chapter 10), never recovered. Delany's honor and pride had prevented her from manipulating her husband to secure a more substantial provision; this had a profound effect on the rest of her life. All that followed was the result of the slender provision made her, and her life is in striking contrast to the life of that other childless younger wife Elizabeth Montagu. She never had enough money, and she spent considerable time making long visits to friends. Financial difficulties nearly made a companion of her, though her position as companion always remained politely unacknowledged; as Montagu had once done, Delany spent a lot of time with the Duchess of Portland. Probably because of her poverty, a serious attraction to Lord Baltimore failed to result in marriage; instead Baltimore apparently tried to make her his mistress.[7] In 1736 she tried unsuccessfully to get an appointment as bedchamber woman to the new Princess of Wales. Then in 1743 a man she had liked before his first marriage, Patrick Delany, offered her a happy marriage of the kind that Hester Thrale and Emily, Duchess of Leinster, made the second time, one that resulted in equality and happiness for both partners because the man was sufficiently inferior in wealth and station. But unlike the other two women, Delany had little money and her new husband was only adequately provided. When she was widowed again in 1768, the situation was as bad as before. She was able to afford a house of her own in London for the winter only by spending the summer at Bulstrode with the duchess. When the duchess died, for the second time Delany was left— probably at her own insistence this time—unprovided for.

In 1785 Delany was where Burney found her, a pensioner of the king and queen at Windsor with an ex officio post as grandmother to the royal family. It is no marvel that Delany and Burney, when they met in 1783, recognized their similarity despite the great disparity in age and no surprise that it was Delany who was primarily responsible for Burney's appointment (entrapment) at court. The similarity of their destinies was entirely owing to a short supply of money. Studying the lives of Delany and Burney, it is less easy to fault Montagu or Chudleigh, after beginning life on somewhat the same course, for having enjoyed a splendid independence in the later years—an independence Delany and Burney suffered more to obtain and obtained to a far lesser degree.

The course of Delany's life was thus shaped in large part by the inimicable presence at a crucial moment of a spy and rival for her husband's regard, a disregarded sister who could reclaim her brother's interest only at the expense of his wife, who therefore had to be made to appear unreliable, unfaithful, and unworthy. Delany, in every way an altruist but young and inexperienced of judgment and judging herself as little deserving of marital reward, was incapable of maneuvering her way past her sister-in-law's plots into her husband's good graces. The situation shows that, given the right (or wrong) disposition of the husband, the influence of the companion could far surpass that of the wife.

A darker version of Delany's tale was that of the famed Lady Cathcart, who, by the combination of a faithless husband and a faithless companion, was incarcerated in Ireland for over twenty years. That this lengthy imprisonment, known to her family, friends, and neighbors, could be relieved only by the death of her husband seems incredible but is true.

Born Elizabeth Malyn in about 1691,[8] the daughter of a wealthy brewer, as a girl she was encountered on horseback in Enfield Chase by Sir Richard Steele, who, unable to dismiss her either from his heart or his head, wrote, "If I were to draw a picture of youth, health, beauty or modesty, I would represent any or all of them in the person of that young woman."[9] She was first married, "to please her parents,"[10] to the rich James Fleet of Tewin, Hertfordshire, the only surviving son of Sir John Fleet, citizen and grocer, member of Parliament, and sheriff of London. He bought the manor of Tewin and various other properties, including Tewin Water, a beautiful estate of about 150 acres, finely timbered, in 1713, probably on the occasion of their marriage.[11] On his death in 1733 (she was already over forty) she married "for money" Captain William Sabine.[12] Left at his death a rich widow and still in possession for life of Tewin Water, she then married in 1739 "for title" Charles, Lord Cathcart, who died the next year, commander in chief of British forces in the West Indies, at Dominica. She was a good match, still a fine woman, and very rich—with a large income for life and a fortune of her own of, probably, ten to twenty thousand; and in each case it was she who had won the marital tontine. Her final choice, made for love, she later said, was because "the devil owed her a grudge, and would punish her for all her sins."[13] Her choice of the sturdy and sexually attractive young Irishman Hugh Maguire, who courted her and with whom she fell in love, was not forgiven by society for the same reason that Hester Thrale's choice of Piozzi was not forgiven: women of independent means might make discreet use of but were not supposed to marry poor and virile men from nations suspected of exporting persons of undue sexual vigor; such women could be motivated only by an unacceptable hunger for carnal gratification and domestic equality.[14] Their marriages, like that of the

Duchess of Manchester in 1743 to the poor but sturdy-legged young Irishman Edward Hussey, aroused wildly rowdy and inimicable responses. By these marriages control of the women and their fortunes was lost to the establishment—which, however, laid claim to Hussey by making him, eventually, the Earl of Beaulieu. To the gratification of almost everyone, therefore, Cathcart's fate proved the foolishness of her assumption that a handsome man in his early thirties could marry a childless widow in her mid-fifties for any purpose but to rob her.

Elizabeth Cathcart could have had no idea who she was dealing with in the charming Maguire, and knowing that she was in control and on her own ground, that her husband had everything to gain while she lived and little at her death, surrounded by familiar servants, she must have felt safe. But she had had no experience with men like Hugh Maguire, who was from an ancient, proud, but impoverished Milesian Irish family; the Maguires had been princes of Fermanagh for hundreds of years. Hugh Maguire was the namesake of the greatest warrior against the English, a sixteenth-century Chief Lord of Fermanagh, but he was the actual descendant of the chief's half-brother Bryan. The seat of the senior branch of Maguires was the ancient castle at Cnocninne on Lough Erne, from which they moved in the late seventeeth century to Enniskillen Castle on the Lough; but Bryan had been granted two thousand acres near Enniskillen and built a small castle, Tempo, as the family seat of this junior branch. Hugh was the grandson of Bryan's grandson, Cuchonnacht, a colonel who had led a regiment of cavalry for James II at the decisive battle of Aughrim against William's forces in 1691, when, the story goes, after having killed almost an entire regiment, he too perished. There was no living in Ireland for the independent, Catholic, and Stuart-supporting Irish, and Cuchonnacht's sons and grandsons survived by fighting wherever fighting forces were being hired. Hugh's father, Bryan, inherited Tempo; and Hugh Maguire, a younger son, went off to fight for the emperor of Austria in the Hungarian service.[15]

The great shift in Maguire's fortunes occurred with his politic decision to capitulate to Protestantism and the Hanoverians. As Walpole told the story, to take up an English commission, he had applied to the bishop of London to *abdicate* his religion. On the bishop's inquiring what his objections to it were, " 'Oh!' he said, 'there were several things he could not swallow'—'several of the doctrines that were too monstrous to be believed.' 'Pray which be they?' 'Why, there's Transubstantiation—and the Trinity.'—My Lord Bishop cried, 'Enough, enough'—

and immediately baptized him a good Protestant in the name of the
Father, and the Son, and the Holy Ghost." [16]

Maguire was, however, cleverer than Walpole suggests, a fine figure
of a man and highly popular in London society. In October 1741, for instance, he and Walpole danced at Sir Thomas Robinson's ball with the
most eligible of London's young women (37:115). Maguire was by this
time an English officer. Much to the amusement of society, he had acquired as his first patroness Lady Brown, the wife of Sir Robert Brown,
then the paymaster of works. In January 1741 she had obtained for him
the lieutenant-colonelcy in a new regiment of foot. Not content with
this, he had the rare modesty, despite his youth, reported Walpole's
cousin Henry Seymour Conway in October 1742, with Lady Brown's
backing, promptly to apply to the king for a regiment of his own (37:132).
The application was successful, and in that same month Maguire was
named a colonel of Marines.[17] He seems thereafter, however, scarcely
to have left London, an expensive environment for young men of fashion, and, Lady Brown being already married to the useful Sir Robert,
he applied himself to the task of marrying someone else with a fortune.

Lady Cathcart, rich, free, and in control of a large fortune, was his
choice and in May 1745 they married in Bath. Her marriage settlement,
signed the day before they married, recited that she enjoyed rents for
life on estates in London, Middlesex, and Hertfordshire (amounting to
over £18,000 a year), was possessed of mortages worth £8,546 and jewels, rings, and plate of very great value, a great quantity of household
goods, and the use for life of Lord Cathcart's house in Dartmouth Street,
Westminister. All these were put in trust for the sole use of Cathcart
and were to be "in no wise subject to the debts, or be under the power
or at the disposal of" Hugh Maguire.[18] Her belief in her own security
led her to unfortunate insouciance: she is reported to have engraved on
her wedding ring the posy, "If I survive, I will have five," but after two
weeks of marriage to have announced that "she never was *really* married before, though she has three times before gone through the ceremony" (30:84, 85).

Walpole aside, the effect Cathcart's marriage had on her acquaintance may be gauged by a similar tone taken on the occasion by her
Hertfordshire neighbor, the Reverend Edward Young, sententious author of the famed *Night Thoughts*. In the early days Young was a cordial
friend, frequently beholden to Cathcart; he had, for instance, entrusted
his stepdaughter Caroline Lee to her at her house in Westminister for
portions of two London seasons and was indebted to her for Caroline's

introduction into society. Though he had disapproved of Cathcart's marriage, he made no immediate show of his disapproval, but on the contrary, when he found himself inconvenienced by the lack of a curate, he
had proposed inducting Maguire into the position, to which Cathcart
objected "yt however well qualified He may be, yet ye World would not
well relish in a Protestant Pulpit so recent a convert from the Church
of Rome."[19] Maguire had apparently made a favorable impression on
Young, but surely his bizarre suggestion that Cathcart's husband should
function as a curate was a gaffe, perhaps a gibe.

"Compassion is not only a Duty, but a Blessing; It is attended with a
Pleasure, not only in common wth all other Virtues, from a consciousness of doing right, but with a Pleasure of its own peculiar growth,
wh the Uncompasionate can never enjoy": thus the benevolent Young
addressed the Duchess of Portland in October 1746 (p. 240). In September he had commenced a letter, "I am too well acquainted with ye
Pains & Infirmities of human nature, not to compassionate those that
in any Degree labour under them" (p. 238). This letter includes, for the
duchess's amusement, news of his having received a letter apparently
from Maguire on the road to Chester announcing and justifying his
abduction of his wife because she had lied to him, perhaps about her
valuable jewels, which she may have promised before marriage to turn
over to him to pay his debts.[20] "If yr Grace had such a Thing as a Flash
of Lightning in ye Corner of your Cubbard it would be ye most proper
Return you could make for my Present. It was indeed a Clap of Thun-
der to Ly C——t who is now panting in the Irish Seas under ye Conse-
quences of it." He had been put in mind of this letter by the duchess's
mention of the Duchess of Manchester's marriage to Hussey. He begs
she keep his having sent the letter a secret, "for I would not appear as a
Confidant in such an Affair; much less as ye Betrayer of the Betrayer."[21]
He continues in the same merciless vein: "How one false Step naturally
betrays us into another? Had her Ladyp [sic] never married her Grandson, she had never been a Lyar; & if she had never been a Lyar, she had
never been Transported; which, in this Case, is, I think, a severer Fate
than that of being Hanged."[22]

In October 1746 Young was able to elaborate and incidentally made
the first recorded reference to Cathcart's companion:

The following pretty Tale for a Tragedy may perhaps be new to Yr Grace.—Ly
C—— at 59 is smitten with ye gay Feathers of 33, & after short ceremoniny of
Billing & Pruning, takes him into her Nest. 33 finds it very well featherd, & had

a great mind to pluck some Plumes of it for his private Use. This made Dame Partlet bristle against him At This the Cocks-comb rose & could not bear it. It came to a little Sparing, War was declard, & 33 must show all his generalship on this Occasion. To this End he thought it prudent to strengthen himself by Allies. And it happened very fortunately for him, that there was a young Princess in ye Family of 18, whom 59 took from ye Dunghill, & tossed her into a Tub of Soapsuds, out of wh, she soon rose, like Venus out of ye sea, the Delight of her Ladysp's Eyes, & ye Confident of her Heart. This Venus fell in love with Mars, wh was very happy for him, for she returned ye favours she receivd from him with ye Key of her Ladyp's Scritore, where He found ye Will, wh has made him run mad. In his Distraction He snatches both away to Ireland, where the young Princess personates her Ladyp, who is kept out of Eyesight, for fear of telling Tales. And as she before discoverd the Undutifullness of her Husband, so very lately are her eyes open as to ye Treachery of her bosom-Friend. And yet none but these two are ever sufferd to come near her. Can your Grace easily feign a greater Picture of Distress? I own I can not. And yet for this terrible Sore, she neither has, nor is like to have, any other Plaister than Potatoes & Milk. (pp. 244–45)

"How dearly do we often pay for the gratification of an idle desire!" is the moral drawn by this Christian clergyman and former neighbor of the victim. He was able to send further details in February 1747: "Madam, I must let you know that I have a new Nighbour at ye House that was my Lady Cathcarts; she is an Irish Lady, & this is ye scheme (viz) she is to have possession of this English Villa in lieu of an old Castle in ye utmost North of Ireland, frowning over ye sea, in which Lady Cathcart is to be Imprisond, till some generous Knight-errant shall come to her Releif, & rescue her immaculate Virginity from the merciless Tyranny of ye Gyant Maguire."[23]

Despite everyone's knowledge of her plight, she was to remain there from 1746 to the death of her husband in 1766. In part this may have been because once in Ireland, she was beyond the reach of a writ of habeas corpus and Maguire was beyond the reach of English law, but to a large extent it was clearly because everyone believed that she deserved what had happened to her, even if it meant her dying in captivity. In fact, her fate was an important object lesson to all such widows as were entrusted with wealth. While the rich Lady Cathcart had managed to control a great estate, marry and enjoy a handsome and dependent young husband, and queen it in society, Young and everyone else had held their hands if not their tongues (and taken her proffered largesse); but to her punishment for such presumption, all—including apparently the Duchess of Portland, who seems, by the continuing of Young's tale, to have registered no objection—subscribed.

Despite her precautions, Cathcart herself had provided Maguire and her companion the opportunity to seize her power. Possessed of enormous *élan vital*, having always been lucky, she had an unwarranted overconfidence in her own powers and apparently assumed she was safe because Maguire would benefit from her wealth only while she lived and her life was accordingly of utmost value to him. But she had too many additional assets at her disposal. On marriage to Maguire, Cathcart provided him, as men often provided their wives, with a luxurious maintenance but not with the access to her possessions that he had anticipated. Becoming the lover and therefore the ally of the beautiful but faithless young companion, he probably encouraged her with promises that after Cathcart's death he would marry her. She provided the means to come at Cathcart's will so that he could discover how she had disposed of her assets, and, having learned he was not the major beneficiary, Maguire is said to have forced his wife at gunpoint to alter her will. Lady Cathcart, alerted to her husband's rapacious motive for having married her, next hid her jewels about her person, plaiting some into her hair, quilting others into her petticoat. One day in the autumn of 1746 the Maguires with the companion, accompanied by his brothers on horseback, went for an airing in the coach before dinner; when Lady Cathcart wanted to turn back lest they be late, Maguire informed her that they were on their way to Chester to embark for Ireland. Three hours after their departure from Tewin, two servants arrived, sent back by Maguire to strip the house of plate, china, furniture, horses, chaises, "and every thing that was good" under the pretext that Maguire's mother was dying at Oxford and Cathcart had determined to stay there for some time.[24]

Cathcart had left sufficient resources at home instantly to rouse rescuers, and an attorney was sent posthaste after them with a writ either of habeas corpus or of *ne exeat regno*. At their Chester inn, while Cathcart was somehow restrained from appearing—perhaps drugged—her companion successfully impersonated her, informing the astonished attorney that she went cheerfully to Ireland of her own free will. The attorney departed, and Maguire sent bullies after him to rob him and gain possession of his writ.[25] In Dublin on October 3 Cathcart, no doubt under duress, executed a deed assigning half her income to Maguire "in consideration of the tender love and affection she bore" him and "in acknowledgment of that tender and affectionate regard which he has always shown for her." After the death of either Cathcart or Maguire, the trustees of her estate—now his allies—were empowered to raise £12,000 to be disposed of by the survivor.[26] From Dublin Cathcart vanished into durance, perhaps first at Maguire's brother's castle at Tempo but later at his uncle's, Castle Nugent, co. Longford. That she survived at all was undoubtedly owing to her income, which guaranteed Maguire at least £1,800 a year while she lived. Of her own half-income she never saw a penny.

A memorial of a deed dated 1778 from the Dublin Registry of Deeds (218226, Maguire to Lady Cathcart) clarifies some of Maguire's dealings with his wife while she was under duress. His elder brother Constantine had, commencing in 1728, several times mortgaged and then remortgaged his possessions at Tempo until he was indebted for £3,340. He had then died intestate leaving his next brother Robert his heir at law, and two younger brothers, Hugh and Philip. Before marrying, Cathcart had assigned all her possessions to two eminently respectable trustees, but on October 3, 1746 she turned them over to three rakish allies of her husband, who relinquished £8,279 of her money to redeem the Tempo mortgage and to purchase "other securities." In June 1751 Maguire and Cathcart in concert moved to foreclose on Robert Maguire, who had evidently not redeemed the new mortgage; apparently Hugh Maguire intended to acquire Tempo for himself. In April 1755 Maguire and Cathcart were awarded £8,118 by the court with interest and costs which were, however, never collected; and Maguire died in 1766 leaving his landed property in Ireland to his nephew Hugh Maguire—son of one of his brothers—and leaving Tempo to trustees who were to pay Cathcart for "her share" of the mortgage money lent. Cathcart in 1772 sued for the 1755 decree to be executed to no avail. In 1777 her husband's nephew Hugh Maguire, now in possession of Tempo, agreed to pay her £10,804 and legal interest then due her and as security granted her the castle and lands of Tempo. She may thereafter have been able to collect the various rents from the land, but she died without having collected her £10,000. The Maguires, however, perhaps by this settlement, were themselves ruined.[27]

In Ireland the companion again impersonated Lady Cathcart for a period, but her ladyship then vanished upstairs from view, and for many years, while Maguire was visited and countenanced by all the local gentry, he regularly at dinner sent his compliments to her ladyship, informed her that the company drank her health, and begged to know if there was anything at table she chose to have to eat. "The answer was always, 'Lady Cathcart's compliments, and she has everything she wants.' "[28] Gentlemen of the neighborhood forbore to ask questions of Maguire, a skilled, intrepid, and trigger-happy duelist who had killed before.

Everyone, it seems, knew the situation and colluded with Maguire. In the matter of the jewels, however, women helped her: Cathcart engaged a beggar woman who passed under her window to deliver the jewels to an acquaintance who received them, kept them safe despite her husband's intervening bankruptcy, and restored them to their owner on her release.

Cathcart was freed after Maguire died in April 1766. Two tales were related of his demise, one, perhaps fictitious, by Maria Edgeworth, who reported that he was challenged by the brother of one of three Irishwomen her hero had engaged to marry on the reportedly imminent death of his wife and was killed. Allegedly Cathcart herself told a different tale: wearied at last by Maguire's threats, she told him of the secret recess at Tewin where the Tewin deeds were kept. He went there to retrieve them, but the old catch was rusty, and, impatiently employing his jackknife, he cut himself and died of lockjaw.[29] On the assurance of Maguire's death, Cathcart was "rescued" by a Mr. Nugent, and Maria Edgeworth describes her as wearing a red wig and with scarcely sufficient clothes to cover her, looking scared, her understanding seemingly stupefied, and claiming that she scarcely knew one human being from another.[30] She was seventy-three; yet she successfully went to Chancery to regain possession of her estate from Joseph Hickey, Maguire's lawyer, and Joseph Steele, the tenant to whom Maguire had leased it, and she danced at Welwyn assembly when she was ninety-five. On the well-publicized subject of the dancing, in December 1786, Walpole sardonically concluded, "It is woeful to have a colt's tooth when folks have no other left" (33:542). She died in 1789, in her ninety-eighth year, leaving a reputation for great charity to the poor and what was left of her possessions to her servants, and was buried at Tewin beside her first husband.[31]

The gothic purport of this tale is so striking that it abstracts the attention from the other aspects of the case. What of Henry Tilney's expostulation to Catherine Morland when she has suspected his father of having perpetrated some such misdeed: "Dear Miss Morland. . . . Remember that we are English, that we are Christians. . . . Does our education prepare us for such atrocities? Do our laws connive at them?"[32] Lady Cathcart had both brother and sisters; everyone knew of her plight. How could she have been left to languish for twenty years, even granted that there was no legal recourse and that society believed she richly deserved her fate? People like Walpole and Young seem to have forestalled any uncomfortable moral response by finding her punishment comical. Patriarchs seem to have found it impossible to set a precedent of undermining patriarchal privilege. Her own family may have considered that once she signed the will in Maguire's favor, her own significance and value had dwindled and that if reclaimed she would have constituted only a dependent nuisance.[33]

The companion in this tale is significant. Her motive was obvious: Maguire offered her the opportunity to turn the tables and take her mistress's place, and she was another grateful subservient whose gratitude was entirely hypocritical. She seems to have been a tool and little more, and if she was the Mary Horton who received an annuity of fifty guineas only till she reached twenty-one or married (at this point the money came virtually from Maguire's pocket), her reward was small enough. But Cathcart's fate hung on her choices. Had she been faithful to her patroness, who had apparently removed her from poverty, she would have reported Maguire's proposals rather than joining him. Had she allied herself with Cathcart, the two women would have been too strong for him. Without her, Maguire would not have been able to find the will, to abduct his wife to Ireland, or to disarm the attorney and the local Irish gentry. At first, she impersonated Lady Cathcart, at the same time isolating her from all other contact. It was the combination against Cathcart that proved too strong for her, and so for the moment the companion's power must have seemed to herself deceptively great.

But the companion's impersonation was known at once, even in London, so possibly it did not long continue. The companion is not noted after Lady Cathcart disappeared in ill health upstairs, and as in the case of Jane Pendarves her ultimate fortune is unknown. Perhaps she was sent away with her £50 annuity; perhaps she stayed on in the house as Maguire's mistress. It seems unlikely that her fate was superior to what it would have been had she remained loyal to Cathcart in London, and her triumphant days were probably not long—and yet, one wonders. Another gothic twist to the tale might read that Elizabeth Cathcart died under her husband's galling treatment and that, to continue to enjoy her rents, Maguire put the companion, a skilled impersonator, into her place once more, that it might have been the companion who was "rescued," so confused that she scarcely knew one human being from another, the companion who on Maguire's premature decease in 1766 seized her own chance and returned to live on Cathcart's rents, who danced at Wellwyn assembly (in the assembly rooms endowed by

Edward Young), and who died, not at ninety-eight but much younger. It
is a fanciful, but I think a feasible twist to the plot, but we cannot know.

In any case, Cathcart's rage, when she first discovered her protégée's
perfidy, must have been mighty, her reconsiderations weighty. Her own
character, so well thought of by her neighbors, so charitable to the poor,
seems to have been that of an ill-considering, superficial, and happy
woman who took her companion's and her fourth husband's professions
of gratitude and love at face value. Perhaps she became belatedly wise
in her incarceration, though there is some reason to believe that she may
have been drugged a considerable portion of the time. She was probably drugged at Chester, where her shrieks would certainly have alerted
the officer, and if she survived to 1766, drugs may have accounted for
her stupefaction on release. In her kindness to Caroline Lee and to her
companion, in the portrait provided by a servant of her last days, in
which processions of pensioners streamed up the avenue to Tewin to receive her charity, there are hints of true altruism, but her career may
also be construed as that of a gay and selfish woman who bought attendance and adoration at no vast cost to herself. She had none of that
deep knowledge of her fellow creatures or their natures without which
we are all imperiled.

Lady Elizabeth Foster was much cleverer than Cathcart's nameless
girl companion. The beautiful Georgiana, Duchess of Devonshire, lived
from 1782 to her death with a companion, Lady Elizabeth, who was
also the mistress of the duke and the mother of two of his children—
reared in the Devonshire nursery with the duchess's own children—
and who succeeded her friend as second duchess in 1809. The story has
often been told,[34] and the question just as often raised as to why the first
duchess put up with the situation, which seems consistently to have elevated the fortunes of Foster above those of her friend in relation to the
duke and their ménage.

The cast of characters in this famous triangle includes three of the
most prominent figures of the period. William Cavendish, fifth Duke of
Devonshire, was very rich and powerful, with an income of £40,000 a
year, Horace Walpole calculated,[35] "a nobleman," said Wraxall, "whose
constitutional apathy formed his distinguishing characteristic." He was
unusually unanimated and unruffled, and he "seemed to be incapable
of any strong emotion, and destitute of all energy or activity of mind."
Wraxall thought, however, that he had an improved understanding,
noting that at his club, Brooks's, all disputes relative to passages of the
Roman poets or historians were referred to him, and judging him, if

not a superior man, at least an honorable and respectable member of society. Despite his "somnolent tranquillity," however, Wraxall judged the duke not insensible to the seduction of female charms.[36]

Lady Georgiana Spencer was one of the most charming women of her age but open, ingenuous, and accustomed from her childhood to being wheedled and manipulated by others, not to have to manipulate others herself. In 1773, when with her parents, Earl and Lady Spencer, she encountered (designedly) the duke at Spa, she was just sixteen. The duke, convinced of the suitability of the marriage, concluded an agreement without bestowing his heart. Unhappily for the brilliantly attractive Georgiana, he had no heart to bestow, having for some time been the slave of Charlotte Spencer, a milliner who had already enjoyed a checkered career.[37] A letter written in October of that year by an interested observer confided: "The young Ladies must for this winter look upon the D. of Devonshire as a lost man, for he has taken Charlotte Spencer (a Lady I presume you know by sight) into keeping selon toutes les formes. I hear She says She has received the *most passionate* Letters from him that ever She read in her Life. He is now at Chatsworth, & it was once reported She was going down to him, but that is not true."[38]

Considering that negotiations between the duke and the Spencers must almost certainly have commenced, the duke's behavior in yielding to a passion for the wrong Spencer constitutes a declaration both of his small interest in and small respect for his intended bride and of his intention as to how he would proceed. Charlotte Spencer's daughter Charlotte Williams, to whom her father was devoted, was born about the time of his marriage. Despite her probable knowledge of the situation, despite her realization that her impulsive and childish daughter was too young to marry, Lady Spencer was so determined upon this brilliant match that she overlooked the duke's amorous involvement as well as his obvious lack of interest in her daughter, and she acceded to his foolish insistence that the marriage take place while Georgiana was still sixteen, consenting to a quiet ceremony on June 5, 1774, two days before Georgiana's seventeenth birthday.

Even before the marriage there was ample evidence of the duke's perverse indifference to his entrancing fiancée. At Bath in May, Delany reported, Georgiana fainted at a ball. Devonshire, at the other end of the room, inquired of the bustle, *"What's that?"* "They told him, and he replied with his usual demureness: I *thought* the noise—was—among—the women!"[39] During the same period Mary Hamilton noted an occasion when the duke "walked between Lady Georgiana & I, we were very *chatty*, but not one word spoke the Duke to his betrothed, nor did one smile grace his dull visage,—notwithstanding his rank & fortune I w^d not marry him—they say he is sensible & has good qualities—it is a pity he is not more ostensibly agreeable,—dear charming Lady Georgiana will not be well matched." [40] The *Town and Country Magazine* noted the paradox, "which is, that after some years intercourse with Miss S———r, who was now rather approaching the decline of beauty, our hero should marry a nobleman's daughter, an universal toast, still in her teens, with every personal accomplishment, who gives the *Ton* wherever she goes, and that he should still be fond of his antiquated (by comparison) Charlotte. . . . That the blooming, the blythe, and beautiful D—— should be neglected for Charlotte S—— is really astonishing!"

As this "Tête-à-Tête" suggests, the situation did not improve after marriage, and Frances Boscawen was to report to Delany on June 16, 1774, "The Duke was at the levee yesterday, and at night at Ranelagh, leaving his fair bride!" [41] Such beginnings, if unremedied, often have long-range effects, and it is the opinion of one of the duchess's biographers, based on the cold, phlegmatic nature of the duke, that the problem was one of sexual incompatibility deriving from the necessity of the duke's being aroused and serviced by a woman experienced in the art, whereas his young wife required initiation by a skillful lover. [42] There is probably some validity to this theory, which would help explain the duke's perverse distaste for his wife and his wife's acceptance of his connections with Charlotte Spencer and Elizabeth Foster.

The duchess's introduction into married and adult life was cruel. She was suddenly deprived of the unusually warm and affectionate home life to which she had been accustomed. She attempted to maintain this life by exchanging letters almost daily with her mother, but from the marriage the principal sustenance she drew was her annual £2,000 pin money. At the same time she was overwhelmed by the flattery of everyone and the addresses of every man but her husband. She became a notable hostess, but her husband preferred to spend the evenings at Brooks's. She became the undisputed leader of fashion, and he remained faithful to Charlotte Spencer. The compulsive gambling that finally ruined her probably had its root in the sudden deprivation of love in her new life and may have been a plea for her husband's attention, but for too long he, perhaps oppressed by his own burden of guilt, simply compressed his lips and paid up.

Other responses of the duchess boded ill. She was sometimes slatternly. Frances Burney, who sacrificed dearly for dress, described her in

1776 walking in the park with two curls unpinned and hanging down, one shoe down at heel, the trimmings of her jacket and coat unsewn in places, her cap awry, her cloak rusty and powdered, half on and half off, wearing a look of innocence and artlessness. She hung upon the arm of the duke, who looked to Burney ugly, tidy, and grave, like a mean shopkeeper's journeyman.[43] In 1777 Lady Sarah Bunbury noted that Georgiana was ruining her health by dining at seven, going to bed at three in the morning and lying abed next day till four, indulging in hysterical fits in the morning, then dancing in the evening, sometimes bathing, riding, and dancing for ten days, then lying in bed the next ten.[44] Her hysterical and convulsive fits became intermittently habitual.

For seven years she failed to produce an heir and was always and everywhere humiliatingly scrutinized for signs of pregnancy. At last in May 1781 the Cavendish family arranged a marriage for the duke's younger brother Lord George Cavendish with Lady Elizabeth Compton, "it being agreed that the Cavendish family must be continued from his loins. *Mme la Duchesse fait des paroles, mais non pas des enfans.*"[45] There was sometimes hope: in March 1782 George Selwyn observed, "The Duchess of Devonshire went sick yesterday from Court."[46] But hopes proved false.

The duchess was still not pregnant when on May 22, 1782, at the request of her mother, who thought it would be a kindness, she took the duke with her to see Lady Erne and Lady Elizabeth Foster, two unhappy daughters of Frederick Hervey, bishop of Derry and Earl of Bristol, both recently separated from their husbands and therefore in ambiguous (not to mention impoverished) positions and in need of respectable protection and countenance. Lady Elizabeth (hereinafter Foster) was one of those enchanting Herveys noted for their personal corruption, charm, and sexual ambivalence. Her great-uncle Harry Hervey had been of the same breed; Samuel Johnson said of him, "He was a vicious man, but very kind to me. If you call a dog Hervey, I shall love him."[47]

If in the wars of love people are either citadels to be besieged or expert besiegers, the duke and duchess were the first, Elizabeth Foster the second. She was a delicate and enchanting beauty, irresistibly attractive, an *allumeuse* by temperament, said Arthur Calder-Marshall, that is, never satisfied till everyone had fallen in love with her.[48] "Lady Elizabeth," said Frances Burney, "has the character of being so alluring that . . . it was the opinion of Mr. Gibbon no man could withstand her, and . . . if she chose to beckon the Lord Chancellor from his Woolsack in full sight of the world, he could not resist obedience."[49] Immediately upon meeting them she practiced her art on both duke and duchess, reducing them to abject slavery and keeping them so for the rest of their lives.

The duke, no longer in Charlotte Spencer's chains, fell wholeheartedly in love and soon enough provided evidence that he experienced no sexual difficulties with Foster. The warmhearted duchess, with no domestic object to love, also fell enamored. The pair invited the Hervey sisters to join them next in Bath. Lady Erne, who had an interest in Methodism, soon disappeared from their lives, but Foster, in critical need of an establishment, was with them to stay.

Though Foster was not in disgrace, she had left a husband who kept their two sons and apparently failed to return her settlement or to provide for her, some indication that he may have been an aggrieved party. Her father the earl-bishop had promised her an allowance of £300 a year, but he was not swift to pay up, and in any case that sum was ridiculously inadequate. Foster from this time lived openly upon the duke, though at first there was some pretense that her money came from the duchess. On her first visit to the Devonshires she had become, as she called herself, "your own poor little Bess."[50] Thereafter she returned with them to London and then went visiting with them to Plympton and to the Spencers at Althorp, despite the protests of the acute Lady Spencer.

Ostensibly Foster had joined the Devonshires as the duchess's friend and companion, but society was not slow to comprehend her relationship with the duke. A weakness in her lungs occasioned the Devonshires' sending Foster abroad for the first time in December 1782. She went with Charlotte Williams and her nurse, Mrs. Garner, professedly in charge of the social education of the child, now about eight. Though the daughter, said Horace Walpole, "of an Earl in lawn sleeves," her father had suffered her "from indigence to accept £300 a year as governess to a natural child."[51] But she required far more than £300, though much of the money sent her was no doubt for traveling expenses for the little party. When she was in debt for £170 at Turin in September 1783, the duchess sent £300 at once, "and then let me know where the other 300 is to be sent, my sweetest love. Do not talk of expence, you w^d break my heart and neither use Canis [the duke] or I like B^r & Sister, if you did not spend. . . . God bless you my angel love, I adore and love you beyond description, but I am miserable till I know you have rec^d this. Canis sends a thousand loves."[52] This money came from Canis, as Foster already knew. Though Burney's middle-class heroine Camilla was to agonize when circumstances forced her indebtedness to Sir Sedley

Clarendel, Foster unabashedly took all the money she could acquire from the duke from 1782 to their marriage in 1809.

But the duchess also adored her new friend. While Foster was abroad, the duchess laid plans for her return, announcing that they would take a small house for Foster nearby but that she must sometimes sleep in her old red room. Yes, replied Foster, "Your scheme about a house for me is just what I wish, but let it be as small and as near you as possible. In the sad world we live in I must not be in D.H. [Devonshire House] for more than a few nights."[53] Although Foster had become the duchess's companion, scandal had apparently already penetrated the trio's secret.

The duchess had also confessed to Foster her vast indebtedness. She was already, at twenty-six, ruinously involved; by 1792 she would owe £62,000 (over $6 million), and from as early as 1779 she was perpetually in agony over her debts. But in the meantime she had produced a daughter. Already pregnant when Foster departed in December 1782, she gave birth to Georgiana on July 12, 1783—not a son but certainly an indication that there might yet be a son. Had the presence of Foster in the family somehow facilitated the pregnancy?

Foster returned to England in July 1784 only to depart again for the Continent in early December, reportedly because she was coughing again but actually because she was pregnant by the duke. Her journals of the period, still extant, were written in a spirit of self-dramatization and self-justification to record the intense interest of her situation and to be read by sympathetic sharers of her suffering who would find therein plenty of reason to excuse her weakness. In a thousand agonies, she blames her predicament in part on the duchess: "Would I could fly the face of human kind—yet I could not bear not to see my loved friend again. She has been my comfort and happiness, tho' her unthinking kindness has hurried me down the precipice."[54]

Foster's daughter, Caroline St. Jules, was born at Vietri, Italy, on August 16, 1785. On August 29 the duchess produced her own second daughter, Harriet; it appears that the two women had conceived almost simultaneously. Again the question arises: had Foster's presence been necessary for the duchess to conceive?[55]

It is unclear when the duchess first learned of the liaison between the duke and Foster and of the birth of Caroline and whether she realized on Foster's return in July 1786 that once again her husband and her dearest friend were lovers. At any rate, in August 1787 it became necessary for Foster to depart again for the Continent. She deplored leaving her friends in another journal intended for their edification: "Oh, it was bitterness of grief to lose her—but him—his last embrace—his last look drew my soul after him—I remained motionless—even now, it is present to me. I see him—he is fixed in my heart—this guilty—heart—Oh, why could I not love him without crime. Why cannot I be his without sin?" (p. 41). And again:

I deserve to suffer, and will not complain—Oh, may I see my beloved friends again, for they are dearer still to me than all else in the world!—She is the kindest, dearest, best most beloved of friends—and he is and must be ever the very soul of my existence—I will cease to live in error with him, tho' with shame and blushes I confess it, one moment passed in his arms, one instant pressed to his heart, effaces every sorrow, every fear, every thought but him—but this must not be, shall not be—no, I'll live for him, but as his friend; still will I share, if he will let me, his every thought, his cares, and his anxieties, or his happiness, still will he find my heart adopt and make its own whatever can interest him, still will his pursuits be mine, whatever he likes or dislikes, will be pleasing or otherwise to me, for not only are my natural inclinations like his, but the instant his are known they become mine without a thought to make them so. (p. 43)

This was not an unusual way for a woman to make her living. The unusual elements of the situation were that because Foster could not marry the duke, she had to sustain her rapturous devotion for years, and she also managed to include the duchess in that rapturous devotion. The cares and anxieties Canis discussed with her concerned his wife, her indebtedness, and her failure to produce a male heir. Playing between the pair of them, Foster convinced each of her indispensability: to the duchess she promised to placate her injured husband; to the duke she counseled patience as the only course that could eventually provide an heir of his own loins to the dukedom. Perhaps the real basis of her power lay in the need the duke and duchess had of someone to mediate between them; alone they were unable to maintain a relationship.

Foster's son Augustus Clifford was born in Rouen on May 26, 1788. Thereafter Foster was more or less domiciled with the Devonshires as the duchess's official friend and companion, and in 1790 her two children by the duke joined the others in the Devonshire nursery.

"Oh, come to me, I die for you," the duchess had written to Foster in July 1786.[56] Was she only expressing her affection, or did she need the presence of Foster to quiet the duke's anger at her debts? For he could not live with Foster unless he lived with the duchess too, which over the years made Foster an extraordinarily expensive mistress. Had the duke repudiated the duchess, her credit would have been cut off, her gambling virtually ended. In the latter part of 1786 the duke did determine to rusticate the duchess but then relented, even though in that year she fell in love with the attractive Charles Grey, seven years her junior.

It would appear that the duke, the duchess, and Foster were bound symbiotically together. For the duchess there was the pleasant combination of mother and father figures that was enjoyed by Lady Holland and by Sophia Baddeley (chapter 9) and Elizabeth Vesey (chapter 10). Here as in the other cases, living with mother and father figures appears to have had an infantilizing effect. As for the duke, what man would object to a domestic harem? Besides the psychological pleasures of the situation, there was the practical benefit: had the duke sent away the duchess, he would have lost Foster, and had he lost Foster, she would have lost Devonshire House and Chatsworth. "Depository of both their thoughts," wrote Foster, "I have sought, when her imprudences have alienated him, to restore him to her, and when my heart has mourned over her avowal of his returning caresses, I have checked and corrected the sensation." Or, as Calder-Marshall has interpreted this passage, "Both the Duke and the Duchess confided in me. When the Duke told me that he was so infuriated by the Duchess's extravagances that he felt he could not go on living with her, I pointed out that unless he was prepared to let the title and estates pass to his brother Lord George he had to beget an heir by the Duchess; and when the Duchess told me that the Duke had resumed sexual intercourse, I as his mistress was upset but suppressed my feelings."[57]

So it may have been the duchess's gambling debts that produced her complaisance about Foster's presence in her home. That the duke should have mistresses everyone took for granted; what scandalized society was the insult to the sanctity of the home that the duke's children by three different mothers should all share the Devonshire nursery. Other theories, like that proposed by Calder-Marshall that the duchess needed Foster's presence to excite the duke to the point of sexual capacity, are at least coherent with the known facts. Twice Foster was on the spot when the duchess became pregnant, and supposedly it happened a third time on the Continent in 1790. A third theory, proposed by Janet Todd, is that the real love affair was between the duchess and Foster, who managed to hoodwink everyone.[58] This, too, is a possibility. Conventional language of sentimental friendship aside, Foster was indeed one of the great loves of the duchess's life—along with her mother and her sister. Why would not the duchess, so hungry for emotional satisfaction, have fallen genuinely in love with the alluring Foster? Some of the duchess's indubitable love poems to Foster survive:

À la beauté enchanteresse,
　　Elle unit l'attrait de l'ésprit;
Par un regard elle interesse,
　　Par un sourire elle seduit.[59]

"Lines to Lady E. Foster, from the Duchess of Devonshire on her apprehension of losing her eyesight" included the following stanzas:

I regret not the freedom of will,
　　Or sigh as uncertain I tread;
I am freer and happier still,
　　When by thee I am carefully led.

Ere my Sight I was doomed to resign,
　　My heart, I surrendered to thee;
Not a Thought or an Action was mine,
　　But I saw as thou bidst me to see.

Thy watchful affection I wait,
　　And hang with delight on thy voice;
And Dependance is softened by fate,
　　Since Dependance on Thee is my Choice. (p. 131)

After the duchess's death, Foster published "Lines to Lady Elizabeth Foster, by Georgiana, Duchess of Devonshire," which apparently accompanied a portrait of Foster:

Untutor'd in the pencil's art
My tints I gather from my heart,
Where truth and love together trace
The various beauties of thy face.
Thy form, acknowledged fair and fine;
Thy brow, where sense and sweetness join;
Thy smile, the antidote to pain;
Thy voice, that never spoke in vain;
As diamonds on the crystal trace
In lines no efforts can efface,
To please for ever is thy lot—
Once seen, once loved, and ne'er forgot.[60]

The lines seem to render the duchess's particular experience with Foster, who had indeed conquered her when only once seen. The duchess, even when deeply troubled by her debts, fleshy, half-blind, and half-distracted, was still a charming woman, and perhaps Foster genuinely loved her; and bisexuality was not unfamiliar to the Herveys. Foster wrote to her son after the duchess's death, "She was the only female friend I ever had," and again, "Our hearts were united in the closest bonds of confidence and love, and the charms of her society, which you so well know how to appreciate, could only be equalled by the divine, the truly angelick qualities of her heart and soul." "Never, I believe," she said again, "were two hearts and minds so united, never did two people think and feel so alike." [61] But at the time she spoke she had set herself the goal of marrying the duke; were these not virtually the same sentiments she had written formerly of the duke, and could she ever be completely genuine?

At any rate, Foster and the duchess were the closest pair of the trio for the rest of the duchess's life. In June 1789, just as the French Revolution was about to begin, the three went inexplicably to Paris, where they saw Caroline St. Jules and Augustus Clifford. In Spa in August the duchess was said to have conceived again. In England it was whispered that Foster was the true mother of the expected infant, but in Paris in May Foster was seen at the Opera, thin as a rail. William-Spencer, sixth Duke of Devonshire, was born on May 21, 1790. Rumors persisted for many years as to the true mother of the boy, and it was noted that he alone of the duchess's children remained devoted to Foster after her marriage to his father, that he forbore ever to marry, and that after his death in 1858 the dukedom went to a cousin—William, the grandson of Lord George Cavendish and Lady Betty Compton, the need for whom was so providently forseen by the Cavendishes. The accuracy of these rumors is somewhat endorsed by Lady Charlotte Bury's remark in 1818 that she thought there was truth in them; she added that the story had been hushed up on the promises of the twenty-eight-year-old duke "that he will never *marry, or pretend to present an heir*." [62] Nor did he marry; and surely if the tale were untrue, he might have quashed it by the obvious expedient of marrying and begetting.

In England in 1791 the duchess became pregnant by Charles Grey under circumstances that precluded the duke's supposing he was the father. As a result, she and Foster—who could not have remained at home alone with the duke—set out for the Continent, where the duchess's daughter Eliza Courtney was born at Aix en Provence on January 20, 1792; the child was subsequently adopted by Charles Grey's parents. The two women, joined at times by Lady Spencer and her ailing younger daughter, Lady Bessborough, wandered over Europe, returning home again only in September 1793. Once again, it would seem, the duke's longing for Foster had purchased the duchess's pardon.

Thereafter the three settled into a fairly comfortable middle age; the physical toll on the duchess, however, suggests her misery. She never ceased to lose enormous sums at the gaming table; she grew fat, coarsened, and lost the sight of an eye. Her death was said to be the result of a fever brought on, Lady Elizabeth said, by "the vexation and agitation of mind caused by a novel published shortly before. . . . A character was introduced in it, supposed to be meant for the Duchess, and who is made to swindle and do all sorts of dishonourable actions; at the same time suffering deep remorse, and struggling against amiable feelings and much natural sensibility."[63] It would be characteristic of the duchess, who had been protected and adored long after she ceased to deserve protection and adoration, to suffer at this exposure of the truth.[64] She died on March 30, 1806, aged forty-eight.

Why, against all reasonable expectation, had the wife and not the mistress of the duke the major disadvantages of the situation? The answer would appear to lie in the manipulative genius of Foster, the duchess's counselor at every turn. Had it not been for Foster, the duke would certainly have rusticated the duchess, which might have shocked her into reform. Instead, the duchess was committed to a cosmetic course of managing from crisis to crisis and letting Foster win the duke's pardon for each frightful peccadillo. Might Foster, had she chosen, have halted the duchess's self-destructive course, or did she encourage it as most advantageous to herself? She was at least on hand, sharing the duchess's every thought, when the duchess was gambling and when she was entering upon an affair with Charles Grey, the effects of which she could not conceal. And then there was the duchess's great need for domestic love, affection, and approval, which Foster fulfilled while doubly ensuring through her own alluring presence and the duchess's deterioration that the duke never would fulfill it. The entire situation was a degenerative cycle from which the duchess had not the courage to escape: the duke's indifference tempted her to fling away his money in revenge, and her gambling debts forced her to accept and rely on the mistress who gave her love and kept the duke placated and indifferent.[65]

If, in regard to the duke's son and heir, the duchess colluded in a fraud, it was because the duke wanted a son of his own to succeed, Foster wanted *her* son to succeed, and the Cavendishes had never been the duchess's friend—she owed them nothing. Besides, her provision of a Cavendish heir would make her mother, to whom she had given so much grief, very happy. She was not a sound reasoner, but certainly her letters show her to have been the feeling and loving member of the three: the duke was cold and apathetic, Foster self-indulgent, selfish, and manipulating. The duchess once explained to her mother,

It has happened to me with people who have influence over me to have perfectly seized the reason of their wishing me to do some one thing or other which I did not like to do, and that tho' they did not disclose their real motive, I have been saying to myself all the time that they have been persuading me, "I know what you are at, & why you wish me to do so and so", and yet with this full conviction instead of owning it & in spite of disliking the thing, I have done it because I was desired, & have pretended to believe every word that was said to me, so that I have actually taken more pains to appear a Dupe than most people do to shew that they can't be outwitted.[66]

Perhaps she is confessing that she always knew more than she pretended to know, which would explain the great toll on her health. Hers was essentially a wasted life: she was a natural-born writer who scribbled verses every day of her life and published a novel, *The Sylph*, in 1779. In it one may find her own apologia. Her heroine, young, inexperienced, and virtuous, is married by a man of fashion who carries her away to London, far from her own family, and continues his dissolute life, attempting to corrupt her as well. But she is watched from afar and protected by a sylph, who eventually unmasks himself as a loving and virtuous man who becomes her second husband. The men who loved the duchess were not interested in the preservation of her virtue. She also undoubtedly needed something serious to do, and she spent her life leading the ton, flinging away her husband's fortune, producing (or not producing) children in questionable circumstances, and longing for love, affection, and understanding.

Miss Bennet in Burney's *Cecilia* (1782) is the fictitious version of these scheming companions, the very model of the wife's companion in league with the husband for nefarious purposes. Life has provided enough examples to support Thrale's charge that Burney as an author acted only as a camera obscura. There is little question that by the time this book was written, the malicious hypocrisy of the subservient self-server was well understood. If Lady Margaret Monckton had not been so mean and reprehensible, she could never have tolerated Miss Bennet, a humble companion "in every sense of the phrase," "low-born, meanly educated, and narrow-minded; a stranger alike to innate merit or acquired accomplishments, yet skilful in the art of flattery, and an adept in every species of low cunning."[67] Nor would she have failed to recognize Miss Bennet's duplicity. With no ostensible status in the world, fawning and cringing before her mistress, Bennet draws satisfaction and self-validation from her behind-the-scenes plottings with Mr. Monckton and her knowledge that she is duping her mistress; probably she also receives pecuniary promises and rewards. We see only two of her actions in Monckton's behalf, but both are evil; Burney refused to exploit the comic or satiric possibilities of Bennet's ridiculous flatteries because Bennet is as satanic an element in the novel as her employer (who has appropriately attended the masquerade as a devil—pp. 107–24). First, Bennet goes as Mr. Monckton's agent to prevent Cecilia's marriage to Delvile (p. 126); then she manipulates the ill Lady Margaret into attending Cecilia to London—where she will die—by convincing her that neither Cecilia nor Monckton wants her to come (p. 719). Lady Margaret, like Charlotte Smith's Mrs. Rayland, or like Lady Cathcart, believes herself invulnerable and believes she is in control. She is unaware of her husband's real desires and his plots against her, does not penetrate into the true character or agenda of her companion, and, in a remarkable case of poetic justice, is shocked to death when her husband tells her for the first and only time exactly what he thinks of her.[68]

Through her alliance with Monckton, Bennet thus acquires the most complete power over her mistress, including even the power (vicariously) of killing her with impunity. The power is substantially ended the moment Monckton's object has been gained; but, like Hugh Maguire, he will always have to satisfy his confederate to keep her mouth closed, and while they both live the inferior holds a dangerous power.

An examination of the means by which a humble companion could enhance her contingent position has suggested several effective measures. The companion might provide double service, undertaking offices in some other humble capacity or functioning as an important executive of confidential business or as confidante and/or sexual partner combined. The more important, confidential, and particular the contribution, the more specially or uniquely adapted the inferior for the task, the higher would be her status. Conversely, little in the position of a simple humble companion recommended her to much respect and consideration.

Burney's analysis of all three figures in the Monckton constellation, like Charlotte Smith's subsequent analysis of the figures in the Rayland-Lennard constellation, reaffirms the apparent conclusion of women writers that because women are not naturally subservient, enforced subservience in hierarchically ordered relationships virtually assures moral damage for everyone concerned. It would remain for philosophers like William Godwin to carry this insight to its natural conclusion and demand equality for everyone for precisely this reason. What had been lacking in literature and polemic, at least in explicit terms, was the demand that such unequal distribution of privilege be ended. Women had instead recommended withdrawing from the world of men to form their own egalitarian societies: from Astell to Wollstonecraft (in *The Wrongs of Women*) this was as far as they could take the remedy. But throughout the century women had been demonstrating the damage done to character by excessive privilege (power over others) and inadequate privilege (lack of power over oneself). One may usefully recall here, too, Burney's demonstration of the hypocrisy of Mr. Tyrold's advice to Camilla and the hypocrisy he enjoins upon her—an indictment of the empowered and the obedient disempowered. In the hands of such writers as Sarah Fielding, Jane Collier, Sarah Scott, and Frances Burney, analyses of hierarchically structured relationships, particularly companionship relationships, were anything but simple.

All four of the patriarchal tools examined in this chapter were willing surrogate tyrants. From the point of view of the recommendation of benevolence or sensibility or, in our terms, altruism to women it is useful to see how dangerous the acceptance of the assignment might be to the designated victims. In actuality the attribute of mature self-determined altruism—as opposed to the childish generosity of the duchess—appears, by fostering the quality of empathy in its possessors, to be of some protection. Neither Cathcart in life nor Lady Monckton in fiction was able to detect the infidelity with which they lived or the traps laid for them. Delany, however, understood exactly the nature of the trap she was in; it was her own probably mistaken and overscrupulous choice not to fight back. The duchess probably knew the truth about her situation but chose to be blinded. The empathetic altruist may be more perceptive but appears to have less recourse, being bound by many moral strictures as well as by consideration for others and the impulse to sacrifice her own best interests for them. Frances Burney's clear recognition of her position at court and her resignation to it is another case in point. But Burney had already dealt with this problem in *Cecilia*. Her conclusion was that sensibility is not to be given up just because it is urged upon women by the patriarchs, just because it may prove dangerous to the possessor; but it must be accompanied by mature reason and experience of the world to guide it properly or it must almost invariably lead to its possessor's victimization. To speak cynically, perhaps here is one important reason for the growing contemporary demand that women take sensibility for their province and leave ratiocination to men, the growing insistence of women such as Mary Wollstonecraft and Ann Radcliffe that women, to become complete human beings, must develop their powers of reasoning.

Having in this chapter examined two relationships in which the husband and companion were lovers, let us turn to a situation in which mistress and companion were lovers and economic allies. Both aspects of this relationship seem to have contributed to an almost equal adjustment of power between the two.

Top, Elizabeth Chudleigh, engraving by S. Bull after a portrait by Sir Joshua Reynolds, c. 1743. Courtesy Print Collection, Lewis Walpole Library, Yale University. *Bottom*, Elizabeth Chudleigh in her masquerade character of Iphigenia at Ranelagh, 1749. Courtesy Print Collection, Lewis Walpole Library, Yale University.

Frances Burney, portrait by Edward F. Burney, c. 1784–85.
By permission of National Portrait Gallery, London.

Facing page: top left, Elizabeth Allen Burney, artist unknown. By permission
of Raymond Paul Martin; *top right*, Queen Charlotte, engraving by Read after
Thomas Gainsborough, 1790. Courtesy Print Collection, Lewis Walpole
Library, Yale University; *bottom*, Hester Lynch Thrale, engraving by
E. Finden after a portrait by Sir Joshua Reynolds, c. 1778. Courtesy Print
Collection, Lewis Walpole Library, Yale University.

Elizabeth Montagu, engraving by Ridley after Sir Joshua Reynolds.
Courtesy Print Collection, Lewis Walpole Library, Yale University.

Mary Delany, by Richard Cosway. Photograph: Courtauld Institute of Art.

Elizabeth Montagu and William Mason, "Abelard and Eloisa," 1778.
Courtesy Print Collection, Lewis Walpole Library, Yale University.

"An ANGEL, gliding on a Sun-beam into Paradice." Milton.

"Down thither prone in flight, Lo Schwelly speeds, & with her brings, the Gems, and Spoils of Heav'n"

Elizabeth Juliana Schwellenberg, "An Angel Gliding on a Sun-Beam into Paradise," by James Gillray, 1791. Courtesy Print Collection, Lewis Walpole Library, Yale University.

Lady Holland coroneted in "The Irish Stubble Goose," 1762. By permission of the Pierpont Morgan Library, New York. The Peel Collection, III.66v.274.

Dr. Samuel Parr, portrait by G. Dawe. By permission of
National Portrait Gallery, London.

Facing page: top, Georgiana, Duchess of Devonshire, with her daughter
Georgiana, portrait by Sir Joshua Reynolds, 1784. Devonshire Collection,
Chatsworth. By permission of the Chatsworth Settlement Trustees.
Photograph: Courtauld Institute of Art; *bottom*, Lady Elizabeth Foster,
afterward Duchess of Devonshire, portrait by Sir Joshua Reynolds, 1787.
Devonshire Collection, Chatsworth. By permission of the Chatsworth
Settlement Trustees. Photograph: Courtauld Institute of Art.

Your Affectᵗ M Carter

From a sketch taken by F. M. Nelthorpe at
St Lawrence Cottage I. of. W. in 1795 when
Mʳˢ Mary Carter was asleep ..

Mary Carter, drawing, 1795. By permission of Lt. Col. R. S. Nelthorpe.

Elizabeth Steele (?), "A Modern Antique" [identified as "Miss Steele" in a contemporary note], 1782. By permission of the Pierpont Morgan Library, New York. The Peel Collection, VIII.49v.168.

Elizabeth Vesey, pastel, artist unknown.
By permission of National Portrait Gallery, London.

Facing page: top, Frances Greville, chalk drawing by Ozias Humphry (?),
1768 (?). Private collection, London. Photograph: Courtauld Institute of Art;
bottom left, Sophia Baddeley, engraving by E. Welch after a portrait by Sir
Joshua Reynolds, 1771. By permission of the Trustees of the British Museum;
bottom right, Georgiana, Countess of Spencer, engraving by S. W. Reynolds
after a portrait by Sir Joshua Reynolds. Courtesy Print Collection, Lewis
Walpole Library, Yale University.

Louisa, Lady Clarges, portrait by Thomas Gainsborough.
By permission of the Victoria Art Gallery, Bath City Council.
Photograph: Courtauld Institute of Art.

Chapter Nine

BUSINESS PARTNERS:
BADDELEY AND STEELE

THE RELATIONSHIP of Sophia Snow Baddeley and Elizabeth Hughes Steele was in part like that of star and personal manager, in part like that of whore and madam; and their seemingly balanced relationship, in its endurance, was more a product of their successful partnership than of their friendship or of the fact that they were lovers. That is, it seems probable that Steele's position as Baddeley's companion was vastly strengthened by her functions as Baddeley's business partner or bawd and as her best friend and lover but that the business function was the basis of their continuing association. Economics was at its root, and it would appear that once Baddeley was no longer able to earn, Steele left her. Moreover, the pair bear out the thesis of chapter 7, that to prosper long, one worked for, rather than against, the establishment. Insofar as the pair worked in behalf of fashionable male society, they prospered. Insofar as they were exploitative and subversive of it, they were doomed to eventual failure.

Baddeley, in her brief heydey (1764–71), was one of the most popular of actresses and singers, and from 1769 to 1773 she was probably the most sought-after courtesan in London. Almost totally lacking in discretion, she skirted disaster during those last four years only because of the vigilant management of Steele, who to her role of formal companion added those of watchdog, financial manager, campaign strategist, and publicist. Steele was well paid, taking whopping fees of her own from the men who courted Baddeley as well as from the sums Baddeley collected; in 1773 she was to claim that the money she had advanced to Baddeley (all acquired after 1769) amounted to £3,000—but she was probably exaggerating. It was important to Steele to suggest, in the six volumes of Baddeley's life which she either authored or dictated,[1] that despite Baddeley's dozens of clients, she was emotionally dependent on Steele.

Baddeley had dependency problems, and certainly she was, according to Steele, dependent on her, habitually clinging about her neck and begging not to be deserted. This triadic relationship of bawd, courtesan, and a succession of lovers is a grotesque reflection of the mother-daughter-father relationship described by Chodorow, so satisfactory (and so infantilizing) to the daughter figure.[2] Certainly Steele functioned as a mother figure. She built Baddeley's image as a love goddess and maintained it as long as she could, meting out her favors so as to increase her desirability. Left to herself, Baddeley would probably much sooner have destroyed herself for the beautiful young men she loved and oftener have disdained the rich, ugly, and older ones who provided her fortune. But though it was always the fashion to call her stupid, with "an understanding which has ever been remarkably shallow,"[3] though she certainly lacked discretion, she probably often only "played dumb," cultivating the appearance of a natural who might be easily overreached—after all, she competently memorized and acted a considerable repertory of leading roles. But Steele never could control Baddeley's profligate extravagance, which, no matter what her income, kept her perpetually in enormous debt. The business enterprise of the two women was in the end destroyed by debt.

In the late eighteenth century, the rich children of men who had amassed great fortunes through questionable means often flung away those fortunes as fast as they could. Ste and Charles Fox are examples, and so is Lord Melbourne, Baddeley's principal keeper. Baddeley may have been a victim of the same syndrome: ill gotten, soon gone. The famous twenty-pound-note story usually associated with Fanny Murray and Kitty Fisher has also been told of Baddeley: presented by an admirer with the note (worth $2,000 today), she is said to have shown her contempt for the paltriness of the sum by clapping it between two pieces of bread and eating it.

The registers of St. Margaret's parish provide substantiation for the opening of Steele's tale. Elizabeth Hughes, daughter of John and Antonetha (in later records Antinetta) was born March 24 and baptized April 1, 1741; Sophia Snow, daughter of John and Jane, was born April 16 and baptized April 18, 1746. John Hughes was the king's slater; John (usually called Valentine) Snow was the king's trumpeter. Sophia was born a white-skinned beauty with a fine style of Grecian face and cultivated an "inexpressibly" soft and feminine air. Endowed with a beautiful singing voice with "an enchanting soft tone," she was, says one source, apprenticed young to Michael Arne, himself a child professional singer, son of the composer Dr. Arne.[4] Supposed to be constitutionally lazy and averse to discipline, delighting most in dress, dissipation, and admiration, she probably early acquired the laudanum habit that would destroy her and that made her appear stupid. Certainly she seems never to have developed career ambitions but always to have been reluctantly driven to use her talents by the ambitions of others.

Information about the relationship between the two women comes almost entirely from Baddeley's memoir, published by Steele in 1787, the year after Baddeley's death.[5] The facts Steele presents, when verifiable, are accurate if vague in date, but there is little opportunity to check the validity of Steele's point of view; we must take what she tells us and assess it, aware that she wrote Baddeley's biography for at least two purposes: to titillate and sell copies and to blackmail former clients, who would have had an opportunity before publication to pay to have their names obliterated. If Steele collaborated with a ghostwriter, he may have had a third purpose, to calumniate certain political figures of the Opposition.[6] But what Steele does reveal is probably close to the truth. When she tattles about a client, she tells all she knows, even publishing his letters. What is distorting is that clients who paid up are not mentioned.

The behavior of the two women is sometimes strangely gilded over, sometimes inconsistently interpreted, sometimes ludicrously moralized or bowdlerized, but the narrative is so hastily thrown together that it often reveals more than Steele intended to tell. Baddeley, of course, would have told the story differently; she hated the parental watchdogs that she seems to have needed, and she ran away from her father, her husband, and, more than once, from Steele. Steele dwells on Baddeley's dependence on her, makes much of her deep love for Baddeley, revels in the contempt of the two women for the men who kept them, and outlines the strategies by which she elevated and maintained Baddeley's market value.

Great courtesans need companions;[7] but Steele was more than maid, chaperone, protectress, and receiver of proffers. In the complex relationship between these two women we can see them using men, expressing contempt for them, floating their business in the patriarchal marketplace, and for a time succeeding brilliantly. Their economic and sexual alliance vastly elevated Steele's power.

The names of the two women could almost have been chosen by Samuel Foote for a farce. By marriage Sophia Snow became Sophia Baddeley (pronounced Badly); her friend Elizabeth Hughes by marriage became Steele, suggestive of her manly fortitude and of the pistols she could so effectually flourish. According to Steele (who ignores the five-year difference in their ages) they were inseparable schoolfellows. Steele tells us little else about herself except that she had married and had children before she took Baddeley in hand in 1769.[8]

Baddeley had been designed by her father for the concert stage, perhaps for the opera. Rebelling against his regimen, she eloped, aged about seventeen, in 1763, with the actor Robert Baddeley. He was about thirty, a clever character actor who had begun life as a cook and valet.[9] In many ways fitted to play the mentor to a young actress, he was also a lover of women, unformed for marital fidelity; he may have eloped with Baddeley simply as a way of acquiring a potentially valuable property.

Robert Baddeley first trained his wife and then procured her an engagement at Drury Lane, where in 1764 she made her debut as Ophelia and went on to play many principal parts. The stage was a display case from which men of fashion often plucked the toast of the moment, and some women probably thought of it only as a necessary preliminary to a career of affluence and ease. Robert Baddeley seems to have made small objection to his wife's love affairs, which commenced almost at once, and his principal concern seems to have been that she share her earnings. Her early affair with the wealthy merchant Mendez[10] was more likely to have been arranged by her husband than herself, and he probably saw some pecuniary advantage in those first years even from her affairs with such lovers as the actors John Edwin and Charles Holland and, after Holland's death, with his attending physician, Dr. Hayes. Her husband's satisfaction with such small fry may have derived from his failure to recognize her great potential, from his inability to control her penchant for good-looking men, or from his realization that more powerful lovers would have removed her from the stage and his control.

Holland was said to have been the first man Baddeley truly loved, and he is said to have perfected her acting style, easy and unembarrassed, with an astonishing power to express the passions of love and grief.[11] Her expression of these excesses on and off the stage apparently made her interesting to ever more powerful men, who valued excess in courtesans. According to Steele's account, Baddeley had already had a fling with Edward, Duke of York, when she separated from her husband by 1767; their legal separation, however, took place in 1770, after Steele had decided to make something of her and it therefore became necessary to invalidate any claim her husband might make to her earnings. Sophia Baddeley had an almost lifetime involvement with two brothers, Captain William Hanger[12] and John Hanger, the latter a dependent elder son who was to succeed his father as Lord Coleraine in 1773.[13]

Her involvement with John, her beloved "Gaby," one of her beautiful young men, was by far the more serious. In 1769 Baddeley, with combined Drury Lane and Ranelagh earnings of twenty pounds a week, was domiciled with Gaby Hanger (hereinafter Hanger) and bearing most of the housekeeping expenses; Hanger had underwritten the coach hire. They were already in debt for £700—Hanger was as extravagant as his mistress—when one day he appeared, announced his father had discovered and forbidden the connection, packed up his clothing, and coolly departed, stopping on his way to inform the coachmaster that he was no longer responsible for the carriage (1:30).

This was the traumatic desertion of Baddeley's life. She loved Hanger. She always tended to be stricken with genuine panic when left alone, and she now went directly to an apothecary, bought three hundred drops of laudanum, and swallowed the lot. She was saved by a trio of doctors and Steele, who now—her motives can only be surmised—left her own husband and children, scraped up the money to settle Baddeley's debts, took a house in fashionable St. James's Place convenient to the men's clubs, hired a carriage, and settled herself and Baddeley in.

Steele did all this, she tells us, on no more than a promise from Baddeley "to attend to her business and give up all thoughts of a person from whom she experienced such unmerited treatment" (1:34). Because she can scarcely expect us to believe that her motive was disinterested friendship or that the bankroll was her own, we are free to surmise that Baddeley's business was now officially that of a courtesan. Many of Steele's errors are errors of omission. Who, in this case, supplied the capital and paid the debts? Either a rich keeper had been found, someone who later paid for Steele's silence, or, more likely, a consortium of young clubmen—a group of whom were always welcome in the house— set her up together, as Kitty Fisher, it was reported, had been kept by a subscription of the whole club at Arthur's.[14] In either case, Steele was a necessary part of the arrangement, paid by Baddeley's lovers to keep her in order.

Though Baddeley hated working in the theater, Steele tried to keep her on advantageous view both on stage and in public. In September 1769, for instance, Baddeley made a prestigious appearance in the title role of Arne's opera *Judith* at the Stratford Shakespeare Festival, caused a sensation by her rendition of "Sweet Willy, O!," and continued to sing at Vauxhall and Ranelagh; all that season and the next she played at Drury Lane. At the same time, with Steele driving, she was to be seen dashing about town in a phaeton or at masquerades—the pair went to one dressed as Juliet and her nurse—or in Hyde Park or at Ranelagh, always beautifully dressed and expensively jeweled.

"To keep a restraint on Mrs. Baddeley, was at times a very difficult task," commented Steele (2:109). When the Drury Lane season ended in 1770, Baddeley pranced off to Ireland with her beloved Gaby, who had discovered either that he could not live without her after all or— Steele's explanation of all his advances—that because of her great éclat, he found it gratifying to display to the world his continuing power over her. Steele always hated Hanger as her most dangerous rival, as probably a sharer in Baddeley's earnings, and as the man whose defection had provided her own opportunity in the first place and whose reappearance could often disrupt her arrangements. She had the pleasure of quoting Baddeley to the effect that Gaby was most in love with his own beauty, always strutting before the glass and admiring his leg or his foot or—when no glass was in view in which to approve his face—his hand (5:111).

Steele may have been right. By her account, Hanger frequently sought Baddeley out in public, desiring her attentions as a way of calling attention to himself and his ineluctable fascination. When Baddeley departed for Ireland with him in the summer of 1770 after having promised Steele to give him up, Steele left their house and took another in King's Road, Chelsea. On her return, Baddeley was almost inconsolable at this desertion, "not able to bear a separation from me," offering again to renounce Hanger, "adding, that whatever prosperous situation she might be in, she would share what she had with me, as she was indebted to me for her happiness, and her life, without my esteem and company, would be intolerable" (1:77). She joined Steele in Chelsea, where in the ensuing year they entertained a variety of fashionable lovers. To keep the market up, Steele dismissed any lover who was not fashionable. In general she chose the applicants, professing to frown on such married supplicants as the Dukes of Ancaster and Northumberland. To others Baddeley granted occasional "interviews," and Steele lists such sharers in her favor as John Damer, Lord March, Lord Palmerston, Lord Pigot, and Sir Thomas Mills, who together may have been her consortium (5:168).

Steele must have realized that Baddeley had to be allowed the gratification of her love affairs with the young men who periodically attracted her passionate admiration and to whom she also may have given money. Hanger took his place at times among this group, but between 1769 and 1773 Baddeley was in love for months each with William Fawkener, Thomas Storer, and a handsome young Oxford student, Joseph Gill.[15]

Steele was clever and capitalized on Baddeley's caprices: because eligible men, like the ugly Charles Fox, could be rejected, it became the thing to be found lounging in her drawing room or to be recognized by her in public. "The notice of Mrs. Baddeley was at that day sufficient to give credit and eclat to a man of the ton" (1:71). To be admitted to her house was a great mark of favor. Sometimes Steele took hundreds of pounds and yielded nothing in return. Sometimes a handsome young man, who had suborned a servant to learn when Steele had stepped out, stormed the citadel and took it at once, as Thomas Storer did (3:69–77).

The women found it easy to supply their wants in those golden days. Once John Damer was shown into the drawing room, where he found upon a table a jeweler's box containing diamond earrings and a price ticket of £250. Recognizing a dun when he saw one, he slipped the sum into the box (2:12). Wherever the women went, admirers offered presents. The acceptance of a gift, however trivial, conferred on the donor a momentary ownership, a sense of mastery. Lord Harrington tried to buy her £56 worth of books (refused); Lord Ancaster proffered a £5 pineapple (accepted) (1:160–61).

In 1771 the pair found their greatest single source of supply in the twenty-five-year-old, excessively rich, delightfully independent, and encouragingly foolish—"not the brightest man of the age," said Steele (1:120)—Peniston Lamb, Lord Melbourne. His father, Matthew Lamb, Steele said, had amassed great sums lending money to the needy, had also lent money to the prosperous, and had left his heir over a million pounds.[16] "Money got over the devil's back is spent under his belly," she added (2:204). Melbourne had bought the Hollands' house in Piccadilly for £16,000 and once told Steele that since his twenty-first birthday he had spent £200,000. In 1769 he had married Elizabeth Milbanke, but he was a married man too rich to ignore. Later Steele would ridicule his frequent references to "dear Betsey," quote his injunction to burn his letters, and print eight of them to demonstrate his inelegant command of the language (1:56, 189–99; 2:41).[17] But that was in the future. In the autumn of 1771 his promise of lavish keeping prompted the indolent Baddeley at last to give up her engagement at Drury Lane, whereupon Steele, who had valued Baddeley's cover as actress, pretended to leave her in a dudgeon and took a house in Grafton Street, at or near Bond Street, at £200, purportedly to let out in lodgings (1:120–21). This house was, it transpired, fortunately far more convenient than the Chelsea house to Melbourne's home in Piccadilly, and soon enough the quarrel was made up, Baddeley was forgiven, and she was ensconced in the

Grafton Street house. That autumn she was beautifully painted by Sir Joshua Reynolds at the expense (35 guineas) of Mr. Hanger.[18] Steele was most relieved to discover that "even in this change of circumstances," Baddeley "escaped the tongue of slander" and remained as fashionable as ever (1:121). But it was undoubtedly Steele's doing that in that season of 1771–72 Baddeley continued to sing at Ranelagh.[19]

Melbourne was so prodigal with his money that for eighteen months he must almost have kept pace with Baddeley's expenditures. These were surely all but unparalleled, for Steele remarks that when the Duke of Northumberland toward the end of the period made an offer of £1,500 a year, this was not a quarter of what Melbourne had provided (3:49). At another point she says of this period that she gave good advice and kept expenses under £10,000 a year (2:150).

These were brilliant days. On one famous occasion in January 1772, when the Pantheon, a fashionable new place of amusement, had opened and the managers had announced their determination to keep out women of dubious character, Captain William Hanger led an army of young military men brandishing swords to force Baddeley's entrance.[20] It was an adventure worth a fortune in publicity, and besides, it had been necessary to gain Baddeley's free access to this new arena for display. Steele may well have been the general behind this exploit, but it was Baddeley who had triumphantly entered the breach, and her heroic leadership procured entrée to the Pantheon for all the fashionable men's favorite women whom the society women had been determined to exclude. In a May masquerade there, one celebrated bawd, Mrs. Mitchell, appeared as a fruitwoman attended by three nosegay girls, while another, Mrs. Kelly, was a lady abbess surrounded by her nuns.[21] Baddeley attended a June masquerade as the celebrated dancer Madam Heinel wearing a shockingly short skirt that displayed a great deal of stocking.[22]

Always on duty and at Melbourne's disposal when he was in town, the two women enjoyed themselves most thoroughly during their "holidays," when he went with Betsey to a watering place, but at any time their pace was hectic. Steele drove them about town in their phaeton always at a full gallop, which Baddeley called "going like herself" (4:165). When they traveled, they went night and day at the full gallop with four horses. According to Steele's account, they might return from Ranelagh or the Pantheon at three in the morning, change clothes and go off alone in the phaeton together for ten or twelve miles to breakfast, spend the morning at exhibitions or auctions, then take airings in Hyde

Park, dress, go to the play, Ranelagh, supper, and Epsom for breakfast, and keep up this pace for five or six days in succession (4:163). These public exhibitions of Baddeley's excesses were symbolically important as advertisements of her impassioned and reckless nature.

Steele appears necessarily to have turned a blind eye toward Baddeley's penchant for beautiful (and impoverished) young men; in her affairs with them, perhaps Baddeley purified herself by giving herself freely or gratified herself by reversing the roles of benefactor and sexual object. Steele enjoyed these flings vicariously or took pleasure in betraying Baddeley's keeper and participated or colluded in some of Baddeley's excursions. Baddeley always made the most of her "holidays," but the two women practiced the worst of their indiscretions out of town, away from their suborned servants. Though in the hire of Baddeley's keeper, Steele enjoyed spiriting Baddeley away to the suburbs for a rebellious frolic, and the two spoke of their clients privately with ridicule and vindictive scorn.

On occasion, the pair enjoyed humiliating a man. The Neapolitan ambassador, unlike true Protestant English gentlemen, was embarrassed by his entrée to the house and always responded to a knock on the door by running to hide himself. One day while he was with them, they arranged for a servant to knock on the door and say Lord March had come. The ambassador ran into the back parlor, where the women crammed him into a cupboard closet so tight that he could not turn around and left him there for half an hour while they laughed till their sides ached. Then the servant slammed the outer door as though March had departed, and they released their diffident visitor. Thereafter Baddeley liked to play the role of the Neapolitan ambassador, a rendition climaxed by cramming herself into the closet. Melbourne too relished the tale, saying to Steele that day when he departed (which take for a specimen of his wit), "Be sure, Steele, keep off all the d——ned dogs till my return, and put the ambassador under lock and key" (4:38–42).

At times Steele seems almost to vaunt the sexual nature of the women's relationship. She had left husband and children to live with Baddeley, though her daughter was at school nearby and had moved in with the women by 1773; the child, probably as a maid (and as Steele's spy), also went to Ireland with Baddeley that year. Steele was careful, however, to lodge her husband and her other children in a house at Henley (at £20 a year), a safe distance from their own arena. She had, and cultivated, a masculine appearance. One of her anecdotes is of a time when she and Baddeley were traveling in France and an innkeeper's daughter, pre-

sumably influenced by the relationship of the two women, became convinced that Steele was a man traveling in disguise in woman's dress and
fell madly in love with her (2:67). Baddeley mischievously encouraged
the girl in her passion until she turned up in Steele's bed and had to be
appeased with a present—a riding crop. There is something amiss about
this tale; it is far more feasible that Steele was actually traveling disguised as a man, for the protection of both women and for convenience.
She affected men's dress, sometimes adopting it for masquerades. Once
she went dressed in a domino with a man's hat and feather; returning
home from another masquerade, she used her truncheon, an adjunct of
her costume, to beat off an assailant. During the worst of their financial
troubles, she once escaped from the bailiffs disguised as a man (6:108–
10). She envisioned herself as an intrepid male. In the summer of 1773,
when to escape her debts Baddeley had stolen secretly to Ireland with the
notorious Colonel Luttrell accompanied by a woman relation of Steele's
as companion, the Danish husband of the companion, exacerbated by
secrecy, demanded at pistol point knowledge of the whereabouts of his
wife. Steele first challenged the Dane to a duel, then took his pistol,
threatened to shoot him, and at last threw it into the street, whereupon
the Dane remarked that she was fitter to be a man than a woman (5:53–
56). Steele's pleasure in recounting the compliment underscores her affectation of male virtues, and she consistently reports her own behavior
to have been firm, courageous, decisive, unintimidated—and manly.

The pair habitually slept together; Steele notes as an exception that
they never slept together on the road (2:71).[23] At home Baddeley could
sleep in a separate chamber only by pleading a headache. She was prone
to headaches. Baddeley, totally resistant to being owned or ruled, was
incapable of fidelity to anyone, and she enjoyed deceiving Steele with
the beautiful young man of the moment. By feigning a headache she
could stay at home while Steele went out and then send word to her
lover to come. On at least one occasion when Steele had to go out alone,
she foiled Baddeley by putting her under the hands of the hairdresser,
a three-hour procedure, and placing a book in her hand. But Baddeley
often managed successful exploits that produced moods of the greatest
glee. On one notable day she enjoyed a delicious infidelity with Thomas
Storer in the morning while Steele was out and in the evening insisted
on going, with Steele's daughter as sole companion, to the women's villa
in Hammersmith to meet the Duke of Northumberland, who turned
out, not unexpectedly, to be so persistent that she yielded to him too (3:
80–86). Because she was still under the protection of Melbourne, and

Steele was paid to be watchdog, this latter was a significant infidelity, which is probably why Steele had carefully dissociated herself from it. The women had taken care that the interview should occur away from Grafton Street but had not considered that Melbourne and Northumberland may have been in collusion to effect a change of keepers, for just at this time Northumberland made generous offers and Melbourne began to prove unforthcoming.

Steele iterates again and again Baddeley's declarations of dependence on her, apparently savoring them. Ignoring the evidence of Baddeley's predilection for dashing young men, she likes to make such claims as that Baddeley "traversed the gay scenes of life, with a heart disengaged from the trammels of love" (1:22). Baddeley's inconsolable response to the loss of Steele when in the summer of 1770 Baddeley went off to Ireland with Gaby and Steele moved to Chelsea was quoted above. When Baddeley quitted Drury Lane in the autumn of 1771 and Steele moved to Grafton Street, Baddeley assured her "that life would be insupportable" without her (1:119). On returning from a naughty excursion with John Damer, Baddeley with a headache rode with him in his carriage while Steele, alone beside them, drove the phaeton in which they had come. Later Baddeley asked pardon for her defection by crying, hanging round Steele's neck, and begging her to swear she would never leave her. " 'When you was from me in the phaeton,' said she, 'I thought my heart would have broke; I looked at you so often, and thought I was without all I valued upon earth' " (5:55–59). Given her usual reason for recourse to a headache, she was probably more absorbed by Damer than she cared to acknowledge, but her avowals at least reveal her need of Steele's continued countenance. When they parted, Baddeley was apt to sob like a child, and she refused to stay in Ireland with Colonel Luttrell in 1773 unless Steele would come there too (4:214–15, 240). On her return to England she again hung round Steele's neck: "I have got you again, my dear Steele, and nothing shall ever part us, even for an instant" (5:60). And so on, culminating in Baddeley's proposal to Steele that they share their fate thenceforward together, for "as to the men, I have been deceived by them, and will endeavour to be even with them, some way or other" (5:175).

Steele too is full of protestations of devotion. Her love for Baddeley was so great that she would endure ruin or give up her life for her (5:205); she had given up her little fortune, forsaken her husband, neglected her family for Baddeley "and given her myself, and would now give up my life, if necessary, to serve her," she averred in their worst troubles (5:221). Baddeley's avowal when she left Steele at last for Stephen Sayre was prophetic: "Life to me without you, will not be worth having" (6:129). Both women were ill for some time after that crucial separation.

Their best of times ended in 1773, when Melbourne, tired of disbursing, racked up the total of Baddeley's expenses and was appalled. He had been prodigal with her, eager to anticipate her demands. To Steele he might say, "So . . . have you not laid out all your cash?" and Steele would reply, "No, my Lord," while Baddeley frowned at her (2:143). The two women had the Grafton Street house, a house at Brighton, and the villa at Hammersmith. When Baddeley wanted anything she had only to say, "My Lord, I wish for such and such a thing, but Mrs. Steele tells me it is extravagant," and Melbourne would reply, "Pray, Mrs. Steele, say nothing about it; I shall not refuse her sweet face any thing" (2:164). But in 1773 Melbourne's money ceased to flow, and as Baddeley continued to compound debts at the old rate, refusing to retrench, the situation grew serious.

Northumberland, an eager suitor, no doubt apprised by Melbourne of his fair chance, now presented retainers of £1,000 to Baddeley and £700 to Steele (3:87–88). The pair might have made a smooth transition to his protection but hesitated fatally at his proffered budget of only £1,500 a year. The duke may also have taken warning when they spent his retainers, which would have been sufficient to pay off nearly half of Baddeley's acknowledged debts. Steele claims she begged the money might go to their creditors but Baddeley insisted the creditors must wait for Melbourne to pay them; she determined to enjoy her money on a jaunt to Portsmouth. Actually it was almost a business necessity to be present at this great event of the summer of 1773, when the king reviewed the fleet and everyone came to watch—and Baddeley was triumphantly established as the personal guest of Admiral Spry and dined every day on his ship.[24] Steele used £130 of her own share to buy Baddeley a pair of bracelets, perhaps to wear on this occasion (3:97–99). In imminent danger of arrest for debt, Baddeley decamped incognito (as "the Hon. Mrs. Steele") to Ireland with Colonel Luttrell that summer, leaving Steele to try to get Melbourne to disburse. Hanger had in the meantime succeeded, as Lord Coleraine, to the family title, but his fortune was spent. Determined to recover the vanished Baddeley, he at last found her in Ireland and dickered with Luttrell. If Baddeley would come back with him to England, he would pay her debts, settle £500 a year on her, and agree never to cohabit; he gave her £500 earnest money, which he had privately determined was all she should ever see. Luttrell agreed but privately arranged with Baddeley that once Coleraine had paid her debts, she would return again to him (5:89–90, 98–99). The conclusion that each man was using Baddeley in an attempt to best the other is compelling and reinforces the notion that the important point of owning the current toast was based on much the same sort of motive.

Back in London Coleraine confined Baddeley, beat her, informed her he would never pay her debts, and, as an alternative solution to her problem, tried to force her to depart with him for France (5:110). Baddeley had fallen prey to Coleraine again and again, even after his first desertion. Throughout the subsequent years, he had beaten her when he could, threatened both women, and once, probably when she was on the manly defense, knocked out one of Steele's teeth (2:138). But the 1773 adventure apparently ended the affair; or perhaps soon thereafter Baddeley, ceasing to be a toast and no longer lavishly generous with her riches, ceased to be an object worthy of her lover's attention.[25]

The women were again in London together, their debts still unpaid, in the autumn of 1773. They now put their affairs into the hands of a man who was almost undoubtedly a new lover, Mr. P., a financial adviser.[26] For some time P., enjoying the situation and perhaps hopeful of forcing Melbourne to disburse, handled the problem so that Baddeley and Steele felt reasonably secure; but at length, unable any longer to stave off their arrest, he persuaded them (Steele says) to sign a note, which resulted in their arrest at his own hands.

In this extremity, neither Melbourne nor Coleraine would assist. A friend to whom Steele extends anonymity got up a subscription for them at his club, to which Charles Fox, the rejected admirer, allegedly put a stop. If the women hoped for a time that their old consortium might come to their aid, their enormous debts provided an insuperable obstacle. John Damer gave them £300 and borrowed another £200 for them.[27] Several respected noblemen subscribed a few pounds each. Baddeley, in a panic, declared she would accept any offer whatsoever, a development that moved Steele delicately to beg that she should never be informed of the issue of such a resolve (6:38–39).

Steele's moral indignation was typically reserved for any slip unworthy of the dignity of a great courtesan or of the devotion of her followers. There was a certain esprit to be maintained by a woman of Baddeley's status, and Steele had always been the confident arbitress and upholder of that esprit. She had fought once to keep Baddeley on the stage and had managed at least to keep her occasionally on the concert platform. Now she knew that Baddeley must not fall into the hands of the wrong class of lovers. The pair had miscalculated in their dealings with the Duke of Northumberland, setting Baddeley's value too high, and ought not to have made the same mistake again; but they did. The Duke of Bolton, inquiring as to the amount of the debts with a mind to settle them, was informed that Baddeley owed £4,000 and an additional £3,000 to Steele, who had advanced her own "fortune" to assist her friend. The duke's natural conclusion was that Baddeley came too dear. Next the women listened to the advances of Mr. Mordecai, a financier, who, on hearing only of the £4,000, withdrew in horror (6:57).

Shaken by these rejections and in desperation, Baddeley now entertained an offer from the handsome and charming Stephen Sayre, an American republican, an associate of John Wilkes, a banking partner in the London firm of Sayre and Purdon, and, fortuitously, in the year 1773 a sheriff of London, who could not pay her debts but could undertake to protect her from arrest. Steele no doubt argued that if Baddeley left the polite world, she could never expect to reenter it. This was a waste: Baddeley, only twenty-seven, might have hoped to enjoy many more years of prosperity. But frightened and in need of protection which Steele could no longer provide, Baddeley fled to Sayre's house in Cleveland Row, St. James's, effecting the separation from her friend which she had sworn never should occur. Steele took and let out two houses in lodgings.

The separation of the two women was prolonged. Baddeley had at least one child by Sayre, who, unable to support her extravagance, collected funds for the payment of her debts from Melbourne and other former friends, but, according to Steele, kept the money himself (though probably to maintain Baddeley). Then, while she was pregnant, in February 1775, the thirty-eight-year-old Sayre effected one of those desertions which Baddeley could not handle psychologically; he married Elizabeth Noel, a forty-seven-year-old London heiress. He moved Baddeley out of his house and into a house at £25 a year "in a by-street, adjourning Rathbone-place, in order to be near him and to save expenses" (6:145). There, very near term, she fell into a state of living in total darkness, without a fire, unable to bear the least noise. She could neither eat nor drink, and she saw no one but Dr. Hunter, who, though unpaid, attended her daily. "At intervals she would talk, but it was only of me, and the love she bore me; that she fancied herself a supernatural being, and sometimes a China jar" (6:146). Her laudanum addiction was evidently serious.

Steele, who had been out of town, reached Baddeley's bedside when she had been in this condition for two months. At the sound of Steele's voice in the darkness, Baddeley cried out for candles so as to see her friend, "and as soon as I was known, she threw herself forwards, kissed me, and clung round my neck." Steele stayed the night and next day wrapped Baddeley up and took her home to nurse her back to health. Baddeley returned to her little house and Sayre's protection for the birth of her child, but Steele says she paid for the necessities. Steele attended her through the birth, and at the end of Baddeley's month took a house for her in Chelsea ("for which I paid forty pounds a year"), "and all this I did in opposition to my friends, who would not have done any thing for me, had they known it" (6:151). Steele says she hired a coach and horses for Baddeley, went every day to see her, and lent her money.

In 1774 Baddeley had returned to the stage, and now she and Steele labored to retrieve their former successes. But their offers were no longer from men of the first fashion; Baddeley had begun the traditional descent through the hands of men ever less influential. One favored lover was Henry Bate, editor of the *Morning Post*. Rude shocks were constantly administered. "Mr Petrie, a Scotch gentleman,"[28] offered a settlement of just £100 a year, which Baddeley tore up only after she had realized that he was engaging for exclusive possession (6:155). Toward the end of 1775, Steele, having given up, left London for almost a year.

In the meantime, with the American war impending, Sayre had been imprisoned in the Tower in October 1775, accused of having plotted to seize the king, take the Tower, and overthrow the government.[29] Once released, he and Purdon filed for bankruptcy in November 1776 and disappeared from Baddeley's life. Through correspondence Steele learned that Baddeley had gone to the actor William Brereton for protection and from him had acquired a venereal disease and that she had next gone to live with the actor-singer Anthony Webster. With Webster Baddeley had three more children and a happy relationship, but in the spring of 1780 he died. All this time she had continued on the stage, but she had lost her looks: Burney's brother Charles in this year describes a beauty with a face "which might enslave a Hermit—it is what Mrs Baddeley's was 12 years ago—before she grew fat."[30]

Steele found Baddeley in the latter part of 1780 in a small house in Pimlico ("twenty-five pounds a year") just delivered of Webster's posthumous child and attended by John, Webster's manservant, "a man genteelly dressed in black; black silk waistcoat and breeches, and a pair of black silk stockings, with his hair well-dressed" (6:166–67). Stupefied by grief at Webster's death, Baddeley confessed to Steele, she had drunk too much brandy at a friend's instigation and had wakened next morning to find John in her bed. "To add to all this," confessed Baddeley, "I am fool enough to like him, in preference to all men" (6:172). The women wept at Baddeley's now irreversible descent, and Baddeley cried, "Oh! my dear Steele, had you been with me, nothing of this kind would ever have happened!" Steele assured her that she loved her still and never would forsake her but to us confides, "This conduct of her's, hurt me beyond measure: to see her attached to a low-bred fellow, not possessed of a shilling, nor in any way to earn his bread, but as a servant; to think that she should thus fall from her splendor, to take up at last, with a man of this stamp, cut me to the soul" (6:180–81). And now Baddeley was dropped by Drury Lane; she had played her last London role. Her anonymous 1780 biographer described her as "scarcely half a degree removed from an idiot. Her eyesight is decayed, her memory extinct, and her whole frame relaxed to a degree of almost infantine imbecillity, by a dreadful and excessive indulgence in love, liqour, lust, and laudanum."[31] Her fall had not gone unnoted, and she was depicted in another popular pamphlet as a portrait of Lais, a wanton female, "the most alluring courtezan of Sicily," but with proportionately exorbitant demands. "An affected innocence of manners, well expressed by the *virgin blush* which at the same time softens her complexion, is the grand object. . . . The back scene is so desolately naked, that . . . we must suppose the good fortune of Lais to have existed only for a period."[32]

She was living with a man who, like Robert Baddeley, had been a servant and hoped to turn actor, and she began to train him as Robert Baddeley had once trained her. Money collected from friends, including Steele, enabled her to take John with her to Ireland in the autumn of 1780 for an acting engagement. "Something tells me," she said to her friend, "I shall never see you more." Apparently Steele intended her readers to assume that they never did see each other more. She may have occupied herself during the women's separation as a bawd. A November 1782 print of a subject identified in an annotation on one of its states as "Miss Steele" depicts a squat woman playing the ace of hearts for money (three guineas lie before her), a concealed spider (to trap flies) dangling from the back of her cap. Though there is no certainty, this may be a portrait of Baddeley's friend—there is no other possible subject named Steele known. If so, Steele may sometimes have had other women under her management, especially during Baddeley's absence.

But although Baddeley never again returned to England, the faithful

Steele had rejoined her by the time she went to play for Tate Wilkinson in Edinburgh in 1783. In that year Wilkinson took her with his company to perform for a week at York Spring Meeting, where she performed with great credit until the last night, when she appeared incapacitated by the laudanum she was then taking in "incredible" quantities. Wilkinson, defending his own fair practice as company manager, noted that though Baddeley was well paid, she was a beggar when it came time to return to Edinburgh; but her friend "Mrs. Stell" was with her, "who I fancy had always occasion for such sums as that unfortunate woman received."[33] It would appear that Steele had a reputation for exploiting Baddeley, and she certainly would now have had no problem in stripping her of her earnings. It is not clear when she finally left Baddeley, who died a pauper in Edinburgh in July 1786, aged just forty. Prematurely old, lame, stupefied by her laudanum habit, she had in her final year been incapable of work and had been supported by the actors' charity.

Despite Steele's vaunted attitude of independence and her pretense to resources of her own, her system of leasing and furnishing houses and letting out lodgings, and the likelihood that her houses were houses of assignation or brothels, she was far from prosperous when she undertook her last project, the compiling and publication of Baddeley's memoirs. Probably she had waited for Baddeley's death to unearth the letters she had carefully preserved, her property in which Baddeley could have disputed. Discreet offers must have been made to many old connections prescribing the terms of her silence. Undoubtedly some men did pay. The book was noticed in the reviews for June and July 1787: "the Memoirs of a frail fair one, communicated by her *friend* and *companion*. . . . The peace of families wantonly sported with."[34]

Steele, who published the memoir for herself, evidently failed to earn enough to retrieve her poor circumstances. She was being hunted for a forgery "committed on a respectable [commercial] house in the city,"[35] was ill, and was in hiding at the Dolphin Inn in Bishopsgate Street when she died there on November 14, 1787; she survived Baddeley by only sixteen months. When her identity was discovered, the old man who had brought her to the inn and had called himself her husband denied any connection with her. She had died after two weeks "in the most extreme agonies and distress," perhaps a suicide, and was buried in Bishopsgate Churchyard, "in a manner rather better than a common pauper."[36]

Not entirely unreasonably, in the "Conclusion" to her tale Steele attributed Baddeley's fate to the viciousness of men. Had Robert Baddeley, she thought, proved a kind and protective husband instead of a

pimp; had Hanger, whom Baddeley deeply loved, not taken her money
and decamped when it was gone; had others lived up to their engagements. . . . And she makes much of Baddeley's tender, loving capacities, though her brief that given the right husband Baddeley would have
proved faithful and never looked elsewhere is not convincing, considering her unstable and inflammatory nature. Underlying all is her conviction that Baddeley was at least safe with her, that the pair had successfully outwitted the men at least for a time, and that Baddeley's talents,
if managed properly, were such as to render her worthy of the world's
homage she had once had. In Steele's view, the inevitable result of a
woman's putting herself into the power of a lover (by living with him—
the ultimate foolhardiness) was a slide toward debilitating lyings-in,
cruel mistreatment, and, in the end, impoverishment.

Janet Todd has noted that manipulative love thrives on displays of
sentiment and is rich in tears and long embraces.[37] Steele inadvertently
makes clear that her relationship with Baddeley was one of manipulative love. Both women were morally immature, selfish, cunning, and
devious. Both were users of others. In their own relationship they capitalized on the possibilities of the tyrant-toady game, Steele playing the
patriarch, like a husband ruling Baddeley and choosing and profiting
from her lovers, while Baddeley played the cajoling, submissive, deceiving, and manipulative wife. At the same time both pretended to the
most delicate sensibility. Baddeley may not have been very clever: the
Town and Country Magazine in 1772 judged her personal attractions to
be overbalanced by "a total want of sentiment [sense], and insipidity in
her conversation, which her admirers are good-natured enough to mistake for simplicity; though the frequent murders she commits upon the
English language sufficiently indicate her want of mental abilities."[38]
An incompetence caused by her addictions might account for her lapses
as well as for her great dependency upon whoever happened to be in
charge.[39] Unluckily, torn between her greedy desire to live luxuriously,
which she could fulfill only by putting herself in Steele's hands and submitting to a pretense of passion for men who did not please her, and her
evident self-contempt for such pretense, which she could combat only
by yielding herself in genuine passion to the poor young men who attracted her, she settled into a way of life in which she swung between
her two conflicting objects—and took opium.

Though Steele's ascendancy and influence over Baddeley probably
depended much on an ability to play the role of the strong and protective
male—quite apart from any sexual alliance between them—another

basis for her power was her ability to make and keep up the best market for Baddeley's wares. The two prospered only by working together.

For a while they appear to have beaten the odds, and the splendid times Steele remembers are usually those when the women were together, alone. But, like the other female coalitions against the patriarchy examined in this book—the Parrs and Mitissa, her mother, and maid—this one too was doomed to ultimate failure. By skillfully keeping up Baddeley's market for a longer period, by avoiding debt, and by putting away money for a modest retirement, the women might have triumphed; but the women elevated by the fashionable male world were deliberately chosen precisely for the recklessness and extravagance of nature that made them reckless and extravagant lovers and displayers of their charms and also made dull prudence impossible to them. Almost all died in a poverty, disorder, and disease that may gratifyingly have signified to the men where, in sober fact and despite the seeming ascendancy of such women, the real power and superiority had always resided. In truth, the women of honor elevated into high fashion by men of fashion were not so much successful career women as clay pigeons tossed sportively up to be shot down in gratification of a pervasive misogyny, counters assigned an arbitrary value for the duration of a game so that the men might vie for possession in yet another contest with one another. The courtesans were intricately enmeshed in a system for controlling and denigrating women even when they seemed in the greatest ascendancy. They were used for punishing those less obliging and possibly less hypocritical women of their keepers' domestic circles, and when they took their elevation seriously, they were punished themselves. It might therefore have been delightful to have seen these women triumph, but it would have been most unlikely. The women chosen for "the game" were not the kind to comprehend it fully. Despite Steele's self-vaunted altruism (a pose not too seriously or consistently kept up), the pair were at heart manipulative users who, like the Parrs, Mitissa, and other preyers on the establishment, only seemed for a time to have triumphed—and subsequently paid for their ambitions.

Of the women to be examined in the final four chapters of this book, all are altruists. When paired, they present models of more or less equal relationships, models of the way in which women, empowered to make their own choices, might also design their marriages. Yet these relationships, anything but dull, differ in a great number of ways.

Chapter Ten

THE DOMESTIC TRIANGLE: THE VESEYS AND HANDCOCK

ALL HAPPY mistress-companion relationships were not happy in the same way. Elizabeth Vesey and her sister-in-law Handcock were probably equal in power, but their complementarity, at first fortuitous, grew absolute, binding them to each other in need. Handcock and Mr. Vesey confined Vesey to perpetual girlhood as Anne Fannen and Fox did Lady Holland.

As with Lord and Lady Holland, Agmondesham and Elizabeth Vesey seemed very much a couple and might easily be misread as partners in a good, "companionate" marriage. But the notion of a close couple living with the wife's companion suggests tension, especially when, as in the Veseys' case, the companion is genteel enough to be a perpetual witness. The wife is tête-à-tête first with the one, then with the other. To the wife the companion is a constant resource, as indirectly she is to the husband as well, if he wants (as Henry Fox and Agmondesham Vesey did) freedom from domestic attendance. Such a triangle might ameliorate marital grievance but must almost certainly weaken the marital bond.

The wife was the companion's first consideration, but in the presence of the husband both wife and companion had to bow to a superior consideration. The husband felt their alliance and knew that the more he availed himself of their preoccupation with each other, the more he kept his affairs to himself, the more likely they would be to discuss him together and to pry. If he could not subvert the companion with his money, power, or sexuality, the best he might manage would be an indifference to the two women and their concerns. Even if the companion were very useful to him in liberating him from wifely demands upon his attention, he might resent her for fortifying his wife above the usual defenseless condition of women. For Mr. Vesey, Handcock may have been all the more irritating because as the sister of Vesey's first husband she was a witness to and relict of that earlier marriage; or he may have been irritated because through her superb competence she rendered his wife increasingly incompetent, increasingly childlike. She probably irritated him for another reason: it is reasonable to assume, from an acquaintance with Mr. Vesey, that he attempted Handcock's virtue, and from an acquaintance with Handcock, that she calmly and without ado rebuffed him.

If the relationship for Mr. Vesey had its irritating aspects, for his wife it must have represented all that it did for Lady Holland and for the Duchess of Devonshire: a recreation of the familial triangle, father, mother, and daughter, which satisfied but seems in all cases to have infantilized the wife. That she had no children by either of her husbands confirmed Vesey in her role as charming, impulsive child, and the efficiency of Handcock, who found her own vocation in managing Vesey's practical affairs, sealed her fate.

The paucity of information about Handcock is amusing and revealing. A record of information about a spinster is useless to patriarchal archives, and I cannot determine which of William Handcock's sisters— Susanna, Dorothy, or Abigail—she was. Information about William Handcock, Vesey's first husband, is meager, for having left neither descendants nor a significant estate, he too is of small interest. He was William Handcock of Willbrook in Westmeath, Esq., member of Parliament for the Irish borough of Fore.[1] His sister was attractive in her youth, when she was dubbed "Fair Tranquillity." She had no great fortune, and what she had was probably converted, in her spinsterhood, into an annuity of about £200.[2] That sum made it convenient for her to live with someone, for it was exactly calculated to enable her to live politely if she could spend it on herself. By temperament she was cheerful, practical, self-abnegating, and self-sacrificing, such a notable woman that it seems odd no one insisted on marrying her. Hymen's loss was Vesey's gain. Handcock and Vesey gradually developed (or shrank) into two halves of a whole, Handcock dubbed by their friends "Body" and Vesey "Soul." Handcock, though full of admirable domestic expedients and salutary advice, never indulged in the feminine passion for letter writing, whereas Vesey was writing perpetually. Vesey's impracticality and unregulated fancy required constant restraint by Handcock's good sense and matter-of-factness.

Vesey's more usual name among her friends, "The Sylph," is another reference to her antithetical character to that of "Body." Clearly the women, and not the married couple, came to make up the primary unit. And Mr. Vesey, left to himself, which he preferred, had full license to confirm and develop his natural tendencies toward selfishness, inconsiderateness, self-indulgence, autocracy, and social success; in time he became known to Vesey's friends as "The Monster," or "The Grand Turk." It is possible that although he appreciated having his wife otherwise occupied than with himself, he disliked her having other resources.

Elizabeth Vesey was born about 1715, probably in Ireland, the youngest daughter of Sir Thomas Vesey, bishop of Ossory, and the descendant of an ancient family. Her mother, Mary Muschamp, had been an heiress.[3] Vesey was a small but lovely girl, and her loveliness survived for a long time unfaded. Even when she was forty-six, in about 1761, Laurence Sterne wrote to her "That you are graceful, & elegant & most desirable &c. &c. every common beholder, who only stares at You as a dutch Boore does at the Queen of Sheba in a puppit Show can readily find out; But that You are sensible, and gentle and tender—& from end to the other of you full of the sweetest tones & modulations, requires a Connoisseur of more taste & feeling—in honest truth You are a System of harmonic Vibrations—You are the sweetest and best tuned of all Instruments—O Lord! I would give away my other Cassoc to touch you."[4]

With a handsome dowry, beauty, charm, and spirit, Elizabeth Vesey was a catch, and she married young. Delany encountered her at a Dublin ball in December 1731 and noted, "Mrs. Hancock's husband is so jealous of her, that she must not dance with an unmarried man."[5] She must have been a flirt, for she flirted all her life, and it seems probable that her husband installed his sister in the household as, if not a spy, a form of ballast. It would be like Vesey to convert the sister to a devoted friend. She had no children with William Handcock, who died in 1741. His sister presided over Vesey for forty-eight years thereafter.

However Handcock arrived at her position in the Vesey household, she probably was early established as Vesey's *gouvernante*. Delany, married to Patrick Delany and living at Delville in Ireland, saw the trio on January 25, 1746: "Last Sunday Mr. and Mrs. Vesey (Mrs. Handcock that was), Miss Handcock, and Mrs. Marley came to dine. I found them in my garden when I came from church."[6] On October 14, 1748, the Delanys returned home from Dangan by way of Lucan, the Vesey estate, and called at two hoping to dine with the Veseys, who, however, were in Dublin. As they turned to depart, Handcock called after them, inviting them to eat a bit of mutton with her. Presiding over her modest meal of a shoulder of mutton and potatoes, Handcock was an emblem of the gentlewomanly companion dining in Spartan fashion at the family's table (2:503). A few days later the Veseys and Handcock went to Delville to stay so as to escape workmen laboring at Lucan; another fine line drawn establishes Handcock as of the family rather than as the housekeeper left at home to cope with the renovations. Fair Tranquillity was still young enough to be "Miss Handcock" when she and the Veseys spent the day at Delville in March 1752 (3:104).

Vesey's vagaries in those early days are not as well chronicled as those of her later life, but she was apparently always spontaneous, impulsive, easily distracted, with a short attention span, and greedily eager for the next treat while dashing from pleasure to pleasure, yet delightfully kind and considerate. In February 1751 the Delanys had set off early to breakfast with the Veseys at Lucan but met them in a coach and four en route to Dublin. Both conveyances stopped, and Vesey insisted on joining the Delanys in their chaise, which had already incorporated one extra passenger on a stool, to return home with them. "Open the door, John," said Vesey to the Delanys' driver. "For what? There is no room for you here." "No matter, I'll find room." Vesey flew into the chaise, the stool's occupant whisked into the dean's lap, and Vesey "nestled herself in so cleverly they had room enough" (3:20). In June Delany found Vesey at Lucan with a whim "to have Indian figures and flowers cut out and oiled, to be transparent, and pasted on her dressing-room windows in imitation of painting on glass," and helped her finish the project (3:39). Already Delany had dubbed Vesey a sylph, protesting that the spirits of the air protected Lucan in a windstorm (3:21). Life at Lucan in those days, Delany thought, was so friendly, easy, and without restraint that it was the place she liked best to be after her own home; she thought they said and did there just as they liked (3:151–52).

Vesey's continuing childlessness helped to maintain her sylphhood; with Handcock to supervise the housekeeping and manage her sister-in-law as well, Vesey had nothing to do except ineptly to coddle her husband and fuss over the ailments of all three and deftly to exercise her social talents. As the years passed, she grew more and more restless; London became increasingly necessary to her; and the trio began their more or less habitual pattern of spending the Irish parliamentary winters (in the odd years) at Lucan or in Dublin and the seasons of the alternate years in London. In London they leased houses in Clarges Street, Bolton Row, then Clarges Street again. At first the Veseys went on almost humbly, almost like obliging protégés of the great Earl and Countess of Kildare, who dominated Irish political life. In May 1759, when Lady Emily Kildare was decorating Carton, the grand new country palace (a project that also kept Anne Fannen busy), the earl, in London, delivered a sheet of Indian wallpaper to Vesey for her to match which ought instead to have gone to his sister-in-law Lady Louisa. But Handcock went off into the city in search of the paper, and, despite dire predictions that the paper could not be matched in England, found two good sheets and had determined upon a second foray "to the last and only place that she had not been at, where there was the least chance of getting any." Lady Emily set the earl, who was oblivious to the hierarchical ranking and respective obligations of women, right as to her original designee for the commission, but, pleased by Handcock's thorough efficiency, noted that if the Veseys had not meant to set out again for Dublin, she should have employed Handcock next about some painted taffeta.[7]

Handcock's sterling qualities had not gone unnoted, and probably during the Irish winter Lady Emily made a closer acquaintance with them. In October 1760, back in London, Vesey lent her to Emily Kildare's (and Lady Caroline Fox's) sister-in-law "Lady George" Lennox for her lying-in. Lady Caroline, who had an eye for such a woman, reported, "I like her of all things; how beautiful and how like Patsy [Emily] she is! She is very pleasing I think, and seems a mighty rational good kind of body to be with them; she is quite an acquisition to the house" (1:298). Handcock stayed with the Lennoxes for a month at least, and in early November Lady Caroline went to court with her—something she could never have done with Fannen and an excellent indication of Handcock's social status and her great value to Vesey. Handcock's heart, characteristically, remained at home with her charge. She had left Lady George laughing and was chagrined on her return to find her patient just getting into bed, where in three-quarters of an hour she was delivered. She had probably gone to court only to oblige and escort Lady Caroline and she was rueful about having misjudged the situation (1:302). Vesey, though perhaps not without some tact and dexterity, managed to retrieve her treasure.

As the long Vesey marriage wore on, it deteriorated from that pleasant early state extolled by Delany. In general Vesey's friends were calculatedly reticent about her husband, whom they found vain, superficial, and profligately faithless. A great-grandson of Charles II through Charles's daughter, the sister of the Duke of Monmouth, he prided himself on his breeding, which kept him tame in domestic bounds. Vesey's friends flattered him, or, like Montagu, carried on flirtations with him, to ensure that he would continue to bring his wife to England for all their sakes. In his later years they concealed their contempt for his "septuagesimal gallantry"[8] and his susceptibility to their manipulation. Montagu was besought by Vesey in May 1781 to "sprinkle some of your intoxicating enchantment upon Mr Vesey that he may not return to Lucan, with the determination of forever."[9]

In the 1760s Vesey, who had gained entrance to Montagu's bluestockings and was equally passionately fond, in her own way, of talk, seized upon the idea and began to establish herself as hostess of her own conversation parties. All the women loved her, and all therefore contrived at her behest to make her husband feel at least equally delightful. Vesey's greatest coup along these lines was to arrange her husband's election in 1773 to Johnson's Club, an endeavor in which she was abetted by Montagu.[10] His considerable elevation of spirits and status after his election ensured their longer and longer sojourns in London.

Agmondesham Vesey was indeed good-humored, sensible, and well-bred, but he was at his best as an acquaintance. In 1774 Elizabeth Carter summed him up as a person of many amiable qualities who would have had more "if he formed his standard of action from his own mind, for I am inclined to think he is not vicious so much from inclination, as from the example of the world. If it was a fashionable thing for wits and scholars, and lord lieutenants, and other distinguished personages, to be true to their wives, probably our friend would not have found him an unfaithful husband" (2:295–96).

How much of Mr. Vesey's adulterous wandering may have been the result of his wife's long relationship, a kind of marriage, to Handcock, cannot be known, but his notorious testament certainly suggests retaliation against them. Vesey, however, was widely considered a devoted and often heartbroken wife. Six months before her husband's death in 1785, Montagu admirably predicted her, and Handcock's, reactions to the departure of the unfaithful one:

According to the most approved method of woefull Widows, she will drink his ashes, or weep all day over his heart in a crystal case, or sit mourning on his monument. She will do all that any illustrious Widow has done. . . . What a task will Mrs. Hancock have in the occasion? who never knew the value of a husband, nor has studied the duty of Widows, but . . . will reckon grief of the deprivation to be merely adequate to the felicity of the possession, and this unsentimental creature will give part of our friends sorrow to the Dairy maid he woed, to the actresses he won, to the kept mistresses he maintain'd, till in short there will be only an ordinary portion of sorrow left to our Sylph.

She added that Mr. Vesey was an amiable man and a comfort to his wife, who, she thought, "loves the companion and esteems the friend, and forgives the infidelities of the Husband."[11]

The worst suspicions of Vesey's friends were confirmed, however, after the conditions of her husband's unaccountably cruel will were revealed. The will was written in late 1772, at a time when Mr. Vesey may simply have wanted to get down the broad outlines of his disposition, and it disposed of Lucan and his other property. He failed to mention his servants or Handcock or his wife. Having taken care of the main business, at a time when his wife was nearly fifty and no heir of his own was to be expected—and perhaps under the influence of a sister-in-law whose family were the main beneficiaries—like many a hedonist, Agmondesham Vesey may have been reluctant to readdress himself to the writing of a definitive will. His oversight may have been less a deliberate act of spite than an action originating in that "strange insensibility with which he seems to neglect every serious consideration," as Elizabeth Carter had expressed it earlier (3:144). But his wife's friends, who had always been infuriated by his insensitive behavior to her, were, at his death, free to express their fury. Carter said he had been endowed with "mere constitutional good humour, and specious civility," and considered that as his mind had been little influenced by religion or religious principles, so his base treatment of his wife was less wonderful (3:244). Frances Burney accounted for Vesey's excess of grief by resorting to some intimation of his eternal damnation: "The *agremens* which she found in the society of Mr. Vesey she regrets the loss of, and he had not those virtues from whence consolation can be drawn. A frippery character, like a gaudy flower, may please while it is in bloom; but it is the virtuous only that, like the aromatics, preserve their sweet and reviving odour when withered." [12]

Mr. Vesey suffered from epilepsy or, as his contemporaries styled it, "fits," and was the object of his wife's probably useless ministrations and great concern. Handcock confined her ministrations only to her mistress and had her hands full. In the letters Vesey wrote Montagu between 1760 and 1786, Handcock, with only one or two exceptions, is noted in her function as child or sick nurse. She appears just bringing Vesey some unpleasant medicine, summoning her to dinner, or objecting to her late hours: "Adieu my d^r Mrs Montagu Mrs Handcock will scold if I sit up till Daylight" (October 10, 1765, "that awkward country Gentlewoman"). Once writing when Handcock had summoned her to supper, Vesey scribbled on: "You may go my d^r Mrs Handcock & sup by yourself as you have often done before while 10 11 12 aclock has found me nail'd to a chair in Hill Street" (Summer 1773, "the pleasure I felt in reading y^r letter").

Vesey suffered, like Montagu, from chronic stomach disorders and treated herself with a bewildering array of remedies and expedients that included a course of river bathing in the Liffey, sea bathing at Scarborough, and various exotic prescriptions—Montagu once suggested that when the doctor prescribed an ordinary course of crushed oyster shell, he had to pretend it was a rare American root.[13] She had, said Carter, "a restlessness of body and mind, which harasses and wears out both," and she was unable to keep faithful to one remedy long enough for it to benefit her (2:108–9). In 1773 Carter hoped that Vesey had recovered from the ill effects of bathing and advised, "Do pray give yourself up a little more to the directions of Mrs. Handcock. Her sober good sense will correct your fancies, and her affection is too strong to suffer her to laugh when there is the least reasonable cause of alarm. By guarding against imaginary distempers you are in perpetual real danger from misapplied and improper remedies."[14]

Handcock must have clucked over Vesey sometimes. One of her medical tenets, often referred to by Carter, had to do with her fear of harm incurred by overindulgence in tea. In 1768 Carter recollects having had her cups of tea limited "and a grave remonstrance from Mrs. Handcock's prudence and sobriety, between every one of them."[15]

Handcock was Vesey's "sister" in eighteenth-century parlance and often went out socially with Vesey or with both Veseys, but although she must have been responsible for arranging Vesey's evening parties, she is almost never mentioned by the illustrious callers at the famous salon, the enchanted blue room in Bolton Row, where were entertained the members of the Club, Montagu, Carter, Hannah More, Burney, and almost every other well-known personage of the time. Her role was as "Body," or as practical arrangements.

She was far more reliable a presence than Vesey's husband. When Vesey wrote to Montagu she almost invariably closed with compliments from both her intimates: "Mr. Vesey, Mrs. Handcock much yours." But often this becomes "Mr Vesey, if he were here would . . . ," "Mr Vesey who is gone to dine . . . & Mrs Hand at Elbow" send compliments. As time passed, Mr. Vesey's absences lengthened; he found himself obliged to spend three days a week in his Dublin office and sometimes for a month in autumn moved to Dublin, leaving Vesey and Handcock solitary at Lucan.

Thus in the autumn of 1765 they endured the "dulness languor & the dreary dripping scene which is gathering about our old walls where Mrs Handcock & I are the only inhabitants" ("that awkward country

Gentlewoman"); in the autumn of 1773, "Mrs Handcock & I have heard enough of the howling wind seldome broke by any human voice for our neighbours as well as family are all gone to Dublin" ("Your letter tho wrote a month ago").

Handcock too suffered from occasional ill health, and whenever her companion fell ill, Vesey was vastly dismayed and fearful of the worst. When Vesey feared, she feared extravagantly and fell naturally into a strain of gothic lamentation. What she feared most was the loss of what she valued most—her reason, her eyesight, Mr. Vesey, Handcock, and her London life. Her fears of four of these losses were prophetic, but she suffered for a long time prematurely. In 1770 Handcock had a bad cold which Vesey promptly diagnosed as paralytic symptoms. "I hope," wrote Carter, "this distemper has no better foundation than her own dozen apoplectick fits. . . . Mrs. Hancock is a most valuable woman on her own account, and her life of unspeakable consequence to dear Mrs. Vesey" (2:70). At this period, with Vesey only in her fifties, it was evident to herself and to her friends that she could not have managed alone and that Mr. Vesey was not a reliable resource.

Though Handcock would not write letters, she may be glimpsed in the letters of others. Once, in a spirit of Irish patriotism, she sent an inquiry through Vesey as to whether Carter had read *The Vicar of Wakefield.* Carter describes her refusing to endorse Vesey's newly invented coffee-pot, which had neither spout, handle, nor lid that would open—"But she is an intolerable common sense woman," said Carter. Once she is detected forbidding Vesey to poach an egg in an expensive cup lest she break it, and once she buys and presents another cup to Carter herself.[16]

Vesey's one prolonged anecdote about Handcock has to do with a night they spent in a simple inn while on a tour together through Dorset in the year 1775. On arrival, coming downstairs from examining their chambers, Mrs. Handcock slipped on a stair:

A faint voice call'd out who is that has fallen is y^r candle out—she ask'd in her turn who are you—an unfortunate Taylor who went a pleasuring upon the water at Portsmouth & fell out of the Boat & lastly being as little used to a coach fell from the top of one & here I lye a Stranger nobody knows me my wife & children in London—Mrs Handcock bid him good night & presently the maid went up & told him a Lady had paid his passage for a place in the inside of the coach— Mrs Handcock pass'd by the door again going to Bed the same voice call'd out again and is that my Dear, heaven bless you I had pawn'd my Watch y^r Charity is not thrown away. (October 2, [1775], Petersfield, "last Night we parted in the Hall at Cowdry")

Vesey adds jocosely, "for my part I believe the Taylor had a red coat & a cocade & that she stumbled at his Door on purpose." The admirable Handcock never saw the man she had rescued. In a few words she discovered the matter, no doubt applied then to the innkeeper to learn more of the tailor's situation, and settled his problem with expedition. With the same competence she arranged Vesey's life.

Once in 1769 Carter describes Handcock, after unwearied endeavors, rescuing a mouse from a cat.[17] On an evening at Lucan after a large party had rambled on the Liffey and done some boating, thoroughly enjoying and wetting themselves, "Mrs Handcock's storehouse was obliged to do the honors of sending the Ladies home with dry shoes & Petticoats" (August 3, 1781, "my d^r friend what have I done"). Vesey, sending Handcock's good wishes in a letter, could add that all of Handcock's wishes were good ones. Vesey once carried four caged nightingales from England to Lucan in hopes of naturalizing them there; "I hope," commented Montagu, "the Hibernians will erect a statue to her with a nightingale on her Head."[18] But Handcock trained the native thrushes at Lucan to come to her windowsill for crumbs.

Medicines and beds were particular provinces of Handcock, as was self-abnegation. Late in their careers—in 1785—Walpole, considering a visit when he could not conveniently return home in the evening, imagined he could hear Handcock "tell me what a nice bed she could fit up in a trice in Mrs. Vesey's closet and how well it should be aired."[19] On August 24, 1780, at Sunning Hill, Handcock insisted, Vesey wrote, that Montagu should come and take her room: "We have a spare Room but as it was over the Kitchen I wou'd not suffer Mrs Handcock to continue in it but it is a good Bed & she can receive no damage,—begs you will do her the pleasure to accept— . . . so pray be assured you can not give Mrs Handcock greater pleasure but take care you do not leave any of y^r visions upon her Pillow tho they all brag of coming out of the Ivory Gate they may have too much trafficing for the cell of fair Tranquility" ("this minute my dear friend I received"). When is Handcock ever glimpsed that she is not in service to someone?

Handcock probably maintained a consistent appearance from year to year. The erratic Vesey vacillated between fat and lean. "How fat she is!" exclaimed Lady Caroline in 1759.[20] In 1767 Vesey wrote to Montagu from Scarborough, "Mr Vesey is flirting with Comptesses at Spa—when he will leave his plump German Ladies to take up a lean wife I don't know" ("I wrote to you my d^r Mrs Montagu"). In November 1770 Carter rejoiced at Vesey's added *embonpoint*, "even if it should reduce her from being a shadowy Sylph, to a mere earthly fat gentlewoman in perfectly vulgar good health" (2:95). And in 1783 Montagu worried about Vesey, who had lost hearing, appetite, spirits, and even her corporal form, which "always mince and delicate, is much shrunk, and I am almost afraid she should melt into air, into thin air."[21]

Vesey's nickname "The Sylph" had less to do with her bulk or lack of it than with her lack of practical good sense and also her lack of moral ballast: though filled with a sensibility and empathy toward others that kept her often in sympathetic joy or distress, her responses were ad hoc, and she neither constructed nor subscribed to any moral or religious system. For this her friends did not precisely blame her, for they recognized the unparalleled goodness and kindness of her heart and the complete absence of envy or malice in her composition, but still on occasion they lectured or tried to enlighten her, for they attributed the depression of her spirits and the inappropriate levity of her pursuits, particularly as she grew older, to a lack of fixed (or Christian) principle. A reliance on Christianity might indeed have steadied and consoled Vesey, who suffered increasingly from depression as she grew older. Her spirits sank when Mr. Vesey came in fatigued from his walk; or they sank for no reason at all. In January 1782, for example, they were "depress'd to such a degree I can not write & fear to communicate the dullness that hangs about me" ("my d^r friends as I was about writing to you").

Handcock's task of regulating Vesey therefore grew increasingly difficult over the years. Fearful for her sanity and her sight in the 1760s, Vesey grew terrified at the prospect of the loss of her faculties as time passed. Her friends laughed at her fears, but she was conscious of lapses that frightened her, and everyone repeated stories of her absentminded gaffes. On one famous occasion she, twice married, addressed Emily, Duchess of Leinster, now remarried to her children's tutor, on the reprehensibility of second marriages; when reminded of the situation, she said simply she had forgotten. Lady Clermont, describing that same evening, noted that while the Duchess of Leinster stayed, Vesey spoke of nothing but second husbands, and after the Princess Dashkov came— she was a coconspirator of Catherine the Great, supposedly implicated in the death of Peter III—of nothing but murder. Wraxall diagnosed Vesey: "Simplicity, accompanied by a sort of oblivious inattention to things passing under her very sight, characterized her." He commented on the occasion of her remarks to Leinster: "There was indeed some decay of mind in such want of recollection."[22] Clearly, she allowed herself to free associate in the presence of guests without check or "recollection"; whether she could recollect herself or not is unclear, but in later years she seems to have lost the ability to resist any whim or impulse. Everyone laughed at her extravagant fancies, and perhaps she enjoyed such attentions. She loved sublime scenery and once, on a cliff at Scarborough, had to be snatched back to safety by Handcock. When her friend Mrs. Henry broke her leg at Lucan and the doctor said she might walk only on gravel, Vesey announced that she would at once order the gardener to gravel the drawing room. Her passion for landscaping found her at Lucan watching trees planted while sitting in a chaise "without Horses a candle to keep me warm & a book to read while the work was going on they will think M.ʳ Vesey had his reason for leaving the Gentlewoman in the Country" (c. February 1782, "I received yʳ bewitching letter").

By the 1770s she had lost her looks. Wraxall noted that she had no personal advantages of manner and no ornaments of dress. Burney in 1779 found her exceedingly well-bred and agreeable but with "the most wrinkled, sallow, time-beaten face I ever saw." [23] And the Burneys were agreed she was no wit. Dr. Burney, writing to Frances Crewe in 1808, said she was without wit and simply brought witty people together.[24] His daughter had made the same judgment thirty years before: "All her name in the world must, I think, have been acquired by her dexterity and skill in selecting parties, and by her address in rendering them easy with one another." [25] But in fact she could be very witty: her wit when she was in spirits flowed lavishly and spontaneously. Many examples are to be found in her letters to Montagu. Wit, after all, depends on free association. When in the winter of 1773–74 Lord Harcourt had great success as lord lieutenant of Ireland after the repressive reign of George Townshend, Vesey explained, "There is an old receipt to gain the affections of a Dog get some one to lock him up strike & beat him & do you come feed stroke & carry him to walk" ("Your letter tho wrote a month ago"). When in spring 1782 Montagu moved from the once-admired house in Hill Street to the new mansion in Portman Square, she wrote, "adieu cold dark dining Room of Hill Street tho your faults were all forgot from 4 to 7—8 & 9 I will give you a kick now you are out of place" ("I have been longing to hear from my dear beloved Friends").

She was known for her "flights," her sustained fancies, many of which are to be found in her letters though she could take wing in speech as well. In 1772, isolated at Lucan in the old mansion built by religious, and longing to be with Montagu and her other friends in London, she wrote

Happy you yᵉ Rooks who are content with yʳ native Bowers & the croking of yʳ fellow citizens & never wish to hear the voice of the nightingale & happy were you yᵉ votaries of Sᵗ Patrick you never pray'd to have yʳ twilight domes

exchanged for painted roofs & gay Pavilions or y^r black letter'd history of the
Martyrs for an elegant composition or to see the table of Y^r Refectories surrounded with Orators Bards & Philosophers—much less did you ever dream of
calling upon y^r sable demure Prioresse the silent observer of superstitious eti-
quette to animate her company with the fire of her own imagination you never
desired to place ye incense pot upon a Tripod or expected the routine of clois-
terd ignorance shou'd assume the modest wisdom of an Athenian Maid. I believe I may as well leave the jack daws & nuns to chatter for themselves—I am
afraid I shall never practice any of the Lessons they might give me. ("I am in
despair my d^r Mrs Montagu")

Just so her prattle must have flowed, full of unexpected turns and sudden felicities, when she was in tune. To her close friends she was a perpetual delight.

From about 1770 to 1785 Vesey's conversation parties were in the
height of fashion; only Montagu's could compete. But Vesey was far too
wise to challenge Montagu. Her own house was comfortable but not
grand, her collations simpler. Instead of copying Montagu's rigid circle,
Vesey appropriately arranged her furniture into little islands for two,
three, four, or five, among which in her later years she would dash, increasingly deaf, wearing her silver ear or extending an ear trumpet, constantly seeking whatever was interesting that might be going forward,
in terror of what she might miss. Montagu described the famous blue
room where, she declared, all people were enchanted,

tho' the magic figure of the circle is vanished, thence; a Philosopher, a fine
Lady, and a Gallant Officer form a triangle in one corner; a Maccaroni, a Poet,
a Divine, a Beauty, and an Otaheite Savage, a wondrous Pentagon in another;
then the Coalition of Parties, professions, and characters which compose the
group standing in the middle of the room; the flying squadrons of casual visi-
tants that are ever coming in and going out! Great Orators play a solo of decla-
mation; Witts lett off epigrams like minute guns; the Sage speaks sentences,
everyone does his best to please the Lady of the enchanting room, "For all con-
tend / To win her grace whom all commend."[26]

A great acquisition to these parties was the members of the Club—including Johnson, Burke, Garrick, Gibbon, Sir Joshua Reynolds, Thomas
Warton, Dr. Burney, Adam Smith, Bishop Percy, and Richard Sheridan, among others—after Mr. Vesey's election to membership in 1773.
In the 1780s Vesey had parties every other Tuesday, the day the Club
members dined together, after which they all came to her "with the
addition of such other company as it is difficult to find elsewhere."[27]
Bennet Langton described a party in 1780 at "Mr. Vesey's," when the

company stood four or five deep around Johnson's chair to hear him talk with Dr. Barnard, the provost of Eton. The company included the Duchess Dowager of Portland, the Duchess of Beaufort, Mrs. Boscawen, Lady Lucan, Lady Clermont, Lord Althorp, Lord Macartney, Sir Joshua Reynolds, Lord Lucan, and Mr. Wraxall.[28]

Mr. Vesey, always frivolous, was in his element in society but, like his wife, apparently remained frivolous too long. Hannah More said of him in 1783, "He is so old and so young, so infirm and so strong. I know not what judgment to form of him. One day in a sickbed, the next at the Opera or Pantheon; one hour in a fit of epilepsy, another in a fit of gallantry! a *cheerful* old age is a fine thing, a *gay* old age a very absurd one!" (1:156). In 1780 Montagu had made much the same observation of her friend: "Mrs. Vesey is more dissipated than a young maccaroni. There is a strange vertigo possesses the present age. It is ever agreeable to see persons advanced in age mix with society, and not plead the privilege of age to avoid performing the little social duties and attentions, but merely to march from 70 to four score in the train of les jeux et les ris is not graceful; it is time to quit the dancing measure and to leave those to trifle with more grace and ease Whom folly pleases, / And whose follies please."[29]

Given Vesey's nature, then, the relationship between herself and Handcock seems easy enough to understand. Handcock's power was in her domestic authority, her ability to make all practical considerations easy; Vesey's power was in her superior position as wife and in her social success. By becoming more and more a specialist in her own occupation, each further empowered the other. Neither was concerned with broadening either her own or the other's interests, abilities, or ambitions. Whether the life of *gouvernante*-housekeeper was really all that Handcock ever desired we cannot tell, and no one has bothered to record anything about her ill health except that in her later years it gave genuine cause for alarm. Clearly, Vesey was not prepared for a fruitful old age and went on forever attempting to live the old, youthful, even childlike life. The relationship between Handcock and Mr. Vesey is more difficult to assess. As Vesey's surrogate mother, Handcock must have detested the selfishness of the man but had to maintain a calm domestic surface and a formal respect. Between the Veseys themselves the problem was complex. Vesey did a great deal of agonizing about her husband's misdeeds to her friends. She must have had periods of anger. There was a domestic crisis when Mr. Vesey, an amateur architect, left his wife and Handcock in London from 1775 to 1777 while he tore down the old house at Lucan and built a new mansion without inviting their participation.[30]

Though Vesey was happy in London, much occurred during this period to upset her. She took a great interest in building and landscaping. She had devised a romantic cottage and a bower at Lucan on the banks of the Liffey. In the 1780s, according to More, Montagu considered finding a cottage near Sandleford for Vesey to fit up (1:212), and when Lord Spencer's house at Wimbledon burned down, Carter said, Vesey wished earnestly to contrive him a new one (2:290). Her interest in Montagu's improvements to her grounds at Sandleford was intense; she followed them on a plan and wrote twice describing them in her mind's eye. When given an opportunity, she was inventive, and when she decorated her new dressing room at Lucan in 1777, she did it "so as mortal dressing room was never yet furnished," said Carter (3:44). Mr. Vesey did not consult her about the new house, and she learned from a plan sent her in December 1775 that she was to have a round room, "like an old parrot in a cage" (2:357). Handcock and Carter, following the usual system, laughed her out of her distresses, offering to add scarlet trimmings to her green gown. But surely Vesey had a genuine grievance. The finished house, Carter thought, was not to her taste: the dear old castle was to her inestimable, "but alas! Mr. Vesey understands her not." It was now "a mere prosaical house, full of mortal comforts and conveniences, without the least particle of romance or sylphery . . . much better adapted to the ordinary wants and purposes of the Right Honourable Agmondesham Vesey, Esq., and privy councillor, than to those of his aetherial partner" (3:39–40).

Mr. Vesey also took the opportunity of his two-year sojourn in Ireland to develop a particularly serious infidelity. It was probably to this reason for his delayed return that Montagu referred in a passage in which she noted that husbands are never in the wrong, for as absolute monarchs have absolute power and can do no injustice, so "if a moment of penitence should happen to Mr. Vesey; Mr. P. will assure him Husbands cannot do wrong and he will say ' 'tis true.' "[31] Carter noted cryptically in July 1777, when Vesey herself returned to Ireland, that uncertainties were now certainties but that at least the young man did not accompany them to Ireland (3:30). The suggestion is perhaps that a long-concealed relationship with a mistress had been discovered and that in the absence of legitimate children, Mr. Vesey had produced one less legitimate, and worse, forced him upon his wife's notice. Another serious possibility was that she had discovered an illicit connection between her husband and his sister-in-law and cousin—her cousin too—Letitia Vesey, so that George Vesey, Letitia's son and Mr. Vesey's designated heir, now almost seventeen, had become an unpleasant object to Vesey.

Whatever the exact truth, the marital relationship had suffered a serious blow, and Mrs. Thrale was convinced in January 1779 that Vesey hated her husband.

Mrs Crewe was saying how happy Mrs Vesey must be to come from Ireland— we all know She hates Ireland—and how delightful it must be to her to see Mrs Montagu again: ay replied I She does adore Mrs Montagu, almost as much as She hates her Husband—but says She it must be uncomfortable too to divide one's self so—I should hate to be living half my Life on one Side the Sea & half o'th'other.—Why really I replied, Mrs Vesey's manner of spending her Time does sometimes put me in Mind of that Heathen Goddess who lived half the Year with *Ceres* in *Heaven*—& the other half with her *Husband* in Hell.[32]

But even before this crisis, Mr. Vesey as a husband had been a perfect autocrat, reinforcing the childlike state in which his wife lived. Vesey has provided us with one small domestic scene at Lucan in the year 1774. She is sitting by her fireside writing to Montagu, to whom Mr. Vesey also owes a letter, though he despairs of penning one worthy—perhaps not of her but of himself—to be displayed in Hill Street.

Here he is with a folio under his arm begging a place by my fire side this 6th of july—what are you doing—writing to Mrs Montagu—how-taking my province—*my province*—you don't deserve it a letter wrote with the wit of greece & the gentilesse of France still unanswered—why *you wretch* that is the very reason tho' my Heart overflow'd my pen despaired of catching the Graces of her style often have I attempted—that Paradise she let down to tempt floated before my Eyes & the difficulty of reaching it I will look no more Lucan country I shall sell you to the first bidder—do so my Dear I am very good you know I must follow where ever you lead. (July 6, 1774, "what my D^r friend has froze y^r Pen")

"You know I must follow where ever you lead." Vesey was denied autonomy by both her husband and her sister-in-law. Mr. Vesey seems rarely to have admitted her to his confidence; she learned, for instance, the final provisions of his will only after his death. During their life together she was, like Montagu, uncertain again and again of traveling plans about which she was not even to inquire so that she (or rather Handcock) must have been sorely inconvenienced in packing or making household arrangements. In 1761 Mr. Vesey, about to depart for Spa, would not say whether his wife was to accompany him. She rarely knew when they would depart for England, when they would embark again for Ireland, or once in the summer of 1783, when they were to go to Margate. All her friends knew and understood his disposition, and Dorothea

Gregory, writing to Montagu from Edinburgh on November 9, 1782, commented on the reported return of Vesey to London: "I rejoice to hear the dear Sylph is returning to the Land of the Living for such England is to her & till orders were actually issued out by the Grand Turk for preparing the house I never knew how to believe that he really meant to restore her to her friends & shall not be perfectly convinced of it till I hear they are landed for I have just as much confidence in (and very near as much esteem) for a weather Cock as for M^r V—" ("a thousand thanks, my Dear Madam").[33]

Nor was his wife ever to be sure about the state of Mr. Vesey's finances (one can hardly call them her own). In about 1780 she was afraid to increase expenses by so much as her own removal from Lucan to Dublin: "Mr Vesey has built a spacious House has portion'd a niece his Brother's Widow now lives out of his fortune his nephew at Academy & to buy into the Army" (c. February 1782, "I received y^r bewitching letter").[34] Perhaps she relied on his firm direction of their affairs and enjoyed his amusing civilities, from which apparently he rarely deviated. But she was also afraid of his autonomous decisions and apparently her wishes (setting aside her judgment) had no authority with him, so she resorted at times to childish schemes and deceits. A letter sent to her in late 1777 from London informed her that a flooding problem in the cellars and kitchen of the Bolton Street house had recurred. Vesey concluded that if her husband heard of it—and he had a hogshead of claret in the cellar—he would give up the house and then of course would never take another and she would be cut off from London. She determined to hide the problem from him and to solve it herself. Consulting with Handcock, she then asked a close friend, Lord Shelburne, who lived nearby and who had the power to interest the commissioner of sewers in the problem, to procure remedies. Shelburne responded positively, but whatever ensued, the Veseys afterward moved to another house in Clarges Street.[35] Her consultation with Handcock, Vesey, and Lord Shelburne behind Mr. Vesey's back—probably typical behavior for Vesey and Handcock and reminiscent of the plots laid to get Mr. Vesey into the Club—suggests a ground for the husband's resentment of his wife and her companion.

It was Handcock, then, and not Mr. Vesey, with whom Vesey discussed and planned her life—as much as lay in her power. And it was Handcock, not Mr. Vesey, with whom Vesey traveled. While Mr. Vesey went to Spa alone, Vesey and Handcock went to Scarborough together. Vesey and Handcock made their Dorset tour while Mr. Vesey was building in

Ireland. A somewhat emblematic event occurred in June 1763, when the trio arrived at Holyhead to embark for Ireland and found a packet waiting. Vesey declared herself too fatigued "to step out of the Coach into the Ship." Mr. Vesey, straining toward Ireland, therefore embarked alone, while Vesey—"my Theseus has abandon'd me"—remained behind in Holyhead with Handcock to rhapsodize over the romantic scenery (June 11, 1763, "sound dies away in the Caverns of Snowden").

In late 1782 the Veseys came to London once more and never contrived to return to Ireland. Mr. Vesey, unregenerate and unrepentant, spent the summers of 1783 and 1784 at Margate, where he gave public breakfasts and attended all the parties and balls. In May 1785 Delany reported that both Veseys and Handcock were in declining health. "Mrs. Handcock . . . supports them with her steady conduct in the best manner she can: but what is *human* support, if we do not look higher!"[36] The Veseys had not acquired religious habits of thought; it is not certain where Handcock stood. Mr. Vesey died soon afterward, in London, on June 3, 1785.

The will appalled the Vesey circle. There were no bequests to servants, no remembrances to friends, and no mention of poor Vesey or her companion. It was noted with indignation that whereas Mr. Vesey had left £1,000 to his trollop, he had left nothing to his wife.[37] Mr. Vesey's will itself does not survive, though the list of his legatees does.[38] No trollop is mentioned, unless she were Letitia Vesey, the widow of his brother George and the mother of his principal heir, Major George Vesey. If Letitia Vesey had indeed been Mr. Vesey's mistress and had therefore influenced his testamentary provisions, Vesey would have had just cause for distress.

Mrs. Howe sent word to Lady Spencer on June 23 that Vesey had the lease of the house in Clarges Street and £500 in money, but all she and Handcock had to live on was £800 a year, a sum that apparently represented the total of Vesey's jointure and Handcock's annuity.[39] On July 26, Lady Lucan, the wife of one of the nephew legatees, reported that Vesey and Handcock would have the house and £1,000 a year and would be able to keep the all-important coach.[40] In September Carter reported that Major George Vesey was maintaining the coach and that the pair would have £900 a year (3:250). Hannah More's comment that "our dear Mrs. Vesey will have a competency, though nothing like the affluence to which she has been accustomed and to which she has so good a right," suggests that much of the money her husband had bequeathed to his brother's family may originally have been her own.

The blow to Vesey was double. The loss of her husband, who had so long dictated the terms of life to her, was disorienting; the insult of the public message that he cared nothing for her comfort or the continuation of her pleasures after he was gone was devastating. She was forced to reevaluate her assessment of her husband and her marriage—surely a task made easier by her many sufferings over his infidelities—and her past life must have crumbled to ashes before her eyes. Montagu, who understood her reaction, called Mr. Vesey's oversight "vile neglect" and thought that if Vesey could forget him, "she would be happier than she has been since we knew her." She considered Mr. Vesey's action comparable to that of the Duchess of Portland, who in the same year failed to provide for her companion of many years, Mary Delany, and said, "nothing . . . c^d heal the wound such unkindness must give."[41]

Vesey's first response was bewildered misery.

My dull Pen has now added melancholy and the Hours that fled with down upon their Wings carry nothing but sorrow & oeconomy for by some misunderstanding of Settlement there is no income comes to me. It certainly was not want of kindness for we never had any cross purposes but lived in Peace and friendship & the last Hours of his life he look'd at me with an affection & drew my Hand to his Heart with such a look when He was deprived of Speech that I can not yet remember it without Tears—yet in the Will there is no income for me tho every thing else that is kind—which as we near Relations [sic] by Kith & still more united by affection which was never broken into by any disagreement—I must impute to it [sic] chance unknown for I am sure it cou'd not originate in his Heart. (July 1785, "my D^r friend I am almost blind")

"Sorrow and oeconomy" seem to have been pretty nearly equal burdens, and the thought occurs that Vesey's almost perpetual tears thereafter may have been in considerable part for her vanished bluestocking parties. This may, in fact, have been Mr. Vesey's revenge.

The virtual marriage between Handcock and Vesey continued to Handcock's death in 1789. Handcock looked after Vesey for as long as she could. At first Vesey appeared to recover. In mid-June Eva Garrick, herself experienced in grieving widowhood, had found Vesey in black gloves and little else that was black. "I am persuaded she perfectly forgot for what reason she wears black gloves as the rest of her Mourning can put her in mind of no loss whatsoever. Mrs. Hancock is determined I believe to wear out her green silk lutestring gown upon this joyful occasion; for she looks more chearful than I ever saw her."[42]

Eva Garrick, like Handcock, apparently knew Mr. Vesey's true value. But then Vesey tumbled over entirely and permanently into the gulf of depression. Perhaps, as she still had Handcock, it was not so much the loss of Mr. Vesey that sunk her as it was the loss of the illusion of his kindness, the patriarchal protection, which if it had stifled her at least always to some extent indulged her. She cried over the public insult of his neglect and the loss of her parties, which were her vocation, and the sense that youth, health, husband, and all pleasure had irrevocably gone; she cried almost without ceasing until her death in 1791.

So Handcock had small joy of her green gown and her liberation from the tyrant. She devoted herself instead to nursing Vesey, who was, everyone recognized, incompetent to look after herself. Handcock fell ill in the latter part of the summer of 1785 and Lady Mt. Edgcumbe reported in September: "I left Mrs. Handcock very ill, and I fear in some danger. If any accident should happen to her, she [Vesey] would die naked and starved."[43] Handcock recovered and in 1786 was arranging small parties in Clarges Street to divert Vesey. Hannah More, who attended them and sometimes took Vesey calling, now named her "poor Mrs. Vesey" and saw that year that her memory was visibly impaired (1: 236–37, 247). There was a party for Frances Burney and Leonard Smelt in March 1787 and another for Burney in May attended only by women friends and, to Vesey, the faithful, always kind Horace Walpole. In 1787 More had lost all hope that Vesey would ever recover. "I never think of her but with sorrow," she wrote to Walpole, "because hers is a distress which leaves one nothing to hope: it is terrible that the only clear idea she has left is a keen sense of all she has lost." What a blessing, she adds, "for Mrs. Vesey that Mrs. Handcock is alive and well! I do venerate that woman beyond words: her faithful, quiet, patient attachment makes all showy qualities and shining talents appear little in my eyes. There is so little parade in her kindness, that I believe she herself never suspects she is making a sacrifice. Such characters are what Mr. Burke calls the 'soft quiet green on which the soul loves to rest.' "[44]

Vesey's friends had recognized that she suffered not only from "low spirits" but also from "decay." Walpole provides a commentary on the progress of her dissolution. In October 1787 he informed More that though there was not a soul in town, Vesey had assured him that the town was very full and she had had a great deal of company. "Her health is re-established, and we must *now* be content that her mind is not restless. My pity now feels most for Mrs Handcock; whose patience is inexhaustible, though not insensible" (31:255). In December he noted that the situation was deplorable, for Vesey was "scarce sensible of anything but her own misery—Oh! yes! momentary gleams of her most constitutional virtue, benevolence, still break out—the sight of those she loves still enliven her for a moment—but she cannot converse with them for two minutes coherently, nor express the glimmerings of ideas she retains. The suffering and patience of Mrs Hancock are not to be described—were it not for her comfort, I could almost wish that very few were admitted to see her friend! Some indeed show they are worthy of performing so respectable a duty" (31:257–58). In February 1788 he said, "Very often do I think with true and tender sorrow of poor dear Mrs. Vesey, or rather Mrs. Handcock, for to her is all one's feeling now due" (31:266). And in August that year he reported that Vesey had grown violent and intractable (31:277).

Handcock was failing all the time; Mr. Vesey's heirs took no responsibility; and in the end the two women were befriended by a benevolent pair who could expect no inheritance, Vesey's cousin Lord Cremorne and his lady, who took them into their house at Chelsea in 1788.[45] Carter saw Vesey there in that year and reported: "The painted glass particularly attracts Mrs. Vesey's notice, and when she sees it, her admiration, her flights of fancy, and brilliancy of expression are almost equal to her best days, but then she again sinks into despondency, and will scarce utter a word" (3:300). In January 1789 the final blow fell: Handcock died. It was possibly the only disloyal act to Vesey she had ever committed. She was not, that is known, memorialized. Hannah More wrote, "It is melancholy to look at the house, where I have seen so many ingenious people, and heard so much pleasant conversation, and made so many friendships, and to think that of its two mistresses, whose faces were never turned towards me but with kindness, who never received me without affection, or parted from me without regret,—one is a corpse, and the other bereft of her faculties; what a call for serious reflection!" (1:304).

In January 1790 Burney wrote to her old friend Dorothea Gregory Alison, "poor poor Mrs. Vesey!—how gone without going!"[46] In September 1790 Carter reported that Vesey had grown thinner and weaker and had lost her appetite. Major George Vesey had been to see her; she had not spoken but had wrung her hands and burst into tears (3:319). Her death in early 1791 was not specifically reported, nor have I discovered her burial place.

Was it simply bad luck that the two devoted women Handcock and Vesey were unable to survive the death of the patriarch to enjoy an autumnal independence? If not, in what way had he, with his inconsequential character, his self-importance, and his autocratic will, insinuated himself so into the life of the two women that they could not manage without him or without a share in his approval? Her husband had belatedly shattered Vesey's belief in the benignity of the universe. To his eternal condemnation, all that Agmondesham Vesey needed to have done was to leave his wife an extra income of £500 a year, which would have diverted income from his sister-in-law's family for an insignificant time; to have left a lesser annuity to Handcock; and to have expressed his love and gratitude to both women for their long service. His failure to remember his servants, however, was also a mark of black ingratitude. It seems unlikely that his failure to make these dispositions was due only to carelessness. Rather he was either expressing a long-unexpressed resentment against his wife and Handcock, or—more likely—he had been got round by his sister-in-law, who wanted both the income and the triumph for herself and her children.

But Mr. Vesey could not dictate his wife's and Handcock's reaction to his action. Why could they not recover? Was it that women who had accepted their roles as contingent could not late in life become independent individuals and were dependent upon the judgment of the patriarch, even of themselves? Vesey had not, like Montagu, inwardly revolted at the wifely role she had to play; she had acquired no ambition to achieve autonomy. Handcock, whether it was necessary or not, had protected her from the effects of her own indiscretions until she could not manage without protection. We can only guess at Handcock's inner life; not a single letter has survived to preserve her voice. But very likely she needed someone to look after who would at the same time validate her as a caretaker, which indicates that she too was a contingent person. Pace Shaftesbury, sensibility, that divine concern for the feelings and concerns of others, with which both women were plentifully supplied, can by no means guarantee happiness—as Frances Greville had already declared (chapter 11). Something else—a strong sense of self, a commitment to a well-regulated mental life—was required.

Chapter Eleven

SENSIBILITY AND ROMANTIC FRIENDSHIP: FRANCES GREVILLE AND LADY SPENCER

As THE EIGHTEENTH CENTURY PROGRESSED, not only was the possession of sensibility a badge of superiority both touted and flaunted, but for women it was becoming de rigueur. In either public or private presentation of themselves, women wished to display the attributes considered appropriate, and for genteel women after the midcentury, sensibility, with its concomitant benevolence (or altruism), was not only the superior moral position but also the only admissible superiority for the submissive gender.[1] This chapter will consider separately two women friends of marked sensibility, some of their responses to that assignment, and some of their companions.

Georgiana Spencer and Frances Greville were sufficiently compatible to be firm friends. Spencer admired and feared Greville for her formidable wit; Greville admired and loved Spencer for her right thinking and kindness. Both women were confirmed in their sensibility, empathizers to the point of pain, willing to help when they could; and each devised a method, involving strict self-control, for avoiding the victimization that could so easily ensue from sensibility, that is, from too much feeling. Both also appear to have avoided taking companions of equal class and age, with whom they might have been closely emotionally involved, but instead chose younger women of inferior class. Their lives suggest that the way women were being reared often was successful in instilling genuine, as well as assumed, sensibility. Women had to become adept at reading the moods, motives, and intentions of men. If a cold insight that facilitated manipulation and necessitated false declarations of loyalty was sometimes the result, so was a warm empathic sympathy. Women who could remain sympathetic, hence vulnerable, to people of so much power as the men who controlled the circumstances of their lives were in peril of total immolation. The defense both Greville and Spencer raised was their own self-control, their eschewal of emotionalism, their reliance on reason.

Greville, by far the cleverer of the two, publicly repudiating the feminine role, defended herself by displaying a brusque, even callous, wit that frightened her acquaintance. She refused to pose as childish or sentimental and no doubt often gave a fair imitation of a person of no sensibility at all. In October 1778 Hester Thrale wrote to Johnson that she had met Greville at Tunbridge and had had an opportunity to observe her closely: "Mrs Greville has a commanding Manner & loud Voice. Why She downs every body I am sure; You never told me that She was so Lofty a Lady, nor did Dr Burney who knows her better. . . . My Master . . . says . . . that I must absolutely add that Mrs Greville is said to have formed her Manner upon yours." Johnson responded that he was glad Thrale had been downed, and he hoped she would come home flexible as a rush; as for Greville, if she copied him she would "lose more credit by want of judgement, than she will gain by quickness of apprehension."[2] The Johnsonian manner was probably habitual to Greville in her middle years; she is certainly the original of Mrs. Selwyn, who "downs everybody" in *Evelina*, and Burney drew another memorable portrait of her in 1814:

To many she passed for being pedantic, sarcastic, and supercilious: as such, she affrighted the timid, who shrunk into silence; and braved the bold, to whom she allowed no quarter. The latter, in truth, seemed to stimulate exertions which brought her faculties into play; and which—besides creating admiration in all who escaped her shafts—appeared to offer herself a mental exercise, useful to her health, and agreeable to her spirits.

Her understanding was truly masculine; not from being harsh or rough, but from depth, soundness, and capacity; yet her fine small features, and the whole style of her beauty, looked as if meant by Nature for the most feminine delicacy: but her voice, which had something in it of a croak; and her manner, latterly at least, of sitting, which was that of lounging completely at her ease, in such curves as she found most commodious, with her head alone upright; and her eyes commonly fixed, with an expression rather alarming than flattering, in examination of some object that caught her attention; probably caused, as they naturally excited, the hard general notion to her disadvantage above mentioned.[3]

In her unfinished novel, Frances Greville provides a patently autobiographical scene at a dinner table where Mrs. Castletown, a version of herself, defends female rationality in a quarrel with the detestable Sir James Saville, who begins the attack.

Mrs Sandford . . . is in my Opinion every thing a Woman ought to be, gentle modest, unpretending, always just as far as she goes, & never attempting to go farther than she ought—

I hope she is pleased with the Encomium Sir but to be sure it might just as well have been given to her Maid or any other illiterate vulgar Woman. It is to very little purpose that she has polished her understanding by an Excellent Education & improved her mind by books if at last she is to have no other merit than Miss of fifteen, & to be able to make the tea well; & tell What a clock it is— . . .

let me tell you Madam it would be very well for many Ladies if they would confine their talents to such humble things & not be eternaly seeking for opportunities to display their Wit at the expence of their Judgments. . . . I allow you what is sometimes called Wit & will raise a laugh in Company which is more *at* you than *with* you, however you may flatter yourself to the Contrary. . . . For my part I hate Sensible Women, & learned Women. . . . Their learning is always inferior to that of a School Boy, & their Sense answers no purpose but to make them presumptuous and dogmatical. They have nothing to do but to be pretty, clean & good humoured—

Obedient you would have added replied Mrs Castletown, & if you could prove to us that Fools were always found to be more governable your argument might, at least in one light, have some weight to it.[4]

Mrs. Sandford then rose and proposed retiring to coffee.

As Jane Spencer has noted, women were in general permitted writing with sensibility rather than "taking over the masculine pen, instrument of rational discourse."[5] That left them in undisputed possession of the province of the sentimental, the romantic, and the gothic modes, all of which, of course, were comparatively despised. Though refined sensibility was awarded complimentary lip service, in actual fact, in its implied failure of reason and fortitude, it was denigrated.[6]

The distance at which Greville held the expression of sentimental distress, even in her writing, can be shown in her unfinished novel, the structure of which is a frame of the letters of two sensible, rational friends—who never indulge in romantic endearments—enclosing a long sentimental tale related by one to the other. The friends begin writing when one remains in London while the other, for economy's sake, goes to live with her husband on his country estate. Mrs. Sandford cheerfully accepts her new situation and cheerfully explores the

possibilities, often comic, of a new and restricted society and new unfamiliar activities. Mrs. Harper wryly comments on the foibles of her
excellent husband. Neither woman will be an easy victim to adversity;
neither will fall sentimentally in love with another man. To ensure comedy, a seventeen-year-old ungainly sister of Sandford's, raised by a vulgar aunt, arrives to embarrass her connections. Women suffer in marriage, but they successfully practice fortitude. Sir James Saville, who
combines the worst traits of Greville's husband, is a widower and can
torment no one but Mrs. Castletown. Mrs. Harper's sister Lady Fairfax, however, is married to another man like Greville, constantly cavil-
ing, but has determined to remain with him to protect her children.
Lady Fairfax is equal to the situation. "When I consider," comments
Mrs. Sandford, "with what easy propriety she always conducts herself,
the placid & serene countenance she comes every where unto all companies, I think she must be more than human, for its plain she feels it all,
since her spirits are conquered tho' her temper is not; & till now I have
imputed her gentle timid, & sometimes, almost dejected Manner . . . to
want of health." This is an accurate portrait of Frances Greville in her
later years; she suffered from want of spirits and from ill health, but she
refused ever to capitulate.

The interpolated tale of Mrs. Mildmay, which fills more than half the
manuscript, is a tale of sensibility but is twice distanced and would then
be further undercut by the misbehavior of Mrs. Mildmay: she tells her
story to Mrs. Sandford, who then writes it to Mrs. Harper. The tale is
further distanced from the world of the two friends because Mrs. Mildmay's father was a city merchant; she comes from quite another place.
The happy family of the Clintons has suffered the loss of the mother, and
because the widower seems unable to function without her, his friends
undertake to find him a second wife. They choose a fortuneless woman
twenty years his junior who has been schooled "from having passed the
best part of her life in nursing an Old Gouty Father." The new Mrs. Clinton at once assumes the role of tyrant, enslaving her husband and tormenting his children.[7] She manages the family income, misusing it for
such purposes as the maintenance of a worthless lover. She falls in love
with her stepdaughter's lover and, when she cannot win him away, con-
trives to make his uncle ship him to the East Indies; as a result her stepdaughter dies. Greville here satirizes the male attitude that submission
can be instilled through tyranny.

The emotional Mrs. Mildmay is full of sensibility and is clearly about to try Mrs. Sandford by making Sandford fall in love with her. Mrs. Castletown warns that "both Men & Women Friends are dangerous things when cultivated to the excess & brought too near home." In the structure and the plot of her novel, Greville is suggesting that a coolly rational, good-humored approach to life is best, and she demonstrates— or was about to demonstrate—how women might deal with difficult husbands and the sentimental distresses imported into their lives by others.

Frances Greville was chief and most famous and probably first of those who publicly repudiated sensibility.[8] Greville's "Ode to Indifference" is first known to have been published in the *Edinburgh Chronicle* in 1759, when she was in her thirties, and appeared frequently thereafter, quite as frequently as Gray's "Elegy." Her ode was also refuted in verses defending sensibility more than a dozen times by authors of both genders.[9] The text of this important work is best rendered from Greville's own manuscript notebook of poems:

Ode to Indifference
Oft I've implor'd the Gods in vain,
  And pray'd 'till I've been weary,
For once I'll seek my suit to gain
  Of Oberon the Fairy.

Sweet airy being Wanton Sprite
  Who liv'st in woods unseen
And oft by Cynthias silver light
  Trip'st gaily o'er the Green

If e'er thy pitying Heart was mov'd
  As ancient Stories tell
And for th'Athenian maid who lov'd
  Thou Sought'st a Wond'rous Spell

Oh Deign once more t'exert thy pow'r
  Haply some Herb or Tree
Sov'reign as Juice from Western Flow'r
  Conceals a Balm for me.

I ask no kind return in Love,
  No tempting charm to please
Far from the Heart such gifts remove
  That sighs for Peace and Ease.

Nor ease nor peace that Heart can know
  Which like the Needle true,

Turns at the touch of Joy or woe,
  But turning trembles too.

Far as distress the Soul can wound
  'Tis pain in each degree
'Tis Bliss but to a certain bound,
  Beyond is Agony.

Then take this treach'rous sense of mind
  Which dooms me still to Smart.
Which pleasure can to pain refine
  To pain new pangs impart.

Oh haste to shed the Sov'reign Balm,
  My shatter'd nerves new string
And for my Guest serenely calm,
  The nymph Indifference bring.

At her approach see Hope see Fear,
  See Expectation fly
With disappointment in the rear,
  That blasts the promis'd Joy.

The tears which pity taught to flow,
  My Eyes shall then disown.
The Heart that throb'd at others woe
  Shall then scarce feel its own.

The Wounds that now each moment bleed
  For ever then shall close
And tranquil days shall still succeed
  To nights of sweet repose.

O Fairy Elf but grant me this,
  This one kind Comfort lend
And so may never fading Bliss
  Thy Flow'ry paths attend.

So may the Glow worms glim'ring light
  Thy tiny footsteps lead
To some new Region of Delight,
  Unknown to Mortal tread.

And be thy Acorn Goblet fill'd
  With Heav'ns ambrosial dew
From sweetest freshest Flowers distill'd
  That shed fresh sweets for you.

> And what of Life remains for me,
>   I'll pass in sober ease,
> Half pleas'd Contented will I be,
>   Content but half to please.[10]

Janet Todd has noted that the ode "did not seem a questioning of sensibility's worth or even a genuine uneasiness at its connection with femininity, but simply an elegant expression of the very quality it decried."[11] But Greville here and habitually does attempt to repudiate sensibility, critiquing it for its dangers even as she simultaneously demonstrates that she cannot repudiate it. The ode is an elegant expression of sensibility, but it is also and simultaneously a reckoning of the misery sensibility bestows on its possessors, a warning of its adverse powers.

The ode, probably written in about 1756, after Greville had been married for eight years to a husband all but pathologically jealous of her literary reputation, was an escapee that naturalized itself in the literary world. Its fame discomposed her stately husband, Fulke Greville, who desired preeminence in poetry as in all else, and its impact may also have offended his pride, for if Frances Burney, Greville's goddaughter and namesake, associated the stimulus that led to composition of the ode with marital disappointment, that explanation occurred to others. Burney wrote in 1768, "Her Ode to Indifference is so excessively pretty that it almost puts me out of conceit with my desire to be favoured with a touch of the power of Cupid, when I happen to recollect it. How she would scorn me if she knew it—but I suppose she did not begin with a passion for Indifference herself—I should not like to be Mr. Greville if he converted her to that side."[12]

The ode was therefore read as a repudiation of romantic love as well as of sensibility, and indeed it was; the very sensible (in two senses) Frances Greville was among the first of her period to identify the ideology of romantic love and sensibility as useful agents of those who profited by the subordination of women. Burney read the poem (or excused it) almost entirely as a plea against romantic love as her reference to "Cupid," above, makes clear. In her father's *Memoirs* (1814) she called the poem "a burst of genius emanating from a burst of sorrow, which found an alleviating vent in a supplication to Indifference." It was "clearly . . . incited by acute disappointment to heart-dear expectations."[13] Burney made her judgment from a full acquaintance with the character of Fulke Greville, of whom she wrote, having alluded to his brief immersion in domestic bliss following his marriage, "but constancy requires virtue to be leagued with the passions." [14]

The frame fiction, the prayer to Oberon, who directed the administration of the love potion in *A Midsummer Night's Dream*, confirms this reading and supports Burney's interpretation that Greville regretted having the attractions and the susceptibility and responsiveness that resulted in her marriage; sexual responsiveness is also part of the sacrifice she wished to make.[15] Mary Poovey has noted this frequent concomitant of sensibility: women's emotional responsiveness to others was assigned to them as their province but also regarded with suspicion because, though if properly cultivated it could lead to benevolence (and selflessness), if improperly or unguardedly cultivated it could quickly degenerate into sexual responsiveness or, even worse, selfish appetite.[16]

To judge from the many responses to the poem, however, Greville's repudiation of sensibility (a word that does not appear in it) was generally read as a repudiation of too much empathy with the woes of others; and, as might have been expected, many women protested at this denigration of the one moral superiority to which they could aspire. But Greville, who had more than sufficient empathy with the woes of others, always detested public displays of a cultivated sentimentality. She disliked Sterne and was suspicious of Rousseau, informing Lady Holland that she disliked his notions about women in *Emile*. [17]

For Greville herself, the ode, whatever else it meant, was a personal declaration of the severance of her identification with her husband, of her independence, which thereafter she maintained as much as possible by living as separately from her husband as she could. Nor would she ever again play the docile, compliant woman, though compliance might be forced upon her. In reaction, when possible, she played the role of domineering conversationalist, giving no quarter to males, something in the style of Mrs. Castletown.

Frances Greville believed in keeping a tight rational control. To her intimate friends, however, as Burney noted, she could expose a genuinely feeling side, and though her letters to Spencer are never romantic, in them she reins in her wit and often expresses an almost wistful esteem to this one friend whom she considered to be almost entirely good. Spencer had a reputation for right thinking and right doing. A word portrait of herself was sent to her in 1780 depicting her as fine, sensible, rational, with beauty, talents, wisdom, and constancy. She was a woman "capable of making the bad good,—the inconstant stable, and the giddy wise; and he, who would wish to see what was most perfect & respectable in the female character, would do well to see & converse with her." [18] Greville was all but awed by her.

In France in 1773, when Lady Spencer distressed Greville by refusing to talk in her daunting presence, Greville wrote to her:

Ever since you took the cards to play the other Night because you said you could not talk before me, I have considered myself as a guilty person labouring under the greatest anxiety lest my crime should be divulged & that I should be banished from Society, & in fact of what Nature must my Devilish Wit be if it reduces you to Silence?

> you who are form'd a thousand ways to Bless
> Whose greatness never yet made others less
> Whose Modest Worth ev'n Vice itself reveres
> Whose Words speak comfort & whose Aspect chears
> Who look through kind Indulgence' milder Eye
> On faults your nice discernment must descry—

and is it this I have reduced to Silence?

> Quick Quick take back your cruel Words again
> The first that e'er you utter'd to give pain
> And let not me alone be doom'd to find
> That once Ev'n generous Spencer was unkind.

I assure you this is no poetical flight but real sober truth.[19]

Nevertheless, though she could be docile before someone like Spencer, Greville's attack was generally formidable. It was she who at Tunbridge in the summer of 1778 took on Elizabeth Montagu in defense of Frances Burney's depiction of the "low" Branghtons in *Evelina*, [20] and she would have defended anywhere the right of a woman writer to indite scenes of delicious low satirical humor.

Frances Macartney, the third of the four daughters of James Macartney, an Irishman of some fortune who lived mostly in London, was, as Burney's description reveals, almost too gifted with beauty, wit, high spirits, and literary talent. When the dashing Fulke Greville saw her, he was determined to have her. For elegance and ton he was the leading fine young man in London, had a fortune besides, and in any case she had fallen in love with him—a mistake she later amply recognized. They were married rather hastily in 1748, and thereafter she had ample leisure to repent while he was at Brooks's or the racecourse throwing away his fortune.

Fulke Greville was an inconstant husband and a compulsive gambler. Even worse, if possible, he was so egomaniacal that he quarreled if anyone had the temerity to differ with him on the smallest point, suffered exquisitely, vociferously, and at length over the smallest inconvenience or cross, and rarely considered anyone's happiness except his own.

His ambition was to rival the illustrious Elizabethan kinsman whose namesake he was (not, as he let it be assumed, his direct descendant) in gentility and accomplishment, so that not only was he the complete sportsman, but he also lusted after literary fame, professing both poetry and philosophy. Had his pretensions been more modest, more adapted to his abilities, his abilities would have appeared respectable and he would not have been certified an overbearing fool. In early life his determined courtliness masked his egomaniacal obsession; in later life he became a caricature of tyrannical will exemplified. In 1770, when James Macartney died, he left an income to his daughter Frances for her life and attempted to ensure that her husband could not touch it. While Fulke Greville knew that she had a penny, he would not leave his wife alone. His threats of abduction if she did not disburse destroyed her chance of peace; she took refuge in Ireland. Her bank records show that even after their separation, he regularly made off with about half of her annual income of £800. Her death in 1789 was certainly hastened by his harrying.

In her frequent separations from her husband and her sojourns away from home even before their official separation in the mid-1780s, Greville was much in need of a companion; but she could neither afford to pay the expenses of another woman of her own class nor in conscience allow such a person to share her troubled existence, her lack of a home, the constant harassment by a man truly not in his right mind. Invitations to stay would also be harder to come by if she were to carry another gentlewoman with her. She did the best she could by using her maid as a companion, and her strong desire to remain autonomous and as self-directed as possible reinforced a decision through which she remained in sole charge. Because of the dual role the maid had to play, Greville was careful in her choices and was willing to put up with deficiency in the usual talent for hairdressing if the maid could only read sensibly to her—for like her friend Lady Holland and so many other women of her age, she suffered sadly from afflictions of the eyes. Evidence of Greville's character and need for privacy is apparent in the extent to which she interested herself in the histories, the families, and the troubles of her maids; she was barred by the rules of class structure from talking about her own life with them, but she could derive satisfaction from sharing their lives.

The first maid of whom we hear is Frances Lowe, who was very satisfactory and who, then only nineteen, was with Greville in January 1774 at Winterslow, the Wiltshire estate of Ste and Lady Mary Fox, when early in the morning of the ninth, after the public presentation of a play, the house, full of family, players, and guests who fled, burned to the ground. Lowe, sleeping in a room with Lady Mary's maid Sally, was awakened by Sally at three in the morning "with a great knock for that she could not speak she was so suffocated."[21] The subsequent behavior of the two maids was so feckless that it was great luck no one in the house died. They got up quietly and went down to the housekeeper's room to sleep, decided next to try the drawing room sofa, found a man sleeping there, went back to their room to see if the smoke had cleared—and met other inmates of the house, one of whom declared that his bed was on fire.

Lowe now ran to Greville and warned her, assuring her she need not hurry, then imploring her to make haste. Greville dispatched Lowe to warn her husband and her nearly grown sons in their rooms and still in her bedgown hurried to the nursery, where she found Lady Mary sitting dazed on the bed of one of her children; picking up the infant, Greville led the rest of the occupants of the nursery from the house. Lowe, burdened with responsibility beyond her capacity and also suffering from smoke inhalation, waked Fulke Greville in a fit of hysterical laughter. It developed that a beam under a fireplace in the house had been smoldering for days. In the early morning hours a battalion of guests emptied the house of furniture, and the house was consumed.

The next morning the Grevilles set out for Wilbury, their nearby Wiltshire home, in borrowed clothing, Greville in her bedgown, two underpetticoats, and someone's old scarlet cloak "half starved with Cold, Fanny [Lowe] & the Boys in another Chaise all of them so singularly drest, she with a great coat of L.ᵈ Pem[broke]'s." Pembroke's greatcoat fell to the silly young maid while Greville shivered in the old scarlet cloak. Perhaps the girl was already ill; whether or not because of smoke inhalation, Fanny Lowe sickened after the fire and in June 1775 Greville had to return her to her mother in London in so bad a way "that I should imagine there are but small hopes of her recovery." She had sent the eminent Dr. Warren to her, and Warren had not quite given her up, but Greville, now at Wilbury, was in sad straits for a maid and was consulting Lady Spencer, a woman who cultivated worthy families that were pools of promising servants, about Sarah Banister, "your little Gentlewoman." Banister was a girl apparently above the usual station for a maid, and she came, Spencer warned, with a wounded heart, but Greville would be glad to have her on trial, "provided she chuses to serve in that capacity & is at all qualified for it by knowing how to dress my hair & make up my caps &c. . . . A very small degree of science in either of these things will satisfy me." Banister should, however, know something of washing small linen and might take a few lessons of Spencer's friseur "just to be able to comb a toupee—& make two curls of a side which is all I ever have." [22]

As Lowe worsened, Greville tried to content herself with little Sarah Banister, who was uncomfortable in the station of a lady's maid but was so much the better qualified as a reader: "I really think there is great merit in this *Duodecimo*, she reads vastly well & enters with great intelligence into the Subjects she reads about, which is much better for me than if she was a mere Automate, & au reste she seems to have so willing a mind to improve in such things as she is not yet perfect in, that I foresee I should have some regret to part with her if she is inclined to live on with me, & can take up with such conditions as I am able to afford" (September 1, 1775).

In the autumn Greville went with her sister Catherine to Ireland; Banister probably went too. In her charge Greville had her thirteen-year-old niece Hester Lyttelton, the daughter of her sister Mary,[23] and Hester's governess, Margaret Planta. Greville, who made her society as she could find it, enjoyed this group. Planta was a great acquisition, "really a treasure," wrote Lady Louisa Conolly to her sister Emily, Duchess of Leinster, "and the only person I ever saw in that station that I should like; she is so exactly what one wants that I cannot help having an eye towards her for you, if ever you should want such a person." Planta was treated by Greville, always a snob to pretentious gentility but an egalitarian with people of merit, as a friend. Lady Louisa describes a "frolic" of her Christmas houseparty at Castletown when everyone put on masquerade disguises and invaded a neighbor's dinner party—Greville, her sister, her niece, Planta, Lady Louisa, and all, as priests, a Flora, nuns, a gypsy.[24]

In Ireland Greville received the news of the death of Frances Lowe and wrote the only epitaph I have seen penned by a mistress for her maid:

Epitaph on Fan: Lowe who died Novem[br] 11th 1775 Aged 21 Years

>Here rests in Peace within this rustick Tomb
>An humble Maid whose Death caused many a tear
>For Earth contains not in her ample Womb
>One that was once more gentle kind or fair—
>Yet Ah! let none lament her early Fate
>And blooming beauties mould'ring in the Grave
>Since Heav'n perhaps in mercy fix'd the date
>To take unsullied back the life it gave.[25]

Lines 6 to 8 of the poem remind that in regard to her servants Greville had always to consider the problems that an inconstant husband and four sons all capable of mischief might pose. Later she was to confess to Spencer that she had once engaged a maid under twenty (which Frances Lowe had also been) and "I do not recollect that my own youth & charms had ever been half so troublesome to me as hers were, & you will readily allow that to have all the plague of those things without the pleasures is a very disagreeable situation" (November 1776).

Back in England, at Bath, Greville had to inform Spencer that after all Sarah Banister would not do in the role of servant.

The plain truth of the matter [is] if she could get her bread by joyning with her sister in the Mantua Making business, or could work with any body in the Milinary way she would do much better than going to Service for tho' she has quite tallents enough to make a good Servant & many more than most have, yet she has a certain turn of mind & temper that will I am afraid always prevent her being pleased & consequently her pleasing others, but if you still wish she should be a Servant, I will not leave off my endeavours to find her a place for I wish the poor little Thing very well independantly of the pleasure it always gives to do any thing you approve of. (November 1776)

Staffing and running a house full of servants in those times cannot have been easy; people looking for service were plentiful, but good servants were scarce and had to be carefully trained. Lady Spencer, who was always helpful to poor families, extended her care to scenting out potentially good servants, sometimes training them and then placing them with her friends. Presumably she found another situation for Sarah Banister, and two years later she recommended Phyllis Knight to Greville. Knight was one of a family of promising young women, probably connections of Dick Knight, formerly the Spencers' famous huntsman at Althorp, or of Francis Knight of St. James's Street, the Spencers' stationery seller.[26] Greville requested that Mrs. Anne, Spencer's first woman, judge whether Phyllis could

get up, as they call it, small linnen work at her needle & dress up caps well enough to be a comfortable Servant to me. with regard to dressing hair if she is not quite without genius she may improve & as I shall not want much of that this Winter, I could more easily dispense with her scavoir faire in that respect, & as to reading it is almost impossible to find in that rank of life one that can read pleasantly till they have been tutor'd by better Masters or Mistresses than they ever get. If they have sense or feeling, as they grow to understand what they read they grow to express it. (November 22, 1778)

Sometimes in the course of their employment servants could be educated far beyond the requirements of their original class, if their employers required more of them, so that although education at the time was thoroughly adapted to maintain class (and gender) differentiation, individual usage could subvert the status quo. What became of Phyllis Knight after ten years in Greville's employment is unknown; but we have seen Fannen grow from a probable position as humble nursery maid to overseer of a great establishment and finally retired woman of independent means (chapter 7); the actress Sarah Siddons, an intimate friend of the great ladies of her time, had begun as a lady's maid. In this chapter we will see Lady Spencer educate a clergyman's daughter to become the well-prepared wife of a nabob. Women like Greville and Spencer were not reluctant to raise their protégées by educating them; and the readings aloud that upper servants were trained to perform must have been as vitally important in their education as the examples shown them by their employers.

Luckily Knight, despite her youth—she was under twenty—proved entirely satisfactory. She joined Greville early in 1779. Greville would have preferred her to stay longer in the Spencer household, where she was receiving expert training, but her temporary maid had a husband who required her at home. In July 1780 Knight went to Dublin with Greville, who found to her great pleasure that although the girl attracted admiration on board ship, her behavior was guarded and exemplary. In 1781 Knight had a long and worrisome illness, which began with a fit of hysterics after a fright. For six weeks Greville both nursed her and tended herself, no easy task at a time when ladies could not lace their own stays or dress their own hair. She feared that Knight would never be fit for service again and begged Spencer to send one of the younger Knights to help with her sister and do the washing. But Knight at length recovered, stayed with Greville to her death, and was remembered in her will.

Greville's and Spencer's troubles over servants—finding them, training them, keeping them in health, and, if they were promising, sometimes moving them onward—illustrate just a little the problems of housekeeping of the time and hint at the communities of women within each household that could cut across classes and provide companionship. For ten years Phyllis Knight was not only the maid but also the companion Greville sorely needed. But she was a companion who answered most practical purposes and demanded a minimum of emotional response. Greville protested against the uncritical acceptance of the burden of sensibility in a variety of ways. She avoided indulgence in emotion and maintained a firm control, if not of the circumstances of her life, at least of her responses to them. She defended wit and humor, attacked stereotypical feminine behavior, and allowed herself masculine forthrightness in conversation.

Probably on her own sixty-first birthday she wrote a set of verses which, significantly, she titled "The Old Man": the objectives she chooses for herself might have been considered too positively assertive from a woman's pen.

> My Sixty Years are roll'd away,
> Nay more, alas! I'm sixty one
> Yet not in darkness ends my day
> Some light still gilds my Horizon
> And to the last expiring spark
> I'll gaily steer my little bark.
>
> To Tyrant age I must submit
> But O avaunt ye hideous crew
> Detested followers of it;
> Think not I'll be a Slave to you;
> Time to my form may be unkind
> But he shall ne'er debase my mind.

Greville had had enough of tyrants and was determined not to lose her mental control and self-possession. In the ensuing stanzas "the old man" vows to remain charitable, unmiserly, uncensorious of lovers, modest about his own wisdom, still capable of enjoying friendship and the making of verses, though inspiration too has fled:

> I still can sing such songs as this
> Without a flight to Helicon.[27]

One suspects that poetic inspiration itself was suspect to the extent that it was not controllable.

Lady Spencer, whom Greville dearly loved, in part because her life, at least after widowhood, was so clearly self-determined, was a far more fortunate woman and far milder and less clever. She also saved most of her correspondence, which provides us with an interesting exploration of her relationship with one of her companions, Elizabeth Preedy. The relationship was in some respects that of a mother and daughter but also grew, unnoted and certainly unplanned by Spencer, both romantic and sentimental. The effect of Spencer's discovery of the unsuspected depth of the relationship is more comic than moving. Spencer, like Greville, needed a companion but preferred young girls with whom intimacy was seemingly far less likely. At one point in her widowhood one of her two best friends—peers, with equal knowledge of the world—offered to come live with her, and she responded with horror. She valued privacy, solitude, and autonomy, and she valued Elizabeth Preedy no less because she herself remained in control in their relationship. The development of the Preedy romance is therefore interesting; moreover, the affair provides an interesting counterpoint to the Montagu-Gregory conflict, for the crux of the problem was the question of marriage for the companion. Once again the mistress was loath to be parted from her ideal consort—but in this case the suitor was very rich, of good character, and not lightly to be spurned.

Georgiana Poyntz, Lady Spencer, had had an unusually good marriage. Elaine Showalter has noted the prevalence of feminized heroes in the novels of nineteenth-century women—men "feminized" into equality through disadvantages such as a physical disability.[28] (A "feminized" male might also be a husband of inferior station or fortune such as those chosen the second time by Hester Thrale, Mary Delany, and the Duchess of Leinster. Burney's husband was "feminized" by refugeeism.) Spencer, who married young and without such considerations, captured the best match of her period, the man who with all his other possessions was also the heir of the great Duchess of Marlborough. But he suffered from two constraints: the eccentric duchess's will forbade him to hold public office so he could not join his fellows in the public arena; and he was a valetudinarian. He was thus disadvantaged very nearly to the level of his wife. In the twenty-eight years of their marriage he was unusually dependent on her companionship, collaboration, and friendship. Because the prescribed distance from political life was the same for both, they shared an active vicarious political life. They were both mild-tempered, congenial people, and they developed together a skill at manipulating local and influencing national politics and a great interest in antiquities and Continental travel. Lady Spencer completed her influence over her husband by becoming a skillful guardian of his health, and they took an equal interest in the celebrated Pytchley Hounds and Althorp Hunt with which they rode. She attested to their compatibility by producing four children (one of whom died young) and in almost every alternate year suffering a miscarriage—in the twenty-third year of her marriage, 1778, a pregnancy and a miscarriage prevented her joining her daughter the Duchess of Devonshire at Tunbridge. The domestic happiness of the pair was certified by the cynical Lord March in 1767: "They are really the happiest people I think I ever saw in the marriage system. *Enfin, c'est le meilleur menage possible.*"[29]

Spencer had the ample means denied to Greville and was a great organizer of charities. In London she had a charitable group into which she enticed many women of fashion and which managed a fund distributed in appropriate sums to worthy objects.[30] This was one of her methods of establishing her sense of control during her marriage. Spencer was devastated by the death of her husband in 1783, when she was forty-six, but took the opportunity to please nobody thenceforward but herself and to revise her life-style as she considered appropriate for a widow. Her son established his own family at Althorp, and she retired to Holywell House in St. Albans, the former home of the first Duke and Duchess of Marlborough. She took a great interest in the occupants of the Marlborough Almshouses in St. Albans, erected by Duchess Sarah herself. In these endeavors she was assisted by the Reverend Benjamin Preedy, formerly master of the St. Albans grammar school and rector of St. Albans,[31] and by his son James, who succeeded him at the school and with whom, whenever possible, Spencer daily read Greek and Latin. Even before her husband's death, after the marriages of her daughters, Spencer had often felt the need of a female companion with whom to walk, read, and discuss domestic affairs. The accomplished Georgiana Shipley, daughter of the bishop of St. Asaph, had for some years spent considerable time with Spencer, but in 1783 she had married. And dating from around the time of the marriage of Spencer's younger daughter Harriet to Lord Duncannon in November 1780, Elizabeth

Preedy, the daughter of the rector, had been making useful visits to Spencer and was helpful during her husband's final illness and after his death.

The Preedy family were protégés (or "clients") of the Spencers, and after Spencer was widowed, the Preedys became better friends than ever. Dr. Preedy had left St. Albans for Brington in Northamptonshire, a Spencer living, before Elizabeth Preedy came to stay with Spencer, but his son James had functioned briefly as headmaster of the school and then apparently filled in as his father's curate at St. Albans.

Elizabeth Preedy was present with Spencer behaving like an exemplary daughter in the years immediately after Lord Spencer's death when Spencer's own two daughters, Georgiana, Duchess of Devonshire, and Lady Harriet Duncannon (in 1793 the Countess of Bessborough), were most worrisome. The contrast between Spencer's life as a widow and the lives of her daughters was great. Both Spencer and her husband had been eager gamblers.[32] To distance herself from that former life, which she may have thought corrupted her daughters, and as a form of conspicuous critique of that life, Spencer emerged from her grief to establish a calm and useful but almost Spartan existence, the prevailing rule of which was to use her time as God would best approve. The time she took for study and self-improvement was never allowed to impinge on her duties to others. Though she did not begrudge frequent visits to London to see her daughters and her grandchildren, she liked best to be at Holywell House. Here she rose early and read history and studied Greek—first the New Testament, then Homer—with James Preedy, followed sometimes by readings in Latin, which she already knew.

Her day was spent calling on or receiving the calls of her many friends or visiting the inmates of "the buildings," her almshouses. She instituted a Sunday school at St. Albans. She was an active and dedicated fisher and a great walker, often walking long distances on her errands. She dined frugally when alone on chicken or an egg with greens, walked again after dinner if there were sufficient warmth and light, and in the evenings preferred to have sermons or history read, though if callers came she obligingly provided cards or other games.[33] She was attempting to take rational control of her own life.

Elizabeth Preedy was a young woman of her daughter's age but of a temperament more like Spencer's, quiet and sedate, and by 1786 Spencer needed a friend of that description. The young social set round the Prince of Wales had become profligate; rumors and scandals about its members tarnished their reputations but could not banish them from society while the prince continued all the more to countenance them. Spencer's daughters were perpetually dismaying and humiliating her. Her beloved daughter Georgiana, the Duchess of Devonshire, was social leader of the prince's set, countenancer and too frequently abettor of its amours. In the spring of 1786 the duchess had seconded her cousin Georgiana Poyntz Fawkener in her love affair with Jack Townshend, and when this niece eloped from William Fawkener, Spencer found herself in the position of trying to undo what her daughter had done. She captured her niece, but the young woman eloped again to go to Townshend in lodgings in Hampstead, sending to her aunt for her clothes. Spencer's anguish over this affair was much exacerbated by her daughter's implication in it; she had to visit her desolated brother and his wife to confer with them in May.

Meanwhile Harriet Duncannon, Spencer's younger daughter, had modeled her marital life on her sister's. During the summer of 1786 there were rumors, untrue but disturbing, that she had run off with a lover. In July 1786 Lady Elizabeth Foster, whom as the duke's mistress Spencer usually refused to meet, had reappeared in England, upon the duchess's urgent request: "Je ne vie pas sans toi!"[34]—perhaps a cry of love or perhaps an admission that she needed Foster to bring the duke round again. In September 1786 the duchess's gambling debts had created a crisis, and Spencer had to journey to Chatsworth to attend deliberations on her fate; the duke wanted to rusticate her, a system which if pursued for a year or two might have saved her. Spencer could not bring herself to agree to a course that would mean public disgrace and found herself for once on the same side as Foster. But the question was debated for some time; in October Spencer's son George, who may have disbursed to help his sister, was retiring to the country to retrench and willing that the duchess should join him there.[35]

Spencer grieved particularly over this most beloved child the duchess, who had now shaken off the maternal influence because of her unhealthy alliance with Elizabeth Foster and the protection and influence of the prince. In his set men almost openly fathered children with their friends' wives, and they shared the favors not only of their wives but also of certain courtesans (one of whom, after making the circuit, married Charles Fox). Gambling was seemingly the only other occupation of the set as they waited for what never did happen, the accession to power of their party with Fox as prime minister. The duchess's terrible addiction, her enormous debts, and her general extravagance were frightening, her recurrent attacks of convulsive fits (hysteria) were frightening, but even more frightening were her unwillingness to control her vices and her recourse to lying about them and about Foster to everyone, including her mother, rather than addressing her problems. As if all that were not enough, in 1786 she had begun the disastrous love affair with Charles Grey, which in 1791 was to end in her pregnancy.

In the peace of Holywell House at St. Albans, Spencer found solace with the quiet Elizabeth Preedy, a girl who was perfectly attuned to the life there. Spencer was given to warm, even romantic attachments. Her attachment to the duchess, her daughter, was also in its way romantic. For years after marriage the duchess had written her mother, her own avowed first love, every day. In August 1781, for instance (some months before she met Foster), she wrote verses which declared that at all times, while dressing, while surrounded by Babel-like voices,

> Whate'er the place, or how or when
> My heart still dictates to my pen
> And keeps its favourite hope in view
> Of vowing every thought to you.[36]

The duchess may have needed to carry an imaginary lover-mentor about with her, rather like the Sylph, but before long her mother's views had become inconvenient; Foster was an ideal replacement. Here, of course, was another reason for Spencer's detestation of Foster. In the difficult years between 1783 and 1786, Preedy steadily gained ground as the substitute for both the dead earl and the delinquent daughter(s), and Spencer's love for Preedy grew considerably more romantic than Spencer realized. The crisis came when Preedy attracted a marriage proposal from a middle-aged and widowed but entirely unobjectionable nabob, Charles Bourchier.[37] Bourchier's reason for making his choice can only be conjectured. No doubt he found Preedy attractive, but middle-aged men of wealth did not marry primarily to gratify a predilection. This was for him a second marriage, he had two young sons, and he required not so much a fortune to establish a second family as an amenable young wife to oversee his first, which now included an aging mother. In Preedy, a companion so satisfying to the Countess Spencer, he could be virtually guaranteed a genuinely amenable young person, he could be assured that she understood the ways of an aristocratic household run with absolute meticulousness, and his wife would have, as he would have, the social countenance of Lady Spencer and her connections, no inconsiderable *douceur*. Bating the lack of fortune, Preedy was an advantageous match. From her own point of view she would cease servicing one mistress and undertake the servicing of a husband, his mother, and two stepsons.

The Preedy family, dependent upon the clerical earnings of the father, had no money of their own, and the wealthy Bourchier, aged forty-seven, must have seemed equally attractive to them. But Spencer and Preedy found their life together so congenial that both were loath to give it up. Moreover, it is apparent that at the first Preedy loved Spencer considerably more than she esteemed Bourchier. In September 1786, while the proposal was pending and no decision had been taken, Spencer had to go to Chatsworth to attend the deliberations about her daughter's possible rustication. Spencer's friend Caroline Howe, who with Lady Clermont remained behind at Holywell, reported, "Poor Miss Preedy retired to her room soon after she saw the last of your chaise. I let her alone about 20 minutes & then visited her, sat & chatted a while with her, & then brought her in to Lady Clermont pretty well composed. I do not wonder at her fondness for you." [38]

From Chatsworth Spencer replied by confiding the news of Bourchier's proposal. Ought Preedy to marry and leave her? "The Difference," she suggested, "is so great between a footing of friendship & a state of dependence—however easy—that one ought not in Conscience to advise her against it." Interestingly, Spencer, whose marital relationship had been one of unusual friendship, made an assessment of marriage as friendship and apparently considered companionship but not marriage as a state of dependency.[39]

Spencer wrote again on September 6 with a fuller explanation—no doubt the affair helped to distract her from her darker and more frustrating preoccupation at Chatsworth—to reveal that Preedy had given Bourchier the answer they had devised, "saying they were too little acquainted with each other to be able to form any Judgment how far such an engagement might promote the happiness of each of them—& that she was herself too happy in her present situation to have any wishes to change it—it ended I believe in his proposing to make her Father a visit at Brington & Consequently I look upon the whole matter as settled."

Spencer was concerned because she was to visit her brother in Norfolk in November and could not manage there (she thought) without Preedy but believed she could not take her away for a prolonged visit at such a crucial period. On September 14 she sent news that "Miss Preedy presents an obstinate silence about her intentions but as she now corresponds with him, or at least he writes to her, & goes to Brington with her Consent, I conclude she is determined." But on September 18 there was more news: Preedy was "sadly agitated & sometimes seems quite determined that nothing shall make her Marry and leave me, at other times she hesitates." And there was a new factor: Preedy had a brother farming at Althorp who was dying and would leave a large family destitute. If he died, Spencer thought, Preedy would marry to soothe her father, who having now met Bourchier, wished her to seize her opportunity. Howe responded from Richmond that the brother was dead but that she herself would prefer Preedy to marry from inclination.

On September 25, Spencer reported, Preedy had written to her. "She doubts if she shall ever feel as strong an affection for anybody as she has for me—& says that the very happy time she has passed with me seems to be sliding from her & she knows not whither she is going. . . . All this confirms the Idea of her intending to Marry."

From Chatsworth Spencer continued to discuss Preedy's affair with her friend while remaining determinedly silent on the subject of her troubles about her daughter. On October 9 she wrote to announce that Preedy had consented to marry in March but wished to visit with Spencer in Norfolk in the interim. Bourchier was to settle £10,000 on Preedy at once and more when he got his money from India. Spencer had replied, instructing her "by no means to put off her Marriage till March as he must now be her first object—& I ought not to have the preference, besides that the living so many months with me is by no means a good way of disposing her more to marry him." She had decided that it would be difficult and against Preedy's preference for her to marry but that she must do it. Whether or not this is precisely how Preedy felt, the two women gradually reached a highly emotional state about the situation, and Spencer began to view herself, if unconsciously, as Bourchier's preferred rival and herself and Preedy almost as the lovers in a romantic tragedy.

At last Bourchier brought Preedy to Spencer in preparation for the Norfolk journey. Spencer's observation of the couple was that she was attentive to him and he adored her. But on October 31 she cheerfully reported to Howe that Preedy was miserable at the thought of leaving her and had offered more than once to end the engagement. In November from North Creek, her brother's home, Spencer wrote that she found Preedy liked Bourchier better than she had thought and "seems to think of her future prospects with less apprehension than at first but her spirits are weak and she is so agitated whenever she talks of parting with me that I am quite fidgetty about it. . . . I can never send her away alone, &

it would not be right I am sure to have him come & fetch her, & see how unwilling she is to go,—the least ill consequence of that, would be his taking an aversion to me." How, then, was the bride to be delivered? On November 10 Spencer responded to Howe, "I do not like your Advice about carrying Miss Preedy to St Albans—she would have all the distress of leaving me & Holywell under Mr Bourchiers & his Mothers Eyes who would neither of them be pleased with her expressing much Concern— at all events they should not see how sorry she can be to leave me & go to him.—She says if she can be alone, or with any body to whom she need not fear showing what she feels for one day after she quits me she is sure shall do very well—I fancy I must get her Brother to meet her." Good news ensued: Mr. Bourchier had sensibly taken a house close to Holywell called Tittenhanger. But on November 29 Spencer wrote, "It is terrify- ing as she say's, to depend for the rest of her life upon a Man, with whose real Character she is so little acquainted, this added to the thoughts of our living asunder, makes us both sometimes good for nothing."

A small comedy followed concerning the silver candlestick Spencer selected as her wedding present to Preedy. Spencer wished to entwine upon it her own initials and Preedy's maiden ones. Howe forbore to suggest that the initials of the bridal couple might be more appropriate but suggested that the candlestick might be engraved with the initials EB and an allusive motto. For the moment, at least, Spencer compro- mised for the initials EP but may have reverted to her original design.

More to-do occurred when in early December Bourchier insisted Preedy must come down to Tittenhanger to settle some arrangements. He came himself and took her away, ostensibly for only a few days. Once she had gone, however, Spencer could not help but think that the problem of separation without offending him because of the strength of Preedy's affection for her had luckily been resolved, and she wrote, "in the strongest manner I can—not absolutely to forbid her—but to repre- sent how much pain she will save us both . . . for her to stay where she is—I quite grieve on my own account . . . but I am really afraid if she comes back it will be too much for her."

Preedy came back. On December 20 Howe responded to a letter of Spencer's (now missing), which apparently suggests that Preedy had been pressured into consenting to marry and that her health was there- fore affected. On December 21 Spencer revealed that she herself had been very low and had had a violent fit of crying. "Miss Preedys going begins to be a serious matter both to her & to me."

On January 1, 1787, the separation had been concerted. Preedy would be taken to Newmarket, where she would be met by Bourchier and his brother. "She will have had the whole day to recover in which I hope will do & when that is once over she will have such a perpetual course of occupations that she will I dare say feel less than she thinks she shall. . . . We both live in dread of Thursday Senni't."

Preedy suffered from a nervous cough. On January 3, Spencer wrote, they were comforting themselves that they would live near each other, meet often, make her father and family happy, and gratify a wealthy man whose comfort depended only on Preedy. But the day before at prayers Preedy had had a violent fit of laughing and crying hysterics. The hysterics continued daily until on January 11 Preedy at last set out.

The question of female hysteria has arisen four times in this single chapter,[40] and perhaps its prevalence may shed some light on the problem. Carroll Smith-Rosenberg has suggested that one cause of such hysteria may be the discontinuity between the demands made on women: on one hand, as proper submissive females to be retiring, passive, and unresourceful; on the other, as the "upper servants" who oversaw the development of children and the running of households, to be forthcoming, active, and resourceful.[41] Both of Greville's maids seem to have suffered fits of hysterics when called upon to act independently in a crisis.[42] If we apply to Smith-Rosenberg for an explanation, might it not be true that as good lesser servants they were too thoroughly accustomed to acting obediently under orders? Both Spencer's daughter and her surrogate daughter, her companion, resorted to hysterics under stress. Might it not be that both were accustomed to following Spencer's stern moral lead and were frightened at having to seize more autonomous control of their lives? Dorothea Gregory (chapter 6) resorted to hysterics when her confrontation over Archibald Alison reached an impasse and a crisis. Gregory was already a notable, independent woman being asked to take direction like a child, marry a child, and remain in the status of a child: might she not have suffered the same conflict in reverse?

Possibly the duchess, only sixteen when she left home to marry and still very much under her mother's direction, felt the want of direction from her indifferent husband and fell into fits when required to exert self-control. No doubt Spencer had provided Preedy with direction as well. There is some hint that in Spencer's thinking Bourchier was to succeed her as mentor, as well as, perhaps, lover, in her tendency to think of herself and him as rivals, in the major consideration she makes of the actual handing over of the bride from herself to him, and in her fears that he may come to resent her influence.

Spencer too may have responded nervously to a sense of loss of control. The day after Preedy departed, Spencer confessed that she was very low. "I have dreaded the loss of her ever since this business has been in view & now I dread still more for I fear her health is declining—I did not know how much I loved her nor did I at all suspect I should feel so much as I have done about her these last eight & forty hours."

In town Preedy visited Howe and was presented with a remedy for the hysterics and the candlestick, of which she kissed the cipher (had Spencer after all stubbornly had their initials intertwined?). Howe wrote that she had heard Bourchier had settled £500 a year on his bride; Spencer replied that it was £600 and £10,000 in the stocks.

Following the wedding, Spencer continued to agonize for some time, fearing that the change would be fatal to Preedy. The cough improved, but within three months she was pregnant. Spencer had great apprehensions, for Preedy was no longer young and by no means strong; moreover, her body had a bony sort of firmness, which Spencer had heard was in childbed always attended with greater pain and difficulty than when the joints were more relaxed. In November Preedy had a healthy daughter christened Georgiana, and Spencer gradually became reassured that her protégée was safe, happy, prosperous, and even likely to live.

Many of Spencer's journals survive, and they assist in the reconstruction of her life. But the journals for the traumatic years 1786 and 1787 do not survive. Through all this time Spencer diverted herself with concern for Preedy and was suffering acutely over the behavior of her daughters but would not risk discussing these affairs in her letters. She may have later discarded her journals of this period as memorials of an epoch she did not care to memorialize. The journal of 1785 shows no signs of the importance of Preedy. At the end of that year Preedy was at Holywell House while Spencer, concerned about the birth of one of Harriet's children, was traveling to and from Cavendish Square. On October 9 Spencer and Preedy walked to the almshouses to visit some of the inmates; Spencer was then absent at her daughter's until the twentieth, when returning to Holywell, "I found Miss Preedy. the Evening was wet. we could not walk but we read till Prayer time." Another week at Cavendish Square was succeeded by a visit to St. Albans from the duchess and her two daughters. In St. Albans members of the Preedy family often came to dine, but Preedy herself is not often mentioned. Perhaps in the year 1786 she grew closer to Spencer. Perhaps Spencer distracted herself from her distresses about the duchess in 1786 by thinking more about Preedy. And perhaps, as she says, she had not realized how much she loved and depended on Preedy until they were faced with separation.

Spencer, who throughout her marriage had accommodated herself to her husband, as well as suffering (after their marriages) the flagrancies of two not very amenable daughters, had doubtless enjoyed the years with Preedy, who had accommodated herself so entirely to her. The 1788 journals reveal that Spencer continued to regret her loss. The Bourchiers lived nearby at Tittenhanger and never neglected Spencer; there was contact between the two houses several times a week and sometimes daily: short visits, long ones, dinners, overnight visits. Despite the speedy appearance of Preedy's daughter Georgiana, Preedy often came to visit the almshouses with Spencer or to sit with her when she was ill—once even at Devonshire House—or to spend the evenings when she was alone. Bourchier also came to dinner or to call. On January 17, 1788, Spencer dined at Tittenhanger and took a walk round the plantation afterward with Bourchier, "much pleased with the Manner in which he spoke of his Wife of his increasing affection for her & of her general Conduct which was pleasing to him & to every body."[43]

On January 25, the Bourchiers' first anniversary, Spencer composed lines for the occasion in her chaise. Then, "M.^{rs} Ch: B.—— came & returned before dinner to Tittenhanger—she has been this day married a year, & seems happy & likely I hope to continue so—which I rejoice at most sincerely tho' I feel every hour the loss of such a Companion. I gave her some lines I had written in the chaise . . . which affected her more than I intended they should. they were on the progress of our friendship."[44]

In the end Spencer let Preedy go and thrive, the proper unselfish choice. On the discovery of the depth of her attachment, she relinquished Preedy, in her sacrifice expressing, like Greville, her distrust of emotional indulgence. Spencer spent her last years subduing herself. Though always kind and right thinking, she was also mightily ambitious, had made an ambitious marriage herself, and had married her daughters ambitiously. She had vastly enjoyed her political influence. Perhaps she saw the early death of her husband and the disastrous careers of her daughters as a punishment. In her widowhood she rigorously disciplined herself and tried to make amends. To relinquish Preedy would have seemed to her all the more right because it required the loss of the good daughter who had comforted her for her prodigals. Faced with a choice of sensibility that represented the difference between the indulgence of selfish emotionalism and the rigorous requirements of altruism, she rejected selfish considerations. Both Greville and Spencer profited by companionship, but though both had important women friends, neither chose companionships in which the companions were equals. They had their own ways of protesting against the stringent definitions of genteel women of their time, and each had the strength to manage largely on her own. They demonstrated the endurance and the fortitude so prized by Burney. And by deliberately tempering their sensibility with rational self-control they managed to become whole persons. Each, however, in her later life, to a greater extent than most women of fashion of the time, lived much of the time without intimate collaboration with their women peers, confining their contacts with them to visits and correspondence. Arguably, combinations of equal women living in close collaboration provided a greater possibility of self-realization to women, as the next two chapters show.

Chapter Twelve

FRIENDS: MOLLY CARTER
AND LOUISA CLARGES

A WOMAN WHO TOOK AS A COMPANION an unmarried social equal, someone
with money of her own, excellent connections, and many of the same
friends, was not disposed toward either termagancy or tyranny. Such a
companion as Mary (or Molly) Carter with money of her own actually
had two advantages over a wife: the money remained her own, and she
could depart with it whenever she chose.

Moll Carter, as she was affectionately known, was a companion with
all these advantages, and in addition she took charge of the motherless
Louisa Clarges when she was in her mid-forties and Louisa was scarcely
in her late teens. The role she filled during the eight or nine years they
lived together was to some extent that of Clarges's mother and guide:
despite social problems of her own, she helped introduce Clarges into
society. There is also the possibility that the two women were lovers—
Carter was generally thought to be a lesbian—but given her maternal
function and the difference in age between the women, that remains an
open question. Clarges was not the sort to need a mother or guide forever, and Carter was not the sort to encourage dependence. The pair
separated, still friends, after Clarges had been fully established on her
own in fashionable society; the separation might have been like that of
mother and adult daughter, of lovers who have outlived their mutual
need, of bear leader and cub who have concluded their travels—any or
all of these.

Carter was an unusual and notable woman, the daughter of a Welsh
family, which in 1729 had bought the estate of Redbourne in Lincolnshire.[1] The youngest of the twelve children of William Carter, member
of Parliament, and his wife and cousin, Sarah Price, she was christened
at Redbourne on January 22, 1731. She was only fourteen when the

nineteen-year-old Charles Burney, sent to Elsham by his master Arne to officiate as musical conductor at the revels of a large houseparty of the young, first met and assessed her, writing later, "Miss Carter, very young, intelligent and handsome, though very pleasing, did not discover herself to be possessed of so large portion of wit, as that for wch she has since been so justly celebrated."[2]

The Carter family circumstances were easy, but with so many children to provide for, money for its unmarried daughters cannot have been plentiful, and no family could afford to establish either younger sons or daughters in the style in which Carter later lived. In 1774 she was living in her own house at 7 Hill Street, Grosvenor Square;[3] in 1778 she rented stables, suggesting that her considerable establishment included a carriage and coachmen, horses, and grooms. Her will (1812) mentions a cook, housekeeper, two maids, and a manservant. Such a life-style required an income of at least £1,000 a year.[4] Given the different circumstances of the spinster daughters of other well-to-do families, one can only wonder at both her income and her independence. She may have acquired other significant sums through inheritance, though to live on her interest at the rate of £1,000 a year she would have needed a fortune of at least £20,000. She may have made fortunate investments. Another interesting possibility, feasible because of her life-style, is that she found a way to be profitably useful in society, sometimes perhaps taking in women like herself not to "lodge" but to live with her; sometimes functioning as she did with Clarges to introduce people into society; sometimes acting—as she also did with Clarges—as a courier and guide on expeditions to the Continent. In any case, she was for her time a remarkable woman.

She also had a remarkable character. Good-humored and strong-minded, she was not inclined to direct the lives of others, in which, however, she took a great friendly interest, always willing to do what she could to oblige or assist. She never displayed malice and was high-spirited with a great sense of fun. She was well-informed and had excellent common sense and judgment. Her empathetic nature gave her genuine sensibility, and she had a "masculine intelligence," a combination that made her a mature altruist with a perfectly developed capacity for self-preservation. She had no faith in limitations set on women and was independent in thought and action. At the end of her life she was to write to Lady Spencer, "I was most assuredly began for a Mule & finished for a Woman."[5]

So far as can be determined, the financial provision made for Carter was not extraordinary. William Carter died in 1744, when Moll was thirteen. His eldest son, Thomas, then about thirty, inherited both Redbourne and responsibility for his mother and siblings. The sum settled on their daughters in William and Sarah Carter's marriage settlement is not mentioned, but some details that are known suggest that the provision for younger daughters was at least £3,000 and perhaps more.[6] No possible provision, however, could have bought Carter even an annuity of £1,000 a year, and that she lived on interest rather than on an annuity is indicated by the sum she had to leave in legacies—almost £7,000 and probably considerably more. When her brother Thomas died in 1767, he left Carter £500 and all that had been left him by his sister Susannah.[7] Unless someone else died making her an absolute heiress—which no one ever implied she was—that is all the money likely to have come to her. So it seems possible that Carter made her own fortune.

At least after 1747, when her brother Thomas entered Parliament, Carter lived with him either at Redbourne or, in the season, in his house in St. James's Street, where with her other unmarried female relations —her sisters and her orphaned niece Charlotte Willoughby—she kept house for him. When Thomas Carter died unmarried in 1767 the estate went to his next brother, the Reverend Robert Carter, with whom his sisters never had much to do; the youngest brother, Roger, was named the contingent heir and beneficiary of a £200 annuity. Molly Carter, now thirty-five and unmarried, would at this point probably have clubbed her income with the incomes of her unmarried sisters and her niece and have taken a house with them, and very possibly this is what she did. Little is heard of her for some time; as a single older woman in society and no heiress, of a family that produced no more political figures or even male heirs, she was of no dynastic and of little social interest.

Some indication that she spent her middle years among her many family connections, gradually extending her acquaintance beyond the family and its friends, is provided in an incomplete letter written late in her life to Lady Spencer, who in those later days (or after 1793) had become her intimate friend. The letter is a brief memoir of Carter's acquaintance with Jane Collier's sister Margaret, whom she had encountered in Ryde on the Isle of Wight in June 1773 while staying with the Charles Gore family, connections from Lincolnshire. Someone, Carter explained, had described Mrs. Collier "as an extraordinary Amiable Benevolent *Character*" so that they all determined to visit her in the miserable cottage in which she was then living. Having found her to be fond of music and with nothing but a dreadful spinet to play on, Mrs. Gore sent her the present of a pianoforte, and Carter sent her some of Handel's works. Some years later Carter returned in two consecutive years and saw her again, then "in *her great Stile*," in much improved conditions.[8]

The sisters of Charles Gore had been girlhood friends of Carter's, and apparently she had kept up the acquaintance. Within a month or so of Carter's visit, the entire Gore family went to Florence and remained on the Continent thereafter for many years. Although Carter was to take possession of her house in Hill Street in 1774, it seems possible that she accompanied the Gores abroad for a year, perhaps as a sort of doyen for the Gore daughters. Perhaps her fee provided her with sufficient funds to take her London house. Her self-assurance when in 1783 she escorted Lady Clarges abroad suggests she had had previous experience.

Her having been abroad at times, or in the country, might help to explain why neither her old friend Charles Burney nor his journalizing daughter Frances ever mentioned her. But another possibility is that she may have been under a cloud such as that hinted at in a letter she wrote to Edward Jerningham. It is certain that she was established in her house in Hill Street by 1774 and that soon after Clarges's marriage in 1777, and perhaps before, she was in charge of the young woman. But in 1778, when she was in Tunbridge with Clarges—who was then a young bride expecting her first child—she went unnoted by the commentators on that exceedingly high-fashion season; nor did she go about with Clarges into society.[9] Why did she stay in the background? She begins to be noticed sparingly in the 1780s, and she was "taken up" by such people as Lady Spencer in the 1790s. But although she was acknowledged as Charles Burney's oldest friend and corresponded with him in their last years, there are no early letters extant and no known Burney references to her London life before the end of the century. All this is mysterious but suggests that a marked deviation from the norm for women caused her to be regarded suspiciously until she was in her sixties and had become an undisputed and interesting "character."

Louisa Skrine Clarges, for whom Carter provided an essential service, is as mysterious a figure as her companion. She was born with few claims to social acceptance and found an establishment greatly beyond her expectations. Her father was the son of a well-known and rich Bath apothecary, her mother, though respectably born, a cast mistress of Lord Sandwich, and her parents married not until she was four.

William Skrine was indulged by his mother after his father's death in 1725, went to Oxford, made aristocratic friends, toured the Continent, rapidly dispersed his large fortune, and was fairly indistinguish-

able—save for the inevitable jokes about his origins—from the other
fashionable rakes of the day, except that he was especially attractive to
and successful with women.[10] Before 1760 he had formed a connection
with Jane Sumner, a woman of beauty, wit, and cultivation, the sister of
Robert Carey Sumner, the master of Harrow, and of William Brightwell
Sumner, an Indian nabob, the niece of John Sumner, canon of Windsor and headmaster of Eton.[11] She had been debauched by the repro-
bate Lord Sandwich and from him had probably obtained an annuity as
well as the diamonds she bequeathed her daughter. Highly intelligent,
she apparently had not repined overmuch at her lost respectability but
took some pleasure in the freedom of "the life." She was described as
the constant companion of the famous Kitty Fisher, a spirited conversationalist who spoke French with great fluency; and she was described
as a "great source of entertainment in Kitty's alliances," being "not only
a professed satyrist, but a woman of learning and an excellent companion." Lord Ligonier often made up their trio, "and some of the merriest
hours of his life he acknowledges to have passed with these two *ladies
of genuine pleasure.*"[12]

More than one man of the period, having run out of funds, as a last
resort married a pensioned-off mistress, but apparently Sumner's income was not sufficient to tempt Skrine to marry her. Louisa was born
on June 6, 1760, and christened at St. George's, Hanover Square, as
Louisa Missington.[13] In 1764 Skrine's good friend William Brightwell
Sumner offered him his sister with a fortune of £10,000. Skrine, in desperate money troubles, accepted, and the pair were married by Robert
Carey Sumner at the church where Louisa had been christened on
May 21, 1764. Soon afterward they departed for the Continent, where
the English in delicate social or financial situations customarily sought
refuge. Jane Sumner was already in precarious health. In the latter part
of 1765 the Skrines were in Turin, and on November 26 Laurence Sterne
and his friend John Errington, passing through the town, witnessed her
will.[14] She died in Rome in February 1766, an event at which Walpole
commented, "I suppose Mr. Skreene is glad of his consort's departure.
She was a common creature, bestowed on the public by Lord Sandwich."[15]

In her brief will Sumner left her diamonds, by her marriage settlement her own, to her daughter, and appointed Skrine Louisa's guardian until his remarriage, in which case he was to be succeeded by her
brother William. Skrine was her executor.

The illegitimate daughters of men of fashion usually inherited the social positions of their mothers with commensurate fortunes.[16] In the case of Louisa Skrine, even the position of her father had not a great deal to recommend it: he had neither family nor (any longer) fortune. Louisa's own fortune, perhaps no more than her mother's diamonds, may have been augmented by her nabob uncle. But to her own brilliant charms (and the sensible family decision to introduce her to society so that she might have an opportunity to show them off) must be credited her brilliant marriage. She was delicately beautiful, sprightly, playful, essentially good, and had an exquisitely trained soprano voice and a "cantabile that would do credit to a composer"; she also played the harpsichord.[17] She was a serious and dedicated musician; music was always her predominant interest. We hear of her first at Brighton, in the summer season of 1777, when she was seventeen. Bath, Tunbridge, or Brighton, where people mixed more informally than in London, would have been the logical place to introduce her, and she must have been there with a woman who could sponsor her; probably Carter or someone like her provided by William Sumner (soon after this time Skrine did remarry) was already on the scene.

At her engagement to the rich Sir Thomas Clarges, Louisa Skrine first burst into notice, having now become of interest to the custodians of the patriarchal record. Sir Thomas, also devoted to music, was of a lineage pleasantly combining the advantages of city money and aristocratic breeding. In 1771 Frances Burney had found him "a modest young baronet" and in 1775 "a young baronet . . . formerly so desperately enamoured of Miss Linley, now Mrs. Sheridan, that his friends made a point of his going abroad to *recover himself.*" He had then barely returned, but she thought "he still retains all the school-boy English *mauvaise honte;* scarcely speaks but to make an answer, and is as shy as if his last residence had been Eaton instead of Paris." [18]

Louisa Skrine had all the attributes of the beautiful Elizabeth Linley, including the delightful soprano voice. Sir Thomas plunged into love a second time, and his guardians may have feared to thwart him again, but more probably the less-than-ideal match proved acceptable to them because it extricated him from an entanglement with the unhappily married Lady Warren.[19] Skrine's father was living respectably enough in Arlington Street, a member of Parliament for the borough of Callington (and so safe from arrest for debt). The powerful Lord Barrington, Skrine's intimate friend and Sir Thomas's uncle, interested himself in the arrangements.

When the engagement was announced, Louisa Skrine was suddenly of consequence, and the scribes set to work. Lady Mary Coke sent her sister word of the engagement on September 25, reminding her that she must remember Mr. Skrine, who married Miss Sumner, kept by Lord Sandwich, and took her abroad to live, where she died. She added that Louisa Skrine was very accomplished and probably had a good fortune. Lady Spencer's correspondents Mrs. Howe and Rachel Lloyd sent her the news, Mrs. Howe on September 29, adding that Skrine was giving his daughter £8,000 at present and that if he did not marry again, she would have a good fortune. From Brighton Lloyd mistakenly announced the wedding on October 16, adding that it was "a match made here this summer. She has but eight thousand pounds, so its a great match for her." The wedding took place at St. George's, Hanover Square, on November 6, which left time for Elizabeth Burges to inform her mother that Miss Skrine had "charm'd him with her musical power—her Mother . . . was a kept mistress to Mr. S, an Apothecary, who afterwards married her."[20]

Tracing the accretion of information here one feels some pity for the girl who thus entered society. She was only seventeen, and a respectably born woman like Carter would have been useful in the new establishment of the couple on Tilney Street.

The brief marriage was happy and productive. In its five years the Clarges had four children and entered into social and political life as well as into the small fashionable London musical circle in which they were happiest. The new Lady Clarges was acceptable if not a great success during the 1778 summer season at Tunbridge, where the Duchess of Devonshire, wearing a regimentally inspired riding habit, presided over the circle of her friends whose militia husbands, under the threat of imminent French invasion, were encamped with thousands of troops at nearby Cox Heath. The duchess, probably on her mother's advice, admitted Clarges, whom she very much liked, into her small circle but stopped short of making a friend of her. It was the way of Opposition hostesses, led by the duchess, especially to woo bright young men, but even when Sir Thomas joined Parliament in 1780 and then in 1781 opposed the American war, the Clargeses did not become intimates of the circle. As for Carter, though her charge was satisfactorily if not brilliantly in countenance, she herself, though present at least part of the summer, seems to have played the retiring role of a true humble companion. The duchess found Clarges, pregnant with her first child, Louisa, in a small set consisting of Lord and Lady Sefton and Mrs. Brudenell, members of London's fashionable musical society.[21]

On July 21 the duchess had encountered Mrs. Brudenell with Clarges, "whom I like vastly," on the Pantiles. On the twenty-fourth, a nasty, rainy day, she drank tea and supped with Lady Sefton and heard Mrs. Brudenell and Clarges sing. "Mrs Brudnel's voice is full and very sweet, but Ly Clarges is sweetness itself tho' her situation makes it rather lower than usual at present." The next day the duchess went on an excursion with her temporary companion-in-residence Lady Clermont, Sir Charles Bunbury, Mr. Grenville, Sir Thomas Clarges, and Lord Sefton, and then to tea at Mrs. Brudenell's, "where we had some charming singing." Then on Sunday Lord and Lady Sefton, Mr. and Mrs. Crewe, and Sir Charles Bunbury dined with the Devonshires and afterward they all drank tea with Lady Clarges, "and she sung delightfully to us." Lady Clermont reported this (as was her wont) to Lady Spencer somewhat differently: their party, she said, "is only dull conversasion the performers Ld & Ly Sefton M.ʳ & Mʳˢ Brudenell S.ʳ Tho.ˢ Ly Clergis M.ʳ Ch.ˢ Bunbery M.ʳ Crawford M.ʳ S.ᵗ John M.ʳ Grenville & M.ʳˢ Crew." Her good report of the duchess is tempered by the news that her rakish friends Lady Melbourne and Lady Jersey would shortly arrive—which arrivals may account for Clarges's eclipse.

Thereafter the Clargeses disappear from the duchess's social notes. Had they left Tunbridge?[22] The Seftons, Mrs. Brudenell, and the Clargeses had given a round of teas; but only the Seftons had been invited to dine with the duchess; and from this time the duchess and Clarges had only a polite—perhaps cordial—acquaintance. It can be safely concluded that as Lady Clarges, Sir Thomas's new wife, Clarges was welcomed into countenance but was not to become an intimate of the great. That she would obviously have children to marry off, and children with sizable fortunes, would have been the point: the Cavendishes would not mingle their bloodstreams with those of the Skrines and Jane Sumner.

Whatever her ambivalent position in the great world, Clarges now immersed herself in the musical scene, making her familiar acquaintance not only among fellow aficionados, but also—indicating that ability and merit rather than blood were her primary considerations—among the most fashionable and gifted of the professional musicians and of such music lovers as Susan Burney, whose delicate beauty and fine voice were apparently similar to her own.[23]

Susan Burney's journals produce a portrait of the nineteen-year-old Clarges in the spring of 1780. At a concert at Lady Hales's on April 26 she found Clarges looking "really beautiful . . . not too highly rouged, her hair most fancifully & becomingly dressed . . . tho' she now shows

her situation very plainly, & all the Eve^g. was making a fuss about her
figure."[24] She was sorry not to have been at home when Susan called
and feared she would drop her: "You . . . will think I am denied—Now
I am really never denied—besides I would not be to you if I was but I
believe that old Porter does not always tell me when you come—I will
scold him when I go home." Later the highly fashionable castrato singer
Pacchierotti made a ridiculous speech to Susan which he desired her to
repeat to Clarges, "to whom he seem'd to think it necessary to talk ab-
surdly, & as she very often does the same thing to *him*, I believe they
frequently *don't* know what to make of each other, but in fact *fun &
Nonsence* are more natural & more becoming to Ly. Clarges, than to
Pacchierotti—she talks at random, & often says strange things from an
impulse nearly irresistable, or wch. she seeks not to resist—but Pactti.
is *striving* to be irrational when in her presence in order to divert her &
never cuts so bad a figure as on these occasions" (f. 129). Later in the
evening another of Pacchierotti's admirers, Louisa Harris,[25] flirted with
him "& Ly. Cl. told me she was so *jealous* at it she *must* hiss her, & so
she did for a little while" (f. 132).

Such sport was habitual to Clarges. On May 5 at another concert she
continued her attack on Louisa Harris, again including Susan Burney
in the fun.

"do you know, s.^d L.^y Cl. to me, that she (meaning Miss L:H:) is now quite
Notorious w.th Pacchierotti—You know we observed her at L.^y Hales's—She was
then pretty bad—but Now really there is no Supporting it—. . . . It's really
being what I call quite *common!*—don't you think so now? Miss L:H: answered
her in the same style—& Mrs Brudenell s.^d they were *both so much in love w.th
Pacchierotti, & so jealous of him,* that she did not know how to keep peace be-
tween them—L.^y Cl: told Miss L:H: She never intended to go anywhere w.th her
again—that she was too bad!—& abused her head dress, &c in *Pacchierotti's*
name—"He says he never saw such an Ugly hat in his life—they don't wear
such things in Italy—& your hair—he has been telling me it's frightful"—So
she ran on, in a comical wild manner.

Next, spying Pacchierotti about to depart, "Lord, s.^d L.^y Cl., Let us all
go & assail him—We can have him nicely up in that corner'—Miss
L:H: urged her on, & Mrs Brudenell followed them laughing." Susan
confessed, "I saw them very busy about him till his Coach was called, &
sh.^d not have been sorry to have been of their party" (ff. 159–60).

The Burney family preserved a packet labeled "A few of the Frisky
Letters of the sportive, heedless, happy, & where she chose it captivating
Lady Clarges."[26] The letters support the characterization of Susan Bur-

ney's journals. The young Clarges was a laughing, giddy girl, beautiful, heedless, and silly, but good-natured, dedicated to music, and willing to take great care in regard to such affairs as the benefits of the singers. Perhaps her apparent heedlessness was a defense against her uncertain social situation. Whether her carelessness was affected or not, she remained throughout her marriage the same heedless girl. Toward the end of 1780 she wrote from Lincoln, where her husband had just been elected to Parliament, of an election ball.[27] She wrote at other times of her passion, shared by Susan and half the rest of musical London, for Pacchierotti, and at some time after October 1782, without betraying trepidation, she notified her friend that in a few days the family should set out for the south of France to seek the recovery of her husband's health.

Sir Thomas's health had been declining for some time, but the young couple had taken insufficient alarm. In August 1780 he was at Scarborough, and in the summer of 1781 he took a house at Salt Hill,[28] both places customarily visited for their healthy air. But at the end of 1780 he endured the rigors of an election and thereafter fulfilled his duties at Westminster. In February 1781 Clarges was recovering from a birth or a miscarriage,[29] and in June she gave a ball.[30] In that same month her husband spoke in Parliament against the prosecution of the American war.

By 1782 the couple seemed established in every way. Clarges had found a niche for herself among the fashionable artistic and musical set, which included Lady Lucan, Lady Home, Lady Mary Duncan, and Lady Edgcumbe, and with them welcomed the astonishing young William Beckford when he burst upon the scene that year. Beckford's first interest at the time was music; he had "very extraordinary talents; he is a perfect master of music, but has a voice, either natural or feigned, of an eunuch," wrote George Selwyn.[31] In April 1782 Beckford composed the music for an operetta with a book by Lady Craven, and the pair produced their work with considerable éclat at Lord March's Queensbury House. Pacchierotti assisted, and fashionable London crowded to the representation. Beckford, who affected to despise the libretto and not much to admire his own music, reported, "Lady Clarges, with one of her arch looks, told me fairly I did not shine. However, when she heard the finales, she exclaimed, 'Thank God!—At least you have made a good end.' "[32]

It was Sir Thomas who was next to have that opportunity. Clarges's enjoyment of her life was interrupted in 1782 by the rapid decline in Sir Thomas's health. Possibly she was the conduit of a tubercular infection deriving from her mother and passed to her husband and children. On

March 15, 1782, Sir Thomas made his last recorded speech in the Commons, this time against the practicality of the American war. A plan to go to the south of France was probably delayed by Clarges's new pregnancy; in July Pacchierotti informed Burney of the birth of her twin sons, adding, "I heard from Sr Thomas, she is pretty well as the children."[33] The birth of the two children further delayed the departure, for Sir Thomas was determined to go *en famille*.

Before they could go, it must have become evident that it was too late. Sir Thomas's death came speedily. In December he was dying, as Pacchierotti informed the Burneys. On Sunday, December 22, the singer called at St. Martin's Street to report that in Sir Thomas's intervals of reason and of ease, he often asked whether Pacchierotti had called to inquire for him. The invalid died on December 23, and on the twenty-ninth Burney noted of Pacchierotti, "He is now so depressed by the loss of his friend, that he cannot, without a sadness too much well to endure, talk or think of him."[34]

It would appear that Clarges had lost a truly kind and compatible husband. At the beginning of 1783 she was a twenty-two-year-old widow with four children under five years of age, and she turned to Carter again, who had probably been sustaining her in her husband's illness, perhaps helping to nurse him. But who would have supposed that, children and all, the pair would next spend three years making the grand tour?

Clarges was now rich. Her husband's will, made on December 8, carefully provided for his children and left his wife the household furnishings and a thousand pounds for her immediate wants, naming her the children's guardian until she remarried.[35] He must therefore have given her a large jointure when they married and have provided for her in other ways, for she was to be in control of what seem almost limitless funds in the next few years, and she died leaving bequests totaling £39,000. These dispositions suggest that he loved her a great deal and feared for her position (and the position of his children) after he had gone. Sir Thomas had stipulated in his will that the Tilney Street lease should be sold, and Carter immediately set about looking for a suitable new house, which suggests that the pair did not immediately conceive the plan of staying abroad for a prolonged period. In the first months of 1783 Carter must have looked over the house in Grosvenor Square, near her own house in Hill Street, in which lived her friend the poet and harpist Edward Jerningham, an important member of London's musical set, for she wrote to him about it in a letter that refers mysteriously to her own fall from social grace and to his former advice that perhaps it would profit her to withdraw herself for a time (during the illness and death of Sir Thomas?). She wrote, "I can not suffer the temples of my head to take their rest without thanking you most kindly for the favor you granted me in seeing *the house* which is charming & w^d Answer in every respect if *we* can afford it. I shall pick the bone you so kindly offer. My premier Pas in the World has been to Lady Salisburys where there was the World his Wife & Children. There is nothing like making yourself scarce; Lady Derby could not have had a more gracious Accueil. Adieu tis Morn & the Cocks crowing. I shall see you I hope tomorrow that is (Tuesday) night." [36]

This letter can probably be dated as somewhat later than a letter of January 6, 1783, to Jerningham from another friend inquiring "why Lady Clarges leaves the house in Tylney Street. Do you know how she is left? I suppose well; as Sir Thomas was very fond of her." To the same letter the writer added a postscript: "Does Miss Carter approve her friend Lord Palmerston's marriage? I am glad to hear that worthy singular woman is in better spirits than when I last heard from her. When I think she is more at liberty, I shall write to her. En attendant, if you see her, tell her . . . how much I love and esteem her." [37]

There is some mystery here. Carter was deeply involved in helping Clarges rearrange her life and had recently been depressed and withdrawn from the world. The natural assumption, given her earlier association with Clarges, is that she had been staying with the family during the period around Sir Thomas's death. Although Clarges must have been in mourning and seclusion in early 1783, Carter had reentered society at one of the great Sunday night routs of Lady Salisbury and, despite Jerningham's prediction that her having been withdrawn for a period would ensure her welcome, had been snubbed. It would therefore seem that Carter may earlier have been under a cloud, which would explain the Burney family's failure—particularly Susan's—to mention her among their acquaintance of the period. Because both Beckford and Gibbon later referred to her as a lesbian, her cloud might well have been of a sexual nature. That would explain Jerningham's support, for the Jerningham circle was artistic, bohemian, and tolerant of homosexuals like (probably) Jerningham himself, Walpole, Walpole's cousin the sculptor Anne Damer, and, perhaps, Carter. There is no hint whether Clarges was under the same cloud. Possibly she was, for Charles Greville's later warning to his uncle Sir William Hamilton suggests that he knew some scandal about her, though the circumstances of her birth may have been what he referred to.

The various charges of lesbianism against Carter, though far clearer, are as difficult to evaluate. How was lesbianism defined in this period? Even if it was defined as a question of orientation or preference rather than of overt sexual practice, determination remains difficult. Was it only her singular self-assurance and competence that led men like Beckford and Gibbon to identify Carter as male? It would be interesting and useful if we could be certain that in Carter we have the portrait of an eighteenth-century lesbian.

Lillian Faderman's point that women who loved other women in preference to men expressed their preference in romantic friendship rather than in overt sexuality in the eighteenth century is a good one,[38] though the sublimation of homoerotic feeling cannot have been invariable, and I suspect that the gentrification of society and the correspondent new assignment of passivity to women were responsible for a general inability at the time to recognize lesbianism with full physical expression where it existed. But in any case we still do not know whether Carter's friendships with women—or with some women—were romantic. What we do know is that she may have irritated Beckford and certainly did irritate Gibbon by behavior they interpreted as masculine self-possession. As Faderman has also pointed out, as long as women appear feminine, "their sexual behavior would be viewed as an activity in which women indulged when men were unavailable. But if one or both of the pair demanded masculine privileges, the illusion of lesbianism as *faute de mieux* behavior was destroyed." It was "the attempted usurpation of male prerogative by women who behaved like men" that disturbed.[39] Certainly Carter disturbed in precisely this way; it was the basis of her often-noted "singularity."

Various motives may have impelled the little group abroad. Clarges endured a second blow and some scandal when on March 8, 1783, William Skrine, who had lost his parliamentary seat in 1780 and had recently lost heavily at Brooks's, shot himself in a tavern in Newgate Street. His hastily written will of February 26 left some entailed properties of which he had been unable to dispose to his elder son William and an annuity to his younger son Julian, with his daughter, Clarges, as contingent legatee. To Clarges he also left his Italian books, no doubt as mementos of her mother.[40] In his pocketbook was also found a declaration that he was the long-undesignated father of Lady Louisa Nugent,[41] which once again set the patriarchy's memorializers to work. Clarges's parents had never been of social assistance to her, and, in his death, her father did her a final disservice.

This last event may have determined Clarges to leave England for a time. The journey had already been planned during her husband's illness, probably by Carter, who still felt equal to undertaking it. Clarges had a new responsibility, now that her husband was dead, to establish her four children in society, and the fresh scandal caused by her father's indebtedness, suicide, and new avowal of unregulated paternity may have alarmed her. For Englishwomen of her class and time, Paris and Versailles were almost a necessary venture: France could ruin the reputation of a charming woman by pronouncing her ordinary but by conferring its approval could propel women such as Lady Clermont into extraordinary repute. It had failed to appreciate Elizabeth Montagu and had made Lady Sarah Bunbury the rage. Clarges had every prospect of becoming a success in Paris, where she would make useful friends and establish a reputation that would serve her well in England. And probably she also longed to make the sort of musical tour of the Continent that her friend Dr. Burney had made in preparation for the first volume of his *General History of Music* (1775). There is one other possible motive for the journey that cannot be entirely discounted: the Continent was the traditional refuge for illicit love.

Jerningham's brother in Paris, "the Chevalier," helped with the arrangements, which proceeded slowly: besides the four small children there must have been a considerable entourage of nurses, maids, and menservants. On October 14 Lady Mary Coke wrote to her sister, "Lady Clarges is going with all her children to Paris and Miss Carter goes with her (you have seen her formerly at Lady Blandford's). Lady Clarges has taken a large house for which she is to pay five and twenty louis d'ors a month, just three hundred guineas [or $30,000] by the year."

Six weeks later they had arrived. Lady Mary notes that from Paris Mrs. Carter had sent Lady Bute a black cloak at the great cost of four and a half guineas—fashionable Englishwomen felt obliged to have their cloaks from Paris—and had announced that they found nothing cheap. A woman singular enough to confess to a healthy appetite, she also complained of "the slender French suppers."[42]

Soon the twenty-three-year-old William Beckford arrived in Paris to resume his friendship with both women. The brilliant Beckford was a homosexual and an enfant terrible, and his naturally mischievous bent was now much exacerbated by his having adopted the hobbies of the protagonists of *Les Liaisons Dangereuses* (1782). But his epistles were always fanciful, and his interpretation of his doings, written for the wife of his cousin, his lover and confederate Louisa Beckford, is adapted to please her. To read his letters to her, one would assume that he never

consorted with his wife, that he frequented the house of the delightful
Lady Clarges for the sole pleasure of speaking enthusiastically to Carter
of his mistress, and that the trio was scarcely civil to the other English
in Paris, and one would never have guessed that he was in Paris with a
pregnant wife or that he was and would remain a devoted friend to the
reckless Lady Craven. Moreover, because he habitually revised his own
letters, long after they had been sent, we cannot be certain what was in
the originals. His first report, in its later revision, reads

The latest arrivals of notoriety from our English world are Lady Clarges—escorted by her faithful Chevalier and Lady Craven by her footman—the former
are caressed and invited to everything by everybody—the latter

> Far from splendour, far from trouble,
> Deeming fame an empty bubble
> Free from Husband, care and strife
> Leads a calm domestic life

And so let her by all means. I will never come within glare again of her magnificent eyes—if I can help it. . . . Most different is the expression our beloved Moli,
as Sacchini calls her, gives her glances when you are the subject of conversation.
The admiration she feels, in all sincerity, for you, is glowing and vehement; but
at the same time, not without a delightful mixture of tenderness. This disposition to talk about you from noon till night is to me all in all—and in order to
profit by it, I am for ever and ever at Lady Clargeses. Her dear little self and her
devoted Moli lead me where they please. I cannot quit them. They are no every
day copies of every day people. Originality marks them for her own, and they
act as that glorious power dictates without submission to any rules that were
ever established. So do I—no wonder we agree so perfectly.

He goes on to describe this trio of originals at the Duchess of Manchester's, wife of the English ambassador, treading over poor Lord St.
Asaph, staring at and pushing past Lady Lucan, refusing an invitation
to supper so as to sample the plebeian night life of Paris, and returning
to Clarges's "to a most comfortable poule au riz and delicious maras-
chino sherbert—which Moli knows how to compound delectably." [43]

Some of this is literally true. Lady Craven, who had eloped to Paris
with her footman, was not included in the parties at the Duchess of Manchester's or at the weekly receptions given the English at the queen's
behest and expense by the Duchesse de Polignac. [44] But Beckford did see
her and always continued to be her friend. Clarges and Carter were a
great success in Paris, but not as a result of snubbing their respectable
compatriots. Lord St. Asaph was probably enamored of Clarges, and

both Carter and Clarges were to remember their friend the Duchess of Manchester in their wills. Beckford's sexual innuendos about Carter—his calling her the "faithful Chevalier" and his suggestion that she felt a special romantic tenderness for Louisa Beckford—are more difficult to assess. He was writing to a confidante and lover who knew his homosexual exploits and who was, at the least, knowledgeable about female homosexuality. How valid, then, is Beckford's contrast of the two couples "of notoriety"—Clarges and Carter, received and courted, and Craven and her footman, ignored and despised? Is this a jest that the homosexual lovers are welcomed, the heterosexual ones rejected? He may even be suggesting that Carter and Clarges had previously been notorious. Evidence has also emerged that in the original draft of this letter Beckford described Carter not as "her faithful Chevalier" but as "Mons. le Chevalier Molly Carter."[45] The unanswerable question, then, is, How much did Beckford actually know about Carter and Clarges, and how much was he making up to titillate his correspondent?[46]

At any rate, there is no question that Carter and Clarges were a great success in Paris and at Versailles. Lady Lucan, who had sponsored the ungrateful Beckford in London, was their friend; her daughter, who was to marry Lady Spencer's son, became their lifelong intimate. They were Beckford's friends, too, though after his great scandal in September of that year, after he had returned home and had been caught in the act with his beloved Kitty Courteney and had fled abroad, he was not again mentioned in connection with Clarges or Carter. Clarges had to consider first the social establishment of her four children; and although it seems probable that homosexuals like Jerningham and Walpole had an informal protective federation, none of them could afford to countenance scandalous behavior.

The inseparable trio was not to be intimate much longer, therefore, when with the painter Hubert Robert they visited the king's menagerie at the Jardin du Roi in Versailles. The visit produced a most wonderful set piece by Beckford, who claims that while the son of the naturalist the Comte de Buffon showed the others round the taxidermical collection, Beckford entranced the famous live lioness, who rolled upon her back, her immense mouth "as red and as large pretty nearly as a heated oven, wide open the whole time as if distended by a fit of laughter," uttering a comfortable chuckling sound. Her astonished keeper invited Beckford to enter her cage, where he smoothed her paws, accepting her state of almost hypnotic ecstasy to the admiration of "forty or fifty voices in chorus! 'What talisman does this young gentleman possess?' " The passage concludes triumphantly: "I had not quitted my beloved's grated boudoir, nor relinquished fondling her lovely paw, when Lady Clarges, Robert, Miss Carter, and the Comte de Buffon came up. I thought poor Lady Clarges would have fainted, so great was her terror at this unexpected spectacle. Her faithful companion bore the strange sight with masculine fortitude."[47]

So much for Beckford's state of mind at the time, palpably productive of fantasies of unnatural and unparalleled sexual powers and of braving death in their application; his disgrace a few months later was almost inevitable. The Beckford episode for Carter and Clarges ended in mid-March, when his wife fell ill and the couple returned home. We can deduce from his remarks about Carter and Clarges that both he and his confidante Louisa perceived or naughtily professed to perceive Carter as the "faithful Chevalier," the "devoted Moli," the "faithful companion," which helps to define her relationship to Clarges, and that both also professed to perceive some element of homoerotic affection for Clarges in "Mons. le Chevalier" of the "masculine fortitude," if not also some idea that Clarges and Carter were a couple in the same sense as Lady Craven and her footman, and with a tinge of the same notoriety.

Carter and Clarges stayed on in Paris at least until late June, waiting for the mountain snows to melt on the passage between France and Italy. They were at Versailles for a magnificent ball given for the king of Sweden and were sufficiently acquainted with the French royal family for Carter in 1793 to lament the death of Madam Elisabeth by guillotine and the continued imprisonment of the dauphin and his sister, "Alas! Alas! I am sadly grieved by report. I shall ever love and pity."[48] Toward the end of this long stay in Paris, in May, Carter wrote a letter to Edward Jerningham in which she finally relinquished the prospect of Clarges's purchasing the lease to his house and summarized their Paris experience. A long letter, it conveys some idea of Carter's singularity. "My Dear Old Scratch For the devil himself coud not have wrote a better Letter, or a worse Hand, dont come, for to go, for to think, I have in the least forgot you or the rest of my good friends. Old England for ever Huzza! Huzza!" Jerningham's brother "the Chevalier" has made their stay pleasant, procuring them not only pleasures "but comforts without end" and has been "more indulgent to us than even a Grandmother." But lately "we begin to fly with our own Wings & at a rare rate we sail I can tell you 'tis hard work to spin my *humming top* after her Lyships Gig, but I keep up as well as I can. she is m.^{ch} admired & with great reason. I lead a pleasant life neither much spoke to or looked at so I have

time for contemplation." Carter notes that it has been deepest winter
till within the week and that expenses have been so great that Clarges
cannot afford to purchase the lease to his house, which is "not only a
bargain, but really a delightful thing. I only hope she may settle in one
as good & that you may part with it to better advantage. I beg a thousand Pardons for not answering your kind Letter sooner but the Answer
was given as soon as possible I do assure you." Had the pair only just
decided to continue their stay abroad? She speaks of going on to Italy as
though Jerningham knew their plans. They must wait for the snows to
melt at the end of June and would still be in Paris for the fetes made on
the occasion of the visit of the king of Sweden, though as vile plebeians
they would not be expected to make themselves ruinously fine.

my agreable Compagne de Voyage has what they call succes etonnant. for my
part I do not please *at all* for I cannot employ that never failing attraction &
the only one I have now in my power *called flattery* which they give & receive
in such large doses it makes me quite sick & does not stay & comfort my old
Stomach like the few nice Grains you sent me in your Letter. . . . *my Spirits* are
a little wore with saying expressing what I do not feel there is sure no work so
hard as that of feigning it is a small degree of prostitution I am tired to Death of
the words Superbe delicieux &c &c, & wish you woud send me a praising ma-
chine that woud fit under my Arm like a Childs Cuckow & then I coud be polite
without much bustle.[49]

Carter adds that she had written most of her letter near three parks and
that it was to have traveled with Lord St. Asaph, "the most agreable Saint
in my Calendar in London ye have married him to Ly Clarges but I dont
believe at present they either mean it." She found not only the singing
in Paris intolerable but also the poultry. And on the next day they were
to spend the evening with the Chevalier to meet Madame de Genlis, the
celebrated author and governor to the sons of the Duc de Chartres.[50]

Clarges and Carter as well had been a great success in Paris; the experiment had been of use to both. The king of Sweden arrived in Paris
on June 7, and the snows of Mt. Cenis had probably melted sufficiently
for a passage at the end of the month. Then the entire entourage made
its way to Turin by the same route described by Mrs. Thrale only a few
months later when she and Piozzi were on their honeymoon travels.
From Lyons one ascended the Alps in chairs carried by natives over
trails that seemed perilous. On the one side were immense cascades
bursting from the mountains and on the other cultivated fields rich
with vineyards. Little towns were stuck in clefts that seemed impossible
to reach, where light clouds sailed beneath the feet of the inhabitants.

Thrale saw chamois and goats, heard of wolves in the mountains, and talked with a man who had killed five bears in his pastures. Atop Mt. Cenis the travelers dined on the pale trout from the lake there and then proceeded downward into Italy, Thrale calling to the chairmen at every peril, "Prenez garde!" and they responding each time coolly, "Qu'est-ce donc, madame?" If Clarges had blanched at the sight of Beckford in the lioness's cage, she would truly have quailed before the dangers of this journey undertaken with four small children, but if the Paris house had indeed been taken for the year, probably the children had been left there under adequate supervision. At last the traveler entered Piedmont, where at Novalesa the hollow sound of the accompanying torrent grew faint, "and the ideas of common life," said Thrale, "catch hold of one again." And so on to Turin.[51]

"This charming town is the *salon* of Italy," said Thrale. If Clarges had been there with her mother in 1765, she must have found it additionally interesting. There was a minor court, that of the Duke of Savoy, who was also the Sardinian king. There was a fashionable circle of English with whom the women made lasting friendships. The English envoy was the Hon. John Trevor, cousin to the Duke of Marlborough. Trevor, wrote the third Lady Holland in 1793, was a man of no judgment, slender talents, harmless foibles, and insipid goodness: "His *ridicules* are a love of dress coats, *volantes*, and always speaking French." Another acquaintance thought him "a perfect gentleman, well bred and kind-hearted and did the honours handsomely."[52] No doubt he was agreeable and good, and Clarges was to leave him £2,000 in her will. Trevor's wife, Harriet Burton, whom he had married in 1773, was the daughter of a rich canon and, according to Lady Holland, was formerly a lover of Charles Fox's, good-natured, a little clever, a little mad, and parsimonious. They lived in a villa on a hill where their chaplain read prayers on Sundays for the benefit of Protestant families.

Also in Turin in the autumn of 1784 were Trevor's elder brother Lord Hampden and his wife, Catherine Graeme, Lady Hampden, a great patroness of singers and musicians;[53] Frederick North, later Lord Guilford; Lord Dungannon; and Francis-William, eldest son and successor to Sir Francis Sykes. At the dull court King Victor Amadeus's Spanish wife spread solemnity and gloom, giving balls at which people were confined to their seats, but the English had entrée to the casino, where there were also balls, and to the houses of some of the nobility and of the diplomats, who habitually met with the English twice a week at the house of the Marchioness St. Gilles.

The susceptible Sir William Hamilton stopped in Turin en route to
Rome and Naples, where he was English envoy, and fell under the spell
of Clarges. Now independently situated because of the death of his wife,
he might, even at fifty-four, have been a man for her to consider: Wraxall
describes him in 1779 as tall, meager, dark, with an aquiline nose and
an air of intelligence blended with distinction.[54] He moved on, having
urged upon Clarges and her companion an invitation to follow him.

From Turin Clarges and Carter moved south to Rome, where again
they encountered Hamilton, who repeated his invitation. After a stay in
Rome of several winter months, they had proceeded to Naples by February 1785. Now ensued a small comedy. Hamilton, who had shared a
great love of music with his first wife, had been predictably enchanted
by Clarges's beauty and her voice; she must, at least with such figures as Hamilton, have played a demure role, for he was persuaded
her temperament was "quiet." Hamilton was ripe for remarriage; but in
England his roué nephew and favorite, Charles Greville, was plotting
to unburden himself of his mistress, Emma Hart, by shipping her to
Hamilton so that he himself could marry an heiress. To do so he would
have to be able to assure the heiress's family both that he was Hamilton's
heir and that Hamilton would never remarry, which was the reason for
encumbering his uncle with Emma Hart. While Greville was attempting to explicate these delicate points to his uncle, Hamilton was proposing—or perhaps not quite proposing—to Clarges. On February 22
he wrote in an embarrassed explanation to Greville, "I like her much in
one of my moments of admiration I sayd to her that I wished she would
take possession of my empty apartments—She gravely answered that
she was much flattered but had resolved never to marry again, the Devil
fetch me if I meant to propose tho I own I often have thought she wou'd
suit me well—Her musical talents you may imagine weigh greatly with
me, & she is gentle."[55]

What was he proposing, if not marriage? Could he possibly have
imagined that because she was the daughter of Jane Sumner, the rich
widow of Sir Thomas Clarges would become his mistress? But in May
he admitted to Mary Hamilton, "If Lady C. had been of the same mind
with me, I verily believe I should have married. I was not in the least in
love, but she seemed the quiet companion that would suit me, particularly as her passion for Musick equals mine."[56] At least, he congratu-
lated himself, he had been spared the trouble of Clarges's four children.

In England Charles Greville quailed at the near-shipwreck of his
plans and wrote suggesting that Emma Hart was as good a choice as

Lady Clarges. "Would your friends have thought L.ʸ C. a more prudent connexion than E.? I know the sentiments of all your friends, & my delicacy prevented my writing on that subject, but I can assure you they feel very happy at the departure of L.ʸ C. I am not sorry, Though I should have been so if it had been Mrs. D. instead of L.ʸ C."[57] Charles Greville's sudden access of delicacy is to be regretted, for otherwise he might have explained his objections to Lady Clarges, to whom he preferred Anne Damer, a great favorite of Hamilton's who had visited Naples the year before: was it Clarges's parentage, or were there rumors about her sexual orientation? There was apparently more against Clarges than Greville's selfish wish that Hamilton take Emma for his mistress to prevent his marrying anyone else. When in 1790 Hamilton was once again disarranging matters by actually *marrying* Emma Hart, William Beckford wrote to Lady Craven that he thought Hamilton might as well have coupled himself in God's name to Lady Clarges: "the *mesalliance* in either case would be glaring."[58]

Meanwhile, from Naples Clarges and Carter were making their way northward through Florence, Bologna, Venice, Padua, and Verona to Lausanne, where they joined a splendid company of English in the autumn of 1785. Edward Gibbon, a resident, lamented the indifferent health that prevented his enjoying the "really good company, people one knows," listing Sir Willoughby and Lady Aston, her brother Lord Northington, Colonel and Mrs. Francis Hale, the Trevors (absent on leave from Turin), and "Lady Clarges and Miss Carter (her *Sappho*)."[59] It is impossible to detect whether the intimation about Carter was considered by Gibbon to be already familiar to Sheffield, whether he meant only that Carter was a lesbian, or whether he meant that she was also involved in a lesbian relationship with Clarges.

Clarges took a house, Petit-Ouchy, at Ouchy, perched at some distance above the lake, but still far below Lausanne.[60] The pleasures of the place were at that time as much in the society as in the scenery, and Carter was to comment sadly when she revisited it with the Palmerstons in 1793, "We went to Lausanne for a few days; we found that place sadly altered, and very dull. The house of Cerjat, that used to be so pleasant a *rendezvous* in the evening, and where I have counted a mixture of fourteen different nations, now a perfect hospital and never opened; Gibbon gone to England, and no society whatever; so that, as much as formerly I was attached to it, I think it would be the last town I could wish to settle at."[61]

From Lausanne, having spent over two years in the completion of their tour, Clarges and Carter made their way back to Paris, where in December they called on Frances Greville and her daughter Frances Crewe in their hotel. On December 28, 1785, Crewe noted in her journal that her assembly the evening before had included the Duc de Guines and several English, including Lady Clarges and "Miss Carter (who is with her)." "I felt very happy on seeing Lady Clarges—we had not met for two years, and there is something in her, I think, very amiable and interesting. . . . Miss Carter my other new acquaintance: and who lives with Lady Clarges, is certainly one of the most independent People I ever saw, but good humoured singular and sensible."[62]

Crewe had not noticed Carter at Tunbridge in 1778 but noticed her now as "singular." But Lady Clermont, who had been at the duchess's elbow at Tunbridge, was at Crewe's elbow now, arranging her Paris-Versailles career (she was not an outstanding success). And Lady Clermont apparently did not think it worth Crewe's while to encumber herself in Paris with Lady Clarges. Crewe neither returned the call nor noted having encountered Clarges and Carter again. It is easy enough to list many of Clarges's friends but more difficult to discern, as can be discerned here, the process of tentative application on her part and perhaps not-so-gentle rebuff with which she must have been distressingly familiar. Lady Clermont was the great confidante of Marie Antoinette and knew Clarges and Carter *had* had a great success at Versailles; but she was almost certainly advising Frances Crewe not to saddle herself with an intimacy that might prove inconvenient in England.

Clarges and Carter remained in Paris again for most of 1786. They were still there in October when the Duc de Nivernois sent Clarges a ballad which she dispatched to London to Walpole.[63] Then they returned to England. In October 1787 Gibbon encountered Clarges with Mrs. Trevor at Tunbridge. He was in a minority of people who disliked Carter, for he noted that she, that *young* and amiable personage, had remained in London.[64]

Soon after the return to London, Carter removed to her own house in Hill Street. Clarges was now a settled woman in her mid-twenties, and her children were past infancy. On her own account she had made many useful friends who could help in future to establish her children. Although the two women could congratulate themselves on their achievement—having made the grand tour together and having scored a general social success—it appears it was also time that they separated, that Lady Clarges managed on her own. They remained excellent friends.

Clarges had sobered and matured. She had apparently had an excellent upbringing and had suffered sufficiently to acquire sensibility. She had ceased to be the giddy schoolgirl, and the years with Moll Carter had made her a sensible woman of reliable judgment. Carter had brought her up to be guided by herself, and she did not choose now to amuse herself in society or to marry a handsome officer, though there was a rumor in 1788 that she was about to marry one, Henry Hervey Aston.[65] Instead, she devoted herself to her children and music. She is only occasionally glimpsed: in March 1788 escorting a young Lausanne acquaintance to Greenwich; in 1792 noted as a close friend of the Chevalier Jerningham; in 1793 visiting Strawberry Hill with Sir George Beaumont and returning in 1796 with Mme de Staremberg; in 1802 attending a card party, as she probably often did, at the Jerninghams.[66]

With three sons and a daughter she had the responsibility to plan for the future of her family, but she was cruelly disappointed, and she never did have to conclude a match for any of them. The first blow occurred when one of her twin boys went to sea as a midshipman on the Marlborough man-of-war and in an engagement with the French on June 1, 1794, was wounded, dying in his twelfth year at Plymouth, having borne his acute sufferings (said the *Gentleman's Magazine*) with infinite heroism; he was buried with military honors on June 25.[67] Two others of her children were to die young, and all were to die unmarried.

In large part, no doubt, to guard the health of her remaining three children, and quite possibly following the advice of Carter, at the end of the century Clarges leased a house in the mountains of Wales at Bennarth, near Conway, in Carnarvonshire, where the air was particularly good and where she thereafter spent the summer months. Perhaps the health of her daughter Louisa was already delicate when in 1803 she lingered in Wales until December.[68] In November 1804 Carter, on a Welsh tour, stayed for weeks with Clarges, whom she found hostess to two of the most eminent musicians of the day who were instructing the family, Giovanni Battista Cimadoro, the composer, and Domenico Dragonetti, a double-bass player and composer. Carter wrote her great-niece Fanny, "I should wish for you here to enjoy our most excellent music from Lady Clarges, and Cimador's singing, Dragonetti, Miss Clarges's harp, and her two sons on the violin; so our evenings pass away, and most happily, without *company* or interruption. Visiting, or rather fidgeting is out of the question" (p. 23). Her stay with Clarges was for three months, she wrote to Lady Spencer, and provided fuller details of their life together,

very seldom visiting but often visited by amiable good people & very conversable *altho* they had never seen London & little heard of it. Our family consisted of herself & Daughter who has the great recourse of playing upon the Harp incomparably as well as Drawing, her two Sons quite her Adorers excellent Violins with a *noted* Viola Dragonetti by Name altogether thickened an Excellent Concert we had a most delightful Organ in a room that is in Miniature more like the Pantheon at Rome than any thing else here we began & ended our Day as we ought upon our Knees the young Men Chaplains & Clerk. This opend to an excellent diverting Library not *quite* so large as Althorp where we breakfasted at 9. & then stumped away to the Mountains dined Early wrote—read Sung & played through the Even till 11 & saluted. The place is more beautiful than pen or pencil can describe from wood Mountain River . . . Ruin & the romantic town of Conway not to mention the very best Kitchen Garden I ever saw *any where* grapes, figs, pineapples." [69]

The one communication from Clarges to Beckford still extant is an aria from Sacchini which she had copied out for him.[70] Her one communication to Walpole still extant is the ballad she sent from the Duc de Nivernois. Editors of Frances Burney take a reference from the later journals to be to a song of Clarges's composition, "Grey of the Mountains." [71] It seems probable that Clarges did compose music, but if so, nothing of her composition has yet been discovered.[72]

Carter spent Christmas in Wales with Clarges and in January 1804 went on to stay with Lord Dungannon, their old Turin acquaintance; from there she reported that Clarges with her daughter and one son, some of the Wynns, and other neighbors were to join them next day and that a production of Blue Beard would be attempted. Soon after, Clarges gave up the house in Wales and took another on Richmond-hill as a more convenient retreat from her London house in South Street, Park Lane, Grosvenor Square (very convenient to Hill Street).

Despite Clarges's precautions, her daughter Louisa fell ill and died on January 11, 1806, aged twenty-seven, in London.[73] Had she never married because of the unlucky descent from Jane Sumner or because of delicate health? Then William, the second twin, aged twenty-four, fell ill. He was a former student of Christ Church, Oxford, had become a Fellow of All Souls, and was, said the *Gentleman's Magazine* at his death on May 8, 1807, a promising young man of excellent character.[74] His weakness, as probably was his sister's, was tubercular; he had been in Portugal for his health but on his return died at Falmouth of "haemoptoe," or hemorrhages of the lung.

Clarges's one remaining child, her eldest son, Sir Thomas, twenty-six when William died, never married, and judging by the provisions of her will, his mother knew that he would never marry. His character remains peculiarly unnoted. He may have shown early and serious signs of the family disease and have lived as a valetudinarian. He died in 1834, leaving his wealth—£10,000 a year in landed property—to kinsmen.[75]

Clarges died at her house in Richmond "of a dropsy" on August 5, 1809, and was buried on August 10 in Petersham churchyard. Her long and interesting will discloses the extent of both her wealth and her acquaintance.[76] To her son Sir Thomas she left £12,000 in the stocks, the interest to go, if he died without heirs, to her half-sister Lady Louisa Nugent, now by marriage a Hervey. An additional £27,000 was distributed in legacies. She remembered each of Lady Louisa's children and her husband; her own husband's near relations the Hares; her father's ward Elizabeth Ann Wilson Smith and her husband, Charles Loraine Smith;[77] her brothers William and Julian Skrine; and Dr. Burney. She left £500 to be divided between Lady Eleanor Butler and Miss Ponsonby, the Ladies of Llangollen, whom she must have known in Wales. She left £400 to Mary Carter. To her valued friend the Hon. John Trevor she left £1,000 for himself and £1,000 for his charities and named him her residuary legatee. To "her dear friend" Harriet, his wife, she left £200. There were many other bequests, including a year's wages to each of her servants. To the Dowager Duchess of Manchester, that other friend from the years in France, she left her Johnson's *Lives of the Poets*, "with prints." She was careful to leave money to married women independent of their husband's control. Her husband, recognizing the difficulties she would encounter, had left her rich, and she understood the value to a woman of money of her own.

The vigorous Molly Carter, on her return from abroad, had led a more active life, but, like Clarges, in her London life she is rarely noticed. Horace Walpole mentioned having dined with her in July 1790 at the Grosvenor Street home of Lady Mary Churchill, with several Churchills and William Fawkener. She maintained her connections with the Jerningham circle, with the Palmerstons, with the friends she made abroad, and particularly with members of her own family. Her surviving sisters and her nieces and nephews loved her and saved her letters. Her favorite niece was Charlotte Willoughby, married to Sir John Nelthorpe of Scawby, Lincolnshire; to Lady Nelthorpe and her four children she left £500 each in her will. Her nephew Charles, Lord Yarborough, son of her favorite sister Eleanor Carter Anderson Vyner, was to be her residuary legatee.

But before her death in 1812, Carter had many active years. She was, as her letters show, an indefatigable traveler and visitor; one wonders when she ever stayed in Hill Street, where, we learn from her will, the housekeeper, Mrs. Long, had been in residence for twenty years. In the years 1792–94 she again went abroad, with Lord and Lady Palmerston. This tour interested the recipients of her letters, some of which were saved, and she was also noted in the journals of fellow travelers. In some ways her social popularity, unprecedently high in her last years, seems to have derived from the cachet of this tour. In October 1792 Lady Holland saw her at Naples with the Palmerstons, as well as the Duchess of Devonshire (in disgrace), with those who had rallied round her, Lady Spencer, the Bessboroughs, and Lady Elizabeth Foster, and in March 1793 Holland set off with the Palmerstons and Carter for Paestum. In Milan in July 1793 she dined with Carter and Sir Benjamin Thompson, Count of Rumford.[78] That same month Carter appeared in a portantine—a sedan chair strung between two horses—accompanied by her maid on horseback in the Italian lake district.[79] If she was indeed taken abroad by the Palmerstons as a social and geographical guide, she at least traveled in comfort. From Verona in October 1793 she recounted her adventures in Switzerland, where they had climbed, she claimed, the highest mountains, straddling on asses and sometimes going on their hands and knees. "Few women but such trampers as we are go there" (p. 6). At Vevay they had visited Mrs. Trevor; then on to Milan, Bergamo, Brescia, and Verona, from which she wrote. They were still to go on to Mantua, Perugia, Florence, and Rome, taking in all places the greatest notice of the antiquities (pp. 5–9). From Venice on June 3, 1794, Carter wrote to Walpole that she had "scampered like a nanny-goat over every mountain that was possible" and that at Monte Cavo she had dug up with her own hands a bit of the remains of the Temple of Jupiter Latialis for him. They had been to visit Sir William Hamilton; and she signed herself "Moll Volatile Evaporated."[80] The Palmerston party returned to England in October 1794.

Until 1806, or well into her seventies, Carter continued to run about the world. Her letters record visits to a host of people that include Walpole's cousin General Conway, Lord Bagot, Lady Spencer, Lady Aylesford, Lord Bulkeley, Lady Clarges, Sir Watkin Williams Wynn, the Duchess of Manchester, Lady Lucan, Lady Mt. Edgcumbe, and Lady Buckingham; it would seem that in her old age she was more the fashion than ever before in her life. The redoubtable Lady Spencer, whom she had encountered abroad, she now addressed in her letters as "Lady Nonsuch," "Cara Miladi," "my dear Deary," or "Bowels of my Affection as we elegantly say in Italian." It was for Spencer that in 1802 she summed herself up: "I was most assuredly began for a Mule & finished for a Woman."

At last, she faltered. A letter to her old friend Charles Burney in 1808 mentions the death of her sister Vyner, whom she had not met in some time but with whom she had exchanged notes every day. She herself, she said, was just like a great turtle, all day unable to move, just able to sit up to meals. Nor was she able to read a note, though she had viewed a comet through an opera glass. An undated scrap to Charles Burney mentions her lack of a manservant to deliver, "having only occasion for Females & have four maids to wait upon little more than a Corpse."[81] She persisted some years in this condition and died at last on May 8, 1812.

Carter had been so well provided with capital that she had not needed to sink her money into an annuity. She left £6,760 in legacies and the rest of her estate—an unspecified sum—to Lord Yarborough. In her will besides those legatees already named, she remembered her servants and many friends, including the Dowager Duchess of Manchester, Lady Lucan, and some of the Palmerston children, but not Sir Thomas Clarges. Among those legatees she shared in common with Lady Clarges were the Duchess of Manchester and Clarges's brother-in-law, Mr. Vincent of Berkeley Square.

Carter desired to be buried in Petersham churchyard and was laid there on May 15, 1812, in "New Ground, No. 1–2, Letters D / E." Clarges had been buried here in "New Ground No. 1, Letter C." The plots must have lain very close together indeed.[82]

Clarges and Carter would both have been identified in their own time as women of sensibility. Neither played victimizer, but neither played victim. Their advantages were not equal, and it appears that they shared advantages to make each other more independent; this is possible only when independence is a desired object. Clarges probably contributed to Carter's financial independence and, insisting that she take an equal part in Continental society, helped her improve her social image so that she became an experienced traveler, Continental guide and a singular woman; Carter encouraged Clarges to travel, encouraged her by risking rejection to make some excellent friends, encouraged her to live as a dedicated musician, to judge for herself. The combination of sensibility and judgment or reason made both women genuine, mature altruists. They lived autonomous lives, but at the expense of avoiding close relationships with men.

The women began with significant differences. Clarges was beautiful, young, charming, rich, and gifted, but vulnerable socially; Carter

was born into the gentry and when the two met was middle-aged, resourceful, witty, good-humored, but perhaps also vulnerable socially.
Instead of leaning on each other for the attributes they lacked, they did
their best to exchange attributes, making each more perfect; and they
worked hard and successfully to build social networks. Learning to acquire another's best attributes rather than simply exploiting them is the
best excuse for marriage. Carter had a green hand and a lucky inability
to accept the idea of limits for women. Under her guidance Clarges
probably extracted the best from her uncomfortable position as semi-
insider, semioutsider, capitalizing on both the advantages and the freedom it offered her.

Other women of even kindlier temperament—one might say of almost
mindlessly kind temperament—such as Elizabeth Vesey and her devoted Handcock—had a far more constraining effect on each other.
Carter and Clarges, in contrast to Vesey and Handcock, usefully demonstrate, if any demonstration were needed, that kindness and empathy
alone imprison women. Money is needed; vision and ambition to en-
large woman's sphere is needed; and physical and mental energy are
needed to undertake the struggle to realize vision and ambition. In all
these respects, Carter and Clarges constituted a remarkably fortunate,
resourceful, and successful combination.

Chapter Thirteen

REFORMERS: SARAH SCOTT
AND BARBARA MONTAGU

SARAH ROBINSON SCOTT was not officially a companion to Lady Barbara Montagu, though Lady Barbara's rank as an earl's daughter led people to think so. Not only were they friends who lived together, but also it was Lady Barbara who accompanied Scott into her marriage, Lady Barbara who encouraged and followed Scott. They were reasonably equal friends but were not even discernibly romantic friends; they were not, apparently, in love with each other. Janet Todd has postulated that low-keyed bonding of women because of need leads rather to political action than to sentiment: "The codes of sentimental friendship, which so successfully free emotion and encourage intense unity, also sap political energy."[1] The bonding of Scott and Lady Bab did release a great deal of political energy.

Somehow these two women, both useless to, even rejects of, the patriarchal system, projected a model of society antithetical to that culture and had the courage to put it into practice. To do this, they had first to undertake a rigorous intellectual analysis of patriarchy and its institutions. That this analysis was a lengthy, ongoing effort not only of Scott and Montagu but of an entire community of single women makes it all the more interesting.

How Sarah Robinson Scott got to the position in which we find her in the 1760s is worth investigating. She had a difficult time growing up. It cannot have been easy to have been junior sister to the dashing Elizabeth Robinson Montagu (chapter 6). Montagu and Scott had been devoted to each other, each the other's best resource while they were growing up. But soon enough they were differentiated. The energetic, ambitious Montagu was first to enter the world, made great friends with Lady Margaret Harley, who became the Duchess of Portland, and spent months away from home with her. Scott, delighted for her sister's happiness, must also have felt desolated and abandoned. Then, in April 1741, when she was twenty, Sarah had smallpox. Hers was a long and severe case, and Elizabeth, who was terrified of the disease, left home and did not see Sarah for a long period—unnecessarily long. After the smallpox, no one again suggested that the sisters were peas in a pod or complimented Sarah's beauty. After Sarah's recovery, Elizabeth did not linger at home in Kent but went to London to stay with the duchess. It was then that Sarah fell in love with writing, as she told Montagu in October 1741: "The love of writing you see, enters into me as soon as you go out of the house; while you are with me I have all I desire, content is then my companion; but when you are gone I can't help writing in hopes you will send me some return for the affection and spirits that are gone with you, all of me that is portable you carry with you." [2]

Just twenty-one, Sarah had a sense of emptiness which only the presence of her sister, her one love object, could satisfy; her language is sexual. She was at that time very near heartbreak, a fact so evident to the Reverend William Freind, who had married their cousin Grace Robinson, that he wrote to Elizabeth about it, pointing out Sarah's loneliness while, though enjoying Elizabeth's success in the world, she saw her lavishing elsewhere the love and attention she once had lavished on Sarah alone.[3] Though Elizabeth Montagu would always feel a special attachment to her sister, her ambition and her vastly enlarged opportunities ensured that Sarah would never again be her only or even her first object. Sarah's gradual disillusionment with Elizabeth became radical. Her portrait of Montagu (as Lady Brumpton) in *A Description of Millenium Hall* (1762) memorializes both her admiration for her sister and the erosion of her esteem:

She was by nature generous and humane, her temper perfectly good; her understanding admirable. She had been educated with great care, was very accomplished, had read a great deal, and with excellent taste; she had great quickness of parts, and a very uncommon share of wit. Her beauty first gained her much admiration; but when she was better known, the charms of her understanding seemed to eclipse those of her person. Her conversation was generally courted, her wit and learning were the perpetual subjects of panegyric in verse and prose, which unhappily served to increase her only failing, vanity. She sought to be admired for various merits. To recommend her person she studied dress, and went to a considerable expence in ornaments. To shew her taste, she distinguished herself by the elegance of her house, furniture, and equipage. To prove her fondness for literature, she collected a considerable library; and to shew that all her esteem was not engrossed by the learned dead, she caressed all living genius's. . . . She aimed at making her house a little academy.[4]

Losing Elizabeth was all the more bitter for Sarah because Elizabeth was virtually all she had had. Though the two Robinson sisters had great advantages of education and some of upbringing, they were seriously disadvantaged by the deficiencies of their parents. Elizabeth Montagu's adopted son characterized her mother, Elizabeth Drake Robinson, as a person "whose frame of mind partook rather of the gentle sedateness of good sense, than of the eccentricities of genius"; her role in her contentious family gave her the name of "the Speaker, from the frequent mediation by which she moderated their eagerness for victory."[5] Mrs. Robinson's mother had married as a second husband the eminent scholar Dr. Conyers Middleton, who took an interest in the development of all the Robinson children. These advantages were offset by Mrs. Robinson's becoming a valetudinarian if not an invalid at the time her daughters were ready to be introduced to the world. Perhaps as a result, the girls were not offered a season in London, which is why Elizabeth made her own arrangements—"*sauve qui peut.*" The situation may also reflect a strain on the family budget because of the pressure of many boys at school, or it may reflect the selfishness of the father, who was dedicated to his own pleasures. But it is astonishing that when Montagu married in 1742, her three youngest brothers, William, Charles, and John, then eighteen, ten, and eight, were said to have been away at school and not to have been at home in five years; after the marriage Edward Montagu provided them with a home for the holidays.[6] This circumstance may help to explain the lifelong mental illness of the youngest child, John Robinson, which was recognized by 1749. The illness of Mrs. Robinson may also have been mental, for she, who brought the estates into the family, ought to have had the influence at least to bring the children home for the school holidays had she been responsible. There may, however, have been other problems to do with Matthew Robinson; none of the children seem to have lived with their father after their mother's death in 1746, and after that date Sarah literally had no home, for she apparently refused to live with the Montagus. Her puzzling rejection of her sister's protection when it would seem she had almost no alternative must be assessed. Would her presence have disturbed the balance of the Montagu household, in which Montagu's attention was concentrated upon her husband and his activities? Or was she refusing to take the path Montagu probably recommended to her of marrying a rich, older man like Edward Montagu?

Sarah Robinson had been christened on March 5, 1721, at Holy Trinity, Goodramgate, York, and apparently was born on September 21, 1720.[7] Mrs. Robinson had inherited the important Kentish estates of East Horton and Mount Morris in the 1720s, but the three boys who followed Sarah were all born in Yorkshire, the last two, Charles and John, in 1732 and 1734 at Swillington, twenty miles southwest of York.[8] In 1736 the family was at Mount Morris, where they remained until 1746, whereupon at Mrs. Robinson's death that estate passed to the eldest son, Matthew, an inhospitable eccentric, who had inherited both the family brilliance and its instability. Matthew apparently did not urge his sister to stay on and be his housekeeper. Having lost his home and his wife, instead of making a home for his children, Sarah's father now moved into lodgings in London with his housekeeper-mistress so that Sarah was no longer able to live with him either.

Sarah Robinson, however, had had her chance in 1742 and again in 1743 to visit Bath in company with a family friend, a well-known doctor's wife, Mrs. Cotes.[9] Sarah never had the glitter, the beauty, or the charm for fashionable life, and childless little Mrs. Cotes, though gay and only about four years Sarah's elder, was a far cry from the Duchess of Portland, but she was well-connected and genteel, and at Bath under her protection Sarah danced at balls, played shuttlecock with assorted young men and women, and learned as Elizabeth had how to be agreeable. At Bath she saw something of George Lewis Scott, the son of friends in Canterbury. Scott had escorted the two women to visit the Montagus at Sandleford in October 1743 (Mrs. Cotes drove) and was probably the suitor Elizabeth then teased about. Sarah responded that he had the highest esteem and benevolence for her, but "I am persuaded he will never go farther and indeed I believe it wou'd be very inconvenient if he shou'd for I find he is very dependent upon his Mamma." [10]

Where precisely Sarah made her home after her mother's death in 1746 can only be surmised: perhaps she had none; perhaps her things were left with the Montagus while she wandered about making visits. In the summer of 1747 she was staying with her cousin Lydia Botham at Albury. Thereafter, in ill health, she spent five weeks at Tunbridge with her favorite brother, Morris, and her father—whom she described as witty at home and abroad and amused and talking bawdy with a favorite widow—and then she went to visit a sister of George Scott's, Callie

Scott Best, at Chilston, Kent. In September she was reduced to asking
her sister to beseech her maid to find some of her warmer clothing because she had no idea where it was. She was managing on an allowance so small that her accounts had to be settled by her father, and
she was constantly worried as to whether he would be "pleased" or not.
Her father's unwillingness to disburse to her would plague her until his
death in 1778 and perhaps afterward.

Meeting Barbara Montagu, known to her family and friends as Lady
Bab, was probably the most significant event in Scott's life. In December 1747 Scott went to Bath with Edward and Elizabeth Montagu. The
Montagus, having lost their infant son in 1744, probably hoped to have
another; Scott may have been in Tunbridge and Bath seeking relief
from the savage headaches that afflicted her. Montagu returned home
in May, but Sarah remained in Bath with a friend, Miss Grinfield. During her stay in Bath she had become intimate with Lady Barbara, a
woman about her age, barely able to maintain herself alone in Bath,
and too young to be living alone. When Miss Grinfield departed, Scott,
who found that Bath agreed with her, was easily persuaded to stay on
with her new acquaintance. She moved into her house in Trim Street in
August 1748 and found the solution to her housing problem so agreeable
that except for a few brief intervals the two women remained together
until Montagu's death in 1765.

Barbara Montagu, one to five years Scott's junior, though an earl's
daughter, was poor. Her father, George Montagu, Earl of Halifax, and
his second wife Lady Mary Lumley, daughter of the Earl of Scarborough, had produced one son, George, who succeeded as earl, and six
daughters, all of whom had to be adequately portioned. The girls had
£5,000 each; by contrast, Scott's portion of one thousand pounds had
not like Barbara Montagu's been turned over to her on her coming of
age and was apparently reserved for her marriage.

Barbara Montagu suffered from a serious heart ailment; Scott would
later mention her severe palpitations.[11] When she died, her cousin
George Montagu wrote Walpole, "She was the one I always loved and
passed all my youth with in daily gaiety and joy, for she had all the wit
and humours of the family, generous, and beneficent; her constitution
so delicate that her life has been a sufferance for many years."[12] Too
frail to think of marriage, she would ordinarily have been expected to
make her home with one of her sisters—Lady Frances Burgoyne, Lady
Betty Archer, Lady Ann Jekyll, or Lady Charlotte Johnston. But her
poor health could not have endured the fashionable lives they led, and

her presence in their establishments would have entailed trouble rather than conferred benefit upon her sisters. She had found that Bath was beneficial to her and inexpensive enough so that she could live there modestly alone, in sufficient style for an earl's invalid daughter. She had an annual income, probably, of about £200.

How much Matthew Robinson contributed to his daughter's maintenance during her first three years in Bath with Barbara Montagu is unknown, but undoubtedly it was the least amount possible. To some extent in these years the world saw Scott as the companion.[13]

Sarah had by this time reached an understanding with George Lewis Scott, with whose family her own had been intimate since their removal to Kent; this relationship may even have been the reason she had separated from her sister, who was very much against the match. George Scott had always been in too precarious a financial position to marry.

George Scott was a tall, burly man, at least twenty-two years Sarah's senior, with formidable talents, excellent connections, and as yet, in his fifties, no income to speak of. His father had been a diplomat and friend to George I; the Princess Sophia was his godmother. He was a member of the bar, a Fellow of the Royal Society, a fine musician and performer on the harpsichord and a historian of music, and "perhaps the most accomplished of all amateur mathematicians who never gave their works to the world." Dr. Burney found him "very sociable and facetious"; an intimate friend praised him as "amiable, honorable, temperate, and one of the sweetest dispositions I ever knew."[14] It is small wonder that Sarah Robinson had grown up admiring him. Yet he may have been constitutionally as well as economically unfit for marriage, if he was the same Mr. Scott whom thirty years later Susan Burney found "a Man of uncommon learning & knowledge wth a puffy fat person, & the manners of a frib."[15] Montagu's vehement opposition may have been because Scott was poor, because she wanted to keep Sarah to herself (as she would try to keep Dorothea Gregory), or perhaps because she knew or suspected something amiss in George Scott, who was well acquainted with that other eminent amateur mathematician Edward Montagu. To her intimate the Duchess of Portland the Reverend Edward Young was to write in January 1751, seemingly in reference to Scott's approaching marriage, "I am, madam, exstremely concerned for ye young Lady You mention; for her Acquaintance with yr Grace obliges me to conclude that she deserves a much better Fate."[16]

By 1749 the couple was awaiting only some source of income for George Scott, while Montagu vehemently protested. To most of their friends her reaction seemed motivated by pride: married to George Scott, her sister would be poor for life. Unmarried to George Scott, however, her sister was at least equally poor. To Scott herself it may have seemed that her situation could scarcely have been worsened by marriage. Moreover, if she married, her father would have to think about mustering up her settlement. In August 1748 Scott had written Montagu a long letter defending herself from various charges angrily leveled: that she had confided her affairs to others, had sent her maid secretly to town on unrevealed commissions, had failed to attend her sister's sickbed. She defended George Scott from an accusation that he wanted to end the sisters' friendship, and she denied having to make any sacrifices for him for which he would have to make her amends. Montagu's charges seem all to have had to do with a sense that her sister no longer put her first or told her everything. The Duchess of Portland quarreled with Montagu about the affair, advising her that Sarah "might wish to obey her in all other respects, but could not control her affections."[17]

In this period, when the pair were engaged and worried about the wherewithal to marry, Scott wrote her first novel, *The History of Cornelia* (1750). To some extent the plot of the novel helps to explicate Scott's own position at the time. Her orphan heroine Cornelia is forced, because of her guardian uncle's incestuous designs, to renounce her identity and her riches to become a wanderer and fugitive. In her wanderings she is consistently the victim of the selfish and irrational passions of both men and women. She is enticed into a brothel and narrowly escapes rape; she is twice imprisoned, once in the secret room of a castle and once in the Bastille. When at last she might have been happy with the worthy man she loves, an enemy traduces him as a libertine and she is forced to renounce him.[18] The novel—or romance—has all the components of a gothic tale except the frisson: the heroine never gives way to terror and remains firmly rational as she persists and conquers. She uses her learning without shame, at one time earning her living as a governess, and on occasion she is able to exert her benevolence. Her character well tested and firmly established, she is at last enabled to marry her lover and move into a safe harbor with him, where they regulate not only their own lives but their entire neighborhood, which is filled with industrious workers and pious, happy children, and they live "in the enjoyment of every social happiness, and in the highest public respect and applause." The plot may have helped to provide an outline for Ann Radcliffe's *Mysteries of Udolpho*, but though Cornelia has all the benevolence of sensibility, she has none of its debilitating imagination.

The story seems to be the story of Scott's own love delayed by the selfish father figure who banished her from home, withheld her inheritance, and forced her to wander and to be imprisoned. Cornelia's response is apparently Scott's response: a determined endurance and resourcefulness permit her to pass successfully through the ordeals that give her the mature experience she needs not only to take control of her own life but also to guide the lives of others. One might wonder whether Matthew Robinson's designs were either emotionally or literally incestuous. And was George Scott impugned as a libertine, and is that what Elizabeth Montagu held against him? What is more ascertainable is that Scott's vision of adult responsibility for women as for men transcended responsibility to the family and included the responsibility to regulate the entire community. It was a vision resulting in part from her sense of her father's selfishness and lack of concern for others, and she would always retain it.

The differences between the two sisters had become irreconcilable. Elizabeth Montagu's desires to regulate were those of the capitalist entrepreneur; Scott's became those of the utopian reformer. If suffering enables empathy with similar sufferers, then Scott's sense of having been left bereft, and not only once, resulted in a need to ensure the absence of bereavement for others; her sense of being without financial resources of her own resulted in her desire to ensure financial security for everyone. She wanted an absolute end to bereavement and financial powerlessness. In one important regard, Scott was like her sister: she struggled to be one of the regulators rather than one of the regulated. But her passion was for justice for everyone, not preeminence for herself. Montagu, forced to admire her, may have recognized that Scott had also chosen the one course that would provide her with a measure of superiority over her brilliant sister. The differences between them made it impossible for them to live together for any significant period.

The History of Cornelia was not very successful and could not have earned much for its author, but preferment for George Scott came suddenly, and, as his wife always claimed, unbidden and unexpectedly. In late 1750 he was named preceptor to the Prince of Wales, later George III.[19] The prince's education had been neglected, and the appointment was a wise one.

Scott now had her doubts that her father would produce her settlement. She wrote to her sister in September 1750, "If my Fathers intention ever comes to a proper birth I shall celebrate his generosity in the words Sr Tommy usd to thank his Barbadous Subjects for their gift, but

I am afraid the Embrio is weak, I expect a miscarriage" ("Dear Sister, I shou'd have answered the letter").[20]

In the period before marriage perhaps Scott felt some misgivings about that state expressed obliquely in comments about her now widowed friend Mrs. Cotes. On December 5, 1748, she had written, "I don't think her likely to marry, & I am very glad of it; she is in my opinion much better form'd for happiness in a single than in a married state" ("Dear Sister, I have been oblig'd to defer answering"). And in September 1750 to further hints about Cotes she responded, "What has Cotes to do to hitch herself to any more strange things? will women never learn to prize the liberty they so seldom can hope to obtain?" (Dear Sister, I shou'd have answer'd the letter you wrote").

Nevertheless into marriage Scott went. Her father seems to have produced the settlement after all, and the couple took a house in Leicester Fields, convenient to Leicester House, the prince's residence; apparently using Scott's dowry, they paid about £480 for the lease and several hundred more for furniture. (This large investment would result in severe bickering later.) Then on June 15, 1751, at St. Michael Bassishaw in London, near Gresham College, they married. Barbara Montagu came to live with them and probably contributed a part of her income to their common maintenance.

It is unlikely that the marriage was successful even at the start. By the autumn Scott, who never did well except in the country with air and space about her, had moved to Chelsea with Barbara Montagu. George Scott, busy with his demanding duties, stayed in Leicester Fields. In April 1752 the marriage ended when Scott's father and brothers came and removed Scott from under her husband's roof.

No wife could ever have effectively removed herself; the fine hand of Elizabeth Montagu is detectable here; given the male loyalties to the patriarchy, who could thereafter have blamed a woman rescued by her own father and brothers? How Matthew Robinson could have been persuaded thus to bestir himself is difficult to know; perhaps he was tender on the subject of the reputation of his family. The precise reason for the debacle will probably never be known. The principals had every possible reason to obscure the truth. The Robinson family had a very fine line to tread: sufficient justification for their extreme interference had to be inferable, but unless they wanted to assume full responsibility for Sarah's future upkeep, George Scott had to be neither mortally offended nor embarrassed, and his sensitive employment could not be jeopardized.[21] Rumors circulated, and Delany wrote an explanation on April 30: "What a foolish choice Mrs. Scot has made for herself! Mrs. Montagu wrote Mrs. Donnellan word that she and the rest of her friends had rescued her out of the hands of a very bad man, but for reasons of interest they should conceal his misbehaviour as much as possible, but intreated Mrs. Don. would vindicate her sister's character wherever she heard her attacked, for she was very innocent."[22]

Annie Raine Ellis 140 years later footnoted a mention of George Lewis Scott without giving her source: "Mr. and Mrs. Scott soon separated. Her friends said that he was a bad man, but did not say why. A rumour spread that he had tried to poison her. His pupil, George III, who always remembered him with affection, said, long afterwards, that it was 'a gross and wicked calumny,' invented by an intriguing upper preceptor, Dr. Hayter, Bishop of Norwich, 'against a man of the purest mind, and most innocent conduct.' "[23]

Four possible explanations seem sufficiently to explain the extreme nature of the Robinson family's action. In a domestic situation, George Scott, like other amiable fellows before him, may have proven physically violent and abusive; indeed, he may have resorted to poison. Second, his sexual predilections may have been the issue. Already fifty-one when he married, he was set in his habits, and though the domestic peculiarities of an aging bachelor would have been tolerated by women of the time, real sexual deviancy—such as (only for instance and not a particular hypothesis) a homosexual relationship with his manservant or molestation of the child labor in the kitchen—would not have been tolerated. Third, he may have had secret libertine inclinations that had resulted in his giving his wife a venereal disease, generally conceded to be a sufficient cause for separation if the wife positively insisted.[24] Finally, the possibility of a sexual relationship between Scott and Montagu, discovered by George Scott, who may then have become violent, cannot be discounted.

We can know George Scott's own partial explanation, produced at Leicester House for the satisfaction of the Princess of Wales. Because Sarah Scott revealed his story with some indignation to her sister, it was apparently not the truth as they saw it—or at least as Sarah Scott had told it. No doubt George Scott's reputation and his desire to remain in employment were first in his consideration when he devised it, but as a gentleman he was also required, even for the sake of his own reputation, to be tender of his wife's character. All of this it must be said he ingeniously contrived. Scott introduces the story by some references to her brother Jack, who was then in confinement for mental aberration.

The mention of that poor Lad puts me in mind of M^r—— story; since he is the foundation of this noble fabrick of his invention; take it as follows. Two or three days before marriage, it seems, his wife told him that she had one thing upon her mind, which she beg'd pardon for not having mention'd before; she had a madness in her family, was sensible she had done wrong to conceal it, but had at last determind for that reason never to marry, as she coud not bear the thought of bringing forth a race of lunatics, but woud always endeavour to preserve his friendship. To this the gentleman generously replied, No Madam, a friendship with me without marriage might hurt your character; which is as dear to me as it can be to yourself, & shall never suffer by me; I can not give up the pleasure of your conversation; therefore we will marry, & I promise you then to confine myself to that friendship you require. To this he bound himself most strictly, & in observance of it never enter'd into the same bed with her, nor offerd any thing improper, except once or twice when warm'd by dalliance into forgetfulness he was asham'd to say he had been too importunate. but she reproved him with so much gentleness & delicacy, as indeed she always did, & represented to him the small estimation in which we ought to hold all sensual pleasure, in so reasonable a light, & reminded him of the sentiments he had profess'd in that respect, that he immediately desisted. Is not the Lady oblig'd to him for representing her as a person of so much delicacy? It is really quite exemplary.

One problem with this tale is that it does not explain the separation or the manner of it; something is missing. To her account Scott adds the princess's response that "if he is in debt to her certain knowledge it is not his fault for he is the best oeconomist breathing but with such a setting out as his wife's, she does not wonder if his fortune was considerably impair'd tho' the time was short" ("My Dear Sister, I am very glad the tulips were proper").

George Scott's version of events emphasizes his own heterosexual normality and his wife's contempt for sexual passion; either emphasis could be contrived to hide an unpalatable truth. The barrenness of the marriage despite its ten-month duration may be suggestive but is not conclusive proof of a *mariage blanc* and not conclusive evidence of psychological or physical deficiency in either partner. What is certain is that Scott's subsequent attitude to her husband, as evidenced by her comments to her sister in letters, was one of distaste, dislike, and distrust. She showed a particular distrust of his word and his behavior in regard to financial matters and the settlement between them.

After the separation Scott was in no position, as she had never been, to fight for financial independence. She had to depend, like Barbara Montagu, on the goodwill and the family pride of the men of the family.

To her additional disadvantage, she took a humble view of her own unmerited advantages over others that made it difficult for her to demand
anything. As she was to write to her sister-in-law in August 1774, when
her fortune had never yet been great, she thought, "As many have not
the good they deserve others have more than they merit; the first may
have some reason to complain but as I come under the latter Class, I can
say nothing against the unequal distribution" ("My Dear Madam, The
head-ache is very apt to interfere").

Her brother Morris, now a competent lawyer and her good friend,
handled the arrangements of the separation, which the family attributed to "disagreement of tempers." George Scott returned half of his
wife's fortune to her father, who pocketed it and resumed the doling
out of allowances. George Scott also, no doubt impressed by the need
for her to remain silent about the reasons for the separation and aware
as well of her important part in obtaining him his appointment, agreed
to allow his wife £100 a year in quarterly payments. (He fell behind,
of course, and on February 3, 1753, she complained that the install-
ment due had not arrived.) Thus the capital remained in the hands of
the men, and the woman was left to rely on the men's pleasure, which
in turn was contingent upon her exemplary behavior. Dependent now
entirely upon her father's and her husband's continued prosperity and
goodwill, Scott probably had an income of well under £200 and was in
real need of Barbara Montagu's protection.[25] She was at last outside the
patriarchal structure, unclaimed by father, brother, or husband, unable
to marry again, with nothing of her own that any man wanted, with no
beauty and no fortune, but almost free and almost secure from starva-
tion. And everyone must have assumed that she would adopt the usual
shadowy half-life of the indigent single gentlewoman. Not at all; she was
to flower into a self-sufficient personage as powerful, in her own way,
as her sister Montagu, as effectual, and considerably more altruistic.

Scott had reached the point of altruistic behavior because of the pain
caused her by Elizabeth Montagu's early rejection of her except as a
humble follower, by her own inability to follow Elizabeth by imitating
her successes, and by her father's lack of concern for her. She was forced
to develop a mode of her own. Marriage might have stifled her development, forcing her to accept direction from her husband and busy herself
with domestic affairs; but all at once she was suddenly no longer, in any
practical sense, married. And now she returned to Bath to a strong influence that would help her codify her convictions and determine to act
on them. Her life had been redirected by a series of circumstances rare

for women of the period yet shared by others, particularly Sarah Fielding and Lady Barbara, of the Bath community she now rejoined. Her
great luck was in finding support among other similar women.

The support came from a remarkable group. The Bath community
was a world of independent-minded women, strong, self-sufficient, and
resourceful. They had been well educated and were neither beauties nor
fortunes. They had suffered rejection and pain, were poor, and enjoyed
the pain and the benefits of liberation from male protection. In Bath
each found a fellowship of other similar women. Of central significance
to them was Sarah Fielding, who had already tested her ideas about
woman's place and man's tyranny in her novels (see chapters 2 and 3),
was probably at the moment that Scott and Montagu returned to Bath
taking an interest in Jane Collier's *Essay on the Art of Ingeniously Tormenting* (1753), was soon to collaborate with Collier on *The Cry* (1754),
and now became the intimate friend of Scott and Lady Barbara.[26] The
group, which may also have included Collier before her death in about
1755, must have analyzed the power structure they began to discern
about them, anatomized it, and resolved to be supportive among themselves both psychologically and financially, to practice an enlightened
benevolence in the community, and insofar as they could, to provide an
example of an alternative way to live. With no modest conception that
genteel women did not put their opinions forward, they encouraged one
another to publish, considering publication an important source of income for their own support and to provide supplies for their benefactions.[27] They were impelled not only by their benevolence but also by
their anger. The alternative life-style, to be most fully expounded in
Scott's *Description of Millenium Hall*, was not the work of a few months;
it was conceived slowly. But it was to incorporate many of what we might
call conservative socialist ideas and was inspired primarily by a detestation of tyranny and an imaginative reconstruction of what genuine
Christianity might produce if it had ever been realized, for it was apparent to these women that genuine Christianity and patriarchy could
not coexist.

Fielding was the theorist of the group, and if Collier joined them,
she must have provided clear insight into tyranny. Scott was to be the
group's most ardent exponent of putting their ideals of a counterculture
into practice. Barbara Montagu followed and supported Scott in her
practical experiments. Elizabeth Cutts was an important member of the
group.[28] So was Miss Arnold, a more shadowy figure.[29] In Batheaston
Margaret Riggs, with her infant daughter, the future Lady Miller, lived

with Margaret Mary Ravaud.[30] This group was mutually supportive in a fluid harmony and as required. They had a variety of coadjutors, temporary affiliates, sympathizers, contributors, and protégées. Nina Auerbach writes that a community of women may suggest the idea of "an antisociety, an austere banishment from both social power and biological rewards."[31] But the Bath community, which might have remained only an antisociety, was far more ambitious in its schemes, wresting considerable social power for its members and planning to enjoy vicariously many biological rewards by furthering the fortunes of other people's children.[32] There was no idea about leveling the class structure in their program; they were not so radical, nor could they have implemented such an idea. Their plan, a product of their own painful experience, was that each person ought to be raised within his or her proper station to a full enjoyment of virtue, prosperity, and productivity. And, as one critic has noted, they may also have intended, through their superior management and vision, to advocate government by women, which *was* a revolutionary idea.[33]

In April 1752, on the implementation of the Scotts' separation (there was never a divorce, which would have been far too costly), Scott and Montagu returned to Bath. At first, puzzlingly, unless some imputation had been made against the women, Scott made a point of living alone. She may have been living temporarily with Barbara Montagu when in about July 1752 she wrote to her sister that she had been looking for a house she could afford but would probably have to be content with lodgings at £25 a year. In the fall she wrote Montagu that she intended to leave her father in quiet possession of her fortune: "After having done so much for peace this is but one small sacrifice more, & what I have so ordered my matters as to bear very well." She describes her household: for both principle's and economy's sake she had begun to employ the handicapped. She had two maids, the first "a well meaning simpleton, who, was not her understanding still in its minority, I might call a Woman; & a more useful Domestic . . . to whom nature instead of the sense of hearing has given numberless virtues, & indeed made almost a miracle for her station" (c. September 1752, "Dear Sister, I did not hear"). Neither could do the shopping so Miss Arnold did that for them.

Montagu now persuaded her father to give Scott the money to buy a house of her own (that is, to buy a long-term lease) despite his proclaimed fears that George Scott could henceforward claim any money or possessions she had. Scott protested that she had desired nothing more than to know that her fortune had been secured to her in her father's will (it was not). But she was grateful and thought the sum of £400 would give her a much prettier house than she could have hired for £50 a year. All went well, for in October 1752 she was settling into her new home, perhaps the house on John Street where she and Montagu were living in 1754, for they soon joined forces again. But in February 1753 she was struggling with her father once more and appealing to Morris to prevent his selling the lease to the house in Leicester Fields and pocketing the money, whereas she wanted to lease it furnished and keep the income. At the same time she feared the new upheavals at Leicester House, which threatened to displace George Scott, would result in the closing in of his creditors, who would then take the furnishings from the house.[34] Luckily Barbara Montagu's finances were stable.

In May 1754 Montagu took the house for which they would be best known, in Batheaston, the village on the Avon two miles from Bath, close to the home of Riggs and Ravaud. They would remain there until 1762, and this was always Scott's favorite home and the place where she instituted her most successful social schemes. Ordinarily they retired to Bath for the winter, where Barbara Montagu profited from drinking the waters. Occasionally, for reasons of health or to visit members of their families, the two women separated, but their separations were brief. The house was convenient, and Barbara Montagu put up a tent at the bottom of the garden from which there was a delightful prospect down a steep descent to the Avon and over valleys and wooded hills. The pleasant walk to Bath wound along the riverbank.

In this community, so much simpler than Bath, Scott and Barbara Montagu set to work devising their new system of life. In October 1755 Montagu visited there and described the house as a kind of convent, "for by its regularity it resembles one," but a cheerful place, and noted that Scott had become a truly serious Christian. "My sister seems very happy, it has pleased God to lead her to truth, by the road of affliction." Scott rose early, read prayers to the household, and then sat down to cut out and prepare work for twelve poor girls whose schooling the two women paid for. To those capable of such improvement, she taught writing and arithmetic. The girls made childbed linen and clothes for the poor of the neighborhood, which were distributed by Scott and Barbara Montagu as they judged best. Scott was always interested in devising schemes of economy based on a benevolent rather than a profit motive, and the idea of teaching poor children to sew and then distributing their products to the poor was typical of her benevolist system of economics. The women also schooled twelve small boys, and on Sunday mornings

Scott had Sunday school for the twenty-four children before they were sent to church. Montagu thanked God that Scott and her friend were not Methodist enthusiasts but went often to the theater and sometimes even to balls and were calm and rational, though she thought they would have done better in the true country away from fashionable Bath life.[35] There were other schemes: poor women of the neighborhood were set to work making mittens and other useful items, which Scott and Montagu then sold to their friends.[36]

They used the publishing world for charitable purposes as well. A long correspondence survives between Barbara Montagu and Samuel Richardson about the production of some elaborately devised sets of cards bearing mathematical, historical, geographical, and other information—probably a learning game—which the women invented and printed up, the proceeds dedicated to help a poor neighbor. When the women arranged for Richardson to publish *The Histories of Some of the Penitents in the Magdalen House* for its author's benefit, Lady Barbara paid his charges.[37] In addition to these labors, Scott was a prolific author after 1753.[38]

This new way of life was the construction of the two women who shared it; Scott, who had superior health and strength, seems more prominent, but it would have been impossible for one woman to manage it alone. The partners were supported by an association of like-minded women who might also join the ménage on occasion. In such a true community, it becomes meaningless to attribute an idea or an action to one member. Scott was particularly dedicated to testing community ideals in practice, more so than Fielding, for instance; but Barbara Montagu might easily have inspired her dedication.

Sarah Fielding, who brought to the group the experience and ideas of the Collier sisters as well as her own, had already propounded a scheme of a community for gentlewomen in *The Countess of Dellwyn*. Janet Todd has in interesting fashion traced eighteenth-century ideals of community through Mary Astell and Lady Mary Wortley Montagu, both of whom recommended something like Protestant nunneries for single women of small fortune, and through David Hume, who saw community as a combination of self and others bonded by a sympathy and tenderness that elided individual differences. And she notes Sarah Fielding's darkening doubt of the safety of community in the second part of *David Simple* (1753).[39] Initially David Simple had believed "tenderness can prevail in a very small secluded community, which avoids the world" but learns that benevolence and tenderness prove insufficient because the community is ultimately dependent upon the vicious who are outside it. But Fielding, buoyed up in Bath by a community of women, did not entirely despair. If her "fellowship of four victimized souls" in *David Simple*, who must travel together into the miseries of Part II, was ineffectual and unable to protect itself, then a larger, more powerful community, well endowed and not only self-supporting but autonomous, powerful enough even to change the vicious world, need not be. If a small group of women might be easily defeated, perhaps a large group could not so easily be. During the 1750s the discussions of the Bath community apparently resumed where Fielding's and Collier's work had left off—with tyranny at least partially anatomized and with some sense of the power any effectual community must have.

After they had made themselves thoroughly conscious of the disastrous permutations of tyrannic behavior throughout their culture—no simple task—the group's visions took the form of utopian schemes within which the needs of the less fortunate classes could be met and ecological systems devised within which all could work in harmony with themselves and nature with equal consideration for all (animal creation included) instead of every creature and object in nature existing for the service and ruthless misuse of an upper class of self-serving and destructive males who could not even make themselves content.

That in the meantime Scott never fully freed herself from her complicated feelings about her sister is evidenced by her translation of a French work, *La Laideur Aimable*, in 1754. Scott and Montagu were consistent patrons of the Bath bookshops, read most current works in English and French, and had a considerable library when Barbara Montagu died in 1765. Scott clearly chose to translate this one work, as *Agreeable Ugliness: or, The Triumph of the Graces*, because of its fable of two sisters. The heroine is her stepmother's "shocking monster" while the younger half-sister is pretty and given first chance to be companion to the distinguished Mademoiselle de Beaumont (read Duchess of Portland); but she flirts, gets into difficulties, and is sent home again. Then the plain one is sent for and soon, in a more kindly atmosphere than her home, develops and is valued for her good parts. After many trials and tests—she has married not the man she loves but the man her father has chosen for her—she is enabled to marry the man of her choice while her pretty sister, who has disgraced herself, retires to a convent.

By 1760 it was apparent to Scott and Barbara Montagu that although Bath did not agree with Scott as well as Batheaston, it was necessary for the health of Montagu; they needed sufficient income to maintain establishments in both places, or they needed to move to Bath, for Montagu's health was deteriorating. Financial necessity and the desire to keep her beloved Batheaston establishment produced further publishing on Scott's part in 1760 and 1761.[40] In 1760 Barbara Montagu had taken a lease on a house in Beaufort Square. In September 1761 she moved to Bath for six weeks. She insisted on Scott's remaining in Batheaston, but they contrived to meet—one or the other walking the two miles along the Avon—every day.

The separation as well as the expense having proved impractical, Scott gave up the house in her beloved village, with all her projects, after the summer of 1762, and the pair compromised on a house that was high and airy in a new street in Bath.[41] Before giving up the house at Batheaston, they had probably put a great deal of effort into obtaining a pension for Montagu, probably through the assistance of her brother, who since the 1750s had enjoyed a pension of £1,500 a year. In April 1763, too late to save the Batheaston lease, Montagu was granted a pension on the Irish establishment of £300 a year, which must have been of considerable assistance to the projects of the pair.[42]

The writing of *A Description of Millenium Hall* (1762) was therefore probably motivated as much by economic necessity as by the desire to proselytize for the group's ideas. Scott's most important book, it describes the discovery by two men of a remarkable community of women, and its development is the gradual revelation of the community plan to the visitors. Millenium Hall is supported by five women modeled on the women of the Bath community and their friends, who are endowed with fortunes sufficient for ambitious experiments. Altogether they have a large estate and £86,000,[43] and Scott is candid throughout the book about financial calculations and costs.

In the course of the women's explication, the history of each of the five is told: each has suffered indignities and assaults at the hands of tyrannical and exploitative men. The struggle against tyranny is the theme of the book. Tyrannies directed at the lower classes, the handicapped, and animals are identified and denigrated. Tyrannies against women are not identified as such but are fulsomely described. One of the women has been forced by a stepmother to marry a truly obnoxious husband who separates her from her devoted friend; her story has some striking parallels to the history of Delany. Another has been reared by a libertine guardian for his own sexual delectation. A third has been nearly decoyed into a spurious marriage with a married suitor.[44] In these tales Scott used the familiar stories circulated in the world of women's talk.

But the tyrannies of men to women, and particularly the tyrannies of marriage, are never definitively labeled; in 1762 one could still not attack marriage overtly.[45] Nor are tyrannies against children identified; it would seem that some prerogatives of the patriarchy were not to be directly attacked.[46]

The efforts of the group at Millenium Hall are a counter to the tyranny of the outer world. Gentlewomen without sufficient income here pool their resources to live in cheerful harmony. The disadvantaged are advantageously employed. The physically handicapped are sheltered from ridicule. Young ladies are boarded and usefully educated. Schools educate poor children. A carpet industry is established. In the neighboring villages the virtuous are encouraged, and presents are given to aid the establishment of young couples.[47]

The book resolutely opposes the altruistic standards of the women of the community to the tyrannies of the patriarchal structure. This is a feminine utopia designed to convert men by showing them a better system; and the revelation, in both senses, to the male visitors is thoroughly convincing to the superior of the two. The one great error of the book's projector(s) is an error common to reformers throughout the later part of the century: a supposition that people can be reasoned into altruistic behavior, reasoned out of their enjoyment of inflicting their power upon others.[48]

This book was, surprisingly, Scott's one great success. It would appear that a considerable reading public recognized the truth of her generally implicit charges. Possibly the time had arrived when female altruism could be recognized as a natural and potentially beneficial phenomenon. Even Matthew Robinson found wit—the only commodity he respected—to commend in it, much to the astonishment of his daughter. It went into its fourth edition in 1778 and has never been forgotten. Perhaps the greatest compliment to it is that, although Scott's authorship has always been known, Oliver Goldsmith and Christopher Smart have been credited with writing it, probably on the grounds that it was an influential book, on a rational plan, and therefore could not be the work of a woman. Horace Walpole noted on his copy of the book that Barbara Montagu had collaborated on it; nothing would be more reasonable than to assume the effort was a joint one, even a group one, though there is little reason to doubt that Scott was the principal author and inditer.

The removal to Bath could not halt the progress of Barbara Montagu's illness, and she died in August 1765. Elizabeth Cutts devoted herself to the pair during the final period. Immediately upon the death, Scott sat down and wrote to her sister a letter beginning, "My Dear Sister will wish to know how I am after the great the irreparable loss she will hear I have sustained, & I wou'd not commit to any other hand the office of telling her that I am better than I cou'd hope after such a grievous shock. . . . Mrs Cutts was with me, & is so every day."

The dispositions of Barbara Montagu's will help to illustrate the life of the women, of their community, and of the network the community sustained; her greatest care was of women in humble circumstances. First, she returned to her brother Halifax the annuity of £100 a year which she had "bought of him during his life"—which would now presumably return to him for the remainder of his own life. She left legacies of £100 to two of her surviving sisters, Ann Jekyll and Betty Archer, and to her niece, the daughter of her sister Frances Burgoyne. The rest of her legacies had to do with her Bath life. The house in Beaufort Square was rented, but she left the remainder of its lease, after its tenant Sarah Morse had departed, to Elizabeth Cutts. Mrs. Anne Aust, living with Sarah Morse, was bequeathed £40 and an annuity of £10 until her son should be able to provide for her. Sarah Fielding, living at Walcot, was bequeathed £10 a year for life and £10 for the rent of garden ground as long as she continued there. A young protégée was left £30 a year for school expenses, £50 to apprentice her, £10 a year for clothing during the apprenticeship, and £150 thereafter to stock a shop. Miss Arnold received the choicest clothing, watches, rings, and garnet earrings, and Montagu's woman servant received £10 and the rest of the clothes. Scott's servant, Mary Aust, got £5, and the cook £10 to apprentice a dependent child whom she boarded out. Mary Groom at Teddington got £4 a year for life. Altogether Montagu left under £1,000 in legacies and annuities that would last for varying periods totaling under £60 a year, all of which had to come out of an estate of £2,900, her remaining capital. It was a careful disposition of what she had to give.[49]

Montagu's trustees were her sister Elizabeth Archer and Scott's brother Charles Robinson, and to them she left the remainder of her fortune and personal estate in trust for Scott "for her Sole and Separate Use to be paid Applied and Disposed of as She shall Solely Direct and Appoint and not to be Subject to the Controul Disposition or Appointment of her Husband." Simple arithmetic indicates that the annuities Montagu left were exactly calculated to absorb the interest of the £2,000 that was not bequeathed in legacies. Scott would not profit until the annuities had expired, but if she outlived the annuitants she would gradually fall heir to at least £60 a year.

A codicil dictates that whenever Montagu's brother Halifax gives Scott a post as keeper of the pheasants and the salary thereof, she wants him to have £100, because then Scott will be enabled to pay all of Montagu's annuities and legacies without spending her own principal. For, she says, she dies possessed of only £2,900 and owing about £50 and the funeral expenses to pay, and Scott will be left with nothing but Montagu's half share in their furniture because all the books are hers already. This is a bribe of £100—to a man who married an heiress of £100,000—but although no doubt Montagu knew her man, there is no evidence that Scott ever obtained the post.

And there is no evidence that Halifax, not named his sister's executor, ever did anything for Montagu from his own pocket. As in the case of so many of the women studied in this work, the more they appear to rely upon themselves and upon one another and to seek their own good, the more disaffected and even vindictive appear to grow the men closest to them. The Parrs, Baddeley and Steele, Vesey and Handcock, and Montagu and Scott all appear to have been paid back in some way for their coalitions by the holders of the purses.

Scott's subsequent life—she lived until 1795—was an exploration of and a dedication to the systems she had established with Barbara Montagu. For a time she continued the pattern of their life together. She had already completed a sequel to *A Description of Millenium Hall* called *The History of Sir George Ellison*—he the more worthy and therefore the convert of the two male visitors to the female utopia. The book is the outline of the manner in which a man could implement the ideals of Millenium Hall. Most significantly, it could be done by a man in an ordinary domestic setting.

Ellison has made his fortune in Jamaica as a merchant, employing servants from England but refusing to endorse slavery, which he finds abhorrent, by buying slaves. When he marries a widow with a valuable plantation, he realizes he cannot abolish slavery even on her (read "his") own estate; his measures therefore become not radical, but ameliorative, his policy gradualism, and against the protests of his wife and her overseer, he introduces every humane expedient. His object becomes "to find a means of rendering our slaves obedient, without violating the laws of justice and humanity." [50] "When you and I are laid in the grave," he instructs his wife, "our lowest black slave will be as great as we are; in the next world perhaps even greater; the present difference is merely adventitious, not natural" (1:27). To mitigate the sufferings of his slaves becomes Ellison's first and then his only object, and his treatment of

them, including two shortened workdays, the remission of work during the heat of the day, and the provision of innocent amusements and
abolition of corporal punishment, is superior to the treatment of many
English farm laborers (1:28–38). Scott's argument, therefore, is that
Ellison's reforms would be both beneficent and practical or economically advantageous because the slaves cease to be rebellious and subversive under his enlightened treatment. At the same time she manages to
underscore the essential point: that blacks were in no way intrinsically
inferior to any other group. By the same lights, neither were women.

For Scott, then, as for Mary Astell fifty years earlier, subordination
seems to be at least formally acknowledged as necessary in this imperfect world, but, significantly, it can be dispensed with in the next perfect
one. Ellison, for the momentary purpose at least, purports to find things
done better in England: "No subordination exists there, but what is for
the benefit of the lower as well as the higher ranks; all live in a state of
reciprocal services, the great and the poor are linked in compact; each
side has its obligations to perform; and if I make use of another man's
labour, it is on condition that I shall pay him such a price for it, as will
enable him to purchase all the comforts of life; and whenever he finds
it eligible to change his master, he is as free as I am" (1:38).[51]

Scott cannot openly call for the end of slavery in Jamaica and cannot openly call for the end of the subordination of the daughter to the
father. (In even her last novel, *A Test of Filial Duty* [1772], she emphasizes, as she does in most of her novels, the duty of a daughter to marry
according to her father's wishes.) Nor can she openly call for the end of
the subordination of the wife to the husband. We can only guess that
she would have liked to. What she always emphasizes is the responsibility of the superior to maintain a loving, beneficent, and nurturing
concern for the inferior and to accept all the responsibilities of stewardship without reveling in any of its incidental perquisites. Her plea for
slaves is therefore of a piece with her implicit plea for wives; but she
never proposes an abolition of rank or station or of the proper responsibilities attached to each. Thus the curricula of the ideal schools for
young women in Ellison's society are carefully thought out and are of
three kinds, one for young ladies with fortunes, another for those without, and a third for the daughters of shopkeepers; and preparation for
very different stations is a first consideration (1:258–66).

On his return from Jamaica, Ellison determines to try the life he has
so admired. He acquires a housekeeper trained at Millenium Hall for
his country estate and begins actively to engage in society. His house is
always crowded with people of all ages, his servants are encouraged to

marry and beget children, and he establishes a school where the young are educated according to their stations. His particular concern is to travel to prisons and release the more worthy of the prisoners for debt, after which he helps them reestablish themselves. He selects a daughter-in-law but then allows his son instead to court a poor girl of his own choice; and when the son has killed the girl's father in a hunting accident, he helps him retrieve the situation and marry the girl anyway. He befriends a peasant couple fortuitously elevated to a dukedom, educating them for their new station. Everywhere he encourages merit, settles family quarrels, and finds niches for displaced persons. Altruistic masters in a world that remains hierarchical are the only solution Scott dares to proclaim. The distinction between the male and the female spheres is marked in these two utopian novels; Ellison can operate from the normal domestic sphere whereas the women of Millenium Hall must forgo marriage and live entirely outside the patriarchal system in order to put their ideas into practice.

In the behalf of the enlightened treatment of women, this novel also provides a precise analysis of the treatment of a Mr. Reynolds's two wives: the first, inferior in understanding and cunning and devious, he had treated with indulgence; the second, a woman of great understanding and honor, he constantly denigrates, refusing ever to grant her wishes. Finding his first wife so inferior to him in intelligence, "he would not so far affront himself, as to believe she could attempt to govern so wise a Being, one of the Lords of the Creation; he therefore was not on his guard against her." His second wife was so beautiful that he married her "in spight of her excellent understanding, which he looked upon as a very alarming circumstance," resolving "to be very watchful in the preservation of his sovereignty. From the day he married her, he has constantly opposed every inclination she has expressed, although it has frequently been agreeable to his own, fearing lest a seeming compliance should encourage an attempt to enslave him. As a handsome woman, he is fond of her, but as a sensible one he envies her; and when he most admires her beauty, he is jealous of her understanding. He is ever caressing, and ever endeavouring to mortify her, by pretending a contempt for her judgment, which he flatters himself will give her a low opinion of it" (1:63). This wife, unlike the first, of course, has no wish to dominate her husband. Here, probably, Scott used experience garnered from her own marriage.

The money from this latest work may perhaps have helped to finance the greatest venture of all. While Scott and Cutts were recovering from their loss in Bath, they were projecting an ambitious experiment, a female utopia founded upon the Millenium Hall scheme though of much more modest dimensions. Sarah Fielding, who in 1767 was perhaps living with Scott,[52] must have helped with the planning. Scott, Cutts, and Arnold were joined in their scheme by a convert, Scott's cousin Grace Robinson Freind, whose son owned an estate at Hitcham in Buckinghamshire, where the women were to make the experiment. That they were to live in community is certain. Probably they were also to begin schools for poor children in the neighborhood and employ poor women to knit as Scott had at Batheaston. In the spring of 1768 they had begun, for Montagu sent them a present of livestock, visited them at Hitcham in April, and also offered to pay the expenses for Fielding to join the community. Fielding, however, was now too near death to go.[53]

Sadly, the plan failed almost at once. It was undoubtedly the inclusion of Grace Robinson Freind, who had not been sufficiently schooled in the Bath community, that was the flaw. The one complaint Scott voiced about her, that Freind invited her daughter to lie in with them without consulting the others first, suggests rather than a lack of charity on Scott's part a sense that Freind, who had provided the estate and had the most money, was unwilling to yield the advantages she imagined these circumstances had conferred. All was not well, and by the summer Scott was so plagued by headaches that she had to fly to Chelsea and the baths of Dr. Dominiceti.[54] The community soon disbanded, and Elizabeth Carter, ironically, attributed its failure to the absence of a proper subordination, or of a proper chain of command, writing to Montagu in December, "You have never told me, that the society at Hitcham was dissolved. My informant makes grievous lamentation for the scandal which she supposes this event will reflect on female friendship." But, she goes on to say, people disagree not because they are men or women, but because they are human, that in families the accepted subordination regulates and determines all, but it is quite different between independent members of a voluntary society.[55] Scott's attempt at a limited eradication of hierarchy was here condemned by one of the most sympathetic of onlookers; but Carter's doubts about that experiment in the removal of hierarchical order underline both the fact that Scott's group did attempt such an experiment, suggesting that it was an ideal of the Bath community, and that it seemed a dubious one to another learned bluestocking. It seems feasible to postulate that the Millenium Hall scheme for gentlewomen and the Hitcham scheme were both tentative or first experiments in the removal of hierarchy.

The Hitcham experiment needs to be more closely studied. Did it fail because any attempt to remove subordination is bound to fail, or because it was undertaken on too limited a scale, was too made up of available bargain components such as Grace Freind? At any rate, this project, conducted when Scott was forty-eight, was her last great effort. Probably still in need of funds, she continued to write. But in her last years she was moderately comfortable. After Edward Montagu died, her sister settled a £200 annuity on her. Then her father died in 1778. His principal concern seems characteristically to have been for the welfare of his housekeeper, Elizabeth Hawkins, to whom he left a £70 annuity and his furniture, recommending her to the kindest care from his children. To Sarah he left not her fortune but the income for life of a leasehold estate in Yorkshire and, in an undated codicil, a further annuity of £50, or £200 outright if his (male) heirs chose to cancel the annuity.[56] Capital was not allowed out of the family, and in this context family was construed to mean the male heirs.

Altogether Scott now had about £400 a year, a respectable competency. She spent much of the remainder of her life with Elizabeth Cutts; they were often with Miss Arnold; and she published no more. In 1787 she took a house at Catton, near Norwich, and died there on November 3, 1795. Her private papers, by her own wish, were destroyed.

Women like Astell and Scott were able to think unhierarchically, to imagine a society without due subordination and to judge that society an improvement over their own, but they began with groups of their own sort of women who might provide leavening action; they did not presume to reorganize society at large. Their insufficiency seems less when we consider that the problem of an egalitarian society still remains unsolved. Hierarchy was at that time still a sacred beast, unchallenged—subscribed to—even by Astell and Wollstonecraft. Despite Scott's failure to endorse more radical reforms, her life can be said to have been that of a political activist. She is certainly the one woman of all those considered here who dared the most in the hope of changing the cruelest aspects of the society in which she lived. The entire Bath community was a female society of an unusually forceful, political nature, a demonstration that an extended group can generate a lot of power, an exemplar to be vaunted and cherished.

Conclusion

WOMEN RESPOND to what appear to be similar situations according to the climate of their time, and when Mary Wollstonecraft became a companion in 1779 she did it in a previously unnoted way. She went to the widowed Mrs. Dawson in Bath not only as a declaration of independence from her family but as a test of her own strength. Wollstonecraft had learned that Mrs. Dawson was a woman "of great peculiarity of temper, that she had a variety of companions in succession, and that no one had found it practicable to continue with her." She took the situation "with a resolution that she would effect . . . what none of her predecessors had been able to do,"[1] that is, to remain and to compel her employer's respect. Her circumstances forced her into depression, but she continued to exercise her powers of judgment and autonomy. She condemned the cruelty of the king, who in a hurry had ridden three horses to death, and accused him of murder, and she noted, "Bound as my power of doing good is, I have sometimes saved the life of a fly, and thought myself of consequence."[2] She clung to her powers of choice, to save flies, judge the king, refuse to enumerate her miseries or indict Mrs. Dawson. William Godwin wrote: "she had reason to consider the account she had received [of Mrs. Dawson as employer] as sufficiently accurate, but she did not relax in her endeavours. By method, constancy, and firmness, she found the means of making her situation tolerable; and Mrs. Dawson would occasionally confess, that Mary was the only person that had lived with her in that situation, in her treatment of whom she had felt herself under any restraint."[3]

She was summoned away from Mrs. Dawson in 1780 to attend her mother in her last illness. The will to succeed and not to succumb or even complain helped Wollstonecraft survive a grueling test that must have given her a confidence in her own fortitude very important to her in subsequent years.

The eighteenth century has been identified by various social historians as a watershed period for social change. Many have noted that it is the period of the development of the less extended, more nearly nuclear family. Foucault has added that as a consequence it is the period in which sexuality became located and nurtured within the family. It is the period in which a new concept of the basic goodness and sensibility of humans was first popularized. It is the period in which the idea of tyranny was explored, if not very objectively, and the period in which to a considerable extent political, if not domestic, inequities of power were recognized and, on occasion, significantly addressed. Not to mention the industrial revolution and the period of colonial expansion.

In terms of democratization, which seems to have required a preliminary or at least a concurrent recognition of tyranny, the period should have a more mixed review than it has generally received. Within the patriarchy the power seeped downward; men protested the absolutism of kings and the unearned privileges of aristocrats, won the right to oversee (that is, to publish the proceedings of) Parliament, and established definitions of tyranny that not only made it possible for ordinary men to protest against interference with their prerogatives as they perceived them but also enabled a large minority to protest the evils of colonialism in America and a smaller minority to protest the institution of slavery.[4] There was no equivalent argument made in behalf of women, and the patriarchal rationale for the suppression of equal rights for women became increasingly more codified, as we have seen in the conduct books for women, the proliferation of which during the course of that century and the next was required to maintain the distinctions supporting male privilege.

For women, then, the century began more advantageously than it ended. Yet somehow, as Wollstonecraft shows us, women's consciousness expanded during that period to recognize that resistance and fortitude were feasible and necessary. At both beginning and end of the century there were protests in behalf of women's rational capacity, but these protests were stronger and more incisive at the beginning, when Astell claimed women's reason equal to men, than at the end, when Wollstonecraft asked for equal opportunity of education for women in order to provide a fair test of their reason. And the long period of virtual silence between 1714 and 1792 made renewed efforts more tentative. Eighteenth-century movements to abolish tyranny, then, apparently benefited only the members of the patriarchy, who characteristically never questioned their right to rule over women and colonials.

Yet despite a climate hostile to women's claiming equal rights and therefore identifying male domination as tyranny, many women began privately to perceive male domination as precisely tyrannic. Woman's ability to reason remained the central issue. Aware that their right to

dominate women, slaves, and colonials inhered principally in their re-
putedly superior reasoning powers, members of the patriarchy exerted
every effort to prove that male reason was superior both by divine mandate and by natural law (rather than by superior and exclusive education), and therefore without guilt they deprived their inferiors of every
educational, professional, and social advantage. If women's *difference* in
respect to reason could be firmly established, then a charge of tyranny
could not be leveled at the patriarch. Not content with the disadvan-
taging of women in society, the conduct-book writers set about to disadvantage them psychologically by instructing them that the way to
please their masters (avoid punishment, gain the most advantageous
marriage, win male attention and approval) was to eschew a display of
reason, feign weakness, and develop an intentionally debilitating sensibility. Wollstonecraft's argument that women should be educated in
kind if not in degree went, therefore, to the heart of the problem.

Women had readily taken to the new opportunity to earn their livings
by writing: this was a career open to them, it could be done at home, and
the only outlay required was for paper and pen. But in the eighteenth-
century climate, women writers worked under a considerable disadvantage. They were forbidden the subject matter and the judgmental forms
of male writers, and the matter and forms of male writers were of course
always accounted superior. Women writers were largely confined to such
genres as the novel and poetry, but forbidden the experience of such
a writer as Henry Fielding and forbidden to write openly about sex as
Manley had done. They were forbidden the judgmental forms of satire
and wit; they were forbidden to indulge in rational argument. Domes-
ticity and domestic relations, sentiment and sensibility, and an endorsement of all patriarchal values and arrangements became their allotted
subjects. And yet within the forms allotted—particularly the sentimental novel and the gothic—some women contrived to enter a plea for a
cessation of the devastating division of male and female into separate
conduits of reason or sensibility. Their heroines typically acquired reason to control their own sensibilities and acquired husbands with sensibility to temper their reason and to ensure that those husbands would
never deteriorate into tyrants.

In the period between Astell and Manley on the one hand and Wollstonecraft on the other, woman's sphere was so definitively identified,
woman's fitness for an unautonomous domestic capacity so unarguable,
that women writers, while confined to writing of the domestic scene,
were also confined to appearing, at least, to endorse it. Often, as Astell

had done, perceiving husbands as tyrannical and marriage as injurious to women, they were prohibited from saying so. The analogy between marriage and the mistress-companion relationship provided an appropriately indirect method of displaying and discussing the damage inflicted by patrons and toadies on one another. Men have consistently denigrated not only the rational but also the moral capacities of women, and have not been sorry to have to denigrate either. An examination of the moral damage suffered by toadies, who must scheme, cheat, and manipulate, can therefore also be indirectly a defense of the basic, intrinsic, moral equality of women and an indictment of the morality and justice of men.

Perhaps most difficult for women writers of the period to manage was the problem of women's sexuality: for virtuous women openly to lay claim to a right to sexuality became impossible, and as only ascertainably virtuous women could hope to publish or at least to sell books, sexuality was permissible only to the "bad" women of their novels' subplots. If, as Foucault has suggested, the family in that period became a hotbed of sexuality, the problem could be modified with least disadvantage to the privileged by curbing the sexuality of the politer class of females in it. Already in the eighteenth century the concept of proper and improper sensibility conveniently divided women into the sexless good ones and the sexual bad ones. The virtuous heroines of women's novels love, and even love passionately, but they appear to save their sexuality for a proper consummation, expressing it only obliquely by fainting, hysterics, or some other intensely emotional display. Hysterics may have become, even as Freud thought, the encoded way of expressing an otherwise inexpressible sexuality, but if so, such hysterics or abandonment of rational control should be read as a language, a sort of signing by the mute, expressing a need for forbidden fulfillment. By patriarchal direction, proper female sexuality, if it existed at all, was to be saved for and confined to marriage. But let us not forget Dr. Gregory's oblique and delicate direction to young women never to let their husbands know how much they "love" them—apparently an instruction never to shock them by a sexual response: truly proper female sexuality was at least not to *seem* to exist. By indirection, then, sexuality in both maidens and wives is exhibited in various forms of emotional display that characteristically suggest illness. For women writers who were assigned feeling as their province, the prohibitions—the "not-saids"—thus presented a staggering challenge, and it is little wonder that the only women who managed to write really first-rate novels were Burney, Radcliffe, and Austen.

Given the society in which the women who are considered in this book lived, their diverse responses to it are illuminating and instructive. Altruism largely unmoderated by reason or judgment was the common ideal presented to women of the time. To meet this ideal, they had to be feeling, generous, self-sacrificing, and natural victims. In this category can be located Lady Caroline Fox (Lady Holland), who was manipulated into an elopement by an unworthy lover who wanted an alliance with her for political reasons and who accordingly convinced her that his health would suffer if she did not marry him at once. The result was that her own health never recovered; her parents too, whether or not because they had been co-opted by Fox, both died early deaths. Lady Caroline remained a child, parented by her husband and her housekeeper. The women of this study who most successfully established such ménages all remained demonstrably immature. Elizabeth Vesey was a senseless altruist, thoroughly without judgment, following her own whim but always sensitive to the needs of others—willing to order the gardener to gravel the drawing room to accommodate a friend's broken leg. She was devoted to a husband who humiliated her with his infidelities when alive and later demonstrated his contempt for her in his will. Sophia Baddeley, who relied upon her friend Steele to complete a ménage with a protean father figure, remained not only a spendthrift but also a thoughtless (though never heartless) soft touch and was financially ruined. Georgiana, the Duchess of Devonshire, was an immature altruist, incapable of regulating her own life, who came to disaster when she replaced her mother's mentoring with that of Lady Elizabeth Foster. All four of these women died, three of them prematurely, at least in part because of their victimization by others who for one reason or another found the relationship with them profitable.

Those who were aware of the dangers of immature altruism could choose to become either tyrants or, most difficult of all, mature altruists. Elizabeth Montagu, Elizabeth Chudleigh, and Elizabeth Steele were all, in their own ways, identifiers with the aggressors. All three prospered as aggressors often do. Like the patriarchs, these women developed their reasoning powers and carefully planned their benefactions so as to get back more than they gave, publicized them so as to get full credit, and rarely—unless it was necessary to maintain their dominance—gave their dependents what they themselves wanted or needed, or what could lead them to independence.

The other corrective to the mindless altruism recommended to women was the development of a kind of reason which would, by weighing the comparative importance of sacrificing for the needs of others against the cost to oneself, enable the altruist to make rational choices—choices that in turn would allow her to continue as an effective altruist instead of immolating herself in destructive relationships useful only to others. These women, who achieved mature reason, could have chosen solely to look after themselves but made the choice to live lives essentially as altruists. They did so because, as experienced victims, they genuinely sought to work out better and alternative social models. But they also chose to live not with victimizers and exploiters but with other mature altruists. They were fully aware of the cost of altruism to themselves, and considered the cost worth the end attained. All were doubtless influenced by the Christian ethic, but not all were like Sarah Scott and presumably Lady Bab Montagu in being serious Christians. Scott and Montagu were poor, but labored so as to give away a large part of their income. Like them Dorothea Gregory repudiated the life-style and the fortune of Elizabeth Montagu. Frances Burney trod a delicate line in search of independence but always erred on the side of generosity, giving up the profits of her first novel to her reckless brother, immolating herself at court for her family, sharing her little pension with a penniless husband. Despite the apparent risks of her great generosity, however, she judged correctly enough to survive and to produce the novels that made her the first woman novelist of the first rank. Lady Spencer, always a woman of sensibility but also a woman of great ambitions, was chastened by the dreadful effects of the brilliant marriages of her daughters into a disciplined and devout style of life. For Elizabeth Preedy, also a mature altruist, Spencer sacrificed to do what was best. Frances Greville was never a Christian believer, but she was an altruist, immature when she married Fulke Greville, gradually maturing, taking Lady Spencer for a model, and joining her in her charitable work. Judging that her husband would willingly dissipate her fortune as he had his own, and that only she could provide for her four sons, she combated him for the last years of her life, which were consequently filled with discomfort and terror. Hers was a war won at the expense of her health and at last of her life. Mary Carter and Lady Clarges demonstrate what two altruists willing to develop one another's potential could accomplish. At the end of their period together both were established in society, Carter financially independent and the beautiful, young, and rich Clarges determined to devote herself to her family and music. Sarah Scott and Barbara Montagu, the most ambitious altruists of all, attempted in both life and literature to construct new models for society.

The problem of the inclusion of full sexuality in the lives of women can also be glanced at here. Open sexuality like Baddeley's of course placed women beyond the limits of polite society. Baddeley functioned as one of the sensuous women of unrestrained sensibility who took the blame for men's own unbridled expression of sexuality. The Duchess of Devonshire and Lady Elizabeth Foster too, like Chudleigh, though protected by the countenance of duke and prince, paid in heavy disapproval for the development of their sensual sensibility. Obviously if a respectable woman enjoyed sex with her husband or anyone else at this period, she did so with extreme circumspection. One suspects that Fox made something of a convert of Lady Caroline, that the Spencers had a happy sexual union, but one can know virtually nothing of that matter between husband and wife.

It can be postulated that women are no more naturally inclined to altruism than are men, but the postulation would be impossible to prove. What is demonstrable is that for the past two hundred years women have been in large part assigned the altruistic roles. The gender assignments of aggressive self-realization, expression, and acquisition on the one hand and altruistic self-sacrifice, silent acquiescence, and generosity on the other were significantly synchronous with Adam Smith's theory of the efficiency of the division of labor. In any case, the eighteenth-century assignment of altruism to women was one of the more serious problems for women of the time. The point that in the course of the century middle- and upper-class women were gradually though rigorously directed toward altruism, through the punishment of self-assertion and the rewarding of sensibility and self-abnegation, is probably unassailable. Mill's comments on what was virtually the pruning, the espaliering (or clipping, patterning, flattening against the wall, and cultivating for their beauty and their fruit) of women—the social rather than the natural selection that was modifying them—are salient.

But the lives and activities of some of the women examined here suggest that true nature will in some fashion out, and that our true natures are genuinely mixed. Passively as many women may have fulfilled their assigned roles, others used them in a variety of patently aggressive ways. Even the most aggressive of industrialists has found relief in altruism, and women have discovered that altruism can be carried to aggressive lengths. In the course of the eighteenth century, women found that the expression of sensibility could go public. They combined in charities and learned about raising and managing money and about persuasive speaking. They undertook public crusades against slavery, prostitution, and in the next century, alcohol consumption. The role of amelioration, originally devised and permitted to smooth over the worst effects of aggression and thus to obviate opposition and rebellion, involves first tacit but then vociferated criticism of that which is to be ameliorated, and women through the assignment of altruism found themselves at last empowered to attack the systems of their oppressors. Through altruism many accomplished women found what had seemingly been denied them: public lives, aggressive self-expression, and the moral high ground.[5]

The Bath community of women is an early example of this phenomenon. Assigned roles as educators, given excellent preparatory educations, Fielding and Collier were led to think about the theory of education, the nature of humans, the faults of existing systems, the possibility of their amelioration, and the construction of alternatives. Through them aggressive opposition was generated and fostered in Sarah Scott, Barbara Montagu, and the rest of the Bath group. The explorations of this book seem to bear out the acknowledgment by these women that both aggression and altruism are inherent in all human creatures, and that constricting assignments of one or the other alone are crippling. But this was the message of many eighteenth-century women writers, most importantly, probably, of Frances Burney, for whom it was a major concern. Now that we have begun to recognize and tolerate difference, to read these women in their lives and their texts for the obliquely expressed and even for the not-saids is instructive, rewarding, and illuminating.

Notes

Works frequently cited in the notes have been identified by the following abbreviations:

BL   British Library
DA   *The Daily Advertiser*
DNB   *Dictionary of National Biography*
GM   *The Gentlemen's Magazine*
IGI   International Genealogical Index of the Church of Jesus Christ of the Latter-Day Saints on microfiche
PCC   Prerogative Court of Canterbury

ONE. Companionship: A Range of Possible Choices

1. Charlotte Smith, *The Old Manor House* (London: Pandora, 1987), pp. 10–11. Subsequent references to this work will be by page number in the text. My thanks to Robert Bataille, who suggested to me that this book might be useful, and to Judith Stanton, who advised me on the subject of Smith and humble companions.

2. Lawrence Stone, *The Family, Sex and Marriage in England, 1500–1800* (New York: Harper & Row, 1977), chap. 8, suggests that in the eighteenth century the patriarchally dominated family was yielding to a new model of companionate marriage; if so, the companion was viewed as the Puritans viewed women (p. 136), as subordinates, second helpers, servants, assistants. Stone does not imply that the term *companionate marriage* was in use during the eighteenth century; but I suggest that in that period the concept of companionship, in terms of a couple in an intense isolated relationship, did not involve equal abilities and equal rights. John R. Gillis in *For Better, for Worse: British Marriages, 1600 to the Present* (New York: Oxford University Press, 1985) also questions Stone's thesis, e.g., pp. 3–5 and 14. He identifies the conjugal marriage as only a new form of tyranny (p. 5), a view with which I concur.

3. *The Autobiography and Correspondence of Mary Granville, Mrs. Delany: With Interesting Reminiscences of King George the Third and Queen Charlotte*, ed. Lady Llanover, 6 vols. (London: Richard Bentley, 1861–62), 3:546–47. Aware that the most effective argument for the subservient position of women derived from the *Book of Genesis*, Delany posed a counterargument from the same source.

4. *Mrs. Montagu, "Queen of the Blues": Her Letters and Friendships from 1762 to 1800,* ed. Reginald Blunt, 2 vols. (London: Constable, 1923), 2:119. On this subject, see also Elizabeth Bergen Brophy, *Women's Lives and the 18th-Century English Novel* (Tampa: University of South Florida Press, 1991), pp. 228–30. Subsequent references to this book will be by page number.

5. Arthur Collier (1707–77), the brother of Jane and Margaret Collier (for whom see chapter 3 and n. 8), specialized in tutoring women to achieve proficiency in the classics; his students included his two sisters, Sarah Fielding, Hester Thrale, and Sophia Streatfeild.

6. *Thraliana: The Diary of Mrs. Hester Lynch Thrale (Later Mrs. Piozzi), 1770–1809,* ed. Katherine C. Balderston, 2 vols. (Oxford: Clarendon Press, 1942), 2: 825–26. Thrale's 1791 entry may be a response ("Well then Philosopher—") to Samuel Johnson's *Rambler* essay 35 (see chapter 7). "Mother" in pickles is a slimy, bacteria-produced substance that forms in the vinegar.

7. Mary Astell, *Some Reflections upon Marriage* (London: John Nutt, 1700), pp. 56–57.

8. Astell's last published work, in 1709, *Bart'lemy Fair: Or, An Enquiry After Wit,* was an attack on Shaftesbury for an expression of irreligious ideas (see Ruth Perry, *The Celebrated Mary Astell, an Early English Feminist* [Chicago: University of Chicago Press, 1986], pp. 223–38). Though she signed her work "Mr. Wotton," she was found out and attacked twice in the *Tatler* as a quaint visionary virgin recluse with a scheme for a college for women that would teach "at least a superficial Tincture of the Antient and Modern Amazonian Tactics" (ibid., p. 229). Perry suggests (p. 231) that Astell probably stopped writing and publishing "because she recognized that the weight of history was against her."

9. For the period after Mary Astell, it becomes increasingly more difficult (though certainly not impossible) to find in women's published writings overt assertions of women's equality and overt criticism of marriage as an institution unfriendly to women. The treatises of "Sophia," *Woman Not Inferior to Man* (1739) and *Women's Superior Excellence over Man* (1740), are obvious anomalies, but, as Moira Ferguson points out (*First Feminists: British Women Writers, 1578–1799* [Bloomington: Indiana University Press, 1985], p. 266), her works are "semi-translations, with substantial additions of her own," of François Poulain de la Barre's *De l'egalité des deux sexes* (1673), a work of an earlier era. Claims of equality and criticism of marriage for women tended to go underground, expressed indirectly or through the subsidiary woman's (or second) plot of their novels and notably through the companionship trope. That criticism of marriage was often privately expressed in letters or journals and was a very real subcurrent of women's lives at the time is clear: see, for an important work in this regard, Brophy, *Women's Lives,* chap. 4.

10. On indirection, see Mary Poovey, *The Proper Lady and the Woman Writer* (Chicago: University of Chicago Press, 1984), pp. 40–47, 243, also p. 253, n. 8, which cites several other important sources. Mary Anne Schofield in *Mask-*

*ing and Unmasking the Female Mind: Disguising Romances in Feminine Fiction,
1713–1799* (Newark: University of Delaware Press; London and Toronto: Associated University Presses, 1990), pp. 9–11, provides a complementary bibliography of work on the secondary "woman's plot."

11. For a full discussion of Griffith's playwriting career that includes an analysis of this episode, see my " 'Depressa Resurgam': Elizabeth Griffith's Playwriting Career," in *Curtain Calls*, ed. Mary Anne Schofield and Cecilia Macheski (Athens: Ohio University Press, 1990), pp. 120–42.

12. Terry Eagleton, *Criticism and Ideology: A Study in Marxist Literary Theory* (London: Verso, 1976), pp. 89–90.

13. Quotations from Thrale's "Children's Book" and from manuscripts of 1817 and 1819 cited by William McCarthy, *Hester Thrale Piozzi: Portrait of a Literary Woman* (Chapel Hill: University of North Carolina Press, 1985), pp. 26–27, 271, n. 34.

14. For a woman's view of the prospect of the permanence of this sort of enforced altruism, see the discussion in chapter 11 of Frances Greville's novel and her portrait of the hypocritically subservient companion who becomes a tyrannical wife. A "toady" or "toad eater" was a humble companion who bore every form of abuse.

15. *Thraliana*, 1:112.

16. Elizabeth Griffith had learned her lesson so well that in her last published work, *Essays, Addressed to Young Married Women* (London: T. Cadell and J. Robson, 1782), she advised wives to indulge their husbands' love of power and authority so as to keep them at home, to review their own faults should their husbands wander, to pretend to be cheerful no matter what their true feelings, never to upbraid, and to hope patient suffering might in the end be rewarded by returning love.

17. Frances Burney, *Diary and Letters of Madame d'Arblay*, ed. Austin Dobson, 6 vols. (London: Macmillan, 1904–5), 2:382. Subsequent references to this work will be by volume and page number in the text.

18. Jane Austen, *Emma*, ed. R. W. Chapman (London: Oxford University Press, 1966), p. 6. Subsequent references to this work will be by page number in the text.

19. Janet Todd, *Women's Friendship in Literature* (New York: Columbia University Press, 1980), p. 277.

20. Lionel Trilling, "Introduction," *Emma* (Boston: Riverside, 1957), pp. x, xxi.

21. Marylea Meyersohn, "Jane Austen's Garrulous Speakers," in *Reading and Writing Women's Lives: A Study of the Novel of Manners*, ed. Bege K. Bowers and Barbara Brothers (Ann Arbor: UMI Research Press, 1990), p. 41; see also her dissertation, "The Uses of Conversation: Rationality and Discourse in Jane Austen" (Columbia University, 1985).

22. The antimarriage plot, in which the marriage is tacked on perforce at

the end, is not uncommon in the novels of eighteenth- and nineteenth-century women. For the analysis of Charlotte Brontë's *Shirley* as a novel of this kind, see Tess Cosslett, *Woman to Woman: Female Friendship in Victorian Literature* (Atlantic Highlands, N.J.: Humanities Press, 1988), pp. 111–37.

23. There is some evidence that Lady Caroline assumed unwomanly prerogative in her comment in a letter to her sister the Duchess of Leinster in 1756: "What possess'd you to send two dogs, dear sis—? You know how Mr Fox hates them, and he grows to have a will of his own (since he is a great man) in private" (*Correspondence of Emily, Duchess of Leinster,* ed. Brian Fitzgerald, 3 vols. [Dublin: Stationery Office, 1949], 1:168). Fox, an asthmatic who probably had reason to hate dogs, had become leader of the House of Commons and secretary of state in 1755.

24. BL Add. Mss 51,414, ff. 168r–168v, Caroline Fox to Henry Fox from Bath, September 1749. Mary Margaret Stewart shared her copy of this letter with me and has been generous with other information.

25. BL Add. Mss 51,414, ff. 172v–174r, Caroline Fox to Henry Fox from Bath, September 14, 1749. Again I am indebted to Professor Stewart for sharing her copy of this letter.

26. *Life and Errors of John Dunton* 2 vols. (London, 1818), 1:310, quoted by Stone, *Family, Sex and Marriage,* p. 241.

27. Charles Pigott, *The Female Jockey Club, or a Sketch of the Manners of the Age,* 7th ed. (London: D. I. Eaton, 1794), p. xxviii.

28. Anthony Ashley Cowper, Third Earl of Shaftesbury, *Characteristics of Men, Manners, Opinions, Times,* Treatise 4, "An Inquiry Concerning Virtue or Merit," book 2, part 1, section 3.

29. For sensibility, see Janet Todd, *Sensibility: An Introduction* (London: Methuen, 1986).

30. Perhaps it is not too fanciful to suggest motives for this odd male predilection for a delicate-looking rather than a robust and healthy wife. Apart from the fact that men have always preferred to have every obvious advantage over women, including those of strength and longevity, apart from the fact that a middle-class wife taken not for production but for show would attest to a man's easy circumstances, it is also possible that a woman who appeared good only for a few years—to produce several heirs and then die—might attract a man who feared a lifetime entrapment, who would be reluctant to leave the encumbrance of a widow's jointure on his estate should he die first, and who from the moment of marriage was in possession of his wife's fortune so that if she died he was free to shop for another. Certainly to appear smaller, women throughout the century wore metal braces that deformed and even killed them (Stone, *Family, Sex and Marriage,* pp. 444–45), and by the end of the century they were drinking noxious poisonous draughts to induce the correct pallor.

31. John Gregory, *A Father's Legacy to His Daughters . . . with the Author's Life. To Which Is Added, Mr. Tyrold's Advice to His Daughter . . . from the Novel*

of "Camilla." By Mrs. D'Arblay. (Poughnill: G. Nicholson, 1809). Dr. Tyrold's letter is chapter 5 of book 5 of Frances Burney's *Camilla; or A Picture of Youth* (Oxford: Oxford University Press, 1983), pp. 355–62. Subsequent references are by page number in the text.

32. Pigott, *Female Jockey Club*, pp. 138–39.

33. The word *altruism* was coined in the nineteenth century by Auguste Comte, who, born in 1798, was an heir to the theories of sensibility. The term *benevolence* becomes unwieldy when substituted for *altruism*, so in discussing the important choice of serving others of many of the women discussed here, I use the anachronistic term *altruism* as more accurately defining what was being asked of them and what they were demanding of themselves.

34. Anna Freud, *The Ego and the Mechanisms of Defense: The Writings of Anna Freud*, 2d ed. rev., vol. 2, trans. Cecil Baines (New York: International Universities Press, 1974). Subsequent references are given in the text.

35. Lillian Feder, "Selfhood, Language, and Reality: George Orwell's *Nineteen Eighty-Four*," *Georgia Review* 37 (Summer 1983): 392–409.

36. Emile Durkheim, *Moral Education: A Study in the Theory and Application of the Sociology of Education* (New York: Free Press of Glencoe, 1961), pp. 255–57.

37. M. T. Ghiselin, *The Economy of Nature and the Evolution of Sex* (Berkeley: University of California Press, 1974), p. 247.

38. J. Philippe Rushton, "The Altruistic Personality," in *Altruism and Helping Behavior: Social, Personality, and Developmental Perspectives*, ed. J. Philippe Rushton and Richard M. Sorrentino (Hillsdale, N.J.: Lawrence Erlbaum Associates, 1981), p. 264.

39. Carol Gilligan, *In a Different Voice: Psychological Theory and Women's Development* (Cambridge, Mass.: Harvard University Press, 1982) and *Mapping the Moral Domain: A Contribution of Women's Thinking to Psychological Theory and Education*, ed. Carol Gilligan, Janie Victoria Ward, and Jill McLean Taylor, with Betty Bardige (Cambridge, Mass.: Harvard University Press, 1988).

40. Nancy Armstrong, *Desire and Domestic Fiction: A Political History of the Novel* (New York: Oxford University Press, 1987), p. 89.

41. For fuller discussions of *Millenium Hall*, see chapters 2 and 13. For a reference to the problem of child beating, see chapter 13, n. 47. Because both wife and child beating were legal, it was necessary to change the law, but first to change the moral preconceptions of the aggressors (that is, the lawgivers) on this topic, an exceedingly delicate and difficult task.

42. See chapter 7, n. 50 and text.

43. Steven Epley, in a study of Mary Hayes, Mary Wollstonecraft, Susanna Rowson, and Hannah More, "Public Voices in Four Women Writers of the 1790's" (Ph.D. dissertation, Columbia University, 1992), has reached much the same conclusion.

TWO. The Socioeconomics

1. Women envied male prerogative in regard to clubs and made various attempts to have their own. The *DA* for July 18, 1745, notes that on the preceding evening a woman belonging to a club of women who dressed as men had sat as chairman, got drunk, abused the watch on her way home at 3 A.M., misused the constable, been detected, and been sent to Bridewell. Whether true or the fabrication of a "paragraph-maker"—a writer who concocted interesting news paragraphs—the story is significant, suggesting both female envy of male-only amusements and male discomfort at this envy. The upper-class female coteries and clubs of the 1770s finally officially established a female prerogative in this regard.

2. Jane Austen, *Northanger Abbey*, ed. R. W. Chapman (London: Oxford University Press, 1972), p. 157. Subsequent references to this work will be by page number in the text.

3. Frances Burney, *Evelina; or the History of a Young Lady's Entrance into the World* (New York: Norton, 1965), pp. 284–87. Subsequent references to this work will be by page number in the text.

4. Hester Lynch [Thrale] Piozzi, *Observations and Reflections Made in the Course of a Journey Through France, Italy, and Germany*, ed. Herbert Barrows (Ann Arbor: University of Michigan Press, 1967), p. 13. A fascination with the strictly female societies of convents was general among Englishwomen abroad, who sometimes formed relationships with the nuns there.

5. If the coup were very considerable, she was hugely anathemized as well. The Duchess of Bedford was excoriated by her unsuccessful rivals for the mean devices by which she secured the Duke of Marlborough for her daughter Caroline in 1762. The duchess of the fourth Duke of Gordon was positively notorious for having married her daughters to the dukes of Bedford, Manchester, and Richmond, and the Marquis of Cornwallis, despite the known tincture of insanity in the Gordon line. She was said to have assured the doubtful marquis that there was actually no drop of Gordon blood in the daughter under consideration. See *The Goodwood Estate Archives*, ed. Timothy J. McCann, 3 vols. (Chichester: West Sussex County Council, 1984), 3: 9–10, and *The Historical and the Posthumous Memoirs of Sir Nathaniel William Wraxall*, ed. Henry B. Wheatley, 5 vols. (New York: Scribner and Welford, 1884), 4:459.

6. Francis Coventry, *The History of Pompey the Little* (New York: Garland, 1974), pp. 42–43. Coventry manages to use Lady Tempest's epithets for her husband of fool and tyrant to indict *her*.

7. Apparently, straightforward arrangements were sometimes made, for Lady Clermont wrote to Lady Spencer, December 9, 1776, that a Mrs. Martyn had invited Miss Erwin to live with her offering £100 a year and £4,000 at her death (BL, Althorp Papers, F124 as provisionally cataloged).

8. See the will of the Earl of Halifax, who died in 1739, PCC Prob 11/696. In

converting eighteenth-century sums to present-day value, I find it convenient to multiply by one hundred and state the resultant sum in dollars. At the present rate of inflation, the resultant sum is now on the conservative side. Appendix IV, p. 951, of Frances Burney, *Cecilia*, ed. Peter Sabor and Margaret Anne Doody (Oxford: Oxford University Press, 1988), suggests multiplying any sum in pounds by at least sixty to reach the value in today's pounds. The two methods are not incompatible.

9. PCC Prob 11/922.

10. PCC Prob 11/913.

11. H. J. Habakkuk, "Marriage Settlements in the Eighteenth Century," *Transactions of the Royal Historical Society* 4th ser., 32 (1950): 21, notes that by the end of the seventeenth century the jointure was conventionally £100 a year for every £1,000 of fortune. Subsequently it tended to lessen. Further information about marriage settlements can be found in Lloyd Bonfield, *Marriage Settlements, 1601–1740: The Adoption of the Strict Settlement* (Cambridge: Cambridge University Press, 1983), and Barbara English and John Saville, *Strict Settlement: A Guide for Historians* (Hull: University of Hull, 1983).

12. On this subject see Susan Staves, "Pin Money," *Studies in Eighteenth-Century Culture* 14 (1985): 47–77. See also Staves, *Married Women's Separate Property in England, 1660–1833* (Cambridge, Mass: Harvard University Press, 1990).

13. See *The Yale Edition of Horace Walpole's Correspondence*, ed. W. S. Lewis, 48 vols. (New Haven: Yale University Press, 1937–83), 17:136, n. 38 and 39, 439, n. 51. Janice Thaddeus suggested I investigate Mary Edwards, who deserves to be the subject of further research.

14. Correspondence between Mrs. Howe and Lady Spencer, January 6, 9, 1782, BL, Althorp Papers, F49.

15. "Miss *Boone* keeps a Monkey; She is a strange Woman, fat, sensual, & gross: tho' accomplished enough as to painting, Working, making Wax Models &c: and is surprizingly handsome too, her immense Magnitude considered—the Men however as I am told now—call her *Baboon*" (*Thraliana*, 1:473). She was the daughter of Daniel and Anne Evelyn Boone and died in 1787 leaving a £10 annuity to her monkey (June 7, 1789, BL, Althorp Papers F63).

16. Sarah Scott, *A Description of Millenium Hall*, ed. Walter M. Crittenden (New York: Bookman Associates, 1955), p. 161. Subsequent references to this work will be by page number in the text.

17. PCC Prob 11/1254. Hester Greville died in 1795.

18. Carolyn Woodward, " 'Feminine Virtue, Ladylike Disguise, Women of Community': Sarah Fielding and the Female I Am at Mid-Century," *Transactions of the Samuel Johnson Society of the Northwest* 15 (1984): 62. The title was intended to read "Womanly Community."

19. In a paper read in Minneapolis in 1990, "Promoting 'This Little Book': Women Novelists and Their Male Mentors in Mid-Century Britain," Wood-

ward noted that following the publication of *The Cry*, Fielding's work became more focused on women's lives and women's agency. She notes the suggestion by J. Paul Hunter, who invokes evidence provided by Sheffield Rogers, that Jane Collier may not have coauthored *The Cry* ("Novels and History and Northrop Frye," *Eighteenth-Century Studies* 24 [Winter 1990–91]: 235 and n. 9); but Woodward inclines, as I do, to believe the women worked together on this important book. In any case, as she pointed out (in a conversation with me), Fielding and Collier were living together with Henry Fielding while it was being written and must have discussed it. What is most important is their construction of a community of women writers (and thinkers about social problems) and their ongoing influence on the Bath community.

20. Amelia Opie, *Adeline Mowbray; or, The Mother and Daughter* (London: Pandora, 1986), p. 248.

21. Thomas Whitehead, *Original Anecdotes of the Late Duke of Kingston and Miss Chudleigh* (London: S. Bladon, 1792), p. 93.

22. *Letters of Sarah Byng Osborn, 1721–1773*, ed. John McClelland (Stanford: Stanford University Press, 1930), p. 106. The will of Lady Ann Jekyll, PCC Prob 11/922, proved 1766, notes that Miss Ann Roberts, to whom she left £600 and her clothes, was her cousin.

23. Lady Louisa Stuart, *Memoire of Frances, Lady Douglas*, ed. Jill Rubenstein (Edinburgh: Scottish Academic Press, 1985), pp. 62–63.

THREE. Satires of Tyrants and Toadeaters: Fielding and Collier

1. Walpole, *Correspondence*, 17:487 and 20:39.

2. Sarah Fielding, *The Adventures of David Simple*, ed. Malcolm Kelsall (London: Oxford University Press, 1969), p. 113. Subsequent references to this work will be by page numbers in the text.

3. Delariviere Manley, *The Adventures of Rivella; or, the History of the Author of the Atalantis* (London, 1714), pp. 31–40; reprinted as *The Novels of Mary Delariviere Manley*, ed. Patricia Koster, 2 vols. (Gainesville, Fla.: Scholars' Facsimiles and Reprints, 1971), 2: 729–856. Subsequent references to this work (as *AR*) will appear by volume and page number in the text. Manley's mistress-companion relationship here is conceived with reference to the Restoration model of the game of love: a short period of favoritism followed by rejection and recourse to a new favorite. The eighteenth-century model was that of marriage: a short honeymoon after which the relationship continued with tyranny and abuse. In the first case the mistress is gratified through a series of "romances," in the second through the abuse of a reliable victim.

4. Delariviere Manley, "The Physician's Stratagem," in *The Power of Love: In Seven Novels* (London: John Barber and John Morphew, 1720), pp. 141–74.

5. Manley, "The Husband's Resentment. In Two Examples," ibid., pp. 229–

71. Though published as late as 1720, and though demonstrating Manley's consciousness that wifely adultery was not acceptable, Desideria attended various ladies for short periods according to the Restoration model of affairs rather than marriage and took a lover in the same spirit.

6. Walpole, *Correspondence*, 19:298.

7. Coventry, *History of Pompey the Little*, p. 43.

8. As in the case of the Fieldings and the Robinsons (Sarah Scott's family), only the boys were provided with professions as a means of livelihood. In all cases the daughters lived in greater penury than their brothers. Arthur Collier became an advocate in Doctors' Commons and was one of the counsels who advised Chudleigh to make her bigamous marriage (chapter 4); Charles Collier was thought to have reached the rank of colonel in the army (see Robert Benson, *Memoirs of the Life and Writings of the Rev. Arthur Collier* [London: Edward Lumley, 1837]). Parish records for Collier's parish, Steeple Langford in Wiltshire, show Arthur born October 13, christened October 27, 1707; Charles christened February 25, 1712; Jane christened January 16, 1715; and Margaret born at Salisbury August 7, 1717, and christened there September 2. For this information I am indebted to Miss Rundle of the Wiltshire County Record Office. See also Robin Jarvis, "Jane Collier," and Amelia Whitehead [Betty Rizzo], "Margaret Collier," in Janet Todd, ed., *A Dictionary of British and American Women Writers, 1660–1800* (Totowa, N.J.: Rowman & Allanheld, 1985).

9. *The Correspondence of Samuel Richardson*, ed. Anne Letitia Barbauld, 6 vols. (London: Richard Phillips, 1804), 4: 371–74 and 6: 79. Subsequent references to this work will be by volume and page number in the text. Lady Bradshaigh had written: "Great learning would make strange work with us. You know we are to submit and obey; and it is as much as ever we can do, often more, in our inferior state of knowledge" (ibid., 6:71). In other words, learning made submission more difficult for women.

10. Martin C. Battestin with Ruthe R. Battestin, *Henry Fielding: A Life* (London: Routledge, 1989), p. 392 and p. 665, n. 218, which notes that Harris's daughter Katherine heard that her father "had written great part of the Art of Tormenting."

11. Susan Forward and Joan Torres, *Men Who Hate Women and the Women Who Love Them* (Toronto: Bantam, 1986), p. 10. Forward and Torres identify as misogynists men who in the eighteenth century might have seemed normal or mildly authoritative patriarchs.

12. Collier's book was advertised as "This Day" in the *DA*, April 19, 1753. Williams's essay is attributed to him in the preface to the *World*, in A. Chalmers, ed., *British Essayists*, vol. 26 (London, 1802), p. xlviii.

13. Sarah Scott, *The History of Sir George Ellison*, 2 vols. (London: A. Millar, 1766), 1:302. Subsequent reference to this work will be by volume and page number in the text.

14. *A Trip to Calais; A Comedy in Three Acts. As Originally Written, and In-*

*tended for Presentation, by the Late Samuel Foote, Esq. To Which is Annexed,
The Capuchin; As it is Performed at the Theatre-Royal in the Haymarket. Altered
from the Trip to Calais by the Late Samuel Foote, Esq. and Now Published by
Mr. Colman.* (London: T. Cadell, 1778), pp. 89–90.

15. In 1775 the Duchess of Kingston stopped the production of "A Trip to
Calais." For details see Mary Megie Belden, *The Dramatic Work of Samuel
Foote* (New Haven: Yale University Press, 1929), pp. 36–49; Simon Trefman,
Sam. Foote, Comedian (New York: New York University Press, 1971), pp. 233–57.

16. Trefman, *Sam. Foote*, pp. 260–61, points out that the original preface to
the play noted that Dashwou'd did "Foote full justice for broadfaced mirth, bit-
ing satire, and basic goodness of disposition."

17. John Pike Emery, *Arthur Murphy* (Philadelphia: University of Pennsylvania Press, 1946), pp. 125–39, and Howard H. Dunbar, *The Dramatic Career of
Arthur Murphy* (New York: Modern Language Association, 1946), pp. 268–90,
discuss Murphy's play, noting its indebtedness to *L'Irrésolu*. Emery points out
that Miss Neville is a new character. Dunbar (pp. 276–77) quotes James Boaden
in his *Memoirs of Mrs. Siddons* as having pointed out the connections between
the termagant-toadeater pairs in Foote's farce and Murphy's comedy, including
Foote's mention of the place "Bromley." He thought Mrs. Bromley strikingly
like Lady Kitty Crocodile in her pretended grief for her dead husband and her
treatment of her companion, but, assuming that Murphy could not have seen
Foote's farce in manuscript, suggested Foote had talked about it in Murphy's
presence. Foote's manuscripts, however, were in the possession of Colman at
Covent Garden before Murphy's play was produced there, and it seems feasible
that Murphy read his close friend Foote's original farce and used the two excised characters with Colman's assent and Foote's blessing. Murphy's adaptation of Lady Kitty would have been Foote's opportunity to have the last word
with the duchess. On Murphy's play see also Robert Donald Spector, *Arthur
Murphy* (Boston: Twayne, 1979), pp. 120–29.

18. Dashwou'd characterizes Mrs. Bromley's pity for Miss Neville as "no more
than the cruel art of tormenting an unhappy dependent upon her generosity";
Lady Bell says of Millamour, "If I could once catch him paying his adoration to
me, my aunt Bromley does not raise and sink Miss Neville's spirits, with such
exquisite skill in the art of tormenting, as I should his" (Arthur Murphy, *Know
Your Own Mind*, in *The Works of Arthur Murphy, Esq.*, 7 vols. [London: T. Cadell,
1786], rpt. as *The Plays of Arthur Murphy*, ed. Richard B. Schwartz, 7 vols. [New
York: Garland Publishing, Inc., 1979], 4:7–182). Subsequent references to this
work will be by page number in the text.

FOUR. Elizabeth Chudleigh and Her Maids of Honor

1. In Chudleigh's generation the Restoration tradition of demirep aristocratic
women still survived among a substantial group that included herself and her

friends Lady Caroline Petersham (later Lady Harrington) and Elizabeth Ashe and such women as Lady Townshend and Lady Rochford. The other "maids" at Prince Frederick's court also gave frequent scandal.

2. Delariviere Manley, *The New Atalantis*, 1:43, in *The Novels of Delariviere Manley*, ed. Koster, 2:770–71. Subsequent references to this work, as *NA*, will be by volume and page number in the text.

3. Henrietta Louise Von Waldner, Baronne d'Oberkirch, *Memoirs of the Baroness d'Oberkirch, Written by Herself*, ed. Count de Montbrison, 3 vols. (London: Colbourn & Co., 1851), 1:225–26. In her last years in Paris Chudleigh wrote a short autobiography (pp. 219–42 in d'Oberkirch) for the baroness, who with her permission kept a copy and later published it. The baroness states plainly that the memoir was already written out and read to her and that she obtained a copy for herself. The memoir she published, however, is in French, like her own journal (translated in the edition noted above). Very probably Chudleigh wrote it in French, which means the version included in Oberkirch's original memoirs is authentic. Chudleigh's holograph apparently does not survive, and it would appear that the baroness's English translator also put Chudleigh's memoir into English, which means it is not her own English. But there seems no real justification for Mavor's asseveration that Chudleigh told her tale and the baroness wrote it down, filling in with details from contemporary accounts (see note 5). This memoir by Chudleigh was written to justify the life of its author "about whom public report has invented a thousand stories" (p. 218). It begins, "The Duchess of Kingston, whose name has for many years resounded through all Europe, has been the victim of calumny and mistaken judgment, without having even felt a desire to justify herself in public opinion: but she now wishes, for the sake of those who love her, to give a short and faithful account of the truth." The account contains inaccuracies. Quotations from this work (*Memoirs*) will henceforward be identified by page number in the text.

4. Edwards is said to have married Lord Anne Hamilton in the Fleet ca. 1731 and then, when he began to waste her fortune, to have paid to have the record of marriage destroyed. Her independence of behavior did not end there: wrote Richard Pococke in 1736, "Ld Anne is turned off, and Mrs. E——ds keeps now a parson. I saw her in her fine coach and six in London, and her little boy, her only child, in it" (*The Travels Through England of Dr. Richard Pococke*, ed. James Joel Cartwright, 2 vols. [London: Camden Society, 1888], 1:vii). The immensely wealthy Mary Edwards, however, though she managed to outwit the husband who would have liked to annex her fortune, was not so foolish as to marry again. Chudleigh, in marrying a second time, committed bigamy, and, in becoming the Duke of Kingston's heir, disinherited his nephews.

5. Chudleigh's twentieth-century biographers have been kinder than her eighteenth- and nineteenth-century ones. Albert Louis Cotton, in "Elizabeth Chudleigh," *GM*, January 1903, delivered one of the last negative verdicts: she "had the temper of a fiend and the manners of a fishwife. She had neither wit nor sense, nor was she ever guilty of an unselfish action" (p. 20). E. Beresford

Chancellor in 1925 placed her in the tradition of English eccentric individual-ists, finding scarcely any other of her century "who set herself so consistently to follow her own desire, or to slight the prejudices and susceptibilities of the world in such a marked degree" ("Elizabeth Chudleigh, Duchess of Kingston," *English Review*, December 1925, pp. 812–21). More recent biographers, perhaps oppressed by models of Victorian womanhood, have fallen under Chudleigh's spell to a considerable extent, appreciating the free spirit while ignoring the vicious aspect of her behavior. These include Charles E. Pearce, *The Amazing Duchess*, 2 vols. (London: Stanley Paul, 1911); Beatrice Curtis Brown, *Elizabeth Chudleigh, Duchess of Kingston* (London: Gerald Howe, 1927); and Elizabeth Mavor, *The Virgin Mistress* (London: Chatto & Windus, 1964).

6. I do not find Elizabeth Chudleigh's baptism on the IGI, but her parents married June 23, 1718, at Chelsea Pensioners Army Hospital. Her brother, who died an army officer in 1741, was born in 1719 (before July 18), and she could have been born no earlier than 1720, the date she herself names in her auto-biography. She was always truthful about her age.

7. *An Authentic Detail of Particulars Relative to the Late Duchess of Kingston* (London: G. Kearsley, 1788), p. 133. This, the earliest life of Chudleigh written after her death, was pirated in the Dublin life (see note 12), which took its title and nothing else from the second London life (see note 15).

8. *The Wentworth Papers, 1705–1739*, ed. James J. Cartwright (London: Wyman and Sons, 1883), p. 420; *A List of the Colonels* . . . (London: Cox, Bat-hurst, and Pemberton, 1740), p. 42, which records Thomas Chudleigh's en-trance in the regiment as an ensign on July 18, 1719.

9. Walpole, *Correspondence*, 24:198.

10. *British Magazine and Review; or Universal Miscellany* 1 (August 1782): 91.

11. Chudleigh had a quick mind. Of herself, she wrote, "She did not get much instruction in her youth, or rather she did not take that which was offered her, for although masters of all kinds were employed for her education, the vivacity of her disposition prevented her from being an attentive pupil; she was not the less all her lifetime considered a person of intelligence and education." The baroness wrote of her, "She is really a most extraordinary woman, who, having lived all her life in the society of learned and celebrated people, has gleaned from all some portion of their knowledge, with which she afterwards adorns her conversation so skilfully, that, at least for a time, she would deceive one as to the extent of what she knew" (*Memoirs*, 1:220–21, 244).

12. *The Life and Memoirs of Elizabeth Chudleigh, Afterwards Mrs Hervey and Countess of Bristol, Commonly Called Duchess of Kingtson* [*sic*] (Dublin: H. Chamberlaine et al., 1789), p. 177.

13. Henry Wilson, "The Duchess of Kingston," in *Wonderful Characters* (New York: Henry Bill, 1848), p. 114. Wilson is, of course, at a distance of a hundred years, elaborating from earlier, also questionable, sources.

14. *Memoirs*, 1:225–26.

15. *The Life and Memoirs of Elizabeth Chudleigh, Afterwards Mrs. Hervey and*

Countess of Bristol, Commonly Called Duchess of Kingston. Written from Authentic Information and Original Documents (London: R. Randall, [1788]), p. 33; Wilson, "Duchess of Kingston," p. 127; "Elizabeth Chudleigh," *DNB*, 4:301. Count Igor Gregor'ivich Chernyshev (as the name is spelled in Walpole, *Correspondence*) had been Russian ambassador to England in 1768–69. In Chudleigh's will she insists at some length that the pictures were only lent and demands their return (PCC Prob 11/1186).

16. *Life and Memoirs* (Dublin, 1789), pp. 176–77.

17. Walpole, *Correspondence*, 20:57.

18. Ibid., p. 49.

19. Published inaccurately in *The Letters of Mrs. Elizabeth Montagu*, ed. Matthew Montagu, 4 vols. (London: T. Cadell and W. Davies, 1809–13), 3:158; reproduced here from the original letter in the Houghton Library, Harvard University, Cambridge, Mass., with permission.

20. *A New Atalantis for the Year One Thousand Seven Hundred and Fifty-eight*, 2d ed. (London: M. Thrush, 1758), p. 126. Subsequent references will be by page number in the text.

21. Walpole, *Correspondence*, 20:57.

22. Ibid., p. 213. Having witnessed this scene, Henry Fox commented to Charles Hanbury Williams, "I am allways glad when the K. do's what He likes to do, and whatever He has a mind to do I hope He will do" (Lewis Walpole Library, CHW 52-10902, pp. 89–90).

23. *British Magazine and Review*, August 1782, p. 88. As an example of Chudleigh's indulgence in intrigue, the *Monthly Magazine*, July 1, 1821, p. 532, charges that she assisted George III, while Prince of Wales, in his amour with Hannah Lightfoot, the Fair Quaker, arranging her marriage to Isaac Axford and then abducting her so that Axford never saw her again.

24. Richardson, *Correspondence*, 3:314.

25. *Thraliana*, 1:32. Walpole noted the print in February 1761: Chudleigh curtsies to the remonstrating princess and replies, "Madame, chacun a son But" (*Correspondence*, 9:338).

26. *Les aventures trop amoureuses ou Elisabeth Chudleigh Ex-Duchesse Douairiere de Kingston, aujourd'hui Comtesse de Bristol et la Marquise de la Touche sur la scene du monde* (London, 1776), pp. 36–37. This long biography deals somewhat inaccurately with the high points of Chudleigh's life but is more concerned with the life of Kingston's mistress, Madam de la Touche, who left her husband to come to England with Kingston and then was sent home again when he fell in love with Chudleigh. Subsequent references to this book will be by page number in the text.

27. *British Magazine*, August 1782, p. 88, and Whitehead, *Original Anecdotes*, Letter V. Subsequent references to this work will be by letter number in the text. Whitehead's work, written in seventeen letters, is summarized and quoted in Pearce, *Amazing Duchess*. Whitehead notes that Elizabeth was reported to have been the child of one of Chudleigh's brothers dead abroad (impossible be-

cause her only brother died in 1741) but was considered the child of the duke and Chudleigh.

28. *Letters from Lady Jane Coke to Her Friend Mrs. Eyre at Derby, edited with notes,* by Mrs. Ambrose Rathborne (London: Swan Sonnenschein, 1899), pp. 105, 110–11, 130.

29. Walpole, *Correspondence,* 38:473; see also *The Letters and Journals of Lady Mary Coke,* 4 vols. (Edinburgh: D. Douglas, 1889–96), 1:18. All had never been smooth sailing. In 1758–59 Sir Charles Hanbury Williams's daughter, Lady Essex, had reported to him a false rumor "that the Duke of Kingston has settled 3000£ a year on Miss Chudleigh & & [*sic*] is going down to Scotland to marry the Dss of Hamilton" (Lewis Walpole Library, CHW 10846, pp. 277–80).

30. *The Letters of Philip Dormer Stanhope, 4th Earl of Chesterfield,* ed. Bonamy Dobree, 6 vols. (London: Eyre and Spottiswoode, 1932), 6:298. Chesterfield noted that "she no more wanted the waters of Carlsbadt than you did"; that there was a trick in the journey somewhere (p. 299).

31. Ibid., p. 300; on October 25, 1765, he noted her recent return to London. Perhaps Chudleigh's secret was that Kingston knew he would have to pay up on his bond if he married anyone else.

32. Whitehead, *Original Anecdotes,* Letter III. Whitehead, formerly the duke's valet, was always inimical to Chudleigh but for the facts that can be checked, proves reliable. The *Monthly Review* (April 1792, pp. 471–72) found his book "a genuine, though a coarse, disclosure of private family anecdotes." He spells the name of her violoncellist "Siprihni," indicating Siprutini, a violoncellist who played in London concerts in 1761–62 and 1764–65, the last of these at the Haymarket on March 11, after which his name disappears from the record (see G. W. Stone, Jr., ed., *The London Stage, 1660–1800,* Part 4, 1747–76, 3 vols. [Carbondale: Southern Illinois University Press, 1962], 2:884, 1102).

33. Jacques Casanova de Seingalt, *The Memoirs of Casanova,* trans. Arthur Machen, 6 vols. (New York: G. P. Putnam's Sons, and London: Elek Books, n.d.), 6:353–60. Casanova also notes, ca. 1764, just missing Chudleigh and the duke at Hanover on their way to Berlin (5:444).

34. For this affair, see Mavor, *Virgin Mistress,* pp. 87–94. Hervey had fallen in love, wished to marry, and therefore collected evidence to sue Chudleigh for divorce on grounds of adultery. Chudleigh, who also wanted to be free to marry Kingston, had no desire to "prove herself a whore" and instead suggested procuring a jactitation of marriage, a nullity decree on grounds that there was no legal proof of marriage. In all likelihood Hervey accepted a large sum—reportedly £14,000—from Kingston to pursue that course, which in the event proved disastrous only because Kingston's heirs-at-law, the Medowses, set out to prove her bigamous. *The Case of the Duchess of Kingston* (London: J. Wheble, 1775), pp. 7–8, gives the verdict in the jactitation suit, which declared the marriage not proven and Chudleigh "a spinster and free from all Matrimonial Contracts (as far as to us yet appears)" and, declaring that Hervey had wickedly and mali-

ciously boasted of his marriage, enjoined silence upon him and fined him £100. The sentence, signed by four doctors of common law, including Arthur Collier, was read at Doctors Commons February 10, 1769. For a full transcription of the trial see *The Trial of Elizabeth Duchess Dowager of Kingston for Bigamy, Before the Right Honourable the House of Peers, in Westminster-Hall, in Full Parliament* (London: Charles Bathurst, 1776).

35. Delany, *Autobiography*, 4:554n. Delany was apparently well informed; since £4,000 was the annual sum left Chudleigh in Kingston's will, it was probably also her allowance during marriage. The inadequacy of the sum to her needs would explain Chudleigh's frequent extortions of large additional sums from the duke.

36. The duke's will (PCC Prob 11/991) left her the same allowance she had always enjoyed, an annual £4,000, which she was to lose should she remarry (the duke was certain she would otherwise soon have fallen prey to a fortune hunter), but also left her all his personal estate absolutely and his real estate (vested in the hands of trustees) for life. The terms of the will do not forthrightly indicate that Chudleigh was to be restricted to her £4,000 allowance, but had she been she could quietly have sold off his valuable personal possessions—his paintings, plate, jewels, china, arrears of rent, and all other effects and personal estate. After his death she pillaged both Thoresby and Kingston House but did it legally.

37. The writ of *ne exeat regno* had been obtained by Kingston's relations, the Medowses, who intended, now that it was established she had not been married to the duke, to contest her retention of her inheritance, and in particular the holding of his real estate in trust to provide her income until her death, after which the second Medows son, Charles, was to inherit. In 1778 they tested the cause by bringing suit to eject the tenant of the Tuns, an inn at Bath, part of the duke's estate (*Bath Chronicle*, June 4, 1778). Eventually they lost their cause. Meanwhile, with Chudleigh to Calais allegedly went the Reverend William Jackson, her secretary and coadjutor, particularly in her struggle with Foote, throughout her English stay (and subsequently, probably, Sophia Baddeley's biographer; see chapter 9). For him see Lucyle Werkmeister, "Notes for a Revised Life of William Jackson," *Notes & Queries* 206 (1960): 62–82; 207 (1961): 16–54, 126–62.

38. Chesterfield, *Letters*, 6:309.

39. The will, with a few minor inaccuracies, was published in *An Authentic Detail*, pp. 128–78. Mavor, *Virgin Mistress*, pp. 193–98, notes that her will, made in France, did not fully comply with French law; that there were strange blanks where the names of principal legatees had not been filled in; and that very few of her testamentary wishes were, in the end, honored. The Russian slaves, for instance, were not freed, nor did they receive the legacies left them.

40. Manley describes an active lesbian court circle in *NA*, 1:575–90, so Chudleigh would have had a model for such activity.

41. E. J. Burford, in *Wits, Wenchers and Wantons* (London: Robert Hale,

1986), pp. 165–66, notes that eighteenth-century lesbian bordellos existed at Mother Courage's in Suffolk Street and Frances Bradshaw's in Bow Street and that Harrington and Ashe were patrons, but he gives no sources. Chudleigh always remained an intimate of the rakish and dissolute Lady Harrington; Casanova first met Chudleigh at Harrington's, and both Harrington and Chudleigh were particular patrons of Madame Cornelys, a former mistress of Casanova's, whose mansion in Soho Square provided rooms for fashionable masquerades and also, apparently, for assignations.

42. Chudleigh appears to have kept no elderly maids. She may have rid herself of superannuated maidens and evaded her responsibility to them, as Foote suggests Kitty Crocodile did, by inciting them through ill treatment to open rebellion and resignation of their positions.

43. Quoted in C. E. Vulliamy, *Aspasia, The Life and Letters of Mary Granville, Mrs. Delany* (London: Geoffrey Bles, 1935), pp. 195–96. Delany noted that six women helped Chudleigh attend the duke's deathbed in state (*Autobiography*, 4:563). By amending the word *ladies* to *misses*, Delany is stressing the youthfulness and the garb of Chudleigh's attendants, not impugning their morals.

44. She sometimes fired these pistols. In 1776 Walpole (*Correspondence*, 24:198) mentions a hole from the ball of a pistol in the ceiling or wainscot at Kingston House produced during one of Chudleigh's habitual threats to murder either the duke or herself.

45. For Montresor see *DNB*, 13:774–75. For Harriet Fielding see Wilbur L. Cross, *The History of Henry Fielding*, 3 vols. (New Haven: Yale University Press, 1918), 3:117–20; Austin Dobson, *Henry Fielding: A Memoir* (New York: Dodd, Mead, 1900), pp. 291–92; F. Homes Dudden, *Henry Fielding: His Life, Works, and Times*, 2 vols. (Hamden, Conn.: Archon, 1966), 1:234.

46. *Life and Memoirs* (London, [1788]), pp. 32–33.

47. *British Magazine*, August 1782, p. 88. Whitehead is the only authority for Elizabeth's last name but is proved correct by the Perlethorpe parish register.

48. I am particularly indebted to Miss N. Corcoran of the Worksop Public Library, Notts, for information about Elizabeth Skinner's burial and about Thoresby.

49. Whitehead (Letter III) notes that Chudleigh tried to convince her attorney Mr. Field to add a codicil to the will that would have canceled "the major part of the will" wherein Bate was a legatee. It must have been the duke's codicils, which left legacies to Bate and Whitehead, that Chudleigh would have wanted canceled. They were not canceled (PCC Prob 11/991). Wilson, "Duchess of Kingston," p. 119, further states that Chudleigh sent for Field when the duke was on his deathbed and attempted to persuade him to present the duke with a new will for his signature, one that would not disinherit her should she remarry, but Field refused. It is equally likely she wanted no deductions, however inconsequential, from her income.

50. Mary Penrose was the granddaughter of one of Chudleigh's first cousins.

For this family see *The Penroses of Fledborough Parish*, ed. A. B. Baldwin (Hull: A. Brown & Sons, 1933); *Letters from Bath, 1766–1767 by the Rev. John Penrose*, ed. Brigitte Mitchell and Hubert Penrose (Gloucester: Alan Sutton, 1983); and *DNB*. Mary Penrose's niece Mary married the Reverend Thomas Arnold and was the mother of Matthew Arnold. Christine North, county archivist for Cornwall, and Adrian Henstock, principal archivist for Notts, provided helpful information about the Penrose family.

51. Trefman, *Sam. Foote*, pp. 223, 231. The season at the Haymarket opened May 15, 1775. The *Town and Country Magazine* for May (pp. 258–59) announced *The Siege of Calais* [*sic*]: "the groundwork of the piece is said to be the denouement of a certain *Double Marriage*, that has lately made so much noise in the polite world, and among the lawyers" (Trefman, *Sam. Foote*, p. 233).

52. *An Authentic Detail*, p. 41, and *Life and Memoirs* (London, [1788]), p. 15. Belden, *Dramatic Work of Samuel Foote*, p. 39, also notes the possibility that Penrose was the informer.

53. In her will, Chudleigh left blanks in the place of the names of many of her principal legatees; apparently wishing to await her final whims as to disposition of her properties and effects, she was overtaken by death before she could attend to this essential matter. She left the names of the first legatees of her paternal estate blank; John Penrose considered going to law for the estate because his was the first actual name mentioned.

54. Mavor, *Virgin Mistress*, p. 195.

55. John Nichols, *Illustrations of the Literary History of the Eighteenth Century*, 8 vols. (London: For the author, by Nichols, son, and Bentley, 1817–58), 1:137 where Daniel Wray, writing in October 1768, referred to an untoward indelicacy perpetrated by a gentleman while Macaulay was present and adds, "I trust the *Maid of Honour* will command more deference and respect."

56. Wilson, "Duchess of Kingston," p. 121.

57. *Memoirs of the Baroness d'Oberkirch*, p. 224.

58. Pearce, *Amazing Duchess*, 2:110–11.

59. Walpole, *Correspondence*, 35:299–301.

60. *St. James's Chronicle*, May 21, 1763.

61. *Letters and Journals of Lady Mary Coke*, 2:200, 261.

62. Lord Chesterfield was not the only one to have known of her pregnancies. Elizabeth Montagu wrote to Elizabeth Carter in December 1768 of Tom Hervey's wife, "She has not had so many children as Virgin C[hudleig]h but I believe has had 3 or four" (*Mrs. Montagu*, ed. Blunt, 1:181). Rumors that she had twins by Augustus Hervey apparently never died; Mavor publishes an illustration of a portrait of a "Miss Hervey," "the reputed 'other twin' of Elizabeth and Augustus Hervey."

FIVE. Frances Burney and the Anatomy of Companionship

1. Osborn File, 47.5, Beinecke Library, Yale University, New Haven, Conn.

2. In a letter to Frances Burney on January 1, 1775, Maria Allen Rishton wrote that her unpleasant brother Stephen had told her "he was sure D." Burney woud never like any of his daughters to be brought up Notably [that is, as accomplished housekeepers]" and he dares say Charlotte, whom Elizabeth Burney was attempting to train early as her right hand, "would soon follow her Sisters" (Berg Collection, New York Public Library). Stephen Allen was echoing his mother's displeasure that Charles Burney kept Frances Burney "so close to writing"—no doubt working on his *General History of Music*—and away from her own exactions, and he was scorning the familial pretension that excused the daughters from household labors.

3. Frances Burney, *Memoirs of Doctor Burney, Arranged from His Own Manuscripts, from Family Papers, and from Personal Recollections, by his Daughter, Madame d'Arblay*, 3 vols. (London: Edward Moxon, 1832), 1:201. Although Burney enjoyed her stepmother's discomfiture, she had probably collaborated in it by sharing an enthusiasm for Sterne's book. In May 1769 she noted that she was about to *charm* herself with it for the third time (*The Early Journals and Letters of Fanny Burney*, ed. Lars E. Troide [Oxford: Clarendon Press, 1988–90], p. 65).

4. *Thraliana*, 1:372.

5. Letter beginning "Thanks for your charming Letter," BL, Barrett Collection.

6. *Thraliana*, 2:562–63.

7. Letter of December 14, 1781, Berg Collection. On August 27, 1782, Burney fiercely indicted "The Lady of the Manor," her "eternal jealousy of our affection and comfort from each other," her invalidism as the only way for her to exact attendance and distinction. "How odious she does make herself, & how universally is she detested" (Unnumbered folio, ibid.).

8. Burney, *Early Journals and Letters*, 2:xiv–xv, 115–29, 135–49, 151–54, 157–58, 163–64.

9. Letter of May 8, 1775, ibid., p. 123.

10. Joyce Hemlow, *The History of Fanny Burney* (Oxford: Clarendon Press, 1958), p. 148. Crisp's reading of the ease with which Burney produced is a gloss on her unobtrusive habits when she was writing. At this time, Burney was making herself ill by trying to finish the book, according to her father's wishes, for publication in early 1781.

11. Hester Thrale, from "Journal of Her Tour in Wales," in *Doctor Johnson and Mrs. Thrale*, ed. A. M. Broadley (London: John Lane, 1910), pp. 171–72, quoted in McCarthy, *Hester Thrale Piozzi*, p. 28. The passage, an incisive illustration of the gendered division of interests of the period, constitutes an important comment on Stone's theory of companionate marriage, for this appears like

a thoroughly "companionate" tour, yet each marriage partner desires a companion of the same sex.

12. A letter draft from Charles Burney to Frances Crewe of October 1807 in Osborn File, 46.75, Beinecke Library, Yale University. He adds, "There must have been something very inoffensive at least, in my conduct & manners among my betters abroad & at home, to be so countenanced."

13. Burney, *Diary and Letters*, ed. Dobson, 1:314. A footnote reads, "Costume was always a trouble to Miss Burney. Mr. R. O. Cambridge of Twickenham affirmed that 'Miss B. had no time to write, for she was always working at her clothes' " (p. 308). Subsequent references to the Dobson edition in this chapter will be by volume and page number in the text.

14. Thrale refers to the tyrannical Mrs. Bromley and her luckless companion Miss Neville in Arthur Murphy's *Know Your Own Mind* (see chapter 3).

15. Undated letters in the Osborn File, 51.27, Beinecke Library, Yale University.

16. Letter of Burney to her father, June 20, 1780, Berg Collection, New York Public Library. Henry Thrale, like Henry Fox (chapter 7) and Agmondesham Vesey (chapter 10), also welcomed the companion as a person who, when present, relieved him of his wife's implicit reproaches and demands for genuine companionship. Burney had therefore to combat the advances of both Thrales.

17. *Thraliana*, 1:443. Lady Louisa was a supercilious snob in *Evelina*.

18. Burney, *Diary and Letters*, ed. Dobson, 2:492, but text amended from MS. in the Berg Collection, New York Public Library.

19. Though Thrale was always publicly appreciative of *Evelina*, privately she considered marriage, rather than a resource to her talent, to be the only sensible establishment for Burney and also considered her not to be a writer of the first class. Before she knew her she judged *Evelina* "flimzy" compared (in order of their merit) to Rousseau, Charlotte Lennox, Smollett, and Fielding. *Cecilia* she later called "the Picture of Life such as the Author sees it: while therefore this Mode of Life lasts, her Book will be of value, as the Representation is astonishingly perfect: but as nothing in the Book is derived from Study, so it can have no Principle of Duration—Burney's Cecilia is to Richardson's Clarissa—what a Camera Obscura in the Window of a London parlour,—is to a view of Venice by the clear Pencil of Cannaletti" (*Thraliana*, 1:329, 536). She missed all that Burney put into both *Evelina* and *Cecilia* by "study"; she never suggested there would be any loss should Burney cease to write; and she did all she could to find her a husband.

20. Kristina Straub, *Divided Fictions: Fanny Burney and Feminine Strategy* (Lexington: University Press of Kentucky, 1987), p. 107. Rose Marie Cutting, in "Defiant Women: The Growth of Feminism in Fanny Burney's Novels," *SEL* 17 (1977): 519–30, first argues for more emphasis on Burney's toughness and less on her decorum; Julia Epstein, in *The Iron Pen: Frances Burney and the Politics*

of Women's Writing (Madison: University of Wisconsin Press, 1989), takes the same view.

21. Letter of Burney to Thrale, August 17, 1781, Berg Collection, New York Public Library. Surely Burney was, for whatever reason, denying the obvious, her stepmother's great jealousy of her social success, including her having all but originated the role in fashionable society of a respectable and entirely acceptable professional woman.

22. Letter in Osborn File, 47.5, Beinecke Library, Yale University.

23. *Evelina*, p. 276.

24. *Cecilia*, p. 11. Subsequent references to this work will be by page number in the text.

25. In drawing a parallel between Miss Bennet, who steals Cecilia's marriage vow, and Elizabeth Burney, I evoke the question of incest, so immanent among the Burneys. Certainly the doctor's relationship with Frances for some time precluded her finding other men attractive. When James eloped with his half-sister Sarah, they may have been "acting out" an already familiar family drama. For the general incestuousness of families, see Michel Foucault, *The History of Sexuality*, Vol. 1 (New York: Pantheon Books, 1978), pp. 108–9, where he notes that from the eighteenth century, when the family became "an obligatory locus of affects, feelings, love," sexuality had its privileged point of development there and that for this reason sexuality is "incestuous" from the start; incest therefore occupies a central place in the family, where "it is constantly being solicited and refused; it is an object of obsession and attraction, a dreadful secret and an indispensable pivot." It is "a thing that is continuously demanded in order for the family to be a hotbed of constant sexual excitement."

26. Burney, *Diary and Letters*, ed. Dobson, 2:304. References again will be made by volume and page numbers in the text. It appears that Burney knew her father would prefer her scribbling about lucrative employment to her scribbling novels. Delany too apparently shared the preference.

27. Burney, *Memoirs*, 3:71, 77–78. See also my " 'The High Road to Eminence': A New Letter from Charles Burney in Norfolk," *Notes & Queries* 231 (March 1986): 61–63, and *The Letters of Dr. Charles Burney*, Vol. 1, 1751–84, ed. Alvaro Ribeiro, S.J. (Oxford: Clarendon Press, 1991), pp. 20–22. Burney's efforts were ongoing and persistent: in the summer of 1783 Thrale for the first time met Shelburne, the prime minister, come to inspect her own garden, seized the occasion to ask him for the post of master to the queen's music for Dr. Burney, and reported, too sanguinely, that she thought he would get it (letter to Burney, Berg Collection, New York Public Library).

28. Mrs. Mayer's companion (chapter 2) vacillates between a costly resistance and an equally costly cowardice; but Burney's failure to resist, though it may have resulted in the same passivity, she herself saw not as cowardice but as "endurance"—an important distinction. The cost to her was in failure not of character but of health.

29. Letter of Burney to her father, December 27, 1790, Berg Collection, New York Public Library.

30. Hemlow, *History of Fanny Burney*, p. 36, n. 7; Margaret Ann Doody, *Frances Burney: The Life in the Works* (New Brunswick: Rutgers University Press, 1988), p. 177.

31. Doody, *Frances Burney*, p. 177.

32. Hemlow, *History of Fanny Burney*, p. 341, n. 2.

33. Burney, *Diary and Letters*, ed. Dobson, 2:382.

34. Hemlow, *History of Fanny Burney*, pp. 214–15. For the affair of Charles Burney, Jr., at Cambridge in 1777, see Ralph S. Walker, "Charles Burney's Theft of Books at Cambridge," *Transactions of the Cambridge Bibliograhical Society* 3 (1962): 313–26.

35. It has become a commonplace observation; see, for instance, Patricia Meyer Spacks, in *Imagining a Self: Autobiography and the Novel in Eighteenth-Century England* (Cambridge, Mass.: Harvard University Press, 1976), e.g., Burney's "novels and journals alike reveal the dynamics of fear in a woman's experience," p. 192; D. D. Devlin, *The Novels and Journals of Fanny Burney* (New York: St. Martin's Press, 1987); Doody, *Frances Burney*, pp. 33–34: "Her courage emerges more in her works than in her life."

36. In "Hubert de Vere" Geralda has ruined her life and driven her lover to madness by marrying Glanville as the price he exacts for sparing the life of her uncle-guardian; in "The Siege of Pevensey" Adela refuses to extricate herself from the most excruciating dangers by marrying her lover without her father's permission, and later, to save her father, she is willing either to marry her persecutor or to immolate herself in a convent. Doody provides a full and excellent analysis of these tragedies, *Frances Burney*, pp. 150–98.

37. Frances Burney, *Camilla; or, A Picture of Youth* (Oxford: Oxford University Press, 1983), p. 45. Subsequent references to this work will be by page number in the text.

38. See Frances Burney, *The Wanderer; or, Female Difficulties* (London: Pandora, 1988). Subsequent references to this work will be by page number in the text. Despite this portrait of the perfect tyrant and the perfectly enduring (but not hypocritically submissive) companion, the Burneys were most conscious of the malice of toadies; Doody calls attention to a manuscript play in the Berg Collection, "The Triumphant Toadeater," in which the toadeater manipulates herself into place as her mistress's heir (*Frances Burney*, pp. 292, 418–19). The play is apparently in the hand of Ralph Broome, the second husband (in 1798) of Charlotte Burney, and is written on a high-grade paper with a distinctive watermark identical to paper he used for other writing in 1798.

39. "At least, thought Juliet [of Mrs. Ireton], I need not give you any lessons in the art of ingeniously tormenting! There you are perfect!" (p. 463). There are other references to Collier.

40. Doody, *Frances Burney*, p. 73.

41. Charles Burney's 1781 letters to and from Lord Findlater in the Osborn File, 47.77/50.129, Beinecke Library, Yale University, suggest the extraordinary extent to which Charles could request and receive—and desperately require—large sums (fifty guineas, for instance) simply on the basis of a short but (suspiciously) warm acquaintance.

42. See Epstein, *Iron Pen*, pp. 53–83.

SIX. Parent and Child: Montagu and Gregory

1. Letter of Dorothy Gregory to Elizabeth Montagu, January 7, 1783, in the Montagu Collection, Huntington Library, San Marino, Calif. Subsequent letters in this series—all letters from Gregory—will be cited by date if known and by the opening words of the letter.

2. *Elizabeth Montagu, The Queen of the Blue-Stockings*, ed. Emily J. Climenson, 2 vols. (London: John Murray, 1906), 1:179. Montagu mentions Gregory in 1744 and notes she had met him even earlier. Portraits by Francis Cotes of Dr. John Gregory (1724–73) and Elizabeth Forbes Gregory (1720–61) are in Fyvie Castle, Scotland.

3. According to a note by Frances Burney on an undated letter from Gregory, Berg Collection, New York Public Library.

4. *Mrs. Montagu*, ed. Blunt, 1:143.

5. An undated letter from Montagu to Dr. Gregory in the Lewis Walpole Library, Yale University, Farmington, Conn.

6. *Mrs. Montagu*, ed. Blunt, 2:363.

7. Unpublished portion of the journal of Frances Burney for April 3, 1780, Berg Collection, New York Public Library, to be published in *Early Journals and Letters*, vol. 4, forthcoming. Subsequent references will be by date in the text.

8. Burney, *Diary and Letters*, ed. Dobson, 1:334. Subsequent references will be by page numbers in the text.

9. Unpublished note from the scrapbooks of Frances Burney in the Berg Collection, New York Public Library. Burney detested complimentary references to *Evelina*, and Gregory probably alludes to a compliment to her "penetration into Characters."

10. Sir Archibald Alison, *Some Account of My Life and Writings*, 2 vols. (Edinburgh: W. Blackwood and Sons, 1883), 1:292.

11. This compliment, not infrequently paid to women of the period, meant that they demonstrated powers of reasoning.

12. Walpole, *Correspondence*, 43:356.

13. *Mrs. Montagu*, ed. Blunt, 2:136. Following references to this work will be by volume and page number in the text.

14. Pigott, *Female Jockey Club*, pp. 189–90. This radical author is so sensi-

tive to any infringement on male prerogatives that in a note he attacks tyranny: "The abuse of power is manifest in every condition of life from a *K——g* to a *Master Chimney-sweeper*, How cautious ought we therefore to be in granting Powers!" He also implies rightly that Montagu is a tyrant: all her decrees pass unanimously in the bluestocking society. But he remains oblivious to the tyrannies practiced routinely upon women. For a kindlier interpretation than Pigott's or my own of Elizabeth Montagu's benefactions see Edith Sedgwick Larson, "A Measure of Power: The Personal Charity of Elizabeth Montagu," *Studies in Eighteenth-Century Culture* 16 (1986): 197–210. Larson, however, still views Montagu's approach to charity as an exercise of power.

15. The IGI reveals that Elizabeth Robinson was christened on October 13, 1718, at Holy Trinity, Goodramgate, York, where from 1717 to 1724 Robert, Sarah, and William were also christened. Her birthday was October 2 so she was probably born on that day in 1718, although 1720 is consistently given as the year of her birth. It was the year of birth of her sister.

16. *Letters of Mrs. Elizabeth Montagu*, 2:317.

17. Letter from Elizabeth Vesey of August 3, 1781, Montagu Collection, Huntington Library ("my d^r friend what have I done"). Other letters from Vesey, cited by date and first words of text, are from the same collection.

18. As Larson notes, Montagu got nothing but her father's bond for £1,000 on her marriage (he later paid up) and Scott also got only £1,000 ("Measure of Power," pp. 201, 204). In Matthew Robinson's will he recites that his own marriage settlement provided the sum of two thousand pounds as "the portions of my younger Children" (PCC Prob 11/1046). The wording seems deliberately confusing: if all but his eldest son got two thousand pounds divided among them, £1,000 was too much; if each was to receive £2,000, £1,000 was too little. As only daughters receive "portions," perhaps "children" here means "daughters." The will claims that more than the sum settled on "such Children" had already been paid them.

19. Lavish new clothes were always worn at court on royal birthdays.

20. *Letters of Mrs. Elizabeth Montagu*, 1:126.

21. Ibid., p. 133.

22. Walpole, *Correspondence*, 9:255. They were probably working on Lyttelton's *Dialogues of the Dead* (1760), to which Montagu contributed three dialogues, possibly even on Lyttelton's history of Henry II (published 1767–71). To the postilion's suspicion must be opposed Lyttelton's asseveration on his deathbed that since his first marriage he had "never had any unchaste connection, with any woman." See Rose Mary Davis, *The Good Lord Lyttelton* (Bethlehem, Pa.: Times Publishing Co., 1939), p. 386.

23. Letters from Vesey to Montagu of August 31, [1783] ("the fatal news at last arrived"); [August 20, 1766], "what can you be employ'd about"; [June 1784], "my beloved Friend I sent you a large parcel." The letters of Vesey to Montagu,

from the Montagu Collection in the Huntington Library, will henceforward be identified in the text by date and opening words, as will the letters of Gregory to Montagu.

24. Hester Chapone, *The Works of Mrs. Chapone*, 4 vols. in 2. (New York: Evert Duyckinck, 1818), 1:135. Mrs. Chapone summed up Gregory's problem astutely in a letter of June 1784: "The situation she was in with Mrs. —— is, of all others, the least favourable to matrimony. Men of small pretensions would not look up to her, and men of great ones would look above her. In effect the experiment has been tried for ten years, and every year makes the chance considerably worse." It was natural, Chapone adds, for Gregory to have lowered her views, and she hopes Montagu's displeasure will not affect her intentions of benefiting her adopted daughter, "for had she been a real daughter, at her time of life, it can hardly be disputed that she had a right to choose for herself" (1:139).

25. Unpublished portion of the journal of Frances Burney for February 8, 1781, Berg Collection, New York Public Library.

26. Davis, *Good Lord Lyttelton*, pp. 261–62. In her own case, however, Montagu understood that while as a wife having no will of her own was a necessity, it was nevertheless a pose difficult to maintain.

27. *Mrs. Montagu*, ed. Blunt, 1:298.

28. Ibid., p. 161.

29. Ibid., p. 44.

30. Ibid., pp. 265–66. Such struggles, of course, were not new to the marriage. In 1754 Frances Boscawen, alone at Hatchlands, summoned Montagu to her, informing her "she might if she would"; Montagu responded that like an oracle Boscawen should read the sentence backward: "she would if she might" (Frances Boscawen, *Admiral's Wife*, ed. Cecil Aspinall-Oglander [London: Longmans, Green, 1940], p. 151).

31. *Mrs. Montagu*, ed. Blunt, 1:287. James Harris, an author and figure in society, had published *Hermes: or, A Philosophical Inquiry Concerning Language and Universal Grammar* (London: Nourse, Vaillant, et al., 1751).

32. *Mrs. Montagu*, ed. Blunt, 1:298.

33. *Lady Louisa Stuart: Selections from her Manuscripts*, ed. Hon. James Home (New York: Harper & Brothers, 1899), pp. 158–59.

34. See the literary portrait of Melissa in Fulke Greville, *Maxims, Characters, and Reflections, Critical, Satyrical, and Moral* (London: J. and R. Tonson, 1756), pp. 44–47.

35. Wraxall, *The Historical and the Posthumous Memoirs*, 1:102.

36. Scott, *Description of Millenium Hall*, p. 151.

37. Richard Cumberland, *The Observer*, 5 vols. (London: C. Dilly, 1786–90), 1:232–43, No. 25.

38. Ibid., 3:84–92, No. 70. The essay concludes, "*This lady should never be seen in a circle.*"

39. *The Life and Poetical Works of James Woodhouse*, ed. R. I. Woodhouse,

2 vols. (London: Leadenhall Press, 1896), 1:68. For an excellent full discussion of Woodhouse's portrait of Montagu, with many insights into her character and behavior, see Katherine G. Hornbeak, "New Light on Mrs. Montagu," in *The Age of Johnson: Essays Presented to Chauncey Brewster Tinker* (New Haven: Yale University Press, 1949), pp. 349–61.

40. For more on Montagu and Woodhouse, see my "The Patron as Poet Maker: The Politics of Benefaction," *Studies in Eighteenth-Century Culture* 20, ed. Leslie Ellen Brown and Patricia B. Craddock (East Lansing, Mich.: Colleagues Press, 1990), pp. 254–58.

41. *Elizabeth Montagu*, ed. Climenson, 1:280. It is not clear why Montagu assumed a sister two years her junior ought to obey her, but it seems probable she assumed that obligations conferred upon her sister, who was in unfortunate circumstances, obliged her complaisance.

42. *Mrs. Montagu*, ed. Blunt, 2:137.

43. *Thraliana*, 1:412.

44. *Mrs. Montagu*, ed. Blunt, 2:361.

45. Ibid., 1:129.

46. Historical Manuscripts Commission, *Calendar of the Manuscripts of the Marquis of Bath* (London: His Majesty's Stationery Office, 1904), 1:342. Catherine Chapone did take the position as governess to the children of the widower John Boyd and married him in 1766 (*Letters from Mrs. Elizabeth Carter, to Mrs. Montagu, Between the Years 1755 and 1800*, 3 vols. [London: F. C. & J. Rivington, 1817], 3:315); in 1775 he became a baronet. The Historical Manuscripts Commission's conjectured date of this letter of 1775 is ten years too late.

47. For this and subsequently cited information about Gregory and his Durham curacy I thank M. C. McCollum, assistant keeper of the Department of Palaeography and Diplomatic, the University of Durham. The *DNB* incorrectly states that Alison was incumbent of Brancepeth.

48. *Mrs. Montagu*, ed. Blunt, 2:136.

49. Ibid., p. 137.

50. Historical Manuscripts Commission, *Calendar of the Manuscripts of the Marquis of Bath*, 1:353–55.

51. William Nairn, ca 1731–1811, Scottish advocate and judge and fifth baronet of Dunsinnan; see *Boswell's Life of Johnson*, ed. G. B. Hill and L. F. Powell, 6 vols. (Oxford: Clarendon Press, 1950), 5:475–76.

52. William Pulteney (1729–1805), born Johnstone, fifth baronet in 1794 and member of Parliament, in 1782 married the daughter and heiress of General Henry Pulteney, Lord Bath's brother and heir and, on becoming heir to the princely Pulteney estates (reputed £20,000 a year), assumed the name.

53. *Mrs. Montagu*, ed. Blunt, 2:175.

54. Ibid., pp. 176–77.

55. For information about Gregory's Northamptonshire living I thank R. Watson and Sue Groves of the Northamptonshire Record Office.

56. Letter in the Osborn File, 3.125, Beinecke Library, Yale University.

57. Walpole, *Correspondence*, 33:446.

58. Letter of March 10, 1785, BL, Althorp Papers, F57.

59. Walpole, *Correspondence*, 34:70.

60. *Lady Louisa Stuart*, p. 161.

SEVEN. Deputy Labor: Empowering Strategies I

1. For an elaboration of this point see Leonore Davidoff and Catherine Hall, *Family Fortunes: Men and Women of the English Middle Class, 1780–1850* (Chicago: University of Chicago Press, 1987).

2. See *The Goodwood Estate Archives*, ed. Francis W. Steer, J. E. Amanda Venables, and Timothy J. McCann, 3 vols. (Chichester: West Sussex County Council, 1972–84). The name Milyard occurs with some frequency in the papers of the seventeenth to nineteenth centuries and is often associated with the Sussex estate of Boxgrove.

3. BL Add. MSS 51427, ff. 43–44v.

4. BL Add. MSS 51424, f. 1.

5. Ibid., ff. 3–4.

6. Princess Marie Liechtenstein, *Holland House*, 2 vols. (London: Macmillan, 1874), 1:56.

7. BL Add. MSS 51414, f. 1.

8. BL Add. MSS 51424, ff. 9–12v. Mary Margaret Stewart, a student of the British Library Holland House collection of manuscripts and of the Charles Hanbury Williams correspondence in the Lewis Walpole Library collection, has generously lent me her notes, which allow me in this and subsequent passages greatly to supplement my own information with hers. The conjecture that Fannen left with Lady Caroline is hers.

9. Williams Correspondence, 48-10914, f. 76, June 14, 1744, Lewis Walpole Library, courtesy of Mary Margaret Stewart. It seems likely that Betty Milward had already joined the new young family.

10. BL Add. MSS 51414, ff. 71–71v.

11. Ibid., ff. 83v–84.

12. Ibid., f. 85.

13. Ibid., f. 89.

14. Ibid., f. 87.

15. BL Add. MSS 51428, ff. 1–2. I am grateful to the British Library for permission to quote this letter in full.

16. BL Add. MSS 51414, ff. 90v–91.

17. Ibid., ff. 132–33.

18. The temptations were serious. In 1759 a steward of Fox's, John Ayliffe, was hanged for having forged Fox's name to a lease (see *GM*, November 1759, pp. 548–49; December 1759, pp. 578–80). He had also fraudulently induced a

former employer to sign a deed of gift to him of £420 a year. His last words were to Mr. Fannen, "a person who had been a principal evidence against him, expressing his obligations to Mr. *Fox*, and requesting to be buried in *Hertford-shire*"; he was carried off in a hearse and four at Fox's expense.

19. See the IGI.

20. BL Add. MSS 51414, ff. 175–76.

21. BL Add. MSS 51415, f. 17. Charles James Fox had been born on January 24, 1749.

22. *Letters of Sarah Byng Osborn*, p. 68.

23. Nancy Chodorow, *The Reproduction of Mothering* (Berkeley: University of California Press, 1978), pp. 126–40.

24. Women's choice of other women as emotional objects would have been even more prevalent among eighteenth-century women, whose lives were shared, more exclusively than the lives of women now, with other women.

25. *Correspondence of Emily, Duchess of Leinster*, 1:252. Tylney, a homosexual émigré who lived most of his life in Florence, was on good terms with the Hollands abroad and may have taken this graceful way of making acquaintance.

26. *The Court and City Register for the Year 1756* (London: J. Barnes et al., n.d.), p. 165, lists her in the post. She kept the office to her death in 1786 (*GM*, October 1786, p. 911).

27. *Correspondence of Emily, Duchess of Leinster*, 2:81.

28. Lady Caroline was elevated into the peerage sui juris as Lady Holland in 1762; Henry Fox became Lord Holland in 1763. She was thenceforward known as Lady Holland.

29. *Correspondence of Emily, Duchess of Leinster*, 1:516.

30. Ibid., p. 441.

31. Ibid., pp. 449–50.

32. Ibid., p. 493.

33. Ibid., 2:205.

34. Chodorow, *Reproduction of Mothering*, p. 167.

35. Quoted by Warren Derry, *Dr. Parr: A Portrait of the Whig Dr. Johnson* (Oxford: Clarendon Press, 1966), p. 22.

36. Charles Pigott, *The Whig Club* (London: B. Crosby, 1794), p. 212; *DNB*, 15:356–64. Pigott, probably familiar with the later Parr domestic scene, would have been a supporter of the doctor, but he clearly mistakes Marsingale's origins. Though she may have been companion to an obscure citizen's widow, she could scarcely have had a cockney accent and may have been responding, through her cheap economies and her possibly embarrassed complaints, to a very narrow supply of housekeeping money on which to entertain numerous visitors. Whether or not she had become the mistress of Askew—aged forty-nine in 1771—cannot be certainly known, but if she were, by marrying her to Parr, Askew committed an ignoble action. In any case Elizabeth Holford Askew, Askew's wife, "a woman of celestial beauty and celestial virtue" (*DNB*) and the

mother of twelve, was far more likely to have been the patroness of Marsingale.

37. Derry, *Dr. Parr*, pp. 22–23.

38. William St. Clair, *The Godwins and the Shelleys: A Biography of a Family* (Baltimore: Johns Hopkins University Press, 1989), p. 128. Subsequent references to the Parrs from St. Clair will be by page numbers in the text.

39. *GM*, July 1810, p. 92. Parr goes on to endorse his daughter's extensive reading in French and English, her judgment, and her becoming resignation to the will of Heaven with which she endured a long and painful illness, "brought upon her by the pressure of domestic sorrow on a constitution naturally weak." Interesting here also is Parr's emphasis on the appropriately weak constitution and his refusal even at this late date to note that she apparently read Greek.

40. Derry, *Dr. Parr*, pp. 201–2.

41. St. Clair, *The Godwins and the Shelleys*, pp. 150–51. Sarah Anne Parr's letters are in the Abinger archive of manuscripts, Bodleian Library, Oxford University, c512, c513, b227/2.

42. Derry, *Dr. Parr*, p. 198.

43. William Field, *Memoirs of Dr. Parr*, 2 vols. (London, 1828), 2:480, quoted ibid., pp. 70–71.

44. *Godwin and Mary: Letters of William Godwin and Mary Wollstonecraft*, ed. Ralph M. Wardle (Lawrence: University of Kansas Press, 1966), p. 85. Subsequent references to this work will be by page number in the text.

45. *The Piozzi Letters*, ed. Edward A. Bloom and Lillian D. Bloom, Vol. 2 (Newark: University of Delaware Press; London and Toronto: Associated University Presses, 1991) p. 472. Apparently in an attempt to assist his daughter, Parr had accompanied her to Wales, where he was no great success. Apart from being a republican in Tory territory, Parr was a stubborn and persistent smoker, which irritated housekeepers. Piozzi's triple pun plays on the secondary meanings of *smoke* as to gather a hint, to grow angry, or to ridicule, and on the French *se moquer de*, meaning to ridicule, and suggests Parr expressed defiance of Sarah's Tory in-laws and did her no good, but rather the converse. Her first child was born the following year at his own home, Hatton.

46. Derry, *Dr. Parr*, pp. 280–82. In comparison to the obituary Dr. Parr wrote for his daughter, that for his wife was short but also charged her death indirectly to the account of the Wynnes: "At Teignmouth, Devon, in consequence of an inflammation upon the lungs, brought on by fatigue, and the affectionate discharge of her maternal duties to a beloved and only remaining daughter, Mrs. Jane Parr, wife of Rev. Dr. Parr, of Hatton, co. Warwick, and niece of the late Tho. Mauleverer, esq. of Arnecliffe, Yorkshire" (*GM*, May 1810, p. 493). The widower deftly avoids noting his own bereavement.

47. Elizabeth Janeway, *Powers of the Weak* (New York: Knopf, 1980), p. 111.

48. *Thraliana*, 2:825–26, entry for 1791, and see chapter 1, n. 6. See also *Thraliana*, 1:222; Henry Thrale received £4,000 for the wood cut on his wife's beloved estate.

49. Smith, *The Old Manor House*, p. 10. Subsequent references to this work will be by page number in the text.

50. John Stuart Mill, *The Subjection of Women*, ed. Susan Moller Okin (Indianapolis: Hackett, 1988), p. 22.

EIGHT. Agents, Rivals, and Spies: Empowering Strategies II

1. The IGI shows that he was christened at St. Gluvias's, Cornwall, on November 11, 1662. See also Romney Sedgwick, *The History of Parliament: The House of Commons, 1715–1754*, 2 vols. (New York: Oxford University Press, 1970), 2:334.

2. The story of Miss Mancel and Mr. Morgan in Sarah Scott's *Description of Millenium Hall* bears some similarity to Delany's story—the coercion to force the young woman to marry the repugnant older man, the disagreeable sister in attendance, and so on. Scott notes that Miss Mancel was threatened into submission by means of unjust innuendo against her character because of a younger man. There was a young lover in the background when Delany married. For an excellent detailed description of Delany's marriages and a reappraisal of Delany see Janice Thaddeus, "Mary Delany, Model to an Age," in *History, Gender, and Eighteenth-Century Literature*, ed. Beth Fowkes Tobin (Athens: University of Georgia Press, forthcoming).

3. Delany, *Autobiography*, 1:34. Subsequent references to this work will be by volume and page number in the text.

4. The question of who reads to whom in this period is interesting; as in the case of Fannen's reading to Lady Holland and John Fannen's reading to Lord Holland (chapter 7) or her maids reading to Mrs. Greville (chapter 11), the reader is the person of lower status.

5. The IGI shows that Jane Pendarves was christened at St. Gluvias's December 11, 1660.

6. I am grateful to Janice Thaddeus, whom I consulted on the subject of Delany's finances.

7. After she was widowed for the first time, Baltimore told Delany he had loved her for five years, then visited her and asked for assurance of her affection and, receiving no satisfaction, left her, never to return. Not long afterward he married an heiress. It seems probable that he meant to make her his mistress from the beginning and, finding that she assumed he was proposing marriage, chose this means to extricate himself. See also Stone, *Family, Sex and Marriage*, who suggests the same interpretation, pp. 312–13.

8. Her father, Thomas Malyn of Battersea, Surrey, died in 1733 leaving an extensive estate to his wife, Valentine, his son Thomas (who inherited the brewery), and three daughters and a granddaughter by a fourth (PCC Prob 11/658/124).

9. Edward Ford, *Tewin-Water, or The Story of Lady Cathcart; Being a Supplement to the "History of Enfield"* (Enfield: J. H. Meyers, 1876), p. 9. This privately

printed memoir of Cathcart contains much information subsequently published in W. J. Hardy, "Lady Cathcart and Her Husbands," *St. Albans and Herts Architectural and Archaeological Society Transactions* n.s., (1898): 119–28, and W. R. Hughes, "The Dowager," *Blackwood's Magazine* 234 (July–December 1933): 119–27. I am indebted to Kathryn M. Thompson of the Hertfordshire County Record Office for copies of the latter two articles.

10. Lady Cathcart's obituary notice, *GM*, August 1789, pp. 766–67, supplies this and many other important details of her history. According to custom, she retained her title after her next marriage to Maguire and was always known as Lady Cathcart.

11. The title deeds are in the Hertfordshire County Record Office (D/EP T2341-7); A. J. Drewery of that office provided this and other archival information. James Fleet, Cathcart's first husband, died only a month after her father in 1733, leaving his wife all his Hertfordshire estates, including the newly repaired and beautified Tewin Water and all his wharves, keys, cellars, vaults, and so on in and about Thames and Fenchurch streets in London. Tewin Water and its furnishings were hers only for life and were to be inventoried and passed down intact, should Cathcart die without heirs, to his next heir, a nephew, under penalties; nor was she to cut any timber (PCC Prob 11/659/149). Fleet could scarcely have guessed that his widow would survive him by fifty-six years. His generous terms suggest that he had received a large settlement with her; no doubt both fathers had hoped to raise a genteel progeny.

12. William Sabine, originally of Tring but then of Tewin, was not rich and probably added little to Cathcart's wealth, but he wrote a brief will proved in April 1738 in which he left everything he owned to his dear and loving wife, Elizabeth Sabine (PCC Prob 11/689/103). The will of Lord Cathcart, who had numerous offspring by a former marriage, does not mention his widow (PCC Prob 11/712/257), but in a marriage settlement he left her the lease of his Dartmouth Street house for life.

13. *GM*, August 1789, pp. 766–67. The contributor of these anecdotes is unknown.

14. After Hester and Gabriel Piozzi had departed for the Continent following their marriage, it was widely reported and believed that once in his power she had been incarcerated by him in Italy. Dr. Johnson anticipated such an end when he warned her to stay at home, noted Mary Stuart's fatal decision to seek shelter in England, and added, "If the parallel reaches thus far; may it go no further. The tears stand in my eyes" (*The Letters of Samuel Johnson with Mrs. Thrale's Genuine Letters to Him*, ed. R. W. Chapman, 3 vols. [Oxford: Clarendon Press, 1952], 3:178).

15. Thomas Maguire, *Fermanagh: Its Native Chiefs and Clans* (Omagh: S. D. Montgomery, 1954); John Lodge, *The Peerage of Ireland*, rev. Mervyn Archdall, 7 vols. (Dublin: James Moore, 1789), 1:230; Mark Bence-Jones, *Burke's Guide to Country Houses*, Vol. 1, *Ireland* (London: Burke's Peerage, 1978), p. 271.

16. Walpole, *Correspondence*, 17:420. References to this work immediately following will be by volume and page number in the text.

17. *GM*, January 1741, p. 51. Eleven new regiments, of which Maguire's was one, had been formed in preparation for the War of the Austrian Succession (*GM*, October 1742, p. 547). Maguire was advanced to the vacated place of colonel of the regiment.

18. Hardy, "Lady Cathcart and Her Husbands," p. 123.

19. *The Correspondence of Edward Young, 1683–1765*, ed. Henry Pettit (Oxford: Clarendon Press, 1971), p. 236. Subsequent references to this work will be by page numbers in the text.

20. Maria Edgeworth lived at Edgeworthstown, co. Longford, not far from Castle Nugent, where Maguire incarcerated Cathcart for some years and the place from which she was released. In Edgeworth's novel *Castle Rackrent* (New York: Century, 1904), p. 18, she provides in a footnote factual evidence about the imprisonment, affirming that she herself ("the editor") knew Colonel Maguire and knew the gentleman who accompanied Cathcart back to England after Maguire's death. She incorporates other elements of Cathcart's story in the novel, in which Cathcart figures as Lady Rackrent; in this fictional permutation of the tale, the details cannot be assumed to be literally true, though they may be. Sir Kit is imprisoning his wife until she yields up her jewels, concealed about her person, as she had promised to do before marriage, to pay his gambling debts. Possibly Maguire had to leave England because those debts remained unpaid, and it is known that Cathcart did retain her jewels. I am indebted to Mitzi Myers for information about the Edgeworths and Nugents in relation to Cathcart.

21. Which of course he was. Everything about Young's tone suggested that he and Portland had discussed Cathcart previously, to her disadvantage, and in justification of Young it might be suggested that perhaps he and his stepdaughter had found that the stepdaughter had been only a justification for Cathcart's enjoying the full gaiety of a London season. Nevertheless, his consistent failure of compassion in regard to Cathcart's literal if not illegal kidnapping is strikingly revelatory of how much such self-gratification on the part of widows as Cathcart had openly boasted of was detested.

22. Cathcart's lie very probably had to do with her jewels, which she had refused to relinquish. Young added a postscript that he had just received news (erroneous) that "the Happy Couple are soon to return from Ireland in perfect Peace." But he hoped that both Cathcart and the Duchess of Manchester were now "as ready to repent of their *Sins* as they are of Their *Follys*" (p. 239).

23. *Correspondence of Edward Young*, p. 267. Young appears to be describing Cnocninne (or Chocninnidh) Castle, the original but now deserted home of the Maguires, erected on a hill of limestone above Lough Erne, rather than Tempo, where he may first have taken her, or Castle Nugent, the owner of which was John Nugent, Maguire's maternal uncle. Fermanagh is in the north of Ireland, though not the extreme north, and not on the sea. The name of Cathcart's

first tenant has apparently not survived, but she may have been the Elizabeth Nugent provided with £500 in Cathcart's 1746 Dublin deed. Two of the tenants of Tewin Water during these years are named in the lists of gamekeepers printed in the *Hertfordshire County Records, Calendars to the Sessions Books, 1752–1799*, ed. William Le Hardy, Vol. 8 (Hertford: Elton Longmore, 1935): in 1755 Lord Oliphant; in 1764 Joseph Hickey (Maguire's attorney); when Cathcart returned, the tenant she evicted was Joseph Steele. In 1766 the occupant was again "Elizabeth, dowager Lady Cathcart, widow."

24. Hughes, "The Dowager," p. 124.

25. *GM*, August 1789, p. 766; Ford, *Tewin-Water*, pp. 28–29; Hardy, "Lady Cathcart and Her Husbands," p. 124; Hughes, "The Dowager," p. 124.

26. Hardy, "Lady Cathcart and Her Husbands," pp. 125–26. A fifty-guinea annuity for a Mary Horton, to be continued until she was twenty-one or married, was also provided; Mary Horton may have been the companion.

27. Cathcart's will (PCC Prob 11/1182/422) leaves several legacies contingent upon the unlikely redemption of this mortgage; see also Hardy, "Lady Cathcart and Her Husbands," p. 127.

28. Edgeworth, *Castle Rackrent*, p. 18n. There is a tradition that Tempo Manor was the setting for Edgeworth's novel, which suggests that it may have been the first place of Cathcart's incarceration. News of Lady Cathcart seems to have become lost to her acquaintance by April 1749, when Young inquired of his stepdaughter, Cathcart's former protégée, who was then in Dublin, "If you learn anything for certain as to Lady Cathcart you will mention it in your next" (Stephen Brown, "A Letter from Edward Young to Caroline Lee Haviland: Some Biographical Implications," *Philological Quarterly* 68 [Spring 1989]: 265). My thanks to James May, who called this reference to my attention.

29. Ford, *Tewin-Water*, pp. 40–41; Hughes, "The Dowager," p. 126.

30. Maguire's death was reported in *GM*, May 1766, p. 247. Edgeworth notes of her hero Sir Kit, "No sooner was it known for certain that he was dead, than all the gentlemen within twenty miles of us came in a body, as it were, to set my lady at liberty, and to protest against her confinement" (p. 22). Elisabeth Inglis-Jones in *The Great Maria: A Portrait of Maria Edgeworth* (London: Faber and Faber, 1959), p. 30, notes that Edgeworth had heard of Cathcart's rescue and her appearance from Mr. Nugent, who took her from her lair, half-stupefied in a red wig and rags, and escorted her back to her friends in England. Mr. Nugent was very possibly the Walter Nugent, Esq., of Carpenterstown, County Westmeath, bred an attorney, who had functioned as a guardian and adviser to Richard Edgeworth (W. J. McCormack, *Ascendancy and Tradition in Anglo-Irish Literary History from 1789 to 1939* [Oxford: Clarendon Press, 1985], pp. 404–5).

31. Lady Cathcart's will, drawn up in 1780, significantly mentions no members of her immediate family except two unmarried nieces, to each of whom she left £200 in Irish money, these like many of her bequests dependent upon the dubious repayment to her of the money she had given Maguire in return for the mortgage on Tempo. She left various modest bequests to a number of

friends and to members of her large staff various furnishings, silver, linen, two chaises and three horses—probably the entire contents of her estate because the reversion to the estate had already been sold, perhaps for cash necessary to support her. Her steward Philip Cosgrove, who had been established as her gamekeeper on her return in 1766, was her sole executor and the residuary legatee (PCC Prob 11/1182/422). Her anonymous biographer in the *GM* would seem to be right in stating that she had not had a great deal of wealth left to leave, but in 1775 she had joined with Fleet's designated heir John Bull to sell the reversion to the estate to the Third Earl Cowper (a sale accomplished in 1782), and she had been able to maintain herself on her estate with an extensive staff and stable. Her tablet in the south pier of the chancel arch at Tewin Church reads, "The Right Honourable Elizabeth, Lady Dowager Cathcart, of Tewin Water, one of the daughters of Thomas Malyn, of Battersea, Esq., and sometime the wife of James Fleet, Esq., of Tewin Water, but afterwards the widow of the Right Honourable Lord Cathcart. She departed this life the 3rd of April, 1789, in the 98th year of her age" (John Edwin Cussans, *History of Hertfordshire*, 8 vols. in 3 [London: Chatto and Windus, 1870–81], Vol. 2, "Hundreds of Hertford," pp. 17, 19).

32. Austen, *Northanger Abbey*, p. 197.

33. Another possibility is suggested by the fact that the character Edgeworth models on Lady Cathcart is a Jew who wears a diamond cross. There is no other indication that I can find that Lady Cathcart was originally Jewish except that her father provided no conventional Christian preamble in his will. But could it be that the idea that she was Jewish, cleverly put about in Ireland by Maguire, might have alienated the sympathy of the Irish Roman Catholics? (Edgeworth has the fictitious husband tormenting his wife by serving bacon at her table.) Fielding glances at the Cathcart story in the episode of the Irish incarceration of Mrs. Fitzpatrick in *The History of Tom Jones* (1749).

34. See bibliographies in Arthur Calder-Marshall, *The Two Duchesses* (London: Hutchinson, 1978), p. 183, and Georgiana Cavendish, Duchess of Devonshire, *Georgiana*, ed. Earl of Bessborough (London: John Murray, 1955), p. 296; also Brian Masters, *Georgiana, Duchess of Devonshire* (London: Hamish Hamilton, 1981).

35. In 1764 Walpole calculated this was the duke's father's income (*Correspondence*, 38:445).

36. Wraxall, *Historical and Posthumous Memoirs*, 3:344.

37. The *Town and Country Magazine*, March 1777, pp. 121–24. This "Tête-à-Tête" says that the duke had been with Spencer for some years before marriage.

38. Letter from Mrs. Burgoyne to the Duchess of Argyll in *Intimate Society Letters of the Eighteenth Century*, ed. Duke of Argyll, 2 vols. (London: Stanley Paul & Co., 1910), 1:176.

39. Delany, *Autobiography*, 4:587.

40. *Mary Hamilton*, ed. Elizabeth Anson and Florence Anson (London: J. Murray, 1925), p. 27.

41. Delany, *Autobiography*, 5:5.

42. Calder-Marshall, *Two Duchesses*, pp. 69–71.

43. *The Early Diary of Frances Burney, 1768–1778*, ed. Annie Raine Ellis, 2 vols. (London: George Bell and Sons, 1907), 2:203–4.

44. Lady Sarah Bunbury to Lady Susan O'Brien, in *The Life and Letters of Lady Sarah Lennox*, ed. Countess of Ilchester and Lord Stavordale, 2 vols. (London: John Murray, 1901), 1:261.

45. Historical Manuscripts Commission, *15th Report, Appendix Part VI, Vol. 42, The Manuscripts of the Earl of Carlisle* (London: Her Majesty's Stationery Office, 1897), p. 485.

46. Historical Manuscripts Commission, *Manuscripts of the Earl of Carlisle*, p. 594.

47. *Boswell's Life of Johnson*, 1:106.

48. Calder-Marshall, *Two Duchesses*, p. 50.

49. Joyce Hemlow, *The History of Fanny Burney* (Oxford: Clarendon Press, 1958), pp. 223–24. In 1791 Burney noted, "Lady Elizabeth has the general character of inheriting all the wit, all the subtlety, all *les agremens*, & all the wickedness of The Herveys" *The Journals and Letters of Fanny Burney*, ed. Joyce Hemlow et al., 12 vols. (Oxford: Clarendon Press, 1972), 1:46.

50. Devonshire, *Georgiana*, p. 53.

51. Walpole, *Correspondence*, 25:455. Walpole adds that the earl-bishop had £25,000 a year.

52. Devonshire, *Georgiana*, p. 64. The trio had pet names for one another: the duke was Canis, the duchess was the Rat, and Foster was Racky, for Raccoon.

53. Ibid., p. 75.

54. Dorothy Margaret Stuart, *Dearest Bess* (London: Methuen, 1955), p. 26. Subsequent references will be by page number in the text.

55. There were persistent rumors that the Prince of Wales considered himself the father of this child. See, for instance, John Wardroper, *Kings, Lords and Wicked Libellers* (London: John Murray, 1973), p. 118. Wardroper reports that a shocked George V burned a packet of the prince's and duchess's letters in 1913.

56. Devonshire, *Georgiana*, p. 109.

57. Calder-Marshall, *Two Duchesses*, p. 85.

58. Suggestion made in conversation.

59. Vere Foster, *The Two Duchesses* (London: Blackie & Son, 1898), p. 131. The duchess, however, ends her poem, "Mortels, craintifs fuyez ses charmes, / Fuyez son pouvoir enchanteur. / La cruelle impose les peines, / Au lieu de donner le bonheur." A subsequent reference to this work is in the text by page number.

60. Elizabeth, Duchess of Devonshire, *Anecdotes and Biographical Sketches* (London, 1863), before title page.

61. Foster, *Two Duchesses*, pp. 281, 289.

62. When the *accoucheur* Sir Richard Croft died in 1818, obituaries revived the story that he had exchanged the children; see the *London Times*, February

16, 1818, and *GM*, March 1818, p. 277. But the duke's failure to marry and his close connection to Foster, whom the duchess's daughters hated, is more compelling evidence. A report in the *GM* for August 1810 (p. 188) that a Cavendish relation had left £700,000 to Lord George and his three sons suggests some attempt to redress an imbalance of justice. To believe this story, however, one would also have to believe that the duchess, if she also had a child, allowed a daughter to be spirited away.

63. The novel in question was T. S. Surr, *A Winter in London*, 3 vols. (London: Richard Phillips, 1806). In it the duchess figures as the Duchess of Belgrave, "A Victim of Fashion," who went straight from the nursery to the summit of fashionable freedom and whose open heart made her everybody's dupe.

64. Charles Pigott, for instance, so censorious of the women of her set in *The Female Jockey Club*, makes of the duchess an undiluted angel, bestowing upon her every possible panegyric, pp. 12–20.

65. In this one instance, Lady Spencer, who did all she could to avoid the scandal of a repudiation of her daughter, probably did her no service. The duke proposed a five-year separation, which might have reformed the duchess (certainly would have ruined her credit and prevented her amassing more debt) and would have separated Foster from the duke.

66. Devonshire, *Georgiana*, p. 77.

67. Burney, *Cecilia*, p. 11. Subsequent references to this work will be by page numbers in the text.

68. Consistent deception is a necessity in any hierarchically structured relationship in which the inferior is not what Dr. Gregory would have called a "natural" woman—or a "natural" inferior of either sex. It is interesting that Foster, who dedicated herself to deceiving and controlling the Duchess of Devonshire, attributed her death to her having been confronted with what was arguably the truth about herself, now made known to everyone. Characteristically, Foster laid the blame on the novel's author.

NINE. Business Partners: Baddeley and Steele

1. John Fyvie, in *Comedy Queens of the Georgian Era* (London: Constable, 1906), p. 232, repeated a conjecture that Alexander Bicknell, who had compiled the six-volume memoir of the actress George Ann Bellamy in 1785, had assisted Steele in the compilation of Baddeley's memoir. The conjecture, generally accepted (see *sub* Baddeley in *DNB*) is unfounded. Baddeley's lover Stephen Sayre, in an 1802 letter to James Madison, identifies Steele's assistant in the project (without naming him) as William Jackson, Chudleigh's secretary and factotum during her trial, who had brought sodomy charges against her opponent Foote to force him to suppress his farce about Chudleigh. Jackson is a likely pros-

pect, and Sayre must have been knowledgeable on this point. John R. Alden, in *Stephen Sayre, American Revolutionary Adventurer* (Baton Rouge: Louisiana State University Press, 1983), p. 28, n. 24, assumes that Sayre, in identifying Steele's coadjutor as "that most infamous of all Ministerial Hirelings," was referring to Bicknell, but he was plainly referring to Jackson. Jackson did take his opportunity to blacken the characters of the Opposition leader Charles Fox, his follower Melbourne, and the republican Sayre, among others.

2. Chodorow, *Reproduction of Mothering*, pp. 126–40. The Duchess of Devonshire and Elizabeth Vesey also seem to some extent to have been infantilized by the same situation. Extrapolating from these four examples, it would seem that, to become mature, the daughter must succeed to the mother role.

3. *Character of the Present Most Celebrated Courtezans. Interspersed with a Variety of Secret Anecdotes Never Before Published* (London: M. James, 1780), p. 30.

4. Ibid., p. 29.

5. *The Memoirs of Mrs. Sophia Baddeley, Late of Drury Lane Theatre. By Mrs. Elizabeth Steele*, 6 vols. (Clerkenwell: For the Author, at the Literary Press, 1787). Subsequent references to this work will be by volume and page number in the text.

6. See note 1.

7. They could become well-known in their own right. The *Public Advertiser*, April 30, 1763, notes, "Yesterday died the celebrated Bett Beuley, late Companion to Kitty Fisher, universally esteemed for her many amiable qualifications."

8. See also Steven Myers, "Elizabeth Steele," in Todd, *A Dictionary of British and American Women Writers, 1660–1800*, pp. 296–97.

9. For Robert and Sophia Baddeley see Philip H. Highfill, Jr., Kalman A. Burnim, and Edward Langhans, *A Biographical Dictionary of Actors, Actresses, Musicians, Dancers, Managers and Other Stage Personnel in London, 1660–1800* 14 vols. to date (Carbondale: Southern Illinois University Press, 1973–), 1:196–208.

10. *Character of the Present Most Celebrated Courtezans* identifies this early lover as the "Policy-Broker J-sh- Mendez," p. 33.

11. Ibid., p. 35.

12. The *Town and Country Magazine*, May 1772, pp. 233–36, published a "Tête-à-Tête" about Baddeley and William Hanger which does not mention either Melbourne or John Hanger.

13. See Walpole, *Correspondence*, 24:235.

14. *Town and Country Magazine*, April 1770, p. 178.

15. Fawkener (see chapter 11 for the unfortunate debacle of his marriage) and Storer were well-known and fashionable young men about town. Joseph Gill, who narrowly escaped ruin at Baddeley's hands, was a twenty-year-old Oxford student in 1773, the son of Thomas Gill of Reading; he took his BCL degree in 1780, his DCL in 1786. See *Alumni Oxonienses, The Members of the University of*

Oxford, 1715–1866, ed. Joseph Foster (London, 1888; 4 vols. in 2 rpt. Nendeln/ Liechtenstein: Krause Reprint, 1968), 2:524.

16. See Sedgwick, *History of Parliament*, 2:195–96.

17. Elizabeth Milbanke, Lady Melbourne, gave her husband as good as she got. The Duchess of Devonshire, her friend, portrays her as Lady Besford in *The Sylph*, 2 vols. (London: T. Lowndes, 1779), where she contributes to the fashionable education of the heroine by explaining, "I never indulged myself with the least liberty with other men, till I had secured my lord a lawful heir. . . . My lord kept a mistress from the first moment of his marriage. What law excludes a woman from doing the same? Marriage now is a necessary kind of barter, and an alliance of families." Lady Melbourne cut it too close, however, by providing her husband with only one true heir; her second son, generally conceded to be the son of Lord Egremont, succeeded to the Melbourne title.

18. The portrait of Baddeley, caressing a favorite cat, which plays with a lock of her hair, is described by Charles Robert Leslie and Tom Taylor, *Life and Times of Sir Joshua Reynolds*, 2 vols. (London: John Murray, 1865), 1:393, and in Algernon Graves and William Vine Cronin, *A History of the Works of Sir Joshua Reynolds, P.R.A.*, 4 vols. (London: H. Graves, 1899–1901), Vol. 1. Jayne Shrimpton of the National Portrait Gallery notes that the present whereabouts of the portrait is unknown. An engraving from the portrait by E. Welsh was published in 1772.

19. The *Town and Country Magazine*, May 1772, p. 236, notes that she was currently singing at Ranelagh.

20. Ibid. gives a slightly different account.

21. Ibid., p. 239.

22. Ibid., June 1772, p. 295.

23. But this seems an exception without point and may have been thrown in by Steele to authenticate her anecdote about the innkeeper's daughter and yet to disguise the fact that she was impersonating a man at the time.

24. Steele only notes the decision to take a jaunt to Portsmouth. Her story is verified by reports of Baddeley having been at Portsmouth with Spry; see Leslie and Taylor, *Life and Times of Sir Joshua Reynolds*, 2:26.

25. Coleraine, more fortunate than Baddeley in debt as in life, protected by class and gender privilege, survived his own financial indiscretions to die unmarried, in Paris, in 1794. At his own death in 1773 his father had left all he could—£1,600 a year—to his wife, but her three sons divested her of it all, and had in 1775 recently forced her to town to display her to their moneylenders as a "good life." Coleraine spent most of the rest of his life comfortably in Paris eluding his debtors (Walpole, *Correspondence*, 24: 235–36; 30:264). His brother William, sixth Baron Coleraine at his death, died unmarried in 1814.

26. This may well have been Bartholomew Coote Purdon, of the Oxford Street bank Sayre and Purdon, who maintained a splendid establishment and at whose home musical London, including the Sheridans and the Duchess of Devonshire, congregated. For him see Alden, *Stephen Sayre*, pp. 33–35. Purdon

with his partner Stephen Sayre was listed as a bankrupt in the *GM*, November 1776. In any case, Mr. P. obviously paid to remain at least ostensibly unidentified by Steele.

27. Those gentlemen friends of Baddeley's who had the good sense not to try to extricate her generally survived and prospered. In August 1776 the generous John Damer shot himself to death in a tavern, having lost £20,000 in one night.

28. Thomas Mortimer, in *The Universal Director; or, The Nobleman and Gentleman's True Guide* . . . (London: J. Coote, 1763), lists a William Petrie and Son, Scotch linen factors, in Tokenhouse-yard.

29. See Alden, *Stephen Sayre*, chaps. 5 and 6.

30. From a long journal letter in the Osborn File, 47.67, Beinecke Library, Yale University, which is printed in the *Aberdeen University Review* 45 (Spring 1973): 1–19.

31. *Character of the Present Most Celebrated Courtezans*, p. 42.

32. *The Picture Gallery, Containing Near Two Hundred Paintings by the Most Distinguished Ladies in Great Britain* (London: G. Kearsley, 1780), p. 10.

33. Tate Wilkinson, *The Wandering Patentee*, 4 vols. (York: For the author, 1795), 2:152. A list of humorous and fictitious book titles in the *Public Advertiser*, December 22, 1779, included "True love indissoluble.—A Poetical attempt,—Mrs. B——d——y.—Laudanum-lane."

34. *Critical Review*, June 1787, p. 480. The critic, in the manner of Elizabeth Foster, assigns the blame for disturbing the peace of families to the revealer of the connections with Baddeley rather than to those who instigated and enjoyed the connections.

35. Sayre, in the letter to James Madison in 1802 in which he attempted to refute the charges made against him in Baddeley's memoirs, noted that "the ostensible author would have been hang'd for forgery, had she not cut her throat." I am grateful to James H. Hutson, chief of the Manuscript Division of the Library of Congress, for providing me with a copy of this letter from that archive.

36. *GM*, November 1787, p. 1053.

37. Todd, *Women's Friendship*, p. 328.

38. *Town and Country Magazine*, May 1772, p. 234n.

39. Baddeley's parents may have been unsympathetic to her style of life and of little help to her after she left them; the apparently mutual desertion of child and parents was not owing to the parents' early deaths, for Steele refers to their visiting her ailing mother, and her father survived until 1770.

TEN. The Domestic Triangle: The Veseys and Handcock

1. William Handcock's nephew was elevated to the peerage as Lord Castlemaine, under which title the Handcock family may be found. Arthur Vicars

edited *Index to the Prerogative Wills of Ireland, 1536–1810* (Dublin, 1897); for William Handcock, who died in 1741, see p. 215. Most of the wills Vicars lists were unfortunately destroyed in the fires of 1922. "Bethams Genealogical Abstracts made from Irish Wills," a manuscript in the National Archives, Four Courts, Dublin, made entirely for genealogical purposes, contains lists of all the names in the wills and notes relationships to the testator but gives no further details. William Handcock made his will on March 2, 1733, probably soon after his marriage, and mentions his wife, Elizabeth, his mother, his three brothers, and his three sisters by name.

2. Handcock left no will that I can discover and probably had converted all she had into an annuity. As Handcock and Vesey between them had £800 or £900 on Mr. Vesey's death, I calculate that Vesey's jointure was probably £500–£600, Handcock's annuity £200–£300.

3. Lodge, *Peerage of Ireland*, 6:33–36.

4. The letter probably dates from 1761; see *Letters of Laurence Sterne*, ed. Lewis Perry Curtis (Oxford: Clarendon Press, 1935), p. 138. Curtis notes that this extraordinary missive is genuine, for there is a copy in Sterne's letterbook.

5. Delany, *Autobiography*, 1:324.

6. Ibid., 2:415. In the next few years Delany vacillates between "Miss" and "Mrs." Handcock, suggesting that Handcock was on the verge of confirmed spinsterhood but not quite arrived. Subsequent references to Delany will be by volume and page number in the text.

7. *Correspondence of Emily, Duchess of Leinster*, 1:74–75, 78, 81, 84. At this time the Kildares also employed an Irish agent named Handcock, certainly some connection. Subsequent references to this work will be by volume and page number in the text.

8. Carter to Montagu, *Letters from Mrs. Elizabeth Carter*, 3:144. Subsequent references will be by volume and page number in the text.

9. "What a Heaven born letter you have wrote." The letters of Elizabeth Vesey to Montagu are among the Montagu Papers in the Huntington Library, San Marino; I am grateful for permission to quote from them. Subsequent references to these letters will be by date and opening words in the text.

10. The eminent members of the Club never knew why they had elected Agmondesham Vesey, a well-bred lightweight, to join them, unless they considered it of sufficient advantage to be privileged members of the Vesey salon. Each member of the Club was supposed to be an authority in some field of learning, and on one occasion Mr. Vesey was named in charge of "Irish antiquities, or Celtick learning," about which he knew little or nothing. Burke proposed him as "good-humoured, sensible, well-bred," with all the social virtues. Montagu had already advised them that he was a man of taste without pretensions, jealousy, or envy (*Boswell's Life of Johnson*, 4:179; 5:108–9).

11. *Mrs. Montagu*, ed. Blunt, 1:183–84.

12. Burney, *Diary and Letters*, ed. Dobson, 2:350–51.

13. Reginald Blunt, "The Sylph," *Edinburgh Review*, October 1925, p. 370.

14. *A Series of Letters Between Mrs. Elizabeth Carter and Mrs. Catherine Talbot, from the Year 1741 to 1770. To Which Are Added, Letters from Mrs. Elizabeth Carter to Mrs. Vesey, Between the Years 1763 and 1787*, 3d ed., 3 vols. (London: F. C. & J. Rivington, 1819), 3:208.

15. Carter, *Series of Letters*, 3:95.

16. Ibid., 3:248–49, 395; *Correspondence of Emily, Duchess of Leinster*, 3:297.

17. Carter, *Series of Letters*, 3:119–20.

18. Blunt, "The Sylph," p. 370.

19. Walpole, *Correspondence*, 31:235.

20. *Correspondence of Emily, Duchess of Leinster*, 1:211.

21. Historical Manuscripts Commission, *Calendar of the Manuscripts of the Marquis of Bath*, 1:350.

22. BL, Althorp Papers F124; Wraxall, *Historical and Posthumous Memoirs*, 1:304. The incident occurred on May 23, 1780.

23. Burney, *Diary and Letters*, ed. Dobson, 1:253.

24. Letter in the Osborn File, 46.76, Beinecke Library, Yale University, dated January 1808.

25. Burney, *Diary and Letters*, ed. Dobson, 1:253. Burney annotated a 1783 note from Vesey in her scrapbook of correspondence as from "the famous Blue Receiver, Mrs. Vesey, who thinks F.B. too ill to Write or answer, yet invites her to 3 following Assemblies" (Berg Collection, New York Public Library).

26. *Mrs. Montagu*, ed. Blunt, 2:58. See also *Elizabeth Montagu*, ed. Climenson, 2:6.

27. William Roberts, *Memoirs of the Life and Correspondence of Mrs. Hannah More*, 2 vols. (New York: Harper & Brothers, 1851), 1:286. Subsequent references to this work will be by volume and page number in the text.

28. *Boswell's Life of Johnson*, 3:425–26.

29. *Mrs. Montagu*, ed. Blunt, 2:95.

30. In consultation for the interiors with Sir William Chambers, James Wyatt, and Michael Stapleton, Vesey himself designed the impressive Palladian villa that replaced the old house, itself a replacement of the castle erected in the seventeenth century by Patrick Sarsfield, Earl of Lucan (d. 1693). Lucan House is presently Ireland's Italian embassy (Bence-Jones, *Burke's Guide to Country Houses*, 1:195).

31. *Mrs. Montagu*, ed. Blunt, 2:358. Mr. P. was probably Agmondesham Vesey's friend Edmund Sexton Pery (1719–1806), speaker of the Irish House of Commons. In 1762 Pery had married as his second wife Elizabeth Vesey's niece and namesake the widow Elizabeth Vesey Handcock, and his visits to London would have made him known to Montagu.

32. *Thraliana*, 1:361.

33. Montagu Papers, Huntington Library.

34. Agmondesham Vesey's youngest brother, George, identified in his May

1967 obituary in the *Gentleman's Magazine* (p. 280) as the accountant general of Ireland, had married Letitia Vesey, another cousin, on January 2, 1755, in Dublin; their daughter Elizabeth was christened November 20, 1755, and married Richard Martin of Dangan on February 8, 1777. Mr. Vesey apparently supported his brother's widow as well as having portioned his niece and paid the school expenses of his nephew George.

35. Letters of November 1777, "my ever Dear Friend I received your letter" and December 12, 1777, "in joy or sorrow in solitude or the bustle of the world." In November 1779 the leasehold for sixty-one years of a spacious house, formerly the Hon. Mrs. Digby's (deceased) on the east side of Clarges Street, Piccadilly, was advertised for sale (*DA*, November 27, 1779); it was this lease Mr. Vesey purchased.

36. Delany, *Autobiography*, 6:256.

37. *Mrs. Montagu*, ed. Blunt, 2:190.

38. Betham's Genealogical Abstracts names the legatees: Letitia Vesey, George Vesey, Elizabeth Vesey Martin, and his nephew Sir Charles Bingham, who in 1776 had become Lord Lucan.

39. Elizabeth Montagu wrote to Sarah Scott on June 26, 1785, that Vesey had got no settlement on her second marriage and that her husband had got her jointure from her first marriage (Montagu Collection, Huntington Library). Most probably the jointure, legally devised to him for life, now reverted to her, and her husband had considered it sufficient income. But there is some likelihood that, complaining of his many expenses and playing on her guilt for not having given him an heir, Mr. Vesey had abstracted other sums from his wife and she now recognized that her own comfortable subsistence had been diverted to her sister-in-law and her children, making it apparent to her where her husband's true affections had resided.

40. BL, Althorp Papers, F58.

41. *Mrs. Montagu*, ed. Blunt, 2:193.

42. Ibid., pp. 367–68. The reference to Handcock's green gown is to the maid Susannah's lack of sorrow at the death of Bobby in *Tristram Shandy* (bk. 5, chap. 7).

43. Lewis Bettany, *Edward Jerningham and His Friends* (New York: Brentano's, 1919), p. 204.

44. Walpole, *Correspondence*, 1:304. In the remainder of this chapter, subsequent references to Walpole will be in the text by volume and page number.

45. Thomas Dawson, Viscount Cremorne, was the son of Vesey's paternal aunt Elizabeth Vesey Dawson (who may have been her godmother) and hence her first cousin. The second Lady Cremorne was Philadelphia-Hannah Freame, a granddaughter of William Penn. Lord Cremorne had acquired a house originally built by the Earl of Huntingdon on the Thames side just west of Battersea Bridge and spent a large sum on the house and grounds and an art collection; Vesey's last home was a good one. After Cremorne's death, Cremorne Gardens

were opened as a sort of Vauxhall but were closed down in 1877 and the ground built over (Henry B. Wheatley, *London Past and Present*, 3 vols. [London: John Murray; New York: Scribner and Welford, 1891], 1:473–74).

46. Letter in the Osborn File, 45.23, Beinecke Library, Yale University.

ELEVEN. Sensibility and Romantic Friendship:
Frances Greville and Lady Spencer

1. For instance, Spacks, *Imagining a Self*, p. 28, suggests that women auto-biographers typically boast of passivity while hiding anger, aggression, and forcefulness, whereas male autobiographers turn a face to the world demon-strating strength. Spacks also introduces the important idea that women writers convey through conventional structures the private intensity of divided impulse (p. 63).

2. *Letters of Samuel Johnson*, 2:262–63. Johnson's remarks suggest (setting aside his "jest" to Thrale about her flexibility) that he considers his own displays of quickness of apprehension entirely inappropriate in a woman.

3. Burney, *Memoirs*, 1:56. Burney designated her mother's understanding as masculine (see *Diary and Letters*, ed. Dobson, 6:400–402). Mrs. Selwyn is also credited with a masculine understanding in *Evelina* (p. 268). In the passage quoted here Burney gives a brief definition of "masculine understanding"; ap-parently no one expected depth, soundness, or capacity from a female of su-perior mentality. Considering the rigid posture imposed upon women by metal braces and stays, Greville's habit of lounging at ease in commodious curves probably also constituted a rebellion against stereotyping. See also her son's at-tribution of a "masculine understanding" to Dorothea Gregory, chapter 6, n. 11. Mary Wollstonecraft finally repudiated such compliments to individual women at the expense of womankind when she refused to call Catherine Macaulay's "a masculine understanding, because I admit not of such an arrogant assumption of reason" [by the male sex] (*A Vindication of the Rights of Woman*, ed. Carol H. Poston, 2nd ed. [New York: Norton, 1988], p. 105).

4. Frances Greville's unfinished manuscript novel is in the possession of her descendant Mary, Duchess of Roxburghe, to whom I am grateful for copies and for permission to quote.

5. Jane Spencer, *The Rise of the Woman Novelist* (Oxford: Basil Blackwell, 1986), p. 79.

6. See, for instance, Alice Browne, *The Eighteenth-Century Feminist Mind* (Detroit: Wayne State University Press, 1987), p. 110; on p. 116 Browne quotes Alexander Jardine (1788): "Many of those female weaknesses which we term delicacy, etc. and pretend to admire, we secretly laugh at;—or when our taste is so far vitiated as really to like them, it is chiefly from their being symptoms of

inferiority and subordination, that soothes and feeds our pride and domineering spirit."

7. The tyranny of the stepmother is a pervasive theme in fiction by women; see, for instance, Fielding's *David Simple* and Sarah Scott's tale of Leonora from *A Journey Through Every Stage of Life*. Besides truly reflecting a frequent state of domestic affairs, it is also a way to expose the hypocrisy of the kindness and submission of many women.

8. See my lives of Greville in Todd, ed., *Dictionary of British and American Women Writers*, pp. 139–40, and in Janet Todd, ed., *British Women Writers: A Critical Reference Guide* (New York: Continuum, 1989), pp. 293–95. See also Roger Lonsdale, ed., *Eighteenth-Century Women Poets: An Oxford Anthology* (Oxford: Oxford University Press, 1989), pp. 190–94; and my forthcoming biography of Greville.

9. For instance, Lady Carlisle's immediate response, "The Fairy's Answer," in *The Lady's Poetical Magazine* (1781) 1:186–88; "Ode to Sensibility" in *The Poetical Calendar* (1763) 11:95–96, and Thomas Tomkins, ed., *Poems on Several Occasions* (1782); one burlesque and one refutation in *Two Odes; to Fortitude and an Easy Chair* (1772); Lady Tuite's "Answer to Mrs. Greville's Prayer for Indifference" in *A Collection of Poems, Mostly Original by Several Hands* (Dublin, 1790); "A Prayer to Sensibility. On Reading Mrs. Greville's Prayer for Indifference" in *An Asylum for Fugitive Pieces* (2d ed., 1795), 3:61–62; Miss Bradford's "Oberon—The Fairy's Answer to Mrs. Greville's prayer for Indifference," MS. in the Bodleian (not Carlisle's version). See also Isobel Grundy, "Indifference and Attachment: An Eighteenth-Century Poetic Debate," *Factotum* 26 (July 1988): 15–16. There is a similar bibliography of imitations of Greville's ode and of verses written in support of indifference.

10. Greville's manuscript volume of her poems is in the possession of the Duchess of Roxburghe, to whom I am grateful for copies and permission to quote.

11. Todd, *Sensibility*, p. 61.

12. *The Early Diary of Frances Burney, 1768–1778*, ed. Annie Raine Ellis, 2 vols. (London: George Bell and Sons, 1907), 1:26; see also Burney, *Early Journals and Letters*, 1:32n.

13. Burney, *Memoirs*, 1:114.

14. Ibid., pp. 71–72.

15. Thrale noted that the ode was a response to the death of Greville's eldest son, Algernon, aged about six, who, she said, had almost recovered from inoculation for smallpox when by accident he took or was given a draft of medicine meant for his father, suffered convulsions for twenty-four hours, and died (*Thraliana*, 1:136). The child was buried at St. James's on May 15, 1756. Thrale adds that soon afterward the Grevilles went abroad to Lorraine, where Greville, after a long conversation with Lord Eglinton about sensibility, sat down and

wrote the ode. There are errors in and problems about Thrale's story, but it suggests that heartbreak for a child's death was an important cause, unless Greville in some way blamed her husband as well.

16. Poovey, *Proper Lady*, p. 18.

17. Rousseau's view was that women were made for the pleasure of men and to be subordinate to them; because they were essentially playthings, learning in them was displeasing. Lady Holland, whose feelings for her childhood friend Greville were markedly ambivalent, had written, "Mrs. Greville admires it but she and several others don't like what he says of women, nor his notions about them, so unwilling are our sex to give up being wits, *bels esprits, politicieux*, gamesters, and fine ladies and to allow a woman shines most in her own sphere," *Correspondence of Emily, Duchess of Leinster*, 1:353.

18. BL, Althorp Papers, F47, Mrs. Howe to Lady Spencer, May 1780. All of Greville's letters to Spencer are from this collection and are quoted here by date. I am grateful to Frances Harris for allowing me early access to these papers and to the British Library for permission to quote from them.

19. BL, Althorp Papers, F104.

20. Hester Thrale wrote to Johnson from Tunbridge on October 19, 1778 "Mrs Montagu cannot bear Evelina—let not that be published—her Silver-Smiths are Pewterers, She says, & her Captains Boatswains" (*Letters of Samuel Johnson*, 2:259). By the following summer Thrale had confided the truth to Frances Burney, who wrote that both Alexander Wedderburne, the attorney general, and Elizabeth Montagu had "cut up" the Branghtons and that Frances Greville had warmly applauded them (Frances Burney, *Diary and Letters of Madame D'Arblay*, ed. Charlotte Barrett, 7 vols. [London, 1842–46], 1:180–81; and see also Burney, *Early Journals and Letters*, Vol. 3, forthcoming). When *Evelina* and Burney became the rage, Montagu's opinion became more favorable.

21. A copy made of Greville's letter to her daughter Frances Crewe written immediately after the fire (on January 10?) is in BL Add. MSS 51452, ff. 72–76. I am obliged to Christopher Wright for having supplied me with a copy of this text.

22. Greville's correspondence quoted here and below is from BL, Althorp Papers, F104.

23. Mary Macartney had married Lord Lyttelton's brother William in 1761 and had died in Jamaica, where he was governor, in 1765.

24. *Correspondence of Emily, Duchess of Leinster*, 3:168, 209.

25. From Greville's manuscript book of poetry (at the end in Frances Crewe's hand), quoted by permission of Mary, Duchess of Roxburghe.

26. The Knight family functioned as important clients of the Spencers, as the Milwards were of the Richmonds (chapter 7), providing a series of good, reliable servants. The responsible female heads of important households had great need of such pools of servants and must have cultivated them as much as possible. On February 12, 1785, Mrs. Howe wrote to Lady Spencer that Lady Harrington

had heard she might have Isabella Knight for her daughter and mentioned that young Lady Middleton had another of the family (BL, Althorp Papers, F57).

27. From her manuscript book of poems, in possession of Mary, Duchess of Roxburghe.

28. Elaine Showalter, *A Literature of Their Own* (Princeton: Princeton University Press, 1977), chap. 5.

29. John Heneage Jesse, *George Selwyn and His Contemporaries,* 4 vols. (New York: Scribner, 1882), 2:213. March does not identify his hosts, but his letter is dated December 31, 1767, and on January 5, 1768, Selwyn told Lord Carlisle that March was still with the Spencers and having a good time (Historical Manuscripts Commission, *15th Report, Appendix Part VI, Vol. 42,* p. 227).

30. Letter of November 4, 1774, BL, Althorp Papers F43.

31. Benjamin Preedy, ca. 1722–96, of Queens College, Oxford, B.A. 1743, M.A. 1772, B.D. and D.D. 1772, was rector of St. Albans and Dunton and of Brington, Northamptonshire, and master of the St. Albans School, where he ran a flourishing boardinghouse until he moved to Brington in 1775. His son James, born ca. 1753, B.A. 1775, Queens College, became rector of Hasleton with Entworth, Gloucester, in 1785, but appears to have remained at St. Albans.

32. George Selwyn noted in 1781 that a fashionable keeper of a faro bank was worn out by being kept up at one lady's house or another until six every morning and named Lady Spencer and her daughter the duchess as two of his chief punters. This may have been in behalf of Lord Spencer, who is consistently named by Selwyn as a gambler at Brooks's till six in the morning (Historical Manuscripts Commission, *15th Report, Appendix Part VI, Vol. 42,* pp. 487, 497).

33. The Spencer journals from which these and many facts that follow are extrapolated are in the Spencer Collection at Chatsworth, Derbyshire; my thanks to Peter Day, keeper of collections, for providing me with copies for the relevant years.

34. Devonshire, *Georgiana,* p. 108.

35. Ibid., p. 111.

36. *Anglo-Saxon Review* 2 (1899):50.

37. Charles Bourchier (1739–1818), known as "Governor" Bourchier, had joined the East India Company as a writer in 1751 and was appointed governor of Madras in 1767, a post he held for three years. Boswell found him in 1781 a man of good sense and observation, therefore very entertaining (*Boswell's Life of Johnson,* 4:88, 489). For the Bourchier family, see "A Genealogical Memoir of a Branch of the Family of Bourchier," in *The Herald and Genealogist,* ed. J. G. Nichols (London: R. C. Nichols & J. B. Nichols, 1874), 8:367–76. His first wife had died in 1784; when he married Preedy he was forty-seven and his two sons were aged nine and six.

38. The correspondence between Spencer and her friends (chiefly Caroline Howe) is from the Althorp Papers, F60–62, and is quoted hereafter by date.

39. Spencer may have considered marrying again, to her devoted friend and correspondent Lord John Cavendish; in 1784 Elizabeth Montagu wrote to her sister: "Should they really marry, I do not believe they will long think they have acted wisely. . . . One woud not put on fetters without some good cause, liberty is so very agreable" (*Mrs. Montagu,* ed. Blunt, 2:178).

40. Frances Lowe and Phyllis Knight, Greville's two maids, the Duchess of Devonshire, and Elizabeth Preedy all suffered fits of hysteria.

41. Carroll Smith-Rosenberg, *Disorderly Conduct: Visions of Gender in Victorian America* (New York: Knopf, 1985), pp. 197–216.

42. Frances Lowe was faced with a burning house; Phyllis Knight's hysteria was the result of a fright of some kind, which no doubt also challenged her fortitude.

43. Spencer journal, 2014.161, Chatsworth.

44. Spencer journal, 2014.162. Spencer had thought of marriage as friendship and of companionship as dependency for the companion. She was therefore speaking of the transition of Preedy from dependent to friend, a transition authorized only by her marriage.

TWELVE. Friends: Molly Carter and Louisa Clarges

1. In 1805 Carter wrote Lady Spencer that her father's mother had made him sell his beautiful place in Wales in the vale of Clwydd, "to reside in flat low frightful Lincolnshire" (BL Althorp, F127, letter of January 24, 1805). She is misidentified in Walpole, *Correspondence,* 11:95 and 42:405. For the Carter family of Kinmel, Denbighshire, see *The Dictionary of Welsh Biography Down to 1940* (London: The Honourable Society of Cymmrodorion, 1959), Appendix, pp. 1113–14, and *Journals of the House of Commons,* April 18, 22, 26, and May 5, 12, 14, 1729. For information about the Carter family in Lincolnshire, I am indebted to Miss G. Moyes of the Lincolnshire Archives Office. See also Sedgwick, *History of Parliament;* 1:533, and *Mrs. Mary Carter's Letters* (London: Clayton and Co., n.d.) containing genealogical notes on the family by the editor "C.H.J.A." (probably Charlotte Johnston Anderson), copies of which are in the British Library and the Lincolnshire Archives Office. Scant attention to such unmarried women as Carter, who have proved of no effectual use to the patriarchy, is usual, but in her case, apart from her family's loyalty, the neglect was possibly punitive as well.

2. *Memoirs of Dr. Charles Burney, 1726–1769,* ed. Slava Klima, Garry Bowers, and Kerry S. Grant (Lincoln: University of Nebraska Press, 1988), p. 51, p. 52, nn. 8, 10.

3. Among the other puzzles about Carter's social standing is that I can discover no connection between her and her neighbor in Hill Street, Elizabeth Montagu.

4. For her will see PCC Prob. 11/1533.

5. BL Althorp, F127, letter of February 23, 1802.

6. Her father's will, PCC Prob. 11/733, recites that originally there was a £1,500 difference between the settlements of the elder and the younger daughters. When he wrote his will, someone had recently died and left the five younger daughters legacies which, he thought, might make up the difference.

7. PCC Prob. 11/929.

8. Carter's letters to Lady Spencer commenced in December 1793, after the two women had met abroad and were both still on the Continent, and are among the Althorp Papers, F 127. Spencer had apparently asked Carter for a memoir of Margaret Collier, who had retired to Ryde for economy's sake in about 1755. Margaret Collier's correspondence with Richardson is in *Correspondence of Samuel Richardson*, 2:59–112.

9. *Mrs. Mary Carter's Letters*, p. 20, recollects in August 1804 that it was twenty-six years since she had been near Cox Heath with Clarges. She is not mentioned by any commentators on that scene.

10. For him see Warren Hunting Smith, "Mr Skrine's Dinner Party," in *Originals Abroad* (New Haven: Yale University Press, 1952), pp. 3–9.

11. For Robert Carey Sumner, see *DNB*, 19:170.

12. See *Notes & Queries*, November 12, 1910, p. 389, which quotes the *Town and Country Magazine*, April 1770, p. 178. Leslie and Taylor, *Life and Times of Sir Joshua Reynolds*, 1:164, provide an advertisement placed by Fisher in the *Public Advertiser*, March 30, 1759, in the Johnsonian style, and suggest it was written by Sumner. It begins, "To err is a blemish entailed upon mortality, and indiscretions seldom or never escape from censure."

13. As Sumner noted in her will, spelling the surname Missenden. Louisa, daughter of William and Jane Missington, born June 6, was baptized July 5, 1760, at St. George's, Hanover Square.

14. PCC Prob. 11/922. "Mr. Screen" subscribed to *The Sermons of Mr. Yorick*. Arthur H. Cash notes that while on these travels Sterne unabashedly solicited subscriptions (*Laurence Sterne: The Later Years* [London: Methuen, 1986], p. 234).

15. Walpole, *Correspondence*, 22:402.

16. Charlotte Williams, the daughter of the Duke of Devonshire and the courtesan Charlotte Spencer, for instance, was married to a man of business about the Chatsworth estate. No attempt was made to elevate her through her marriage into the fashionable world; but Foster had also indicated very early that the child had no great qualifications for it. Clarges as a girl exhibited every qualification.

17. "Amateur Musicians," *London Chronicle*, January 13, 1787, p. 44.

18. See Burney, *Early Journals and Letters*, 1:148 and n. 18, and 249, n. 59. See also Burney, *Early Diary*, 1:116–17; 2:57. By the summer of 1777 Sir Thomas was not so shy that he had not attracted some attention.

19. On July 10, Mary Curzon announced that Sir George and Lady Warren were to part because she had taken so much to Sir Thomas Clarges, "they say

not so much out of vice as determin'd to do something to get rid of Sir George" (*Dear Miss Heber: An Eighteenth Century Correspondence*, ed. Francis Bamford [London: Constable, 1936], p. 8). Sir George Warren and Lady Warren had appeared in the ecclesiastical court to air their marital grievances in 1771–72 and then reconciled; Curzon's note sheds new light on the *Annual Register* verdict (1804) that after 1772 they "renewed their conjugal endearments and lived together" until the death of Sir George in 1801 (*Annual Register*, p. 68). The threatened entanglement may have persuaded Sir Thomas's guardians to marry him safely off, disregarding the disadvantages of the bride's heredity.

20. Unpublished journals of Lady Mary Coke; BL, Althorp Papers, F44, F125; Malcolm Elwin, *The Noels and the Milbankes* (London: Macdonald, 1967), p. 82.

21. The duchess wrote a continuing journal letter from Tunbridge to her mother; this and what follows is from Letter 217 in the Chatsworth MSS. I am indebted to Peter Day, keeper of collections at Chatsworth, for providing me with many copies. Lady Sefton was Isabella Stanhope, daughter of Lady Harrington; Mrs. Brudenell was Ann Legge, sister of Lord Dartmouth.

22. Louisa Clarges may have gone to London or elsewhere in preparation for the birth of her first child; I have not found the records of the christenings of any of her children.

23. Susan Burney described a visit to Streatham in 1779 when she sang and "Miss Thrale said I sung like *Lady Clarges*. . . . My father said Mr. Skrine thought our faces alike" (Burney, *Early Diary*, 2:258). Annie Raine Ellis (ibid., 1:57n.) says Sir Thomas married a lady beloved by Dr. Burney "as resembling his Susan (who was her dear friend) in person, voice, and musical taste and skill."

24. Susan Burney's 1780 journal in the BL, Egerton 3691, f. 127. Subsequent references to this journal will be by folio number in the text. Clarges was pregnant at this time.

25. Louisa Harris (1753–1826), an accomplished singer and an important member of London musical society, was the daughter of James Harris of Salisbury. Just before her death, in spring 1809, Clarges gave a drawing of the poet Cowper by either Thomas Lawrence or his sister to this lifelong friend (Douglas Goldring, *Regency Portrait Painter: The Life of Sir Thomas Lawrence, P.R.A.* [London: Macdonald, 1951], p. 103).

26. BL, Egerton 3700A, ff. 64–72.

27. Was Sir Thomas's standing for Lincoln of Carter's contrivance? The other representative for Lincoln, from 1774–84, was Robert Vyner of Gautby, her sister Eleanor's second husband, like Sir Thomas an independent Whig.

28. Elwin, *The Noels and the Milbankes*, p. 162; Historical Manuscripts Commission, *15th Report, Appendix, Part VI, Vol. 42*, p. 508.

29. Frances Burney wrote to Susan on February 3, 1781, "I am very glad you found Lady Clarges so comfortable" (Berg Collection, New York Public Library). Clarges was noticeably pregnant in April 1780 so it would seem that

she probably had two pregnancies within a short period, one of which miscarried. The child born was her eldest son, Thomas, later Sir Thomas.

30. Historical Manuscripts Commission, *15th Report, Appendix, Part VI*, *Vol. 42*, p. 480.

31. Ibid., p. 572.

32. J. W. Oliver, *The Life of William Beckford* (Oxford: Oxford University Press, 1937), p. 115.

33. Letter of July 20, 1782, Osborn File, 50.136, Beinecke Library, Yale University. That the Clargeses had intended to take Carter with them is somewhat confirmed by news sent on October 19, 1782, by Dorothea Gregory to Elizabeth Montagu from the Smelts in Langton, Yorkshire, when she was on her way northward to Edinburgh: they had heard Miss Carter was to go to Paris, "but none of the Company could give any account of why she was going or with whom" (Montagu Papers, Huntington Library). Everyone assumed that "Miss Carter" designated Elizabeth Carter, the famous bluestocking.

34. Burney, *Diary and Letters*, ed. Dobson, 2:151, 167.

35. PCC Prob. 11/1099.

36. Jerningham Collection, JE185, Huntington Library. I am grateful to the Huntington for permission to quote this letter in full. Mary Amelia Hill, wife of the seventh earl of Salisbury, was an important society figure who, to the disapproval of the bishops, had card parties on Sunday evening—Carter was apparently fond of cards. Lady Derby had been ostracized by many since the birth in 1779 of her daughter by the Duke of Dorset. Jerningham had lived with his mother in Grosvenor Square since the death of his father in 1774. He was contemplating a move after her death, which occurred in September 1785, after which his address was Green Street, Grosvenor Square.

37. Bettany, *Edward Jerningham*, p. 157. The writer was Marianne Dorothy Harland, daughter of Admiral Sir Robert Harland (*DNB*); see Bettany, pp. 145–62. She had a musical genius for all keyed instruments, played the German harp, and sang. She married William Dalrymple, brother of the Fifth Earl of Stair, and died in 1785 ("Amateur Musicians," *London Chronicle*, January 18, 1787, p. 59; February 1, 1787, p. 111).

38. According to Lillian Faderman, *Surpassing the Love of Men* (New York: William Morrow, 1981), pp. 17–20, the romantic friendship of the eighteenth century would probably have been the lesbianism of today but was often at that time not explicitly sexual. Though providing much useful information, her work seems biased through special pleading, constructed to identify the romantic friendships of eighteenth- and nineteenth-century women as essentially lesbian, in response to Elizabeth Mavor, *The Ladies of Llangollen* (London: Michael Joseph, 1971), who established the concept of romantic friendship as romantic love between women not sexually expressed, an argument constructed to relieve her subjects of the onus of the charge of lesbianism. Chodorow is useful on this point when she suggests that because of the essentially triadic nature of

their early relationships, women usually establish men as their sexual objects but maintain women as their emotional objects (*Reproduction of Mothering*, pp. 140, 193, 199). Delariviere Manley outlined the problem in her own terms in a speech by Astrea: "If only tender *Friendship*, inviolable and sincere, be the regard, what can be more meritorious? . . . But if they carry it a length beyond what *Nature* design'd, and fortifie themselves by these new-form'd *Amities* against the *Hymeneal Union*, or give their *Husbands* but a second place in their *affections* and *Cares*, 'tis wrong and to be blam'd" (Manley, *New Atalantis*, 2: 57–58, in Koster, 1: 589–90). In general in the eighteenth-century women's romantic friendship was highly valorized and judged as touchingly meritorious.

. 39. Faderman, *Surpassing the Love of Men*, p. 17.

40. PCC Prob. 11/1101.

41. Lady Louisa (1757–1841), like Clarges spirited, beautiful, and with an exquisite soprano voice, in addition a harpist, had been born to Lady Berkeley while she was married to her second husband, Robert Nugent, but Nugent disclaimed the child, nicknaming her "Chance." Through her mother, Lady Berkeley, Lady Louisa was also half-sister to Lady Craven. See also Walpole, *Correspondence*, 24:418, and Martin Sherlock, *Letters from an English Traveller* (London: J. Nichols et al., 1780; rpt. New York: Garland, 1971), pp. 120–23, wherein Sherlock aroused the national pride of his *GM* reviewer by his fulsome praises of Lady Louisa at seventeen (see *GM*, December 1779, p. 602; January 1780, p. 30). The second of these reviews quoted from Sherlock's *New Letters from an English Traveller*, noting Lady Louisa's "generosity and delicacy of sentiment in which you will distinguish her father and mother." These praises of her may have inspired Skrine's proud acknowledgment. Lady Louisa married Admiral Sir Eliab Hervey.

42. Photostats of manuscript journals, Lewis Walpole Library. Lady Mary assumed her sister remembered Lady Clarges but had to remind her she had seen Carter, probably often, at the weekly card parties of Lady Blandford (which Walpole also attended). Her implication is that a woman past childbearing age of no great fortune and no dynastic significance is of small importance except to fill in a card table. But she also seems unaware of any cloud attached to Carter.

43. Letter of January 27, 1784, Oliver, *Life of Beckford*, pp. 165–71.

44. Lady Craven had taken a house at Versailles. In March 1783 Lady Bristol wrote to her daughter Lady Elizabeth Foster, then in Paris, "You must have no intercourse there [with Lady Craven] at all. She is quite undone, and has not an atom of character left" (George Paston [Emily Morse Symonds], "Lady Craven," in *Little Memoirs of the Eighteenth Century* [New York: E. P. Dutton, 1901], pp. 143–44).

45. Guy Chapman, *Beckford* (New York: Charles Scribner's Sons, 1937), p. 327.

46. In his letters to Louisa Beckford (as well probably as in his own mind) Beckford was at this period fulsomely indulging a homoerotic strain; in the let-

ter draft quoted by Chapman (note 45 above), for instance, he describes the Duchess of Manchester's son, "a fair stripling who looks as if he had been naughty at Harrow."

47. Chapman, *Beckford*, p. 174.

48. Walpole, *Correspondence*, 42:407.

49. Carter apparently refers to a mechanism like that of the cuckoo clock.

50. Jerningham Collection, JE186, Huntington Library. The epistolary styles of Carter and Clarges are suggestively similar: Clarges in 1780 had written to Susan Burney, "Huzza huzza, I am so happy Pachierotti has arrived safe, sweet Creature!" And she is playful in a similar fashion: "I very imprudently told Sr Thos Dr Burney sent me his Love & he begs he will meet him in Hyde Park next Monday before it is light, he will take the Mayor of Lincoln for his second Dr Burney may choose his. I am very sorry for what I have done. pray pray forgive me" (BL, Egerton 3700A).

51. Piozzi, *Observations and Reflections Made in the Course of a Journey Through France, Italy, and Germany*, pp. 20–23.

52. *The Journal of Elizabeth Lady Holland*, ed. Earl of Ilchester, 2 vols. (London: Longmans, Green, 1908), 1:154; *The Early Married Life of Maria Josepha Lady Stanley*, ed. Jane Adeane (London: Longmans, Green, 1899), p. 40.

53. "Amateur Musicians," *London Chronicle*, January 13, 1787, p. 44, describes Lord Hampden as a flautist who knew a little of the fiddle and the tenor, no brilliant performer, but the owner of the best arranged private collection of music in the kingdom. The generally misogynistic Charles Pigott, in *The Female Jockey Club*, described Lady Hampden, subsequently a lifelong friend of Clarges, as an imbecile who entertained a host of "fiddlers, *sopranos*, and musicians of all descriptions," "a patroness of musical science" (pp. 153–67).

54. Wraxall, *Historical and Posthumous Memoirs*, 1:163–64.

55. BL Add. MSS 42,071, f. 2, quoted inaccurately in Brian Fothergill, *Sir William Hamilton, Envoy Extraordinary* (New York: Harcourt, Brace & World, 1969), p. 204. I am grateful to Elizabeth Brophy for checking this transcription for me. "Amateur Musicians," *London Chronicle*, February 1, 1787, p. 111, notes that Hamilton played the fiddle and the tenor and owned several curious old instruments from the best makers; in 1787 the violinist and composer Felice de Giardini was living with him.

56. Flora Fraser, *Emma, Lady Hamilton* (New York: Knopf, 1987), p. 54.

57. Letter of Charles Greville, May 5, 1785, *The Collection of Autograph Letters and Historical Documents Formed by Alfred Morrison (Second Series, 1882–1893)* (Privately printed, 1893), 3, 101. Quoted save for the last sentence by Fothergill, *Sir William Hamilton*, p. 209.

58. Chapman, *Beckford*, p. 235.

59. *The Letters of Edward Gibbon*, ed. J. E. Norton, 3 vols. (New York: Macmillan, 1956), 3:33.

60. "Diary of Sir Charles Blagden," ed. G. R. de Beers, *Notes and Records of*

the Royal Society 8 (1950): 77. Colonel Henri de Molin de Montagny had two houses at Ouchy, Ouchy and Petit-Ouchy, in which, respectively, the Duchess of Devonshire and her mother Lady Spencer were to live in 1792. The house, later also inhabited by Mme de Staël, was rechristened L'Elysée and was still standing in 1950.

61. *Mrs. Mary Carter's Letters*, p. 7.

62. Frances Crewe, "A Journal Kept at Paris from December 24th 1785 to March 10th 1786," BL Add. MSS 37926, ff. 25–26.

63. A note from Clarges to Walpole announcing that she is sending him his packet and has been happy to serve him is preserved with the ballad in the front of a copy of Nivernois's translation into French of Walpole's *Essay on Modern Gardening* in the Lewis Walpole Library.

64. Gibbon, *Letters*, 3:72. Gibbon wrote in French: "cette *jeune* et gentille personne Mademoiselle Carter."

65. Anthony Storer to William Eden, *The Journal and Correspondence of William, Lord Auckland*, ed. Bishop of Bath and Wells, 4 vols. (London: Richard Bentley, 1861–62), 1:464. Henry Hervey Aston, cousin of Clarges's Lausanne acquaintance Sir Willoughby Aston, as well as a cousin of Lady Elizabeth Foster's father, was an army officer given to adventurous incidents who died in a duel in 1798; see Walpole, *Correspondence*, 25:565–66; 33:482.

66. D. M. Low, *Edward Gibbon* (New York: Random House, 1937), p. 317; *The Jerningham Letters*, ed. Egerton Castle, 2 vols. (London: Richard Bentley, 1896), 2:67, 211; Walpole, *Correspondence*, 12:243, 252.

67. *GM*, June 1794, p. 582.

68. *Mrs. Mary Carter's Letters*, p. 15. Subsequent references to this work will be in the text by page number.

69. BL, Althorp Papers, F 127.

70. MS. Beckford, f. 4, in the Beckford Papers, Bodleian Library.

71. Burney, *Journals and Letters*, 5:387, and n. 6.

72. The Music Library of the British Library has no compositions by Lady Clarges but does own a manuscript "Sei canzoncine . . . per uso di Mi Lady Clarges," the work of Giuseppe Millico, transcribed for Clarges by Dr. Burney (Add. MSS 11,591), and a collection of anonymous operatic fragments in the hand of Dragonetti, including one, "Deliro—fremo" known to have belonged to Clarges (Add. MSS 17,830). R. J. Chesser of the Music Library was kind enough to provide this information.

73. *GM*, January 1806, p. 93.

74. *GM*, May 1807, p. 493.

75. For him see John Burke and John Bernard Burke, *A Genealogical and Heraldic History of the Extinct and Dormant Baronetcies of England, Ireland, and Scotland*, 2d ed. (London, 1841; rpt. London and Baltimore: Burke's Peerage/ Genealogical Publishing Co., 1985).

76. *GM*, August 1809, p. 788; PCC Prob. 11/1501.

77. E. W. Ainley Walker, *Skrine of Warleigh* (Taunton: Wessex Press, 1936),

p. 103, states that William Skrine was also the father of Elizabeth Ann Wilson, an error repeated in subsequent publications. She was the natural daughter and the heiress of Crayle Crayle, Esq. (d. 1780), who had married William Skrine's sister Elizabeth; William Skrine acted as one of her guardians. Her marriage settlement, D/39/28 in the Buckinghamshire Record Office, elucidates the family situation. In 1781 she married Charles Loraine Smith. Clarges left £400 to him, £200 to her.

78. Elizabeth, Lady Holland, *Journal*, 16, 1:59.

79. Brian Connell, *Portrait of a Whig Peer* (London: Andre Deutsch, 1957), p. 288.

80. Walpole, *Correspondence*, 42:405–7.

81. Letter in the Osborn File, 48.15, Beinecke Library, Yale University, and in the collection of John Comyn, Esq.

82. For this information I am grateful to Karen Reader and Michael Page of the Surrey Record Office. The plan of Petersham churchyard is no longer among the church records, but the new ground was purchased and opened in 1802, and, as Michael Page notes, if a grid system was employed, as seems likely, the two plots lay very close together if not side by side.

THIRTEEN. Reformers: Sarah Scott and Barbara Montagu

1. Todd, *Women's Friendship in Literature*, p. 358.

2. Walter Marion Crittenden, *The Life and Writings of Mrs. Sarah Scott, Novelist* (Philadelphia: University of Pennsylvania Press, 1932), p. 17.

3. Letter in the Lewis Walpole Library, Farmington, Conn. For William Freind, see *DNB*, 7:685–86.

4. Scott, *Description of Millenium Hall*, pp. 148–49.

5. *Letters of Mrs. Elizabeth Montagu*, 1:7.

6. *Elizabeth Montagu*, ed. Climenson, 1:121.

7. The IGI reveals the record of her baptism; her birthday was September 21, so presumably she was born on that day in 1720. Her sister Elizabeth was christened on October 13, 1718, and her birthday was apparently October 2 in that year. The absence of a meaningful parental presence is indicated by Sarah's confusion about her birth date. In September 1750 she wrote to Elizabeth to ask, "Pray tell me how old I am this month, for I have wish'd myself younger till I believe I have persuaded my self out of my age." She had no one but Elizabeth to ask, and Elizabeth apparently subtracted two years from both their ages. The letters of Sarah Scott to her sister Elizabeth Montagu are in the Huntington Library, San Marino, among the Montagu Papers. I refer to her letters by date and opening words and am grateful to Mary L. Robertson, curator of manuscripts at the Huntington Library, for providing me copies and for permission to quote from them.

8. IGI.

9. Williamina-Dorothy Cheselden (ca. 1716–63) was the daughter of the noted surgeon William Cheselden; she married Charles Cotes, M.D. (ca. 1703–48), former Fellow of All-Souls College, Oxford, and member of Parliament for Tamsworth, 1735–47, of the Cotes family of Woodcote, Salop, and was left a widow and childless on his death on March 21, 1748 (see John Nichols, *Literary Anecdotes of the Eighteenth Century*, 6 vols. [London: Nichols, Son, and Bentley, 1812–16], 4:622–24; Sedgwick, *History of Parliament*). Climenson, in *Elizabeth Montagu* (1:95) mistakenly identifies Mrs. Cotes as sister of Henry, Viscount Irvine. Mrs. Cotes was as much in need of a proper companion with whom to travel as Sarah Robinson was of a patroness; on August 10, 1750, Montagu wrote Scott from Tunbridge that she was sorry poor Mrs. Cotes had such a strange girl with her; she had made herself the jest of the place and it was not creditable to appear with such a person.

10. Letter of October 1743 in the W. S. Lewis Walpole Library, Farmington, Conn.

11. In a letter to Montagu of October 1765, after Lady Bab's death, Scott noted that her friend had palpitations "to a most extraordinary degree." One of her remedies was musk: the *OED* cites a 1471 prescription of musk in hot wine "if his herte quake."

12. Walpole, *Correspondence*, 10:169.

13. Sarah Byng Osborn, providing news of the Montagu daughters in October 1750, noted, "Lady Bab at Bath: her Miss Robinson's Mr. Scott is made Preceptor to Prince George" (*Letters of Sarah Byng Osborn*, p. 70).

14. *DNB*, 17:961.

15. BL, Egerton, 3691, f. 60. There were other Mr. Scotts, but George Lewis may be indicated here. "Frib" generally meant a frivolous, trivial person, but it could have a secondary meaning of effeminate: "Fribble. An effeminate fop; a name borrowed from a celebrated character of that kind, in the farce of Miss in her Teens, written by Mr. Garrick" (*1811 Dictionary of the Vulgar Tongue* [Northfield, Ill.: Digest Books, 1971]). Susan Burney may have been speaking from some knowledge about Scott.

16. *Correspondence of Edward Young*, p. 358.

17. The letter of August 20, 1748 begins, "Dear Sister, we left Ladbury last Wednesday," *Elizabeth Montagu*, ed. Climenson, 1:280. It is interesting that both Montagu and the duchess seem to consider it proper that Sarah should obey her elder married sister.

18. As a test of reason in control of sensibility; Ann Radcliffe uses the same test of Emily in *The Mysteries of Udolpho* (Oxford: Oxford University Press, 1970).

19. The family's story was that the Jacobite Lord Bolingbroke had forwarded the nomination unknown to George Scott. The truth probably was that James Cresset, secretary and favorite to the Princess of Wales, secured the appointment; he was now married to Scott's cousin and intimate connection, Anne Robinson Knight.

20. Sir Thomas Robinson, brother of Anne Robinson Cresset and Grace

NOTES TO PAGES 303-307

Robinson Freind, had from 1742 to 1747 been governor of Barbados, where he quarreled with the assembly about his salary and did extensive building for which ultimately he himself had to pay; he was recalled in 1747 (see *DNB*, 17: 49–50). Two addresses in Robinson's defense from His Majesty's Council at Barbados, one to the king, one to Robinson, are recorded in the *GM*, December 1747, pp. 557–58, but his "words of thanks" to his subjects are not. Once again Scott employs curiously sexual language. In regard to Scott's settlement, her father did eventually give her £1,000.

21. The importance of protecting George Scott's reputation is illustrated by the size of the income provided him by the Crown till his death; the £100 a year promised his wife might be viewed as her share for collusive silence. When his appointment as tutor to the prince ended in 1755, George Scott was granted a pension of £500 a year, which ceased in February 1758, when he was appointed a commissioner of the excise at £1,000 a year—the prince "thinking derogatory to his dignity, to suffer a person to remain unprovided for, who once had the honour of being concerned in his education" (Lewis Namier, *The Structure of Politics at the Accession of George III*, 2 vols. [London: Macmillan, 1957], 2:539, n. 1).

22. Delany, *Autobiography*, 3:115.

23. Ellis, in Burney, *Early Diary*, 1:53n. For the reference to Bishop Hayter, see n. 34.

24. Lady Frances Williams in 1742 separated from Charles Hanbury Williams and Lady Diana Bolingbroke in 1765 separated from Lord Bolingbroke on these grounds.

25. Her husband fared considerably better. After his death in 1780 Christie and Answell disposed of his effects at auction in his house "on the North Side of Leicester Square": household furniture, a "capital Library of Books, consisting of the valuable and scarce Works of the most esteemed Authors in fine Preservation," and the lease of another house in Charlotte Street (*DA*, February 3, 1781). His wife was not mentioned in his will.

26. They had probably known each other for some time. Miss Cutts, Dr. Cotes, Mrs. Anne Robinson Knight, and "Miss Sally Robinson" (as well as Miss Chudleigh) subscribed to Fielding's *Familiar Letters Between the Principal Characters in David Simple* in 1747. But Fielding's move to Bath occurred after she tried the waters in early summer of 1754 and found they agreed with her; she was settled in Bath with improved health in December 1756 (Richardson, *Correspondence*, 2:68–70, 101). At about this time Fielding and Margaret Collier may have made a joint decision not to take positions as governesses again: in November 1755 feelers were put out in vain hopes Fielding would accept such a position (ibid., 4:109) and Margaret Collier moved to Ryde, where she could live independently on a pittance.

27. For these projects see T. C. Duncan Eaves and Ben D. Kimpel, *Samuel Richardson: A Biography* (Oxford: Clarendon Press, 1971), pp. 462–65, 698–700, 702–3.

28. Elizabeth Cutts was long a member of the Bath community and was fairly

well-known to society. She was probably the sister of Mordecai Cutts, Esq., of Thorne, Yorkshire, a subscriber to some of the community members' publications. In April 1765 she briefly (and improbably) attracted the flirtatious attentions of Laurence Sterne (Cash, *Laurence Sterne*, p. 207), and she subscribed to his sermons. In 1775 she published verses, *Almeria: or Parental Advice: A Didactic Poem. Addressed to the Daughters of Great Britain and Ireland, By a Friend to the Sex*, to benefit "two worthy people." Cash, p. 207, identifies her as Scott's companion, which after the death of Barbara Montagu she sometimes was (as was Miss Arnold), though only in a fully egalitarian sense.

29. Miss Arnold is connected in a Fielding subscription list (1762) to a Mr. Arnold of Wells, probably Christopher Arnold, Esq. (1757). William Adams, Esq. and Mrs. Adams subscribed (1757, 1762). For copies of Fielding's subscription lists, I am grateful to Carolyn Woodward.

30. Margaret Piggott Riggs (ca. 1714–88) was the widow of Edward Riggs; their daughter Anna (1741–81), later Lady Miller of Batheaston vase fame, grew up among the Bath community women; Scott mentioned her having smallpox as a child. In 1775 Walpole described Riggs as "an old rough humourist who passed for a wit" (*Correspondence*, 39:240–41). Margaret Mary Ravaud, her longtime friend and companion, was also a friend and correspondent of Delany, who referred to her as "my niece." Dr. Richard Pococke visited "Mrs. Ravoe" in 1754 in their newly built "very good" house, "highly finish'd," the side of the hill to the road improved in "beautiful lawn, walks, garden, cascades, a piece of water and a stream running thro' the garden" (*Travels*, 2:33). Elizabeth Carter, visiting them in June 1759, found them "very agreeable people" in "one of the most enchanting spots I ever beheld" (*Letters from Mrs. Elizabeth Carter*, 1:48).

31. Nina Auerbach, *Communities of Women: An Idea in Fiction* (Cambridge, Mass.: Harvard University Press, 1978), p. 3.

32. Their ideas about molding society were fully expressed in *A Description of Millenium Hall*.

33. Todd, *Women's Friendship in Literature*, p. 344.

34. The upheavals resulted from a struggle for power between the prince's governor and preceptor (Lord Harcourt and Bishop Hayter, who got most of the stipends) and his subgovernor and subpreceptor (Andrew Stone and Scott, who did most of the work). Cresset supported Stone and Scott. Hayter probably used the story of Scott's having poisoned his wife at this juncture. For details see John Brooke, *King George III* (New York: McGraw-Hill, 1972), pp. 35–43; Walpole, *Correspondence*, 20:203, 323, 342. Though also accused of Jacobitism, Scott remained in place as subpreceptor until 1755; and he was never disgraced.

35. *Letters of Mrs. Elizabeth Montagu*, 3:335–37.

36. Ibid., 4:17.

37. Eaves and Kimpel, *Samuel Richardson*, pp. 463–64.

38. Scott's nine known works are listed in Crittenden's preface to *A Description of Millenium Hall*, pp. 21–22. In her letters she mentions work on at least one not in this known list.

39. Todd, *Sensibility*, pp. 27, 89, 96.

40. *The History of Gustavus Erickson, King of Sweden* by "Henry Augustus Raymond, Esq." (1761); *The History of Mecklenburgh*—from which the new queen came—(1762); *A Description of Millenium Hall* (1762).

41. Crittenden seems to suggest some peculiarity of temperament as the explanation for Scott's frequent moves. They are far more likely to have been the result of the ever-present requirement for economy and the location most beneficial to the health of one or the other of the women. Moves were frequent enough to make the whereabouts in Bath of the two sometimes unclear. Barbara Montagu had taken a house in Beaufort Square and owned the lease at her death, but the house was rented. Lady Frances Williams had found the pair in Bath in lodgings in December 1760, Lady Bab too ill and depressed to see her (Letter to Montagu of November 19, 1760, in W. S. Lewis Walpole Library, Farmington, Conn.).

42. For Halifax's generous pension, see Namier, *Structure of Politics*, 2:539ff. For Montagu's, see *Calendar of Home Office Papers of the Reign of George III, 1760–[1775] Preserved in Her Majesty's Public Record Office*, 4 vols. (London: Longman, 1878–99), 1763, 1:374. It may be unnecessary here to point out the disparity between the sums deemed necessary for men and for women at the same social level; see also note 25: George Scott allowed his wife £100 from an income of £500, and presumably also from an income of £1,000.

43. Crittenden's calculations in his preface to *A Description of Millenium Hall*, pp. 20–21.

44. This story, that of Lady Mary Jones, pp. 132–53, has no obvious connections with Lady Bab, but Lady Bab's mother was named Mary and her mother had the surname Jones; the name seems to constitute a matrilineal naming.

45. Scott made her position clear, however obliquely. In *The History of Sir George Ellison*, 1:18–19, her exemplary hero has married a widow with a Jamaica plantation and "perhaps few have more severely lamented their being themselves enslaved by marriage, than he did his being thus become the enslaver of others."

46. Margaret Collier had made it clear to Richardson (*Correspondence*, 2:62) that although Sarah Fielding disapproved of "corporeal severities" for schoolchildren, and even though her book *The Governess* (1749), ostensibly for children, contained "many a sly hint" for their governesses, she avoided this sensitive issue in her book because "there is no occasion that she should teach the children so punished that their punishment is wrong." Collier was reviewing the proofs of Fielding's book for Richardson, who had wished to enter some proscription against corporeal severity. This was a delicate issue, involving, ultimately, patriarchal prerogative, and physical abuse of both women and children was on the list of unbroachable subjects. The women apparently feared that a direct attack on corporeal punishment might discredit other more acceptable pedagogical reforms.

47. Some evidence that *Millenium Hall* had a practical influence exists: Eliza-

beth Montagu reported in 1783 that her friends the Cholmleys at Househam, Yorkshire, had "built a village very near their house, and fitted up and furnished the houses with all the decent comforts humble life requires, and these habitations are bestowed on their old or married servants who are obliged to retire. The children of the latter are taught to read, write, cast accounts, sew, knit, spin, etc., at a school established by Mr. Cholmley, and well regulated and frequently inspected by Mrs. Cholmley" (Historical Manuscripts Commission, *Calendar of the Manuscripts of the Marquis of Bath*, 1:349).

48. Here is an early example of a naive attitude shared by the proponents of the American and French Revolutions; see, for instance, William Godwin's *Enquiry Concerning Political Justice* (1793).

49. PCC Prob. 11/913/15.

50. Scott, *History of Sir George Ellison*, 1:24. Subsequent references to this work will be by volume and page number in the text. Matthew Gregory ("Monk") Lewis, author of *The Monk*, was in 1816 to establish similar reforms on his plantations in Jamaica: he abolished harsh punishments, decreased the labor, and increased the comforts and holidays of his slaves.

51. Ellison's moderate enlightenment continues in England, where against all custom, his "house contained also many children of inferior rank; his servants had intermarried, the blacks with blacks, the white servants with those of their own colour: for though he promoted their marrying, he did not wish an union between those of different complexions, the connection appearing indelicate and almost unnatural" (2:48). Once again it is not clear whether Scott was inditing her own opinion or modulating it to forestall destructive negative criticism.

52. *Letters from Mrs. Elizabeth Carter*, 1:371; on November 25, 1767, Carter noted, Mrs. Scott had as her companion Sarah Fielding, who was dying. The implication is that they lived together.

53. Fielding died on April 9, 1768, as Scott's community was establishing itself at Hitcham; she was buried at Charlcombe, near Bath.

54. *Mrs. Montagu*, ed. Blunt, 1:175. Dr. Bartholomew Dominiceti had petitioned in 1767 for a patent for his "method of making the arbitrarily heated and medicated baths, pumps, and stoves, both moist and dry, and a variety of fumigations from herbs, seeds, &c., and an infinite variety of machines for applying the above to the human body." (See *Calendar of Home Office Papers*, 1766–69, 2:268.) Formerly a bankrupted druggist and apothecary at Bristol (*DA*, May 24, 1762), Domeniceti became famous for his baths at Chelsea.

55. *Letters from Mrs. Elizabeth Carter*, 2:16–17.

56. PCC Prob 11/1046.

CONCLUSION

1. William Godwin, *Memoirs of the Author of A Vindication of the Rights of Woman*, ed. Gina Luria (New York: Garland Publishing Inc., 1974), p. 25.

2. *Collected Letters of Mary Wollstonecraft*, ed. Ralph M. Wardle (Ithaca: Cornell University Press, 1979), p. 74.

3. Godwin, *Memoirs*, p. 26.

4. The *OED* shows a definition of tyranny that in Chaucer's time, following Greek authority, already connoted absolute sovereignty, but had no invariable moral connotation: thus Creon heals the city of Thebes with his tyranny (or inescapable decrees). It came gradually to have its modern meaning; Hobbes, no libertarian, in 1651 noted "From Aristotle's civil philosophy, they have learned, to call all manner of common-wealths but the popular . . . tyranny."

5. Though beyond the scope of this book to develop, two points about the recrudescence of interest in altruism may perhaps be briefly noted here. If some efficient insect societies have armies of different kinds of aggressors to defend the group and to feed it, and cadres of caregivers to administer to those armies, possibly humans have utilized the same model—though this theory about altruism is not presently in credit. Theoreticians about altruism today—psychologists, philosophers, and most notably educators—often attribute the explosion of work on the subject to the traumas of the second world war, during which, in a climate of a frenzied murderous aggression, some people inexplicably risked and gave their lives to save others upon whom they might safely have turned their backs. They fail to note that the explosion of interest in the subject really occurred after the commencement of the modern women's movement. An equally probable occasion for concern about altruism was that the women's movement of the 1960s signaled the end of women's unconscious acceptance of their assigned roles. A second effect of the threatened defalcation of women from their traditional assignment is the emerging insistence that men become more caring. For extensive bibliographies of recent discussions about altruism, only as examples, see those in J. Philippe Rushton and Richard M. Sorrentino, eds., *Altruism and Helping Behavior: Social, Personality, and Developmental Perspectives* (Hillsdale, N.J.: Lawrence Erlbaum Associates, 1981); Carolyn Zahn-Waxler, E. Mark Cummings, Ronald Ionnotti, eds., *Altruism and Aggression: Biological and Social Origins* (Cambridge: Cambridge University Press, 1986); Samuel P. Oliner and Pearl M. Oliner, *The Altruistic Personality* (New York: The Free Press, 1988).

Bibliography

Manuscript Sources

Henry W. and Albert A. Berg Collection, New York Public Library, Astor, Lenox, and Tilden Foundations, New York. By permission.
> "Hubert de Vere." Manuscript tragedy by Frances Burney.
> Letters of Frances Burney to Dr. Charles Burney, June 20, 1780, December 27, 1790.
> Letter of Frances Burney to Susan Burney, February 3, 1781.
> Letter of Frances Burney to Susan Burney, December 14, 1781.
> Letter of Frances Burney to Hester Thrale, August 17, 1781.
> Letters of Dorothea Gregory (Alison) to Frances Burney.
> Letter of Maria Allen Rishton to Frances Burney, January 1, 1775.
> Letter of Hester Thrale to Frances Burney, Summer 1783.
> Letter of Elizabeth Vesey to Frances Burney, 1783.
> Manuscript journals and letters of Frances Burney.
> "The Siege of Pevensey." Manuscript tragedy by Frances Burney.
> "The Triumphant Toadeater." Manuscript play, probably by Capt. Ralph Broome, 1798.

Bodleian Library, Oxford University, Oxford, England. By permission of the Keeper of Western Manuscripts.
> Letters of Sarah Anne Parr to William Godwin, Dep c512, c513, b227/2 (with permission of Lord Abinger).
> MS Beckford, f. 4. Aria from Sacchini copied by Louisa Clarges.

British Library, London. By permission of the British Library Board.
> Add. MSS 11591. "Sei canzoncine . . . per uso di Mi Lady Clarges" by Millico, transcribed by Dr. Charles Burney.
> Add. MSS 17830. Operatic fragment transcribed by Dragonetti for Lady Clarges.
> Add. MSS 37926, ff. 25–26. Frances Crewe, "A Journal Kept at Paris from December 24th 1785 to March 10th 1786."
> Add. MSS 42071, f. 2. Letter of Sir William Hamilton to Charles Greville, February 22, 1785.
> Add. MSS 51414, ff. 1, 71–71v, 83v–84, 85, 87, 89, 90v–91, 132–33, 175–76. Letters of Caroline and Henry Fox, Holland House Papers.

Add. MSS 51415, f. 17. Letter of Caroline to Henry Fox, Holland House Papers.

Add. MSS 51424, ff. 1, 3–4, 9–12v. Holland House Papers.

Add. MSS 51427, ff. 43–44v. Holland House Papers.

Add. MSS 51428, ff. 1–2. Holland House Papers.

Add. MSS 51452, ff. 72–76. Holland House Papers.

Althorp Papers. The correspondence of Georgiana, Countess of Spencer. F43–44, F49–63, F104, F124–25, F127.

Barrett Collection. Letter of Frances Burney to Hester Thrale, July 1781.

Egerton 3691. Susan Burney's extant 1780 journal.

Egerton 3700A, ff. 64–72. Letters of Lady Clarges to Susan Burney.

Buckinghamshire Record Office, Aylesbury, Bucks.

D/39/28. Marriage settlement of Elizabeth Ann Wilson.

Devonshire Collections, Chatsworth, Derbyshire. By permission of the Duke of Devonshire and the Trustees of the Chatsworth Settlement. Devonshire MSS, Chatsworth, 1st series

Spencer Collection, 2014.141–2014.162. Journals of Georgiana Spencer, Countess Spencer.

Letter 217. Georgiana, Duchess of Devonshire to Lady Spencer.

Hertfordshire County Record Office, Hertford, Herts.

D/EP T2341-7. Fleet-Cathcart deeds for Tewin Water.

Houghton Library, Harvard University, Cambridge, Massachusetts. By permission of the Houghton Library.

Letter of Elizabeth Montagu, May 1749.

Huntington Library, San Marino, California. By permission.

Jerningham Collection

JE185–186. Letters of Mary Carter to Edward Jerningham.

Montagu Collection

Letters of Dorothea Gregory to Elizabeth Montagu, 1782–83.

Letters of Elizabeth Montagu to Sarah Scott.

Letters of Sarah Scott to Elizabeth Montagu, 1747–53 and October 1765.

Letters of Elizabeth Vesey to Elizabeth Montagu.

Irish Registry of Deeds, Dublin.

218226. Memorial of Maguire-Cathcart deed of December 10, 1778.

Manuscript Division, Library of Congress, Washington, D.C.
Manuscript Division, James Madison Papers, Reel 7.
Letter of Stephen Sayre to James Madison, March 10, 1802.

National Archives, Four Courts, Dublin.
Betham's Genealogical Abstracts made from Irish Wills.

Osborn File, Beinecke Library, Yale University, New Haven, Connecticut. By permission of Yale University Library.
Letter of James Beattie to James Gregory, June 1790, 3.125.
Letters of Dr. Charles Burney to Mary Carter, December 29, 1811 and January 4, 1812, 46.61.
Letters of Dr. Charles Burney to Frances Crewe, October 1807 and January 1808, 46.75, 46.76.
Journal letter of Charles Burney, D.D., to Charlotte, Susan, and Frances Burney, June 28–August 6, 1780, 47.67.
Letter of Charles Burney, D.D., to Frances Burney, November 1781, 47.5.
Letters of Charles Burney, D.D., to and from Lord Findlater, 1781, 47.77/50.129.
Letter of Frances Burney to Dorothea Gregory Alison, January 1790, 45.23.
Letter of Mary Carter to Dr. Charles Burney, 1808, 48.15.
Seven letters of Elizabeth Chudleigh to Bell Chudleigh from Russia, undated, 7.313.
Letter of Gaspar Pacchierotti to Frances Burney, July 1782, 50.136.
Letters of Hester Thrale to Dr. Charles Burney, undated [1780], 51.27.

Public Record Office, London.
Prerogative Court of Chancery wills.

Lewis Walpole Library, Yale University, Farmington, Connecticut. By permission of Yale University Library.
Photostatic copies of unpublished journals of Lady Mary Coke.
MISC. MSS. Letter of Dr. William Freind to Elizabeth Montagu, 1741.
MISC. MSS. Letter of Elizabeth Montagu to Dr. John Gregory, undated.
MISC. MSS. Letter of Sarah Robinson to Elizabeth Montagu, 1743.
Charles Hanbury Williams Correspondence, CHW 48-10914, f. 76; 52-10902, ff. 89–90; 10846, pp. 77–80.
Letter of Lady Frances Williams to Elizabeth Montagu, November 19, 1760.

PRIVATE COLLECTIONS

From a family collection in the possession of John Comyn, Esq. By permission.
Letter of Mary Carter to Dr. Charles Burney, undated.

Douglas and Angus Estates, Scotland. By permission.
  Unpublished journals of Lady Mary Coke.

In the possession of Mary, Duchess of Roxburghe. By permission.
  Manuscript unfinished novel of Frances Greville.
  Notebook of poems by Frances Greville.

Holkham Estate Office, Wells-Next-the-Sea, Norfolk. By permission.
  Holkham transcripts of Lady Mary Coke's journals.

Primary Works

Astell, Mary. *Some Reflections upon Marriage.* London: John Nutt, 1700.
Auckland, William, First Baron. *The Journal and Correspondence of William, Lord Auckland.* Edited by the Bishop of Bath and Wells. 4 vols. London: Richard Bentley, 1861–62.
Austen, Jane. *Emma.* Edited by R. W. Chapman. London: Oxford University Press, 1966.
——. *Northanger Abbey.* Edited by R. W. Chapman. London: Oxford University Press, 1972.
An Authentic Detail of Particulars Relative to the Late Duchess of Kingston. London: G. Kearsley, 1788.
Les aventures trop amoureuses ou Elisabeth Chudleigh Ex-Duchesse Douairiere de Kingston, aujourd'hui Comtesse de Bristol et la Marquise de la Touche sur la scene du monde. London, 1776.
Baddeley, Sophia. *See* Steele, Elizabeth.
Blagden, Sir Charles. "Diary of Sir Charles Blagden." Edited by G. R. de Beers. *Notes and Records of the Royal Society* 8 (1950): 65ff.
Boscawen, Frances. *Admiral's Wife.* Edited by Cecil Aspinall-Oglander. London: Longmans, Green, 1940.
Boswell, James. *Boswell's Life of Johnson.* Edited by G. B. Hill and L. F. Powell. 6 vols. Oxford: Clarendon Press, 1950.
Bunbury, Lady Sarah. *The Life and Letters of Lady Sarah Lennox.* Edited by the Countess of Ilchester and Lord Stavordale. 2 vols. London: John Murray, 1901.
Burney, Dr. Charles. *A General History of Music, from the Earliest Ages to the Present Period.* 4 vols. London, 1776–89. Reprint. New York: Dover, 1957.
——. *The Letters of Dr. Charles Burney.* Vol. 1, 1751–84. Edited by Alvaro Ribeiro, S.J. Oxford: Clarendon Press, 1991.
——. *Memoirs of Dr. Charles Burney, 1726–1769.* Edited from Autograph fragments by Slava Klima, Garry Bowers, and Kerry S. Grant. Lincoln: University of Nebraska Press, 1988.
Burney, Frances. *Camilla; or, A Picture of Youth.* Edited by Edward A. Bloom and Lillian D. Bloom. Oxford: Oxford University Press, 1983.

———. *Cecilia; or Memoirs of an Heiress.* Edited by Peter Sabor and Margaret Anne Doody. Oxford: Oxford University Press, 1988.

———. *Diary and Letters of Madame d'Arblay.* Edited by Charlotte Barrett. 7 vols. London, 1842–46.

———. *Diary and Letters of Madame d'Arblay.* Edited by Austin Dobson. 6 vols. London: Macmillan, 1904–5.

———. *The Early Diary of Frances Burney, 1768–1778.* Edited by Annie Raine Ellis. 2 vols. London: George Bell and Sons, 1907.

———. *The Early Journals and Letters of Fanny Burney.* Edited by Lars E. Troide. Vols. 1–2. Oxford: Clarendon Press, 1988–90.

———. *Evelina; or the History of a Young Lady's Entrance into the World.* New York: Norton, 1965.

———. *The Journals and Letters of Fanny Burney (Madame d'Arblay), 1791–1840.* Edited by Joyce Hemlow et al. 12 vols. Oxford: Clarendon Press, 1972–84.

———. *Memoirs of Doctor Burney, Arranged from His Own Manuscripts, from Family Papers, and from Personal Recollections, by His Daughter, Madame d'Arblay.* 3 vols. London: Edward Moxon, 1832.

———. *The Wanderer; or, Female Difficulties.* London: Pandora, 1988.

Carter, Elizabeth. *Letters from Mrs. Elizabeth Carter, to Mrs. Montagu, Between the Years 1755 and 1800.* 3 vols. London: F. C. & J. Rivington, 1817.

———. *A Series of Letters Between Mrs. Elizabeth Carter and Mrs. Catherine Talbot, from the Year 1741 to 1770. To Which Are Added, Letters from Mrs. Elizabeth Carter to Mrs. Vesey, Between the Years 1763 and 1787.* 3d ed. 3 vols. London: F. C. & J. Rivington, 1819.

Carter, Mary. *Mrs. Mary Carter's Letters.* Edited by C.H.J.A. London: Clayton and Co., n.d.

Casanova, Jacques, de Seingalt. *The Memoirs of Casanova.* Translated by Arthur Machen. 6 vols. New York: G. P. Putnam's Sons, and London: Elek Books, n.d.

The Case of the Duchess of Kingston. London: J. Wheble, 1775.

Cavendish, Elizabeth Foster, Duchess of Devonshire. *Anecdotes and Biographical Sketches.* London, 1863.

Cavendish, Georgiana Spencer, Duchess of Devonshire. *Georgiana.* Edited by the Earl of Bessborough. London: John Murray, 1955.

———. "Selections from the Letters of Georgiana Duchess of Devonshire." Edited by Louise Fredericke Auguste Von Alten, Duchess of Devonshire. *Anglo-Saxon Review* 1 (June 1899): 225–42; 2 (September 1899): 21–89.

———. *The Sylph.* 2 vols. London: T. Lowndes, 1799.

Chalmers, A., ed. *British Essayists*, Vol. 26. London, 1802.

Chapone, Hester. *The Works of Mrs. Chapone.* 4 vols. in 2. New York: Evert Duyckinck, 1818.

Character of the Present Most Celebrated Courtezans. Interspersed with a Variety of Secret Anecdotes Never Before Published. London: M. James, 1780.

Chesterfield, Philip Dormer Stanhope, Fourth Earl. *The Letters of Philip Dormer*

Stanhope, 4th Earl of Chesterfield. Edited by Bonamy Dobree. 6 vols. London: Eyre and Spottiswoode, 1932.

Coke, Lady Jane. *Letters from Lady Jane Coke to Her Friend Mrs. Eyre at Derby, edited with notes, by Mrs. Ambrose Rathborne.* London: Swan Sonnenschein, 1899.

Coke, Lady Mary. *The Letters and Journals of Lady Mary Coke.* 4 vols. Edinburgh: D. Douglas, 1889–96.

The Collection of Autograph Letters and Historical Documents Formed by Alfred Morrison (Second Series, 1882–1893). 3 vols. Privately printed, 1882–93.

Collier, Jane. *An Essay on the Art of Ingeniously Tormenting, with Proper Rules for the Exercise of that Pleasant Art. Humbly Addressed in the First Part, to the Master, Husband, &c.; in the Second Part, to the Wife, Friend, &c. With some General Instructions for Plaguing All Your Acquaintance.* London: A. Millar, 1753. [Numerous subsequent editions].

The Court and City Register for the Year 1756. London: J. Barnes et al., [1756].

Coventry, Francis. *The History of Pompey the Little.* New York: Garland, 1974.

Cowper, Anthony Ashley, Third Earl of Shaftesbury. *Characteristics of Men, Manners, Opinions, Times,* treatise 4, "An Inquiry Concerning Virtue or Merit," book 2, part 1, section 3. [Numerous editions].

Cumberland, Richard. *The Observer: Being a Collection of Moral, Literary, and Familiar Essays.* 5 vols. London: C. Dilly, 1786–90.

[Cutts, Elizabeth]. *Almeria: or Parental Advice: A Didactic Poem. Addressed to the Daughters of Great Britain and Ireland, by a Friend to the Sex.* London: E. and J. Rodwell, 1775.

Dear Miss Heber: An Eighteenth Century Correspondence. Edited by Francis Bamford. London: Constable, 1936.

Delany, Mary. *The Autobiography and Correspondence of Mary Granville, Mrs. Delany: With Interesting Reminiscences of King George the Third and Queen Charlotte.* Edited by Lady Llanover. 6 vols. London: Richard Bentley, 1861–62.

Dunton, John. *The Life and Errors of John Dunton, Citizen of London; With the Lives and Characters of More Than a Thousand Contemporary Divines, and Other Persons of Literary Eminence . . .* 2 vols. London: J. Nichols, Son, and Bentley, 1818.

Edgeworth, Maria. *Castle Rackrent.* New York: Century, 1904.

Field, William. *Memoirs of Dr. Parr.* 2 vols. London, 1828.

Fielding, Sarah. *The Adventures of David Simple.* Edited by Malcolm Kelsall. London: Oxford University Press, 1969.

——. *The Cry, a New Dramatic Fable.* London: R. and J. Dodsley, 1754.

——. *Familiar Letters Between the Principal Characters in David Simple.* 2 vols. London: A. Millar, 1747.

——. *The Governess: or, Little Female Academy.* London: Richardson, 1749.

——. *The History of the Countess of Dellwyn. Two Volumes. By the Author of David Simple.* London: A. Millar, 1759.

Fitzgerald, Emily, Countess of Kildare and (1760) Duchess of Leinster. *Correspondence of Emily, Duchess of Leinster.* Edited by Brian Fitzgerald. 3 vols. Dublin: Stationery Office, 1949.

Foote, Samuel. *A Trip to Calais; A Comedy in Three Acts. As Originally Written, and Intended for Presentation, by the Late Samuel Foote, Esq. To Which is Annexed, The Capuchin; As it is Performed at the Theatre-Royal in the Haymarket. Altered from the Trip to Calais by the Late Samuel Foote, Esq. and Now Published by Mr. Colman.* London: T. Cadell, 1778.

Gibbon, Edward. *The Letters of Edward Gibbon.* Edited by J. E. Norton. 3 vols. New York: Macmillan, 1956.

Godwin, William. *An Enquiry Concerning Political Justice, and Its Influence on General Virtue and Happiness.* 2 vols. London: G. G. J. and J. Robinson, 1793.

——. *Memoirs of the Author of A Vindication of the Rights of Woman.* Edited by Gina Luria. New York: Garland Publishing Inc., 1974.

Godwin, William, and Mary Wollstonecraft. *Godwin and Mary, Letters of William Godwin and Mary Wollstonecraft.* Edited by Ralph M. Wardle. Lawrence: University of Kansas Press, 1966.

The Goodwood Estate Archives. Edited by Francis W. Steer, J. E. Amanda Venables, and Timothy J. McCann. 3 vols. Chichester: West Sussex County Council, 1972–84.

Gregory, John. *A Father's Legacy to His Daughters.* London: W. Strahan, 1774. [Numerous subsequent editions].

——. *A Father's Legacy to His Daughters . . . with the Author's Life. To Which Is Added, Mr. Tyrold's Advice to His Daughter . . . from the Novel of "Camilla." By Mrs. D'Arblay. . . .* Poughnill: G. Nicholson, 1809.

Greville, Fulke. *Maxims, Characters, and Reflections, Critical, Satyrical, and Moral.* London: J. and R. Tonson, 1756.

Griffith, Elizabeth. *Essays, Addressed to Young Married Women.* London: T. Cadell and J. Robson, 1782.

Hamilton, Mary. *Mary Hamilton.* Edited by Elizabeth Anson and Florence Anson. London: J. Murray, 1925.

Harris, James. *Hermes: or, A Philosophical Inquiry Concerning Language and Universal Grammar.* London: Nourse, Vaillant, et al., 1751.

Historical Manuscripts Commission. *Calendar of the Manuscripts of the Marquis of Bath.* London: His Majesty's Stationery Office, 1904.

——. *15th Report, Appendix Part VI, Vol. 42, The Manuscripts of the Earl of Carlisle.* London: Her Majesty's Stationery Office, 1897.

Holland, Elizabeth, Baroness. *The Journal of Elizabeth Lady Holland.* Edited by the Earl of Ilchester. 2 vols. London: Longmans, Green, 1908.

Intimate Society Letters of the Eighteenth Century. Edited by the Duke of Argyll. 2 vols. London: Stanley Paul & Co., 1910.

The Jerningham Letters. Edited by Egerton Castle. 2 vols. London: Richard Bentley, 1896.

Johnson, Samuel. *The Letters of Samuel Johnson with Mrs. Thrale's Genuine Let-*

ters to Him. Edited by R. W. Chapman. 3 vols. Oxford: Clarendon Press, 1952.

Journals of the House of Commons, 1729.

Knight, Cornelia, and Thomas Raikes. *Personal Reminiscences by Cornelia Knight and Thomas Raikes.* Edited by Richard Henry Stoddard. New York: Scribner, Armstrong, 1875.

A List of the Colonels. . . . London: Thomas Cox, 1740.

Lyttelton, George, First Baron Lyttelton. *Dialogues of the Dead.* London: W. Sandby, 1760.

Manley, Delariviere. *The Novels of Mary Delariviere Manley.* Edited by Patricia Koster. 2 vols. Gainesville, Fla.: Scholars' Facsimiles and Reprints, 1971.

———. *The Power of Love: In Seven Novels.* London: John Barber and John Morphew, 1720.

Montagu, Elizabeth. *Elizabeth Montagu, the Queen of the Blue-Stockings.* Edited by Emily J. Climenson. 2 vols. London: John Murray, 1906.

———. *The Letters of Mrs. Elizabeth Montagu.* Edited by Matthew Montagu. 4 vols. London: T. Cadell and W. Davies, 1809–13.

———. *Mrs. Montagu, "Queen of the Blues": Her Letters and Friendships from 1762 to 1800.* Edited by Reginald Blunt. 2 vols. London: Constable, 1923.

More, Hannah. *See* Roberts, William.

Mortimer, Thomas. *The Universal Director; or, The Nobleman and Gentleman's True Guide. . . .* London: J. Coote, 1763.

Murphy, Arthur. *Know Your Own Mind: A Comedy, Perform'd at the Theatre-Royal, in Covent-Garden.* London: T. Becket, 1778.

A New Atalantis for the Year One Thousand Seven Hundred and Fifty-eight, 2d ed. London: M. Thrush, 1758.

Oberkirch, Henrietta Louise Von Waldner, Baronne d'. *Memoirs of the Baroness d'Oberkirch, Written by Herself.* Edited by the Count de Montbrison. 3 vols. London: Colbourn & Co., 1851.

Opie, Amelia. *Adeline Mowbray; or, The Mother and Daughter.* London: Pandora, 1986.

Osborn, Sarah Byng. *Letters of Sarah Byng Osborn, 1721–1773.* Edited by John McClelland. Stanford: Stanford University Press, 1930.

Penrose, John. *Letters from Bath, 1766–1767, by the Rev. John Penrose.* Edited by Brigitte Mitchell and Hubert Penrose. Gloucester: Alan Sutton, 1983.

The Picture Gallery, Containing Near Two Hundred Paintings by the Most Distinguished Ladies in Great Britain. London: G. Kearsley, 1780.

Pigott, Charles. *The Female Jockey Club, or a Sketch of the Manners of the Age.* 7th ed. London: D. I. Eaton, 1794.

———. *The Whig Club.* London: B. Crosby, 1794.

Piozzi, Hester Lynch Thrale. *See* Thrale, Hester.

Pococke, Richard, D.D. *The Travels Through England of Dr. Richard Pococke.* Edited by James Joel Cartwright. 2 vols. London: Camden Society, 1888.

Radcliffe, Ann. *The Mysteries of Udolpho.* Oxford: Oxford University Press, 1970.

Richardson, Samuel. *The Correspondence of Samuel Richardson.* Edited by Anna Letitia Barbauld. 6 vols. London: Richard Phillips, 1804–6.

Roberts, William. *Memoirs of the Life and Correspondence of Mrs. Hannah More.* 2 vols. New York: Harper & Brothers, 1851.

Scott, Sarah. *A Description of Millenium Hall.* Edited by Walter M. Crittenden. New York: Bookman Associates, 1955.

————. *History of Cornelia.* London: A. Millar, 1750.

————. *The History of Gustavus Erickson, King of Sweden.* By Henry Augustus Raymond, Esq. London: A. Millar, 1761.

————. *The History of Mecklenburgh.* London: J. Newbery, 1762.

————. *The History of Sir George Ellison.* 2 vols. London: A. Millar, 1766.

————. *A Journey Through Every Stage of Life. By a Person of Quality.* 2 vols. London: A. Millar, 1754.

Sherlock, Martin. *Letters from an English Traveller.* London: J. Nichols et al., 1780. Reprint. New York: Garland, 1971.

————. *New Letters from an English Traveller.* London: J. Nichols et al., 1781.

Smith, Charlotte. *The Old Manor House.* London: Pandora, 1987.

"Sophia." *Woman Not Inferior to Man: or, A Short and Modest Vindication of the Natural Rights of the Fair-Sex to a Perfect Equality of Power, Dignity, and Esteem, with the Men.* London: John Hawkins, 1739.

————. *Women's Superior Excellence over Man: or, A Reply to the Author of a Late Treatise, Entitled Men Superior to Women.* London, 1740.

Stanley, Maria Josepha, Baroness. *The Early Married Life of Maria Josepha Lady Stanley.* Edited by Jane Adeane. London: Longmans, Green, 1899.

Steele, Elizabeth. *The Memoirs of Mrs. Sophia Baddeley, Late of Drury Lane Theatre. By Mrs. Elizabeth Steele.* 6 vols. Clerkenwell: For the Author at the Literary Press, 1787.

Sterne, Laurence. *Letters of Laurence Sterne.* Edited by Lewis Perry Curtis. Oxford: Clarendon Press, 1935.

————. *The Life and Opinions of Tristram Shandy, Gentleman.* Edited by Melvyn New and Joan New. 3 vols. Gainesville: University Presses of Florida, [1978] c. 1984.

Stuart, Lady Louisa. *Lady Louisa Stuart: Selections from Her Manuscripts.* Edited by Hon. James Home. New York: Harper & Brothers, 1899.

————. *Memoire of Frances, Lady Douglas.* Edited by Jill Rubenstein. Edinburgh: Scottish Academic Press, 1985.

Surr, T. S. *A Winter in London.* 3 vols. London: Richard Phillips, 1806.

Thrale, Hester (later Piozzi). "Journal of Her Tour in Wales." In *Doctor Johnson and Mrs. Thrale,* edited by A. M. Broadley, pp. 158–219. London: John Lane, 1910.

————. *Observations and Reflections Made in the Course of a Journey Through France, Italy, and Germany.* Edited by Herbert Barrows. Ann Arbor: University of Michigan Press, 1967.

———. *The Piozzi Letters*. Edited by Edward A. Bloom and Lillian D. Bloom. Vol. 2, 1792–98. Newark: University of Delaware Press, 1991.

———. *Thraliana: The Diary of Mrs. Hester Lynch Thrale (Later Mrs. Piozzi) 1770–1809*. Edited by Katherine C. Balderston. 2 vols. Oxford: Clarendon Press, 1942.

The Trial of Elizabeth Duchess Dowager of Kingston for Bigamy, Before the Right Honourable The House of Peers, in Westminster-Hall, in Full Parliament. London: Charles Bathurst, 1776.

Walpole, Horace. *The Yale Edition of Horace Walpole's Correspondence*. Edited by W. S. Lewis. 48 vols. New Haven: Yale University Press, 1937–83.

Whitehead, Thomas. *Original Anecdotes of the Late Duke of Kingston and Miss Chudleigh*. London: S. Bladon, 1792.

Wilkinson, Tate. *The Wandering Patentee*. 4 vols. York: For the Author, 1795.

Wollstonecraft, Mary. *Collected Letters of Mary Wollstonecraft*. Edited by Ralph M. Wardle. Ithaca: Cornell University Press, 1979.

———. *A Vindication of the Rights of Woman*. 2d ed. Edited by Carol H. Poston. New York: Norton, 1988. *See also* Godwin, William.

Woodhouse, James. *The Life and Poetical Works of James Woodhouse*. Edited by R. I. Woodhouse. 2 vols. London: Leadenhall Press, 1896.

Wraxall, Sir Nathaniel William. *The Historical and the Posthumous Memoirs of Sir Nathaniel William Wraxall*. Edited by Henry B. Wheatley. 5 vols. New York: Scribner and Welford, 1884.

Young, Edward. *The Correspondence of Edward Young, 1683–1765*. Edited by Henry Pettit. Oxford: Clarendon Press, 1971.

Secondary Works

Alden, John R. *Stephen Sayre, American Revolutionary Adventurer*. Baton Rouge: Louisiana State University Press, 1983.

Alison, Sir Archibald. *Some Account of My Life and Writings*. 2 vols. Edinburgh: W. Blackwood and Sons, 1883.

Alumni Oxonienses, The Members of the University of Oxford, 1715–1866. Edited by Joseph Foster. 4 vols. in 2. London, 1888. Reprint. Nendeln/Liechtenstein: Krause Reprint, 1968.

"Amateur Musicians." *London Chronicle*, January 13, 18, February 1, 1787.

Annual Register, 1804.

Armstrong, Nancy. *Desire and Domestic Fiction: A Political History of the Novel*. New York: Oxford University Press, 1987.

Auerbach, Nina. *Communities of Women: An Idea in Fiction*. Cambridge, Mass.: Harvard University Press, 1978.

Bath Chronicle, June 4, 1778.

Battestin, Martin, with Ruthe R. Battestin. *Henry Fielding: A Life*. London: Routledge, 1989.

Belden, Mary Megie. *The Dramatic Work of Samuel Foote*. New Haven: Yale University Press, 1929.

Bence-Jones, Mark. *Burke's Guide to Country Houses*. Vol. 1, *Ireland*. London: Burke's Peerage, 1978.

Benson, Robert. *Memoirs of the Life and Writings of the Rev. Arthur Collier*. London: Edward Lumley, 1837.

Bettany, Lewis. *Edward Jerningham and His Friends*. New York: Brentano's, 1919.

Blunt, Reginald. "The Sylph." *Edinburgh Review* 242 (October 1925): 364–79.

Boaden, James. *Memoirs of Mrs. Siddons. Interspersed with Anecdotes of Authors and Actors*. 2 vols. London: H. Colburn, 1827.

Bonfield, Lloyd. *Marriage Settlements, 1601–1740: The Adoption of the Strict Settlement*. Cambridge: Cambridge University Press, 1983.

British Magazine and Review; or Universal Miscellany, August 1782.

Brooke, John. *King George III*. New York: McGraw-Hill, 1972.

Brophy, Elizabeth Bergen. *Women's Lives and the 18th-Century English Novel*. Tampa: University of South Florida Press, 1991.

Brown, Beatrice Curtis. *Elizabeth Chudleigh, Duchess of Kingston*. London: Gerald Howe, 1927.

Brown, Stephen. "A Letter from Edward Young to Caroline Lee Haviland: Some Biographical Implications." *Philological Quarterly* 68 (Spring 1989): 263–71.

Browne, Alice. *The Eighteenth-Century Feminist Mind*. Detroit: Wayne State University Press, 1987.

Burford, E. J. *Wits, Wenchers and Wantons*. London: Robert Hale, 1986.

Burke, John, and John Bernard Burke. *A Genealogical and Heraldic History of the Extinct and Dormant Baronetcies of England, Ireland, and Scotland*. 2d ed. London, 1841. Reprint. London: Burke's Peerage/Genealogical Publishing Co., 1985.

Calder-Marshall, Arthur. *The Two Duchesses*. London: Hutchinson, 1978.

Calendar of Home Office Papers of the Reign of George III, 1760–[1775] Preserved in Her Majesty's Public Record Office. Edited by Joseph Redington (Vols. 1–2), Richard Arthur Roberts (Vols. 3–4). London: Longman, 1878–99.

Cash, Arthur H. *Laurence Sterne: The Later Years*. London: Methuen, 1986.

Chancellor, E. Beresford. "Elizabeth Chudleigh, Duchess of Kingston." *English Review* 41 (December 1925): 812–21.

Chapman, Guy. *Beckford*. New York: Charles Scribner's Sons, 1937.

Chodorow, Nancy. *The Reproduction of Mothering*. Berkeley: University of California Press, 1978.

Connell, Brian. *Portrait of a Whig Peer*. London: Andre Deutsch, 1957.

Cosslett, Tess. *Woman to Woman: Female Friendship in Victorian Literature*. Atlantic Highlands, N.J.: Humanities Press, 1988.

Cotton, Albert Louis. "Elizabeth Chudleigh." *Gentleman's Magazine*, January 1903, pp. 20–35.

Critical Review, June 1787.

Crittenden, Walter Marion. *The Life and Writings of Mrs. Sarah Scott, Novelist.* Philadelphia: University of Pennsylvania Press, 1932.

Cross, Wilbur L. *The History of Henry Fielding.* 3 vols. New Haven: Yale University Press, 1918.

Cussans, John Edward. *History of Hertfordshire.* 8 vols. in 3. London: Chatto and Windus, 1870–81.

Cutting, Rose Marie. "Defiant Women: The Growth of Feminism in Fanny Burney's Novels." *SEL* 17 (1977): 519–30.

Daily Advertiser, 1730–1808.

Davidoff, Leonore, and Catherine Hall. *Family Fortunes: Men and Women of the English Middle Class, 1780–1850.* Chicago: University of Chicago Press, 1987.

Davis, Rose Mary. *The Good Lord Lyttelton.* Bethlehem, Pa.: Times Publishing Co., 1939.

Derry, Warren. *Dr. Parr: A Portrait of the Whig Dr. Johnson.* Oxford: Clarendon Press, 1966.

The Dictionary of Welsh Biography Down to 1940. London: The Honourable Society of Cymmrodorion, 1959.

Dobson, Austin. *Henry Fielding: A Memoir.* New York: Dodd, Mead, 1900.

Doody, Margaret Anne. *Frances Burney: The Life in the Works.* New Brunswick: Rutgers University Press, 1988.

Dudden, F. Homes. *Henry Fielding: His Life, Works, and Times.* 2 vols. Hamden, Conn.: Archon, 1966.

Dunbar, Howard H. *The Dramatic Career of Arthur Murphy.* New York: Modern Language Association, 1946.

Durkheim, Emile. *Moral Education: A Study in the Theory and Application of the Sociology of Education.* New York: Free Press of Glencoe, 1961.

Eagleton, Terry. *Criticism and Ideology: A Study in Marxist Literary Theory.* London: Verso, 1976.

Eaves, T. C. Duncan, and Ben D. Kimpel. *Samuel Richardson: A Biography.* Oxford: Clarendon Press, 1971.

1811 Dictionary of the Vulgar Tongue. Northfield, Ill.: Digest Books, 1971.

Elwin, Malcolm. *The Noels and the Milbankes.* London: Macdonald, 1967.

Emery, John Pike. *Arthur Murphy.* Philadelphia: University of Pennsylvania Press, 1946.

English, Barbara, and John Saville. *Strict Settlement: A Guide for Historians.* Hull: University of Hull, 1983.

Epley, Steven. "Public Voices in Four Women Writers of the 1790's." Ph.D. dissertation, Columbia University, 1992.

Epstein, Julia. *The Iron Pen: Frances Burney and the Politics of Women's Writing.* Madison: University of Wisconsin Press, 1989.

Faderman, Lillian. *Surpassing the Love of Men.* New York: William Morrow, 1981.

Feder, Lillian. "Selfhood, Language, and Reality: George Orwell's *Nineteen Eighty-Four.*" *Georgia Review* 37 (Summer 1983): 392–409.

Ferguson, Moira, ed. *First Feminists: British Women Writers, 1578–1799.* Bloomington: Indiana University Press, 1985.

Ford, Edward. *Tewin-Water, or The Story of Lady Cathcart; Being a Supplement to the "History of Enfield."* Enfield: Privately printed, 1876; copy in BL.

Forward, Susan, and Joan Torres. *Men Who Hate Women and the Women Who Love Them.* Toronto: Bantam, 1986.

Foster, Vere. *The Two Duchesses.* London: Blackie & Son, 1898.

Fothergill, Brian. *Sir William Hamilton, Envoy Extraordinary.* New York: Harcourt, Brace & World, 1969.

Foucault, Michel. *The History of Sexuality,* Vol. 1. New York: Pantheon Books, 1978.

Fraser, Flora. *Emma, Lady Hamilton.* New York: Knopf, 1987.

Freud, Anna. *The Ego and the Mechanisms of Defense: The Writings of Anna Freud.* 2d ed. rev., Vol. 2, trans. Cecil Baines. New York: International Universities Press, 1974.

Fyvie, John. *Comedy Queens of the Georgian Era.* London: Constable, 1906.

"A Genealogical Memoir of a Branch of the Family of Bourchier." In *The Herald and Genealogist,* edited by J. G. Nichols, 8: 362–76. London: R. C. Nichols & J. B. Nichols, 1874.

Gentleman's Magazine, 1731–1914.

Ghiselin, M. T. *The Economy of Nature and the Evolution of Sex.* Berkeley: University of California Press, 1974.

Gilligan, Carol. *In a Different Voice: Psychological Theory and Women's Development.* Cambridge, Mass.: Harvard University Press, 1982.

Gilligan, Carol, Janie Victoria Ward, Jill McLean Taylor, with Betty Bardige, eds. *Mapping the Moral Domain: A Contribution of Women's Thinking to Psychological Theory and Education.* Cambridge, Mass.: Harvard University Press, 1988.

Gillis, John R. *For Better, for Worse: British Marriages, 1600 to the Present.* New York: Oxford University Press, 1985.

Goldring, Douglas. *Regency Portrait Painter: The Life of Sir Thomas Lawrence, P.R.A.* London: Macdonald, 1951.

Graves, Algernon, and William Vine Cronin. *A History of the Works of Sir Joshua Reynolds, P.R.A.* 4 vols. London: H. Graves, 1899–1901.

Habakkuk, H. J. "Marriage Settlements in the Eighteenth Century." *Transactions of the Royal Historical Society* 4th ser., 32 (1950): 15–30.

Hardy, W. J. "Lady Cathcart and Her Husbands." *St. Albans and Herts Architectural and Archaeological Society Transactions* n.s. 1 (1898): 119–28.

Hemlow, Joyce. *The History of Fanny Burney.* Oxford: Clarendon Press, 1958.

Hertfordshire County Records, Calendars to the Sessions Books, 1752–1799. Edited by William Le Hardy. Vol. 8. Hertford: Elton Longmore, 1935.

Highfill, Philip H., Jr., Kalman A. Burnim, and Edward Langhans. *A Biographical Dictionary of Actors, Actresses, Musicians, Dancers, Managers, and Other*

Stage Personnel in London, 1660–1800. 14 vols. to date. Carbondale: Southern Illinois University Press, 1973–.

Hornbeak, Katherine G. "New Light on Mrs. Montagu." In *The Age of Johnson: Essays Presented to Chauncey Brewster Tinker.* Pp. 349–61. New Haven: Yale University Press, 1949.

Hughes, W. R. "The Dowager." *Blackwood's Magazine* 234 (July–December 1933): 119–27.

Hunter, J. Paul. "Novels and History and Northrop Frye." *Eighteenth-Century Studies* 24 (Winter 1990–91): 225–41.

Inglis-Jones, Elisabeth. *The Great Maria: A Portrait of Maria Edgeworth.* London: Faber and Faber, 1959.

Janeway, Elizabeth. *Powers of the Weak.* New York: Knopf, 1980.

Jesse, John Heneage, ed. *George Selwyn and His Contemporaries; with Memoirs and Notes.* 4 vols. New York: Scribner, 1882.

Larson, Edith Sedgwick. "A Measure of Power: The Personal Charity of Elizabeth Montagu." In *Studies in Eighteenth-Century Culture,* edited by O. M. Brack, Jr., 16: 197–210. Madison: University of Wisconsin Press, 1986.

Leslie, Charles Robert, and Tom Taylor. *Life and Times of Sir Joshua Reynolds.* 2 vols. London: John Murray, 1865.

Liechtenstein, Princess Marie. *Holland House.* 2 vols. London: Macmillan. 1874.

The Life and Memoirs of Elizabeth Chudleigh, Afterwards Mrs. Hervey and Countess of Bristol, Commonly Called Duchess of Kingston. Written from Authentic Information and Original Documents. London: R. Randall, [1788].

The Life and Memoirs of Elizabeth Chudleigh, Afterwards Mrs. Hervey and Countess of Bristol, Commonly Called Duchess of Kingston. Dublin: H. Chamberlaine et al., 1789.

Lodge, John. *The Peerage of Ireland.* Revised by Mervyn Archdall. 7 vols. Dublin: James Moore, 1789.

London Times, February 16, 1818.

Lonsdale, Roger, ed. *Eighteenth-Century Women Poets: An Oxford Anthology.* Oxford: Oxford University Press, 1989.

Low, D. M. *Edward Gibbon.* New York: Random House, 1937.

McCarthy, William. *Hester Thrale Piozzi: Portrait of a Literary Woman.* Chapel Hill: University of North Carolina Press, 1985.

McCormack, W. J. *Ascendancy and Tradition in Anglo-Irish Literary History from 1789 to 1939.* Oxford: Clarendon Press, 1985.

Maguire, Thomas. *Fermanagh: Its Native Chiefs and Clans.* Omagh: S. D. Montgomery, 1954.

Masters, Brian. *Georgiana, Duchess of Devonshire.* London: Hamish Hamilton, 1981.

Mavor, Elizabeth. *The Ladies of Llangollen.* London: Michael Joseph, 1971.

———. *The Virgin Mistress.* London: Chatto and Windus, 1964.

Meyersohn, Marylea. "Jane Austen's Garrulous Speakers." In *Reading and*

Writing Women's Lives: A Study of the Novel of Manners, edited by Bege K. Bowers and Barbara Brothers, pp. 35–47. Ann Arbor: UMI Research Press, 1990.

———. "The Uses of Conversation: Rationality and Discourse in Jane Austen." Ph.D. dissertation, Columbia University, 1985.

Mill, John Stuart. *The Subjection of Women*. Edited by Susan Moller Okin. Indianapolis: Hackett, 1988.

Monthly Magazine, July 1, 1821.

Monthly Review, 1749–1844.

Myers, Steven. "Elizabeth Steele." In *A Dictionary of British and American Women Writers, 1660–1800*, edited by Janet Todd, pp. 296–97. Totowa, N.J.: Rowman & Allanheld, 1985.

Namier, Lewis. *The Structure of Politics at the Accession of George III*. 2 vols. London: Macmillan, 1957.

Nichols, John. *Illustrations of the Literary History of the Eighteenth Century*. 8 vols. London: For the author, by Nichols, son, and Bentley, 1817–58.

———. *Literary Anecdotes of the Eighteenth Century*. 6 vols. London: Nichols, son, and Bentley, 1812–16.

Oliver, J[ohn] W[alter]. *The Life of William Beckford*. Oxford: Oxford University Press, [1937].

Paston, George. *See* [Symonds, Emily Morse].

Pearce, Charles E. *The Amazing Duchess*. 2 vols. London: Stanley Paul, 1911.

The Penroses of Fledborough Parish. Edited by A. B. Baldwin. Hull: A. Brown & Sons, 1933.

Perry, Ruth. *The Celebrated Mary Astell, an Early English Feminist*. Chicago: University of Chicago Press, 1986.

Poovey, Mary. *The Proper Lady and the Woman Writer*. Chicago: University of Chicago Press, 1984.

Public Advertiser, March 30, 1759, April 30, 1763, December 22, 1779.

Rizzo, Betty. " 'Depressa Resurgam': Elizabeth Griffith's Playwriting Career." In *Curtain Calls*, edited by Mary Anne Schofield and Cecilia Macheski, pp. 120–42. Athens: Ohio University Press, 1990.

———. " 'The High Road to Eminence': A New Letter from Charles Burney in Norfolk." *Notes & Queries* 231 (March 1986): 61–63.

———. "The Patron as Poet Maker: The Politics of Benefaction." In *Studies in Eighteenth-Century Culture*, edited by Leslie Ellen Brown and Patricia B. Craddock, 20: 241–66. East Lansing, Mich.: Colleagues Press, 1990.

Rushton, J. Philippe. "The Altruistic Personality." In *Altruism and Helping Behavior: Social, Personality, and Developmental Perspectives*, edited by J. Philippe Rushton and Richard M. Sorrentino, pp. 251–66. Hillsdale, N.J.: Lawrence Erlbaum Associates, 1981.

St. Clair, William. *The Godwins and the Shelleys: A Biography of a Family*. Baltimore: Johns Hopkins University Press, 1989.

St. James's Chronicle, May 21, 1763.

Schofield, Mary Anne. *Masking and Unmasking the Female Mind: Disguising Romances in Feminine Fiction, 1713–1799*. Newark: University of Delaware Press; London: Associated University Presses, 1990.

Sedgwick, Romney. *The History of Parliament: The House of Commons, 1715–1754*. 2 vols. New York: Oxford University Press, 1970.

Showalter, Elaine. *A Literature of Their Own*. Princeton: Princeton University Press, 1977.

Smith, Warren Hunting. *Originals Abroad*. New Haven: Yale University Press, 1952.

Smith-Rosenberg, Carroll. *Disorderly Conduct: Visions of Gender in Victorian America*. New York: Knopf, 1985.

Spacks, Patricia Meyer. *Imagining a Self: Autobiography and the Novel in Eighteenth-Century England*. Cambridge, Mass.: Harvard University Press, 1976.

Spector, Robert Donald. *Arthur Murphy*. Boston: Twayne, 1979.

Spencer, Jane. *The Rise of the Woman Novelist*. Oxford: Basil Blackwell, 1986.

Staves, Susan. *Married Women's Separate Property in England, 1660–1883*. Cambridge, Mass.: Harvard University Press, 1990.

————. "Pin Money." In *Studies in Eighteenth-Century Culture*, edited by O. M. Brack, Jr., 14: 47–77. Madison: University of Wisconsin Press, 1985.

Stone, George Winchester, Jr., ed. *The London Stage, 1660–1800*. Part 4, 1747–76. 3 vols. Carbondale: Southern Illinois University Press, 1962.

Stone, Lawrence. *The Family, Sex and Marriage in England, 1500–1800*. New York: Harper & Row, 1977.

Straub, Kristina. *Divided Fictions: Fanny Burney and Feminine Strategy*. Lexington: University Press of Kentucky, 1987.

Stuart, Dorothy Margaret. *Dearest Bess*. London: Methuen, 1955.

[Symonds, Emily Morse]. *Little Memoirs of the Eighteenth Century*. New York: E. P. Dutton, 1901.

Thaddeus, Janice. "Mary Delany, Model to an Age." In *History, Gender, and Eighteenth-Century Literature*, edited by Beth Fowkes Tobin. Athens: University of Georgia Press, forthcoming.

Todd, Janet. *Sensibility: An Introduction*. London: Methuen, 1986.

————. *Women's Friendship in Literature*. New York: Columbia University Press, 1980.

————, ed. *British Women Writers: A Critical Reference Guide*. New York: Continuum, 1989.

————, ed. *A Dictionary of British and American Women Writers, 1660–1800*. Totowa, N.J.: Rowman & Allanheld, 1985.

Town and Country Magazine, April 1770; May, June 1772; May 1775; March 1777.

Trefman, Simon. *Sam. Foote, Comedian.* New York: New York University Press, 1971.

Trilling, Lionel. "Introduction." In Jane Austen, *Emma.* Boston: Riverside, 1957.

Trumbach, Randolph. *The Rise of the Egalitarian Family: Aristocratic Kinship and Domestic Relations in Eighteenth-Century England.* New York: Academic Press, 1978.

Vicars, Arthur, ed. *Index to the Prerogative Wills of Ireland, 1536–1810.* Dublin: E. Ponsonby, 1897. Reprint. Baltimore: Genealogical Publishing Co., 1989.

Vulliamy, C[olwyn] E[dward]. *Aspasia, The Life and Letters of Mary Granville, Mrs. Delany (1700–1788).* London: Geoffrey Bles, 1935.

Walker, E. W. Ainley. *Skrine of Warleigh.* Taunton: Wessex Press, 1936.

Walker, Ralph S. "Charles Burney's Theft of Books at Cambridge." *Transactions of the Cambridge Bibliographical Society* 3 (1962): 313–26.

———. "Charles Burney's Tour in the North-East of Scotland, 1780." Edited by Ralph S. Walker. *Aberdeen University Review* 45 (Spring 1973): 1–19.

Wardroper, John. *Kings, Lords and Wicked Libellers.* London: John Murray, 1973.

The Wentworth Papers, 1705–1739. Edited by James J. Cartwright. London: Wyman and Sons, 1883.

Werkmeister, Lucyle. "Notes for a Revised Life of William Jackson." *Notes & Queries* 206 (1960): 62–82; 207 (1961): 16–54, 126–62.

Wilson, Henry. *Wonderful Characters.* New York: Henry Bill, 1848.

Woodward, Carolyn. "'Feminine Virtue, Ladylike Disguise, Women of Community': Sarah Fielding and the Female I Am at Mid-Century." *Transactions of the Samuel Johnson Society of the Northwest* 15 (1984): 57–71.

———. "Promoting 'This Little Book': Women Novelists and Their Male Mentors in Mid-Century Britain." Paper presented at conference of American Society for Eighteenth-Century Studies, Minneapolis, 1990.

Annotated Index

Holroyd, John Baker,(*cont'd*)
1735–1821 (statesman), 287
Home, Countess of. *See* Ramey, Abigail
Horner, Elizabeth Strangways, 1723–92
(m. [1736] Stephen Fox, Baron [1741]
and Earl of Ilchester [1756]), 10, 54
Horton, Mary, fl. 1745–46 (?Lady
Cathcart's companion), 179–83, 360
(n. 26)
Howard, Frederick, 5th Earl of Carlisle
(1758), 1748–1825, 373 (n. 29)
Howe, Caroline, ca. 1721–1814 (m. [1742]
John Howe of Hanslope, Bucks.):
reports to Lady Spencer, 35, 139, 235,
260–61, 273; letters from Lady
Spencer, 260–64
Hughes, Antinetta, fl. 1740s (mother of
Elizabeth), 200
Hughes, Elizabeth, 1741–87 (companion
and bawd to Sophia Baddeley; m. ——
— Steele), 22, 199–217 passim, 315, 324,
365 (nn. 23, 24), 366 (n. 35); *The
Memoirs of Mrs. Sophia Baddeley*
(1787), 201
Hughes, John, fl. 1720–40 (the king's
slater; father of Elizabeth), 200
Hume, David, 1711–76 (philosopher;
historian): *Enquiry Concerning the
Principles of Morals* (1740), 19, 310
Hunter, J. Paul, 336 (n. 19)
Hunter, William, M.D., 1718–83
(physician), 212
Huntingdon, Earl of. *See* Hastings,
Francis
Hurd, Dr. Richard, 1720–1808 (bishop of
Worcester [1781]; bishop of Lichfield
[1774]), 138
Hussey, Edward (in 1749 Hussey-
Montagu), Baron Beaulieu (1762), Earl
of Beaulieu (1784), 1720–1802, 176, 178
Hysterics. *See* Women: and hysterics

Identification with the aggressor, 19, 22,
80, 95, 324
Ilchester, Countess of. *See* Horner,
Elizabeth Strangways

Ilchester, Earl of. *See* Fox Strangways,
Stephen
Imperiale, Michele, Prince of Francavilla,
d. 1782, 69
Incest, 302, 321, 348 (n. 25)
Inchbald, Elizabeth. *See* Simpson,
Elizabeth
Indirection. *See* Woman's (secondary)
plot
Influence of women authors on one
another. *See* Women authors

Jackson, Rev. William, ca. 1737–95
(newspaper editor; author; Irish
revolutionary): relations with
Chudleigh, 343 (n. 37); author of
Baddeley's memoir, 363–64 (n. 1)
James II, King of England, 1633–1701,
176
Janeway, Elizabeth, 160
Jardine, Alexander, d. 1799, 370–71 (n. 6)
Jekyll, Lady Ann. *See* Montagu, Ann
Jekyll, Joseph, ca. 1714–52 (of Dallington,
Northamptonshire), 32
Jennings, Sarah, 1660–1744 (m. [ca. 1677]
John Churchill, 1st Earl of
Marlborough [1689], 1st Duke of
Marlborough [1702]), 255, 256
Jerningham, Charles ("the Chevalier"),
1742–1814 (French officer; Chevalier de
Barfort), 280, 283–84, 289, 291
Jerningham, Edward, 1727–1812 (poet;
harpist; brother of Charles), 270,
277–78, 282–84, 289, 291, 377 (n. 36)
Jerningham, Lady. *See* Plowden, Mary
Jersey, Countess of. *See* Twysden, Frances
Joe (servant to Henry Fox), 149
John (coachman to Patrick Delany), 221
John (manservant to Anthony Webster;
lover of Sophia Baddeley), 213–14
Johnson, Samuel, LL.D., 1709–84
(lexicographer; author), 155, 187;
Taxation No Tyranny, 11; *Rambler 35*,
22, 143, 144, 160–62, 163, 166–67, 330
(n. 6); friend of the Thrales, 89, 90, 93,